Arguing About Human Nature

Arguing About Human Nature covers recent debates—arising from biology, philosophy, psychology, and physical anthropology—that together systematically examine what it means to be human. Thirty-five essays—several of them appearing here for the first time in print—were carefully selected to offer competing perspectives on twelve different topics related to human nature. The context and main threads of the debates are highlighted and explained by the editors in a short, clear introduction to each of the twelve topics. Authors include Louise M. Anthony, Patrick Bateson, David J. Buller, John Dupré, Paul E. Griffiths, Sally Haslanger, Nancy Holmstrom, R.C. Lewontin, Ron Mallon, Kim Sterelny and E.O. Wilson.

Suggested Reading lists offer curious readers new resources for exploring these debates further. *Arguing About Human Nature* is the first volume of its kind, designed to introduce to an interdisciplinary student audience some of the most important arguments on the subject generated by scientific research and philosophical reflection.

Stephen M. Downes is Professor of Philosophy at the University of Utah.

Edouard Machery is Associate Professor of History and Philosophy of Science at the University of Pittsburgh.

Arguing About Philosophy

This exciting and lively series introduces key subjects in philosophy with the help of a vibrant set of readings. In contrast to many standard anthologies which often reprint the same technical and remote extracts, each volume in the *Arguing About Philosophy* series is built around essential but fresher philosophical readings, designed to attract the curiosity of students coming to the subject for the first time. A key feature of the series is the inclusion of well-known yet often neglected readings from related fields, such as popular science, film and fiction. Each volume is edited by leading figures in their chosen field and each section carefully introduced and set in context, making the series an exciting starting point for those looking to get to grips with philosophy.

Available:
Arguing About Metaethics
Edited by Andrew Fisher and Simon Kirchin

Arguing About the Mind
Edited by Brie Gertler and Lawrence Shapiro

Arguing About Art 3rd Edition
Edited by Alex Neill and Aaron Ridley

Arguing About Knowledge
Edited by Duncan Pritchard and Ram Neta

Arguing About Law
Edited by John Oberdiek and Aileen Kanvanagh

Arguing About Metaphysics
Edited by Michael Rea

Arguing About Religion
Edited by Kevin Timpe

Arguing About Political Philosophy
Edited by Matt Zwolinski

Arguing About Language
Edited by Darragh Byrne and Max Kolbel

Arguing About Bioethics
Edited by Stephen Holland

Arguing About Science
Edited by Alexander Bird and James Ladyman

Arguing About Human Nature
Edited by Stephen M. Downes and Edouard Machery

Forthcoming:
Arguing About Political Philosophy, second edition
Edited by Matt Zwolinski

Arguing About Ethics
Joshua Glasgow

Arguing About Human Nature

Contemporary Debates

Edited by

**Stephen M. Downes and
Edouard Machery**

Routledge
Taylor & Francis Group

NEW YORK AND LONDON

First published 2013
by Routledge
711 Third Avenue, New York, NY 10017

Simultaneously published in the UK
by Routledge
2 Park Square, Milton Park, Abingdon, Oxon OX14 4RN

Routledge is an imprint of the Taylor & Francis Group, an informa business

Library of Congress Cataloging in Publication Data has been applied for

ISBN: 978–0–415–89439–5 (hbk)
IBSN: 978–0–415–89440–1 (pbk)

Typeset in Joanna
by RefineCatch Limited, Bungay, Suffolk

SFI Certified Sourcing
www.sfiprogram.org
SFI-00453

Printed and bound in the United States of America
by Edwards Brothers, Inc.

Contents

Acknowledgments

We would like to thank John Dupré, Paul Griffiths, Sally Haslanger, Jonathan Kaplan, Ron Mallon, Richard Samuels, Kim Sterelny, Steve Stich, Rob Wilson and our anonymous referees for their helpful comments and suggestions about the table of contents of this volume. Thanks to Andy Beck for overseeing this project from beginning to end and thanks to Heather Cushing for her work on production and Allyson Moyer and Joann McIntyre for their help in gathering original materials. Finally, thanks to Elizabeth Cashdan, Rachel Cooper, Nancy Holmstrom, and Kim Sterelny for writing new pieces for this volume.

Stephen M. Downes and Edouard Machery
January 23, 2013

INTRODUCTION

PHILOSOPHERS, PSYCHOLOGISTS, POLITICAL SCIENTISTS, and so on have long been drawn to the debate over whether we are products of nature or nurture. A cursory look at the contents of this book might suggest that we have already picked a side in this debate, but this impression would be mistaken. Here we present the controversies that have raged over human nature since the re-introduction of evolutionary theory into the debate about nature and nurture in the 1970s. The evolutionary approach does not close the book on nature vs. nurture; instead, it provides a whole host of conceptual tools and perspectives to apply to this debate and structure it. The post-sociobiology discussion of human nature, we would argue, is full of rich and nuanced ideas about human nature, and recent work in cross-cultural anthropology and psychology as well as cross-cultural genetics brings a whole wealth of empirical data to this discussion that we think cannot be ignored and that stimulates plenty of disagreement.

Of course, the post-sociobiology discussion of human nature invokes all manner of traditional philosophical issues, such as nativism vs. empiricism, essentialism vs. antiessentialism, as well as more technical and local issues in the sciences and social sciences. On the other hand, understanding human nature in the light of this wealth of new empirical evidence is a very different project than that facing philosophers such as Rousseau or Kant, not to mention Plato! Just consider his slightly outdated hypothesis about the origins of our shared bodily features:

> [The gods] copied the shape of the universe and fastened the two divine orbits of the soul into a spherical body, which we now call the head; [. . .] they then put the body together as a whole to serve the head [. . .] and to prevent the head from rolling about on the earth [. . .] they provided that the body should act as a convenient vehicle. It was therefore given height and grew four limbs which could bend and stretch, and with which it could take hold of things and support itself.[1]

For much of the history of Western philosophy, the project of understanding human nature was indistinguishable from the project of understanding the soul, and this project was typically conducted by means of a priori arguments and reasoning. The characteristics and divisions of the soul are of far more interest to Plato than the "vehicle" that transports it around the world. Following up on, and reacting to, Plato's distinction between the intellect, the appetite(s), and the passions, philosophical speculation on the division of the soul (or later the mind) occupied an important place in the Western tradition up to and through the Modern period. Aristotle's proposal on the division of the soul substantially differed from Plato's: For him, while all living things have souls, plants have a nutritive and reproductive soul only, animals

have this soul as well as sentience and self-motion, and humans, all that and the intellect. Centuries later, Descartes distinguished between rational thought, imagination,
and the passions. He also delineated the soul as a separate substance, intimately
connected with the body, but of an entirely different order of existence. While
Descartes had a keen interest in physiology and in many of what later became identified as separate sciences, given his clear distinction between souls and bodies, he
could see none of these inquiries as appropriate to the study of the nature of our soul.

The study of human nature in the Western philosophical tradition has not always
involved the application of reason to the task of characterizing the divisions of the
soul. Hobbes, an empiricist and trenchant materialist, rejected the very notion of a
soul and introduced his concept of human nature in the course of developing his
political theory. For Hobbes, in a nutshell, we are all more or less equal in terms of
physical strength and intellect, and we all compete with one another for what we
desire, which inevitably leads to the "endeavour to destroy or subdue one another."
Government is justified by appeal to the "state of nature" that would result from all
of us acting in this way—viz. in accordance with our natures: Only a sufficiently
forceful government, or ruler, can prevent the misery that would prevail in the state of
nature. Rousseau also presented and defended an account of human nature in the
context of a political theory, but he did not share Hobbes' vision of human nature: For
him, civilization has corrupted people's original goodness.

Hume too had what we might now call a naturalistic approach to understanding
human nature, and, in the introduction of *A Treatise of Human Nature*, he called for
the development of a "science of Man" based on "a cautious observation of human
life" instead of a priori arguments and reasoning. Where Hobbes needed an account
of human nature to anchor his political theory, Hume was more interested in the
empirical study of our minds and our behavior for its own sake. Perhaps for this
reason, his account of human psychology was more nuanced than Hobbes'. On the
other hand, while he was certainly a keen observer of the workings of the human
mind, his observations were not always systematic, and some were tinged with considerable bias. For example, according to Hume, tales of miracles abound most among
the "ignorant and barbarous" rather than amongst the civilized.[2] Similar ethnocentric musings are the mainstay of many discussions of human nature in the Western
tradition up through the early twentieth century.

Kant's *Anthropology from a Pragmatic Point of View*[3] can be viewed as picking
up where Hume left off, continuing the collection of ad hoc and often extremely
biased observations about human nature. Unlike Hume, Kant does not envision a
systematic "science of Man"; his aim is more practical: He wants to show how we
must be civilized or educated in order to resist our "animal tendency to yield passively
to the attractions of comfort and well-being, which [we] call happiness." Thus, part
of his job in the *Anthropology* is to delineate this animal tendency and all our other
inclinations. Along the way, he attempts to establish the key differences between men
and women and between the various peoples on earth. These purported differences
are often stipulative or drawn from dubious sources, including Hume, who Kant
repeatedly cites (sometimes incorrectly) as an expert on topics such as what annoys
"women (even old maids)" and national character.[4] What we see in both Hume and

Kant are the beginnings of anthropology and comparative psychology, but neither project is guided by a scientific theoretical framework.

Near the conclusion of *The Origin of Species,* Darwin made the following bold prediction:

> In the distant future I see open fields for far more important researches. Psychology will be based on a new foundation, that of the necessary acquirement of each mental power and capacity by gradation. Light will be thrown on the origin of man and his history.[5]

Darwin recognized the potential of his own evolutionary theory as a foundation for the empirical study of human behavior and culture. He devoted much of *The Descent of Man*[6] to defending the very idea that humans are a product of evolution, and, in doing so, he sets himself apart from his contemporaries, including Alfred Russell Wallace, who developed the notion of evolution at the same time as Darwin, but did not believe that human psychological traits were a product of evolution. Darwin also presented his theory of sexual selection in *The Descent of Man,* and applied it to humans.

Darwin presented his own observations of people from around the world and collected those of other anthropologists, explorers, naturalists, and philosophers. He used his observations of differences between different peoples and variation within populations around the world differently than Hume or Kant did. In both *The Origin of Species* and *The Descent of Man* Darwin aimed to establish the pervasiveness of variation in order, first, to argue against the idea of species as fixed types and, second, to establish that variation along with differential reproduction is the engine of evolutionary change. Although Darwin introduced and defended the key insight that humans, and hence many of our traits, result from evolutionary change, he fell short of providing a systematic evolutionary anthropology or evolutionary psychology. Many of his observations about the differences between sexes and peoples are colored with gender and ethnocentric bias, and they do not constitute a significant advance over Hume and Kant.

Empirical observations relevant to understanding human nature have become much more systematic than those offered by Hume, Kant, or even Darwin, and they are now complemented by experimental work in psychology, genetics, and other scientific disciplines. The more systematic observations are made in the service of scientific inquiry such as comparative psychology or evolutionary anthropology. The underlying philosophical questions may often be the same as those that Hume and Kant posed, but the way in which they must be faced, informed by all this empirical work, has changed drastically. Philosophers and other theorists interested in human nature (including psychologists, anthropologists, etc.) can no longer afford to speculate about human nature from their armchair; rather, they must get acquainted with, understand, and integrate the empirical findings that accumulate in psychology, ethology, sociology, anthropology, genetics, biology, etc. A tall order!

From one perspective, we humans have an awful lot in common, perhaps so much so that we can reasonably talk, as Donald Brown does, of "Universal People,"[7] a theoretical group who have all and only the characteristics that all of us share. From another perspective, we are all quite different, and these differences seem so overwhelming as to rule out any reasonable talk of commonalities or universality. Although we present these debates here against the background of recent and contemporary comparative psychology and evolutionary anthropology (among other fields), the issues at stake are those that have been pursued in Western philosophy for thousands of years.

Notes

1   Plato *Timaeus and Critias,* translated by Desmond Lee. London: Penguin Classics, 1965, p. 61.
2   Hume, D., *Treatise on Human Nature.* Oxford: Oxford University Press, 1739–40/2001.
3   Kant, E., *Anthropology from a Pragmatic Point of View.* Cambridge: Cambridge University Press, 1798/2006.
4   Ibid., pp. 210 and 213.
5   Darwin, C., *The Origin of Species.* London: Penguin Classics, 1859/1985, p. 458.
6   Darwin, C., *The Descent of Man.* New York: Prometheus Books, 1874/1998.
7   Brown, D. E., *Human Universals.* New York: McGraw-Hill, 1991.

PART I

Human Nature and Evolution

Topic 1 EVOLUTION AND HUMAN NATURE

DARWIN LAID THE FOUNDATION for the application of evolutionary theory to the understanding of human nature in *The Origin of Species* and moved this inquiry forward to some degree in *The Descent of Man*. The critical response to Darwin in the late nineteenth century was mostly over the very idea of our existence being a result of evolution. When E. O. Wilson concluded his work on sociobiology with a chapter on humans and then followed it up with a book entitled *On Human Nature*, the critical response was directed at the particular way in which Wilson applied evolution to the understanding of human nature. In a way, all the debates presented in this volume can be seen as responses to the various claims that Wilson made. Some aim to refine and develop Wilson's ideas and insights and some vehemently reject his ideas. The focus of this section is the relations between evolutionary theory and concepts of human nature.

Wilson's aim was to explain all of human behavior and culture in terms of evolution. In this section we first present key elements of Wilson's project. He introduces sociobiology—the application of ecology, ethology, and genetics to the understanding of social behavior—and argues that sociobiology will reveal our nature. Wilson argues that not only are traits such as eye color genetically determined but so are our social behaviors. He defends a form of genetic determinism (a concept debated in depth in a later section of this volume) in part via comparative ethology—the study of animal behavior. He concludes that human behavior is both clearly separate from that of other animals, and particularly of our closest relatives, the Great Apes, but also clearly derives from the behavior of these other animals, particularly their social behavior. As Wilson puts it, "human behavior is organized by some genes that are shared with closely related species and others that are unique to the human species." Wilson presents a challenge for sociobiology, which is to establish that evolutionary biology applies to humans and the study of human nature.

David Hull takes up Wilson's challenge but turns things around. Hull argues that evolutionary theory does not make room for a frequently defended concept of human nature: "All organisms that belong to *Homo Sapiens* as a biological species are essentially the same." So for Hull, evolutionary biology has no room for what was understood by many to be a biological concept of human nature. Hull concludes that we should make a place for the variability in the species *Homo sapiens*, which he takes not to be an accident, but an essential feature of any species. David Buller updates and elaborates on Hull's thesis. Where Hull was responding to sociobiologists and philosophers who supported this view, Buller responds to evolutionary psychologists, whose work descends from sociobiology, but departs from it in key ways. The concept of human nature that Buller sees as key to evolutionary psychology also has the unacceptable essentialism that Hull revealed in earlier concepts of human nature.

Buller also argues, like Hull, that this concept of human nature does not fit well within evolutionary theory.

In the final two essays in this section we see two different types of pleas for a concept of human nature. Edouard Machery argues that an explanatorily useful notion of human nature can be salvaged and that this concept sits well with evolutionary biology. To establish this, Machery responds to criticisms such as Hull's and Buller's. The key move in Machery's response is to distinguish between essentialist and nomological notions of human nature and to demonstrate that the Hull- and Buller-style criticisms apply only to the former but not to the latter. He goes on to argue that the nomological notion of human nature does helpful explanatory work, even in evolutionary biology. Finally, Elizabeth Cashdan, in her new essay for this volume, develops a concept of human nature that is applicable in the context of the massive variation within our species that Hull emphasized.

Suggested Further Reading

Degler, C. N. (1991) *In Search of Human Nature: The decline and revival of Darwinism in American social thought*. New York: Oxford University Press.

Ghiselin, M. T. (1997) *Metaphysics and the Origins of Species*. Albany, NY: State University of New York Press.

Griffiths, P. E. (2009) Reconstructing human nature. *Arts: The Journal of the Sydney University Arts Association*, 31: 30–57.

Griffiths, P. E. (2011) Our plastic nature. In S. Gissis and E. Jablonka (Eds.), *Transformations of Lamarckism: From subtle fluids to molecular biology* (pp. 319–330). Cambridge, MA: MIT Press.

Lewens, T. (2009) What is wrong with typological thinking? *Philosophy of Science*, 76: 355–371.

Lewens, T. (2012) Human nature: The very idea. *Philosophy & Technology*, 25: 459–474.

Linquist, S., Machery, E., Griffiths, P. and Stotz, K. (2011) Exploring the folkbiological conception of human nature. *Philosophical Transactions of the Royal Society B*, 366: 444–453.

Machery, E. (2012) Reconceptualizing human nature: Response to Lewens. *Philosophy & Technology*, 25: 475–478.

Mayr, E. (1976) Typological versus populational thinking. In E. Mayr (Ed.), *Evolution and the Diversity of Life* (pp. 26–29). Cambridge, MA: Harvard University Press.

Pinker, S. (2003) *The Blank Slate: The modern denial of human nature*. New York: Penguin.

Powell, R. (2012) Human nature and respect for the evolutionary given: Comment on Lewens: The very idea. *Philosopy & Technology*, 25: 485–493.

Prinz, J. (2012) *Beyond Human Nature*. New York: W. W. Norton & Company.

Ramsey, G. (2012) Human nature can inform human enhancement: A commentary on Tim Lewen's Human Nature: The Very Idea. *Philosopy & Technology*, 25: 479–483.

Samuels, R. (2012) Science and human nature. *Royal Institute of Philosophy Supplement*, 70: 1–28.

Sober, E. (1980) Evolution, population thinking, and essentialism. *Philosophy of Science*, 47: 350–383.

Stotz, K. (2010) Human nature and cognitive-developmental niche construction. *Phenomenology and the Cognitive Sciences*, 9: 483–501.

Walsh, D. (2006) Evolutionary essentialism. *The British Journal for the Philosophy of Science*, 57: 425–448.

Chapter 1

Edward O. Wilson

ON HUMAN NATURE

Thousands of species are highly social. The most advanced among them constitute what I call the three pinnacles of social evolution in animals: the corals, bryozoans, and other colony-forming invertebrates; the social insects, including ants, wasps, bees, and termites; and the social fish, birds, and mammals. The communal beings of the three pinnacles are among the principal objects of the new discipline of sociobiology, defined as the systematic study of the biological basis of all forms of social behavior, in all kinds of organisms, including man. The enterprise has old roots. Much of its basic information and some of its most vital ideas have come from ethology, the study of whole patterns of behavior of organisms under natural conditions. Ethology was pioneered by Julian Huxley, Karl von Frisch, Konrad Lorenz, Nikolaas Tinbergen, and a few others and is now being pursued by a large new generation of innovative and productive investigators. It has remained most concerned with the particularity of the behavior patterns shown by each species, the ways these patterns adapt animals to the special challenges of their environments, and the steps by which one pattern gives rise to another as the species themselves undergo genetic evolution. Increasingly, modern ethology is being linked to studies of the nervous system and the effects of hormones on behavior. Its investigators have become deeply involved with developmental processes and even learning, formerly the nearly exclusive domain of psychology, and they have begun to include man among the species most closely scrutinized. The emphasis of ethology remains on the individual organism and the physiology of organisms.

Sociobiology, in contrast, is more explicitly hybrid discipline that incorporates knowledge from ethology (the naturalistic study of whole patterns of behavior), ecology (the study of the relationships of organisms to their environment), and genetics in order to derive general principles concerning the biological properties of entire societies. What is truly new about sociobiology is the way it has extracted the most important facts about social organization from their traditional matrix of ethology and psychology and reassembled them on a foundation of ecology and genetics studied at the population level in order to show how social groups adapt to the environment by evolution. Only within the past few years have ecology and genetics themselves become sophisticated and strong enough to provide such a foundation.

Sociobiology is a subject based largely on comparisons of social species. Each living form can be viewed as an evolutionary experiment, a product of millions of years of interaction between genes and environment. By examining many such experiments closely, we have begun to construct and test the first general principles of genetic social evolution. It is now within our reach to apply his broad knowledge to the study of human beings.

Sociobiologists consider man as though seen through the front end of a telescope, at a greater than usual distance and temporarily diminished in size, in order to view him simultaneously with an array of other social experiments. They attempt to place humankind in its proper place in a catalog of the social species on Earth. They agree with Rousseau that "One needs to look near at hand in order to study men, but to study man one must look from afar."

This macroscopic view has certain advantages over the traditional anthropocentrism of the social sciences. In fact, no intellectual vice is more crippling than defiantly self-indulgent anthropocentrism. I am reminded of the clever way Robert Nozick makes this point when he constructs an argument in favor of vegetarianism. Human beings, he notes, justify the eating of meat on the grounds that the animals we kill are too far below us in sensitivity and intelligence to beat comparison. It follows that if representatives of a truly superior extraterrestrial species were to visit Earth and apply the same criterion, they could proceed to eat us in good conscience. By the same token, scientists among these aliens might find human beings uninteresting, our intelligence weak, our passions unsurprising, our social organization of a kind already frequently encountered on other planets. To our chagrin they might then focus on the ants, because these little creatures, with their haplodiploid form of sex determination and bizarre female caste systems, are the truly novel productions of the Earth with reference to the Galaxy. We can imagine the log declaring "A scientific breakthrough has occurred; we have finally discovered haplodiploid social organisms in the one- to ten-millimeter range." Then the visitors might inflict the ultimate indignity: in order to be sure they had not underestimated us, they would simulate human beings in the laboratory. Like chemists testing the structural characterization of a problematic organic compound

by assembling it from simpler components, the alien biologists would need to synthesize a hominoid or two.

This scenario from science fiction has implications for the definition of man. The impressive recent advances by computer scientists in the design of artificial intelligence suggests the following test of humanity: that which behaves like man is man. Human behavior is something that can be defined with fair precision, because the evolutionary pathways open to it have not all been equally negotiable. Evolution has not made culture all-powerful. It is a misconception among many of the more traditional Marxists, some learning theorists, and a still surprising proportion of anthropologists and sociologists that social behavior can be shaped into virtually any form. Ultra-environmentalists start with the premise that man is the creation of his own culture: "culture makes man," the formula might go. Theirs is only a half truth. Each person is molded by an interaction of his environment, especially his cultural environment, with the genes that affect social behavior. Although the hundreds of the world's cultures seem enormously variable to those of us who stand in their midst, all versions of human social behavior together form only a tiny fraction of the realized organizations of social species on this planet and a still smaller fraction of those that can be readily imagined with the aid of sociobiological theory.

The question of interest is no longer whether human social behavior is genetically determined; it is to what extent. The accumulated evidence for a large hereditary component is more detailed and compelling than most persons, including even geneticists, realize. I will go further: it already is decisive.

That being said, let me provide an exact definition of a genetically determined trait. It is a trait that differs from other traits at least in part as a result of the presence of one or more distinctive genes. The important point is that the objective estimate of genetic influence requires comparison of two or more states of the same feature. To say that blue eyes are inherited is not meaningful without further qualification, because blue eyes are the product of an interaction between genes and the largely physiological environment that brought final coloration to the irises. But to say that the *difference* between blue and brown eyes is based wholly or partly on differences in genes is a meaningful statement because it can be tested and translated into the laws of genetics. Additional information is then sought: What are the eye colors of the parents, siblings, children, and more distant relatives? These data are compared to the very simplest model of Mendelian heredity, which, based on our understanding of cell multiplication and sexual reproduction, entails the action of only two genes. If the data fit, the differences are interpreted as being based on two genes. If not, increasingly complicated schemes are applied. Progressively larger numbers of genes and more complicated modes of interaction are assumed until a reasonably close fit can be made. In the example just cited, the main differences between blue and brown eyes are in fact based on two genes, although complicated modifications exist that make them less than an ideal textbook example. In the case of the most complex traits, hundreds of genes are sometimes involved, and their degree of influence can ordinarily be measured only crudely and with the aid of sophisticated mathematical techniques. Nevertheless, when the analysis is properly performed it leaves little doubt as to the presence and approximate magnitude of the genetic influence.

Human social behavior can be evaluated in essentially the same way, first by comparison with the behavior of other species and then, with far greater difficulty and ambiguity, by studies of variation among and within human populations. The picture of genetic determinism emerges most sharply when we compare selected major categories of animals with the human species. Certain general human traits are shared with a majority of the great apes and monkeys of Africa and Asia, which on grounds of anatomy and biochemistry are our closest living evolutionary relatives:

- Our intimate social groupings contain on the order of ten to one hundred adults, never just two, as in most birds and marmosets, or up to thousands, as in many kinds of fishes and insects.
- Males are larger than females. This is a characteristic of considerable significance within the Old World monkeys and apes and many other kinds of mammals. The average number of females consorting with successful males closely corresponds to the size gap between males and females when many species are considered together. The rule makes sense: the greater the competition among males for females, the greater the advantage of large size and the less influential are any disadvantages accruing to bigness. Men are not very much larger than women, we are similar to chimpanzees in this regard. When the sexual size difference in human beings is plotted on the curve based on other kinds of mammals, the predicted average number of females per successful male turns out to be greater than one but less than three. The prediction is close to reality; we know we are a mildly polygynous species.
- The young are molded by a long period of social training, first by closest associations with the mother, then to an increasing degree with other children of the same age and sex.
- Social play is a strongly developed activity featuring role practice, mock aggression, sex practice, and exploration.

These and other properties together identify the taxonomic group consisting of Old World monkeys, the great apes, and human beings. It is inconceivable that human beings could be

10   *Edward O. Wilson*

socialized into the radically different repertories of other groups such as fishes, birds, antelopes, or rodents. Human beings might self-consciously *imitate* such arrangements, but it would be a fiction played out on a stage, would run counter to deep emotional responses and have no chance of persisting through as much as a single generation. To adopt with serious intent, even in broad outline, the social system of a nonprimate species would be insanity in the literal sense. Personalities would quickly dissolve, relationships disintegrate, and reproduction cease.

At the next, finer level of classification, our species is distinct from the Old World monkeys and apes in ways that can be explained only as a result of a unique set of human genes. Of course, that is a point quickly conceded by even the most ardent environmentalists. They are willing to agree with the great geneticist Theodosius Dobzhansky that "in a sense, human genes have surrendered their primacy in human evolution to an entirely new, nonbiological or superorganic agent, culture. However, it should not be forgotten that this agent is entirely dependent on the human genotype." But the matter is much deeper and more interesting than that. There are social traits occurring through all cultures which upon close examination are as diagnostic of mankind as are distinguishing characteristics of other animal species—as true to the human type, say, as wing tessellation is to a fritillary butterfly or a complicated spring melody to a wood thrush. In 1945 the American anthropologist George P. Murdock listed the following characteristics that have been recorded in every culture known to history and ethnography:

Age-grading, athletic sports, bodily adornment, calendar, cleanliness training; community organization, cooking, cooperative labor, cosmology, courtship, dancing, decorative art, divination, division of labor, dream interpretation, education, eschatology, ethics, ethnobotany, etiquette, faith healing, family feasting, fire making, folklore, food taboos,

funeral rites, games, gestures, gift giving, government, greetings, hair styles, hospitality, housing, hygiene, incest raboos, inheritance rules, joking, kin groups, kinship nomenclature, language, law, luck superstitions, magic, marriage, mealtimes, medicine, obstetrics, penal sanctions, personal names, population policy, postnatal care, pregnancy usages, property rights, propitiation of supernatural beings, puberty customs, religious ritual, residence rules, sexual restrictions, soul concepts, status differentiation, surgery, tool making, trade, visiting, weaving, and weather control.

Few of these unifying properties can be interpreted as the inevitable outcome of either advanced social life or high intelligence. It is easy to imagine nonhuman societies whose members are even more intelligent and complexly organized than ourselves, yet lack a majority of the qualities just listed. Consider the possibilities inherent in the insect societies. The sterile workers are already more cooperative and altruistic than people and they have a more pronounced tendency toward caste systems and division of labor. If ants were to be endowed in addition with rationalizing brains equal to our own, they could be our peers. Their societies would display the following peculiarities:

Age-grading, antennal rites, body licking, calendar, cannibalism, caste determination, caste laws, colony-foundation rules, colony organization, cleanliness training, communal nurseries, cooperative labor, cosmology, courtship, division of labor, drone control, education, eschatology, ethics, etiquette, euthanasia, fire making, food taboos, gift giving, government, greetings, grooming rituals, hospitality, housing, hygiene, incest taboos, language, larval care, law, medicine, metamorphosis rites, mutual regurgitation, nursing castes, nuptial flights, nutrient eggs, population policy, queen obeisance, residence rules, sex determination, soldier castes, sisterhoods, status differentiation, sterile workers, surgery, symbiont care, tool making, trade, visiting, weather control.

and still other activities so alien as to make mere description by our language difficult. If in addition they were programmed to eliminate strife between colonies and to conserve the natural environment they would have greater staying power than people, and in a broad sense theirs would be the higher morality.

Civilization is not intrinsically limited to hominoids. Only by accident was it linked to the anatomy of bare-skinned, bipedal mammals and the peculiar qualities of human nature.

Freud said that God has been guilty of a shoddy and uneven piece of work. That is true to a degree greater than he intended: human nature is just one hodgepodge out of many conceivable. Yet if even a small fraction of the diagnostic human traits were stripped away, the result would probably be a disabling chaos. Human beings could not bear to simulate the behavior of even our closest relatives among the Old World primates. If by perverse mutual agreement a human group attempted to imitate in detail the distinctive social arrangements of chimpanzees or gorillas, their effort would soon collapse and they would revert to fully human behavior.

It is also interesting to speculate that if people were somehow raised from birth in an environment devoid of most cultural influence, they would construct basic elements of human social life *abinitio*. In short time new elements of language would be invented and their culture enriched. Robin Fox, an anthropologist and pioneer in human sociobiology, has expressed this hypothesis in its strongest possible terms. Suppose, he conjectured, that we performed the cruel experiment linked in legend to the Pharaoh Psammetichus and King James IV of Scotland, who were said to have reared children by remote control, in total social isolation from their elders.

Would the children learn to speak to one another?

I do not doubt that they *could* speak and that, theoretically, given time, they or their offspring would invent and develop a language despite their never having been taught one. Furthermore, this language, although totally different from any known to us, would be analyzable to linguists on the same basis as other languages and translatable into all known languages. But I would push this further. If our new Adam and Eve could survive and breed—still in total isolation from any cultural influences—then eventually they would produce a society which would have laws about property, rules about incest and marriage, customs of taboo and avoidance, methods of settling disputes with a minimum of bloodshed, beliefs about the supernatural and practices relating to it, a system of social status and methods of indicating it, initiation ceremonies for young men, courtship practices including the adornment of females, systems of symbolic body adornment generally, certain activities and associations set aside for men from which women were excluded, gambling of some kind, a tool- and weapon-making industry, myths and legends, dancing, adultery, and various doses of homicide, suicide, homosexuality, schizophrenia, psychosis and neuroses, and various practitioners to take advantage of or cure these, depending on how they are viewed.

Not only are the basic features of human social behavior stubbornly idiosyncratic, but to the limited extent that they can be compared with those of animals they resemble most of all the repertories of other mammals and especially other primates. A few of the signals used to organize the behavior can be logically derived from the ancestral modes still shown by the Old World monkeys and great apes. The grimace of fear, the smile, and even laughter have parallels in the facial expressions of chimpanzees. This broad similarity is precisely the pattern to be expected if the human species descended from Old World primate ancestors, a demonstrable fact, and if the development of human social behavior retains even a small degree of genetic constraint, the broader hypothesis now under consideration.

The status of the chimpanzee deserves especially close attention. Our growing knowledge of these most intelligent apes has come to erode to a large extent the venerable dogma of the uniqueness of man. Chimpanzees are first of all remarkably similar to human beings in anatomical and physiological details. It also turns out that they are very close at the molecular level. The biochemists Mary-Claire King and Allan C. Wilson have compared the proteins encoded by genes at forty-four loci. They found the summed differences between the two species to be equivalent to the genetic distance separating nearly indistinguishable species of fruit flies, and only twenty-five to sixty times greater than that between Caucasian, Black African, and Japanese populations. The chimpanzee and human lines might have split as recently as twenty million years ago, a relatively short span in evolutionary time.

By strictly human criteria chimpanzees are mentally retarded to an intermediate degree. Their brains are only one-third as large as our own, and their larynx is constructed in the primitive ape form that prevents them from articulating human speech. Yet individuals can be taught to communicate with their human helpers by means of American sign language or the fastening of plastic symbols in sequences on display boards. The brightest among them can learn vocabularies of two-hundred English words and elementary rules of syntax, allowing them to invent such sentences as "Mary gives me apple" and "Lucy tickle Roger." Lana, a female trained by Beatrice and Robert Gardner at the University of Nevada, ordered her trainer from the room in a fit of pique by signalling, "You green shit." Sarah, a female trained by David Premack, memorized twenty-five hundred sentences and used many of them. Such well educated chimps understand instructions as complicated as "If red on green (and not vice versa) then you take red (and not green)" and "You insert banana in pail, apple in dish." They have invented new expressions such as "water bird" for duck and "drink fruit" for watermelon, essentially the same as those hit upon by the inventors of the English language.

Chimpanzees do not remotely approach the human child in the inventiveness and drive of their language. Evidence of true linguistic novelty is, moreover, lacking: no chimp genius has accomplished the equivalent of joining the sentences "Mary gives me apple" and "I like Mary" into the more complex proposition "Mary's giving me apple is why I like her." The human intellect is vastly more powerful than that of the chimpanzee. But the capacity to communicate by symbols and syntax does lie within the ape's grasp. Many zoologists now doubt the existence of an unbridgeable linguistic chasm between animals and man. It is no longer possible to say, as the leading anthropologist Leslie White did in 1949, that human behavior is symbolic behavior and symbolic behavior is human behavior.

Another chasm newly bridged is self-awareness. When Gordon G. Gallup, a psychologist, allowed chimps to peer into mirrors for two or three days, they changed from treating their reflection as a stranger to recognizing it as themselves. At this point they began to use the mirrors to explore previously inaccessible parts of their own bodies. They made faces, picked bits of food from their teeth, and blew bubbles through their pursed lips. No such behavior has ever been elicited from monkeys or gibbons presented with mirrors, despite repeated trials by Gallup and others. When the researchers dyed portions of the faces of chimpanzees under anesthesia, the apes subsequently gave even more convincing evidence that they were self-aware. They spent more time at the mirrors, intently examining the changes in their appearance and smelling the fingers with which they had touched the altered areas.

If consciousness of self and the ability to communicate ideas with other intelligent beings exist, can other qualities of the human mind be far away? Premack has pondered the implications of transmitting the concept of personal death to chimpanzee, but he is hesitant. "What if, like man," he asks,

> the ape dreads death and will deal with this knowledge as bizarrely as we have? . . . The desired objective would be not only to communicate the knowledge of death but, more important, to find a way of making sure the apes' response would not be that of dread, which, in the human case, has led to the invention of ritual, myth, and religion. Until I can suggest concrete steps in teaching the concept of death without fear, I have no intention of imparting the knowledge of mortality to the ape.

And what of the social existence of the chimpanzees? They are far less elaborately organized than even the hunter-gatherers, who have the simplest economic arrangements of all human beings. Yet striking basic similarities exist. The apes live in troops of up to fifty individuals, within which smaller, more casual groups break off and reunite in shifting combinations of individuals over periods as brief as a few days. Males are somewhat larger than females, to about the same degree as in human beings, and they occupy the top of well-marked dominance hierarchies. Children are closely associated with their mothers over a period of years, sometimes even into maturity. The young chimpanzees themselves remain allied for long periods of time; individuals on occasion even adopt younger brothers or sisters when the mother dies.

Each troop occupies a home range of about twenty square miles. Meetings between neighboring troops are infrequent and usually tense. On these occasions nubile females and young mothers sometimes migrate between the groups. But on other occasions chimpanzees can become territorial and murderous. At the Gombe Stream Reserve in Tanzania, where Jane Goodall conducted her celebrated research, bands of males from one troop, encroaching on the home range of an adjacent, smaller troop, attacked and occasionally injured the defenders. Eventually the residents abandoned their land to the invaders.

Like primitive human beings, chimpanzees gather fruit and other vegetable foods primarily and hunt only secondarily. The difference between their diets is one of proportion. Where all of hunter-gatherer societies considered together derive an average of 35 percent of their calories from fresh meat, chimpanzees obtain between 1 and 5 percent. And whereas primitive human hunters capture prey of any size, including elephants one hundred times the weight of a man, chimpanzees rarely attack any animal greater than one-fifth the weight of an adult male. Perhaps the most remarkable form of manlike behavior among chimpanzees is the use of intelligent, cooperative maneuvers during the hunt. Normally only adult males attempt to pursue animals—another humanoid trait. When a potential victim, such as a vervet or young baboon, has been selected, the chimpanzees signal their intentions by distinctive changes in posture, movement, and facial expression. Other males respond by turning to stare at the target animal. Their posture is tensed, their hair partially erected, and they become silent—a conspicuous change from the human observer's point of view, because chimpanzees are ordinarily the noisiest of animals. The state of alertness is broken by a sudden, nearly simultaneous pursuit.

A common strategy of the hunter males is to mingle with a group of baboons and then attempt to seize one of the youngsters with an explosive rush. Another is to encircle and stalk the victim, even while it nervously edges away. At the Gombe Stream Reserve an enterprising male named Figan tracked a juvenile baboon until it retreated up the trunk of a palm tree. Within moments other males that had been resting and grooming nearby stood up and walked over to join the pursuit. A few stopped at the bottom of the tree in which the baboon waited, while others dispersed to the bases of adjacent trees that might have served as alternate routes of escape. The baboon then leaped onto a second tree, whereupon the chimpanzee stationed below began to climb quickly toward it. The baboon finally managed to escape by jumping twenty feet to the ground and running to the protection of its troop nearby.

The distribution of the meat is also cooperative, with favors asked and given. The begging chimpanzee stares intently while holding its face close to the meat or to the face of the meat eater. It may also reach out and touch the meat and the chin and lips of the other animal, or extend an open hand with palm upward beneath his chin. Sometimes the male holding the prey moves abruptly away. But often he acquiesces by allowing the other animal to chew directly on the meat or to remove small pieces with its hands. On a few occasions males go so far as to tear off pieces of meat and hand them over to supplicants. This is a small gesture by the standards of human altruism but it is a very rare act among animals—a giant step, one might say, for apekind.

Finally, chimpanzees have a rudimentary culture. During twenty-five years of research on free-living troops in the forests of Africa, teams of zoologists from Europe, Japan, and the United States have discovered a remarkable repertory of tool use in the ordinary life of the apes. It includes the use of sticks and saplings as defensive weapons against leopards; the hurling of sticks, stones, and handfuls of vegetation during attacks on baboons, human beings, and other chimpanzees; digging with sticks to tear open termite mounds and "fishing" for the termites with plant stems stripped of leaves and split down the middle; prying open boxes with sticks; and lifting water from tree holes in "sponges" constructed of chewed leaves.

Learning and play are vital to the acquisition of the tool-using skills. When two-year-old chimpanzee infants are denied the opportunity to play with sticks their ability to solve problems with the aid of sticks at a later age is reduced. Given access to play objects, young animals in captivity progress through a relatively invariant maturation of skills. Under two years of age they simply touch or hold objects without attempting to manipulate them. As they grow older they increasingly employ one object to hit or prod another, while simultaneously improving in the solution of problems that require the use of tools. A similar progression occurs in the wild populations of Africa. Infants as young as six weeks reach out from their mother's clasp to fondle leaves and branches. Older infants constantly inspect their environment with their eyes, lips, tongues, noses, and hands, while periodically plucking leaves and waving them about. During this development they advance to tool-using behavior in small steps. One eight-month-old infant was seen to add grass stems to his other toys—but for the special purpose of wiping them against other objects, such as stones and his mother. This is the behavior pattern uniquely associated with termite "fishing"—by which the apes provoke the insects into running onto the object and then quickly bite or lick them off. During play, other infants prepared grass stalks as fishing tools by shredding the edges off wide blades and chewing the ends off long stems.

Jane Goodall has obtained direct evidence of imitative behavior in the transmission of these traditions. She observed infants watch adults as they used tools, then pick the tools up and use them after the adults had moved away. On two occasions a three-year-old youngster was seen to observe his mother closely as she wiped dung from her bottom with leaves. Then he picked up leaves and imitated the movements, even though his bottom was not dirty.

Chimpanzees are able to invent techniques and to transmit them to others. The use of sticks to pry open food boxes is a case in point. The method was invented by one or a few individuals at the Gombe Stream Reserve, then evidently spread through the troop by imitation. One female new to the area remained hidden in the bushes while watching others trying to open the boxes. On her fourth visit she walked into the open, picked up a stick, and began in poke it at the boxes.

Each tool-using behavior recorded in Africa is limited to certain populations of chimpanzees but has a mostly continuous distribution within its range. This is just the pattern expected if the behavior had been spread culturally. Maps of chimpanzee tool-using recently prepared by the Spanish zoologist Jorge Sabater-Pi might be placed without notice into a chapter on primitive culture in an anthropology textbook. Although most of the evidence concerning invention and transmission of the tool-using methods is indirect, it suggests that the apes have managed to cross the threshold of cultural evolution and thus, in an important sense, to have moved on into the human domain.

This account of the life of the chimpanzee is meant to establish what I regard as a fundamental point about the human condition: that by conventional evolutionary measures and the principal criteria of psychology we are not alone, we have a little-brother species. The points of similarity between human and chimpanzee social behavior, when joined with the compelling anatomical and biochemical traces of relatively recent genetic divergence, form a body of evidence too strong to be dismissed as coincidence. I now believe that they are based at least in part on the possession of identical genes. If this proposition contains any truth, it makes even more urgent the conservation and

closer future study of these and the other great apes, as well as the Old World monkeys and the lower primates. A more thorough knowledge of these animal species might well provide us with a clearer picture of the step-by-step genetic changes that led to the level of evolution uniquely occupied by human beings.

To summarize the argument to this point; the general traits of human nature appear limited and idiosyncratic when placed against the great backdrop of all other living species. Additional evidence suggests that the more stereotyped forms of human behavior are mammalian and even more specifically primate in character, as predicted on the basis of general evolutionary theory. Chimpanzees are close enough to ourselves in the details of their social life and mental properties to rank as nearly human in certain domains where it was once considered inappropriate to make comparisons at all. These facts are in accord with the hypothesis that human social behavior rests on a genetic foundation—that human behavior is, to be more precise, organized by some genes that are shared with closely related species and others that are unique to the human species. The same facts are unfavorable for the competing hypothesis which has dominated the social sciences for generations, that mankind has escaped its own genes to the extent of being entirely culture-bound.

Let us pursue this matter systematically. The heart of the genetic hypothesis is the proposition, derived in a straight line from neo-Darwinian evolutionary theory, that the traits of human nature were adaptive during the time that the human species evolved and that genes consequently spread through the population that predisposed their carriers to develop those traits. Adaptiveness means simply that if an individual displayed the traits he stood a greater chance of having his genes represented in the next generation than if he did not display the traits. The differential advantage among individuals in this strictest sense is called genetic fitness. There are three basic components of genetic fitness: increased personal survival, increased personal reproduction, and the enhanced survival and reproduction of close relatives who share the same genes by common descent. An improvement in any one of the factors or in any combination of them results in greater genetic fitness. The process, which Darwin called natural selection, describes a tight circle of causation. If the possession of certain genes predisposes individuals toward a partic- ular trait, say a certain kind of social response, and the trait in turn conveys superior fitness, the genes will gain an increased representation in the next generation. If natural selection is continued over many generations, the favored genes will spread throughout the population, and the trait will become characteristic of the species. In this way human nature is postulated by many sociobiologists, anthropologists, and others to have been shaped by natural selection.

It is nevertheless a curious fact, which enlarges the difficulty of the analysis, that socio- biological theory can be obeyed by purely cultural behavior as well as by genetically constrained behavior. An almost purely cultural sociobiology is possible. If human beings were endowed with nothing but the most elementary drives to survive and to reproduce, together with a capacity for culture, they would still learn many forms of social behavior that increase their biological fitness. But as I will show, there is a limit to the amount of this cultural mimicry, and methods exist by which it can be distinguished from the more structured forms of biological adaptation. The analysis will require the careful use of techniques in biology, anthropology, and psychology. Our focus will be on the closeness of fit of human social behavior to sociobio- logical theory, and on the evidences of genetic constraint seen in the strength and automatic nature of the predispositions human beings display while developing this behavior.

Let me now rephrase the central proposition in a somewhat stronger and more interesting form: if the genetic components of human nature did not originate by natural selection, fundamental evolutionary theory is in trouble. At the very least the theory of evolution would have to be altered to account for a new and as yet unimagined form of genetic change in popula- tions. Consequently, an auxiliary goal of human sociobiology is to learn whether the evolution of human nature conforms to conventional evolutionary theory. The possibility that the effort will fail conveys to more adventurous biologists a not unpleasant whiff of grapeshot, a crackle of thin ice.

We can be fairly certain that most of the genetic evolution of human social behavior occurred over the five million years prior to civilization, when the species consisted of sparse, relatively immobile populations of hunter-gatherers. On the other hand, by far the greater part of cultural evolution has occurred since the origin of agriculture and cities approx- imately 10,000 years ago. Although genetic evolution of some kind continued during this latter, historical sprint, it cannot have fashioned more than a tiny fraction of the traits of human nature. Otherwise surviving hunter-gatherer people would differ genetically to a significant degree from people in advanced industrial nations, but this is demonstrably not the case. It follows that human sociobiology can be most directly tested in studies of hunter-gatherer soci- eties and the most persistent preliterate herding and agricultural societies. As a result, anthro- pology rather than sociology or economics is the social science closest to sociobiology. It is in anthropology that the genetic theory of human nature can be most directly pursued.

The power of a scientific theory is measured by its ability to transform a small number of axiomatic ideas into detailed predictions of observable phenomena; thus the Bohr atom made modern chemistry possible, and modern chemistry recreated cell biology. Further, the validity of a theory is measured by the extent to which its predictions successfully compete with other theories in accounting for the phenomena; the solar system of Copernicus won over that of Ptolemy, after a brief struggle. Finally, a theory waxes in influence and esteem among scientists as it assembles an ever larger body of facts into readily remembered and usable explanatory schemes, and as newly discovered facts conform to its demands: the round earth is more plausible than a flat one. Facts crucial to the advancement of science can be obtained either by experiments designed for the purpose of acquiring them or from the inspired observation of undisturbed natural phenomena. Science has always progressed in approximately this opportunistic, zig-zagging manner.

In the case of the theory of the genetic evolution of human nature, if it is ever to be made part of real science, we should be able to select some of the best principles from ecology and genetics, which are themselves based on the theory, and adapt them in detail to human social organization. The theory must not only account for many of the known facts in a more convincing manner than traditional explanations, but must also identify the need for new kinds of information previously unimagined by the social sciences. The behavior thus explained should he the most general and least rational of the human repertoire, the part furthest removed from the influence of day-to-day reflection and the distracting vicissitudes of culture. In other words, they should implicate innate, biological phenomena that are the least susceptible to mimicry by culture.

These are stern requirements to impose on the infant discipline of human sociobiology, but they can be adequately justified. Sociobiology intrudes into the social sciences with credentials from the natural sciences and, initially an unfair psychological advantage. If the ideas and analytical methods of "hard" science can be made to work in a congenial and enduring manner, the division between the two cultures of science and the humanities will close. But if our conception of human nature is to be altered, it must be by means of truths conforming to the canons of scientific evidence and not a new dogma however devoutly wished for.

Incest taboos are among the universals of human social behavior. The avoidance of sexual intercourse between brothers and sisters and between parents and their offspring is everywhere achieved by cultural sanctions. But at least in the case of the brother-sister taboo, there exists a far deeper, less rational form of enforcement: a sexual aversion automatically develops between persons who have lived together when one or all grew to the age of six. Studies in Israeli kibbutzim, the most thorough of which was conducted by Joseph Shepher of the University of Haifa, have shown that the aversion among people of the same age is not dependent on an actual blood relationship. Among 2,769 marriages recorded, none was between members of the same kibbutz peer group who had been together since birth. There was not even a single recorded instance of heterosexual activity, despite the fact that the kibbutzim adults were not opposed to it. Where incest of any form does occur at low frequencies in less closed societies, it is ordinarily a source of shame and recrimination. In general, mother-son intercourse is the most offensive, brother-sister intercourse somewhat less and father-daughter intercourse the least offensive. But all forms are usually proscribed. In the United States at the present time, one of the forms of pornography considered most shocking is the depiction of intercourse between fathers and their immature daughters.

What advantage do the incest taboos confer? A favored explanation among anthropologists is that the taboos preserve the integrity of the family by avoiding the confusion in roles that would result from incestuous sex. Another, originated by Edward Tylor and built into a whole anthropological theory by Claude Lévi-Strauss in his seminal *Les Structures Elémentaires de la Parenté*, is that it facilitates the exchange of women during bargaining between social groups. Sisters and daughters, in this view, are not used for mating but to gain power.

In contrast, the prevailing sociobiological explanation regards family integration and bridal bargaining as by-products or at most as secondary contributing factors. It identifies a deeper, more urgent cause, the heavy physiological penalty imposed by inbreeding. Several studies by human geneticists have demonstrated that even a moderate amount of inbreeding results in children who are diminished in overall body size, muscular coordination, and academic performance. More than one hundred recessive genes have been discovered that cause hereditary disease in the undiluted, homozygous state, a condition vastly enhanced by inbreeding. One analysis of American and French populations produced the estimate that each person carries an average of four lethal gene equivalents; either four genes that cause death outright when in the homozygous state, eight genes that cause death in fifty percent of homozygotes, or other, arithmetically equivalent combinations of lethal and debilitating effects. These high numbers, which are typical of animal species, mean that inbreeding carries a deadly risk. Among 161 children born to Czechoslovakian women who had sexual relations with their fathers, brothers, or sons, fifteen were stillborn or died within the first year of life, and more than 40 percent suffered from various physical and mental defects, including severe mental retardation, dwarfism, heart and brain deformities, deaf-mutism, enlargement of the colon, and urinary-tract abnormalities. In contrast, a group of ninety-five children born to the same women through nonincestuous relations were on the average as normal as the population at large. Five died during the first year of life, none had serious mental deficiencies, and only five others had apparent physical abnormalities.

The manifestations of inbreeding pathology constitute natural selection in an intense and unambiguous form. The elementary theory of population genetics predicts that any behavioral

tendency to avoid incest, however slight or devious, would long ago have spread through human populations. So powerful is the advantage of outbreeding that it can be expected to have carried cultural evolution along with it. Family integrity and leverage during political bargaining may indeed be felicitous results of outbreeding, but they are more likely to be devices of convenience, secondary cultural adaptations that made use of the inevitability of outbreeding for direct biological reasons.

Of the thousands of societies that have existed through human history, only several of the most recent have possessed any knowledge of genetics. Very few opportunities presented themselves to make rational calculations of the destructive effects of inbreeding. Tribal councils do not compute gene frequencies and mutational loads. The automatic exclusion of sexual bonding between individuals who have previously formed certain other kinds of relationships—the "gut feeling" that promotes the ritual sanctions against incest—is largely unconscious and irrational. Bond exclusion of the kind displayed by the Israeli children is an example of what biologists call a proximate (near) cause; in this instance, the direct psychological exclusion is the proximate cause of the incest taboo. The ultimate cause suggested by the biological hypothesis is the loss of genetic fitness that results from incest. It is a fact that incestuously produced children leave fewer descendants. The biological hypothesis states that individuals with a genetic predisposition for bond exclusion and incest avoidance contribute more genes to the next generation. Natural selection has probably ground away along these lines for thousands of generations, and for that reason human beings intuitively avoid incest through the simple, automatic rule of bond exclusion. To put the idea in its starkest form, one that acknowledges but temporarily bypasses the intervening developmental process, human beings are guided by an instinct based on genes. Such a process is indicated in the case of brother-sister intercourse, and it is a strong possibility in the other categories of incest taboo.

Hypergamy is the female practice of marrying men of equal or greater wealth and status. In human beings and most kinds of social animals, it is the females who move upward through their choice of mates. Why this sexual bias? The vital clue has been provided by Robert L. Trivers and Daniel F. Willard in the course of more general work in sociobiology. They noted that in vertebrate animals generally, and especially birds and mammals, large, healthy males mate at a relatively high frequency while many smaller, weaker males do not mate at all. Yet nearly all females mate successfully. It is further true that females in the best physical condition produce the healthiest infants, and these offspring usually grow up to be the largest, most vigorous adults. Trivers and Willard then observed that according to the theory of natural selection females should be expected to give birth to a higher proportion of males when they are healthiest, because these offspring will be largest in size, mate most successfully, and produce the maximum number of offspring. As the condition of the females deteriorates, they should shift progressively to the production of daughters, since female offspring will now represent the safer investment. According to natural-selection theory, genes that induce this reproductive strategy will spread through the population at the expense of genes that promote alternative strategies.

It works. In deer and human beings, two of the species investigated with reference to this particular question, environmental conditions adverse for pregnant females are associated with a disproportionate increase in the birth of daughters. Data from mink, pigs, sheep, and seals also appear to be consistent with the Trivers-Willard prediction. The most likely direct mechanism is the selectively greater mortality of male fetuses under adversity, a phenomenon that has been documented in numerous species of mammals.

Let me now try to answer the important but delicate question of how much social behavior varies genetically *within* the human species. The fact that human behavior still has structure based on physiology and is mammalian in its closest affinities suggests that it has been subject to genetic evolution until recently. If that is true, genetic variation affecting behavior might even have persisted into the era of civilization. But this is not to say that such variation now exists.

Two possibilities are equally conceivable. The first is that in reaching its present state the human species exhausted its genetic variability. One set of human genes affecting social behavior, and one set only, survived the long trek through prehistory. This is the view implicitly favored by many social scientists and, within the spectrum of political ideologies that address such questions, by many intellectuals of the left. Human beings once evolved, they concede, but only to the point of becoming a uniform, language-speaking, culture-bearing species. By historical times mankind had become magnificent clay in the hands of the environment. Only cultural evolution can now occur. The second possibility is that at least some genetic variation still exists. Mankind might have ceased evolving, in the sense that the old biological mode of natural selection has relaxed its grip, but the species remains capable of both genetic and cultural evolution.

The reader should note that either possibility—complete cultural determination versus shared cultural and genetic determination of variability within the species—is compatible with the more general sociobiological view of human nature, namely that the most diagnostic features of human behavior evolved by natural selection and are today constrained throughout the species by particular sets of genes.

These possibilities having been laid out in such a textbook fashion. I must now add that the evidence is strong that a substantial fraction of human behavioral variation is based on genetic differences among individuals. There are undeniably mutations affecting behavior. Of these changes in the chemical composition of genes or the structure and arrangement of chromosomes, more than thirty have been identified that affect behavior, some by neurological disorders, others by the impairment of intelligence. One of the most controversial but informative examples is the XYY male. The X and Y chromosomes determine sex in human beings; the XX combination produces a female, XY a male. Approximately 0.1 percent of the population accidentally acquires an extra Y chromosome at the moment of conception, and these XYY individuals are all males. The XYY males grow up to be tall men, the great majority over six feet. They also end up more frequently in prisons and hospitals for the criminally insane. At first it was thought that the extra chromosome induced more aggressive behavior, creating what is in effect a class of genetic criminals. However, a statistical study, by Princeton psychologist Herman A. Witkin and his associates, of vast amounts of data from Denmark has led to a more benign interpretation. XYY men were found neither to be more aggressive than normal nor to display any particular behavior pattern distinguishing them from the remainder of the Danish population. The only deviation detected was a lower average intelligence. The most parsimonious explanation is that XYY men are incarcerated at a higher rate because they are simply less adroit at escaping detection. However, caution is required. The possibility of the inheritance of more specific forms of predisposition toward a criminal personality has not been excluded by this one study.

In fact, mutations have been identified that do alter specific features of behavior. Turner's syndrome, occurring when only one of the two X chromosomes is passed on, entails not just a lowered general intelligence but a particularly deep impairment in the ability to recall shapes and to orient between the left and right on maps and other diagrams. The Lesch-Nyhan syndrome, induced by a single recessive gene, causes both lowered intelligence and a compulsive tendency to pull and tear at the body, resulting in

self-mutilation. The victims of these and other genetic disorders, like the severely mentally retarded, provide extraordinary opportunities for a better understanding of human behavior. The form of analysis by which they can be most profitably studied is called genetic dissection. Once a condition appears, despite medical precautions, it can be examined closely in an attempt to pinpoint the altered portion of the brain and to implicate hormones and other chemical agents that mediated the change without, however, physically touching the brain. Thus by the malfunctioning of its parts the machine can be diagrammed. And let us not fall into the sentimentalist trap of calling that procedure cold-blooded; it is the surest way to find a medical cure for the conditions themselves.

Most mutations strong enough to be analyzed as easily as the Turner and Lesch-Nyhan anomalies also cause defects and illnesses. This is as true in animals and plants as it is in human beings, and is entirely to be expected. To understand why, consider the analogy of heredity with the delicate construction of a watch. If a watch is altered by randomly shaking or striking it, as the body's chemistry is randomly transformed by a mutation, the action is far more likely to impair than to improve the accuracy of the watch.

This set of strong examples, however, leaves unanswered the question of the genetic variation and evolution of "normal" social behavior. As a rule, traits as complex as human behavior are influenced by many genes, each of which shares only a small fraction of the total control. These "polygenes" cannot ordinarily be identified by detecting and tracing the mutations that alter them. They must be evaluated indirectly by statistical means. The most widely used method in the genetics of human behavior is the comparison of pairs of identical twins with pairs of fraternal twins. Identical twins originate in the womb from a single fertilized ovum. The two cells produced by the first division of the ovum do not stick together to produce the beginnings of the fetus but instead separate to produce the beginnings of two fetuses. Because the twins originated from the same cell, bearing a single nucleus and set of chromosomes, they are genetically identical. Fraternal twins, in contrast, originate from separate ova that just happen to travel into the reproductive tracts and to be fertilized by different sperm at the same time. They produce fetuses genetically no closer to one another than are brothers or sisters born in different years.

Identical and fraternal twins provide us with a natural controlled experiment. The control is the set of pairs of identical twins: any differences between the members of a pair must be due to the environment (barring the very rare occurrence of a brand-new mutation). Differences between the members of a pair of fraternal twins can be due to their heredity, their environment, or to some interaction between their heredity and environment. If in a given trait, such as height or nose shape, identical twins prove to be closer to one another on the average than are fraternal twins of the same sex, the difference between the two kinds of twins can be taken as prima facie evidence that the trait is influenced to some degree by heredity. Using this method, geneticists have implicated heredity in the formation of a variety of traits that affect social relationships: number ability, word fluency, memory, the timing of language acquisition, spelling, sentence construction, perceptual skill, psychomotor skill, extroversion-introversion, homosexuality, the age of first sexual activity, and certain forms of neurosis and psychosis, including manic-depressive behavior and schizophrenia.

There is a catch in these results that render them less than definitive. Identical twins are regularly treated alike by their parents, more so than fraternal twins. They are more frequently dressed alike, kept together for longer times, fed the same way, and so on. Thus in the absence of other information it is possible that the greater similarity of identical twins could, after all, be due to the environment. However, there exist new, more sophisticated techniques that can take account of this additional factor. Such a refinement was employed by the psychologists John C. Lochlin and Robert C. Nichols in their analysis of the backgrounds and performances of 850 sets of twins who took the National Merit Scholarship test in 1962. Not only the differences between identical and fraternal twins, but also the early environments of all the subjects were carefully examined and weighed. The results showed that the generally closer treatment of identical twins is not enough to account for their greater similarity in general abilities, personality traits, or even ideals, goals, and vocational interests. The conclusion to be drawn is that either the similarities are based in substantial part on genetic closeness, or else environmental factors were at work that remained hidden to the psychologists.

My overall impression of the existing information is that *Homo sapiens* is a conventional animal species with reference to the quality and magnitude of the genetic diversity affecting its behavior. If the comparison is correct, the psychic unity of mankind has been reduced in status from a dogma to a testable hypothesis.

I also believe that it will soon be within our power to identify many of the genes that influence behavior. Thanks largely to advances in techniques that identify minute differences in the chemical products prescribed by genes, our knowledge of the fine details of human heredity has grown steeply during the past twenty years. In 1977 the geneticists Victor McKusick and Francis Ruddle reported in *Science* that twelve hundred genes had been distinguished; of these, the position of 210 had been pinpointed to a particular chromosome, and at least one gene had been located on each of the twenty-three pairs of chromosomes. Most of the genes ultimately affect anatomical and biochemical traits having minimal influence on behavior. Yet some do affect behavior in important ways, and a few of the behavioral mutations have been closely linked to known biochemical changes. Also, subtle behavioral controls are known that incorporate alterations in levels of hormones and transmitter substances acting directly on nerve cells. The recently discovered enkephalins and endorphins are protein-like substances of relatively simple structure that can profoundly affect mood and temperament. A single mutation altering the chemical nature of one or more of them might change the personality of the person bearing it, or at least the predisposition of the person to develop one personality as opposed to another in a given cultural surrounding. Thus it is possible, and in my judgment even probable, that the positions of genes having indirect effects on the most complex forms of behavior will soon be mapped on the human chromosomes. These genes are unlikely to prescribe particular patterns of behavior; there will be no mutations for a particular sexual practice or mode of dress. The behavioral genes more probably influence the ranges of the form and intensity of emotional responses, the thresholds of arousals, the readiness to learn certain stimuli as opposed to others, and the pattern of sensitivity to additional environmental factors that point cultural evolution in one direction as opposed to another.

It is of equal interest to know whether even "racial" differences in behavior occur. But first I must issue a strong caveat, because this is the most emotionally explosive and politically dangerous of all subjects. Most biologists and anthropologists use the expression "racial" only loosely, and they mean to imply nothing more than the observation that certain traits, such as average height or skin color, vary genetically from one locality to another. If Asians and Europeans are said to differ from one another in a given property, the statement means that the trait changes in some pattern between Asia and Europe. It does not imply that discrete "races" can be defined on the basis of the trait, and it leaves open a strong possibility that the trait shows additional variation within different parts of Asia and Europe. Furthermore, various properties in anatomy and physiology—for example, skin color and the ability to digest milk—display widely differing patterns of geographical ("racial") variation. As a consequence most scientists have long recognized that it is a futile exercise to try to define discrete human races. Such entities do not in fact exist. Of equal importance, the description of geographical variation in one trait or another by a biologist or anthropologist or anyone else should not carry with it value judgments concerning the worth of the characteristics defined.

Now we are prepared to ask in a more fully objective manner: Does geographical variation occur in the genetic basis of social behavior? The evidence is strong that almost all differences between human societies are based on learning and social conditioning rather than on heredity. And yet perhaps not quite all. Daniel G. Freedman, a psychologist at the University of Chicago, has addressed this question with a series of studies on the behavior of newborn infants of several racial origins. He has detected significant average differences in locomotion, posture, muscular tone of various parts of the body, and emotional response that cannot reasonably be explained as the result of training or even conditioning within the womb. Chinese-American newborns, for example, tend to be less changeable, less easily perturbed by noise and movement, better able to adjust to new stimuli and discomfort, and quicker to calm themselves than Caucasian-American infants. To use a more precise phrasing, it can be said that a random sample of infants whose ancestors originated in certain parts of China differ in these behavioral traits from a comparable sample of European ancestry.

There is also some indication that the average differences carry over into childhood. One of Freedman's students, Nova Green, found that Chinese-American children in Chicago nursery schools spent less of their time in approach and interaction with playmates and more time on individual projects than did their European-American counterparts. They also displayed interesting differences in temperament:

Although the majority of the Chinese-American children were in the "high arousal age," between 3 and 5, they showed little intense emotional behavior. They ran and hopped, laughed and called to one another, rode bikes and roller-skated just as the children did in the other nursery schools, but the noise level stayed remarkably low and the emotional atmosphere projected serenity instead of bedlam. The impassive facial expression certainly gave the children an air of dignity and self-possession, but this was only one element affecting the total impression. Physical movements seemed more coordinated, no tripping, falling, bumping or bruising was observed, no screams, crashes or wailing was heard, not even that common sound in other nurseries, voices raised in highly indignant moralistic dispute! No property disputes were observed and only the mildest version of "fighting behavior," some good natured wrestling among the older boys.

Navaho infants tested by Freedman and his coworkers were even more quiescent than the Chinese infants. When lifted erect and pulled forward they were less inclined to swing their legs in a walking motion; when put in a sitting position, their backs curved; and when placed on their stomachs, they made fewer attempts to crawl. It has been conventional to ascribe the passivity of Navaho children to the practice of cradleboarding, a device that holds the infant tightly in place on the mother's back. But Freedman suggests that the reverse may actually be true: the relative quiescence of Navaho babies, a trait that is apparent from birth onward, allows them to be carried in a confining manner. Cradleboarding represents a workable compromise between cultural invention and infant constitution.

Given that humankind is a biological species, it should come as no shock to find that populations are to some extent genetically diverse in the physical and mental properties underlying social behavior. A discovery of this nature does not vitiate the ideals of Western civilization. We are not compelled to believe in biological uniformity in order to affirm human freedom and dignity. The sociologist Marvin Bressler has expressed this idea with precision: "An ideology that tacitly appeals to biological equality as a condition for human emancipation corrupts the idea of freedom. Moreover, it encourages decent men to tremble at the prospect of 'inconvenient' findings that may emerge in future scientific research. This unseemly anti-intellectualism is doubly degrading because it is probably unnecessary."

I will go further and suggest that hope and pride and not despair are the ultimate legacy of genetic diversity, because we are a single species, not two or more, one great breeding system through which genes flow and mix in each generation. Because of that flux, mankind viewed over many generations shares a single human nature within which relatively minor hereditary influences recycle through ever changing patterns, between the sexes and across families and entire populations. To understand the enormous significance of this biological unity, imagine our moral distress if australopithecine man-apes had survived to the present time, halfway in intelligence between chimpanzees and human beings, forever genetically separated from both, evolving just behind us in language and the higher faculties of reason. What would be our obligation to them? What would the theologians say—or the Marxists, who might see in them the ultimate form of an oppressed class? Should we divide the world, guide their mental evolution to the human level, and establish a two-species dominion based on a treaty of intellectual and technological parity? Should we make certain they rose no higher? But even worse, imagine our predicament if we coexisted with a mentally superior human species, say *Homo superbus*, who regarded us, the minor sibling species *Homo sapiens*, as the moral problem.

Chapter 2

David L. Hull

ON HUMAN NATURE

Generations of philosophers have argued that all human beings are essentially the same, that is, they share the same nature, and that this essential similarity is extremely important. Periodically philosophers have proposed to base the essential sameness of human beings on biology. In this paper I argue that if "biology" is taken to refer to the technical pronouncements of professional biologists, in particular evolutionary biologists, it is simply not true that all organisms that belong to Homo sapiens as a biological species are essentially the same. If "characters" is taken to refer to evolutionary homologies, then periodically a biological species might be characterized by one or more characters which are both universally distributed among and limited to the organisms belonging to that species, but such states of affairs are temporary, contingent, and relatively rare. In most cases, any character universally distributed among the organisms belonging to a particular species is also possessed by organisms belonging to other species, and conversely any character that happens to be limited to the organisms belonging to a particular species is unlikely to be possessed by all of them.

The natural move at this juncture is to argue that the properties which characterize biological species at least "cluster." Organisms belong to a particular biological species because they possess enough of the relevant properties or enough of the more important relevant properties. Such

unimodal clusters do exist, and might well count as "statistical natures," but in most cases the distributions that characterize biological species are multimodal, depending on the properties studied. No matter how desperately one wants to construe biological species as natural kinds characterizable by some sort of "essences" or "natures," such multimodal distributions simply will not do. To complicate matters further, these clusters of properties, whether uni- or multi-modal, change through time. A character state (or allele) which is rare may become common, and one that is nearly universal may become entirely eliminated. In short, species evolve, and to the extent that they evolve through natural selection, both genetic and phenotypic variation are essential. Which particular variations a species exhibits is a function of both the fundamental regularities which characterize selection processes and numerous historical contingencies. However, variation as such is hardly an accidental characteristic of biological species. Without it, evolution would soon grind to a halt. *Which* variations characterize a particular species is to a large extent accidental; *that* variation characterizes species as such is not.

The preceding characterization depends on the existence of a criterion for individuating species in addition to character covariation. If species are taken to be the things which evolve, then they can and must be characterized in terms of ancestor-descendant relations, and in sexual species these relations depend on mating. The organisms that comprise sexual species form complex networks of mating and reproduction. Any organism that is part of such a network belongs to that species even if the characters it exhibits are atypical or in some sense aberrant. Conversely, an organism that happens to exhibit precisely the same characters as an organism belonging to a particular species might not itself belong to that species. Genealogy and character covariation are not perfectly coincident, and when they differ, genealogy takes precedence. The priority of genealogy to character covariation is not negated by the fact that species periodically split or bud off additional species. To the extent that speciation is "punctuational," such periods will be short and involve only a relatively few organisms, but inherent in species as genealogical entities is the existence of periods during which particular organisms do not belong unequivocally to one species or another. *Homo sapiens* currently is not undergoing one of these periods. The genealogical boundaries of our species are extremely sharp. The comparable boundaries in character space are a good deal fuzzier. As a result, those who view character covariation as fundamental and want our species to be clearly distinguishable from other species accordingly are forced to resort to embarrassing conceptual contortions to include retardates, dyslexics, and the like in our species while keeping bees and computers out.

The preceding observations about species in general and *Homo sapiens* in particular frequently elicit considerable consternation. Biological species cannot possibly have the characteristics that biologists claim that they do. There must be characteristics which all and only people exhibit, or at least *potentially* exhibit, or which all *normal* people exhibit—at least potentially. I continue to remain dismayed at the vehemence with which these views are expressed in the absence of any explicitly formulated biological foundations for these notions. In this paper I argue that

biological species, including our own, do have the character claimed by evolutionary biologists and that attempts to argue away this state of affairs by reference to "potentiality" and "normality" have little if any foundation in biology. Perhaps numerous ordinary conceptions exist in which an organism that lacks the genetic information necessary to produce a particular enzyme nevertheless possesses this enzyme potentially. I am equally sure that there are conceptions of normality according to which worker bees are abnormal. But these ordinary conceptions have no foundation in biology as a technical discipline. To make matters even worse, I do not see why the existence of human universals is all that important. Perhaps all and only people have apposable thumbs, use tools, live in true societies, or what have you. I think that such attributions are either false or vacuous, but even if they were true and significant, the distributions of these particular characters is largely a matter of evolutionary happenstance. I for one would be extremely uneasy to base something as important as human rights on such temporary contingencies. Given the character of the evolutionary process, it is extremely unlikely that all human beings are essentially the same, but even if we are, I fail to see why it matters. I fail to see, for example, why we must all be essentially the same to have rights.

To repeat, in my discussion of human nature, I am taking "human" to refer to a particular biological species. This term has numerous other meanings which have little or nothing to do with DNA, meiosis, and what have you. Nothing that I say should be taken to imply anything about ordinary usage, commonsense conceptions, or what "we" are inclined to say or not to say. In particular I am not talking about "persons." The context of this paper is biology as a scientific discipline. Within biology itself several different species concepts can also be found. I am concerned only with those doctrines which claim to be based on the nature of *Homo sapiens* as a biological species. Those authors who are not interested in what biologists have to say about biological species or who are content with conceptual pluralism for the sake of conceptual pluralism will find nothing of interest in this paper.

Universality and Variability

All concepts are to some extent malleable and data can always be massaged, but in some areas both activities are more narrowly constrained than in others. For example, it is much harder to argue for genetic than for cultural universals because the identity of alleles is easier to establish than the identity of cultural practices. However, if biological species are characterized by a particular sort of genetic variability, then one might be justified in exposing claims that cultural traits are immune to a similar variability to closer scrutiny. I certainly do not mean to imply by the preceding statement that I think that cultural variability is in any sense caused by genetic variability. Rather, the reason for introducing the topic of genetic variability is that geneticists have been forced to acknowledge it in the face of considerable resistance, the same sort of resistance that confronts comparable claims about cultural variability. If there are any cultural universals, one of them is surely a persistent distaste for variability. But if genetic variability characterizes species even though everyone is absolutely certain that it does not, then possibly a similar variability characterizes cultures even though the parallel conviction about cultures is, if anything, stronger.

For example, Kaplan and Manners remark that a

> number of anthropologists have even attempted to compile lists of universal cultural characteristics. Presumably such cultural universals reflect in some sense the uniform psychological nature of man. But the search for cultural universals has

invariably yielded generalizations of a very broad, and sometimes not particularly illuminating nature—such as, all cultures prefer health to illness; or, all cultures make some institutional provision for feeding their members; or, all cultures have devices for maintaining internal order.[1]

Massive evidence can be presented to refute the claim that all human beings have essentially the same blood type. A parallel response to the claim that all cultures prefer health to illness is more difficult because of the plasticity of such terms as "health" and "illness." My argument is analogical. Both population geneticists and anthropologists have been strongly predisposed to discount variability. Genetics is sufficiently well developed that geneticists have been forced to acknowledge how variable both genes and traits are, both within species and between them. The social sciences are not so well developed. Hence, it is easier for them to hold fast to their metaphysical preferences.

One reason for anthropologists searching so assiduously for cultural universals is the mistaken belief that some connection exists between universality and innateness. For example, in a paper on the *human* nature of human nature, Eisenberg states that "one trait common to man everywhere is language; in the sense that only the human species displays it, the capacity to acquire language must be genetic."[2] In the space of a very few words, Eisenberg elides from language being common to man everywhere (universality), to the capacity to acquire language being unique to the human species (species specificity), to its being genetic. Human language is not universally distributed among human beings. Some human beings neither speak nor understand anything that might be termed a "language." In some sense such people might not be "truly" human, but they still belong to the same biological species as the rest of us. Among these people, some may be incapable of acquiring language because they lack the necessary neural equipment, and in some cases this state of affairs is straight-forwardly genetic. They are potential language users in the sense that if they had a different genetic make-up and were exposed to the appropriate sequences of environments, then they would have been able to acquire language skills similar to those possessed by the rest of us. But this same contrary-to-fact conditional can be applied to other species as well. In this same sense, chimpanzees possess the capacity to acquire language.

Conversely, any attempt to define language use in such a way as to exclude the abilities of other species results in an even larger percentage of the human race being denied this capacity as well. But regardless of the actual distribution of language use or the capacity for language use, nothing is implied about any "genetic basis" for language capacity. Blood type in human beings is about as genetic as any trait can be and yet it is extremely variable. Blood type can be made universal among human beings only by defining it in terms of having some blood type or other—a disjunctive character. For example, at the ABO locus, four different types exist: A, B, AB, and O. Hence, all people have the same blood-type at this locus just in case they have one of these types. If one of these alleles were to be lost or another to crop up, the disjunction need only be contracted or expanded accordingly. This strategy is universality made easy. However, it should be noted that even if this all-purpose strategy were adopted, these disjunctively-characterized traits have a temporal dimension.

Except in the preceding vacuous sense, blood type in human beings is anything but universal. Different people have different blood types, and the combinations of these blood types vary in different populations. An allele which is common in one population may be rare in another, and vice versa. But, one might complain, there must be some blood type which is at least prevalent among the human race. Sometimes certain alleles are widely distributed. In other cases no allele even reaches the fifty percent level. At the ABO locus the frequencies are A (0.447), B (0.082), AB (0.034), and O (0.437) among the white population in England. However, at the MNS locus for this same population, the frequency of the most common genotype is only 0.260. Of course, these frequencies are quite different in other populations, such as Basques and Navahos. Yet blood types is as genetic as any trait can get.

To complicate matters even further, the allelic frequencies at the dozen or so loci known to influence blood type vary independently of each other. Given the most common genotype at each of these loci, only one-fifth of one percent of the world's population is likely to possess the most common genotype at all of these loci (Lewontin 1982). In short, if blood type has anything to do with human nature, only one person in 500 is truly human. However, blood type is hardly the sort of character which advocates of human nature are likely to emphasize. In order to be human, people must be capable of rationality, lying, feeling guilty, laughing, etc. And these characters are both unique to and universally distributed among human beings. Once again, our application of these terms tends to be so selective that it is impossible to say. Those who insist on the uniqueness of humankind dismiss anything that organisms belonging to other species do or do not do with considerable ease. Although an ape might succeed in solving problems that many human beings cannot solve, in no way can these primates be said to "think." The traits (and genes) which characterize all species save our own vary statistically. For some reason those characters which make us what we truly are happen to be universally distributed among all members of our species (at least potentially among normal human beings) and absent in all other species. I find this coincidence highly suspicious.

One reason for insisting on the existence of cultural universals is the mistaken belief that universally distributed characters are liable to have a more determinate genetic basis than those that are distributed in more complex patterns. Another is the desire to formulate laws using these cultural universals. Kinds are easy enough to come by. The difficult task is to discover kinds which function in natural regularities. Even if we grant anthropologists their cultural universals, nothing yet has come of them. In response to the preceding sorts of considerations, Gould complains of "our relentless search for human universals and our excitement at the prospect that we may thereby unlock something at the core of our being."[3] If evolutionary theory has anything to teach us it is that variability is at the core of our being. Because we are a biological species and variability is essential to biological species, the traits which characterize us are likely to vary, our own essentialist compulsions notwithstanding (see also Dupré 1986).

To repeat, some properties may characterize all human beings throughout the existence of our species. After all, we all have some mass or other, but possessing mass can hardly fulfill the traditional functions assigned to human nature because it characterizes all species, not just our own. Some traits may also be unique to our species at the moment, though possibly not universal. For example, we can successfully mate only with other human beings, although a surprisingly high percentage of human beings are sterile. They cannot have been able to mate successfully with an organism belonging to another species. Some mate with other members of our own species. But for several million years, no one has been able to mate successfully with an organism belonging to another species. Some combination or combinations of traits must be responsible for this reproductive gap. But once again, these traits are not likely to fulfill the traditional functions of human nature. If all and only human beings were able to digest Nutrasweet, this ability would still not be a very good candidate for the property which makes us peculiarly human.

Potentiality and Normality

Most phenotypic traits are highly variable both within and between species. In some species there is more intraspecific variation than interspecific variation. Reverting to the genetic level does not help. In fact, it only reaffirms the preceding observations. Zebras and horses look very much alike, but genetically they are quite different. Human beings and chimpanzees look quite different, but genetically we are almost identical. On one estimate, 30% of the genes at loci which code for structural genes in human beings are polymorphic, and in any one individual roughly 7% of the loci are heterozygous, while human beings differ from chimpanzees at only 3% of loci. The usual response to these and other observations about patterns of phenotypic and genetic variability within and between species is to discount them. What do biologists know about biology? Organisms that lack a particular trait actually possess it potentially or else are abnormal for not possessing it.

Sometimes the claim that an organism which lacks a trait nevertheless possesses the capacity for such a trait makes sense. Reaction norms are frequently quite broad. In a variety of environments organisms with a particular genotype exhibit character C, in others C', in others, C'', and so on. They have what it takes to exhibit any one of these character states depending on the environments which they confront. For example, on rare occasions children are raised in near total social isolation until adulthood. As a result they cannot speak or understand any human language, nor can they at this late date be taught one. At one time they had the potentiality for language use but now lack it. On equally rare occasions babies are born with little in the way of a cerebrum. If there is a significant sense in which they nevertheless retain the potentiality for language use, it eludes me. Perhaps such unfortunates are not persons, but they belong unproblematically to *Homo sapiens* as a biological species. Similar observations hold for every other characteristic suggested for distinguishing human beings from other species, whether that characteristic be biochemical, morphological, psychological, social or cultural. In this respect rationality is no different from apposable thumbs.

The more usual way to discount the sort of variation so central to the evolutionary process is to dismiss it as "abnormal." Normality is a very slippery notion. It also has had a long history of abuse. Responsible authorities in the past have argued in all sincerity that other races are degenerate forms of the Caucasian race, that women are just incompletely formed men, and that homosexuals are merely deviant forms of heterosexuals. The normal state for human beings is to be white, male heterosexuals. All others do not participate fully in human nature. That white, male heterosexuals make-up only a small minority of the human race did not give these authorities pause. But the failings of past generations are always easier to see than our own. Few responsible people today are willing to argue in print that blacks are abnormal whites or that women are abnormal men, but it seems quite natural to most of us to consider homosexuals abnormal heterosexuals. Heterosexuality is the normal state programmed into our genes. It needs no special explanation. Normal genes in a wide variety of normal environments lead most children quite naturally to prefer members of the opposite sex for sexual and emotional partners. Homosexuality, to the contrary, is an abnormal deviation which needs to be explained in terms of some combination of defective genes and/or undesirable environments. Such a view is central to several present-day psychological theories. Certainly nothing that a biologist might say about reaction norms, heterozygote superiority or kin selection is liable to dislodge the deeply held intuitions upon which these theories are based—and this is precisely what is wrong with deeply held intuitions.

However, just because a particular notion has been abused in the past, it does not follow that it totally lacks substance. As much of a curse as racism has been and continues to be, biologists are unable to characterize the human species as a homogeneous whole. As a biological species we are seamless but not homogeneous. Various groups of people at a variety of levels of generality exhibit statistical differences. *Homo sapiens* is polytypic. Even so, perhaps one or more biologically respectable notions of "normality" and "abnormality" might be discoverable. The three most common areas of biology in which one might find a significant sense of these notions are embryology, evolutionary biology, and functional morphology.

From conception until death, organisms are exposed to sequences of highly variable environments. The phenotype exhibited by an organism is the result of successive interactions between its genes, current phenotypic make-up and successive environments. The reaction norm for a particular genotype is all possible phenotypes that would result given all possible sequences of environments in which the organism might survive. Needless to say, biologists know very little about the reaction norms for most species, our own included. To estimate reaction norms, biologists must have access to numerous genetically identical zygotes and be able to raise these zygotes in a variety of environments. When they do, the results are endlessly fascinating. Some reaction norms are very narrow, i.e., in any environment in which the organism can develop, it exhibits a particular trait and only that trait. Sometimes reaction norms turn out to be extremely broad. A particular trait can be exhibited in a wide variety of states depending on the environments to which the organism is exposed. Sometimes a reaction norm starts off broad but rapidly becomes quite narrow. Some reaction norms are continuous; others disjunctive. Sometimes most organisms occupy the center of the reaction norm; sometimes they are clustered at either extreme, and so on. Everything that could happen, in some organism or other does happen.

In spite of all the preceding, the conviction is sure to remain that in most cases there must be some normal developmental pathway through which most organisms develop or would develop if presented with the appropriate environment, or something. But inherent in the notion of a reaction norm is alternative pathways. Because environments are so variable in both the short and long term, developmental plasticity is absolutely necessary if organisms are to survive to reproduce. Any organism that can fulfill a need in only one way in only a narrowly proscribed environment is not likely to survive for long. Although there are a few cases in which particular species can fulfill one or two functions in only highly specialized ways, both these species and their specialized functions are relatively rare.

But, one might complain, there must be some significant sense of "normal development." There is a fairly clear sense of "normal development," but it is not very significant. As far as I can see, all it denotes is that developmental pathway with which the speaker is familiar in recent, locally prevalent environments. We find it very difficult to acknowledge that a particular environment which has been common in the recent past may be quite new and "aberrant" given the duration of the species under investigation. Throughout most of its existence, a species may have persisted in very low numbers and only recently boomed to produce high population density, and high population density might well switch increasing numbers of organisms to quite different developmental pathways. During this transition period, we are likely to look back on the old pathway as "normal" and decry the new pathway as "abnormal," but as we get used to the new alternative, just the opposite intuition is likely to prevail. Although the nuclear family is a relatively new social innovation and is rapidly disappearing, to most of us it seems "normal." Any deviation from it is sure to produce humanoids at best.

From the evolutionary perspective, all alleles which we now possess were once more than just rare: they were unique. Evolution is the process by which rare alleles become common, possibly universal, and universally distributed alleles become totally eliminated. If a particular allele must be universally distributed among the organisms belonging to a particular species (or at least widespread) in order to be part of its "nature," then natures are very temporary, variable things. From the human perspective, evolutionary change might seem quite slow. For example, blue eyes have existed in the human species from the earliest recorded times, and yet less than 1% of the people who belong to the human species have blue eyes. Because people with blue eyes can see no better than people with brown eyes, one plausible explanation for the increase of blue eyes in the human population is sexual selection. It might well take thousands of generations for a mutation to replace what was once termed the "wild-type" and become the new "wild type." Early on one allele will surely be considered natural, while later on its replacement will be held with equal certainty to be natural. Human memory is short. From the evolutionary perspective, claims about "normal" genes tend to be sheer prejudice arising from limited experience.

If by "human nature" all one means is a trait which happens to be prevalent and important for the moment, then human nature surely exists. Each species exhibits adaptations, and these adaptations are important for its continued existence. One of our most important adaptations is our ability to play the knowledge game. It is important that enough of us play this game well enough because our species is not very good at anything else. But this adaptation may not have characterized us throughout our existence and may not continue to characterize us in the future. Biologically we will remain the same species, the same lineage, even though we lose our "essence." It should also be kept in mind that some non-humans play the knowledge game better than some humans. If those organisms that are smarter than some people are to be excluded from our species while those people who are not all that capable are kept in, something must be more basic than mental ability in the individuation of our species. Once again, I am discussing *Homo sapiens* as a biological species, not personhood. Although in a higher and more sophisticated sense of "human being" retardates are not human beings, from the crude and pedestrian biological perspective, they are unproblematically human.

The central notion of normality relative to human nature, however, seems to be functional. When people dismiss variation in connection with human nature, they usually resort to functional notions of normality and abnormality. Perhaps someone has produced a minimally adequate analysis of "normal function," but I have yet to see it. As the huge literature on the subject clearly attests, it is difficult enough to give an adequate analysis of "function," let alone "normal function." In general, structures and functions do not map neatly onto each other, nor can they be made to do so. A single structure commonly performs more than one function, and conversely, a single function can be fulfilled by more than one structure. If one individuates structures in terms of functions and function in terms of structures, then the complex mapping of structures and functions can be reduced, possibly eliminated, but only at considerable cost. For example, no matter how one subdivides the human urogenital system, there is no way to work it out so that a particular structure is used for excretion and another structure is used for reproduction. No amount of gerrymandering succeeds without extreme artificiality. Nor has anyone been able to redefine functional limits so that excretion and reproduction turn out to count as a single function.

Like it or not, a single structure can perform more than one function, and one and the same function can be performed by more than one structure. Nor is this an accidental feature of organisms. In evolution, organisms must make do with what they've got. An organ evolved to perform one function might be commandeered to perform another. For example, what is the normal function of the hand? We can do many things with our hands. We can drive cars, play the violin, type on electronic computers, scratch itches, masturbate, and strangle one another. Some of these actions may seem normal; others not, but there is no correlation between commonsense notions of normal functions and the functions which hands were able to fulfill throughout our existence. Any notion of "the function of the hand" which is sufficiently general to capture all the things that we can do with our hands is likely to be all but vacuous and surely will make no cut between normal and abnormal uses. About all a biologist can say about the function of the human hand is that anything that we can do with it is "normal." A more restricted sense of normality must be imported from common sense, society, deeply held intuitions, or systems of morals. Some might argue that this fact merely indicates the poverty of the biological perspective. If so, so be it, but this is the topic of my chapter.

A few additional examples might help to see the huge gap that exists between biological senses of "function" and the various senses of this term as it is used in other contexts. A major topic in the biological literature is the function of sexual reproduction. What is the function of sex? The commonsense answer is reproduction, but this not the answer given by biologists. Biologically, first and foremost, the primary function of sex is to increase genetic heterogeneity. "But that is not what I mean! When I say that the biological function of sex is reproduction, I do not mean 'biological' in the sense that biologists use this term but in some other, more basic sense." Is being sexually neuter functionally normal? Well, it is certainly normal among honey bees. Most honey bees are neuter females. Many species, especially social species, exhibit reproductive strategies that involve some organisms becoming non-reproductives. What counts in biological evolution is inclusive fitness. It is both possible and quite common for organisms to increase their inclusive fitness by not reproducing themselves. "But I am talking about human beings, not honey bees." From the perspective of commonsense biology, human non-reproductives such as old maids and priests may be biologically abnormal, but from the perspective of professional biology, they need not be.

Finally, having blue eyes is abnormal in about every sense one cares to mention. Blue-eyed people are very rare. The inability to produce brown pigment is the result of a defective gene. The alleles which code for the structure of the enzyme which completes the synthesis of the brown pigment found on the surface of the human iris produce an enzyme which cannot perform this function. As far as we know, the enzyme produced performs no other function either. However, as far as sight is concerned, blue eyes are perfectly functional, and as far as sexual selection is concerned downright advantageous. What common sense has to say on these topics, I do not know. My own commonsense estimates about what "we" mean when "we" make judgments on such topics depart so drastically from what analytic philosophers publish on these topics that I hesitate to venture an opinion lest I mark myself as being linguistically abnormal.

Conclusion

Because I have argued so persistently for so long that particular species lack anything that might be termed an "essence," I have gotten the reputation of being totally opposed to essentialism. To the contrary, I am rather old fashioned on this topic (see Dupré 1986 for a more contemporary view). In fact, I think that natural kinds do exist and that they exhibit characters which are severally necessary and jointly sufficient for

membership. More than this, I think that it is extremely important for our understanding of the natural world that such kinds exist. All I want to argue is that natural kinds of this sort are very rare, extremely difficult to discover, and that biological species as evolving lineages do not belong in this category. Just because one thinks that species are not natural kinds, it does not follow that one is committed to the view that there are no natural kinds at all. One misplaced example does not totally invalidate a general thesis.

In fact I think that the species category might very well be a natural kind and that part of its essence is variability. If variability is essential to species, then it follows that the human species should be variable, both genetically and phenotypically, and it is. That *Homo sapiens* exhibits considerable variability is not an accidental feature of our species. Which particular variations we exhibit is largely a function of evolutionary happenstance; the presence of variability itself is not. Nor does it help to switch from traditional essences to statistically characterized essences. If the history of phenetic taxonomy has shown anything, it is that organisms can be subdivided into species as Operational Taxonomic Units in indefinitely many ways if all one looks at is character covariation. Compared to many species, our species is relatively isolated in character space. Perhaps a unimodal distribution of characters might be found which succeeds in placing all human beings in a single species and in keeping all non-humans out. If so, this too would be an evolutionary happenstance and might well change in time.

But why is it so important for the human species to have a nature? One likely answer is to provide a foundation for ethics and morals. If one wants to found ethics on human nature and human nature is to be at least consistent with current biological knowledge, then it follows that the resulting ethical system will be composed largely of contingent claims. The only authors of whom I am aware who acknowledge this state of affairs and are still willing to embrace the consequences that flow from it are Michael Ruse and E. O. Wilson. Ruse and Wilson propose to base ethics on the epigenetic rules of mental development in human beings. They acknowledge that these rules are the

> idiosyncratic products of the genetic history of the species and as such were shaped by particular regimes of natural selection. . . . It follows that the ethical code of one species cannot be translated into that of another. No abstract moral principles exist outside the particular nature of individual species.[4]

Although Ruse and Wilson are willing to grant that morality is "rooted in contingent human nature, through and through," they argue that morals are not relative to the individual human being because human cultures

> tend to converge in their morality in the manner expected when a largely similar array of epigenetic rules meet a largely similar array of behavioural choices. This would not be the case if human beings differed greatly from one another in the genetic basis of their mental development.[5]

The number of genes which influence our mental development have to be at least as large as those that determine blood type. Unless there is evidence to the contrary, the most reasonable hypothesis is that the same sort of variability and multiplicity that characterizes the genes which code for blood type also characterize those genes which code for our mental development. However, perhaps the genetic basis for mental development is a happy exception. Perhaps we all do possess a largely similar array of epigenetic rules based on largely similar genetic make-ups. If so, this too is an accident of our recent evolutionary history, and once again ethics is being based on an evolutionary contingency. Ruse and Wilson agree. Because their

view is empirical, they "do not exclude the possibility that some differences might exist between large groups in the epigenetic rules governing moral awareness."[6]

Although I feel uneasy about founding something as important as ethics and morality on evolutionary contingencies, I must admit that none of the other foundations suggested for morality provides much in the way of a legitimate sense of security either. But my main problem is that I do not see the close connection which everyone else sees between character distributions, admission to the human species, and such things as human rights. Depending on what clustering technique one uses, the human species can be subdivided into a variety of "races." Roughly fifty percent of human beings are male and fifty percent female. The number of intersexes is quite small. Estimates of the percentage of human beings who engage in sexual activity and pair bond exclusively or primarily with members of their own sex vary from five to ten percent. These percentages may vary from society to society and from time to time. I do not see that it matters. All the ingenuity which has been exercised trying to show that all human beings are essentially the same might be better used trying to explain why we must all be essentially the same in order to have such things as human rights. Why must we all be essentially the same in order to have rights? Why cannot people who are essentially different nevertheless have the same rights? Until this question is answered, I remain suspicious of continued claims about the existence and importance of human nature.

Notes

1 Kaplan and Manners 1972, p. 151.
2 Eisenberg 1972, p. 126.
3 Gould 1986, p. 68.
4 Ruse and Wilson 1986, p. 186.
5 Ibid., p. 186.
6 Ibid., p. 188.

References

Dupré, J. (1986) Sex, gender, and essence. *Midwest Studies in Philosophy* 11: 441–457.

Eisenberg, L. (1972) The human nature of human nature. *Science* 176: 123–128.

Gould, S. J. (1986) Evolution and the triumph of homology, or why history matters. *American Scientist* 74: 60–69.

Kaplan, D. and Manners, R. A. (1972) *Culture Theory.* Englewood Cliffs, NJ: Prentice-Hall, Inc.

Lewontin, R. C. (1982). *Human Diversity.* New York: Scientific American Library.

Ruse, M. and Wilson, E. O. (1986) Moral philosophy as applied science: A Darwinian approach to the foundations of ethics. *Philosophy* 61: 173–192.

Chapter 3

David J. Buller

ADAPTING MINDS
Evolutionary Psychology and the Persistent Quest for Human Nature

In what follows I am to engage some broader theoretical issues related to Evolutionary Psychology's advertisement that it is "the new science of human nature."

Some of the theoretical issues examined here are absolutely central to Evolutionary Psychology's claim that there is a universal human nature. That is, the very idea of a universal human nature stands or falls with some of the theoretical arguments considered here. Other theoretical issues engaged are more properly "philosophical," since they concern the broader conceptual framework in which the idea of a universal human nature is situated and interpreted. While these Issues may be less central to Evolutionary Psychology's narrowly focused *scientific project* of discovering universal psychological adaptations and understanding how: they function, they are nonetheless significant. For, in developing and promoting their account of human nature, Evolutionary Psychologists have often endorsed positions on broader philosophical issues, and the positions they've endorsed form part of a widely held, "commonsense" understanding of the idea of human nature. Consequently, it is important to understand both why their philosophical positions are wrong and how those positions help motivate the quest for human nature.

Throughout the discussion of these various theoretical issues, I will be focused on a single theme—that the idea of a universal human nature is deeply antithetical to a truly evolutionary view of our species. Indeed, I will argue, a truly *evolutionary* psychology should abandon the quest for human nature and with it any attempt to discover universal laws of human psychology. As the evolutionary biologist Michael Chiselin so pithily puts it: "What does evolution teach us about human nature? It tells us that human nature is a superstition."[1] In other words, the idea of human nature is an idea whose time has gone.

Human Nature: The Very Idea

Let's begin by examining what it *means* to talk of human nature. One possibility is that the concept of human nature could refer to the totality of human behavior and psychology. In this broad sense, human nature would simply be whatever humans happen to do, think, or feel, regardless of whether different humans do, think, or feel differently. If one person is violent, violence is part of human nature, even if another person is not violent. If one person is kind, kindness is part of human nature, despite another person's inveterate unkindness, which is also part of human nature. In this very broad sense, the concept of human nature has no particular *theoretical* meaning; it is merely an abbreviated way of talking about the rich tapestry of human existence. And, if this is what one means by human nature, no one can quibble about the existence of human nature, since the mere existence of humans guarantees the existence of human nature.

But, traditionally, the concept of human nature has never meant simply *whatever* people happen to do, think, or feel. Regardless of the details of the theory of human nature in which it featured, the concept of human nature has traditionally referred to *some* of the things that people do but not to others, to *some* of the things that people think and feel but not to others. Theories of human nature have differed over precisely which aspects of human behavior and psychology constitute human nature, but they have all used the concept of human nature to pick out only a small part of everything about humanity that meets the eye. That is, regardless of the theory of human nature in which it featured, the concept of human nature has traditionally designated only a proper subset of human behavior and mentation, which was claimed to belong to human beings *by their nature* as opposed to behavior and mentation that was claimed not to be owing to or in accordance with that nature. And there are three noteworthy features of this traditional concept of human nature.

First, the concept of human nature has always refered to what is distinctively human about us, to what distinguishes humans from the other animals on the planet. This aspect of its meaning put the *human* in the concept of human nature, and it is what David Buss alludes to when he writes that "humans also have a nature—*qualities that define us as a unique species.*"[2]

Second, the concept of human nature has typically referred only to *biologically based* behavioral or psychological characteristics of human beings. This aspect of its meaning put the *nature* in the concept of human nature and human *nature* has always been contrasted with human *culture*. As the philosopher Peter Loptson puts it, the characteristic that constitute human nature form a "single unitary nature that humans have, common and generic to all societies they have

formed."[3] These characteristics thus form "a fixed unchangeable nature or 'essence' that human beings have," which "is independent of culture."[4] Accordingly, the characteristics that constitute human nature are a consequence solely of our biological properties, whereas characteristics that result from "socialization" in one's culture are not part of human nature. Eating is part of human nature, since it is a biological function, but using a fork to eat is not part of human nature, since fork users are so only by virtue of having been socialized in fork-using cultures. Thus, in accordance with the traditional concept of human nature, culture has been viewed as an "unnatural" imposition that typically transforms, represses, or corrupts what is biologically "natural" for humans.

Third, the biologically grounded characteristics constitutive of human nature have traditionally been assumed to be *universal* among humans. As the philosopher Roger Trigg expresses it:

> The concept [of human nature] has implications, particularly that we can assume similarities merely on the basis of membership of one biological species. We will then all have some tendencies, and some likes and dislikes, in common simply because of our common humanity.[5]

In sum, then, regardless of the particular theory of human nature in which it featured, the concept of human nature has traditionally designated biologically based, as opposed to culturally instilled, behavioral and psychological characteristics that are presumed to be universal among, and distinctive to, human beings. Because of this, traditional arguments that there is no human nature have tended to emphasize culture over "nature," to argue that humans are what they are principally because of their cultural socialization and that there is no human "nature" that strongly channels or constrains socialization.

Evolutionary Psychology's conception of human nature is but a minor variation on the traditional concept. Evolutionary Psychologists are clearly committed to the idea that human nature consists of psychological characteristics that are universal among humans. Tooby and Cosmides frequently speak of "the psychological universals that constitute human nature,"[6] and they claim that "theories of human nature make claims about a universal human psychology."[7] Further, Evolutionary Psychologists claim that the psychological universals constitutive or human nature evolved during our lineage's stint as hunter-gatherers, which was well after our lineage diverged from that of our nearest relatives, the chimpanzees. Consequently, our putative psychological universals are supposed to have evolved during hominid history; and, since we are the only surviving hominid species, these putative universals are unique to us and serve to distinguish us from other species. This is why Buss refers to the psychological universals that constitute human nature as the "qualities that define us as a unique species."

However, the contrast between nature and culture that provides the traditional concept of human nature with some of its meaning, and that provides the basis for the traditional arguments that there is no human nature, isn't part of Evolutionary Psychology's conception of human nature. There are two primary reasons for this. First, as we will see in greater detail later in the chapter, Evolutionary Psychologists contend that much of the content in human cultures across the globe is determined by universal psychological characteristics of humans. Evolutionary Psychologists argue that the cultural universality of marriage, for example, is the result of psychological universals that impel people to seek out and remain in long-term reproductive unions. If aspects of culture are determined by universals of human psychology in this way, and if psychological universals constitute human nature, then at least some aspects of culture are manifestations of human nature, rather than "unnatural" external constraints or impositions upon human nature.

Second, from a broad evolutionary standpoint, human culture as a whole is not opposed to human biology, but is part of it. From this standpoint, the practices that constitute human cultures differ only in degree of complexity, not in kind, from the web-spinning habits of spiders. For evolutionary biology is concerned to explain the emergence and characteristics of the various forms of life on our planet, and everything that we humans do we do as the living creatures that evolutionary biology studies. Whatever their potentially detrimental consequences, nuclear power plants differ only in degree of complexity, and degree of manipulation of nature, from beaver dams. And just as beaver dams are unproblematically a consequence of beaver biology, nuclear power plants are a consequence of ours. Within everything that is part of human biology, however, distinctions can he drawn between aspects of human life that are genetically transmitted across generations and aspects of human life that are transmitted in other ways, just as we can draw a *biological distinctions* between genotype and phenotype. Accordingly, the biologist John Bonnel defines *culture* as "the transfer of information by behavioral means, most particularly the process of teaching and learning," which he distinguishes from "the transmission of genetic information passed by the direct inheritance of genes from one generation to the next."[8] In this sense, culture is present in a vast array of species, and its evolution predated the emergence of modern humans. Thus, *culture is a biological phenomenon*, in the very broadest sense of the word *biology*, despite not being a genetically determined or genetically transmitted phenomenon. Consequently, the traditional arguments that there is no human nature, because humans are what they are due to cultural socialization rather than biology, rest upon a false dichotomy.

Although Evolutionary Psychology's conception of human nature doesn't involve the traditional dichotomy between human biology (nature) and human culture, it is highly dependent on a dichotomy between different biological characteristics of humans. As Tooby and Cosmides say, "the concept of a universal human nature," as employed in Evolutionary Psychology, is "based on a species-typical collection of complex *psychological adaptations*."[9] Evolutionary Psychology's conception of human nature is thus restricted to universal *adaptations*, which constitute only a proper subset of the biological characteristics to which the traditional concept of human nature has applied. If there are universal psychological characteristics that evolved under genetic drift, for example, these would not count as part of human nature for Evolutionary Psychologists, although they would for traditional theories that include in human nature all universal biological traits. Consequently, the contrast between nature and culture that is part of the meaning of the traditional concept of human nature is replaced within Evolutionary Psychology's conception of human nature by the contrast between traits that are universal adaptations and traits that aren't. In sum, then, according to Evolutionary Psychologists, human nature consists of a set of psychological adaptations that are presumed to be universal among, and unique to, human beings.

In the remainder of this chapter. I will argue that Evolutionary Psychology's theory of human nature is multiply problematic. For the most part, these problems are shared by the traditional concept of human nature. So, while my arguments will be directed at Evolutionary Psychology, they will apply in most instances to the traditional concept of human nature as well. For Evolutionary Psychology and the traditional concept of human nature share the idea that human nature consists of universal biological characteristics that "define us as a unique species." *In this sense*, I will argue, there simply is no such thing as human nature. But, since the dichotomy between nature and culture is a false one, I will not be arguing that Evolutionary Psychology's theory of human nature is wrong because it mistakenly emphasizes biology over culture. Rather, I will argue that the idea that there are universal biological characteristics that "define us as a unique species" simply *gets biology wrong* in a number of important ways. To begin exploring these arguments, let's return to Evolutionary Psychology's reasons for claiming that there is a universal human nature.

Evolutionary Psychologists offer two arguments for the existence of a universal human nature. One of these I called "the argument from sexual recombination," which contends that the genetics of adaptation necessitates the species universality of all complex adaptations. Elsewhere I demonstrated a variety of problems with this argument, and I showed how selection can, and frequently does, maintain polymorphisms of complex adaptations within populations. Contrary to the argument from sexual recombination, there is nothing in the nature of adaptation, or of the evolutionary process more generally, that necessitates a universal human nature as Evolutionary Psychologists conceive it. In other words, there are a variety of adaptational and genetic "natures" in human populations. But, while Evolutionary Psychologists typically take the argument from sexual recombination to be a definitive theoretical proof of the existence of a universal human nature, I don't think that that argument accounts for the intuitive pull that the idea of a universal human nature has enjoyed among Evolutionary Psychologists and their followers. That intuitive pull, I believe, is primarily due to another argument that Tooby and Cosmides offer, which I call "the argument from *Gray's Anatomy*." The argument from *Gray's Anatomy* is largely an appeal to common sense, and it thereby garners tremendous intuitive credibility for Evolutionary Psychology's claim that there is a universal human nature, since it makes the denial of that claim seem quite literally incredible.

The argument from *Gray's Anatomy* is compellingly simple, though not, I will argue, simply compelling. Tooby and Cosmides put it as follows:

> the fact that any given page out of *Gray's Anatomy* describes in precise anatomical detail individual humans from around the world demonstrates the pronounced monomorphism present in complex human physiological adaptations. Although we cannot yet directly "see" psychological adaptations (except as described neuroanatomically, no less could be true of them.[10]

Selection, in other words, has designed a universal human anatomy and physiology. As Tooby and Cosmides say, humans have a "universal architecture," in the sense that "everyone has two eyes, two hands, the same set of organs, and so on."[11] Since selection has presumably designed our minds as well as our bodies, the argument goes, we should expect selection to have designed a system of psychological adaptations that is just as universal as the anatomical and physiological adaptations described in *Gray's Anatomy*. Indeed, Tooby and Cosmides boldly claim that,

> just as one can now flip open *Gray's Anatomy* to any page and find an intricately detailed depiction of some part of our evolved species-typical morphology, we anticipate that in 50 or 100 years one will be able to pick up an equivalent reference work for psychology and find in it detailed information-processing descriptions of the multitude of evolved species-typical adaptations of the human mind.[12]

Despite its intuitive pull, however, the argument from *Gray's Anatomy* is multiply problematic, and it provides no reason to believe that there will ever be a reference work for psychology containing detailed descriptions of universal and species-typical psychological adaptations. I will discuss just five problems with the argument from *Gray's Anatomy*.

First, the argument relies on a questionable analogy between anatomy and psychology. Even if selection has designed a universal human anatomy, that fact alone doesn't justify the inference that selection has designed a universal human psychology. The features of the environment to which aspects of our anatomy have adapted are, for the most part, relatively stable and relatively simple. For example, the composition of the air, to which our lungs are adapted and whose contents they process, has been relatively stable throughout our evolutionary history. Recent problems with air pollution have precipitated changes in the chemical composition of the air we breathe, but our lungs still process the core chemicals in our air to which they are adapted. In contrast, the human mind has evolved to be responsive to rapidly changing environmental conditions. So the selection pressures that drove psychological evolution differ from those that drove anatomical evolution. Further, the selection pressures that drove most of the evolution of human intelligence stemmed primarily from human social life, rather than from the physical environment. But social life doesn't present a uniform condition to which a trait must adapt, in the way that the air presented a relatively uniform condition to which lungs had to adapt. Instead, human social life is characterized by behavioral variation. As a result, the fittest response to the complexities of human social life depends on the behavioral strategies of other humans in the population. This creates frequency-dependent selection, which can result in the evolution of adaptive psychological differences between individuals. Thus, there are reasons why minds could exhibit adaptive differences when and where bodies don't. So, even if there is a universal human anatomy, it doesn't follow that there must be a universal human psychology.

Second, the argument from *Gray's Anatomy* appeals to similarities among people at a relatively coarse scale. But, as the evolutionary biologist David Sloan Wilson points out, "uniformity at the coarsest scale does not imply uniformity at finer scales."[13] Every human may have a brain with two hemispheres, a cortex, an occipital lobe, and so on, just as "everyone has two eyes, two hands, the same set of organs, and so on." But the uniformity at this scale doesn't entail uniformity with respect to psychological mechanisms at a more micro level. Since Evolutionary Psychologists claim that our universal psychological adaptations are modules, which are highly specialized "minicomputers," the universal psychological adaptations they postulate are actually much smaller-scale brain mechanisms than the anatomical structures in the brain that are possessed by most humans. Thus, in order to demonstrate that there are universal psychological adaptations, Evolutionary Psychologists would need to demonstrate psychological uniformity at a much finer scale than that addressed by the argument from *Gray's Anatomy*.

Third, the "coarsest scale" which the argument from *Gray's Anatomy* appeals is incommensurate with Evolutionary Psychologists' understanding of human nature as constituted by "qualities that define us as a unique species. "For the universals appealed to in these arguments typify the whole primate order and sometimes the whole class of mammals and even all vertebrates. For example, all primates have two hands, all mammals have lungs, and all vertebrates have two eyes, a heart, a liver, and a stomach. So the analogical appeal to the coarsest scale of uniformity within our species ("everyone has two eyes, two hands, the same set of organs, and so on") supports no conclusions about universal psychological adaptions that "define us as a unique species," since uniquely human adaptations would have had to evolve during human evolutionary history. Hence, the appeal to very coarse-scale common characteristics supports no conclusion about distinctively *human* universals.

The fourth problem, related to the third, is that the basic structural plan that typifies the "universal architecture" of our species—and that, at ever coarser scales of description, typifies the body plan of our order (primate), class (mammal), and subphylum (vertebrate)— consists primarily of features that have *persisted* down lineages and through speciations for tens to hundreds of millions of years. Although selection probably played a role in designing the basic body plan that now characterizes humans, it did not design that structural plan during human history, but rather during the history of the common ancestor of humans and other primates, mammals, or vertebrates. Consequently, even though all humans may have two eyes, two hands, one nose, and a mouth, it doesn't follow that similarly universal adaptations emerged during comparatively recent human evolutionary history.

Finally, strictly speaking, there is no single human anatomy and physiology possessed by all humans around the world of which *Gray's Anatomy* provides a "detailed" and "precise" description. Approximately 0.25 percent of all humans are born with only one kidney, rather than two, yet nonetheless live reasonably healthy lives. Others are born with three kidneys, yet still live healthy lives (although there are no solid estimates of the incidence of this phenomenon). In addition, somewhere between

> one in every 8,000 to 25,000 people is born with a condition known as situs inversus, in which the positions of all the internal organs are reversed relative to the normal situation (situs solitus): the person's heart and stomach lie to the right, their liver to the left, and so on. (The organs are also mirror images of their normal structures.)[14]

There is no more precise estimate of the incidence of situs inversus because it creates no medical complications, so it is typically discovered only incidentally to routine physical examination (if sought) or medical treatment for some other condition. At the physiological level, there are four main blood types in humans (A, B, AB, and O), which are genetically coded for at a single locus. If we move from the four blood types coded for at that one locus to examine broader categories of blood type, there are more than twenty additional blood types in humans. And, moving to the outside of the body, approximately one in every fifteen hundred infants is born with ambiguous genitalia, which do not allow the assignment of a sex. Thus, the idea that *Gray's Anatomy* provides *a single* "detailed" and "precise" picture of the anatomy and physiology of every human on earth is plausible only if one ignores known facts about human anatomical and physiological variation. Although most of us are pretty much the same in a lot of "coarse" details, we are not all cast from the same anatomical and physiological mold, so there is no reason to think that there is a single psychological mold from which we are all cast. Despite its intuitive appeal, the argument from *Gray's Anatomy* provides no good reason to believe in the existence of a universal human nature.

Essentialism, Part I: "Normal" People

Of course, there is an obvious rejoinder to this last argument. No Evolutionary Psychologist really believes that literally all human beings on earth have precisely the same anatomy or that every single human being on earth possesses all of the characteristics that constitute human nature. Rather, as Cosmides and Tooby say, "a scientific definition of *human nature*" concerns "the uniform architecture of the human mind and brain that reliably develops in *every normal human* just as do eyes, fingers, arms, a heart, and so on."[15] So, *of course* there are some human beings born with only one or with three kidneys, just as some human beings are born without arms. And *of course* there are some human beings born with their organs reversed, just as some human beings are born with three copies of the

twenty-first chromosome (which results in Down syndrome). But such individuals are "abnormal," either because of an unusual genetic condition or because of exposure to some "environmental insult" during development. And the concept of an anatomical universal architecture, like the concept of universal human nature, is not intended to apply to cases of developmental "abnormality." Such concepts are intended, rather, to capture only what *all normal human beings* have in common. Thus, the obvious rejoinder goes, pointing out that some human beings depart from the "universal architecture" described in *Gray's Anatomy* doesn't constitute a valid objection to the argument from *Gray's Anatomy*, since that argument presupposes only that *Gray's Anatomy* provides a "precise" and "detailed" description of the anatomy of all *normal* human beings.

It should be clear at this point that any reasonable claim that there exists a universal human nature must be committed to some distinction between normality and abnormality. For, strictly speaking, there are *no* characteristics that are universally distributed among all and only human beings. So any claim about universality must refer only to characteristics that are universally distributed among "normal" humans, rather than characteristics that are distributed among all humans, and the "abnormal" must be conceived as not partaking of human nature. Accordingly, people who don't possess the characteristics definitive of some theory's concept of a universal human nature don't actually constitute counterexamples to the claim that there is a universal human nature, because those who are "abnormal" simply don't count.

This distinction between normality and abnormality, on which all claims regarding a universal human nature must depend, is part and parcel of a doctrine known as *essentialism*. In general, essentialism is a view about what makes *distinct individual entities* of the same kind into distinct individual entitles *of the same kind*. Essentialism is the view that there are certain characteristics that *define* a kind, so that two different entitles belong to the same kind just in case they both possess the characteristics definitive of that kind. For example, two objects are both samples of the kind *platinum* just in case both of those objects are composed of atoms with atomic number 78. Having atomic number 78 is the characteristic that defines the kind *platinum*, it is the *essence* of platinum. Consequently, any two entitles with atomic number 78 are instances of platinum, regardless of whatever other properties (size, shape, or overall weight) they may have. Kinds, such as platinum, that are defined by essential characteristics, which any object must possess to be a member of that kind, are known as *natural kinds*.

While essentialism is comfortably at home in the lable of elements, it has also been applied to biological classification at least since the time of Aristotle. Within biological classification, essentialism becomes the view that species are natural kinds. Accordingly, species are defined by characteristics that serve to differentiate them from all other species, and those characteristics are taken to constitute the essence of a species. An organism belongs to a particular species, then, by virtue of possessing the characteristics definitive of that species. But the philosopher of biology Elliott Sober points out that essentialism regarding species typically involves more than the minimal claim that species are defined by sets of unique characteristics. According to Sober, a species essence does not simply constitute a condition that is necessary and sufficient for membership in that species, but plays an explanatory role as well. As Sober says:

The essentialist hypothesizes that there exists some characteristic unique to and shared by all members of *Homo sapiens* which *explains why they are the way they are*. A species essence will be a causal mechanism that acts on each member of the species, making it the kind of thing that it is.[16]

That Evolutionary Psychology is committed to essentialism regarding species, and that its essentialism underlies its conception of human nature, is often explicit when Evolutionary Psychologists wax theoretical about *Homo sapiens* and human nature. The passage quoted earlier from Buss, in which he speaks of human nature as consisting of "qualities that *define us as a unique species*," is clearly committed to essentialism regarding species. From the opposite side of the same viewpoint, Cosmides and Tooby write: "By virtue of being members of the human species, all humans are expected to have the same adaptive mechanisms."[17] In other words, membership in the same species entails the shared possession of the essential characteristics definitive of the species. Elsewhere, in a clear expression of the essentialist view that species are natural kinds, Cosmides and Tooby say,

the species-typical genetic endowments of species, and the common ancestry of larger taxa do cause an indefinitely large set of similarities to be shared among members of a natural kind, as does a common chemical structure for different instances of a substance.[18]

Finally, tying essentialism directly to the concept of human nature, the Evolutionary Psychologist Donald Brown writes: "Universals of essence at the level of the individual collectively constitute human nature."[19]

But how can essentialism regarding species be reconciled with the existence of organisms that appear to belong to *Homo sapiens* even though they don't possess all of the "qualities that define us as a unique species"? If species are natural kinds, so that an organism is a member of a species if and only if it possesses the characteristics essential to that species, and if some people don't actually possess all the characteristics that define human nature, which is the essence of *Homo sapiens*, aren't those people not actually human beings? Isn't essentialism committed to claiming that people who lack a characteristic essential to the human species simply aren't human? And, if so, how can essentialism integrally involve a distinction between "normal" and "abnormal" human beings? Aren't "abnormal" humans not actually human, so that, strictly speaking, there is no such thing as an "abnormal" human?

Throughout the history of essentialism there has been a tension between essentialism regarding species and apparent variation within species. The usual way of resolving this tension is to conceive of a species' essence as a *causal mechanism* that produces the phenotypic characteristics considered definitive of membership in that species. This involves what Sober calls the "Natural State Model." According to the Natural State Model,

> there is a distinction between the *natural state* of a kind of object and those states which are not natural. These latter are produced by subjecting the object to an *interfering force*. . . . The cause for this divergence from what is natural is that these objects are acted on by interfering forces that prevent them from achieving their natural state by frustrating their natural tendency. Variability within nature is thus to be explained as a deviation from what is natural.[20]

When applied within biology, the Natural State Model entails that "there is one path of fractal development which counts as the realization of the organism's natural state, while other developmental results are consequences of unnatural interferences."[21] The Natural State Model consequently explains variation in a species as a result of causal interactions between an essential developmental mechanism and potentially interfering forces.

The distinction between "normal" and "abnormal" characteristics of members of a species derives from the Natural State Model. For, according to the Natural State Model, each member of a species possesses the causal mechanism that produces that species' essential characteristics. When not interfered with, the causal essence of a species thus produces normal members of that species. But various factors can prevent the causal mechanism from producing its normal results, and when it is prevented from doing so it results in species members with abnormal characteristic. Thus, according to this version of essentialism, abnormal humans are still human, since despite their abnormal phenotypes they still possess the developmental mechanism considered essential to humans.

Evolutionary Psychology's essentialism, and hence its conception of human nature, is clearly committed to the Natural State Model. Although Evolutionary Psychologists typically identify human nature with a cluster of psychological (phenotypic) adaptations, in a more guarded moment Tooby and Cosmides indicate that their concept of a "universal human nature" is intended to apply primarily at the developmental level and only secondarily at the phenotypic level:

> when we use terms such as "evolved design," "evolved architecture," or even "species-typical," "species-standard," "universal," and "panhuman," we are not making claims about every human phenotype all or even some of the time; instead, we are referring to the existence of evolutionarily organized developmental adaptations, whether they are activated or latent. Adaptations are not necessarily expressed in every individual. . . . For this reason, adaptations and adaptive architecture can be discussed and described at (at least) two levels (1) the level of reliably achieved and expressed organization has for example, in the realized structure of the eye), and (2) at the level of the developmental programs that construct such organization.[22]

Thus, universal developmental programs are the causal mechanism that produces "the species-standard physiological and psychological architecture visible in all humans raised in normal environments."[23]

In addition, the more guarded identification of "universal human nature" with "universal developmental programs" underlies Evolutionary Psychologists' commitment to the idea that some aspects of human nature are sexually dimorphic and age differentiated. For Evolutionary Psychologists argue that the sexes have faced different selection pressures, which designed some adaptive morphological and psychological sex differences, and that differences in selection pressures faced across the life cycle created age-differentiated adaptive "coordinated design differences." These adaptive sex and age differences, however, result from universal developmental adaptations, which are programmed to produce sex-specific adaptations in response to the presence or absence of the SRY gene and to bring age-specific adaptations "on line" and take them "off line" at appropriate ages.

Despite the existence of adaptive age and sex differences, Evolutionary Psychologists are nonetheless committed to the idea that there are certain things that all humans share. First, all humans share the "universal developmental programs" that produce programmed sex and age differences. And, second, these universal development programs produce some morphological and psychological characteristics that are not sex or age differentiated. The latter constitute "the species-standard physiological and psychological architecture visible in all humans raised in normal environments." This "architecture" is "normal," or the "natural state" for humans, and departure from that natural state is presumed to be caused by forces—for example, genetic mutation or "environmental insult"—that interfere with developmental programs and thereby produce "abnormalities." Similarly, there are male and female "architectures" that are "normal," or the "natural state," for human males and human females, and departures from those natural states are caused by interference

with universal developmental programs. Consequently, departures from human nature (or male nature or female nature) at the phenotypic level are due to causal interaction between "interfering forces" and a universal human nature at the level of developmental mechanisms.

There are, however, several problems with Evolutionary Psychology's essentialism. There are problems with the Natural State Model, on which the distinction between "normal" and "abnormal" phenotypes depends, and there are problems with essentialism regarding species more generally. These problems don't so much show that the Natural State Model and essentialism can't possibly be right, but they point up that both are inconsistent with contemporary theory and practice within biology. In other words, the Natural State Model and essentialism can't be founded in contemporary evolutionary biology; there is simply nothing evolutionary about them. And any psychological theory that claims to be *evolutionary* must trade in theoretical constructs that can be founded in evolutionary biology. Further, as we will see in the next section, when essentialism regarding species is abandoned, the prospects for the kind of "science of the mind" that Evolutionary Psychology envisions providing disappear with it. In the remainder of this section, let's examine the problems with the Natural State Model.

As we have seen, according to the Natural State Model there is one path of development that results in the "normal" or "natural" state for the organism, and other paths of development are the result of "interfering forces." "Put slightly differently," as Sober says "for a given genotype, there is a single phenotype which it can have that is the natural one. Or, more modestly, the requirement might be that there is some restricted range of phenotypes which count as natural."[24] The problem with this view is that there is no basis in genetics for the idea that a genotype is associated with a phenotype that is "natural" for it to produce. As Sober says, when one looks to genetic theory for a conception of the relation between genotype and phenotype, one finds no such distinction between natural state and states which are the results of interference. One finds, instead, the *norm of reaction*, which graphs the different phenotypic results that a genotype can have in different environments.[25]

For example, the norm of reaction for a particular genetic strain of corn would be a graph showing the different heights that corn of that genotype would have in each of a range of environments, where the different environments could be characterized by differences in amount of rainfall and sunlight. That is, the norm of reaction would be a graphed function showing that corn with genotype G_1, has height phenotype P_1 in environment E_1, phenotype P_2 in environment E_2, phenotype P_3 in environment E_3, and so on. But nothing in the norm of reaction would identify any particular height as "natural" for corn of that genotype. There are simply different heights that corn of that genotype can have under a range of different environmental conditions.

Of course, there may be a phenotype that is the *statistically most frequent* phenotype produced by a particular genotype. And it makes perfect sense to speak of that statistically most frequent phenotype as the "normal" phenotype for that genotype—as long as we bear in mind that by "normal" we mean only what is statistically most frequent. But this sense of "normal" is not at all the sense that has always been intended by proponents of the Natural State Model. For, in this statistical conception of "normal," a diseased phenotype can be normal for a population. If a virus has reached epidemic proportions in a population, for example, it can be statistically normal for members of that population to be diseased. But no proponent of the Natural State Model would consider disease to be the "natural state" for members of that population, despite its frequency in the population. The Natural

State Model is after a more robust notion of "normal" phenotype, one that would pick out a phenotype as normal regardless of whether that phenotype is prevalent or even represented at all in a population. But the norm of reaction, which is the geneticist's way of understanding the relation between genotype and phenotype, simply doesn't underwrite such a robust notion of "normal" or "natural" phenotype for a genotype.

Since the norm of reaction doesn't privilege any particular phenotype as "normal" or "natural," but simply identifies which phenotypes result in which environments, one way to save the Natural State Model would be to provide some independent justification for identifying one of the environments specified in the norm of reaction for a genotype as the "natural environment" for that genotype (or identifying a restricted range of environments as being "natural environments"). Derivatively, then, a "natural" phenotype for that genotype would be a phenotype that develops in a "natural environment" for that genotype.

This would be the obvious move for Evolutionary Psychologists to make, since it fits quite naturally with their overall theoretical framework. For, as Tooby and Cosmides say, "the species-standard physiological and psychological architecture" is the architecture that is "visible in all humans *raised in normal environments*."[26] And the "normal environments" are clearly those that closely resemble the environment of evolutionary adaptedness (EEA), the statistical composite of the environments in which our adaptations evolved and to which they are adapted. Indeed, in one of the earliest discussions of the EEA in the Evolutionary Psychology literature, Donald Symons refers to the environments that compose the EEA as the "natural environments" for humans, which he characterizes as "environments to which ancestral populations were exposed for sufficient lengths of time to become adapted to them."[27] Thus, Evolutionary Psychologists could argue, of all the environments specified in the norm of reaction for a genotype, those that closely resemble the EEA are the "natural environments" for that genotype. So, of all the phenotypes specified in a norm of reaction, those that develop in "natural environments" are "normal" phenotypes.

There are, however, two problems with this attempts to specify natural environments for development and, derivatively, to define "normal" phenotypes. First, the EEA is supposed to be a natural environment because that is the environment to which we are adapted, the environment for which we are "designed." But we must bear in mind precisely what talk of being "adapted to" and "designed for" an environment means. These expressions appear to describe some direct relationship between our traits (or genotypes) and the environment; but they to fact do not. For selection never "designs" traits for particular environments in isolation from competing traits. To say that a trait is "adapted to" or "designed for" a particular environment is simply shorthand for saying that the trait was *selected over alternative traits* in that environment. And that in turn, simply means that individuals with that trait had higher average fitness in that environment than individuals with alternative traits. Thus, to say that a trait is "adapted to" or "designed for" a particular environment emphatically does *not* mean that the trait is a perfect "fit" for that environment, that the trait is the fittest of all possible traits in that environment, or that the trait has higher fitness in that environment than in any other.

If the motivation for identifying a genotype's "natural environment" with its EEA is that the EEA is the environment in which the genotype made the greatest contribution to fitness (by producing a trait that enhanced fitness), then there are undoubtedly other environments that would be better candidates for a genotype's "natural environment." For example, the EEA of a genotype is simply the environment in which that genotype had *higher fitness than available*

alternative genotypes in the population. In a different environment, the genotype may have had an even greater fitness advantage over those alternatives. So why not identify the "natural environment" of a genotype with the environment in which the genotype has its highest fitness? Similarly, had a genotype competed in its EEA against a different set of alternative genotypes, one of those alternatives may have had higher fitness than the genotype that was actually selected. Why should a genotype's EEA be the "natural environment" for *that genotype* rather than for some other genotype that would have had higher fitness in that environment? Had a mutation occurred that improved the human eye so that it could see as well at night as during the day, for example, the genotype for that supereye would have been selected over the genotype for the typical human eye in the EEA of the human eye. Why should the EEA of the human eye be the "natural environment" for the human eye rather than for the supereye that would have been selected in that environment had in actually been present in our ancestral population? If a genotype's "natural environment" is defined in terms of a genotype's fitness, there are no principled grounds on which to identify as a genotype's natural environment its EEA rather than an alternative environment in which it would have higher fitness, or to identify a genotype's EEA as *its* natural environment, rather than that of an alternative genotype that would have had higher fitness in that environment. Thus, it is arbitrary to call a genotype's EEA its "natural environment."

Second, calling the EEA the "natural environment" involves defining "natural environment" in terms of *selection*, since the EEA of a trait or genotype is the environment in which it was selected over alternatives. This presumes that what is selected for is somehow more "in accordance with nature" than what is selected against or what is neither selected for nor against. But nothing in evolutionary theory justifies privileging selection in this way.

Evolution is change in gene or genotype frequencies across generations in a lineage, and evolutionary theory is concerned to explain *all* such changes. Selection is just *one* of the causes of evolution. Evolution is also caused by mutation, recombination, genetic drift, and migration into and out of populations, and evolutionary theory encompasses these as well. In addition, a trait can increase in frequency because of selection, but it can also increase in frequency because of genetic drift or migration, and evolutionary theory will be there to explain all such changes. Evolutionary theory also explains why traits decrease in frequency and why they sometimes disappear from populations entirely. It also explains why entire species go extinct. All of these processes are natural, each is every bit as real as the others, and evolutionary theory is designed to explain them all, without privileging the process of selection. Thus, an environment in which a trait or genotype is selected for is no more natural than an environment in which it is selected against.

Now, it is true that selection plays a particular explanatory role within evolutionary theory. If we want to explain the process of *adaptation*, selection will be central and indispensable to that explanation. And this fact no doubt underlies Evolutionary Psychology's idea that the EEA is the "natural environment." But, again, adaptation is just one process among many in evolution, and nothing in evolutionary theory privileges the process of adaptation over other processes by considering it more natural than other processes. Similarly, nothing in evolutionary theory privileges traits that are adaptations over traits that are not by considering them a more natural part of an organism's endowment than traits that are not adaptations. We do, of course, appeal to evolutionary theory and the process of selection in order to answer the question, Why is this highly articulated and apparently well designed trait so prevalent in this population? But we also appeal to evolutionary theory to answer the question, Why do humans

have an appendix when it serves no apparent function? Which kind of question we ask reflects only *our explanatory interests*. Nothing in evolutionary theory itself justifies the conviction that one question is more important than the other or that one question better reflects what is "natural." Rather, the conviction that one question is more significant than the other is a theoretical vestige of an outdated worldview, as I will argue in greater detail in the final section of this chapter.

Thus, there are no principled reasons deriving from evolutionary theory to designate certain environments in a norm of reaction as "natural environments." And this means that there are no principled reasons deriving from evolutionary theory to designate certain phenotypes in a norm of reaction as "normal" phenotypes. Our best *biological* understanding of the relation between genotype and phenotype is reflected only in the norm of reaction itself, a simple mapping of environments onto phenotypes for any given genotype. The distinction between "normal" and "abnormal" phenotypes, which is central to the Natural State Model, can't be drawn by the norm of reaction. That distinction is imposed on biological theory from a nonbiological worldview.

But the Natural State Model presupposes not only that each genotype is associated with a normal phenotype, which is the organism's natural state, but that for any locus that codes for a trait there is a normal genotype for an organism to have at that locus. That normal genotype is, of course, the genotype that produces the organism's normal phenotype, and alternate genotypes at the same locus are abnormal because they produce abnormal phenotypes. Again, however, there is nothing in genetic theory that allows for a distinction between "normal" and "abnormal" genotypes (unless, again, by "normal" one simply means the genotype that is most common in a population).

The fact is that substantial genetic variation exists in natural populations, human populations included. A genetic analysis of thirty species of mammal found that, on average, those species were genetically polymorphic—that is, more than one genotype occurred—at approximately 20 percent of their loci.[28] While this analysis didn't provide an estimate of the overall genetic polymorphism within humans, a global genetic study of human populations found that the average heterozygosity in human populations ranges from 21 percent to 37 percent.[29] That is, the average percentage of loci at which individuals in a population are heterozygous is anywhere between 21 and 37 percent of loci, depending on the population; the lowest average heterozygosity is found in New Guinea and Australia, and the highest average heterozygosity is found in the populations of the Middle East, western Asia, and southern, central, and eastern Europe. Heterozygote mating produces genotype polymorphisms, even when heterozygotes mate with homozygotes. Thus, the high degree of heterozygosity in human populations sustains a prodigious amount of genetic variation in human populations. And genetic theory doesn't label some of the genetic variants "normal" and others "abnormal." From the standpoint of population genetics, there are simply a variety of genotypes that change in frequency across generations. A new mutation, which may or may not increase in frequency under selection, is no more or less normal than a statistically more frequent allele at the same locus. Any distinction between "normal" and "abnormal" genotypes must be imposed on genetic theory from a nonbiological perspective.

Therefore, the Natural State Model, on which any distinction between "normal" and "abnormal" human characteristics must rely, has no basis in biology. Nothing in biology justifies viewing certain phenotypes, but not others, as the "normal" phenotypes for a genotype, and nothing in biology justifies viewing certain genotypes, but not others, as the "normal" genotypes for humans. There is substantial variation in human populations at both the phenotypic and genetic levels, and our best biological theories to date simply do not partition that variation into "normal" and "abnormal" variants. As Sober so nicely puts it: "Our current theories of biological variation provide no more role for the idea of a natural state than our current physical theories do for the notion of absolute simultaneity."[30] To the extent that Evolutionary Psychology's theory of a universal human nature relies on the Natural State Model for a distinction between "normality" (which exemplifies human nature) and "abnormality" (which does not), its theory of human nature has no foundation in biology.

Essentialism, Part II: Species

The problems with the Natural State Model, however, are merely symptoms of deeper problems with essentialism itself. The distinction between "normal" and "abnormal," which characterizes the Natural State Model, is necessary only if one is antecedently committed to the view that there are certain characteristics that all and only humans share. For, since the claim that there are characteristics that *literally* all and only humans share is an obvious empirical falsehood, it becomes necessary to retreat to the less robust claim that there are characteristics that all and only *normal* humans share. But, if we are not driven to formulate our understanding of species in terms of what *all and only* members of a species have in common, we don't need a category or "abnormal" to which to relegate the individuals in a species that happen to lack one or more of the characteristics we take to be essential to a species, and we then don't need a category of "normal" to contain the individuals that do happen to possess those characteristics. It is essentialism that forces these categories on us by mandating that our understanding of species in general, and of human beings in particular, be formulated as a claim about what *all and only* certain organisms have in common.

But essentialism about species is absolutely and completely wrong. Essentialism about species takes each species to be a *natural kind*, which is defined by a set of essential properties. This has two significant implications. First, it implies that species are *individuated*—i.e., distinguished from one another—by virtue of their essential properties. If species A and species B are defined by different sets of essential properties, then they are distinct species; if they are defined by the same set of essential properties, then they are, in fact, the same species. Accordingly, every species has its own essence, which is distinct from the essence of any other species, just as every element in the table of elements has its own essential atomic number, which is distinct from the essential atomic numbers of all other elements. Second, it implies that an organism belongs to a species by virtue of possessing the properties essential to that species. If a certain set of characteristics defines a species, then any organism possessing those characteristics belongs to that species, and any organism lacking them doesn't, regardless of what else may be true of those organisms. Thus, the essence of a species constitutes the criterion for belonging to that species, just as atomic number constitutes the criterion for being a particular element.

These implications of the view that species are natural kinds do not accord with the way that biologists individuate species or the way that they assign individual organisms to species. To see why, let's first get a handle on how species are understood according to theory and practice within biology, then let's examine how the view that species are natural kinds conflicts with the biological understanding of species.

When viewed within a relatively brief interval of evolutionary time, a species, in the biological sense, is a group of *interbreeding populations*. When some organisms in one population reproduce with organisms in another population, the genes from the former population are introduced into the latter population, where those genes can

then spread as the organisms in the latter population continue to reproduce. When interbreeding occurs between two populations in this way there is *gene flow* between those populations' gene pools. And when there is gene flow between populations, the interbreeding populations constitute a single species.

However, each of the interbreeding populations that constitute a species itself belongs to a lineage, a temporally extended sequence of populations, the later of which are descended by reproduction from the earlier. Consider two currently interbreeding populations. Do all the descendent populations in their respective lineages also belong to the same species? That depends. If the populations in those lineages continue to interbreed, then both lineages, not just their earlier populations, belong to the same species. Of course, it needn't be the case that there be continual interbreeding between the populations in two lineages, only that there be at least periodic interbreeding between the populations in those lineages. When there is at least periodic interbreeding between the populations in two or more lineages, those lineages are *reproductively interwoven* (by periodic gene flow) across evolutionary time, and they consequently belong to the same species over a longer stretch of evolutionary time.

However, there may come a time at which populations in two reproductively interwoven lineages become *reproductively isolated* from one another (due, for example, to geographic separation). When populations become reproductively isolated, no further gene flow occurs between them, and those populations then belong to different species. So, lineages can be reproductively interwoven over long stretches of evolutionary time, but then reach a point at which they *branch* because populations in those lineages become reproductively isolated. When this branching occurs, the previously existing species is replaced by two (or more) daughter species. This is much like how the letter Y consists of three line segments, where each line segment represents a distinct species. In the species case, of course, the vertical line segment, in the Y is actually one of the diagonal line segments of another Y, so that the representation of how species have diverged over evolutionary time requires an elaborate branching structure. This elaborate branching structure is the "tree of life," which is the goal of biological classification. The tree of life shows how each species is descended from an earlier species, and each node (each point at which a branching occurs) in the tree of life represents a point at which populations become reproductively isolated.

Thus, in the biological sense, a species is a group of reproductively interwoven lineages that lie on a single "line" segment in the tree of life. Each organism in one of these reproductively interwoven lineages is thus descended from earlier organisms in those lineages, and ultimately the genealogy of each organism is traceable to organisms in the ancestral population that started a new branch in the tree of life. When the genealogy of each organism in a group of reproductively interwoven lineages is traced in its entirety, it will crisscross the genealogies of the other organisms in those lineages, and the network of all such genealogies will constitute an elaborate *genealogical means* within which each organism is situated. All the organisms in this genealogical nexus will be descended from common ancestors in the population that founded the species, and the genealogical nexus will display the manner in which they are all related. And, according to biological classification, two organisms that are situated within a common genealogical nexus, which lies on a single segment in the tree of life, are classified as belonging to the same species, regardless of the characteristics those organisms happen to possess.

We are now in a position to see how the biological concept of a species conflicts with the view that species are natural kinds. First, what matters for assigning an organism to a species is the *genealogical nexus* in which it is situated (that is, from which organisms it was descended), not the particular traits it happens to possess. This principle of classification differs sharply from that involved in determining the natural kind to which a particular substance happens to belong. If two samples of liquid contain two parts hydrogen and one part oxygen, bonded in the right way, they both belong to the kind *water*, regardless of how those two samples of liquid happened to come about. One sample may have been produced in a lab by a chemist, and the other may have been scooped out of a river. The provenance of the samples is completely inessential to whether they are samples of water. All that matters is whether the samples have the same *intrinsic properties*. This is because water *is* a natural kind. But, when it comes to determining the species to which an organism belongs, provenance trumps intrinsic properties. Thus, species, *as biologists understand them*, do not exhibit the features of natural kinds.

Second, according to the view that species are natural kinds, if species A and species B possess the same essential characteristics, then they are the same species. But this doesn't accord with practices of biological classification. According to biological classification, if all humans ceased to exist today, *Homo sapiens* would be extinct. If, after millions of years, creatures came to roam our planet that were exactly like us, filling a "precise and detailed description" from *Gray's Anatomy*, and behaved like us in every respect, they would nonetheless not be *Homo sapiens*. Similarly, if we discovered such creatures in another galaxy, they would not be *Homo sapiens* if they had evolved independently of us. For, as biologists see them, terrestrial species are branches in the tree of life that represents the evolution of all living creatures from the first life form on earth. Accordingly, regardless of whether two distinct branches are perfectly identical in all their observable characteristics, they are nonetheless two distinct branches, just as identical twins are two different organisms despite their similarity. So, when one branch on the tree of life terminates, no other branch that may happen to grow further up the tree will be the same branch, regardless of whether it perfectly resembles the lower, terminated branch. This is the significance behind the slogan "extinction is forever." For species are not individuated by their characteristics, they are individuated as segments in the tree of life. If species were individuated by their characteristics, as natural kinds are, then even if a species ceased to exist it could reemerge later, provided that organisms evolved later that possessed the same characteristics as those that had died earlier. Thus, again, *as biologists understand them*, species don't exhibit the features of natural kinds.

Third, species evolve. In fact, one and the same species may evolve so significantly that characteristics that typify a species at one time period cease to typify it at a later time, and another set of characteristics may become typical of that species. If species were natural kinds, however, a species could not undergo such significant change. A lineage undergoing such significant change would have to be classified as one species before the change and another species after it, since the different sets of typical characteristics would constitute the essences of different species. By analogy, given the right chemical intervention, a volume of carbon monoxide could be transformed into carbon dioxide. But it would not be the same *kind* of gas through the change. That is, the kind carbon monoxide *itself* wouldn't become the kind carbon dioxide, but rather a volume of gas would be transformed from an instance of the natural kind *carbon monoxide* into an instance of the natural kind *carbon dioxide*. The natural kinds themselves would remain unchanged. Similarly, if species were natural kinds, a sufficient degree of evolution would simply transform a species into another, distinct natural kind. But, as biologists understand them, species can be radically overhauled by evolution, yet nonetheless remain *one and the same* species. Provided that the evolutionary change occurs *within* a single branch of

the tree of life, the lineage is classified as the same species, no matter how radical the evolutionary change. Evolutionary change creates new species only if the change results in the *branching* of a lineage (the reproductive isolation and splitting of two populations). So, again, *as biologists understand them*, species don't exhibit the features of natural kinds.

Indeed, this last point generates something of a dilemma for the essentialist view that species are natural kinds. Consider the dilemma with respect to Evolutionary Psychology's view of *Homo sapiens*. According to Evolutionary Psychologists, there are "qualities that define us as a unique species," but these qualities evolved during our species' history. Evolutionary Psychologists maintain that our "species-typical architecture" consists of adaptations that evolved to fixation during the Pleistocene and that, by the end of the Pleistocene some 10,000 years ago. Those adaptations reflected "completed rather than ongoing selection."[31] But *Homo sapiens* emerged some 150,000 years ago. So, during at least some of our species' evolutionary history, the qualities that purportedly "define us as a unique species" did not typify our species at all, since they had not yet evolved. In order for those qualities to evolve, however, there had to be sufficient *variation* in our species, since evolution can only occur if there is variation. Thus, during a significant stretch of our evolutionary history, *Homo sapiens* had to be characterized by variation rather than by "the qualities that define us as a unique species."

Here, then, is the dilemma. Evolutionary Psychologists must claim either that we are the same species now that we were 150,000 years ago or that we aren't. If Evolutionary Psychologists claim that we are the same species now that we were 150,000 years ago, before the "qualities that define us as a unique species" became "species typical," then those qualities do not, in fact, "define us as a unique species." For, in that case, *Homo sapiens* would have become a unique species before it was characterized by those qualities—indeed, it would have become a unique species despite being characterized by variation. Thus, because Homo Sapiens remained the same species both before and after the emergence of its alleged "species-typical architecture," no such architecture is essential to the species. On the other hand, if Evolutionary Psychologists claim that we are not the same species now that we were 150,000 years ago, because 150,000 years ago our lineage did not possess the "qualities that define us as a unique species," then Evolutionary Psychology's demarcation of Homo sapiens is directly at odds with the standard biological demarcation of our species. In that case, whatever Evolutionary Psychologists are talking about, they can't be talking about human beings *as a biological species*, since Homo sapiens is a term of biological art. Clearly this horn of the dilemma is unacceptable, especially for any psychological theory that claims to be evolutionary. So the only viable option is to grasp the first horn of the dilemma. Grasping that horn, however, requires giving up the idea that species are natural kinds.

But, if species aren't natural kinds, if they aren't what they are because of particular essential qualities that define them each as unique species, what are they? The answer to this question comes from the work of the evolutionary biologists Ernst Mayr and Michael Ghiselin and the philosopher of biology David Hull. As they have shown, the only metaphysical category that exhibits the properties biologists ascribe to species is the category of *individual*. The fact that species are individuals, rather than natural kinds, however, remains little known and little appreciated outside of biology proper. Indeed, Mayr has bemoaned the fact that, although taxonomic biologists are effectively unanimous in rejecting the idea that species are natural kinds, accepting that they are individuals instead, cognate areas of inquiry have failed to absorb the idea and its implications. With characteristic spunk, Hull echoes, then responds to, the "considerable consternation" voiced by those who find it difficult to accept that species are individuals rather than natural kinds:

Biological species cannot possibly have the characteristics that biologists claim they do. There must be characteristics that all and only people exhibit or at least *potentially* exhibit, or all *normal* people exhibit at least potentially. I continue to remain dismayed at the vehemence with which these views are expressed in the absence of any explicitly formulated biological foundations for these notions.[32]

Hull lampoons these views as exemplary of the attitude, "What do biologists know about biology."[33] In an attempt to break this impasse, let's examine more closely the idea that species are individuals.

The first task is to get clear about what *individuals* are and how they differ from natural kinds. There are three primary characteristics that define the concept of an individual, three things that make something an individual entity. Individuals, are spatiotemporally localized (hence discrete), spatiotemporally continuous, and cohesive. An organism is, by everyone's measure, a paradigm example of an individual, so let's examine these three properties of individuals by seeing how they are exemplified by organisms.

First, each individual is spatiotemporally localized. That is, each individual has a beginning and an end in time, and each individual occupies a specific region of space. For example, an organism's spatial and temporal location constitute the *boundaries* of that organism. No two distinct organisms have precisely the same boundaries, and numerically the same organism cannot have two distinct sets of boundaries (two distinct locations in space and time). Even though a parasite organism may reside within a host organism, it nonetheless occupies a region of space that is properly contained within the region of space occupied by its host. The parasite does not occupy precisely the same region of space as its host. Further, parasite and host virtually never begin and cease to exist at precisely the same moments in time. Thus, organisms are *discrete*: There are points in space and time at which an organism begins and ends, and these points are different from the points at which another organism begins and ends. As Ghiselin says,

> an individual occupies a definite position in space and time. It has a beginning and an end. Once it ceases to exist it is gone forever. In a biological context this means that an organism never comes back into existence once it is dead.[34]

In this respect, individuals differ from kinds. The individual members of a kind are located at particular regions of space-time, but the kind itself has no particular location in spacetime. Further, since kinds are constituted by their members, kinds are not discrete. The same individuals can belong to more than one kind, in which case the kinds to which they belong overlap rather than having discrete boundaries. Indeed, two different kinds can have precisely the same members, in which case they overlap one another completely.

Second, each individual is spatiotemporally continuous. Each individual exists continuously between its beginning and end in time, and at every moment of its existence it occupies the same or contiguous regions of space. Given its spatiotemporal continuity, an individual's existence can be plotted as a "spacetime worm," a single unbroken line, however squiggly, through the three dimensions of space and the fourth of time. For example, we often identify an organism as the same organism solely because of its spatiotemporal continuity, since in many cases the same individual organism undergoes radical change over time. As Mayr points out, "that caterpillar and butterfly are the same individual is inferred not from any similarity in their appearance but from this continuity."[35] In this respect, also, individuals differ from kinds or classes. A kind is not spatiotemporally continuous, since a kind is constituted by its individual members, and those members are frequently scattered across disparate regions of spacetime. Indeed, kinds are potentially unlimited, in that members of a kind can come into and go out of existence in remote reaches of the universe at any time. Due to some bizarre chemical catastrophe, for example, all water could cease to exist today, but tomorrow we could synthesize more water in a lab. The kind *water* would thus not exhibit temporal continuity. Similarly, even if the only water in existence today were in Brazil, and the only water in existence tomorrow were in Scotland, the Brazilian and Scottish substances would both be water despite the fact that the kind *water* would not exhibit spatial contiguity. This is because all that matters with respect to whether liquids are water is that they possess the tight chemical structure, and individual samples of liquid can share that structure without being continuous with one another in time or contiguous with one another in space.

Third, each individual is a cohesive whole. For example, although each individual organism is composed of parts (organs, cells, and so on), and can be broken down into its parts, those parts are not a mere collection, but are *organized* and *functionally integrated*. Indeed, what makes the parts of an organism parts of that organism is the fact that they are functionally integrated with other parts of the organism, the fact that they contribute to the organization that makes up that organism. The functional integration of an organism's parts consists in the fact that those parts causally interact with one another, on a local level, in ways that help to sustain the organism over time and in ways that they do not causally interact with the parts of any other organism. In addition, the parts of an organism need not resemble one another in any respect in order to be parts of the same organism and contribute to its functional organization. Your left lung doesn't resemble your right femur in any interesting respect, and they don't have to share any particular properties in order to be parts of your body. In this respect, again, individuals differ from kinds. The individual members of a kind are not members of that kind because they are functionally integrated or organized in any particular fashion. Rather, individuals are members of the same kind simply by virtue of their similarity to one another.

As Mayr, Ghiselin, and Hull have shown, given the role that the species concept plays in biological theory, species exhibit each of the three characteristics definitive of individuals, just as organisms do. First, each species is spatiotemporally localized, occupying the region of spacetime that is circumscribed by its temporal beginning and end and its spatial borders. More important, each species has a definite location in the tree of life, a definite segment of the tree, with a definite beginning and end. No two species can occupy the same segment of the tree of life, and no one species can occupy two distinct segments. For, as we have seen, when a species goes extinct, numerically the same species cannot come into existence later. Even if other, identical organisms were to come into existence later, they would be classified by biologists as a new species, not as a continuation of the earlier species. Species, then, are spatiotemporally localized and discrete.

Second, each species is spatiotemporally continuous. Each species exists continuously from its temporal beginning to its end, and each species as a whole is spread over the same or contiguous regions of space for every moment of its existence. In this respect, like an organism, a species' existence can be plotted as a "space-time worm." Further, as Hull points out, the organisms that make up a species are related by descent.

> But descent presupposes replication and reproduction, and these processes in turn presuppose spatiotemporal proximity and continuity. When a single gene undergoes replication to produce two new genes, or a single cell undergoes miltotic division to produce two new cells, the end products are

spatiotemporally continuous with the parent entity. In sexual reproduction, the propagules, if not the parent organisms themselves, must come into contact. The end result is the successive modification of the same population.[36]

Thus, species are spatiotemporally continuous.

Third, species are unified, cohesive wholes, held together by the organizational glue of reproduction. For species consist of interbreeding populations, and both individual populations and groups of interbreeding populations are united by the *reproductive interactions* of organisms. As Mayr points out, this is due to the fact that the organisms that compose a species develop "from the joint gene pool of the species, and that they jointly contribute their genotypes to form the gene pool of the next generation."[37] The contribution of genotypes to the next generation, however, involves a great many causal interactions among organisms. The organisms in a population must structure a great many of their activities around the pursuit of sex with conspecifics, the act of sex with conspecifics, the incubation or gestation of the embryonic products of sex, and the care and production of live offspring. These causal interactions on a local level between the organisms involved in reproductive activities produce a cohesiveness within populations and species that is much like the functional organization of an organism (which derives from local causal interactions between its parts). Thus, species are unified, cohesive wholes.

Species, then, exhibit all the properties that are definitive of individuals. But, if species are individuals, just like organisms, how are we to understand the relation between organisms and species? According to essentialism, the only individuals are organisms, and species, as natural kinds, are classes of individuals that are united by a shared set of essential properties. Organisms are thus *members* of the classes that are their species. In this respect, essentialists see the relation between organisms and species as just like the relation between organisms and higher taxa such as orders and phyla. In the essentialist's view, higher taxa are also classes of the same individuals that are members of species, but those individuals are united in orders, and so on, by sharing increasingly more inclusive sets of essential properties. In the view that species are individuals, however, organisms are *parts of* species in precisely the way that cells are parts of organisms. In other words, organisms compose a species in precisely the way that cells compose a body.

The parallel between cell/organism and organism/species is worth belaboring for a moment. Cells are clearly individuals. They are spatiotemporally localized (discrete), spatio-temporally continuous, and cohesive. Yet these individuals are unproblematically parts of another, larger individual (an organism). But what makes the cells in an organism all parts of the same, larger individual? It is *not* shared properties that makes cells all parts of the same organism. The cells in your body, for example, aren't cells of *the same body* because they have the same genetic makeup. For, in fact, many of them don't. In the process of mitosis which created all the cells in your body, mutations occur. As a result, there are genetic differences among many of the cells in your body. They are, nonetheless, all *cells of your body*. Conversely, the cells in the bodies of identical (monozygotic) twins are genetically identical, with the exception of the cells in each twin that contain mutations. But two genetically identical cells from the bodies of two twins are not cells of the same body, despite their genetic identity. So, the genetic makeup of a cell, and its genetic similarity to other cells, is not what determines which body a cell belongs to. Rather, the cells in your body are cells of *your body* because they satisfy two conditions. First, they all descended, via iterated rounds of cell division, from the same zygote. For every cell in your body, there is an unbroken chain of descent via cell division that links it with the same

zygote. And, second, those cells that are parts of your body are so because they are causally integrated into the overall organization that makes up your body.

In the same way, organisms that belong to the same species need not share any properties. Sharing properties is not what determines whether two organisms belong to the same species, even if those organisms do share a significant number of properties. In fact, in many cases, organisms that belong to the same species do not resemble one another much at all. For example, we encountered *Paracerceis sculpta*, a species in which males come in three "morphs" that pursue different mating strategies. Large males are many times the size of small males, and they possess spiked "horns" where small males have only little nubs. Judging by shared properties, the two would be classified as different species, yet they belong to the same species. In addition, in some species in which developmental plasticity is common, individual organisms develop to mimic the appearance of other species. In such cases, different organisms in the species can develop to mimic distinct species, thereby having more observable characteristics in common with those other species than with one another. Thus, similarity is only *incidental* to belonging to the same species; it is not a criterion of it.

Indeed, not only need there be no shared properties among the organisms in a species, but the fact that species are reproductively organized individuals ensures the maintenance of variation among the organisms in a species. For, in meiosis, the early stage of sexual reproduction, gametes are created that contain only half of an organism's genes, and two gametes often contain different halves of an organism's genes. New organisms, or zygotes, are formed by a process that is, in effect, the random sampling of the parental gametes. This ensures that offspring are never genetically identical to either parent, so that every organism in a species (except for monozygotic siblings) is genetically unique. Further, an organism's development is the result of interactions between its genes and its environment, and no two organisms share precisely the same history of interactions with the environment. Consequently, each organism's unique genome encounters a unique environment during development, and the interactions between genome and environment ensure that each organism develops to be phenotypically unique. Of course, the organisms in a species do tend to share a lot of genes, and their developmental environments are often similar in gross outline, so these processes also tend to create some relatively widespread similarities, among organisms in the same species *in certain respects*. But, *on the whole*, each organism is phenotypically unique. Thus, the fact that species are reproductively organized individuals actually serves to guarantee and maintain significant genetic and phenotypic variation among the organisms in a species.

One thing that makes this viewpoint difficult to accept is the prevalence of "field guides" of various sorts—for example, Peterson's *Field Guide to Western Birds*. In field guides (or in dictionaries), you find species apparently defined by certain clusters of "field marks." For example, you will find a list of characteristics that identity the rose-breasted grosbeak: Males have a black head and upperparts, white belly, and a bright splash of red on the breast. This gives the impression to the nonspecialist that these characteristics are the qualities that define the rose-breasted grosbeak as a unique species. But this is mistaken. These characteristics are merely *markers*, which aid in identifying the species to which a bird belongs. They do not *define* the species. In the same way, "yellow house on the corner" can be a marker for identifying the house at 17 Primrose Lane, but it is not definitive of that house, since the house could be repainted, or even moved to another location, yet retain its identity as a unique individual house. Indeed, even though reliance on field guides can induce the conviction that species are defined by the char-

acteristics associated with a species' name in a field guide, a little reflection on their use can actually disabuse one of that conviction. The female common redpoll, for example, shares none of the characteristics that "define" the male of the species; instead, it more closely resembles the female pine siskin, which in turn doesn't much resemble the male pine siskin. Nonetheless, field guides are very clear about the species to which the females belong, and they are not classified in those species because of their distinguishing marks. Thus, field marks are rules of thumb for identifying the species of an organism; they should not be conflated with defining characteristics of a species.

Species, then, are larger-scale individuals than organisms, but they are individuals in the same sense that organisms are. And conspecific organisms are *parts* of the same species, in the same sense in which two cells can be parts of the same body. The fact that you and I belong to *Homo sapiens*, then, *does not entail* that "we can assume similarities merely on the basis of membership of one biological species."[38] Similarly, the fact that my heart and my thumbnail both belong to my body does not entail that there are properties they must share. Thus, when Cosmides and Tooby claim that, "by virtue of being members of the human species, all humans are expected to have the same adaptive mechanisms," they are simply wrong.[39] They misunderstand the nature of species, they misunderstand what's involved in two organisms' belonging to the same species, and they fail to understand how the reproductive organization of a species/individual serves to maintain variation among the organism/parts of that species/individual.

But what does the fact that species are individuals and not natural kinds have to do with human nature? What does the fact that organisms are parts of larger individuals, rather than members of a natural kind, have to do with human nature? The implications of these facts for the idea of human nature are surprisingly direct. If species are individuals, and organisms are parts of those individuals, then organisms do not belong to the same species because of shared possession of a set of characteristics that is purportedly the essence of that species. Shared characteristics are not *definitive* of belonging to the same species, they are *incidental* to belonging to the same species. Indeed, since organisms belong to the same species by virtue of being situated within a common genealogical nexus, there need be no characteristics that are shared by all the organisms that belong to a species. Thus, if human nature is supposed to be a set of "qualities that define us as a unique species," there is no human nature. As Hull says, if species are individuals, "then particular organisms belong in a particular species because they are part of that genealogical nexus, not because they possess any essential traits. No species has an essence in this sense. Hence there is no such thing as human nature."[40]

But the fact that species are individuals, rather than natural kinds, has additional implications. Evolutionary Psychologists envision that their "new science of the mind" will discover the "Darwinian algorithms" that are processed by universal psychological mechanisms. This discovery would demonstrate to us the universal functioning of the human mind, and the descriptions of that functioning would constitute *laws of thought* or *psychological laws*. The fact that species are individuals, however, entails that there can be no such species-specific psychological laws. To see why, let's begin by examining the nature of laws of nature.

Laws of nature are exceptionless universal generalizations. That is, a law of nature applies to all objects, at any point in space and at any time, that possess the properties mentioned in the law. As such, laws of nature mention no specific individuals. For example, Newton's law of gravitation states that two bodies attract one another with a force that is proportional to the product of their masses divided by the square of the distance between them. Although this law applies to any two bodies in the universe, it makes no mention of any specific individual body. As Ghiselin puts it, "although there are laws about celestial bodies in general, there is no law of nature for Mars or the Milky Way."[41] The reason is that laws of nature are designed to capture *regularities* in nature, and regularities involve the *repetition of nonunique properties* or events. While unique individuals can instantiate a regularity, they do so only insofar as they possess properties that are also possessed by other individuals—in particular, the properties mentioned in the law stating the regularity, in other words, only the *nonunique features* of unique individuals—only those features of an individual that are *or could be* possessed by other individuals—fall under laws of nature. Thus, Ghiselin says, "there are no laws for individuals as such, only for classes of individuals."[42]

However, there aren't laws of nature for just *any* classes of individuals. For example, each individual gold watch is a member of the class of watches and a member of the class of gold things. There are no laws of nature that apply to individual gold watches by virtue of their being *watches*, but there are laws of nature that apply to them by virtue of their being *gold*. This is because, although *watch* is a kind, it is not a *natural* kind; *gold*, on the other hand, is a natural kind. Kinds, in general, are defined by properties, so that an individual is a member of a kind just in case it possesses the property or properties that define the kind. Some properties, however, are such that their different instances don't exhibit precisely the same patterns of causal interaction with other objects. Watches, for example, come in many shapes and sizes, and they are made of many different materials. So the different instances of the property *watch* tend to exhibit different patterns of causal interaction with other objects. Some tarnish or scratch in certain conditions, whereas others don't. Other properties, though, are such that their different instances exhibit the same patterns of causal interaction with certain other properties. Each sample of gold, for example, exhibits a range of causal interactions with certain other properties that is also exhibited by every other sample of gold, since the essence of gold (its atomic number) features in deep and robust regularities in nature. The properties that exhibit uniform patterns of causal interaction with other properties are the ones that define natural kinds. Thus, since laws of nature describe exceptionless causal regularities in nature, and since the properties that define natural kinds are properties that interact in regular ways, the classes of individuals to which laws of nature apply are natural kinds. In short, laws of nature serve to capture the regular interactions among the natural kinds that make up our world.

Laws of nature, then, apply to individuals only insofar as those individuals exemplify the natural kinds over which the laws generalize. Given this fact, could there be laws of *specifically human* biology or psychology? That is, could a science that studies properties that are necessarily unique to a single species discover laws of nature that necessarily apply to that species and that species only? There are two ways in which this question can be taken, but the answer in each case is no.

On the one hand, if we are asking whether there could be laws of nature that apply to our species as a whole, and only to our species, the answer is no because *Homo sapiens* is an individual, not a natural kind, and there are no laws of nature that apply exclusively to a single individual. On the other hand, if we are asking whether there could be laws of nature that apply to individual human beings insofar as they possess properties that uniquely *define Homo sapiens*, the answer is still no. For, since *Homo sapiens* is an individual, not a natural kind, individual human beings are not human beings by virtue of instantiating the natural kind *Homo sapiens*. Rather, individual human beings are all human beings by virtue of being *parts* of the same genealogical nexus. And, as we have seen, the individuals that constitute the parts of another, larger individual are not parts of that individual by virtue of being members of the same natural kind.

There are, however, two respects in which this argument must be qualified. First, although there are no laws of nature that apply *exclusively* to human beings, there are laws of nature that apply to *Homo sapiens*. For *Homo sapiens* is a species, and the category of *species* is a natural kind. That is, there are laws of biology, including the laws of evolution, that apply to *all* species. But, the properties that make *Homo sapiens* a *unique* species—the properties that make it a unique segment in the tree of life—will not figure in these laws. Rather, insofar as laws of evolution apply to *Homo sapiens*, they apply to *Homo sapiens* because of properties that it shares with other species—in particular, the properties essential to the natural kind *species*.

Second, although there are no laws of nature that apply exclusively to *Homo sapiens*, there are many laws of nature that apply to individual human beings. The laws of physics and chemistry apply to individual human beings, and there are laws of biology, including the laws of genetics, that apply to individual human beings. But these laws apply to individual human beings only insofar as humans exemplify properties that are not exclusive to human beings, but that are (or could be) possessed by much larger classes that include human beings. The laws of mechanics, for example, apply to individual human beings, but they apply to us as objects with mass, and mass is not unique to human beings. Similarly, the laws of genetics apply to individual human beings, but they apply to us as developmental systems or as sexually reproducing organisms, and these properties are not unique to humans. Thus, the laws of nature that do apply to individual human beings are not candidates for scientific laws of *human nature*, since they are laws that do not apply exclusively to human beings.

There are, however, more specific reasons why there can be no scientific laws exclusive to human psychology. For, if there were psychological laws that applied exclusively to humans, those laws would have to generalize over natural kinds, and those natural kinds would have to be human psychological mechanisms (or aspects of their functioning). In other words, in order for there to be psychological laws, human psychological mechanisms would have to be natural kinds. But, since psychological mechanisms are phenotypic traits, the question of whether psychological mechanisms form natural kinds is really the question of the logic underlying the classification of phenotypic traits. In particular, it is the question of the criteria involved in classifying a trait of two different organisms as "the same" trait (in this case, classifying psychological mechanisms in two individuals as "the same" psychological mechanism). If traits were natural kinds, the criterion involved in classifying a trait of two different organisms as the same trait would simply be whether those two traits shared certain essential properties—namely, the properties definitive of that natural kind of trait. Again, this would be identical to the logic involved in classifying two samples of platinum as the same substance; the two samples are the same substance if they are both composed of atoms with atomic number 78. But this is never the logic involved in the biological classification of a trait in two organisms as instances of the same trait. Indeed, there are two distinct ways of classifying traits as "the same" in biology and neither of these ways involves identifying shared essential properties, such as could feature in laws of nature.

The traits of two organisms are grouped as "the same" trait by virtue of being either *homologies* or *analogies* (also known as *homoptasies*). Traits of two organisms are *homologous* if those traits derived, possibly with modification, from an equivalent trait in the common ancestor of those organisms.[43] The ancestral trait is determined to be "equivalent" to the derived traits just in case it occupied the same position relative to other parts of the body and had similar connections with those other body parts. For example, the human eye is homologous to the eye of a cat, since the human eye and the cat eye derived from an equivalent eye of an ancestor of both humans and cats, although eyes in both lineages were modified after their divergence. Similarly, human limbs and cat limbs are homologous, since they were both derived from the limbs of a common ancestor. This is the sense in which the human eye and the cat eye are both eyes. As the evolutionary biologist Gunter Wagner puts it:

> A large number of characters are certainly derived from the same structure in a common ancestor and are therefore undoubtedly homologous. One simply cannot escape the conclusion that the brain of a rat and a human are actually the "same" in spite of their obvious differences.[44]

In contrast, traits of two organisms are *analogous* if those traits have a similar structure or function, but evolved in those organisms' lineages independently of one another. The human eye and the octopus eye are not derived from the eye of a common ancestor, since the common ancestor to humans and octopuses had no eyes. The human eye and the octopus eye have structural and functional similarities, however, so the human eye is analogous to the octopus eye. Similarly, the wings of the black-capped chickadee are analogous to the wings of the mosquito, since wings evolved separately in birds and insects. They are nonetheless both wings, because of their structural and functional similarities.

Thus, when two organisms are said to have "the same" trait, it means that those organisms possess either homologous traits or analogous traits. There is no other sense, in biology, in which two organisms can be said to have "the same" trait. This is true not only of trait comparisons between species, as in the examples above, but of trait comparisons within a species as well. Your eyes and my eyes are homologous, because they were derived from the eyes of a common ancestor. Of course, the common ancestor from which you and I derived our eyes was far more recent than the common ancestor from which human eyes and cat eyes were derived. Nonetheless, the sense in which your eyes and my eyes are "the same" is that our eyes are homologous. Indeed, all of the traits that you and I share and that are described in "precise anatomical detail" by *Gray's Anatomy* are homologies.

Homologous traits, however, are not classified together by virtue of shared characteristics, let alone by virtue of shared essential characteristics. The human brain and the cat brain are homologous despite many structural differences, and the hind limbs of the crocodile and those of the starling are homologous despite sharing virtually no interesting properties. The same is true of homologous traits *within* species. The eyes of each individual human are not human eyes because they share properties essential to being a human eye, but because they are homologies, traits derived from an equivalent eye in a common ancestor. Indeed, "deformed" eyes, which lack some of the properties of eyes detailed in *Gray's Anatomy*, are nonetheless eyes. And the eyes of the blind are human eyes despite not performing the typical visual function of eyes. Further, male nipples and females nipples are all nipples because they are homologous traits, not because of shared morphological or functional properties (which, in fact, they do not share). This is because, as Wagner says, "homology is assessed regardless of shape or function."[45] In fact, homology is assessed in precisely the way that the species classification of two organisms is assessed—genealogically. Traits of two organisms are homologies if they were derived from an equivalent trait in a common ancestor, regardless of whether they share properties, just as two organisms belong to the same species if they descended from a

common ancestor in that species, regardless of whether they share properties. In short, homologies, like the organisms of a species, are unified by descent, not by shared properties.

Two individual instances of a trait (in two distinct organisms), then, are not classed together as homologous by the same logic as two samples of platinum are classed together as the same substance. Instances of natural kinds, like platinum, are classed together because of their intrinsic properties, regardless of their provenance. If we froze the universe at a particular moment of time, for example, we could identify every instance of platinum simply by determining whether objects were composed of atoms with atomic number 78. But, in that frozen instant, we would not be able to identify every instance of a particular homology. For history is everything with respect to determining whether two individual instances of a trait are homologous. Your eyes and my eyes are homologous ("the same") not because of properties they share *at this instant*, but because of chains of descent that reach back from each of us into the past and converge upon a common ancestor. Our eyes are not "the same" because they are connected by common properties at this moment, but because they are connected by that historical V of descent, with our common ancestor located at the apex. Thus, the logic by which traits are classified as "the same" (homologous) in biology is very different from the logic by which two entities are classified as instances of the same natural kind. In short, "the same" trait in organisms of the same species are homologies, and homologies are not natural kinds.

If many humans share "the same" psychological mechanism, then what makes their psychological mechanisms the same is their derivation from a common ancestor, not any properties they may happen to share. But no phenotypic traits are inherited directly, by being directly copied as wholes from one generation to another. They are, instead, constructed anew in each generation through the process of development. Indeed, like all phenotypic characteristics of individual human beings, psychological mechanisms develop via the interaction between an individual human's unique genome and the unique sequence of environments to which that individual's genome is exposed. And this process consistently produces variation among the psychological mechanisms possessed by humans, just as it consistently produces variation among all phenotypes. Despite these variations, however, psychological mechanisms in different individual humans remain "the same" mechanism. For what makes them the same is that they are derived from a common ancestor, even if they have been modified in the process. Thus, human psychological mechanisms are not natural kinds, they are homologies, which may exhibit significant variation despite being "the same." Consequently, there can be no *laws* of *human* psychology, since laws of nature apply only to natural kinds.

This doesn't mean, however, that we can't make discoveries regarding human psychology, and it doesn't mean that human minds exhibit no regularities. Even if there are no laws of nature that apply to single individuals as such, individuals can nonetheless be *described*. There are no laws of nature that pertain to you and only you, but those who know you well can give richly detailed descriptions of your physique and personality. And those descriptions can convey to others a great deal of knowledge about you as an individual. Similarly, although there can be no laws of nature that pertain exclusively to human psychology, psychology may one day provide us with richly detailed descriptions of human minds. And some of those descriptions may prove general enough to apply to vast segments of our species *for a particular period of time*. In other words, psychology may one day provide us with descriptions of some very widespread regularities among the minds of our conspecifics. But

those descriptions will never achieve the status of laws of nature, since laws of nature apply only to instances of natural kinds. Insofar as psychology concerns itself with distinctively *human* cognition and emotion, it must begin to conceive of itself as being in the business of providing *descriptions* of *homologous characteristics*, rather than being in the business of providing laws of thought in the way that physics provides laws of mechanics or chemistry provides laws of chemical bonding.

To conclude, then, since *Homo sapiens* is an individual, not a natural kind, there is no such thing as human nature. And, since human psychological mechanisms are homologies, human psychological mechanisms do not form natural kinds. Consequently, there are no laws of nature that pertain exclusively to human minds, so Evolutionary Psychology can never fulfill its promise to be the "new science of human nature" by discovering the psychological laws that govern the functioning of evolved psychological mechanisms. A truly *evolutionary* science of human psychology will not only abandon the quest for human nature, but, with it, the quest to be a science in the model of physics or chemistry.

Notes

1 Ghiselin 1997, p. 1.
2 Buss 1999, p. 47; emphasis added.
3 Loptson 1995, p. 1.
4 Loptson 1995, p. 19.
5 Trigg 1988, p. 4.
6 Tooby and Cosmides 1990a, p. 19.
7 Tooby and Cosmides 1990a, p. 18.
8 Bonner 1980, p. 9.
9 Tooby and Cosmides 1990a, p. 17; emphasis added.
10 Tooby and Cosmides 1992, p. 38.
11 Tooby and Cosmides 1992, p. 78.
12 Tooby and Cosmides 1992, pp. 68–69.
13 Wilson 1994, p. 224.
14 Izpisúa Belmonte 1999, p. 47.
15 Cosmides and Tooby 1997, p. 72; emphasis added.

16 Sober 1994, p. 205; emphasis added.
17 Cosmides and Tooby 1992, p. 211.
18 Cosmides and Tooby 1994, p. 101.
19 Brown 1991, p. 50.
20 Sober 1994, p. 210.
21 Sober 1994, p. 222.
22 Tooby and Cosmides 1992, p. 82.
23 Tooby and Cosmides 1992, p. 78.
24 Sober 1994, p. 222.
25 Sober 1994, p. 222.
26 Tooby and Cosmides 1992, p. 78; emphasis added.
27 Symons 1979, p. 32.
28 Lewontin 1995, p. 41.
29 Cavalli-Sforza, Menozzi, and Piazza 1994, p. 141.
30 Sober 1994, p. 214.
31 Tooby and Cosmides 1990b, pp. 380–381.
32 Hull 1989a, p. 12; emphasis added.
33 Hull 1989a, p. 17.
34 Ghiselin 1997, p. 41.
35 Mayr 1988, p. 343.
36 Hull 1989b, p. 85.
37 Mayr 1988, p. 344.
38 Trigg 1988, p. 4.
39 Cosmides and Tooby 1992, p. 211; emphasis added.
40 Hull 1978, p. 358.
41 Ghiselin 1997, p. 45.
42 Ghiselin 1997, p. 45.
43 See Futuyma 1998, p. 109.
44 Wagner 1989, p. 51.
45 Wagner 1989, p. 51.

References

Bonner, John T. (1980). The Evolution of Culture in Animals. Princeton, NJ: Princeton University Press.

Brown, Donald E. (1991). Human Universals. New York: McGraw-Hill.

Buss, David M. (1999). Evolutionary Psychology: The new science of the mind. Boston, MA: Allyn and Bacon.

Cavalli-Sforza, L. Luca, Paolo Menozzi, and Alberto Piazza (1994). The History and Geography of Human Genes. Princeton, NJ: Princeton University Press.

Cosmides, Leda, and John Tooby (1987). From evolution to behavior: Evolutionary psychology as the missing link. In J. Dupré (ed.), The Latest on the Best: Essays on evolution and optimality (pp. 277–306). Cambridge, MA: MIT Press.

Cosmides, Leda, and John Tooby (1992). Cognitive adaptations for social exchange In J. H. Barkow, L. Cosmides, and J. Tooby (eds.), The Adapted Mind: Evolutionary psychology and the generation of culture (pp. 163–228). New York: Oxford University Press.

Cosmides, Leda, and John Tooby (1994). Origins of domain specificity: The evolution of functional organization. In L. A. Hirschfeld, and S. A. Gelman (eds.), Mapping the Mind: Domain specificity in cognition and culture (pp. 85–116). New York: Cambridge University Press.

Cosmides, Leda, and John Tooby (1997). The modular nature of human intelligence. In A. B. Scheibel and J. W. Schopf (eds.), The Origin and Evolution of Intelligence (pp. 71–101). Sudbury, MA: Jones and Bartlett.

Futuyma, Douglas J. (1998). Evolutionary Biology (3rd ed.). Sunderland, MA: Sinauer Associates.

Ghiselin, Michael T. (1997). Metaphysics and the Origin of Species. Albany, NY: State University of New York Press.

Hull, David L. (1978). A matter of individuality. Philosophy of Science, 45: 335–360.

Hull, David L. (1989a). On human nature. In The Metaphysics of Evolution (pp. 11–24). Albany, NY: State University of New York Press.

Hull, David L. (1989b). The ontological status of species as evolutionary units. In The Metaphysics of Evolution (pp. 79–88). Albany NY: State University of New York Press.

Izpisúa Belmonte, Juan Carlos (1999). How the body tells left from right. Scientific American, 280(6): 46–51.

Lewontin, Richard (1995). Human Diversity. New York: Scientific American Library.

Loptson, Peter (1995). Theories of Human Nature. Peterborough, Canada: Broadview Press.

Mayr, Ernst (1988). The ontology of the species taxon. In Toward a New Philosophy of Biology: Observations of an evolutionist (pp. 335–358). Cambridge, MA: Harvard University Press.

Sober, Elliott (1994). Evolution, population thinking, and essentialism. In From a Biological Point of View: Essays in evolutionary philosophy (pp. 201–232). New York: Cambridge University Press.

Symons, Donald (1979). The Evolution of Human Sexuality. New York: Oxford University Press.

Tooby, John, and Leda Cosmides (1990a). On the universality of human nature and the uniqueness of the individual: The role of genetics and adaptation. *Journal of Personality*, 58: 17–67.

Tooby, John, and Leda Cosmides (1990b). The past explains the present: Emotional adaptations and the structure of ancestral environments. *Ethology and Sociobiology*, 11: 375–424.

Tooby, John, and Leda Cosmides (1992). The psychological foundations of culture. In J. H. Barkow, L. Cosmides and J. Tooby (eds.), *The Adapted Mind: Evolutionary Psychology and the generation of culture*

(pp. 19–136). New York: Oxford University Press.

Trigg, Roger (1988). *Ideas of Human Nature: An historical introduction*. Oxford, UK: Blackwell.

Wagner, Gunter P. (1989). The biological homology concept. *Annual Review of Ecology and Systematics*, 20: 51–69.

Wilson, David Sloan (1994). Adaptive genetic variation and human evolutionary psychology. *Ethology and Sociobiology*, 15: 219–235.

Chapter 4

Edouard Machery

A PLEA FOR HUMAN NATURE

The notion of human nature has fallen into disrepute in various quarters and a remarkable number of charges have been filed against it. Some social critics have alleged that it contributes to the justification of oppressive social norms, while some philosophers, such as Sartre, have challenged it on metaphysical grounds.[1] More seriously, prominent philosophers of biology have argued that the notion of human nature is incompatible with modern evolutionary biology. In a well-known article, David Hull writes (1986):

> All the ingenuity which has been exercised trying to show that all human beings are essentially the same might be better used trying to explain why we must all be essentially the same in order to have such things as human rights ... Until this question is answered, I remain suspicious of continued claims about the existence and importance of human nature.[2]

Evolutionary biologist Michael Ghiselin concurs (1997):

> What does evolution teach us about human nature? It tells us that human nature is a superstition.[3]

And, more recently, David Buller has attacked evolutionary psychologists for endorsing the notion of human nature (2005):

> The idea of a universal human nature is deeply anthetical to a truly evolutionary view of our species ... A truly *evolutionary* psychology should abandon the quest for human nature and with it any attempt to discover universal laws of human psychology.[4]

While some criticisms of the notion of human nature might well be justified, I argue in this article that many charges filed by philosophers of biology are unwarranted. Because Hull's (1986) article is the source of many attacks against the notion of human nature in the philosophy of biology, I focus exclusively on it here. For the sake of space, I do not elaborate on the positive arguments for the notion of human nature.

Here is how I will proceed. In the first section, I characterize in some detail two distinct notions of human nature—an essentialist notion and a nomological notion. In the second section, I show that Hull's objections invalidate the essentialist notion of human nature, but not the nomological notion. Finally, I reply to two objections.

Two Notions of Human Nature

It is important to realize that there are many ways to construe human nature and that the arguments for and against human nature often bear on specific construals rather than on human nature in general. In this section, I describe two distinct construals.

According to the essentialist notion of human nature, human nature is the set of properties that are separately necessary and jointly sufficient for being a human. Furthermore, the properties that are part of human nature are typically thought to be distinctive of humans.

Philosophers and scientists have proposed numerous candidate properties for inclusion in human nature, so construed. In the *Discourse on Method*, Descartes argued that language, understood as the capacity to express and understand an infinite number of sentences, was distinctive of humans, in contrast to animals and machines (1637/1987):

> We can certainly conceive of a machine so constructed that it utters words and even utters words which correspond to bodily actions causing a change in its organs (e.g., if you touch it in one spot it asks what you want of it, if you touch it in another, it cries out that you are hurting it, and so on). But, it is not conceivable that such a machine should produce different arrangements of words so as to give an appropriately meaningful answer to whatever is said in its presence, as the dullest of men can do.[5]

Reason, morality, humor, and knowledge of death have also been proposed by philosophers and scientists as good candidates for belonging to human nature.

The essentialist notion of human nature is plausibly rooted in folk biology. Folk biology is the intuitive body of knowledge about animals, plants, biological properties, and biological events (death, disease, etc.) that people spontaneously rely on when they reason about biological matters. An important component of folk biology is the belief that each species is characterized by a distinctive set of properties, which develop endogenously and are transmitted across generations.[6] Because humans are just one species, believing that humans share a set of necessary and jointly sufficient properties, which set them apart from other species, seems to be a natural extension of this component.

Noteworthily, even if the essentialist notion of human nature is truly rooted in folk biology, it does not seem to be widespread across cultures and times, in contrast to other components of folk biology. When one looks at how people have thought about humans across cultures and times, one typically finds an emphasis on what distinguishes humans into distinct groups, rather than an emphasis on what is common to and distinctive of humans. To give a single example, during the last decades of the nineteenth century and the first decade of the twentieth century, European and American psychologists, sociologists, anthropologists, and biologists developed various pseudo-scientific racial classifications of humans that were allegedly grounded in what was then understood of human evolution.

The nomological notion of human nature stands in sharp contrast to the essentialist notion. According to this second notion, human nature is the set of properties that humans tend to possess as a result of the evolution of their species. According to this notion, being bipedal is part of human nature, because most humans are bipedal animals and because bipedalism is an outcome of the evolution of humans. The same is true of biparental investment in children, fear reactions to unexpected noise, or the capacity to speak. According to this construal, describing human nature is thus equivalent to what ornithologists do when they characterize the typical properties of birds in bird fieldguides.

Although I do not have the space to elaborate on this point here, it is important to see that the nomological notion of human nature inverts the Aristotelian relation between nature and generalization. For Aristotle, the fact that humans have the same nature explains why many generalizations can be made about them. For me, on the contrary, the fact that many generalizations can be made about humans explain in which sense there is a human nature.

It is worth highlighting the contrast between the nomological notion and the essentialist notion of human nature. Most important, according to the former notion and in contrast to the latter notion, human nature does not define membership in the human species: the properties that are part of human nature are neither necessary nor jointly sufficient for being a human. Although biparental investment in children might be part of human nature (according to the nomological notion of human nature), membership in the human species has nothing to do with biparental investment in children.

Because the properties that belong to human nature are not definitional, they are not necessarily possessed by all humans. Although the capacity to speak is part of human nature, not all humans are able to speak, because the development of this capacity requires exposure to language. Not all humans have fear reactions, because the amygdala of some humans is impaired, following brain traumas or particular developmental trajectories. What is required of the properties that are part of human nature is that they be shared by most humans, as a result of a specific causal process—the evolution of humans. Relatedly, the properties that are part of human nature do not have to be possessed only by humans. For instance, like humans, many animals react fearfully to unexpected noises. Finally, the properties that are part of human nature are not permanent; human nature might change.

Two additional points should be noted. First, nothing is said about the nature of the evolutionary processes in the proposed characterization of human nature. The traits that are part of human nature can be adaptations, by-products of adaptations, outcomes of developmental constraints, or neutral traits that have come to fixation by drift. In addition, human nature is not normative; there is nothing wrong in not

having the properties that are part of human nature.

According to the nomological characterization of human nature, bimodal traits are not part of human nature (because they are not widely shared among humans in general). Thus, if males and females have different evolved mating psychologies, the properties of male and of female mating psychologies are not part of human nature. One could alternatively propose to include in human nature all the properties that humans have because of the evolution of their species, *whether these properties are shared by most humans or only by some subset of humans*. Then, males' and females' evolved mating psychologies would be part of human nature (supposing that they really differ). To support this alternative proposal, one could push the analogy between human nature and the description of birds in fieldguides, noting that fieldguides usually characterize a species with pictures of males, females, and members of geographic subspecies.

Although this alternative proposal is perfectly coherent, I would like to resist it, because it is useful to have a notion that picks out the similarities between humans, particularly their psychological and behavioral similarities. Much of the social sciences attempt to characterize and explain differences between humans. Differential psychology (e.g., personality psychology) focuses on individual differences, while much of anthropology focuses on cultural differences. In addition, cultural and individual differences are more salient to common sense than similarities. The notion of human nature is thus a useful counterpoint to the widespread neglect of the similarities between humans.

Hull's Arguments

Hull's (1986) main argument against the notion of human nature is straightforward:

Generations of philosophers have argued that all human beings are essentially the same, that is, *they share the same nature* . . . Periodically a biological species might be characterized by one or more characters which are both universally distributed among and limited to the organisms belonging to that species, but *such states of affairs are temporary, contingent and relatively rare.* (my italics)[7]

This argument is rooted in the understanding of the nature of species that emerges from Darwinian population thinking.[8] According to evolutionary biologists, membership in a given species is not defined by the possession of specific (intrinsic) properties. Thus, an animal is not a dog in virtue of having a given set of properties. As a result, the biological notion of species does not entail that conspecifics share a set of (intrinsic) properties.

Furthermore, as Hull rightly emphasizes, evolutionary biologists insist on the variability of conspecifics. Because developmental conditions vary, it is biologically unlikely that all conspecifics share a given property, when in addition to being universal, this property is supposed to distinguish conspecifics from the members of other species. To focus on humans, it is hard to find any property that is both distinctive of humans and common to all humans. Furthermore, even if a property were both distinctive and universal, this state of affairs would be contingent. It would not be a necessary property for being a human.

The way biologists conceive of species clearly invalidates the essentialist notion of human nature, but certainly not the nomological notion of human nature described above, for according to the latter notion, the properties that constitute human nature are not definitional and they need not be universal among humans or distinctive of humans. Thus, Hull's argument leaves the nomological notion of human nature unscathed.

In addition to the argument summarized above, Hull also argues against a revision of the essentialist notion of human nature (1986):

Nor does it help to switch from traditional essences to *statistically characterized essences*. If the history of phenetic taxonomy has shown anything, it is that *organisms can be subdivided into species as Operational Taxonomic Units in indefinitely any ways if all one looks at is covariation.* (my italics)[9]

The reply Hull is considering here goes as follows. Rather than characterizing human nature as a set of properties possessed by all humans and only by humans, one might propose that human nature is the set of properties such that an animal is a human if and only if it possesses a sufficient number of these properties. According to this reply, the properties that constitute human nature need not be universal. Hence, this notion would be consistent with Hull's emphasis that it is biologically unlikely that all and only humans share a given trait. To counter this reply, Hull notes that it has turned out to be impossible to define the membership in species by means of clusters of properties. He concludes that appealing to a cluster of properties in order to flesh out the notion of human nature is of no help to defend this notion.

Like Hull's first argument, this second argument fails to invalidate the nomological notion of human nature. According to this notion, the properties that constitute human nature are not conditions of membership in the human species. Hence, whether or not one can define membership in the human species by means of a cluster of properties has no bearing whatsoever on the value of the nomological notion of human nature.

To summarize, Hull's arguments invalidate the essentialist notion of human nature and variants of this notion. Because species are historical entities and because conspecifics vary, one cannot characterize membership in the human species by means of a definition or by means of a cluster of properties. But, this conclusion does not mean that humans have no nature, if one construes human nature as those properties that humans tend to possess as a result of the evolution of their species. This notion of human nature is consistent with the historical nature of species and with the variability of the traits possessed by conspecifics.

Two Objections

In the last section of this chapter. I consider two objections against the nomological notion of human nature. Both objections grant that some properties are common among humans as a result of the evolution of their species, but question the identification of human nature with this set of property.

A Canada-dry Notion?

One might first argue that the nomological notion of human nature is a "Canada-dry" notion: it looks like human nature, but it isn't.[10] For, the critic might go on, the nomological notion of human nature is unable to fulfill any of the roles that the traditional notion of human nature—the very notion attacked by Hull, Ghiselin, or Buller—was supposed to fulfill. According to this notion of human nature and in contrast to the essentialist notion, the properties that are part of human nature neither distinguish humans from other animals, nor define humans, nor determine what a normal human looks like. If this objection were correct, my criticism of Hull's arguments would be a pyrrhic victory: I would have shown that there is a notion of human nature that is not invalidated by these arguments—just one that is not worth fighting for.

This objection ought to be resisted. The notion of human nature has played many roles in the history of philosophy and in the history of science. The nomological notion of human nature certainly fails to fulfill some of these roles, as noted by the present objection. But it does fulfill other roles, which have traditionally

motivated the notion of human nature. Particularly, saying that humans have a nature entails that humans form a class that is of importance for biology. The members of this class tend to have some properties in common in virtue of evolutionary processes. Furthermore, saying that a given property, say a behavior, such as biparental investment, or a psychological trait, such as outgroup bias, belongs to human nature is to say that this trait is common among humans and that its occurrence among humans can be explained in evolutionary terms. This is also to say that some kinds of explanation for the occurrence of this trait among humans are inappropriate. Particularly, this is to reject any explanation to the effect that its occurrence is exclusively due to enculturation or to social learning.

Do All Traits Belong to Human Nature?

The nomological notion of human nature makes sense only if not all properties of humans are part of human nature. This necessary condition is easily fulfilled because many properties are not widespread among humans and, as a result, are not good candidates for being part of human nature. For instance, the belief that the son of a god died on a cross in Jerusalem is shared by (only) one human out of six and is thus not a good candidate for being part of human nature.

In addition to this easily fulfilled necessary condition, it should also be the case that not all properties that are common among humans are part of human nature. It might seem natural to argue that this condition is also easily fulfilled because not all properties that are common among humans are common because of some evolutionary processes. Among the common properties of humans, those that are not common because of some evolutionary processes are not part of human nature, according to the nomological notion of human nature. For example, the belief that water is wet is not part of human nature, in spite of being common, because this belief is not the result of some evolutionary processes. Rather, people learn that water is wet.

The second objection considered in the third section denies that one can tease apart in this manner those traits that are common among humans and that are part of human nature and those traits that are common among humans without being part of human nature. The reason is that evolutionary processes causally contribute to any property that is common to humans. To see this, consider again the belief that water is wet. People acquire this belief by experiencing the wetness of water or, to put it differently, they acquire this belief by individual learning. Now, people would not be able to form this belief if humans had not evolved the sense of touch and the capacity to form beliefs about the qualitative properties of substances. Because of the truth of this counterfactual, evolutionary processes seem to be among the causes of the belief that water is wet. Since this argument can be generalized to every property common among humans, it seems that human nature includes all these properties—suggesting that the nomological notion of human nature is too inclusive.

It is probably correct that evolutionary processes causally contribute to the existence of any trait that is common among humans. But only some of these traits can be explained by reference to evolutionary processes. That is, only some of them are the object of ultimate explanations. What distinguishes these traits from the traits that are not the object of ultimate explanations is that they have an evolutionary history. Saying that a trait has an evolutionary history is to say something stronger than the fact that it has perdured across generations. Humans have probably believed that water is wet for a very long time, although this belief has no evolutionary history. For this trait is not a modification of a distinct, more ancient trait. By contrast, human shame is probably a modification of an emotion that existed among the last common ancestors of humans and of the great apes.

Thus, the second objection considered in the third section ought also to be resisted. By appealing to the notion of ultimate explanation, one can tease apart the traits that are part of human nature from those traits that are merely common among humans, in spite of evolutionary processes causally contributing to all human traits.

Conclusion

The significance of Hull's influential attack against the notion of human nature is limited. It decisively invalidates the essentialist notion of human nature, a notion that might be rooted in folk biology. However, it leaves the nomological notion of human nature entirely unscathed: humans have many properties in common as a result of the evolution of their species. Importantly, because this notion of human nature is probably the relevant one for understanding sociobiologists', such as E. O. Wilson, and evolutionary psychologists' interest in human nature, Hull's attack fails to undermine their scientific projects.

Notes

1 Sartre (1958) wrote that "there is no human nature. Man first of all exists . . . and defines himself afterwards" (p. 28).
2 Hull 1986, pp. 11–12.
3 Ghiselin 1997, p. 1.
4 Buller 2005, p. 419.
5 Descartes 1637/1987, p. 187.
6 See for example Atran 1990.
7 Hull 1986, p. 3.
8 Mayr 1976.
9 Hull 1986, p. 11.
10 From an old French advertisement for the ginger-ale soda Canada Dry: "It looks like alcohol, it has the taste of alcohol, but isn't."

References

Atran, S. (1990) *Cognitive Foundations of Natural History: Towards an anthropology of science.* Cambridge: Cambridge University Press.

Buller, D. J. (2005) *Adapting Minds*. Cambridge, MA: MIT Press.

Descartes, R. (1637/1985) *Discourse on the method* (R. Stoothoff, Trans.). In J. Cottingham, R. Stoothoff and D. Murdoch (Eds.), *The Philosophical Writings of Descartes* (pp. 111–151). Cambridge: Cambridge University Press.

Ghiselin, M. T. (1997) *Metaphysics and the Origins of Species*. Albany, NY: State University of New York Press.

Hull, D. L. (1986) On human nature. *PSA: Proceedings of the Biennal Meeting of the Philosophy of Science Association*, 2, 3–13.

Sartre, J.-P. (1958). *Existentialism and Humanism* (P. Mairet, Trans.). London: Methuen.

Chapter 5

Elizabeth Cashdan

WHAT IS A HUMAN UNIVERSAL?
Human Behavioral Ecology and Human Nature

In 1991 the cultural anthropologist Don Brown bucked anthropology's tabula rasa tradition by identifying over 300 "human universals"—individual and sociocultural traits that are found in every known human society (Brown 1991; universals enumerated in Pinker 2003). The items he identified include both psychological traits (e.g., wariness around snakes, sweets preferred, sexual jealousy) and sociocultural ones (e.g., territoriality, females do more direct childcare, food sharing). Because they are universal, it is plausible that these traits have a biological basis and that they are evolved features of a universal human nature.

What, then, of the many domains where cultures differ? The assumption is often made that human nature is found solely in its universals—in the traits found in every society. A trait that is found in some societies and not others is then assumed to be culturally constructed and without an evolutionary foundation.

Behavioral ecologists hold a different view: because human nature evolved to be flexible in predictable ways, the task of understanding human nature requires that we understand how evolution shaped that variation. The assumption is not just that we evolved to respond flexibly, but that selection shaped the nature and direction of that flexibility. To a behavioral ecologist, then, the predictable, patterned nature of that response is the universal we must understand. In this view, we cannot understand our universal

human nature without understanding the variability in its expression.

The concept is clarified by viewing variation as a norm of reaction—the pattern of expression of a genotype across a range of environments. The increase in a person's skin pigmentation as a function of exposure to sunlight (tanning) is a norm of reaction, as is the percentage of male and female leopard geckos hatched at different incubation temperatures (see Figure 5.1). Although gecko families vary in the the strength of their response to temperature, the patterning

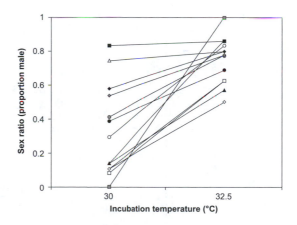

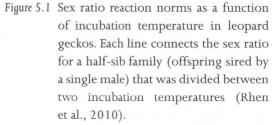

Figure 5.1 Sex ratio reaction norms as a function of incubation temperature in leopard geckos. Each line connects the sex ratio for a half-sib family (offspring sired by a single male) that was divided between two incubation temperatures (Rhen et al., 2010).

of the response is similar: it is part of leopard gecko nature for more males to be born when the temperature is warmer, within this range of temperatures.

Figure 5.2 shows another example, from a brilliant study of soapberry bug mating behavior by Carroll & Corneli (1999). A male soapberry bug may stay attached to his mate after mating in order to guard her against other suitors. If there are many more males than females (high sex ratio), this makes adaptive sense: he gains more by keeping other males away than he loses in forgone mating opportunities. But if eager suitors are less numerous (lower sex ratio), he gains little by mate-guarding and should instead leave after mating and search for another mate. The upper figure shows the mate-guarding response of male Oklahoma

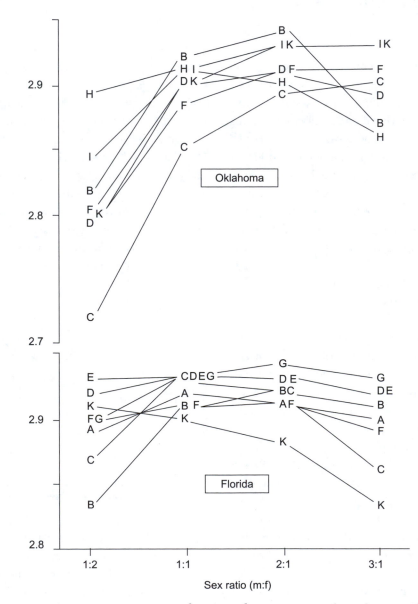

Figure 5.2 Mate-guarding reaction norms as a function of sex ratio in soapberry bugs in Oklahoma (top) and Florida (bottom) (Carroll & Corneli, 1999).

soapberry bugs (each line is a family of half-sibs) to experimental changes in the sex ratio. Mate-guarding increases as the sex ratio increases. Although each family has a slightly different reaction norm, they are similar enough to indicate a general feature of what we might call Oklahoma soapberry bug nature. An observer will see different behaviors in different environments, but the responsiveness—the shape of the reaction norm curve—is "universal."

At least, it is universal in Oklahoma. The lower figure shows that soapberry bug families from Florida do not alter their mate-guarding appreciably, irrespective of experimental changes in the sex ratio. Why not? In Florida, the climate, hence the sex ratio, is less variable than in Oklahoma. In Oklahoma, a facultative (plastic, flexible) response makes adaptive sense, because an individual bug could find himself in a variety of environments and he will reproduce better if he can respond to those changes. For the Florida bugs, living in their equable environment, there is no advantage to such flexibility, and in that population, the flexible response did not evolve (Carroll and Corneli, 1999).

Soapberry bugs occupy a range of environments, but the range is nothing compared to that of humans, who live in every part of the planet and whose environments include novel ones that they constructed for themselves. The principle illustrated in the previous example, therefore, is even more important when discussing human nature. To a human behavioral ecologist, then, human nature is not limited to human universals, as that phrase is usually understood. The human universal is the shape of the response, and the task is to understand how selection pressures shaped it.

This perspective on human nature derives from the anthropologists' knowledge of human variation and the ecological focus of the parent discipline of behavioral ecology. Most human behavioral ecologists were trained as cultural anthropologists, which gives them an unequaled knowledge of the breadth and regularities of

human variation. They know, better than anyone, that people living in developed, industrialized states (the usual subjects of human social science) represent only a very small part of the range of human variation, and that those societies are in many respects quite unusual. The nature of the parent discipline of behavioral ecology also shapes their perspective of human nature. Human behavioral ecology's modus operandi is to model optimal outcomes by considering the costs and benefits of different strategies and how they trade off against one another. Doing this forces an explicit consideration of the ecological factors that shape those costs and benefits, and how they vary across environments.

In what follows I will consider examples which illustrate the following implications of this view of human nature: (1) human and non-human animal behavior can be understood using the same evolutionary theoretical perspective, and, in some cases, models (hence human nature is seen as part of the evolved natural world), (2) viewing behavioral variation as a reaction norm provides guidance on how policy can address the darker side of human nature, and (3) the individual-maximizing process of natural selection has created a remarkably altruistic, cooperative human nature. I will not, in this essay, attempt to review the field of human behavioral ecology generally, which has been done admirably elsewhere (Borgerhoff Mulder, 2003; Cronk, 1991; Laland & Brown, 2011; Smith et al., 2001; Winterhalder & Smith, 2000). However, several points should be made first about the assumptions under which behavioral ecologists operate.

Human nature, broadly speaking, encompasses the ways in which people think, feel, and act. However, thoughts and feelings are themselves "invisible" to natural selection, since they can only affect survival or reproduction by motivating behavior. An emotion, no matter how strongly felt, is irrelevant to evolution if it does not cause an observable change. For this reason, human behavioral ecologists are largely unconcerned with psychological mechanisms, and focus instead on the behavioral outcomes that selection can act upon.

For somewhat different reasons, human behavioral ecologists also are largely unconcerned with genetic mechanisms. Although biologists studying the behavioral ecology of other species are increasingly interested in the genetic basis of flexible responses, these are difficult to study in people, and we know very little about the genetics underlying human nature and behavior. Human behavioral ecologists therefore typically adopt a "phenotypic gambit" that assumes there has been sufficient genetic variation and time for competing selection pressures to have resulted in the evolution of better-adapted phenotypes. Behavioral ecologists who work with humans also typically hold the working assumption (not belief) that the human behavioral differences they observe are the facultative expression of a largely shared genotype.

Finally, human behavioral ecologists assume that human nature is adaptive (fitness-enhancing), and that selection will lead to optimal outcomes. These optimal outcomes are modeled as the best outcome possible given resource constraints and tradeoffs between competing demands. The assumption of optimality is less a matter of belief about human nature than it is a useful working assumption. Behavioral ecologists know, as well as anyone, that people sometimes do maladaptive things (although they do not expect maladaptive outcomes to be common), and they also know the reasons why evolution sometimes leads to sub-optimal outcomes. But it is a reasonable and powerful working assumption in generating and testing hypotheses about the functions of, and selection pressures on, human behavior—hence how human nature came to be. This is best demonstrated by example, so we will consider several, beginning with mating and marriage.

Mating and Marriage: Biological Models can Explain a lot about Human Cultural Behavior

Marriage is universal, but variable, across human societies, and our understanding of what forms are natural or normal have both moral overtones and policy implications. The ethnographic database makes it clear that human nature encompasses marriages that are both monogamous and polygynous, and even, under very rare and special circumstances, polyandrous. What behavioral ecology adds to this pluralistic view of mating and marriage is the specification that men and women will adjust their mating and marriage choices to environmental circumstances in predictable ways, and that those choices will be optimal from the perspective of enhancing reproductive success.

What is the optimal number of wives (assuming a man is legally allowed to have more than one)? It depends. Both time and resources are limited and subject to tradeoffs, and these tradeoffs apply across species. If a male spends time guarding one mate, he has less time available to pursue others. If he spends resources (energy or money) trying to attract and monopolize additional mates, he has less to invest in his current offspring. Like the soapberry bugs, therefore, a human male with few alternative mating opportunities may do better to stay with his mate (not only to keep other suitors away but also, in the case of humans, to invest in his offspring and enhance their reproductive success).

This argument has been used to explain differences in mating and marriage among two groups of South American foragers, the monogamous Hiwi and the polygynous Ache. Among the Hiwi, a comparative shortage of reproductive-aged women and lower fertility promotes monogamous pair bonds and men directing more of their resources to provisioning their family, even though that effort has a modest effect on children's survival compared to that of Ache men. Ache men, in contrast, have relatively more opportunities for new matings and added paternity, and so they can gain more reproductive success by searching for new mates, and marriage is less durable than among the Hiwi (Hurtado and Hill 1992; see also Blurton Jones et al., 2000). Cross-national data (Trent & South, 1989) and historical trends (Guttentag & Secord, 1983; Pedersen, 1991) also find that high sex-ratio societies, in which men more than women must compete for mates, are associated with more stable marriages and lower divorce rates.

Mating and marriage decisions are complex, not least because women and men often want different things and the outcome must consider the strategic decisions of both. Where women can choose their own mates, mating patterns may be driven more by female choice. Polygyny can be in a woman's interests if by being the second wife of a wealthy man she can end up with more resources (after division among wives) than she could by being the sole wife of a pauper. This argument (formalized as the "polygyny threshold" model) was initially developed to explain mating patterns in birds, but was also used successfully to explain who married whom among the agro-pastoral Kipsigis. Borgerhoff Mulder (1990) showed that having co-wives imposes reproductive costs on Kipsigis women, which they try to minimize by judicious marital choices. The Kipsigis women she studied (or their parents acting on their behalf) chose men who had the most acres available after division among existing wives (consistent with the female-choice polygyny threhold model), not the most acres overall (the latter would suggest instead that the wealthiest men were able to control the outcome).

These examples illustrate both limitations and contributions of human behavioral ecology to an understanding of human nature. Because it follows the phenotypic gambit, human behavioral ecology is agnostic about the mechanisms that lead to these patterns, so has little to say about them. Does the choice of mate arise from conscious consideration of the pros and cons of each option? Or from innate preferences, such that fitness-enhancing mates look sexier and

more attractive? Or (most likely) both? For the answer to that question, you will need to ask the evolutionary psychologists—it is simply not a focus of human behavioral ecology. Behavioral ecology does show that (1) marriage choices are consistent with models of adaptive behavior (i.e., behavior that enhances the fitness of the people making them), (2) the diversity of mating and marriage patterns is, therefore, not divorced from nature but rather is a predictable manifestation of it, and (3) models from biology, which were developed for other species, are surprisingly successful in explaining these cultural patterns. The last point underlies the fact that human nature is one manifestation of animal nature.

Life History and Parenting: What the Human Behavioral Ecology Perspective Implies about Problematic Behavior

It is part of human nature for a mother to love her children, but it is also part of human nature that such love is not unconditional. Humans are unusual primates in this respect. The primatologist Sarah Hrdy (2009) has pointed out that in most other primates a mother gives birth only when her other offspring are independent, and unconditional nurture for each new arrival is the norm. This is not true for humans, who differ from other primates in having a long period of childhood dependency together with interbirth intervals that are short compared to those of our closest primate relatives. One result of having to take care of several children simultaneously is that human mothers face allocation decisions most other primate mothers do not, and withdrawal of investment, including even infanticide, is part of the human condition. Another consequence is that human mothers, unlike other primate mothers, need and get help with child-rearing from other relatives (the industrialized world is an exception to this otherwise universal feature).

Behavioral ecologists have shown that a mother's reproductive decisions are sensitive to factors that would maximize the fitness returns on her investment: the condition of the infant, the mother's social and economic support, and her other options. Because a woman's reproductive options diminish with age, the probability that she will terminate investment in an offspring also declines with age. Figure 5.3 shows this pattern in a

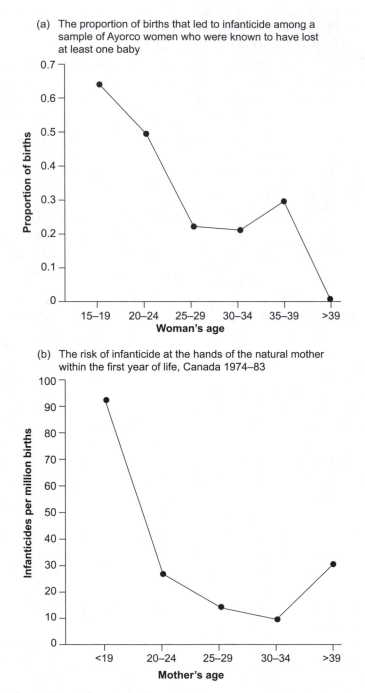

Figure 5.3 Risk of infanticide as a function of mother's age among (a) the Ayoreo (n = 141 births) and (b) Canada (Daly & Wilson, 1988).

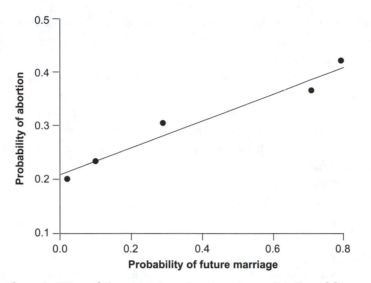

Figure 5.4 Age-specific probability of abortion plotted against the probability of future marriage during the reproductive life span (ages 16–40 years) of single women. England and Wales 1991 (Lycett & Dunbar, 1999).

population of forager-farmers, the Ayoreo (Bugos & McCarthy, 1984), and modern Canada (Daly & Wilson, 1988). The opportunity costs are greater and the age effect steeper for single women than for married women, since men are less likely to marry a woman with children sired by another man, other things equal. This tradeoff is illustrated in Figure 5.4, which shows that the probability of terminating a pregnancy is a linear function of the probability of future marriage (data from England and Wales, Lycett & Dunbar 1999).

Views of human nature have implications for policy, since behavior that is pathological is addressed by trying to change the individual, while a normal but undesired aspect of human nature (i.e., one that lies within the norm of reaction of most of the population) is more profitably addressed (if one wishes to) by changing the circumstances that favor it. By viewing behavior such as child neglect and even infanticide as a fitness-maximizing response to resource constraints and competing demands, the behavioral ecologist would be hesitant to label such behavior as pathological, and more likely to suggest that we ameliorate the situation by addressing the constraints and competing demands that made such choices adaptive. She would also be aware that a single mother who struggles without kin help is in an unnatural situation, although a common one in modern industrial societies, and would suggest policies that change the circumstances to resemble those to which we are normally adapted. While models in human behavioral ecology may seem cold-blooded, therefore, the policy implications of its approach are likely to be both humane and progressive.

Generosity

When Dawkins (2006 [1976]) coined the term "selfish gene" he was describing the fact that any gene that promotes reproductive success in the body it finds itself in will help itself to spread in the population. Genes may be selfish in this sense, but they can spread by promoting altruistic as well as selfish behavior. From Dawkins's gene-centric perspective, a gene that is shared by two individuals through common descent will be favored if those individuals behave altruistically toward each other. Kin selection, which is built on this idea, is the reason many species exhibit behavior that is altruistic (in the technical sense of an act that favors the recipient at some cost to the altruist). Altruism toward kin is an evolved part of human nature also, but humans are unusual in the scope of their unselfish behavior, which is extended far beyond the usual explanatory reach of kin selection. Understanding how selection has favored such behavior is a major part of the recent hunan behavioral ecology research agenda.

Generosity to non-kin can confer long-term benefits (even though at a short-term cost) if the altruist can be sure that a favor given now will be reciprocated at some future time when he needs the help (reciprocal altruism). Such a system is vulnerable to cheaters, so people are expected to be careful about who they are generous to, limiting their generosity to people who have shared with them in the past or who have a reputation for having been generous with others. Experimental games have shown that decision rules of conditional generosity can outcompete selfish behavior. A second way in which generosity to non-kin can confer benefits to the altruists is through advertising the donor's resources or abilities (e.g., the philanthropist who gets his name on a building).

Both of these explanations, and others, have been evaluated by behavioral ecologists, particularly in the context of food sharing. Supportive evidence for the role of reciprocity comes from evidence that food sharing among both Ache and Hiwi is contingent on past behavior (people share more with those who have shared with them) (Gurven, 2006), and that Ache who produced and shared more than average also received more food when they were injured or sick (Gurven et al., 2000). There is also evidence for sharing as advertisement. Some foragers, especially young males, target hard-to-get and large game, which is shared more widely than other resources. The behavior is costly, but pays indirect fitness benefits, chiefly by enhancing mating opportunities for good hunters, even where the sharing is not contingent (Hawkes & Bliege Bird, 2002; Smith & Bird, 2000; Smith et al., 2003). In the case of both reciprocity and showing off, the generosity is real but ultimately enhances the fitness of the donor. Food sharing is one of Don Brown's human universals, but, like most universals, it is exhibited strategically, and we will not understand human nature without understanding that variability and the reasons for it.

Explaining variation in generosity is a major focus of research in behavioral ecology. Figure 5.5 shows how results of an economic sharing game (the "dictator" game) vary with the market integration of the society. In this game, two anonymous players are given a sum of money and one of them (the "dictator") is given the right to allocate whatever fraction of it he wants to the other (the recipient). The recipient can do nothing to punish the dictator for meager offers, yet in no society do people, on average, fail to give something (the reason for this persistent but uneconomical behavior is still being debated). Interestingly, the two groups with the lowest (least generous) offers are Hadza foragers and Tsimane forager-farmers, both of whom depend heavily on sharing in their daily lives and are far more dependent on it than people in the U.S., who anchor the high end by offering nearly a 50–50 split. Group size is also a strong predictor of generosity in this game, with large groups being more generous. Henrich et al. (2010) reach beyond the usual evolutionary mechanisms and models of behavioral ecology to explain this counter-intuitive result, arguing that large-scale market exchange is possible only in groups where norms of fairness and trust among strangers have spread through social means.

Most of the behavioral ecology research on this topic continues to be agnostic about

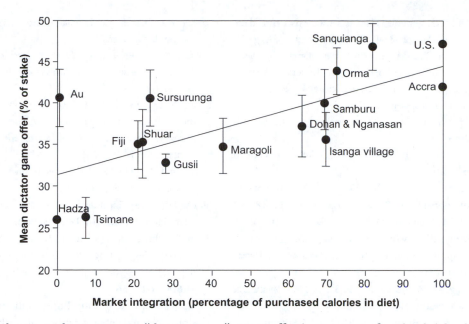

Figure 5.5 Sharing in the anonymous "dictator game": Mean offer (as a percent of total stake) by degree of market integration of fifteen traditional societies and the US (Henrich et al., 2010).

mechanisms, but this is starting to change. Behavioral ecologists and evolutionary psychologists are working together to understand the evolution of the cognitive specializations that makes us such an unusually cooperative species. Cooperation on a larger scale, involving such phenomena as ethnocentrism, fairness to strangers in market societies, and large-scale warfare, are likely to require the understanding of new mechanisms involving cultural as well as genetic transmission, and this is another new and growing area that is expanding the field of human behavioral ecology. It is also an area of active collaboration between human behavioral ecologists and other social scientists, especially experimental economists. Human behavioral ecologists sometimes grumble that these sister disciplines are largely "ecology free" and give insufficient attention to the real range of human variation, and that evolutionary psychologists in particular give inadequate attention to tradeoffs among competing aims, but the trend is clearly toward an integration of the human evolutionary sciences. Substantive differences in the disciplinary views of human nature stem from historical differences in the populations studied and the models and methods employed, and are likely to be short-lived as these complementary strengths are pooled through collaboration.

References

Blurton Jones, N., Marlowe, F., Hawkes, K., & O'Connell, J. (2000). Paternal investment and hunter-gatherer divorce rates. In L. Cronk, N. Chagnon, & W. Irons (Eds.) *Adaptation and Human Behavior: An anthropological perspective* (pp. 69–90). Hawthorne, NY: Aldine de Gruyter.

Borgerhoff Mulder, M. (1990). Kipsigis women's preferences for wealthy men: evidence for female choice in mammals? *Behavioral Ecology and Sociobiology*, 27(4), 255–264.

Borgerhoff Mulder, M. (2003). Human behavioral ecology. In *Encyclopedia of Life Sciences*. Nature Publishing Group.

Brown, D. (1991). *Human Universals.* Temple University Press.

Bugos, P., & McCarthy, L. (1984). Ayoreo infanticide: A case study. *Infanticide: Comparative and evolutionary perspectives*, (pp. 503–520).

Carroll, S., & Corneli, P. (1999). The evolution of behavioral norms of reaction as a problem in ecological genetics: Theory, methods, and data. In S. A. Foster & J. A. Endler (Eds.) *Geographic Variation in Behavior: Perspectives on evolutionary mechanisms* (pp. 52–68). New York: Oxford University Press.

Cronk, L. (1991). Human behavioral ecology. *Annual Review of Anthropology*, 20, 25–53.

Daly, M. Wilson, M. (1988). *Homicide*. Piscataway, NJ: Aldine.

Dawkins, R. (2006 [1976]). *The Selfish Gene*. Oxford University Press.

Gurven, M. (2006 [1976]). The evolution of contingent cooperation. *Current Anthropology*, 47(1), 185.

Gurven, M., Allen-Arave, W., Hill, K., & Hurtado, M. (2000). It's a wonderful life signaling generosity among the Ache of Paraguay. *Evolution and Human Behavior*, 21(4), 263–282.

Guttentag, M., & Secord, P. (1983). *Too Many Women?: The sex ratio question*. Sage Publications.

Hawkes, K., & Bliege Bird, R. (2002). Showing off, handicap signaling, and the evolution of men's work. *Evolutionary Anthropology: Issues, News, and Reviews*, 11(2), 58–67.

Henrich, J., Ensminger, J., McElreath, R., Barr, A., Barrett, C., Bolyanatz, A., Cardenas, J., Curven, M., Gwako, E., Henrich, N., et al. (2010). Markets, religion, community size, and the evolution of fairness and punishment. *Science*, 327(5972), 1480.

Hrdy, S. (2009). *Mothers and Others: The evolutionary origins of mutual understanding*. Cambridge, MA: Belknap Press.

Hurtado, A., & Hill, K. (1992). Paternal effect on offspring survivorship among Ache and Hiwi hunter-gatherers: Implications for modeling pair-bond stability. In B. S. Hewlett (Ed.) *Father-child Relations: Cultural and biosocial contexts* (pp. 31–55). Aldine de Gruyter.

Laland, K., & Brown, G. (2011). *Sense and Nonsense: Evolutionary perspectives on human behaviour*. Oxford University Press.

Lycett, J., & Dunbar, R. (1999). Abortion rates reflect the optimization of parental investment strategies. *Proceedings of the Royal Society of London. Series B: Biological Sciences*, 266(1436), 2355–2358.

Pedersen, F. (1991). Secular trends in human sex ratios. *Human Nature*, 2(3), 271–291.

Pinker, S. (2003). *The Blank Slate: The modern denial of human nature*. Harmondsworth: Penguin Books.

Rhen, T., Schroeder, A., Sakata, J., Huang, V., & Crews, D. (2010). Segregating variation for temperature-dependent sex determination in a lizard. *Heredity*, 106(4), 649–660.

Smith, E., & Bird, R. (2000). Turtle hunting and tombstone opening: Public generosity as costly signaling. *Evolution and Human Behavior*, 21(4), 245–261.

Smith, E., Bird, R., & Bird, D. (2003). The benefits of costly signaling: Meriam turtle hunters. *Behavioral Ecology*, 14(1), 116.

Smith, E., Mulder, M., & Hill, K. (2001). Controversies in the evolutionary social sciences: A guide for the perplexed. *Trends in Ecology & Evolution*, 16(3), 128–135.

Trent, K., & South, S. (1989). Structural determinants of the divorce rate: A cross-societal analysis. *Journal of Marriage and the Family*, (pp. 391–404).

Winterhaider, B., & Smith, E. (2000). Analyzing adaptive strategies: Human behavioral ecology at twenty-five. *Evolutionary Anthropology: Issues News and Reviews*, 9(2), 51–72.

Topic 2   A STONE-AGE MIND?

T HE DEBATE IN THIS SECTION PITS different views about the way in which our make-up has been influenced by evolutionary changes, including about the times at which those evolutionary changes occur. Thus, this debate does not take place between those for and those against the role of evolution in the production of human mental make-up. Rather, proponents of a role for evolution in the shaping of human minds debate about what exactly that role should be.

One bold empirical hypothesis about why we are the way we are is the "stone age mind" hypothesis: We behave the way we do because the mind is a collection of features that adapted early humans to fit their environment. The hypothesis has many adherents among psychologists and philosophers, but also experiences strong resistance, particularly from evolutionary anthropologists and philosophers. In the first article of this section, evolutionary psychologists John Tooby and Leda Cosmides present a classic defense of the "stone age mind" hypothesis. The idea that the mind is a collection of adaptations for an environment from a particular time in our history is described as a central tenet of their overall approach to explaining and under-standing human behavior: evolutionary psychology. Debates rage over evolutionary psychology, and several of those debates are presented in other sections of this volume. In this section, philosopher Stephen Downes challenges the "stone age mind" hypothesis and presents an alternative hypothesis about how evolution contributes to the production of human traits.

Suggested Further Reading

Barkow, J., Cosmides, L. and Tooby, J. (Eds.) (1992) *The Adapted Mind*. New York: Oxford University Press.

Boyd, R. and Richerson, P. J. (2005) *Not by Genes Alone: How culture transformed human evolution*. Chicago, IL: University of Chicago Press.

Buller, D. (2005) *Adapting Minds*. Cambridge, MA: MIT Press.

Buss, D. (Ed.) (2005) *The Handbook of Evolutionary Psychology*. Hoboken, NJ: Wiley.

Cronk, L., Chagnon, N. and Irons, W. (Eds.) (2000). *Adaptation and Human Behavior: An anthropological perspective*. Hawthorne, NY: Aldine de Gruyter.

Daly, M. and Wilson, M. I. (1999) Human evolutionary psychology and animal behaviour. *Animal Behaviour*, 57: 509–519.

Downes, S. M. (2005) Integrating the multiple biological causes of human behavior. *Biology and Philosophy*, 20: 177–190.

Dunbar, R. and Barrett, L. (Eds.) (2009) *Oxford Handbook of Evolutionary Psychology*. Oxford: Oxford University Press.

Dupré, J. (2001) *Human Nature and the Limits of Science*. Oxford: Oxford University Press.

Foley, R. (1996) The adaptive legacy of human evolution: A search for the environment of evolutionary adaptedness. *Evolutionary Anthropology*, 4: 194–203.

Laland, K. N. and Brown, G. R. (2002) *Sense and Nonsense: Evolutionary perspectives on human behaviour*. Oxford: Oxford University Press.

Lloyd, E. A. (1999) Evolutionary psychology: The burdens of proof. *Biology and Philosophy*, 14: 211–233.

Machery, E. and Barrett, C. (2006) Debunking *Adapting Minds*. *Philosophy of Science*, 73: 232–246.

Machery, E. and Cohen, K. (2012) An evidence-based study of the evolutionary behavioral sciences. *British Journal for the Philosophy of Science*, 63: 177–226.

Richardson, R. C. (2007) *Evolutionary Psychology as Maladapted Psychology*. Cambridge, MA: MIT Press.

Shettleworth, S. J. (2010) *Cognition, Evolution, and Behavior*. New York: Oxford University Press.

Smith, E. A., Borgerhoff Mulder, M. and Hill, K. (2000) Evolutionary analyses of human behaviour: A commentary on Daly and Wilson. *Animal Behaviour*, 60: F21–26.

Tooby, J. and Cosmides, L. (1992) The psychological foundations of culture. In J. Barkow, L. Cosmides and J. Tooby (Eds.), *The Adapted Mind: Evolutionary psychology and the generation of culture* (pp. 19–136). New York: Oxford University Press.

Chapter 6

Leda Cosmides and John Tooby

EVOLUTIONARY PSYCHOLOGY

A Primer

Introduction

The goal of research in evolutionary psychology is to discover and understand the design of the human mind. Evolutionary psychology is an *approach* to psychology, in which knowledge and principles from evolutionary biology are put to use in research on the structure of the human mind. It is not an area of study, like vision, reasoning, or social behavior. It is a *way of thinking* about psychology that can be applied to any topic within it.

In this view, the mind is a set of information-processing machines that were designed by natural selection to solve adaptive problems faced by our hunter-gatherer ancestors. This way of thinking about the brain, mind, and behavior is changing how scientists approach old topics, and opening up new ones. This chapter is a primer on the concepts and arguments that animate it.

Debauching the Mind: Evolutionary Psychology's Past and Present

In the final pages of the *Origin of Species*, after he had presented the theory of evolution by natural selection, Darwin (1859) made a bold prediction: "In the distant future I see open fields for far more important researches. Psychology will be based on a new foundation, that of the necessary acquirement of each mental power and capacity by gradation."[1] Thirty years later, William James tried to do just that in his seminal book, *Principles of Psychology*, one of the founding works of experimental psychology (James, 1890). In *Principles*, James talked a lot of "instincts". This term was used to refer (roughly) to specialized neural circuits that are common to every member of a species and are the product of that species' evolutionary history. Taken together, such circuits constitute (in our own species) what one can think of as "human nature".

It was (and is) common to think that other animals are ruled by "instinct" whereas humans lost their instincts and are ruled by "reason", and that this is why we are so much more flexibly intelligent than other animals. William James took the opposite view. He argued that human behavior is more flexibly intelligent than that of other animals because we have *more* instincts than they do, not fewer. We tend to be blind to the existence of these instincts, however, precisely because they work so well—because they process information so effortlessly and automatically. They structure our thought so powerfully, he argued, that it can be difficult to imagine how things could be otherwise. As a result, we take "normal" behavior for granted. We do not realize that "normal" behavior needs to be explained at all. This "instinct blindness" makes the study of psychology difficult. To get past this problem, James suggested that we try to make the "natural seem strange":

It takes . . . a mind debauched by learning to carry the process of making the natural seem strange, so far as to ask for the *why* of any instinctive human act. To the metaphysician alone can such questions occur as: Why do we smile, when pleased, and not scowl? Why are we unable to talk to a crowd as we talk to a single friend? Why does a particular maiden turn our wits so upside-down? The common man can only say, *Of course we smile, of course* our heart palpitates at the sight of the crowd, *of course* we love the maiden, that beautiful soul clad in that perfect form, so palpably and flagrantly made for all eternity to be loved! (William James, 1890)

In our view, William James was right . . . Many psychologists avoid the study of natural competences, thinking that there is nothing there to be explained. As a result, social psychologists are disappointed unless they find a phenomenon "that would surprise their grandmothers", and cognitive psychologists spend more time studying how we solve problems we are bad at, like learning math or playing chess, than ones we are good at. But our natural competences—our abilities to see, to speak, to find someone beautiful, to reciprocate a favor, to fear disease, to fall in love, to initiate an attack, to experience moral outrage, to navigate a landscape, and myriad others—are possible only because there is a vast and heterogeneous array of complex computational machinery supporting and regulating these activities. This machinery works so well that we don't even realize that it exists—we all suffer from instinct blindness. As a result, psychologists have neglected to study some of the most interesting machinery in the human mind. . . . An evolutionary approach provides powerful lenses that correct for instinct blindness. It allows one to recognize what natural competences exist, it indicates that the mind is a heterogeneous collection of these competences and, most importantly, it provides positive theories of their designs. . . .

The Standard Social Science Model

Applying evolutionary biology to the study of the mind has brought most evolutionary psychologists into conflict with a traditional view of its structure, which arose long before Darwin. This view is no historical relic: it remains highly influential, more than a century after Darwin and William James wrote.

Both before and after Darwin, a common view among philosophers and scientists has been that the human mind resembles a blank slate, virtually free of content until written on by the hand of experience. According to Aquinas (following Aristotle) there is nothing in the intellect that was not previously in the senses. Working within this framework, the British Empiricists and their successors produced elaborate theories about how experience, refracted through a small handful of innate mental procedures, inscribed content onto the mental slate. David Hume's view was typical, and set the pattern for many later psychological and social science theories: ". . . there appear to be only three principles of connexion among ideas, namely *Resemblance*, *Contiguity* in time or place, and *Cause or Effect*."[2]

Over the years, the technological metaphor used to describe the structure of the human mind has been consistently updated, from blank slate to switchboard to general purpose computer, but the central tenet of these Empiricist views has remained the same. Indeed, it has become the reigning orthodoxy in mainstream anthropology, sociology, and most areas of psychology. According to this orthodoxy, all of the specific content of the human mind originally derives from the "outside"—from the environment and the social world—and the evolved architecture of the mind consists solely or predominantly of a small number of general purpose mechanisms that are content-independent, and which sail under names such as "learning," "induction," "intelligence," "imitation," "rationality," "the capacity for culture," or simply "culture."

According to this view, the same mechanisms are thought to govern how one acquires a language, how one learns to recognize emotional expressions, how one thinks about incest, or how one acquires ideas and attitudes about friends and reciprocity—everything but perception. This is because the mechanisms that govern reasoning, learning, and memory are assumed to operate uniformly, according to unchanging principles, regardless of the content they are operating on or the larger category or domain involved. (For this reason, they are described as *content-independent* or *domain-general*.) Such mechanisms, by definition, have no pre-existing content built-in to their procedures, they are not designed to construct certain contents more readily than others, and they have no features specialized for processing particular kinds of content. Since these hypothetical mental mechanisms have no content to impart, it follows that all the particulars of what we think and feel derive externally, from the physical and social world. The social world organizes and injects meaning into individual minds, but our universal human psychological architecture has no distinctive structure that organizes the social world or imbues it with characteristic meanings. According to this familiar view—what we have elsewhere called the Standard Social Science Model—the contents of human minds are primarily (or entirely) free social constructions, and the social sciences are autonomous and disconnected from any evolutionary or psychological foundation (Tooby & Cosmides, 1992).

Three decades of progress and convergence in cognitive psychology, evolutionary biology, and neuroscience have shown that this view of the human mind is radically defective. Evolutionary psychology provides an alternative framework that is beginning to replace it. On this view, all normal human minds reliably develop a standard collection of reasoning and regulatory circuits that are functionally specialized and, frequently, domain-specific. These circuits organize the way we interpret our experiences, inject certain recurrent concepts and motivations into our mental life, and provide universal frames of meaning that allow us to understand the actions and intentions of others. Beneath the level of surface variability, all humans share certain views and assumptions about the nature of the world and human action by virtue of these human universal reasoning circuits.

Back to Basics

When rethinking a field, it is sometimes necessary to go back to first principles, to ask basic questions such as "What is behavior?" "What do we mean by 'mind'?" "How can something as intangible as a 'mind' have evolved, and what is its relation to the brain?" The answers to such questions provide the framework within which evolutionary psychologists operate. We will try to summarize some of these here.

Psychology is that branch of biology that studies (1) brains, (2) how brains process information, and (3) how the brain's information-processing programs generate behavior. Once one realizes that psychology is a branch of biology, inferential tools developed in biology—its theories, principles, and observations—can be used to understand psychology. Here are five basic principles—all drawn from biology—that EPs apply in their attempts to understand the design of the human mind. The Five Principles can be applied to any topic in psychology. They organize observations in a way that allows one to see connections between areas as seemingly diverse as vision, reasoning, and sexuality.

Principle 1. The Brain is a Physical System. It Functions as a Computer. Its Circuits are Designed to Generate Behavior that is Appropriate to your Environmental Circumstances

The brain is a physical system whose operation is governed solely by the laws of chemistry and physics. What does this mean? It means that all of your thoughts and hopes and dreams and feelings are produced by chemical reactions going on in your head (a sobering thought). The brain's function is to process information. In other words, it is a computer that is made of organic (carbon-based) compounds rather than silicon chips. The brain is comprised of cells: primarily neurons and their supporting structures. Neurons are cells that are specialized for the transmission of information. Electrochemical reactions cause neurons to fire.

Neurons are connected to one another in a highly organized way. One can think of these connections as circuits—just like a computer has circuits. These circuits determine how the brain processes information, just as the circuits in your computer determine how it processes information. Neural circuits in your brain are connected to sets of neurons that run throughout your body. Some of these neurons are connected to sensory receptors, such as the retina of your eye. Others are connected to your muscles. Sensory receptors are cells that are specialized for gathering information from the outer world and from other parts of the body. (You can feel your stomach churn because there are sensory receptors on it, but you cannot feel your spleen, which lacks them.) Sensory receptors are connected to neurons that transmit this information to your brain. Other neurons send information from your brain to motor neurons. Motor neurons are connected to your muscles; they cause your muscles to move. This movement is what we call *behavior*.

Organisms that don't move, don't have brains. Trees don't have brains, bushes don't have brains, flowers don't have brains. In fact, there are some animals that don't move during certain stages of their lives. And during those stages, *they* don't have brains. The sea squirt, for example, is an aquatic animal that inhabits oceans. During the early stage of its life cycle, the sea squirt swims around looking for a good place to attach itself permanently. Once it finds the right rock, and attaches itself to it, it doesn't need its brain anymore because it will never need to move again. So it eats (resorbs) most of its brain. After all, why waste energy on a now useless organ? Better to get a good meal out of it.

In short, the circuits of the brain are designed to generate motion—behavior—in response to information from the environment. The function of your brain—this wet computer—is to generate behavior that is appropriate to your environmental circumstances.

Principle 2. Our Neural Circuits were Designed by Natural Selection to Solve Problems that our Ancestors faced During our Species' Evolutionary History

To say that the function of your brain is to generate behavior that is "appropriate" to your environmental circumstances is not saying much, unless you have some definition of what "appropriate" means. What counts as appropriate behavior?

"Appropriate" has different meanings for different organisms. You have sensory receptors that are stimulated by the sight and smell of feces—to put it more bluntly, you can see and smell dung. So can a dung fly. But on detecting the presence of feces in the environment, what counts as appropriate behavior for you differs from what is appropriate for the dung fly. On smelling feces, appropriate behavior for a female dung fly is to move toward the feces, land on them, and lay her eggs. Feces are food for a dung fly larva—therefore, appropriate behavior for a dung fly larva is to eat dung. And, because female dung flies hang out near piles of dung, appropriate behavior for a male dung fly is to buzz around these piles, trying to mate; for a male dung fly, a pile of dung is a pick-up joint.

But for you, feces are a source of contagious diseases. For you, they are not food, they are not a good place to raise your children, and they are not a good place to look for a date. Because a pile of dung is a source of contagious diseases for a human being, appropriate behavior for you is to move away from the source of the smell. Perhaps your facial muscles will form the cross-culturally universal disgust expression as well, in which your nose wrinkles to protect eyes and nose from the volatiles and the tongue protrudes slightly, as it would were you ejecting something from your mouth.

For you, that pile of dung is "disgusting". For a female dung fly, looking for a good neighborhood and a nice house for raising her children, that pile of dung is a beautiful vision—a mansion. (Seeing a pile of dung as a mansion—*that's* what William James meant by making the natural seem strange).

The point is, environments do not, in and of themselves, specify what counts as "appropriate" behavior. In other words, you can't say "My environment made me do it!" and leave it at that. In principle, a computer or circuit could be designed to link *any* given stimulus in the environment to any kind of behavior. Which behavior a stimulus gives rise to is a function of the neural circuitry of the organism. This means that if you were a designer of brains, you could have engineered the human brain to respond in any way you wanted, to link any environmental input to any behavior—you could have made a person who licks her chops and sets the table when she smells a nice fresh pile of dung.

But what did the actual designer of the human brain do, and why? Why do we find fruit sweet and dung disgusting? In other words, how did we get the circuits that we have, rather than those that the dung fly has?

When we are talking about a home computer, the answer to this question is simple: its circuits were designed by an engineer, and the engineer designed them one way rather than another so they would solve problems that the engineer *wanted* them to solve; problems such as adding or subtracting or accessing a particular address in the computer's memory. Your neural circuits were also designed to solve problems. But they were not designed by an engineer. They were designed

by the evolutionary process, and natural selection is the only evolutionary force that is capable of creating complexly organized machines.

Natural selection does not work "for the good of the species", as many people think. As we will discuss in more detail below, it is a process in which a phenotypic design feature *causes its own spread through a population* (which can happen even in cases where this leads to the extinction of the species). In the meantime (to continue our scatological examples) you can think of natural selection as the "eat dung and die" principle. All animals need neural circuits that govern what they eat—knowing what is safe to eat is a problem that all animals must solve. For humans, feces are not safe to eat—they are a source of contagious diseases. Now imagine an ancestral human who had neural circuits that made dung smell sweet—that made him want to dig in whenever he passed a smelly pile of dung. This would increase his probability of contracting a disease. If he got sick as a result, he would be too tired to find much food, too exhausted to go looking for a mate, and he might even die an untimely death. In contrast, a person with different neural circuits—ones that made him avoid feces—would get sick less often. He will therefore have more time to find food and mates and will live a longer life. The first person will eat dung and die; the second will avoid it and live. As a result, the dung-*eater* will have fewer children than the dung-*avoider*. Since the neural circuitry of children tends to resemble that of their parents, there will be fewer dung-eaters in the next generation, and more dung-avoiders. As this process continues, generation after generation, the dung-eaters will eventually disappear from the population. Why? They ate dung and died out. The only kind of people left in the population will be those like you and me—ones who are descended from the dung-avoiders. No one will be left who has neural circuits that make dung delicious.

In other words, the reason we have one set of circuits rather than another is that the circuits that we have were better at solving problems that our ancestors faced during our species' evolutionary history than alternative circuits were. The brain is a naturally constructed computational system whose function is to solve adaptive information-processing problems (such as face recognition, threat interpretation, language acquisition, or navigation). Over evolutionary time, its circuits were cumulatively added because they "reasoned" or "processed information" in a way that enhanced the adaptive regulation of behavior and physiology.

Realizing that the function of the brain is information-processing has allowed cognitive scientists to resolve (at least one version of) the mind/body problem. For cognitive scientists, *brain* and *mind* are terms that refer to the same system, which can be described in two complementary ways—either in terms of its physical properties (the brain), or in terms of its information-processing operation (the mind). The physical organization of the brain evolved because that physical organization brought about certain information-processing relationships—ones that were adaptive.

It is important to realize that our circuits weren't designed to solve just any old kind of problem. They were designed to solve *adaptive* problems. Adaptive problems have two defining characteristics. First, they are ones that cropped up again and again during the evolutionary history of a species. Second, they are problems whose solution affected the *reproduction* of individual organisms—however indirect the causal chain may be, and however small the effect on number of offspring produced. This is because differential reproduction (and not survival *per se*) is the engine that drives natural selection. Consider the fate of a circuit that had the effect, on average, of enhancing the reproductive rate of the organisms that sported it, but shortened their average lifespan in so doing (one that causes mothers to risk death to save their children, for example). If this effect persisted over many generations, then its frequency in the

population would increase. In contrast, any circuit whose average effect was to decrease the reproductive rate of the organisms that had it would eventually disappear from the population. Most adaptive problems have to do with how an organism makes its living: what it eats, what eats it, who it mates with, who it socializes with, how it communicates, and so on. The only kind of problems that natural selection can design circuits for solving are adaptive problems.

Obviously, we are able to solve problems that no hunter-gatherer ever had to solve—we can learn math, drive cars, use computers. Our ability to solve other kinds of problems is a side-effect or by-product of circuits that were designed to solve adaptive problems. For example, when our ancestors became bipedal—when they started walking on two legs instead of four—they had to develop a very good sense of balance. And we have very intricate mechanisms in our inner ear that allow us to achieve our excellent sense of balance. Now the fact that we can balance well on two legs while moving means that we can do other things besides walk—it means we can skateboard or ride the waves on a surfboard. But our hunter-gatherer ancestors were not tunneling through curls in the primordial soup. The fact that we can surf and skateboard are mere by-products of adaptations designed for balancing while walking on two legs.

Principle 3. Consciousness is just the Tip of the Iceberg; most of what goes on in your Mind is Hidden from you. As a Result, your Conscious Experience can Mislead you into Thinking that our Circuitry is Simpler that it Really is. Most Problems that you Experience as Easy to Solve are very Difficult to Solve— they Require very Complicated Neural Circuitry

You are not, and cannot become, consciously aware of most of your brain's ongoing activities.

Think of the brain as the entire Federal Government, and of your consciousness as the President of the United States. Now think of your**self**—the self that you consciously experience as "you"—as the President. If you were President, how would you know what is going on in the world? Members of the Cabinet, like the Secretary of Defense, would come and tell you things—for example, that the Bosnian Serbs are violating their cease-fire agreement. How do members of the Cabinet know things like this? Because thousands of bureaucrats in the State Department, thousands of CIA operatives in Serbia and other parts of the world, thousands of troops stationed overseas, and hundreds of investigative reporters are gathering and evaluating enormous amounts of information from all over the world. But you, as President, do not—and in fact, cannot—know what each of these thousands of individuals were doing when gathering all this information over the last few months—what each of them saw, what each of them read, who each of them talked to, what conversations were clandestinely taped, what offices were bugged. All you, as President, know is the final conclusion that the Secretary of Defense came to based on the information that was passed on to him. And all he knows is what other high level officials passed on to him, and so on. In fact, no single individual knows *all* of the facts about the situation, because these facts are distributed among thousands of people. Moreover, each of the thousands of individuals involved knows all kinds of details about the situation that they decided were not important enough to pass on to higher levels.

So it is with your conscious experience. The only things you become aware of are a few high level conclusions passed on by thousands and thousands of specialized mechanisms: some that are gathering sensory information from the world, others that are analyzing and evaluating that information, checking for inconsistencies, filling in the blanks, figuring out what it all means. It is important for any scientist who is studying the human mind to keep this in mind. In figuring out how the mind works, your conscious experience of yourself and the world can suggest some valuable hypotheses. But these same intuitions can seriously mislead you as well. They can fool you into thinking that our neural circuitry is simpler that it really is. . . . Our conscious experience of an activity as "easy" or "natural" can lead us to grossly underestimate the complexity of the circuits that make it possible. Doing what comes "naturally", effortlessly, or automatically is rarely simple from an engineering point of view. To find someone beautiful, to fall in love, to feel jealous—all can seem as simple and automatic and effortless as opening your eyes and seeing. So simple that it seems like there is nothing much to explain. But these activities feel effortless only because there is a vast array of complex neural circuitry supporting and regulating them.

Principle 4. Different Neural Circuits are Specialized for Solving Different Adaptive Problems

A basic engineering principle is that the same machine is rarely capable of solving two different problems equally well. We have both screw drivers and saws because each solves a particular problem better than the other. Just imagine trying to cut planks of wood with a screw driver or to turn screws with a saw.

Our body is divided into organs, like the heart and the liver, for exactly this reason. Pumping blood throughout the body and detoxifying poisons are two very different problems. Consequently, your body has a different machine for solving each of them. The design of the heart is specialized for pumping blood; the design of the liver is specialized for detoxifying poisons. Your liver can't function as a pump, and your heart isn't any good at detoxifying poisons.

For the same reason, our minds consist of a large number of circuits that are *functionally specialized*. For example, we have some neural circuits whose design is specialized for vision. All they do is help you see. The design of other neural circuits is specialized for hearing. All they do is detect changes in air pressure, and extract information from it. They do not participate in vision, vomiting, vanity, vengeance, or anything else. Still other neural circuits are specialized for sexual attraction—i.e., they govern what you find sexually arousing, what you regard as beautiful, who you'd like to date, and so on.

We have all these specialized neural circuits because the same mechanism is rarely capable of solving different adaptive problems. For example, we all have neural circuitry designed to choose nutritious food on the basis of taste and smell—circuitry that governs our food choice. But imagine a woman who used this same neural circuitry to choose a mate. She would choose a strange mate indeed (perhaps a huge chocolate bar?). To solve the adaptive problem of finding the right mate, our choices must be guided by *qualitatively different standards* than when choosing the right food, or the right habitat. Consequently, the brain must be composed of a large collection of circuits, with different circuits specialized for solving different problems. You can think of each of these specialized circuits as a mini-computer that is dedicated to solving one problem. Such dedicated mini-computers are sometimes called *modules.* There is, then, a sense in which you can view the brain as a collection of dedicated mini-computers—a collection of modules. There must, of course, be circuits whose design is specialized for integrating the output of all these dedicated mini-computers to produce behavior. So, more precisely, one can view the brain as a collection of dedicated mini-computers whose operations are *functionally integrated* to produce behavior. . . .

Principle 5. Our Modern Skulls House a Stone-Age Mind

Natural selection, the process that designed our brain, takes a long time to design a circuit of any

complexity. The time it takes to build circuits that are suited to a given environment is so slow it is hard to even imagine—it's like a stone being sculpted by wind-blown sand. Even relatively simple changes can take tens of thousands of years.

The environment that humans—and, therefore, human minds—evolved in was very different from our modern environment. Our ancestors spent well over 99% of our species' evolutionary history living in hunter-gatherer societies. That means that our forebearers lived in small, nomadic bands of a few dozen individuals who got all of their food each day by gathering plants or by hunting animals. Each of our ancestors was, in effect, on a camping trip that lasted an entire lifetime, and this way of life endured for most of the last 1.0 million years.

Generation after generation, for 1.0 million years, natural selection slowly sculpted the human brain, favoring circuitry that was good at solving the day-to-day problems of our hunter-gatherer ancestors—problems like finding mates, hunting animals, gathering plant foods, negotiating with friends, defending ourselves against aggression, raising children, choosing a good habitat, and so on. Those whose circuits were better designed for solving these problems left more children, and we are descended from them.

Our species lived as hunter-gatherers 1,000 times longer than as anything else. The world that seems so familiar to you and me, a world with roads, schools, grocery stores, factories, farms, and nation-states, has lasted for only an eyeblink of time when compared to our entire evolutionary history. The computer age is only a little older than the typical college student, and the industrial revolution is a mere 200 years old. Agriculture first appeared on earth only 10,000 years ago, and it wasn't until about 5,000 years ago that as many as half of the human population engaged in farming rather than hunting and gathering. Natural selection is a slow process, and there just haven't been enough generations for it to design circuits that are well-adapted to our post-industrial life.

In other words, our modern skulls house a stone age mind. The key to understanding how the modern mind works is to realize that its circuits were not designed to solve the day-to-day problems of a modern American—they were designed to solve the day-to-day problems of our hunter-gatherer ancestors. These stone age priorities produced a brain far better at solving some problems than others. For example, it is easier for us to deal with small, hunter-gatherer-band sized groups of people than with crowds of thousands; it is easier for us to learn to fear snakes than electric sockets, even though electric sockets pose a larger threat than snakes do in most American communities. In many cases, our brains are *better* at solving the kinds of problems our ancestors faced on the African savannahs than they are at solving the more familiar tasks we face in a college classroom or a modern city. In saying that our modern skulls house a stone age mind, we do not mean to imply that our minds are unsophisticated. Quite the contrary: they are very sophisticated computers, whose circuits are elegantly designed to solve the kinds of problems our ancestors routinely faced. ...

Although the hominid line is thought to have evolved on the African savannahs, the **environment of evolutionary adaptedness**, or EEA, is not a place or time. It is the statistical composite of selection pressures that caused the design of an adaptation. Thus the EEA for one adaptation may be different from that for another. Conditions of terrestrial illumination, which form (part of) the EEA for the vertebrate eye, remained relatively constant for hundreds of millions of years (until the invention of the incandescent bulb); in contrast, the EEA that selected for mechanisms that cause human males to provision their offspring—a situation that departs from the typical mammalian pattern—appears to be only about two million years old.

The Five Principles are tools for thinking about psychology, which can be applied to any topic: sex and sexuality, how and why people cooperate, whether people are rational, how babies see the world, conformity, aggression, hearing, vision, sleeping, eating, hypnosis, schizophrenia and on and on. The framework they provide links areas of study, and saves one from drowning in particularity. Whenever you try to understand some aspect of human behavior, they encourage you to ask the following fundamental questions:

1.   Where in the brain are the relevant circuits and how, physically, do they work?
2.   What kind of information is being processed by these circuits?
3.   What information-processing programs do these circuits embody? and
4.   What were these circuits designed to accomplish (in a hunter-gatherer context)?

Conclusion

William James's view of the mind, which was ignored for much of the 20th century, is being vindicated today by evolutionary psychologists. ... Their focus on adaptive problems that arose in our evolutionary past has led evolutionary psychologists to apply the concepts and methods of the cognitive sciences to many nontraditional topics: the cognitive processes that govern cooperation, sexual attraction, jealousy, parental love, the food aversions and timing of pregnancy sickness, the aesthetic preferences that govern our appreciation of the natural environment, coalitional aggression, incest avoidance, disgust, foraging, and so on. By illuminating the programs that give rise to our *natural* competences, this research cuts straight to the heart of human nature.

Notes

1   Darwin 1859, p. 458.
2   Hume 1977/1784, p. 14.

References

Hume, D. (1977/1748). *An Enquiry Concerning Human Understanding*. E. Steinberg (Ed.). Indianapolis, IN: Hackett.

James, W. (1890). *Principles of Psychology*. London. MacMillan

Tooby, J., & Cosmides, L. (1992). The psychological foundations of culture. In J. Barkow, L. Cosmides and J. Tooby (Eds.), *The Adapted Mind*. Oxford: Oxford University Press, pp. 19–136.

Chapter 7

Stephen M. Downes

THE BASIC COMPONENTS OF THE HUMAN MIND WERE NOT SOLIDIFIED DURING THE PLEISTOCENE EPOCH

Introduction

There are a number of competing hypotheses about human evolution. For example, *Homo habilis* and *Homo erectus* could have existed together, or one could have evolved from the other, and paleontological evidence may allow us to decide between these two hypotheses (see, e.g., Spoor et al., 2007). For most who work on the biology of human behavior, there is no question that human behavior is in some large part a product of evolution. But, there are competing hypotheses in this area as well. Some claim that human behavior is produced by a collection of psychological mechanisms, for the most part, and that these mechanisms are adaptations that arose in the Pleistocene Epoch (e.g., Buss, 2007; Tooby & Cosmides, 1992). The claim is important and testable (although, more difficult to test than the above-mentioned hypotheses about origins); but importantly, it is only one among many hypotheses about the evolutionary origins of human behavior. While I think that there may be components of our behavior that are best explained by appealing to processes or mechanisms that arose in the Pleistocene, I think that human behavior is a result of evolutionary processes both *much older* and *more recent* than the Pleistocene. I also maintain that much of human behavior, and the mechanisms underlying it, could still be subject to evolutionary change. The aim of this paper is to provide some arguments

for the view that the basic components of the human mind have a long evolutionary history that stretches up to the present, and that will carry on into the future. In supporting this position, I will also provide some arguments against the thesis that the basic components of the human mind are a product of the Pleistocene Epoch.

At the outset, I need to make clear what I am *not* claiming. I do not challenge the view that human behavior has evolutionary roots and that evolutionary biology can be usefully brought to bear in explaining large amounts of our behavior. Some who challenge sociobiology and evolutionary psychology in all their many guises simply reject the thesis that our behavior is a product of evolution. Sometimes this rejection is founded on methodological issues. For example, Richard Lewontin (1998) espouses a particularly strong skepticism about the possibility of explaining human behavior in evolutionary terms, on the grounds that the relevant hypotheses are hard to formulate in a useful way and even harder to test. Others reject the thesis on the grounds that it requires genetic determinism, a position that many in the social sciences reject. I do not think that providing evolutionary explanations of our behavior requires an adherence to genetic determinism. I also do not reject the thesis that some of our behavior may result from evolutionary processes that occurred during the Pleistocene Epoch. It follows directly from the thesis I defend—viz., human behavior is the product of evolutionary processes long before, throughout, and after the Pleistocene—that some of our behavior could be a result of mechanisms produced by evolutionary processes during the Pleistocene. The thesis I reject is that the Pleistocene was the epoch during which *all* our important and defining psychological characteristics evolved.

Next, we need to get clearer about what exactly the relevant thesis claims as well as what variants of the thesis arise in the literature. The thesis is a driving theoretical claim in the work of Evolutionary Psychologists. David Buller (2000, 2005) distinguishes Evolutionary Psychologists from evolutionary psychologists and others who work in the biology of human behavior, for example human behavioral ecologists. Evolutionary Psychologists defend a specific set of theoretical claims about the evolution and structure of the human mind and, hence, about the origin and explanation of human behavior. According to these researchers, human behavior is best understood as the product of a large collection of psychological mechanisms, often called modules, each of which is an adaptation that arose in response to environmental challenges during the Pleistocene Epoch. The period during which these psychological adaptations arose is also often called the Environment of Evolutionary Adaptedness (EEA), a term introduced by John Bowlby (1969, 1973), and later extended and carefully characterized by Donald Symons (1979, 1992). Valerie Starratt and Todd Shackelford make the following useful distinction:

> The EEA is not a place or a time in history, but a statistical composite of the selection pressures (i.e., all environmental characteristics influencing the ability of individuals of a species to survive and reproduce) operating on the adaptations that characterize a species' ancestral past. . . . The Pleistocene is the period of time hypothesized to contain the EEAs of the majority of human-specific adaptations.[1]

What is at stake in the debate is the time during which crucial evolutionary changes occurred in the human lineage, and from here on I will refer to the Pleistocene rather than the EEA.

There are a number of alternative forms that the relevant thesis—viz., the human mind is a product of one particular evolutionary period, the Pleistocene—can take:

1. A general version, whereby *all* components of the human mind are products of the Pleistocene. This version is clearly false and is agreed to be false by nearly all those working in the biology of human behavior, including Evolutionary Psychologists.
2. A trivial version, whereby all components of the human mind that arose as adaptive responses to challenges our human ancestors faced in the Pleistocene evolved in the Pleistocene. This is likely true, but uninformative and question begging.
3. A basic components version, whereby the key distinguishing components of the human mind, or the uniquely human components of the mind, arose in the Pleistocene. Suitably refined, this latter thesis is up for grabs empirically, and is the thesis rejected here.

In what follows, I introduce the relevant thesis and review human evolutionary history. I go on to review William Irons' arguments against the Pleistocene mind thesis, and then add some new examples and some new theoretical approaches to strengthen his arguments. Finally, I introduce an analogy that helps to reinforce the positive thesis of this paper, which is that human psychology is a product of evolutionary processes that took place long before, during, and after the Pleistocene, and will likely continue into the future.

The Pleistocene Mind Thesis and our Evolutionary History

Here is Symons' (1979) account of the Pleistocene mind thesis:

> Large-brained hominids with advanced tool technologies have existed for more than one million years. . . . For over 99% of this period humans lived in small nomadic groups without domesticated plants or animals. This hunting and gathering way of life is the only stable, persistent adaptation humans have ever achieved . . . it is generally agreed that insufficient time has elapsed since the invention of agriculture 10,000 years ago for significant change to have occurred in human gene pools. . . . Humans can thus be said to be genetically adapted to a hunting and gathering way of life.[2]

Here is another nice clear statement of the thesis at stake, from John Tooby and Leda Cosmides:

> [T]he evolved structure of the human mind is adapted to the way of life of Pleistocene hunter gatherers and not necessarily to our modern circumstances. . . . The few thousand year since the scattered appearance of agriculture is only a small stretch in evolutionary terms, less than 1% of the two million years our ancestors spent as Pleistocene hunter-gatherers.[3]

Both authors locate evolutionary change in our lineage in the Pleistocene, and both indicate that evolution is unlikely to have occurred *since* this period, for slightly different reasons.

At this point, it is worth briefly reviewing a little of the relevant evolutionary history at stake. The Cenozoic era, starting around 65 million years ago (mya), is divided into two periods: the Tertiary and Quaternary. The later Quaternary period is divided into two epochs: the Pleistocene, which runs from 1.8 (mya) to 10,000 years ago and is further subdivided into the Lower (.5–.25 mya), Middle (.25–.06 mya), and Upper (.06–.01 mya) Paleolithic, and the Holocene, which runs from .01 mya to the present. The first human ancestors, the Australopithecines, arose in the Pliocene, the last period of the tertiary quarter of the Cenozoic.

The standard story of human evolution as evidenced by the fossil record has the following highlights: at around 4.0 mya, bipedalism arises in the hominid lineage; at 2.0 mya widespread use of stone tools is found; at 1.6 mya *Homo erectus* arises (*Homo habilis* is also dated to around this period); at 1.5 mya some argue that *Homo erectus* uses fire; at .23 mya conservative paleontologists agree fire is controlled; at around .2 mya *Homo sapiens* arises; at .02 mya mil *Homo sapiens* are painting cave walls; at 0.01 mya the first permanent human settlements are formed; at 0.006 mya the first writing is produced. The evolution of brain size throughout this period is also instructive: From 3–4 mya *Australopithecus afarensis* exist with a cranial volume of around 450 cc; the later *Australopithecus africanus*, 3–2 mya, have a cranial volume of 500 cc; *Homo habilis*, 2.5–1.5 mya, have an increased cranial volume of 800 cc; *Homo erectus*, 2–.3 mya, have larger brains still inferred from their 900–1,200 cc cranial volume; and finally *Homo sapiens* have a cranial volume of 1,500 cc measured in specimens from .12 mya.

All the above changes in the human lineage are evolutionary changes of interest, and some can certainly be used to infer changes in our ancestors' psychology during this period. Evolutionary Psychologists emphasize the period from some time after the time stone tools emerged to the point at which the first settlements were developed as the crucial period of human evolutionary history from the point of view of the evolution of our psychological traits. What will be emphasized in the next two sections is that, although some important evolutionary events happened during this period, other periods of evolutionary history are just as important for our understanding of how human psychology arose.

Behavioral Ecologists' Response to the Stone Age Mind Thesis

William Irons (1998) presents several arguments against the thesis that the human mind is a product of evolutionary changes that occurred *only* during the Pleistocene Epoch. Irons' response is typical of others in his field of behavioral ecology and, in part, reflects important methodological and theoretical differences between behavioral ecologists and Evolutionary Psychologists.[4] First, Irons argues that Tooby and Cosmides' claim that our ancestors spent two million years as hunter gatherers is misleading. The paleontological evidence (briefly summarized above) reveals a large number of hominid species appearing and disappearing during the Pleistocene. By the end of this period, *Homo sapiens* are established with their respective way of life, but this way of life may have varied greatly from that of other hominids during this period. Irons (1998) concludes that "saying that human beings were Pleistocene hunter-gatherers for one or two million years creates a false picture of stasis during this period".[5] His next argument concludes that it is mistaken to assume that no evolutionary change could have happened in the 10,000 years of the Holocene leading up to the present. I will pursue this argument, in detail, in the next section and expand it to take into account some theoretical thinking that is different from Irons'.

There is a key difference between Irons' approach and that of Evolutionary Psychologists. Behavioral ecologists seem committed to the view that present fitnesses "caused the origin of an adaptation".[6] In contrast, Evolutionary Psychologists argue that their approach, via the concept of the EEA, maintains a more reasonable stance toward accounting for adaptation: adaptations arise, via natural selection, in response to specific environments at specific times. The

environment that early humans were exposed to during the Pleistocene was the environment that fueled the evolutionary changes that we now see reflected in our current suite of psychological mechanisms. The behavioral ecology approach, so this line of criticism goes, is committed to considering the reproductive consequences of current behavior and factoring this into an account of the adaptiveness of the behavior. This criticism could simply hinge on the distinction between traits that are *adaptations*, or products of natural selection, and traits that are *adaptive*, or those that fit the organism well to a specific feature of its environment.[7] This distinction is part of what the critics have in mind.

The other dimension to the disagreement is that Irons, along with other behavioral ecologists, sees current environments as providing important explanatory insight into various behavioral, as well as morphological, traits. Irons counters by explaining that an adaptation need not be the same thing as providing the causal story of its origin. As a result, "if the form of an adaptation is stable for a very long time and the environment to which it is adjusted is stable, then measures of current fitness can play a logical role in explaining the maintenance of this adaptation".[8] This is not all that Irons and behavioral ecologists are after. They clearly hold the view that evolution in human traits occurred before the Pleistocene, during the Pleistocene, and after the Pleistocene. Their methodology, which includes an emphasis on relations between behavioral traits and current fitness, permits both hypotheses about the stability of traits since the Pleistocene and hypotheses about subsequent evolutionary changes among humans.

Evolutionary Psychologists are committed to the view that all the important evolutionary changes that resulted in the suite of behaviors (and their underlying psychological mechanisms) that we now have occurred during the Pleistocene. The behavioral ecologists' response is that this position limits Evolutionary

Psychologists' range of hypotheses about the evolution of human traits.

An Example and some Alternate Theoretical Directions

In the previous section, I pointed out that Irons' claims that evolution could have taken place during the last 10,000 years, and, of course, if this is right, then the Pleistocene mind thesis could be undermined. He supports this claim with evidence from evolutionary changes in other organisms that have happened in much shorter time spans than this. But evolutionary rates in other animals need not be applicable to humans, and whether or not such rates of evolutionary change occur in nature is an empirical issue. The view that evolution occurred in humans in the last 10,000 years gains a great deal of support from work cited by Peter Richerson and Robert Boyd (2005) concerning human lactose tolerance. I first review this example, and then look at some of the implications of the example for the view that our minds are a product of the Pleistocene Epoch.[9]

The brief sketch of human evolution above reveals that permanent human settlements, evidenced by permanent dwelling structures and domesticated animals and plants, arose 11,000 to 10,000 years ago. Richerson and Boyd argue that during the period since the domestication of animals, human lactose tolerance evolved. The way in which this occurred on their view was via gene/culture co-evolution. The actions of humans in domesticating animals and living with them produced a new selection pressure, and that cultural selection pressure contributed to the increased fitness of individuals who could digest lactose. This trait emerged in humans after the Pleistocene Epoch.

First, we should note that lactose tolerance is not a psychological mechanism, but is a clear case of a human specific evolutionary change that has occurred recently. So while the example is not a case of a human psychological

mechanism arising after the Pleistocene, it is a case of evolutionary change occurring at a more rapid rate than that assumed by Evolutionary Psychologists and the relevant change occurs in the human lineage. Second, it is important to understand the mode of evolutionary explanation that Peter Richerson and Robert Boyd explicitly adopt: gene/culture co-evolution. In the previous section, we saw that behavioral ecologists emphasize different aspects of evolutionary explanation than Evolutionary Psychologists and that this, in part, leads to the disagreement between them over the evolutionary relevance of the Pleistocene Epoch. Analogously, Richerson and Boyd's (2005) commitment to a different theoretical framework leads them to emphasize different explanatory aspects of evolutionary theory.

In arguing against the approach of Evolutionary Psychologists, they maintain: "[C]ulturally evolved traits affect the relative fitness of different genotypes in many ways",[10] and this leads them to oppose the view that "cultural evolution is molded by our evolved psychology, but not the reverse".[11] The target here is the evolution of specific human forms of cooperation and moral norms. Boyd and Richerson argue that Evolutionary Psychologists, via the Pleistocene Epoch thesis, are committed to a view that human forms of cooperation and moral norms arise as a result of psychological mechanisms that were adaptations in earlier humans, which arose as a response to the challenges of small-group living in the Pleistocene environment. Here is Tooby and Cosmides' version of that point:

[T]hings that are cultural in the sense of being organized, contentful, and shared among individuals may be explained in a number of different ways. Within-group commonalities may have been evoked by common circumstances impacting universal architectures. An even larger proportion of organized, contentful, and shared phenomena may be explained as the expression of our universal psychological and physiological architectures in interaction with the recurrent structure of the social or non-social world.[12]

In contrast, Richerson and Boyd's view opens up the possibility that, as various new human cultural formations arose, they played an important role in producing subsequent changes in human psychological makeup via gene/culture co-evolution.

A related line of evolutionary thinking to Richerson and Boyd's gene/culture co-evolution view is niche construction. Rather than focusing exclusively on relations between human cultural products and subsequent evolutionary change, niche constructionists point to the way in which many organisms actively construct aspects of their own niches and, as a result, change the selective environment that impacts upon them (examples are abundant, but include nest building, dam building, and the building of colony dwelling structures). In Kim Sterelny's (2003) hands, human downstream niche construction provides numerous ways in which to impact upon evolutionary change in the human lineage, specifically with respect to the production of novel behavioral repertoires. Gene/culture co-evolution theorists and niche constructionists are more inclined to think of the Holocene as the period during which the most and the most rapid evolutionary change occurred in the human lineage, as opposed to the view that no evolutionary change occurred in this period. As a result, these theorists reject the thesis that the human mind is a product of evolutionary processes that occurred during the Pleistocene.

An Instructive Analogy: The Evolution of the Human Hand

There are many obvious reasons why we focus a great deal of attention on the evolution of human psychological traits. The wide variety of complex cognitive capacities that our minds support are, in large part, responsible for the huge array of unique behaviors we have come up with in our massively varied and challenging environments. But, there are other traits that enable us to get ahead in our complex world. If we were brains in vats, we wouldn't be doing much running, throwing, fishing, sewing, and even playing chess. I contend that the way in which we approach the explanation of the evolution of human behavior and human mental capacities should be consistent with the way in which we approach the evolution of any trait or cluster of traits. A brief reflection on an account of the evolution of the human hand illustrates the points that I want to make here.

Our hands allow us to perform many tasks that our nearest primate relatives are unable to do: sewing, making fish hooks and fishing nets, tying knots, playing instruments, rolling cigarettes, etc. Our hands evolved from mammal forefeet, and their basic structure owes a lot to this ancestry. The hand did not evolve in response to a particular environmental stimulus at any particular time. Rather, various selection pressures, including bipedalism, the occupation of niches with widely varying food resources, and our own niche construction, led to the musculature and bone structure that supports the range of activities for which human hands can be used. One hypothesis about a component of human hand evolution is that it is driven, in large part, by the activities of throwing and clubbing. The idea is that throwing and clubbing pre-date stone tool use, and the throwing and clubbing grips are present in all humans from *Australopithecus* onwards but in no ape lineages (Young, 2003). This account, if correct, takes care of some of the specific morphological and functional attributes of the hand, but by no means all. If we had hands adapted for clubbing and nothing more, we would have a hard time repairing fishing nets with a small bone needle (or making the needle in the first place). The throwing and clubbing account does, however, present a useful hypothesis about an important part of our evolutionary history, the point at which our lineage diverged from that of the rest of the great apes.

And this account also illustrates the point that, in giving an evolutionary account of the suite of traits an organism has, many periods of evolutionary history are relevant; some in quite deep evolutionary time, and some in very recent evolutionary history. There is no *one* evolutionary period in which a set of adaptive problems arose that hands had to face, and I would argue, analogously, that there is no *one* evolutionary period in which the suite of adaptive problems arose that shaped our minds.

Obviously, our brains are far more complicated than our hands; but a similar story should be told about their evolution. Rather than one evolutionary period providing a source of specific selection pressures that produced local adaptive response in brain machinery, the brain's evolution was driven by bipedalism, increased and varied food resources, leading to more use of vision, competition between con-specifics, the need for strategic food gathering (e.g., coordinated hunting), larger group size, and more complex cooperation and coordination problems, including tracking dominance hierarchies, and so on. Crucially, also, the brain's evolution is determined, in part, by the evolution of the hand. The more fine-grained motor skills our hands are capable of, the more monitoring of these skills is required by the brain. The full story of the evolution of the human mind will include components that account for our lineage's divergence from that of the rest of the great apes and components that account for our predictable psychological responses to aspects of large highly complex social groups. Components of this account will come from various times in our evolutionary history, including the Pleistocene, but also including times long before and long after this period.

Conclusions

Here, I have not contended that evolution is irrelevant to our understanding of our mental capacities. Rather, I have presented some arguments that cast doubt on the view that our minds are a suite of adaptive mechanisms which arose only during the Pleistocene Epoch. The broader context for this conclusion is that a complete account of human evolution will be drawn from numerous research programs in the biology of human behavior. One such program is Evolutionary Psychology, but the contribution of this research program to understanding human evolution is limited by an adherence to the thesis that our minds are a product of the Pleistocene Epoch. Actually, more is gained by rejecting this thesis than by retaining it.

Postscript

Evolution of any trait occurs only if there is available variation. Variation in beak shape in finches or variation in running speed in zebras, as long as this variation results in a variation in fitness, leads to selection of one of the variants over others. The relevant variation must also be heritable. One important way in which variation can be heritable is when genetic variation underlies variation in traits. What distinguishes the position I support above from that of prominent Evolutionary Psychologists is that I maintain that there is still a significant amount of genetic variation in humans. As a result of this, it seems reasonable to argue that there can have been recent evolutionary changes in human traits, including psychological traits. Starratt and Shackelford disagree. They say:

> Additionally, geneticists investigating human genetic diversity report that 80% of all genetic differences are among individuals within the same population. In contrast, variations among populations of different continents account for only about 10% of all

genetic differences. This suggests that most genetic variation occurred before modern humans migrated out of Africa roughly 100,000 years ago (see Owens & King, 1999, for a brief overview). If the bulk of our species' genetic makeup has remained relatively constant over the last 100,000 years, it is not unreasonable to argue that our psychological design (which is built by our genes) has remained relatively constant over the last 10,000 years.[13]

Who is right?

In a sense we are both right. John Hawks et al. (2007) report a fair amount of recent genetic variation, some of which they argue is adaptive. They do not have to demonstrate that all human genetic variation arose after the Pleistocene to show that there is potential for the evolution of new traits. Rather, they merely need to present evidence of significant genetic variation occurring in recent years. My argument above is that not all significant evolution of human psychological traits took place in the Pleistocene. The way this discussion impacts on the argument is that it helps establish that the claim that there was human evolution *after* the Pleistocene is a reasonable one to make. The research project of Evolutionary Psychology can be expanded in exciting ways if these new findings in genetics help us discover the evolutionary origins of some of our psychological traits.

Notes

1   Starratt and Shackleford 2009, p. 231.
2   Symons 1979, p. 35.
3   Tooby and Cosmides 2005, p. 5.
4   The presentation here closely follows the presentation in an earlier piece on this topic (Downes, 2001).
5   Irons 1998, p. 195.
6   Irons 1998, p. 196.
7   Sober 2000, p. 85.
8   Irons 1998, p. 196.
9   For many more examples of recent human evolution, see Hawks et al. (2007).
10   Richerson and Boyd 2005, p. 193.
11   Richerson and Boyd 2005, p. 194
12   Tooby and Cosmides 1992, pp. 117–18.
13   Starratt and Shackleford 2009, p. 232.

References

Bowlby, J. (1969). *Attachment and Loss, Vol. I: Attachment.* New York: Basic Books.

Bowlby, J. (1973). *Attachment and Loss, Vol. II: Separation, anxiety, and anger.* New York: Basic Books.

Buller, D. (2000). Evolutionary psychology: A guided tour. In M. Nani and M. Marraffa (Eds.), *A Field Guide to the Philosophy of Mind.* Available at: http://host.uniroma3.it/progetti/kant/field/ep.htm (accessed May 1, 2009).

Buller, D. (2005). *Adapting Minds: Evolutionary psychology and the persistent quest for human nature.* Cambridge, MA: MIT Press.

Buss, D. (2007). *Evolutionary Psychology: The new science of the mind.* Boston: Allyn & Bacon.

Downes, S. (2001). Some recent developments in evolutionary approaches to the study of human behavior and cognition. *Biology and Philosophy,* 16: 575–595.

Hawks, J., Wang, E. T., Cochran, G. M., Harpending, H. C., & Moyzis, R. K. (2007). Recent acceleration of human adaptive evolution. *Proceedings of the National Academy of Sciences (USA),* 104: 20757–20762.

Hrdy, S. (1999). *Mother Nature: Maternal instincts and how they shape the human species.* New York: Ballantine Books.

Irons, W. (1998). Adaptively relevant environments versus the environment of evolutionary adaptedness. *Evolutionary Anthropology,* 6: 194–203.

Lewontin, R. (1998). The evolution of cognition: Questions we will never answer. In D. Scarborough and S. Sternberg (Eds.), *Methods, Models, and Conceptual Issues* (pp. 107–132). Cambridge, MA: MIT Press.

Owens, K., & King, M. (1999). Genomic views of human history. *Science,* 286: 451–453.

Richerson, P., & Boyd, R. (2005). *Not by Genes Alone: How culture transformed human evolution.* Chicago, IL: University of Chicago Press.

Sober, E. (2000). *Philosophy of Biology.* Boulder, CO: Westview Press.

Spoor, F., Leakey, M. G., Gathogo, P. N., Brown, F. H., Antón, S. C., McDougall, I., et al. (2007). Implications of new early *Homo* fossils from Ileret, east of Lake Turkana, Kenya. *Nature*, 448: 688–691.

Starratt, V. G., & Shackleford, T. K. (2009). The basic components of the human mind were solidified during the Pleistocene epoch. In F. J. Ayala and R. Arp (Eds.), *Contemporary Debates in Philosophy of Biology* (pp. 231–242). Oxford: Wiley Blackwell.

Sterelny, K. (2003). *Thought in a Hostile World: The evolution of human cognition.* Oxford, UK: Blackwell.

Symons, D. (1979). *The Evolution of Human Sexuality.* Oxford: Oxford University Press.

Symons, D. (1992). On the use and misuse of Darwinism in the study of human behavior. In H. Barkow, L. Cosmides and J. Tooby (Eds.), *The Adapted Mind* (pp. 137–162). New York: Oxford University Press.

Tooby, J., & Cosmides, L. (1992). The psychological foundations of culture. In H. Barkow, L. Cosmides and J. Tooby (Eds.), *The Adapted Mind* (pp. 19–136). New York: Oxford University Press.

Tooby, J., & Cosmides, L. (2005). Conceptual foundations of evolutionary psychology. In D. Buss (Ed.), *The Handbook of Evolutionary Psychology* (pp. 5–67). Hoboken, NJ: Wiley.

Young, R. (2003). Evolution of the human hand: The role of throwing and clubbing. *Journal of Anatomy*, 202: 165–174.

Topic 3 INNATENESS

BIOLOGISTS, PSYCHOLOGISTS, AND PHILOSOPHERS who believe that human beings share a nature that can be scientifically determined often (but not always) hold that many traits that are part of human nature are innate, as some of the essays in this volume illustrate (e.g., Cosmides & Tooby, 1997 in the previous section 1). And, regularly, pop-science books or articles in the science pages of newspapers and magazines claim that violence, racism, religion, etc. are innate, genetic, or hardwired—one suspects that these terms are near synonyms for lay people. For instance, in an article published in *The New York Times* (07/04/2011), science writer Natalie Angier writes that "Darwinian-minded analysts argue that Homo sapiens have an innate distaste for hierarchical extremes, the legacy of our long nomadic prehistory as tightly knit bands living by veldt-ready team-building rules." Lay people seem to be particularly receptive to claims about the innateness of human characteristics, particularly when those are socially significant. (Curiously, there is little lay interest in the innateness of color perception.)

These claims raise a number of questions. First and foremost, what does it mean to say that a trait is innate? This question may be asked about the use of "innate" among lay people, among scientists, or even among scientists in a specific discipline (say, in cognitive psychology or in evolutionary psychology) since "innate" could mean different things in different disciplines. Alternatively, instead of asking what "innate" actually means, one may be more interested in focusing on what it *should* mean. Instead of being descriptive, one's account would then be prescriptive: It would be a proposal for reform.

Once this question has been answered, we can then ask whether the notion of innateness is scientifically acceptable or whether it should be rejected. The notion of innateness can be confused or, if it is not confused, it can embody assumptions about the biological and psychological world that are inconsistent with current scientific knowledge.

Finally, supposing that the notion of innateness (perhaps some reformed notion of innateness or a notion used in some particular scientific discipline) is scientifically acceptable, we want to know whether many traits are innate and, of course, which ones are.

Paul Griffiths argues that to say that a trait is innate amounts to asserting that it is the expression of the nature of the relevant species, e.g., of human nature. Traits that express the nature of a species tend to be "developmentally fixed": They are hard to change, they do not respond to changes in the environment; they are also species-typical: They are shared by most conspecifics in most environments; and they are "the intended outcome" of development: They are how conspecifics are meant to be. According to Griffiths, the notion of innateness is part of our folkbiology, which is by and large impervious to progress in evolutionary and developmental biology. Strikingly, Griffiths concludes that scientists should stop using the term "innate." As he puts it memorably,

> Substituting what you actually mean whenever you feel tempted to use the word "innate" is an excellent way to resist this slippage of meaning. If a trait is found in all healthy individuals or is pancultural, then say so. If it has an adaptive-historical explanation, then say that. If it is developmentally canalized with respect to some set of inputs or is generatively entrenched, then say that it is. If the best explanation of a certain trait difference in a certain population is genetic, then call this a genetic difference. If you mean that the trait is present early in development, what could be simpler than to say so?

Richard Samuels's essay is in part a response to Griffiths's argument (see also Andre Ariew's and Fiona Cowie's alternatives to this eliminativist conclusion). Samuels argues that cognitive psychologists, such as, e.g., Elizabeth Spelke and Susan Carey, have developed a distinct, coherent, and useful notion of innateness: A trait is innate if and only if it is primitive—viz. its existence cannot be explained in psychological terms—and if it is acquired "in the normal course of events," as Samuels puts it.

Elizabeth Spelke and Katherine Kinzler's essay attempts to answer the third question. They review the empirical evidence about the innate human cognitive endowment—what they call "core knowledge." The view that humans possess numerous innate psychological capacities and are born with a substantial amount of innate knowledge is part of mainstream cognitive developmental psychology. While Spelke and Kinzler endorse this view, they also leave room for learning and cultural influence.

Suggested Further Reading

Ariew, A. (1996) Innateness and canalization. *Philosophy of Science,* 63: S19–S27.

Carey, S. (2009) *The Origin of Concepts.* New York: Oxford University Press.

Carruthers, P., Laurence, S. and Stich, S. (2005–2009) *The Innate Mind, vols. 1–3.* Oxford: Oxford University Press.

Cowie, F. (1999) *What's Within? Nativism reconsidered.* Oxford: Oxford University Press.

Elman, J., Bates, E., Johnson, M., Karmiloff-Smith, A., Parisi, D. and Plunkett, K. (1996) *Rethinking Innateness: A connectionist perspective.* Cambridge, MA: MIT Press.

Gottlieb, G. (2007) Probabilistic epigenesis. *Developmental Science,* 10: 1–11.

Griffiths, P. E. (2009) The distinction between innate and acquired characteristics. In E. N. Zalta (Ed.), *Stanford Encyclopedia of Philosophy,* www.plato.stanford.edu/entries/innate-acquired/

Griffiths, P. E. and Machery, E. (2008) Innateness, canalization, and "biologicizing the mind". *Philosophical Psychology,* 21: 397–414.

Griffiths, P. E., Machery, E., and Linquist, S. (2009). The vernacular concept of innateness. *Mind and Language,* 24: 605–630.

Johnson, M. H. and de Haan, M. (2011) *Developmental Cognitive Neuroscience*, 3rd edn. Malden, MA: Wiley-Blackwell.

Lehrman, D. S. (1953) Critique of Konrad Lorenz's theory of instinctive behavior. *Quarterly Review of Biology*, 28: 337–363.

Linquist, S., Machery, E., Griffiths, P. E. and Stotz, K. (2011) Exploring the folkbiological conception of human nature. *Philosophical Transactions of the Royal Society B*, 366: 444–453.

Mameli, M. and Bateson, P. (2006) Innateness and the sciences. *Biology and Philosophy*, 22: 155–188.

Medin, D. and Atran, S. (2004) The native mind: Biological categorization and reasoning in development and across cultures. *Psychological Review*, 111: 960–983.

Oyama, S. (1990) The idea of innateness: Effects on language and communication research. *Developmental Psychobiology*, 23: 741–747.

Oyama, S., Griffiths, P. E. and Gray, R. D. (2001) *Cycles of Contingency: Developmental systems and evolution*. Cambridge, MA: MIT Press.

Samuels, R. (2002) Nativism in cognitive science. *Mind and Language*, 17: 233–265.

Spencer, J. P., Blumberg, M. S., McMurray, B., Robinson, S. R., Samuelson, L. K. and Tomblin, J. B. (2009). Short arms and talking eggs: Why we should no longer abide the nativist–empiricist debate. *Child Development Perspectives*, 3: 79–87.

Stich, S. P. (1975) The idea of innateness. In S. P. Stich (Ed.), *Innate Ideas* (pp. 1–22). Los Angeles, CA: University of California Press.

Wimsatt, W. C. (1986) Developmental constraints, generative entrenchment, and the innate-acquired distinction. In W. Bechtel (Ed.), *Integrating Scientific Disciplines* (pp. 185–208). Dordrecht: Martinus-Nijhoff.

Chapter 8

Elizabeth S. Spelke and Katherine D. Kinzler

CORE KNOWLEDGE

Introduction

Cognitive science has been dominated by two views of human nature. On one view, the human mind is a flexible and adaptable mechanism for discovering regularities in experience: a single learning system that copes with all the diversity of life. On the competing view, the human mind is a collection of special-purpose mechanisms, each shaped by evolution to perform a particular function. The first view traces back to Enlightenment thinkers such as Locke (1689) and Hume (1748) and has been invigorated more recently by cognitive psychologists and neural network theorists (e.g. Rumelhart & McClelland, 1985; Hinton, 1993). The second view was inspired by Darwin (1871) and gained prominence with the rise of evolutionary psychology (e.g. Cosmides & Tooby, 1994; Pinker, 2002). Much public discussion has focused on the diverging ways in which these views explain human behavior. Does a given ethnic group excel in mathematics because its members have studied more diligently, or because they have inherited greater talent? Do some adolescents join violent gangs because they learned aggressive behavior from their communities, or because they inherited a predisposition toward intergroup competition? Behind these specific questions lies a more general concern: To what degree can we human beings determine our fates and choose our futures? With enough cognitive work, can any person develop her mathematical talents and control her aggression?

Developmental science was born from these concerns, and its research bears on these questions. We believe its research has shown that both these views are false: humans are endowed neither with a single, general-purpose learning system nor with myriad special-purpose systems and predispositions. Instead, we believe that humans are endowed with a small number of separable systems of core knowledge. New, flexible skills and belief systems build on these core foundations.

Studies of human infants and non-human animals, focused on the ontogenetic and phylogenetic origins of knowledge, provide evidence for four core knowledge systems (Spelke, 2004). These systems serve to represent inanimate objects and their mechanical interactions, agents and their goal-directed actions, sets and their numerical relationships of ordering, addition and subtraction, and places in the spatial layout and their geometric relationships. Each system centers on a set of principles that serves to individuate the entities in its domain and to support inferences about the entities' behavior. Each system, moreover, is characterized by a set of signature limits that allow investigators to identify the system across tasks, ages, species, and human cultures.

The core system of object representation has been studied most extensively. It centers on the spatio-temporal principles of cohesion (objects move as connected and bounded wholes), continuity (objects move on connected, unobstructed paths), and contact (objects do not interact at a distance) (Aguiar & Baillargeon, 1999; Leslie & Keeble, 1987; Spelke, 1990). These principles allow human infants as well as other animals to perceive object boundaries, to represent the complete shapes of objects that move partly or fully out of view, and to predict when objects will move and where they will come to rest. Some of these abilities are observed in the absence of any visual experience, in newborn human infants or newly hatched chicks (Valenza, Leo, Gava & Simion, 2006; Regolin & Vallortigara, 1995; Lea, Slater & Ryan, 1996). Even infants with months of visual experience do not, however, have more specific cognitive systems for representing and reasoning about ecologically significant subcategories of inanimate objects such as foods or artifacts (Shutts, 2006), or systems for reasoning about inanimate, non-object entities such as sand piles or liquids (Huntley-Fenner, Carey & Solimando, 2002; Rosenberg & Carey, 2006; Shutts, 2006). Moreover, infants are able to represent only a small number of objects at a time (about three; Feigenson & Carey, 2003). These findings provide evidence that a single system, with signature limits, underlies infants' reasoning about the inanimate world.

By focusing on these signature limits, investigators of animal cognition have discovered the same core system of object representation in adult non-human primates (Hauser & Carey, 2003; Santos, 2004). Like human infants, monkeys' object representations obey the continuity and contact constraints (Santos, 2004) and show a set size limit (of four; Hauser & Carey, 2003). Investigators of cognitive processes in human adults have discovered that the same system governs adults' processes of object-directed attention (see Scholl, 2001, for discussion). Human adults are able to attend to three or four separately moving objects, for example,

when the objects' boundaries and motions accord with the cohesion and continuity constraints. Adults fail to track entities beyond this set size limit, and they fail to track entities that do not obey the spatiotemporal constraints on objects (Scholl & Pylyshyn, 1999; vanMarle & Scholl, 2003; Scholl, Pylyshyn & Feldman, 2001; Marino & Scholl, 2005). Of course, adults also have developed knowledge of more narrow domains of objects such as foods and tools (Keil, Smith, Simons & Levin, 1998; Lavin & Hall, 2001; Santos, Hauser & Spelke, 2001). When attentional resources are stretched, however, the properties that mark these finer distinctions often fail to guide object representations, whereas core properties continue to do so (Leslie, Xu, Tremoulet & Scholl, 1998).

If the core system of object representation is constant over human development, then one would expect that system to be universal. Recent studies of the Piraha, a remote Amazonian group, support that suggestion. The Piraha have been reported to differ dramatically from most other contemporary human groups in their language, culture, and cognitive abilities. For example, their language has been said to lack number words beyond "two" or resources to distinguish past from present, and it may lack basic syntactic devices of recursion and quantification (Everett, 2005). Nevertheless, the Piraha distinguish objects from non-object entities (Everett, 2005), and they track objects with the signature set-size limit (Gordon, 2004).

A second core system represents agents and their actions. Spatio-temporal principles do not govern infants' representations of agents, who need not be cohesive (Vishton, Stulac & Calhoun, 1998), continuous in their paths of motion (Kuhlmeier, Bloom & Wynn, 2004), or subject to contact in their interactions with other agents (Spelke, Phillips & Woodward, 1995). Instead, the intentional actions of agents are directed to goals (Woodward, 1999), and agents achieve their goals through means that are efficient (Gergely & Csibra, 2003). Agents also interact contingently (Johnson, Booth & O'Hearn, 2001; Watson, 1972) and reciprocally (Meltzoff & Moore, 1977). Agents do not need to have perceptible faces (Johnson, Slaughter & Carey 1998; Gergely & Csibra, 2003). When they do, however, infants use their direction of gaze to interpret their social and non-social actions (Hood, Willen & Driver, 1998; Johnson et al., 1998), even as newborns (Farroni, Massaccesi, Pividori & Johnson, 2004). In contrast, infants do not interpret the motions of inanimate objects as goal-directed (Woodward, 1998), and they do not attempt to mirror such actions (Meltzoff, 1995).

Goal-directedness, efficiency, contingency, reciprocity, and gaze direction provide signatures of agent representations that allow for their study in non-human animals and in human adults. Newly hatched chicks, rhesus monkeys, and chimpanzees are sensitive to what their predators or competitors can and cannot see (Agrillo, Regolin & Vallortigara, 2004; Flombaum & Santos, 2005; Hare, Call & Tomasello, 2001). These studies accord well with the physiological signatures of "mirror neurons", observed in captive monkeys, which selectively respond to specific actions performed by the self and others (see Rizzolatti, Fogassi & Gallese, 2002, for a review). Mirroring behavior and neural activity occurs in human adults as well (Iacoboni, Woods, Brass, Bekkering, Mazziotta & Rizzolatti, 1999), and representations of goal-directed action guide adults' intuitive moral reasoning (Cushman, Young & Hauser, 2006). Together, these findings provide evidence for a core system of agent representation that is evolutionarily ancient and that persists over human development.

The core number system is structured around principles that contrast with both the object and the agent systems, and it shows its own distinctive signature limits. Three competing sets of principles have been proposed to characterize this system (Dehaene & Changeux, 1993; Meck & Church, 1983; Church & Broadbent, 1990). Because each of these proposals accounts for the primary properties of numerical representations, their relative merits continue to be debated (see Izard & Dehaene, 2008; Gallistel & Gelman, 1992). There is broad agreement, however, on three central properties of core number representations. First, number representations are imprecise, and their imprecision grows linearly with increasing cardinal value. Under a broad range of background assumptions, Izard (2006) has shown that this "scalar variability" produces a ratio limit to the discriminability of sets with different cardinal values. Second, number representations are abstract: they apply to diverse entities encountered through multiple sensory modalities, including arrays of objects, sequences of sounds, and perceived or produced sequences of actions. Third, number representations can be compared and combined by operations of addition and subtraction.

Number representations with these properties have now been found in human infants, children, and adults, and in adult non-human primates. Infants discriminate between large numbers of objects, actions, and sounds when continuous quantities are controlled, and their discrimination shows a ratio limit (Xu & Spelke, 2000; Xu, Spelke & Goddard, 2005; Wood & Spelke, 2005; Lipton & Spelke, 2003, 2004; Brannon, Abbott & Lutz, 2004). Infants also can add and subtract large numbers of objects (McCrink & Wynn, 2004). Adult monkeys and humans discriminate between large numbers of sounds, with a ratio limit (Hauser, Tsao, Garcia & Spelke, 2003; Barth, Kanwisher & Spelke, 2003), and they add and subtract large numbers as well (Flombaum, Junge & Hauser, 2005). In adults and children, cross-modal numerical comparisons are as accurate as comparisons within a single modality (Barth et al., 2003; Barth, La Mont, Lipton & Spelke, 2005). The precision of numerical representations increases with development, from a ratio of 2.0 in 6-month-old infants to a ratio of 1.15–1.3 in human adults, depending on the task (van Oeffelin & Vos, 1982; Izard, 2006).

Because core representations of number are present throughout development, they should also be present in all cultures, independently of formal education in mathematics. Studies of the Munduruku, a second remote Amazonian group with no verbal counting routine, no words for exact numbers beyond "three", and little formal instruction, support this prediction. The Munduruku discriminate between large numbers with a ratio limit on precision, as accurately as do educated adults in France (Pica, Lemer, Izard & Dehaene, 2004). Further, both Munduruku adults and US preschool children who have received no instruction in mathematics can perform approximate addition and subtraction on large approximate numerosities: they can add two successively presented arrays of objects and explicitly judge whether their sum is more or less numerous than that of a third array of objects (Pica et al., 2004; Barth, LaMont, Lipton, Dehaene, Kanwisher & Spelke, 2006) or sequence of sounds (Barth et al., 2005).

The last system of core knowledge captures the geometry of the environment: the distance, angle, and sense relations among extended surfaces in the surrounding layout. This system fails to represent non-geometric properties of the layout such as surface color or odor, and it fails under some conditions to capture geometric properties of movable objects. When young children or non-human animals are disoriented, they reorient themselves in accord with layout geometry (Hermer & Spelke, 1996; Cheng, 1986; see Cheng & Newcombe, 2005, for review). Children fail, in contrast, to orient themselves in accord with the geometry of an array of objects (Gouteux & Spelke, 2001), and they fail to use the geometry of an array to locate an object when they are oriented and the array moves (Lourenco, Huttenlocher & Vasilyeva, 2005). Under some circumstances, children and animals who are disoriented fail to locate objects in relation to distinctive landmark objects and surfaces, such as a colored wall (Margules &

Gallistel, 1988; Wang, Hermer & Spelke, 1999; Lee, Shusterman & Spelke, 2006). When disoriented children and animals do use landmarks, their search appears to depend on two distinct processes: a reorientation process that is sensitive only to geometry and an associative process that links local regions of the layout to specific objects (Cheng, 1986; Lee et al., 2006).

Human adults show much more extensive use of landmarks, but they too rely primarily on surface geometry when they are disoriented under conditions of verbal or spatial interference (Hermer-Vazquez, Spelke & Katsnelson, 1999; Newcombe, 2005). Recent studies of the Munduruku suggest that sensitivity to geometry is universal, and that it allows children and adults with little or no formal education to extract and use geometric information in pictures as well as in extended surface layouts (Dehaene, Izard, Pica & Spelke, 2006).

In summary, research on non-human animals and on human infants, children, and adults in diverse cultures casts doubt on both of the dominant views of human nature. This research suggests that the human mind is not a single, general-purpose device that adapts itself to whatever structures and challenges the environment affords. Humans learn some things readily, and others with greater difficulty, by exercising more specific cognitive systems with signature properties and limits. The human mind also does not appear to be a "massively modular" collection of hundreds or thousands of special-purpose cognitive devices (Fodor, 2000). Rather, the mind appears to be built on a small number of core systems, including the four systems just described.

Are there other core knowledge systems, with roots in our evolutionary past, that emerge in infancy and serve as foundations for learning and reasoning by children and adults? Recently, we have begun to investigate a fifth candidate system, for identifying and reasoning about potential social partners and social group members.

The social interactions of humans with other humans are a salient feature of every human community, whose adult members show cooperation, reciprocity, and group cohesion. Research in evolutionary psychology suggests that people are predisposed to form and attend to coalitions (Cosmides & Tooby, 2003). A rich and longstanding literature in social psychology confirms this predisposition to categorize oneself and other humans into groups. Any minimal grouping, based on race, ethnicity, nationality, religion, or arbitrary assignment, tends to produce a preference for the in-group, or *us*, over the out-group, or *them*. This preference is shown by adults and children alike, who show parallel biases toward and against individuals based on their race (e.g. Baron & Banaji, 2006).

Studies of infants suggest that these tendencies emerge early in development. Three-month-old infants show a visual preference for members of their own race compared to members of a different race (Kelly, Quinn, Slater, Lee, Gibson, Smith, Liezhong & Pascalis, 2005; Bar-Haim, Ziv, Lamy & Hodes, 2006). This preference is influenced by infants' experience, for it depends both on the race of the infant's family members and the predominance of that race in the larger community. Israeli infants from Caucasian families prefer to look at Caucasian over African faces, Ethiopian infants from African families prefer to look at African over Caucasian faces, and Israeli infants from African families, living in a predominantly Caucasian culture, show no consistent face preferences (Bar-Haim et al., 2006). Infants also look preferentially at faces of the same gender as their primary caregiver (Quinn, Yahr, Kuhn, Slater & Pascalis, 2002).

Race and gender may not be the most powerful or reliable cues to social group membership, however. In the environments in which human social groups evolved, contact with perceptibly different races rarely would have occurred (Cosmides & Tooby, 2003), and all human communities would have contained people of both genders. A better source of information for group membership might come from the language that people speak, and especially from the accent with which they speak it.

Until recently in human history, languages varied markedly across human groups, even groups living in quite close proximity (e.g. Braudel, 1988). From birth, moreover, infants show a preference for the sound of their native language over a foreign language (Mehler, Jusczyk, Lambertz & Halsted, 1988; Moon, Cooper & Fifer, 1993). We have asked, therefore, whether infants use language to categorize unfamiliar people, and whether they prefer people who speak their native language.

In one series of studies (Kinzler & Spelke, 2005), 6-month-old infants were presented with films of the faces of two women who were bilingual speakers of English and Spanish. After the women spoke to the infants in alternation, one in English and the other in Spanish, the two women were presented side by side, smiling without speaking. Although each woman had spoken Spanish to half the infants and English to the others, infants tended to look longer at the woman who had spoken to them in English, their native language.

Further studies revealed that this preference extends to older ages and guides behaviors that are more directly social. For example, 12-month-old infants in Boston were presented with a native speaker of English and a native speaker of French who spoke to them in alternation, while eating two different foods. When later given a choice between the two foods, infants reached preferentially for the snack offered by the English speaker (McKee, 2006).

These findings suggest that the sound of the native language provides powerful information for social group membership in infancy. Together with the studies of infants' sensitivity to race, they raise the possibility that a fifth core knowledge system, distinguishing potential members of one's own social group from members of other groups, may guide infants' and children's learning about the social world.

Core systems for representing objects, actions, numbers, places, and social partners may provide some of the foundations for uniquely human cognitive achievements, including the acquisition of language and other symbol systems, the development of cognitive skills through formal instruction, and the emergence and growth of cooperative social networks. Because learning of words and expressions depends on one's pre-existing concepts, core concepts figure importantly in children's word learning (see Bloom, 2000). Similarly, recent research suggests that core geometric representations guide developing understanding of maps, even in remote cultures with no formal instruction (Dehaene et al., 2006). Core representations of number support preschool children's mastery of counting (Wynn, 1990; Carey, 2001; Spelke, 2003) and older children's and adults' learning and performance of symbolic arithmetic (Dehaene, 1997; Feigenson, Dehaene & Spelke, 2004). Finally, a core system for representing potential social partners may guide infants' and children's "cultural learning" (Tomasello, 1999): their acquisition of skills and behaviors that sustain life within a particular human group. In all these cases, core knowledge systems may support and advance human cognitive development, because the principles on which they are based are veridical and adaptive at the scales at which humans and other animals perceive and act on the world.

Nevertheless, core systems of representation also can lead humans into cognitive errors and maladaptive actions. At the smallest and largest scales that science can probe, objects are not cohesive or continuous, and space is not Euclidean or three-dimensional. Mathematicians have discovered numbers beyond the reach of the core domains, and astute social observers find many cases where human intentions depart, either deliberately or inadvertently, from their overt, goal-directed actions. The gaps and inaccuracies in core representations cause problems for adults and children alike, who are prone to errors in reasoning about properties of object mechanics, non-Euclidean geometry, or numbers that violate the principles of core knowledge (e.g. McCloskey, 1983; Randall, 2005; Gelman, 1991).

The most serious errors may spring from the system for identifying and reasoning about the members of one's own social group. A predisposition for dividing the social world into *us* vs. *them* may have evolved for the adaptive purpose of detecting safe and trustworthy social partners, but it can be misemployed in modern, interconnected and multicultural societies. It even may support the ravages of discord, violence and warfare among individuals, groups and nations. For example, we need not look far to discover linguistic differences leading to social conflicts and intolerance. In US history, the tongues of slaves who spoke no English were severed, Russian speakers were executed following the Alaskan purchase, and the speaking of German in public was forbidden during World War II (Shell, 2001). A look abroad provides innumerable examples of warfare waged across linguistic lines.

Despite these examples, we believe that the strongest message, from human history and developmental science alike, is positive. Although core conceptions are resilient, they can be overcome. The history of science and mathematics provides numerous examples of fundamental conceptual changes that occurred as thinkers became aware of the mismatches between the principles governing their reasoning and the world of phenomena they sought to understand. Despite the pull of core conceptions of Euclidean geometry and object mechanics, cosmologists and particle physicists can test whether space is non-Euclidean and has higher dimensions (e.g. Randall, 2005) and they can use conceptions of massless, discontinuously moving particles to make predictions of astonishing precision (Hawking, 2002).

Conceptual change, moreover, is not the exclusive province of academic science. Preschool children change their conceptions of numbers when they learn to count (Spelke, 2000), and they change their conceptions of agents when they learn about biological processes like eating and breathing (Carey, 1985, 2001).

If core conceptions of social partners lead to errors and harmful conflicts, they too should be open to change, because understanding of human cognitive development yields insight into its malleability. For example, 3-month-old infants' preference for own-race faces is moderated by exposure to other-race faces (Bar-Haim et al., 2006), and biased attitudes toward members of other groups are moderated by certain types of inter-group contact (Pettigrew & Tropp, 2006). Thus, even the deepest-rooted biases are not set in stone. As warring groups in contemporary societies gain ever-greater means for mutual destruction, studies of the conditions that fuel or moderate the development of inter-group bias could be of great importance.

References

Agrillo, C., Regolin, L., & Vallortigara, G. (2004). Can young chicks take into account the observer's perspective? *27th Annual Meeting of the European Conference on Visual Perception (ECVP)*, Budapest.

Aguiar, A., & Baillargeon, R. (1999). 2.5-month-old infants' reasoning about when objects should & should not be occluded. *Cognitive Psychology*, 39: 116–157.

Bar-Haim, Y., Ziv, T., Lamy, D., & Hodes, R. (2006). Nature & nurture in own-race face processing. *Psychological Science*, 17: 159–163.

Baron, A., & Banaji, M. (2006). The development of implicit attitudes: evidence of race evaluations from ages 6 and 10 and adulthood. *Psychological Science*, 17: 53–58.

Barth, H., Kanwisher, N., & Spelke, E. (2003). The construction of large number representations in adults. *Cognition*, 86: 201–221.

Barth, H., La Mont, K., Lipton, J., & Spelke, E.S. (2005). Abstract number and arithmetic in young children. *Proceedings of the National Academy of Sciences*, 39: 14117–14121.

Barth, H., La Mont, K., Lipton, J., Dehaene, S., Kanwisher, N., & Spelke, E. (2006). Non-symbolic arithmetic in adults & young children. *Cognition*, 98: 199–222.

Bloom, P. (2000). *How Children Learn the Meanings of Words*. Cambridge, MA: The MIT Press.

Brannon, E., Abbott, S., & Lutz, D. (2004). Number bias for the discrimination of large visual sets in infancy. *Cognition*, 93: B59–B68.

Braudel, F. (1988). *The Identity of France* (S. Reynolds, trans.). London: Collins (original work published 1986).

Carey, S. (1985). *Conceptual Change in Childhood*. Cambridge, MA: Bradford Books, MIT Press.

Carey, S. (2001). Evolutionary & ontogenetic foundations of arithmetic. *Mind & Language*, 16: 37–55.

Cheng, K. (1986). A purely geometric module in the rat's spatial representation. *Cognition*, 23: 149–178.

Cheng, K., & Newcombe, N. (2005). Is there a geometric module for spatial orientation? Squaring theory & evidence. *Psychonomic Bulletin & Review*, 12: 1–23.

Church, R., & Broadbent, H. (1990). Alternative representations of time, number, and rate. *Cognition*, 37: 55–81.

Cosmides, L., & Tooby, J. (1994). Origins of domain specificity: the evolution of functional organization. In L.A. Hirschfeld & S.A. Gelman (Eds.), *Mapping the Mind: Domain specificity in cognition and culture* (pp. 85–116). New York: Cambridge University Press.

Cosmides, L., Tooby, J., & Kurzban, R. (2003). Perceptions of race. *Trends in Cognitive Sciences*, 7: 173–179.

Cushman, F., Young, L., & Hauser, M.D. (2006). The role of conscious reasoning and intuition in moral judgments: testing three principles of harm. *Psychological Science*, 17: 1082–1089.

Darwin, C. (1871). *The Descent of Man, and Selection in Relation to Sex*. London: J. Murray.

Dehaene, S. (1997). *The Number Sense: How the mind creates mathematics*. New York: Oxford University Press.

Dehaene, S., & Changeux, J. (1993). Development of elementary numerical abilities: a neuronal model. *Journal of Cognitive Neuroscience*, 5: 390–407.

Dehaene, S., Izard, V., Pica, P., & Spelke, E.S. (2006). Core knowledge of geometry in an Amazonian indigene group. *Science*, 311: 381–384.

Everett, D. (2005). Cultural constraints on grammar and cognition in Pirahã: another look at the design features of human language. *Current Anthropology*, 46: 621–634.

Farroni, T., Massaccesi, S., Pividori, D., & Johnson, M. (2004). Gaze following in newborns. *Infancy*, 5: 39–60.

Feigenson, L., & Carey, S. (2003). Tracking individuals via objectfiles: evidence from infants' manual search. *Developmental Science*, 6: 568–584.

Feigenson, L., Dehaene, S., & Spelke, E. (2004). Core systems of number. *Trends in Cognitive Sciences*, 8: 307–314.

Flombaum, J., Junge, J., & Hauser, M. (2005). Rhesus monkeys (*Macaca mulatta*) spontaneously compute addition operations over large numbers. *Cognition*, 97: 315–325.

Flombaum, J., & Santos, J. (2005). Rhesus monkeys attribute perceptions to others. *Current Biology*, 15: 447–452.

Fodor, J. (2000). *The Mind Doesn't Work that Way: The scope and limits of computational psychology*. Cambridge, MA: The MIT Press.

Gallistel, C., & Gelman, R. (1992). Preverbal and verbal counting and computation. *Cognition*, 44: 43–74.

Gelman, R. (1991). Epigenetic foundations of knowledge structures: initial and transcendent constructions. In S. Carey & R. Gelman (Eds.), *The Epigenesis of Mind: Essays on biology and cognition* (pp. 293–322). Hillsdale, NJ: Lawrence Erlbaum Associates.

Gergely, G., & Csibra, G. (2003). Teleological reasoning in infancy: the naïve theory of rational action. *Trends in Cognitive Sciences*, 7 (7): 287–292.

Gordon, P. (2004). Numerical cognition without words: evidence from Amazonia. *Science*, 306: 496–499.

Gouteux, S., & Spelke, E. (2001). Children's use of geometry and landmarks to reorient in an open space. *Cognition*, 81: 119–148.

Hare, B., Call, J., & Tomasello, M. (2001). Do chimpanzees know what conspecifics know? *Animal Behavior*, 61: 139–151.

Hauser, M., & Carey, S. (2003). Spontaneous representations of small numbers of objects by rhesus macaques: examinations of content and format. *Cognitive Psychology*, 47: 367–401.

Hauser, M.D., Tsao, F., Garcia, P., & Spelke, E.S. (2003). Evolutionary foundations of number: spontaneous representation of numerical magnitudes by cotton-top tamarins. *Proceedings of the Royal Society, London, B*, 270:1441–1446.

Hawking, S.W. (2002). *On the Shoulders of Giants: The great works of physics and astronomy*. Philadelphia, PA: Running Press Book Publishers.

Hermer, L., & Spelke, E. (1996). Modularity and development: the case of spatial reorientation. *Cognition*, 61: 195–232.

Hermer-Vazquez, L., Spelke, E., & Katsnelson, A. (1999). Sources of flexibility in human cognition: dual-task studies of space and language. *Cognitive Psychology*, 39: 3–36.

Hinton, G.E. (1993). How neural networks learn from experience. In *Mind and Brain: Readings from the Scientific American magazine* (pp. 113–124). New York: Freeman/Times Books/Henry Holt & Co.

Hood, B.M., Willen, J.D., & Driver, J. (1998). Adults' eyes trigger shifts of visual attention in human infants. *Psychological Science*, 9, 131–134.

Hume, D. (1748). *An Enquiry Concerning Human Understanding*. L.A. Selby-Bigge & P.H. Nidditch (Eds.), (1975 edn.). Oxford: Clarendon Press.

Huntley-Fenner, G., Carey, S., & Solimando, A. (2002). Objects are individuals but stuff doesn't count: perceived rigidity and cohesiveness influence infants' representations of small groups of discrete entities. *Cognition*, 85: 203–221.

Iacoboni, M., Woods, R., Brass, M., Bekkering, H., Mazziotta, J., & Rizzolatti, G. (1999). Cortical mechanisms of human imitation. *Science*, 286: 2526–2528.

Izard, V. (2006). Interactions entre les representations numeriques verbales et non-verbales: études théoriques et expérimentales. Unpublished doctoral dissertation, Université Paris VI, Paris.

Izard, V., & Dehaene, S. (2008) Calibrating the number line. *Cognition*, 106: 1221–47.

Johnson, S., Booth, A., & O'Hearn, K. (2001). Inferring the goals of a nonhuman agent. *Cognitive Development*, 16: 637–656.

Johnson, S., Slaughter, V., & Carey, S. (1998). Whose gaze will infants follow? The elicitation of gaze-following in 12-month-olds. *Developmental Science*, 1: 233–238.

Kelly, D., Quinn, P., Slater, A.M., Lee, K., Gibson, A., Smith, M., Ge, Liezhong, & Pascalis, O. (2005). Three-month-olds, but not newborns, prefer own-race faces. *Developmental Science*, 8: F31–F36.

Keil, F., Smith, W., Simons, D., & Levin, D. (1998). Two dogmas of conceptual empiricism: implications for hybrid models of the structure of knowledge. *Cognition*, 65: 103–135.

Kinzler, K.D., & Spelke, E.S. (2005). The effect of language on infants' preference for faces. Poster presented at the Biennial Meeting of the Society for Research in Child Development, Atlanta, GA.

Kuhlmeier, V., Bloom, P., & Wynn, K. (2004). Do 5-month-old infants see humans as material objects? *Cognition*, 94: 95–103.

Lavin, T.A., & Hall, D.G. (2001). Domain effects in lexical development: learning words for foods and toys. *Cognitive Development*, 16: 929–950.

Lea, S., Slater, A., & Ryan, C. (1996). Perception of object unity in chicks: a comparison with the human infant. *Infant Behavior and Development*, 19: 501–504.

Lee, S.A., Shusterman, A., & Spelke, E.S. (2006). Reorientation and landmark-guided search by young children: evidence for two systems. *Psychological Science*, 17: 577–582.

Leslie, A., & Keeble, S. (1987). Do six-month-old infants perceive causality? *Cognition*, 25: 265–288.

Leslie, A., Xu, F., Tremoulet, P., & Scholl, B. (1998). Indexing and the object concept: developing "what" and "where" systems. *Trends in Cognitive Sciences*, 2: 10–18.

Lipton, J., & Spelke, E. (2003). Origins of number sense: large-number discrimination in human infants. *Psychological Science*, 14: 396–401.

Lipton, J., & Spelke, E. (2004). Discrimination of large and small numerosities by human infants. *Infancy*, 5: 271–290.

Locke, J. (1689). *An Essay Concerning Human Understanding*. Available through L.A. Selby-Bigge (Ed.), Project Gutenberg, LA, 2006.

Lourenco, S., Huttenlocher, J., & Vasilyeva, M. (2005). Toddlers' representations of space. *Psychological Science*, 16: 255–259.

McCloskey, M. (1983). Intuitive physics. *Scientific American*, 248: 122–130.

McCrink, K., & Wynn, K. (2004). Large-number addition and subtraction by 9-month-old infants. *Psychological Science*, 15: 776–781.

McKee, C. (2006). The effect of social information on infants' food preferences. Unpublished honors thesis, Harvard University, April 2006 (K. Shutts, K. Kinzler, and E. Spelke, advisors).

Margules, J., & Gallistel, C. (1988). Heading in the rat: determination by environmental shape. *Animal Learning and Behavior*, 16: 404–410.

Marino, A., & Scholl, B. (2005). The role of closure in defining the "objects" of object-based attention. *Perception and Psychophysics*, 67: 1140–1149.

Meck, W.H., & Church, R.M. (1983). A mode control model of counting and timing processes. *Journal of Experimental Psychology: Animal Behavior Processes*, 9: 320–334.

Mehler, J., Jusczyk, P., Lambertz, G., & Halsted, N. (1988). A precursor of language acquisition in young infants. *Cognition*, 29: 143–178.

Meltzoff, A. (1995). Understanding the intentions of others: re-enactment of intended acts by 18-month-old children. *Developmental Psychology*, 31: 838–850.

Meltzoff, A., & Moore, M. (1977). Imitation of facial and manual gestures by human neonates. *Science*, 198: 75–78.

Moon, C., Cooper, R., & Fifer, W. (1993). Two-day-olds prefer their native language. *Infant Behavior and Development*, 16: 495–500.

Newcombe, N. (2005). Evidence for and against a geometric module: the roles of language and action. In J. Rieser, J. Lockman, & C. Nelson (Eds.), *Action as an Organizer of Learning and Development* (pp. 221–241). Minneapolis, MN: University of Minnesota Press.

Newcombe, N.S., & Huttenlocher, J. (2000). *Making Space: The development of spatial representation and reasoning*. Cambridge, MA: MIT Press.

Pettigrew, T.F., & Tropp, L.R. (2006). A meta-analytic test of intergoup contact theory. *Journal of Personality and Social Psychology*, 90: 751–83.

Pica, P., Lemer, C., Izard, V., & Dehaene, S. (2004). Exact and approximate arithmetic in an Amazonian indigene group. *Science*, 306: 499–503.

Pinker, S. (2002). *The Blank Slate: The modern denial of human nature*. New York: Viking.

Quinn, P., Yahr, J., Kuhn, A., Slater, A., & Pascalis, O. (2002). Representation of the gender of human faces by infants: a preference for female. *Perception*, 31: 1109–1121.

Randall, L. (2005). *Warped Passages*. New York: Ecco Press.

Regolin, L., & Vallortigara, G. (1995). Perception of partly occluded objects by young chicks. *Perception and Psychophysics*, 57: 971–976.

Rizzolatti, G., Fogassi, L., & Gallese, V. (2002). Motor and cognitive functions of the ventral premotor cortex. *Current Opinion in Neurobiology*, 12: 149–161.

Rosenberg, R., & Carey, S. (2006). Infants' indexing of objects vs. non-cohesive entities. Poster presented at the Biennial meeting of the International Society for Infant Studies.

Rumelhart, D.E., & McClelland, J.L. (1985). Distributed memory and the representation of general and specific information. *Journal of Experimental Psychology: General*, 114: 159–188.

Santos, L. (2004). "Core knowledges": a dissociation between spatiotemporal knowledge and contact-mechanics in a non-human primate? *Developmental Science*, 7: 167–174.

Santos, L., Hauser, M., & Spelke, E. (2001). Recognition and categorization of biologically significant objects by rhesus monkeys (*Macaca mulatta*): the domain of food. *Cognition*, 82: 127–155.

Scholl, B. (2001). Objects and attention: the state of the art. *Cognition*, 80 (1): 1–46.

Scholl, B., & Pylyshyn, Z. (1999). Tracking multiple items through occlusion: clues to visual object-hood. *Cognitive Psychology*, 2: 259–290.

Scholl, B., Pylyshyn, Z., & Feldman, J. (2001). What is a visual object? Evidence from target merging in multiple object tracking. *Cognition*, 80: 159–177.

Shell, M. (2001). Language wars. *CR: The New Centennial Review*, 1: 1–17.

Shutts, K. (2006). Properties of infants' learning about objects. Unpublished doctoral dissertation, Harvard University.

Spelke, E.S. (2000). Core knowledge. *American Psychologist*, 55: 1233–1243.

Spelke, E.S. (2003). What makes humans smart? Core knowledge and natural language. In D. Gentner & S. Goldin-Meadow (Eds.), *Language in Mind* (pp. 277–311). Cambridge, MA: MIT Press.

Spelke, E.S. (2004). Core knowledge. In N. Kanwisher & J. Duncan (Eds.), *Attention and Performance, vol. 20: Functional neuroimaging of visual cognition*. Oxford: Oxford University Press.

Spelke, E., Phillips, A., & Woodward, A. (1995). Infants' knowledge of object motion and human action. In D. Sperber, D. Premack, & A. Premack (Eds.), *Causal Cognition: A multidisciplinary debate* (pp. 44–78). Oxford: Clarendon Press/Oxford University Press.

Spelke, E.S. (1990). Principles of object perception. *Cognitive Science*, 14: 29–56.

Tomasello, M. (1999). *The Cultural Origins of Human Cognition*. Cambridge, MA: Harvard University Press.

Valenza, E., Leo, I., Gava, L., & Simion, F. (2006). Perceptual completion in newborn human infants. *Child Development* 77: 1810–1821.

Van Oeffelen, M., & Vos, P. (1982). A probabilistic model for the discrimination of visual number. *Perception and Psychophysics*, 32: 163–170.

vanMarle, K., & Scholl, B. (2003). Attentive tracking of objects versus substances. *Psychological Science*, 14: 498–504.

Vishton, P.M., Stulac, S.N., & Calhoun, E.K. (1998). Using young infants' tendency to reach for object boundaries to explore perception of connected-ness: rectangles, ovals, and faces. Paper presented at the International Conference on Infant Studies, Atlanta, Georgia.

Wang, R., Hermer, L., & Spelke, E. (1999). Mechanisms of reorientation and object localization by children: a comparison with rats. *Behavioral Neuroscience*, 113: 475–485.

Watson, J.S. (1972). Smiling, cooing, and "The Game". *Merrill-Palmer Quarterly*, 18: 323–339.

Wood, J., & Spelke, E. (2005). Infants' enumeration of actions: numerical discrimination and its signature limits. *Developmental Science*, 8: 173–181.

Woodward, A. (1998). Infants selectively encode the goal object of an actor's reach. *Cognition*, 69: 1–34.

Woodward, A. (1999). Infants' ability to distinguish between purposeful and non-purposeful behaviors. *Infant Behavior and Development*, 22 (2): 145–160.

Wynn, K. (1990). Children's understanding of counting. *Cognition*, 36: 155–193.

Xu, F., & Spelke, E. (2000). Large number discrimination in 6-month-old infants. *Cognition*, 74, B1–B11.

Xu, F., Spelke, E., & Goddard, S. (2005). Number sense in human infants. *Developmental Science*, 8: 88–101.

Chapter 9

Paul E. Griffiths

WHAT IS INNATENESS?

What is Innateness?

In molecular developmental biology innateness seems as antiquated a theoretical construct as instinct and equally peripheral to any actual account of gene regulation or morphogenesis. In behavioral ecology, some authors regard the innateness concept as irretrievably confused and the term "innate" as one that all serious scientific workers should eschew[1] whilst others claim that the popular demand to know if something is "in our genes" is best construed as a question about whether a trait is an adaptation.[2] In cognitive psychology, however, whether a trait is innate is still regarded as a significant question and is often the subject of heated debate.[3] In an attempt to clarify what is at issue in these debates, philosophers have proposed numerous analyses of the concept of innateness. Some years ago, Stephen Stich defined innateness as the disposition to appear in the normal course of development, that is, to be part of the typical or normal phenotype of that kind of organism.[4] More recently, André Ariew has analyzed innateness in terms of developmental canalization, a phenomena which he uses to clarify the intuitive idea that the innate traits are insensitive to variation in the developmental environment.[5] William Wimsatt has explicated innateness using his concept of "generative entrenchment": innate traits are those upon which many other features of the organism are built and whose presence is therefore essential for normal development.[6] Fiona Cowie and Richard Samuels have both offered methodological analyses of innateness.[7] Samuels argues that innate traits are "psychological primitives"—traits that are mentioned in psychological explanations but which are not amenable to the explanatory strategies that define psychology as a scientific domain. Psychology appeals to innate traits in its explanations, but the explanation of the innate traits themselves lies outside psychology. Cowie identifies a number of different roles that the innateness concept has played in particular episodes in the history of philosophy and psychology, one of which resembles that described by Samuels. In my view, each of these proposals correctly identifies a belief or an intellectual strategy that lies behind the use of the term "innate" in certain specific research contexts. None of them, however, is an adequate account of the concept of innateness.

In an earlier work I have argued, following a number of developmental psychologists and behavioral ecologists,[8] that the concept of innateness conflates a number of independent biological properties and is thus a confusing and unhelpful notion with which to understand behavioral or cognitive development.[9] Three broad ideas are bundled together in the innateness concept:

- Developmental fixity
- Species nature
- Intended outcome

For reasons that will become clear below, all three terms refer to clusters of related ideas and show up in different forms in different historical, cultural and intellectual contexts. "Developmental fixity" means that the trait is in some sense "hard to change": it is insensitive to environmental inputs in development; its development is or appears goal-directed, so that when prevented from developing in one way it develops in another; changing it disrupts or impairs development. "Species nature" means that innate traits reflect what it is to be an organism *of that kind*, with consequent associations of typicality or universality. "Intended outcome" means that innate traits are how the organism is *meant* to develop: To lack them is to be malformed; upbringings that disrupt them are simply "bad rearing", as Konrad Lorenz used to say. This intentional or normative element of the innateness concept is today usually assimilated to the idea of design by natural selection: innate traits are those that the organism is *designed* to possess or which are *programmed* in its genes. In my earlier work I identified scientific descendants of these three clusters of ideas, namely, being insensitive to environmental factors in development, being universal in the species (I now prefer the vaguer phrase "species-typical") and being the product of adaptive evolution. I argued that because these three are empirically disassociated, a theoretical construct that conflates them is undesirable. In particular, such a construct will give rise to illicit inferences from the presence of one biological property to the presence of the others.

In this chapter I want to simultaneously defend my earlier view and offer a deeper diagnosis of the problem. The innateness concept is an expression of "folk essentialism"—a distinctive feature of pre-scientific thought about animate things ("folkbiology"). Folk essentialism understands biological species as the manifestation of underlying "natures" shared by all members of a species. The three aspects of the innateness concept that I identified are all elements of folk essentialism. Since folk essentialism is both false and fundamentally inconsistent with the Darwinian view of species, it should be rejected. However, folk essentialism is at the very least a widespread human cognitive trait, probably pancultural, and quite possibly a canalized outcome of cognitive development. Because "innate" is a common term whose vernacular meaning embodies this way of thinking about living systems, attempts to stipulate a new, restricted meaning for this word are unlikely to be successful. In any case, proposals for linguistic form should be formulated with the intention of promoting a more accurate understanding of living systems, not preserving intuitions that reflect folkbiology. The several proposed explications listed above each describe a genuine biological property and several others are needed to adequately describe all the phenomena that innateness has been invoked to explain. Therefore, I suggest, the use of new, neutral terms for each of these several properties is preferable to trying to retain the term "innate" for one or more of them.

Innateness in Behavioral Science

Patrick Bateson lists seven different senses in which the term "innate" has been used in animal behavior studies:[10]

- Present at birth
- A behavioral difference caused by a genetic difference
- Adapted over the course of evolution
- Unchanging through development
- Shared by all members of the species
- Not learned
- A distinctly organized system of behavior driven from within[11]

To this list we can add an eighth sense, that of being something that can be taken as given with respect to the set of causal factors currently under investigation. This sense is particularly prevalent in psychology, where "innate" traits are those that are to be explained biologically rather than psychologically.[12] Bateson's sixth sense, in which the innate traits are simply the complement of the learnt traits, is perhaps an instance of this eighth sense, reflecting the domination of psychology by learning theory in the period when ethology was reviving the concept of an innate trait.[13] The use of innateness in this last sense as a way to block a demand for explanation can make ascriptions of innateness the subject of considerable controversy, especially when scientists disagree about explanatory priorities or disciplinary boundaries. This is one reason why the reintroduction of the innateness concept to animal behavior studies by Konrad Lorenz and other early ethologists[14] provoked immediate hostility from developmental psychobiologists.[15] Developmental scientists rejected the innateness concept for the same reason they had rejected the instinct concept earlier in the century—these concepts are used to signal that the traits in question can be treated as given and developmental scientists are engaged in elucidating their origins!

However, the disagreement between Lorenz and his critics was not merely a clash between competing explanatory interests and disciplinary orientations. Developmentally oriented scientists argued that ethologists were using the innateness concept to make invalid inferences via fallacies of ambiguity. The properties of developmental fixity, universality, and evolutionary origin were freely inferred from one another when developmentalists knew them to be empirically disassociated. The traditional notion of universality itself conflates the two very different properties of being *monomorphic* and being *pancultural*. A trait is monomorphic if only one form of that trait is found in a species—the inability to synthesize vitamin C and the elevation of the heart rate in fear are monomorphic human traits. In contrast, a trait is pancultural if it is found in all cultures. Many pancultural traits, such as hair color and susceptibility to early-onset diabetes, are *polymorphic*: more than one form of the trait exists in the same species. Neither being monomorphic nor being pancultural has any very strong connection to being the result of adaptive evolution. Evolution is as capable of producing polymorphisms as monomorphisms, and some non-adaptive evolutionary mechanisms, such as developmental constraint, are likely to produce monomorphic traits. All healthy human beings have the same arrangement of bones in their limbs, an arrangement they share with the whole vast group of tetrapods, but the very ubiquity of this arrangement is strong evidence that humans do not have it because of its adaptive value. Nor need evolved traits be pancultural, as evolutionary psychologists are fond of pointing out. Different cultural environments can systematically induce different developmental outcomes.[16] In this respect different cultures can resemble the different ecological zones that induce the same species of plant to develop into different ecomorphs, for example, a low-growing shrub at high altitudes and an upright tree at lower altitudes.

The relationship between having an evolutionary explanation and exhibiting developmental fixity is equally problematic. There is no intrinsic tendency for evolved traits to be buffered against variation in environmental inputs to development. Developmental psychobiologists since Lehrman have documented innumerable cases in which evolved developmental outcomes require a rich and highly specific developmental environment. In rhesus macaques, for example, the recognition of emotional expressions in conspecifics and the ability to cooperate in agonistic interaction depend on infant social interaction for their development.[17] These findings throw no doubt whatever on the claim that these abilities in adult macaques are the result of adaptive evolution. The constructive role of environmental factors in the development of evolved traits should come as no surprise. Selection cannot favour a trait that compensates for the loss of a developmental input that is, as a matter of fact, reliably available. Evolution does not anticipate future contingencies. In fact, such alternative developmental pathways will be dismantled by mutation if a developmental input becomes readily available, as happened in the primate lineage with the pathway used by most other mammals to synthesize their own vitamin C.[18]

Finally, as developmental scientists have reiterated ever since Lehrman, universality and developmental fixity cannot be equated. Ariew uses this point to argue against Stich's earlier analysis of the innateness concept: The fact that a trait is invariant across normal environments leaves it entirely open whether this is because the trait is insensitive to environmental factors or because the causally relevant factors are invariant across normal environments.[19] In this argument, of course, Ariew is using intuitions driven by one element of the innateness concept (developmental fixity) to argue against an explication that focuses on another (universality/species typicality). Ariew's argument is correct, but Stich could equally well reply by using intuitions about species-typicality to argue against Ariew's explication in terms of developmental fixity. The fundamental physiological and mental traits that depend on environmental vitamin C for their development, for example, are intuitively innate.

In the light of the developmental critique of the innateness concept, some ethologists rejected it entirely, as can be seen in Bateson's work[20] and in that of Robert A. Hinde.[21] Others used the notion of a genetic program to allow them to ignore development in the context of studying evolution while admitting that evolved phenotypic traits are contingent upon a host of other factors in development. Konrad Lorenz took this route in his later work, denying that phenotypic traits could be meaningfully

described as innate and asserting instead that: "certain parts of the information which underlie the adaptedness of the whole, and which can be ascertained by the deprivation experiment, are innate".[22] Something like this approach has become orthodox in contemporary behavioral ecology although it is now more usual to say directly that a trait is programmed in the genes than to make a detour through the concept of innateness.[23]

Folkbiology and Folk Essentialism

The tern "folkbiology" refers both to pre-scientific thought about the animate realm and to the field that studies such thought.[24] Research in folkbiology is conducted by cognitive anthropologists who set out to describe and explain patterns of reasoning about the living world in various human cultures and by cognitive psychologists who study the emergence of these patterns of reasoning in children and their manifestation in adults under controlled conditions. Folkbiological research in cognitive anthropology has revealed some apparently pancultural features of human thought about the animate realm.[25] Although classifications of living things are culturally specific, the form of these classifications is the same everywhere. Organisms are classified hierarchically, with five distinctive taxonomic levels: Folk kingdom (e.g., plant, animal); life form (e.g., tree, mammal); generic species (e.g., oak, dog); folk specific (e.g., white oak, poodle); folk varietal (e.g., spotted white oak, toy poodle). This hierarchical taxonomy is used in inductive inference: The degree of confidence with which observed properties of one organism are projected to another organism is predicted by their taxonomic distance from one another in the local scheme of classification. Categories at the generic-species level are inductively privileged: Higher-level categories support fewer and weaker inductive inferences while lower-level categories add little to the strength or number of inferences. Generic species are thus the level at which folk biological reasoning operates most powerfully.

Folkbiology research by cognitive psychologists has produced a number of intriguing results. Children think in distinctive ways about the cognitive domain of living things, a domain which itself seems to develop in a distinctive manner from an earlier domain of animate (self-moving) things which includes some things that are not alive and excludes plants.[26] Children of kindergarten age presume that each kind of organism possesses some unobservable property that explains the distinctive observable properties of that kind of organism and which preserves the specific identity of an organism through massive changes in its observable properties.[27] This pattern of reasoning is very different with the same children's reasoning about artifacts. The specific identity of artifacts depends on their observable properties and, as children develop further, on those observable properties most relevant to the performance of their intended function. Specific identity is not preserved through change in these observable features: A screwdriver ground down to make an awl is not still "really" a screwdriver. The pattern of thought that seems to imply the existence of some underlying, unobservable property that guarantees identity has been labeled "psychological essentialism" by Douglas Medin,[28] but here I will refer to it as "folk essentialism":

> People act as if things (e.g., objects) have essences or underlying natures that make them the things that they are. Furthermore, the essence constrains or generates properties that may vary in their centrality.[29]

There is considerable controversy about whether these results should be interpreted as support for the existence of a "theory" of living things in young children or for "beliefs" about species and their essences.[30] This, fortunately, is an issue that does not need to be settled for the purposes of this chapter. I can also remain agnostic on the question of how specific the essentialistic pattern of inference is to the biological domain and certain others.[31] All I require for my argument here is that there exists an essentialist strategy of explanation in folkbiology. Just as Scott Atran has argued that the hierarchical taxonomy of early modern biology was derived from folk taxonomy,[32] I argue that a cluster of biological concepts, such as the pre-Darwinian concept of species, the concept of human nature, and the innateness concept, derive from essentialism in folkbiology. They reflect a way of thinking about living systems whose continuing grip on us is explained by the fact that it develops long before we are exposed to scientific biology.

Innateness and Folk Essentialism

It is uncontroversial that the scientific concept of species emerged smoothly from the pre-scientific practice of categorizing organisms into folk species. Folkbiological species categories are understood in terms of an underlying essence which is shared by all members of the species and which makes each individual the kind of organism that it is. This is precisely the "typological" perspective on species that Darwin had to displace in order to establish the gradual transformation of one species into another. Species are not types to which individual organisms more or less imperfectly conform, but abstractions from the pools of overlapping variation that constitute the actual populations of that species, a perspective that Ernst Mayr christened "populational thinking".[33] Folk taxonomy allows traditional societies to interact effectively with the common plants and animals of their region because at a particular time and place species often are clearly separated from one another. The limitations of folk taxonomy become apparent when working on larger geographical and temporal scales. Many species grade into one another spatially, and all do so temporally. When individuals exist who are intermediate between two species due to hybridization or incomplete speciation, it is senseless to ask whether these individuals are "really" of one species or the other. That question presumes that the species is more than an abstraction from the varied individuals that compose it.

Elliott Sober has argued that the crucial element of Mayr's distinction between "typological" and "populational" perspectives lies in their approach to individual variation.[34] The typological perspective sees variation as deviation from a "natural state" that is the same for all individuals of that kind. Variant individuals are understood in terms of the natural state that they have failed to achieve. The Darwinian approach to variation, in contrast, regards species as pools of variation, has no concept of ideal type and treats the current average, modal or typical organism as a temporary reflection of an ongoing process of change. Unlike the typological perspective, the populational perspective does not lead to the expectation that species will be confined within a "circle of variation," as so many of Darwin's critics supposed must be the case. Looked at in this light, Darwin's achievement lies as much in having transformed the question of the origin of species as in having answered it. The original "mystery of mysteries"[35] was why different ideal types of organism are realized in different historical epochs. In Darwin's hands, the question became how individual organisms, albeit clustered together as groups of more or less similar organisms, are succeeded by slightly different individual organisms. Throughout his work, Darwin can be found arguing against the idea that there is a normal or ideal type of each species. In *Descent of Man*, for example, he argues that medical representations of human anatomy are merely useful abstractions from a mass of slightly different arrangements of parts, and even slightly different collections of parts.[36]

Folkbiology regards essences as common to all members of a species and uses a natural-state

model of variation in which variant individuals are seen as deviations from an ideal type. This much is supported by empirical research, as I briefly described in the last section. But I suggest that there are other aspects of folk essentialism that have been less thoroughly investigated. First, essences are conceived as striving to realize themselves. A trait linked to an organism's essence will tend to reassert itself when the distorting influence that prevented its development is removed. Second, essences have normative overtones, so that variant individuals are not merely different but deviant. Individuals who deviate from their natural state are not as healthy and flourishing as normal individuals and no good can come of such deviation from the natural course of things. These claims are, of course, testable by the usual methods of folkbiology and cognitive developmental psychology, but in the absence of an existing empirical literature I can only provide anecdotal evidence in their support.[37] Consider one of the most enduring of science fictions, H. G. Wells's *The Island of Dr Moreau*, in which the eponymous scientist sets out to turn animals into men. Dr Moreau's creations tend to revert to their original type, even in modern retellings of the story in which he has transformed their genomes! Eventually, they become monsters and destroy him. First published in the 1890s, *Dr Moreau* was a response to the new science of developmental mechanics (*Entwicklungsmechanik*), as well as a reflection of contemporary revulsion at the use of vivisection. Ten years earlier, scientists such as Wilhelm Roux had set out to transform embryology from a descriptive to an experimental science, manipulating physical and chemical variables to uncover their role in development and throw light on the mechanisms of cell differentiation and morphogenesis. Some of their results were the very stuff of science fiction, as when Hans Driesch succeeded in cloning the sea urchin by mechanically separating the products of the first cell division. Surely the production of humans in the laboratory was only a few years away! In the novel, Dr Moreau exploits the mechanical "laws of growth" envisioned by scientists like Roux to redirect the development of his animals toward the human form. The novel has been filmed three times,[38] and by 1996 Moreau had become a genetic engineer, manipulating the DNA of his unfortunate victims. It is striking that Wells's plot is as satisfying to contemporary audiences, against this very different scientific background, as it was over a century ago. "The laws of growth" and "the genes" can play exactly the same role as extraordinarily powerful tools for deflecting nature from its course, but which are unable to change the essence of the organism. Moreau continues to lament that continual intervention is needed to prevent "the beast" from reasserting itself, and his vision of creating an exact human copy still ends in death at the hands of his unnatural creations. The first of the two ideas that drive the plot forward, the idea of the essence reasserting itself, seems to me an inevitable concomitant of the explanatory role of essences in folkbiology. Essences explain the fact that all members of a species resemble one another because the essence *generates* the resemblance. The children in one of Frank C. Keil's experiments are sure that a raccoon manipulated to resemble and behave like a skunk will give birth to baby raccoons, presumably because it will pass on to them the essence of raccoon rather than that of skunk.[39] The generative power of essences is primarily used to explain reproduction, but it also explains *regeneration*, as when dyed hair grows back in its natural color or a coppiced tree grows new trunks. It is this capacity for regeneration that is, I suggest, the folkbiological basis for the reversion of Moreau's creations. The second idea, that individuals who deviate from their natural state are malformed or monstrous is all too familiar. The idea that health, happiness and morality can all be achieved by living in accordance with our nature did not need Rousseau to give it currency.

I have suggested that folk essentialism involves belief in unobservable essences shared by all members of a species, which explain the normal characteristics of the species, which reassert themselves when these characteristics are interfered with and deviation from which is viewed as normatively wrong. This complex of ideas can be conveyed in our own case by the term "human nature". Human nature is both evidenced by and used to explain universal (or typical) human traits: "jealousy is found in all cultures—it's part of human nature." Human nature is used to argue for the futility of interference: "It's no use trying to remove gender differences, they're part of human nature." Finally, the idea that ethical questions can be investigated by asking what it is to be truly or fully human has had followers from Aristotle to contemporary "perfectionism".[40] The idea of human nature is, I suggest, the application of folk essentialism to our own case. Human nature is also a near synonym for the *innate* features of human beings. If you give a popular-science talk and assert that, for instance, addictive behaviour is part of human nature, you can count on your audience interpreting this to mean that addictive behaviour is innate. It is hard to change, found in all cultures, and so forth. Conversely, if something is innate, then it is at least reasonable to refer to it as a part of human nature. I think this is true even of diseases that are described as innate. We are "naturally" disposed to suffer from some diseases, such as those of old age. If innateness differs from human nature it is, perhaps, in having weaker normative overtones. I conclude, then, that the vernacular concept of innateness is also an expression of folk essentialism.

Doing without Innateness

The innateness concept continues to promote the conflation of different biological properties in the ways that brought it into disrepute in animal behaviour studies fifty years ago. Innateness allows writers to move illicitly from the view that a trait has an adaptive history to the view that it is insensitive to environmental influences in development. Popular discussions of rape or sexual jealousy inspired by contemporary evolutionary psychology assume that we have to live with these aspects of "human nature" despite the clearest theoretical commitment by evolutionary psychologists to the dependence of evolved traits on the developmental environment. Conversely, developmental fixity is seen as a precondition of evolutionary explanation despite the massive evidence to the contrary. Social constructionists applaud research that shows developmental plasticity because they believe it removes the trait in question from the biological realm. In another set of invalid inferences, universality, in either of its senses, is taken to be the hallmark of adaptive evolution, hence the efforts devoted by some evolutionary psychologists to documenting universality and by social constructionists to documenting cultural difference. The continuing focus on universality against the background of universal acceptance that evolution produces polymorphic outcomes is, I believe, due in no small part to the continuing use of theoretical constructs like innateness and human nature that conflate these distinct biological properties.

It is, of course, possible to define "innate" in a way that makes use of only some limited set of its connotations. But all three aspects of the innateness concept are important and however the term "innate" is redefined, terms will be needed to refer to the aspects of the concept this stipulation has excluded. In fact, each of these three broad ideas needs to be further subdivided to mark critical biological distinctions. Furthermore, "innateness" is a term in common use, and one that represents a highly intuitive way of thinking about living systems. This existing system of thought acts as a sink that draws new, stipulative usages back towards the established use. Substituting what you actually mean whenever you feel tempted to use the

word "innate" is an excellent way to resist this slippage of meaning. If a trait is found in all healthy individuals or is pancultural, then say so. If it has an adaptive-historical explanation, then say that. If it is developmentally canalized with respect to some set of inputs or is generatively entrenched, then say that it is. If the best explanation of a certain trait difference in a certain population is genetic, then call this a genetic difference. If you mean that the trait is present early in development, what could be simpler than to say so? If, finally, you want to "blackbox" the development of a trait for the purposes of your current investigation then saying so will prevent your less methodologically reflective colleagues from supposing that you think the trait is . . . innate.

Notes

1 Bateson, 1991; Bateson and Martin, 1999
2 Symons, 1992, p. 141
3 Cowie, 1999
4 Stich, 1975
5 Ariew, 1996; Ariew, 1999
6 Wimsatt, 1986, 1999
7 Cowie, 1999; Samuels, 2002
8 Elements of this critique have been made many times by many authors in the last sixty years. I myself was drawing on (Bateson, 1991; Gray, 1992; Johnston, 1987; Lickliter and Berry, 1990; Oyama, 1990).
9 Griffiths, 1997
10 Bateson, 1991, p. 21
11 A conception of the unit of mental evolution from classical ethology which resonates strongly with the idea of a "mental module" found in contemporary evolutionary psychology (Barkow, Cosmides, and Tooby, 1992).
12 Samuels, 2002
13 See, e.g., Tinbergen, 1957
14 Schiller, 1957
15 Johnston, 2001; Lehrman, 1953
16 Tooby and Cosmides, 1992
17 Mason, 1985
18 Jukes and King, 1975
19 Ariew, 1999, p. 134

20 Bateson, 1983, 1991

21 Hinde, 1968

22 Lorenz, 1965, p. 40.

23 The "genetic program" idea has some pitfalls of its own. See Oyama 2000a, b; Oyama, Griffiths and Gray, 2001; Griffiths, 2001.

24 Medin and Atran, 1999

25 Atran, 1990, 1999; Berlin, 1992, 1999; Coley et al., 1999

26 Carey, 1985, 1988

27 Keil, 1989

28 Medin and Ortony, 1989

29 Medin, 1989, 1476

30 Downes, 1999

31 Gelman & Hirschfeld, 1999

32 Atran, 1990

33 Mayr, 1976

34 Sober, 1980

35 The phrase is Sir John Herschel's and occurs in a call to biologists to resolve the great question of the origin of species (Herschel, 1966 [1830]). It is used without acknowledgement on the first page of *Origin of Species* (Darwin, 1964 [1859]).

36 Darwin, 1981 [1871], pp. 107–11

37 What follows looks very much like a traditional "analysis" of the concepts of essence, human nature and innateness by appeals to "linguistic intuition". I am, indeed, trying to analyse these concepts, but I make no pretension to have access to a special realm of conceptual truths. This is speculative folkbiology built on anecdotal evidence.

38 In 1932 as *Island of the Damned* with Charles Laughton in the title role, and twice under its original title, with Kirk Douglas as the 70s Moreau still resorting to vivisection and Marlon Brando in 1996 injecting his victims with human DNA.

39 Keil, 1989

40 Hurka, 1993

References

Ariew, A. (1996). Innateness and canalization. *Philososophy of Science*, 63 (3 [Supplement]): S19–S27.

Ariew, A. (1999). Innateness is canalization: In defense of a developmental account of innateness. In V. G. Hardcastle (Ed.), *Where Biology Meets Psychology: Philosophical essays* (pp. 117–138). Cambridge, MA: M.I.T. Press.

Atran, S. (1990). *Cognitive Foundations of Natural History: Towards an anthropology of science*. New York: Cambridge University Press.

Atran, S. (1999). Itzaj Maya folkbiological taxonomy: Cognitive universals and cultural particulars. In D. L. Medin and S. Atran (Eds.), *Folkbiology* (pp. 119–203). Cambridge, MA: M.I.T. Press.

Barkow, J. H., Cosmides, L., & Tooby, J. (Eds.) (1992). *The Adapted Mind: Evolutionary psychology and the generation of culture*. Oxford: Oxford University Press.

Bateson, P. P. G. (1983). Genes, environment, and the development of behaviour. In P. Slater and T. Halliday (Eds.), *Genes, Development and Learning* (pp. 52–81). Oxford: Blackwell.

Bateson, P. P. G. (1991) Are there principles of behavioural development? In P. Bateson (Ed.), *The Development and Integration of Behaviour* (pp. 19–39). Cambridge: Cambridge University Press.

Bateson, P. P. G., & Martin, P. (1999). *Design for a Life: How behavior and personality develop*. London: Jonathan Cape.

Berlin, B. (1992). *Ethnobiological Classification*. Princeton, NJ: Princeton University Press.

Berlin, B. (1999). How a folkbiological system can be both natural and comprehensive: One Maya indian's view of the plant world. In D. L. Medin and S. Atran (Eds.), *Folkbiology* (pp. 71–89). Cambridge, MA: M.I.T. Press.

Carey, S. (1985). *Conceptual Change in Childhood*. Cambridge, MA: M.I.T. Press.

Carey, S. (1988). Conceptual differences between children and adults. *Mind and Language*, 3: 167–181.

Coley, J. D., Medin, D. L., Proffitt, J. B., Lynch, E., & Atran, S. (1999). Inductive reasoning in folkbiological thought. In D. L. Medin and S. Atran (Eds.), *Folkbiology* (pp. 205–232). Cambridge, MA: M.I.T. Press.

Cowie, F. (1999). *What's Within? Nativism reconsidered*. Oxford: Oxford University Press.

Darwin, C. (1964 [1859]). *On The Origin of Species: A facsimile of the first edition*. Cambridge, MA: Harvard University Press.

Darwin, C. (1981 [1871]). *The Descent of Man and Selection in Relation to Sex* (Facsimile of the first edition). Princeton, NJ: Princeton University Press.

Downes, S. M. (1999). Can scientific development and children's cognitive development be the same process? *Philosophy of Science*, 66 (4): 565–578.

Gelman, S. A., & Hirschfeld, L. A. (1999). How biological is essentialism? In J. L. Medin and S. Atran (Eds.), *Folkbiology* (pp. 403–446). Cambridge, MA: M.I.T. Press.

Gray, R. D. (1992). Death of the gene: developmental systems strike back. In P. E. Griffiths (Ed.), *Trees of Life: Essays in philosophy of biology* (pp. 165–210). Dordrecht: Kluwer.

Griffiths, P. E. (1997). *What Emotions Really Are: The problem of psychological categories*. Chicago, IL: University of Chicago Press.

Griffiths, P. E. (2001). Genetic information: A metaphor in search of a theory. *Philosophy of Science*, 68 (3): 394–412.

Herschel, J. (1966 [1830]). *Preliminary Discourse on the Study of Natural Philosophy*. New York: Johnson Reprint Corp.

Hinde, R. A. (1968). Dichotomies in the study of development. In J. M. Thoday and A. S. Parkes (Eds.), *Genetic and Environmental Influences on Behaviour* (pp. 3–14). New York: Plenum.

Hurka, T. (1993). *Perfectionism*. New York: Oxford University Press.

Johnston, T. D. (1987). The persistence of dichotomies in the study of behavioural development. *Developmental Review*, 7: 149–182.

Johnston, T. D. (2001). Towards a systems view of development: an appraisal of Lehrman's critique of Lorenz. In S. Oyama, P. E. Griffiths and R. D. Gray (Eds.), *Cycles of Contingency: Developmental systems and evolution* (pp. 15–23). Cambridge, MA: M.I.T. Press.

Jukes, T. H., & King, J. L. (1975). Evolutionary loss of ascorbic acid synthesizing ability. *Journal of Human Evolution*, 4: 85–88.

Keil, F. C. (1989). *Concepts, Kinds and Cognitive Development*. Cambridge, MA: Bradford Books/M.I.T. Press.

Lehrman, D. S. (1953). Critique of Konrad Lorenz's theory of instinctive behavior. *Quarterly Review of Biology*, 28(4): 337–363.

Lickliter, R., & Berry, T. (1990). The phylogeny fallacy. *Developmental Review*, 10: 348–364.

Lorenz, K. (1965). *Evolution and the Modification of Behavior* (US edition). Chicago, IL: University of Chicago Press.

Mason, W. A. (1985). Experiential influences on the development of expressive behaviors in rhesus monkeys. In G. Zivin (Ed.), *The Development of Expressive Behavior* (pp. 117–152). New York: Academic Press.

Mayr, E. (1976). Typological versus populational thinking. In E. Mayr (Ed.), *Evolution and the Diversity of Life* (pp. 26–29). Cambridge, MA: Harvard University Press.

Medin, D. L. (1989). Concepts and conceptual structure. *American Psychologist*, 44(12): 1469–1481.

Medin, D. L., & Atran, S. (Eds.) (1999). *Folkbiology*. Cambridge, MA: M.I.T. Press.

Medin, D. L., & Ortony, A. (1989). Psychological essentialism. In S. Vosniadou and A. Ortony (Eds.), *Similarity and Anological Reasoning* (pp. 175–195). Cambridge: Cambridge University Press.

Oyama, S. (1990). The idea of innateness: Effects on language and communication research. *Developmental Psychobiology*, 23(7): 741–747.

Oyama, S. (2000a). *Evolution's Eye: A systems view of the biology–culture divide*. Durham, NC: Duke University Press.

Oyama, S. (2000b). *The Ontogeny of Information: Developmental systems and evolution*, 2nd revised edn. Durham, NC: Duke University Press.

Oyama, S., P. E. Griffiths, & R. D. Gray (Eds.) (2001). *Cycles of Contingency: Developmental systems and evolution*. Cambridge, MA: M.I.T. Press.

Samuels, R. (2002). Nativism in cognitive science. *Mind and Language*, 17: 233–265.

Schiller, D. H. (Ed.) (1957). *Instinctive Behavior: The development of a modem concept*. New York: International Universities Press.

Sober, E. (1980). Evolution, population thinking and essentialism. *Philosophy of Science*, 47(3): 350–383.

Stich, S. P. (1975). The idea of innateness. In S. P. Stich (Ed.), *Innate Ideas*. Los Angeles, CA: University of California Press.

Symons, D. (1992). On the use and misuse of Darwinism in the study of human behavior. In J. H. Barkow, L. Cosmides and J. Tooby (Eds.), *The Adapted Mind: Evolutionary psychology and the generation of culture* (pp. 137–159). Oxford: Oxford University Press.

Tinbergen, N. (1957). Preface. In C. H. Schiller (Ed.), *Instinctive Behavior: The development of a modem concept* (pp. xv–xix). New York: International Universities Press.

Tooby, J., & Cosmides, L. (1992). The psychological foundations of culture. In J. H. Barkow, L. Cosmides and J. Tooby (Eds.), *The Adapted Mind: Evolutionary psychology and the generation of culture* (pp. 19–136). Oxford and New York: Oxford University Press.

Wimsatt, W. C. (1986). Developmental constraints, generative entrenchment and the innate-acquired distinction. In W. Bechtel (Ed.), *Integrating Scientific Disciplines* (pp. 185–208). Dordrecht: Martinus Nijhoff.

Wimsatt, W. C. (1999). Generativity, entrenchment, evolution, and innateness: philosophy, evolutionary biology, and conceptual foundations of science. In V. G. Hardcastle (Ed.), *Where Biology Meets Psychology: Philosophical essays* (pp. 139–79). Cambridge, MA: M.I.T. Press.

Chapter 10

Richard Samuels

INNATENESS IN COGNITIVE SCIENCE

Innateness hypotheses have played a pivotal role in the development of cognitive science and have been invoked to explain a broad array of psychological phenomena, including theory of mind (Leslie 2000), arithmetic (Butterworth 1999; Lipton and Spelke 2003), folk physics (Johnson 2000) and language (Chomsky 2000; Stromswold 2000). In spite of their prominence, however, it remains obscure how such hypotheses—and the notion of innateness on which they depend—ought to be understood.

Troubles with the notion of innateness are hardly novel. As far back as the 18th century, the empiricist philosopher David Hume complained that it was both ill-defined and permitted those incautious enough to use it to 'draw out their disputes to a tedious length, without ever touching the point in question' (Hume 1983). Yet the need for a satisfactory account of innateness has become even more pressing in recent years. One reason is that the emergence of novel experimental techniques, especially in developmental neuroscience, has made it harder to determine what should count as evidence for or against innateness (Pallas 2001; Elman et al. 1996; Marcus 2001; Samuels 1998).

Perhaps even more importantly, however, the very idea of innateness has increasingly come under attack from those—such as developmental systems theorists—who view it as scientifically unnecessary or even incoherent (Oyama 2000; Griffiths 2002); and this attitude is very much reflected in large regions of contemporary biology where talk of innateness has fallen into disrepute (Johnson 1997).

Such considerations provide cognitive scientists who aim to characterize our innate cognitive endowment with a strong motive to clarify the notion of innateness on which such inquiries depend. In this chapter I survey and assess current efforts to understand innateness. Although no entirely satisfactory account exists as yet, I maintain that, contrary to what many appear to suppose, the notion of innateness used in cognitive science may turn out to be neither identical to familiar commonsense conceptions of innateness nor borrowed from other scientific disciplines, such as genetics or developmental biology. Instead, the notion used by cognitive scientists may reflect the specific explanatory concerns and theoretical commitments of cognitive science itself.

Innateness and Commonsense

In contrast to earlier attempts to understand innateness (Stich 1975), recent efforts have been largely unconcerned with 'ordinary language conceptual analysis'—that is, roughly speaking, with characterizing the meaning of our 'commonsense' concept of innateness. The rejection of this project is twofold. First, the newer accounts tend to focus on the notion of innateness as it figures in science—in particular, cognitive science—as opposed to ordinary discourse. Second, they are far less concerned with defining the meaning of the term 'innate' than with explaining its role and significance within the sciences.

The default assumption is that scientific practices *track* some theoretically important property and that the goal of an account of innateness is to identify what that property might be. Even so, many familiar proposals draw on the commonsense connotations of the term 'innate'; and it is important to see why such claims are unsatisfactory as accounts of the notion used in cognitive science.

Innateness as Non-acquisition

A familiar claim about innate traits is that they are not acquired. On this view, for example, the thesis that universal grammar is innate amounts to the claim that it is a non-acquired cognitive structure. As stated, however, this account is unsatisfactory, although not because it is false, but because it is vacuous. The problem is that there are lots of different notions of acquisition and it is far from clear which is relevant to understanding innateness. To characterize innateness in terms of nonacquisition thus merely trades one problem for an equally difficult one—namely, explicating the relevant sense in which innate traits are not acquired.

By way of illustration, consider the following 'minimal notion' of acquisition: a characteristic is acquired by an object (e.g. an organism) if and only if there is some period of time when the object has the characteristic in question but some *prior* period when it does not. This is a perfectly sensible notion of acquisition and yet clearly insufficient for drawing the innate/non-innate distinction because, in this minimal sense, all cognitive structures are acquired. Human cognitive structures are traits of biological organisms and it is entirely plausible to maintain that there is a point sufficiently early in development when humans lack any cognitive

structures whatsoever. (A blastula is, for example, a ball of cells altogether lacking in cognitive characteristics.) In which case, if innate traits are just the ones that are not acquired (in the minimal sense), then there are obviously no innate cognitive traits whatsoever.

Of course, the conclusion to draw is not that innateness claims are trivially false or that they cannot be characterized in terms of some notion of (non-) acquisition. Rather, all that follows is that something more *substantial* than the minimal notion is required. But what more is needed? What additional constraints are required to develop a satisfactory account of innateness? This is, in effect, the issue that all accounts of innateness need to address.

Innateness as Presence at Birth

One familiar suggestion is that innate traits must satisfy certain temporal constraints: in particular that they must be present at birth or 'inborn'. (This is tantamount to claiming that innate traits are the ones that are acquired, in the minimal sense, by the time of birth.) Yet despite its long philosophical heritage and inclusion in dictionary definitions, this view is unsatisfactory. For although presence at birth may be evidence of innateness, it is strictly speaking neither necessary nor sufficient. It is not sufficient because prenatal learning is possible (Gottlieb 1997; Lecanuet et al 1993). In which case, the paradigmatic example of traits that are not innate—namely, learned traits—can be present at birth.

Nor is presence at birth necessary for innateness because, as Descartes observed almost four centuries ago, innate characteristics can be acquired (in the minimal sense) quite late in development. This point is commonly made by analogy with non-psychological traits—such as pubic hair and other secondary sexual characteristics—that are plausibly innate but clearly not present at birth. According to nativists in cognitive science, what goes for morphological traits is true of psychological ones as well. Alan Leslie and his collaborators have maintained, for example, that the innateness of a theory of mind mechanism is wholly consistent with the thesis that it develops postnatally (Scholl and Leslie 1999). Similarly, concept nativists very frequently endorse the view that innately specified concepts can be the product of postnatal maturation (Chomsky 2000; Fodor 2000).

Innateness as the Product of Internal Causes

Another common claim is that innate characteristics are the products of internal causes as opposed to external or environmental ones (Godfrey Smith 1996). In their influential book *Rethinking Innateness*, for example, Jeffrey Elman and his coauthors maintain that a trait is innate if and only if it is 'the product of interactions internal to the organism' (Elman et al. 1996).

Literally construed, however, this proposal is unsatisfactory. Like virtually all contemporary theorists, nativists wholeheartedly accept the Interactionist Thesis that cognitive characteristics are caused jointly by both internal and environmental factors (Karmiloff-Smith 1998; Fodor 1998). Indeed, this is little more than a banal truism that holds for all human traits. A foetus does not develop arms and legs, for example, without exchanging oxygen, water and nutrients with its mother; and a neonate does not develop teeth and hair without breathing, drinking and eating: all of which involve interaction with an environment external to the organism.

In addition to these merely nutritive contributions, however, nativists very frequently insist that the environment—and indeed environmentally derived information—has a more specific role to play in the development of innate cognitive structure. In particular, a common claim by nativists is that environmental factors act as inputs to 'triggering' processes—roughly speaking, 'brute-causal', non-psychological processes that eventuate in innate cognitive

structures (Fodor 1981). It is, to be sure, notoriously unclear what triggering is supposed to be (Cowie 1999); and no doubt this is a failing on the part of nativists. But it is one thing to accuse nativists of insufficient clarity and quite another to insist that they hold the deeply implausible view that environmental factors play no role in the development of innate traits. The former accusation is warranted; the latter merely turns nativism into a strawman: a position that is easily refuted but accepted by no one.

Innateness and Biology

If commonsense seems unlikely to furnish cognitive science with a satisfactory notion of innateness, then perhaps we should look to contemporary biology. To anyone with even a passing awareness of recent 'nature–nurture' debates, this might appear an attractive strategy. In particular, it might seem that contemporary biology has constructed—or, at any rate, is close to constructing—a notion of genetic determination that permits a thoroughly modern and scientific account of innateness (Fodor 2000).

Alas, matters are not so straightforward. Although biology in general and genetics in particular are central to the study of human cognition, it is not at all clear that they yield an unproblematic notion of genetic determination that maps smoothly onto the concept of innateness used by cognitive scientists. Instead, what one finds in biology is an altogether messier situation: one in which the notion of genetic determination remains both vague and highly contentious whereas other, more precisely defined genotype–phenotype relations fail to map smoothly onto the notion of innateness.

Innateness as Genetic Determination

According to genetic accounts of innateness, a phenotypic trait is innate (for a particular organism) only if it is determined by genetic factors. But how are we to understand the notion of genetic determination? Historically, there have been two dominant proposals: a 'causal account' on which traits are genetically determined if caused (in the appropriate way) by genetic factors (Lorenz 1957; Plotkin 1997), and a 'representational account' on which traits are genetically determined if represented in (or encoded by) the genes (Fodor 1998; Bates et al. 1998). Neither strategy has met with much success.

The principal problem with the causal approach is that no one has been able to explain what the *appropriate* causal relation between genes and innate traits is supposed to be. The obvious candidate is that innate traits must be caused entirely by genetic factors. This is, for example, a view that the ethologist Konrad Lorenz sometimes appeared to endorse (Lorenz 1957). But the folly of this proposal has long been recognized, as complex biological traits are not caused by genes alone but depend on interactions between genetic and non-genetic factors (Lehrman 1953). This is simply a variant of the Interactionist Thesis mentioned earlier. Moreover, other attempts to characterize genetic determination in terms of genetic causation have been similarly unsuccessful (Block 1981; Griffiths and Sterelny 1999).

Nor have attempts to provide a representational account of genetic determination proven any easier. The least contentious, although still far from straightforward, sense in which genes represent anything, is the familiar thesis that DNA contains a 'coded representation' of proteins (Lewin 2002). Yet even if such claims are relatively unproblematic, what is required is not merely an account of how genes code for proteins, but an account on which genes can represent complex phenotypic traits, such as cognitive structures. As developmental systems theorists are fond of pointing out, however, no such notion of representation appears to exist (Oyama 2000). Suppose, for example, one adopts an account of representation on which a gene (or suite of genes) represents a phenotypic

trait if and only if the trait causally covaries with it. This is, in effect, an application of the standard mathematical notion of information. But this proposal is unsatisfactory because it seems overwhelmingly likely that all traits causally covary with both genetic and environmental factors, in which case all traits will be represented in both the environment and the genome (Griffiths and Sterelny 1999). So the question is: What alternative notion of representation (information or coding) would capture an appropriate notion of genetic representation? At present, no satisfactory proposal exists (but see Godfrey Smith 1999 for a useful discussion of recent efforts and Khalidi 2002 for a recent informational approach to innateness that aims to avoid the sort of problem discussed here).

Innateness as Developmental Invariance

Problems with the notion of genetic determination have led some theorists to explore alternative ways in which the conceptual resources of biology might be brought to bear on understanding innateness. Among the most common of these are so-called 'invariance accounts' (for further proposals see Box 10.1). Such proposals differ in detail, but they all share the idea that innate traits are developmentally invariant with respect to some appropriate range of environments. The philosopher of biology Elliott Sober provides a representative formulation when he suggests that 'a phenotypic trait is innate for a given genotype if and only if that phenotype will emerge in all of a range of developmental environments', roughly, the *normal* environments for organisms with that genotype (Sober 1999).

The invariance account possesses several notable virtues. For example, it captures the commonly held view that innate traits are developmentally stable. Moreover, in conjunction with widely held assumptions about intraspecies genotypic similarity, it explains why innate traits are often universal in the sense of being possessed by all (normally functioning) members of the species. Still, the account is not without its problems. In particular, it appears to have the highly implausible consequence that traits can be both learned and innate—a result that is strongly at variance with the notion of innateness as used by cognitive scientists. The problem arises in the case of traits that are highly invariant, although only because the environmental conditions required to learn them are ubiquitous. So, for instance, it is plausible to maintain that pretty much every human acquires the belief that water is wet under normal environmental conditions and, moreover, that we learn it. But if this is so, then the belief that water is wet can be both learned and innate on the invariance account: a conclusion that might suffice to show that the account is untenable (Samuels 2002).

Box 10.1 Other biologically inspired accounts of innateness

The main text omits several biological accounts of innateness that have been suggested in recent years. In what follows I briefly consider two such proposals: the view of innateness as canalization and the view that innateness can be characterized in terms of the notion of heritability from quantative genetics.

Innateness as Canalization

On this view, a trait of an organism (with a given genotype G) is innate to the extent that it is 'canalized' in organisms with G; and the trait is canalized to the extent that its development is *insensitive* to the range of environmental conditions under which it emerges (Ariew 1996; 1999). So, for example, my possession of legs is (highly) innate on this view because, for organisms with the same genotype as me, the development of legs is highly insensitive to variation in environmental conditions.

The canalization account is a close relative of the invariance approach and, as such, inherits the virtues of that approach. Moreover, by requiring that the development of innate traits is insensitive to environmental variation—as opposed to merely invariant across environments—it appears to avoid the objection that I leveled against the invariance account (but see Samuels 2007), for a discussion of this claim). Even so, the canalization account has been criticized on several grounds. One common concern is that it threatens to trivialize debate over innateness (Cowie 1999). In brief, the worry is that assessments of canalization depend on what sorts of environmental variability one takes to be relevant to the process at hand; and this, in turn, appears to depend on the explanatory interests of those who use the concept of canalization in the first place. The concern is thus that disputes over innateness end up merely reflecting differences of explanatory emphasis.

Innateness as High Heritability

On this view, a trait is innate if and only if it is highly heritable—roughly speaking, variation within the population with respect to this trait is disproportionately due to genetic differences as opposed to environmental ones.

On the face of it, this account is an attractive one because it both preserves the intuition that innate traits are in some way determined by the genes and accords well with the tendency of cognitive scientists to invoke heritability studies—especially on twins—in support of innateness hypotheses (Stromswold). Yet while high heritability might be evidence of innateness, I deny that it *defines* what innateness is. Perhaps the most obvious problem is that high heritability is not necessary for innateness (Sober 2001). This is clearest in the case of traits—such as opposable thumbs in humans—that are near fixation and so possessed by all 'normal' members of a population. As standardly defined, heritability is the proportion of overall phenotypic variation that is due to genetic variation (i.e. Vg/Vp). So, where there is no phenotypic variation (as with opposable thumbs) the denominator Vp is zero and the heritability of the trait is not even defined. The obvious response is to enlarge our population to include organisms that do not possess the trait. But this can lead to some highly implausible consequences. Suppose, for example, that humans only lack opposable thumbs when a drug taken by the mother during pregnancy disrupts fetal development (Ariew 1996). In such cases, phenotypic variation is due to environmental differences. Hence, the trait will have a low heritability and not be innate (see Ariew 1996 for further discussion of the problems).

Innateness and Cognitive Science

If the above arguments are to be believed, then the prospects of providing an account of innateness in terms of genetic determination are unpromising, and the invariance alternative yields consequences that are at odds with how the notion of innateness functions in cognitive science. This clearly does not exhaust the full range of ways in which biological concepts might be invoked to characterize innateness (see Box 10.1 for further examples). But the track record to date is rather bleak, and this might suggest the need to look elsewhere for an account of innateness. In the remainder of this article, I consider the possibility that the notion of innateness used by cognitive scientists should be understood (at least partially) in terms of concepts that derive from psychology or even from cognitive science itself.

Innateness as Not Learned

This suggestion is hardly a novel one. Indeed, among the most common characterizations of innate traits is that they are the ones that are not learned. This view has some notable strengths, such as explaining why learned traits are not innate and why learnability arguments—arguments purporting to show that a given trait cannot be learned—support innateness hypotheses. But there are also some obvious worries with this formulation. A first and, I think, relatively minor one is that it yields counterintuitive results when applied to non-psychological traits. A patch of sunburn, for example, is not learned and yet it is surely not innate either. But even if we restrict our attention to those traits that concern us most—namely cognitive traits—the account will only be of use if some appropriate notion of learning can be identified, and this is not a straightforward task because the term 'learning' turns out to be almost as slippery as 'innateness' (Samuels 2002).

Innateness as Psychological Primitiveness

A more recent but closely related suggestion is that innate cognitive structures are 'psychologically primitive' in (roughly) the sense that they are not acquired by cognitive/psychological processes (Cowie 1999; Samuels 2002). To put the proposal in a slightly different way: although innate cognitive structures are acquired in the minimal sense, it is not at the cognitive/psychological level(s) of explanation—but some lower (biological) level—that an account of how they are acquired is to be found. In short, innate cognitive structures are the ones whose acquisition psychology cannot explain.

One central reason for developing this psychological primitiveness account of innateness is to handle the sorts of difficulties that plague other accounts (see Samuels 2002 for detailed discussion). But another reason is that it might help to explain the peculiar significance of innateness hypotheses to cognitive science. As mentioned earlier, many areas of biology have dispensed with the notion of innateness altogether—in large measure because it no longer plays any useful theoretical role (Johnson 1997). Why then should it continue to have a foothold in the cognitive sciences? One possibility is that this is an unfortunate oversight that should be remedied immediately (Oyama 2000). But if the present proposal is correct, then the notion of innateness in fact functions to frame two issues of genuine importance to psychology and cognitive science. First, it delimits the scope of psychological explanation: once we know that a given structure is innate, we also know that our scientific psychology should not—indeed cannot—be expected to explain how it was acquired and that we must instead look to biology or some other science for an explanation. Second, discovering which structures are innate also furnishes us with the resources—the 'building blocks'—from which to construct developmental psychological theories. Such theories must, on pain of regress, presuppose the existence of structures whose acquisition is not explained by psychology. So, if we know that a given structure is innate, then it can be invoked by psychological theories to explain the development of other psychological traits.

In its present form, however, the psychological primitiveness account still will not do. One problem too complex to consider here is that the account presupposes some appropriate distinction between psychological/cognitive levels of explanation and other levels of scientific explanation; and although it is widely assumed in cognitive science that some such distinction exists, it is far from straightforward how best to draw it. A second problem that I will discuss briefly is that, in its present form, the proposal over-generalizes by incorrectly characterizing some cognitive structures as innate even though no one would count them as such. This problem is clearest in the case of psychological effects that result when environmental insults

produce brain lesions. In such cases, cognitive scientists are not at all inclined to view the outcomes as innately specified even though the explanation is likely to be a neurobiological rather than a psychological one.

How might this over-generalization problem be addressed? One plausible response is to add an extra clause to the account, such as the following 'normalcy condition': A cognitive structure is innate for a given organism only if they would acquire it in the normal course of events. No doubt, there is much that could be done to clarify what counts as 'a normal course of events' (Stich 1975; Lloyd 1994), and perhaps this might be done by invoking the notions of developmental invariance or canalization discussed earlier in the article. For present purposes, however, I leave such matters of detail to one side and focus instead on two more general points. First, adding a normalcy condition seems like the *right* kind of strategy for addressing the over-generalization problem. This is because the cases that seem to pose a problem for the primitiveness view (e.g. psychological effects resulting from environmentally produced brain lesions) are clear instances of abnormal development.

Second, although it would be desirable to provide a more precise account of normalcy, I suggest that the task is no more pressing in the present context than it is in most other areas of science. My reason for saying this is that all sciences—with the possible exception of physics—typically assume some largely unarticulated set of normal conditions in formulating their laws and generalizations. In the jargon of philosophy, they are *ceteris paribus* generalizations that apply only when all else is equal (Carroll 2003; Cartwright 2002). Much the same is likely to be true of innateness hypotheses in developmental psychology and other areas of cognitive science. In effect, they are generalizations that, like virtually all other scientific generalizations, tacitly assume some set of background normal conditions. On this view, notions of normalcy are no more important to understanding innateness hypotheses in cognitive science than they are to understanding hypotheses in geology, economics or, for that matter, aerodynamics.

Conclusion

In this article I reviewed some of the more prominent accounts of innateness and sketched their various strengths and weaknesses. It was argued that proposals drawing on either the commonsense connotations of 'innate' or the conceptual resources of biology are unlikely to prove satisfactory, and that this might indicate that the notion of innateness used by cognitive scientists is not simply borrowed from elsewhere but internal to cognitive science itself. Finally, a specific account of innateness was outlined—the psychological primitiveness account—that takes this suggestion seriously. Although I do not expect the reader to be convinced by the above brief comments, I do hope to stimulate a more systematic debate about innateness; one that does not simply reiterate firmly entrenched opinions on the matter, but critically assesses the role and significance that the notion of innateness does and should have for cognitive science.

References

Ariew, A. (1996). Innateness and canalization. *Philos. Sci.*, 63: S19–S27.

Ariew, A. (1999). Innateness is canalization: in defense of a developmental account of innateness. In V. Hardcastle (Ed.), *Where Biology Meets Psychology* (pp. 117–138). Cambridge, MA: MIT Press.

Bates, E. et al. (1998). Innateness and emergentism. In W. Bechtel and G. Graham (Eds.), *A Companion to Cognitive Science* (pp. 590–601). Blackwell.

Block, N. (1981). Introduction: what is innateness? In N. Block (Ed.), *Readings in the Philosophy of Psychology*, Vol. 2 (pp. 279–281). London: Methuen.

Butterworth, B. (1999). *The Mathematical Brain*, Macmillan.

Carroll, J. (2003). Laws of nature. In E. Zalta (Ed.), *The Stanford Encyclopedia of Philosophy*, http://plato.stanford.edu/entries/laws-of-nature

Cartwright, N. (2002). In favor of laws that are not ceteris paribus after all. *Erkenntnis*, 57: 425–439.

Chomsky, N. (2000). *New Horizons in the Study of Language and Mind*, Cambridge University Press.

Cowie, F. (1999). *What's Within? Nativism Reconsidered*. Oxford University Press.

Elman, J. et al. (1996). *Rethinking Innateness: A connectionist perspective on development*. Cambridge, MA: MIT Press.

Fodor, J. (1981). The present status of the innateness controversy. In J. Fodor (Ed.), *RePresentations: Philosophical essays on the foundations of cognitive science* (pp. 257–316). MIT Press

Fodor, J. (1998). *In Critical Condition*. MIT Press.

Fodor, J. (2000). Doing without what's within. *Mind*, 110: 99–148.

Godfrey Smith, P. (1996). *Complexity and the Function of Mind in Nature*. Cambridge University Press.

Godfrey-Smith, P. (1999). Genes and codes: lessons from the philosophy of mind? In V. Hardcastle (Ed.), *Where Biology Meets Psychology* (pp. 305–331). Cambridge, MA: MIT Press.

Gottlieb, G. (1997). *Synthesizing Nature–Nurture: Prenatal roots of instinctive behavior*. Erlbaum.

Griffiths, P. (2002). What is innatness? *Monist*, 85: 70–85.

Griffiths, P., & Sterelny, K. (1999). *Sex and Death: An introduction to philosophy of biology*, Chicago, IL: University of Chicago Press.

Hume, D. (1983). *A Treatise of Human Nature*. Oxford University Press.

Johnson, M. (1997). *Developmental Cognitive Neuroscience*. Blackwell.

Johnson, S. (2000). The development of visual surface perception: insights into the ontogeny of knowledge. In C. Rovee-Collier, (Eds.), *Progress in Infancy Research*, Vol. 1 (pp. 113–154). Erlbaum.

Karmiloff-Smith, A. (1998). Development itself is the key to understanding developmental disorders. *Trends Cogn. Sci.* 2, 389–398.

Khalidi, M.A. (2002). Nature and nurture in cognition. *Br. J. Philos. Sci.*, 251–272.

Lecanuet, J.P. et al. (1993). Prenatal discrimination of a male and female voice uttering the same sentence. *Early Development and Parenting*, 2: 212–228.

Lehrman, D.S. (1953). Critique of Konrad Lorenz's theory of instinctive behaviour. *Q. Rev. Biol.*, 28: 337–363.

Leslie, A. (2000). 'Theory of mind' as a mechanism of selective attention. In M. Gazzaniga (Ed.), *The New Cognitive Neuroscience* (pp. 1235–1247). Cambridge, MA: MIT Press.

Lewin, B. (2002). *Genes VII*. Oxford University Press.

Lipton, J.S., & Spelke, E. (2003). Origins of number sense: large number discrimination in human infants. *Psychol. Sci.*, 14: 396–401.

Lloyd, E. (1994). Normality and variation: the human genome project and the ideal human type. In D. Hull and M. Ruse (Eds.), *The Philosophy of Biology* (pp. 552–566). Oxford University Press.

Lorenz, K. (1957). The nature of instinct. In C. H. Schiller (Ed.), *Instinctive Behavior: The development of a modern concept* (pp. 129–175). International University Press.

Marcus, G.F. (2001). *The Algebraic Mind*. Cambridge, MA: MIT Press.

Oyama, S. (2000). *Evolution's Eye*. Duke University Press.

Pallas, S.L. (2001). Intrinsic and extrinsic factors that shape neocortical specification. *Trends Neurosci.*, 24: 417–423.

Plotkin, H. (1997). *Evolution in Mind*. Harmondsworth: Penguin.

Samuels, R. (1998). What brains won't tell us about the mind: A critique of the neurobiological argument against representational nativism. *Mind Lang*, 13: 548–570.

Samuels, R. (2002). Nativism in cognitive science. *Mind Lang*, 17, 233–265.

Samuels, R. (2007). Is innateness a confused notion? In P. Carruthers, S. Laurence, and S. Stich (Eds.) *The Innate Mind: Foundations and the future* (pp. 17–36), Oxford, Oxford University Press.

Scholl, B. J., & Leslie, A. M. (1999). The innate capacity to acquire a 'theory of mind': Synchronic or diachronic modularity? *Mind Lang*. 14: 131–153.

Sober, E. (1999). Innate knowledge. In E. Craig (Ed.), *Routledge Encyclopedia of Philosophy*, Vol. 4 (pp. 794–797), Routledge.

Sober, E. (2001). Separating nature and nurture. In D. Wasserman and R. Wachbroit (Eds.), *Genetics and Criminal Behavior: Methods, meanings and morals* (pp. 47–78), Cambridge University Press.

Stich, S. (1975). Introduction. In S. Stich (Ed.), *Innate Ideas* (pp. 1–22), University of California Press.

Stromswold, K. (2000). The cognitive neuroscience of language acquisition. In M. Gazzaniga (Ed.), *The New Cognitive Neuroscience* (pp. 855–870). Cambridge, MA: MIT Press.

Topic 4 GENETIC DETERMINISM

GENETIC DETERMINISTS HOLD THAT all human characteristics arise from our genetic make-up. One way of understanding this claim is that each of our traits is the result of the expression of a gene (or collection of genes) during our development. Another way of understanding the claim is that variation in human traits is best explained by genetic differences. There are well-established cases of single genes being responsible for human traits, and there are also some cases in which heritability analyses have helped us understand variation in traits in terms of genetic variation. The strongest form of genetic determinism holds that all traits result from genes or that all variation is explained in terms of genetic variation. Opponents of genetic determinism range from environmental determinists at one extreme to interactionists—human traits are a product of genes and environment—who occupy a middle ground. There are very few people who occupy a genuine environmental determinist position, which would entail that genes play no role in the production of human traits. There are certainly those who argue that the role of genes is greatly overestimated, even by interactionists who claim to hold a neutral position. Members of this latter camp often identify as developmentalists or developmental systems theorists.

In this section we hear from Thomas Bouchard, a proponent of the view that much of human variation can be traced to genetic variation. His view is supported by his many years of work on human twins, separated at birth. Bouchard and his colleagues have found remarkable similarities between identical twins brought up in different homes, leading them to the view that our traits are largely genetically determined. Bouchard and other behavioral genetics researchers study the variation in our traits via heritability analysis. These analyses involve the application of statistical techniques to apportion the variation in traits to genes and environment. Bouchard and his colleagues believe that these analyses reveal that many human traits have genetic bases, even traits such as religiosity and conservatism.

Patrick Bateson is strongly opposed to the genetic determinist position that Bouchard defends. He is highly critical of heritability studies, believing that they are useful for animal breeders but not for the study of human traits. The developmental systems view Bateson defends places strong emphasis on the many different environments that contribute to our varied traits, for example, the amniotic environment, our varied nutritional regimens, and our different cultures. Developmental systems theorists such as Bateson hold that understanding the complex interplay between the huge number of influences on our developmental trajectories is the key to explaining the variation in human traits.

Philip Kitcher endorses an interactionist view, which he believes to be a true compromise as well as the appropriate evolutionary view. He rejects the excesses of both strong genetic determinism and the opposite extremes of both developmental systems and environmental determinism. He devotes much of his energy to resisting the developmental systems view, but, like Bateson, he is wary of giving too much weight to heritability studies.

Suggested Further Reading

Cranor, C. F. (1994) *Are Genes Us?* New Brunswick, NJ: Rutgers University Press.

Downes, S. M. (2010) Heritability, in Edward N. Zalta (Ed.), *The Stanford Encyclopedia of Philosophy*, http://plato.stanford.edu/entries/heredity/

Flint, J., Greenspan, R. J. and Kendler, K. S. (2010) *How Genes Influence Behavior*. Oxford: Oxford University Press.

Kaplan, J. (2000) *The Limits and Lies of Human Genetic Research*. New York: Routledge.

Kitcher, P. (1996) *The Lives to Come*. New York: Simon and Schuster.

Harpending, H. and Cochran, G. (2002) In our genes. *Proceedings of the National Academy of Sciences of the United States of America*, 99: 10–12.

Nisbett, R. (2010) *Intelligence and How to Get It: Why schools and cultures count*. New York: W. W. Norton & Company.

Rutter, M. (2006) *Genes and Behavior: Nature–nurture interplay explained*. Malden, MA: Blackwell Publishing.

Sarkar, S. (1998) *Genetics and Reductionism*. Cambridge: Cambridge University Press.

Sesardic, N. (2005) *Making Sense of Heritability*. Cambridge: Cambridge University Press.

Chapter 11

Thomas J. Bouchard, Jr.

GENETIC INFLUENCE ON HUMAN PSYCHOLOGICAL TRAITS

Among knowledgeable researchers, discussions regarding genetic influences on psychological traits are not about whether there is genetic influence, but rather about how much influence there is, and how genes work to shape the mind. As Rutter (2002) noted, "Any dispassionate reading of the evidence leads to the inescapable conclusion that genetic factors play a substantial role in the origins of individual differences with respect to all psychological traits, both normal and abnormal".[1] Put concisely, all psychological traits are heritable. Heritability (h^2) is a descriptive statistic that indexes the degree of population variation in a trait that is due to genetic differences. The complement of heritability ($1 - h^2$) indexes variation contributed by the environment (plus error of measurement) to population variation in the trait. Studies of human twins and adoptees, often called behavior genetic studies, allow us to estimate the heritability of various traits. The name behavior genetic studies is an unfortunate misnomer, however, as such studies are neutral regarding both environmental and genetic influences. That they repeatedly and reliably reveal significant heritability for psychological traits is an empirical fact and one not unique to humans. Lynch and Walsh (1998) pointed out that genetic influence on most traits, as indexed by estimates of heritability, is found for all species and observed that "the interesting questions remaining are, How does the

magnitude of h^2 differ among characters and species and why?"[2]

Why Study Genetic Influences on Human Behavioral Traits?

A simple answer to the question of why scientists study genetic influences on human behavior is that they want a better understanding of how things work, that is, better theories. Not too many years ago, Meehl (1978) argued that "most so-called 'theories' in the soft areas of psychology (clinical, counseling, social, personality, community, and school psychology) are scientifically unimpressive and technologically worthless".[3] He listed 20 fundamental difficulties faced by researchers in the social sciences. Two are relevant to the current discussion: heritability and nuisance variables. The two are closely related. Nuisance variables are variables assumed to be causes of group or individual differences irrelevant to the theory of an investigator. Investigators seldom provide a full theoretical rationale in support of their choice of nuisance variables to control. As Meehl pointed out, removing the influence of parental socioeconomic status (SES; i.e., treating it as a nuisance variable) on children's IQ, when studying the causes of individual differences in IQ, makes the assumption that parental SES is exclusively a source of environmental variance, as opposed to being confounded with genetic influence.[4]

Meehl argued that this example "is perhaps the most dramatic one, but other less emotion-laden examples can be found on all sides in the behavioral sciences".[5] His point was that knowledge of how genetic factors influence any given measure (e.g., SES) or trait (e.g., IQ) will allow scientists to develop more scientifically impressive and worthwhile theories about the sources of individual differences in psychological traits.

Evidence of genetic influence on a psychological trait raises a series of new questions regarding the sources of population variance for that trait. All the questions addressed in quantitative genetics (Lynch & Walsh, 1998) and genetic epidemiology (Khoury, 1998) become relevant. What kind of gene action is involved? Is it a simple additive influence, with the effects of genes simply adding up so that more genes cause greater expression of the trait, or is the mode of action more complex? Are the effects of genes for a particular trait more pronounced in men or women? Are there interactions between genes and the environment? For example, it has been known for a long time that stressful life events lead to depression in some people but not others. There is now evidence for an interaction. Individuals who carry a specific genetic variant are more susceptible to depression when exposed to stressful life events than individuals who do not carry the genetic variant (Caspi et al., 2003). Are there gene-environment correlations? That is, do individuals with certain genetic constitutions seek out specific environments? People who score high on measures of sensation seeking certainly, on average, tend to find themselves in more dangerous environments than people who score low for this trait.

Estimates of the Magnitude of Genetic Influence on Psychological Traits

Table 11.1 reports typical behavior genetic findings drawn from studies of broad and relatively representative samples from affluent Western societies. In most, but not all, of these studies,

Table 11.1 Estimates of Broad Heritability and Shared Environmental Influence and Indications of Nonadditive Genetic Effects and Sex Differences in Heritability for Representative Psychological Traits

Trait	Heritability	Nonadditive genetic effect	Shared environmental effect	Sex differences in heritability
Personality (adult samples)				
Big Five				
Extraversion	.54	Yes	No	Perhaps
Agreeableness (aggression)	.42	Yes	No	Probably not
Conscientiousness	.49	Yes	No	Probably not
Neuroticism	.48	Yes	No	No
Openness	.57	Yes	No	Probably not
Big Three				
Positive emotionality	.50	Yes	No	No
Negative emotionality	.44	Yes	No	No
Constraint	.52	Yes	No	No
Intelligence				
By age in Dutch cross-sectional twin data				
Age 5	.22	No	.54	No
Age 7	.40	No	.29	No
Age 10	.54	No	.26	No
Age 12	.85	No	No	No
Age 16	.62	No	No	No

Age 18	.82	No	No	No
Age 26	.88	No	No	No
Age 50	.85	No	No	No
In old age (> 75 years old)	.54–.62	Not tested	No	No
Psychological interests				
Realistic	.36	Yes	.12	NA
Investigative	.36	Yes	.10	NA
Artistic	.39	Yes	.12	NA
Social	.37	Yes	.08	NA
Enterprising	.31	Yes	.11	NA
Conventional	.38	Yes	.11	NA
Psychiatric illnesses (liability estimates)				
Schizophrenia	.80	No	No	No
Major depression	.37	No	No	Mixed findings
Panic disorder	.30–.40	No	No	No
Generalized anxiety disorder	.30	No	Small female only	No
Phobias	.20–.40	No	No	No
Alcoholism	.50–.60	No	Yes	Mixed findings
Antisocial behavior				
Children	.46	No	.20	No
Adolescents	.43	No	.16	No
Adults	.41	No	.09	No
Social attitudes				
Conservatism				
Under age 20 years	.00	NR	Yes	NR
Over age 20 years	.45–.65	Yes	Yes in females	Yes
Right-wing authoritarianism (adults)	.50–.64	No	.00–.16	NA
Religiousness				
16-year-olds	.11–.22	No	.45–.60	Yes
Adults	.30–.45	No	.20–.40	Not clear
Specific religion	Near zero	NR	NA	NR

Note. NA = not available; NR = not relevant

estimates of genetic and environmental influences were obtained from studies of twins. Because the studies probably undersampled people who live in the most deprived segment of Western societies, the findings should not be considered as generalizable to such populations.

Personality

Psychologists have developed two major schemes for organizing specific personality traits into a higher-order structure, the Big Five and the Big Three. As Table 11.1 shows, the findings using the two schemes are much the same. Genetic influence is in the range of 40 to 50%, and heritability is approximately the same for different traits. There is evidence of nonadditive genetic variance. That is, genes for personality, in addition to simply adding or subtracting from the expression of a trait, work in a more complex manner, the expression of a relevant gene depending to some extent on the gene with which it is paired on a chromosome or on genes located on other chromosomes. Research has yielded little evidence for significant shared environmental influence, that is, similarity due to having trait-relevant environmental influences in common. Some large studies have investigated whether the genes that influence personality traits differ in the two sexes (sex limitation). The answer is no. However, sometimes there are sex differences in heritability.

Mental Ability

Early in life, shared environmental factors are the dominant influence on IQ, but gradually genetic influence increases, with the effects of shared environment dropping to near zero (see the twin studies in Table 11.1). Although not reported here, adoption studies of (a) unrelated individuals reared together and (b) adoptive parents and their adopted offspring have reported similar results—increasing genetic influence on IQ with age and decreasing shared environmental influence. Results from two twin studies of IQ in old age (over 75) are reported in Table 11.1. Both studies found a substantial level of genetic influence and little shared environmental influence. The results do, however, suggest some decline in heritability when compared with results for earlier ages. There is no evidence for sex differences in heritability for IQ at any age.

Psychological Interests

Heritabilities for psychological interests, also called vocational or occupational interests, are also reported in Table 11.1. These heritabilities were estimated using data gathered in a single large study that made use of a variety of samples (twins, siblings, parents and their children, etc.) gathered over many years. All respondents completed one form or another of a standard vocational interest questionnaire. There is little variation in heritability for the six scales, with an average of .36. As with personality traits, there is evidence for nonadditive genetic influence. Unlike personality, psychological interests show evidence for shared environmental

influence, although this influence is modest, about 10% for each trait.

Psychiatric Illnesses

Schizophrenia is the most extensively studied psychiatric illness, and the findings consistently suggest a very high degree of genetic influence (heritability of about .80), mostly additive genetic influence, with no shared environmental influence. There do not appear to be gender differences in the heritability of schizophrenia. Major depression is less heritable (about .40) than schizophrenia. Men and women share most, but not all, genetic influences for depression. Panic disorder, generalized anxiety disorder, and phobias are moderately heritable, and the effect is largely additive, with few if any sex differences. The heritability of alcoholism is in the range of .50 to .60, mostly because of additive genetic effects. Findings regarding the possibility of sex differences in the heritability of alcoholism are mixed.

Antisocial behavior has long been thought to be more heritable in adulthood than childhood. The results of a recent analysis do not support that conclusion. The genetic influence is additive and in the range of .41 to .46. Shared environmental influences decrease from childhood to adulthood, but do not entirely disappear in adulthood. There are no sex differences in heritability.

Social Attitudes

Twin studies reveal only environmental influence on conservatism up to age 19; only after this age do genetic influences manifest themselves. A large study (30,000 adults, including twins and most of their first-degree relatives) yielded heritabilities of .65 for males and .45 for females. Some of the genetic influence on conservatism is nonadditive. Recent work with twins reared apart has independently replicated these heritability findings. Conservatism correlates highly, about .72, with right-wing authoritarianism, and that trait is also moderately heritable.

Religiousness is only slightly heritable in 16-year-olds (.11 for girls and .22 for boys in a large Finnish twin study) and strongly influenced by shared environment (.60 in girls and .45 in boys). Religiousness is moderately heritable in adults (.30 to .45) and also shows some shared environmental influence. Good data on sex differences in heritability of religiousness in adults are not available. Membership in a specific religious denomination is largely due to environmental factors.

A Note on Multivariate Genetic Analysis

In this review, I have addressed only the behavior genetic analysis of traits taken one at a time (univariate analysis). It is important to recognize that it is possible to carry out complex genetic analyses of the correlations among traits and compute genetic correlations. These correlations tell us the degree to which genetic effects on one score (trait measure) are correlated with genetic effects on a second score, at one or at many points in time. The genetic correlation between two traits can be quite high regardless of whether the heritability of either trait is high or low, or whether the correlation between the traits is high or low. Consider the well-known positive correlation between tests of mental ability, the evidentiary base for the general intelligence factor. This value is typically about .30. The genetic correlation between such tests is, however, much higher, typically closer to .80. Cooccurrence of two disorders, a common finding in psychiatric research, is often due to common genes. The genetic correlation between anxiety and depression, for example, is estimated to be very high. Multivariate genetic analysis of behavioral traits is a very active domain of research.

Concluding Remarks

One unspoken assumption among early behavior geneticists, an assumption that was shared by most for many years, was that some psychological traits were likely to be significantly influenced by genetic factors, whereas others were likely to be primarily influenced by shared environmental influences. Most behavior geneticists assumed that social attitudes, for example, were influenced entirely by shared environmental influences, and so social attitudes remained largely unstudied until relatively recently. The evidence now shows how wrong these assumptions were. Nearly every reliably measured psychological phenotype (normal and abnormal) is significantly influenced by genetic factors. Heritabilities also differ far less from trait to trait than anyone initially imagined. Shared environmental influences are often, but not always, of less importance than genetic factors, and often decrease to near zero after adolescence. Genetic influence on psychological traits is ubiquitous, and psychological researchers must incorporate this fact into their research programs else their theories will be "scientifically unimpressive and technologically worthless," to quote Meehl again.

At a fundamental level, a scientifically impressive theory must describe the specific molecular mechanism that explicates how genes transact with the environment to produce behavior. The rudiments of such theories are in place. Circadian behavior in humans is under genetic influence (Hur, Bouchard, & Lykken, 1998), and some of the molecular mechanisms in mammals are now being revealed (Lowrey & Takahashi, 2000). Ridley (2003) and Marcus (2004) have provided additional examples of molecular mechanisms that help shape behavior. Nevertheless, the examples are few, the details are sparse, and major mysteries remain. For example, many behavioral traits are influenced by nonadditive genetic processes. These processes remain a puzzle for geneticists and evolutionists, as well as psychologists, because simple additive effects are thought to be the norm. We also do not understand why most psychological traits are moderately heritable, rather than, as some psychologists expected, variable in heritability, with some traits being highly heritable and others being largely under the influence of the environment. It seems reasonable to suspect that moderate heritability may be a general biological phenomenon rather than one specific to human psychological traits, as the profile of genetic and environmental influences on psychological traits is not that different from the profile of these influences on similarly complex physical traits and similar findings apply to most organisms.

Notes

1   Rutter 2002, p. 2.
2   Lynch and Walsh 1998, p. 175.
3   Meehl 1978, p. 806.
4   See Evans 2004 Figure 1 for a recent commission of this error.
5   Meehl 1978, p. 810.

References

Bouchard, T. J., Jr. and McGue, M. (2003) Genetic and environmental influences on human psychological differences. *Journal of Neurobiology*, 54:4–45.

Caspi, A., Sugden, K., Moffitt, T. E., Taylor, A., Craig, I. W., Harrington, H., McClay, J., Mill, J., Martin, J., Braiwaite, A. and Poulton, R. (2003) Influence of life stress on depression: Moderation by a polymorphism in the 5-HTT gene. *Science*, 301:386–389.

Evans, G. W. (2004) The environment of childhood poverty. *American Psychologist*, 59:77–92.

Hur, Y.- M., Bouchard, T. J., Jr. and Lykken, D. T. (1998) Genetic and environmental influence on morningness-eveningness. *Personality and Individual Differences*, 25:917–925.

Khoury, M. J. (1998) Genetic epidemiology. In K. J. Rothman and S. Greenland (Eds.), *Modern Epidemiology* (pp. 609–622). Philadelphia, PA: Lippincott-Raven.

Lowrey, P. L., & Takahashi, J. S. (2000) Genetics of the mammalian circadian system: Photic entrainment, circadian pacemaker mechanisms, and postranslational regulation. *Annual Review of Genetics*, 34:533–562.

Lynch, M. and Walsh, B. (1998) *Genetics and Analysis of Quantitative Traits*. Sunderland, MA: Sinauer.

Marcus, G. (2004) *The Birth of the Mind: How a tiny number of genes creates the complexities of human thought*. New York: Basic Books.

Meehl, P. E. (1978) Theoretical risks and tabular asterisks: Sir Karl, Sir Ronald, and the slow progress of soft psychology. *Journal of Consulting and Clinical Psychology*, 46: 806–834.

Ridley, M. (2003) *Nature via Nurture: Genes, experience and what makes us human*. New York: HarperCollins.

Rutter, M. (2002) Nature, nurture, and development: From evangelism through science toward policy and practice. *Child Development*, 73:1–21.

Chapter 12

Patrick Bateson

BEHAVIORAL DEVELOPMENT AND DARWINIAN EVOLUTION

The One True Cause

The effectiveness of education, the role of parents in shaping the characters of their children, the causes of violence and crime, and the roots of personal unhappiness are self-evidently matters of huge importance. And, like so many other fundamental issues about human existence, they all relate to behavioral development. The catalog continues. Do bad experiences in early life have a lasting effect? Is intelligence in the genes? Can adults change their attitudes and behavior? When faced with such questions, many people want simple answers. They want to know what really makes the difference. Explanations in terms of combinations of conditions is perceived as wooly, obscurantist, and running counter to the successful analytical programs of science.

The search for simple environmental origins, which had wide appeal in the mid-twentieth century, has been partly superseded by an equally skewed belief in the overriding importance of genes. If pressed, scientists may concede that their talk of genes "for" shyness, maternal behavior, promiscuity, verbal ability, criminality, or whatever, is merely a shorthand. They may nonetheless try to legitimize the language of genes "for" behavior, by pointing to seemingly straightforward examples like the genes for eye color. Nonetheless, the notion of genes "for" behavior undoubtedly corrupts understanding.

A single developmental ingredient, such as a gene or a particular form of experience, might produce an effect on behavior, but this certainly does not mean that it is the only thing that matters. Even in the case of eye color, the notion that the relevant gene is the cause is misconceived, because all the other genetic and environmental ingredients that are just as necessary for the development of eye color remain the same for all individuals. A more honest translation of the "gene for" terminology would be something like: "We have found a particular behavioral difference between individuals which is associated with a particular genetic difference, all other things being equal." The media and the public might start to get the message if plain language like this were used routinely.

Fortunately, it no longer seems obscure to many others to refer to developmental processes as systems. I like to think that this change in thinking may reflect commonplace experience. From an early age many people are exposed to computer games, in which outcomes depend on a combination of conditions. Children playing such games meet, for instance, in the dungeon of the dark castle a dragon that can only be killed with a special sword that had to picked up on the top of the crystal mountain; in doing so, they have begun to accustom themselves to the contextual conditional character of the real world. The linear thinking of a previous generation, with every event having a single cause, is slowly being replaced by an understanding of coordinated process. That, at least, is my optimistic view. In what follows I shall consider why systems approaches are essential to an understanding of behavioral development. I shall also argue that they can be successfully married to a Darwinian approach to evolution and to current utility, often viewed as antagonistic to the developmental systems thinking.

How Much Nature, How Much Nurture?

The importance of both genes and environment to the development of all animals, including humans, is obvious enough. This is true even for apparently simple physical characteristics, let alone complex psychological variables. Take shortsightedness, for example. Myopia runs in families but is segregated from other characteristics, suggesting that it is genetically inherited. But it is also affected by the individual's experience. Both a parental history of myopia and, to a lesser extent, the experience of spending prolonged periods studying close-up objects will predispose a child to become shortsighted (Zadnik 1997).

Different styles of doing science are brought into play when dealing with a case like the development of myopia, in which different types of factor affect the outcome. Those who have an aversion to systems thinking sometimes like to present the purely statistical approach as the only scientific solution to the age-old problem of the relative contributions of the different factors. The question becomes: "How much of the variation between individuals in a given character is due to differences in their genes, and how much is due to differences in their environments?" The suggested answer, satisfying old-style linear thinking, was provided by a measure called "heritability." The meaning of heritability is best illustrated with an uncontroversial characteristic such as height, which is clearly influenced by both the individual's family background (supposedly genetic influences) and nutrition (environmental influences). The variation between individuals in height that is attributable to variation in their genes may be expressed as a proportion of the total variation within the population sampled. This index is known as the heritability ratio. The higher the figure, which can vary between 0 and 1.0, the greater the contribution of genetic variation to individual variation in that characteristic. So, if people differed in height solely because they differed in their genes, the heritability of height would be 1.0; if, on the other hand, variation in height arose entirely from individual differences in environmental factors such as nutrition, then the heritability would be 0.

Calculating a single number to describe the relative contribution of genes and environment has obvious attractions. Estimates of heritability are of undoubted value to animal breeders, for example. Given a standard set of environmental conditions, the genetic strain to which a pig belongs will predict its adult body size better than other variables such as the number of piglets in a sow's litter. If the animal in question is a cow and the breeder is interested in maximizing its milk yield, then knowing that milk yield is highly heritable in a particular strain of cows under standard rearing conditions is important.

But behind the deceptively plausible ratios lurk some fundamental problems. For a start, the heritability of any given characteristic is not a fixed and absolute quantity—tempted though many scientists have been to believe otherwise. Its value depends on a number of variable factors, such as the particular population of individuals that has been sampled. For instance, if heights are measured only among people from affluent backgrounds, then the total variation in height will be much smaller than if the sample also includes people who are small because they have been undernourished. The heritability of height will consequently be larger in a population of exclusively well-nourished people than it would be among people drawn from a wider range of environments. Conversely, if the heritability of height is based on a population with relatively similar genes—say, native Icelanders—then the figure will be lower than if the population is genetically more heterogeneous; for example, if it includes both Icelanders and African pygmies. Thus, attempts to measure the relative contributions of genes and environment to a particular characteristic are highly dependent on who is measured and in what conditions.

Another problem with heritability is that it says nothing about the ways in which genes and environment contribute to the biological and psychological cooking processes of development. This point becomes obvious when considering the heritability of a characteristic such as "walking on two legs." Humans walk on fewer than two legs only as a result of environmental influences such as war wounds, car accidents, disease, or exposure to teratogenic toxins before birth. In other words, all the variation within the human population results from environmental influences, and consequently the heritability of "walking on two legs" is zero. And yet walking on two legs is clearly a fundamental property of being human, and is one of the more obvious differences between humans and other great apes such as chimpanzees or gorillas. It obviously depends heavily on genes, despite having a heritability of zero. Low heritability clearly does not mean that development is unaffected by genes.

If a population of individuals is sampled and the results show that one behavior pattern has a higher heritability than another, this merely indicates that the two behavior patterns have developed in different ways. It does not mean that genes play a more important role in the development of behavior with the higher heritability. Important environmental influences might have been relatively constant at the stage in development when the more heritable behavior pattern would have been most strongly affected by experience.

Yet another serious weakness with heritability estimates is that they rest on the extraordinary assumption that genetic and environmental influences are independent of one another and do not interact. The calculation of heritability assumes that the genetic and environmental contributions can simply be added together to obtain the total variation. In many cases this assumption is clearly wrong. For example, in one study of rats the animals' genetic background and their rearing conditions were both varied; rats from two genetically inbred strains were each reared in one of three environments, differing in their richness and complexity (Cooper and Zubek 1958). The rats' ability to find their way through a maze was measured later in their lives. Rats from both genetic strains performed equally badly in the maze if they had been reared in a poor environment (a bare cage) and equally well if they had been reared in a rich environment filled with toys and objects. Taken by themselves, these results implied that the environmental factor (rearing conditions) was the only one that mattered. But it was not that simple. In the third type of environment, where the rearing conditions were intermediate in complexity, rats from the two strains differed markedly in their ability to navigate the maze. These genetic differences only manifested themselves behaviorally in this sort of environment. Varying both the genetic background and the environment revealed a statistical interaction between the two influences.

An overall estimate of heritability has no meaning in a case such as this, because the effects of the genes and the environment do not simply add together to produce the combined result. The effects of a particular set of genes depend critically on the environment in which they are expressed, while the effects of a particular sort of environment depend on the individual's genes. Even in animal breeding programs which use heritability estimates to practical advantage, care is still needed. If breeders wish to export a particular genetic strain of cows that yield a lot of milk, they would be wise to check that the strain will continue to give high milk yields under the different environmental conditions of another country. Many cases are known where a strain that performs well on a particular measure in one environment does poorly in another, while a different strain performs better in the second environment than in the first.

A further point about the mutual actions of individual on the environment and environment on the individual is brought out nicely by the example of myopia already briefly mentioned. Nesse and Williams (1994) point out that the growth of the cornea is affected by the sharpness of the image on the retina. Objects close to the eye, such as books, cause the cornea to grow so that the image of print is less fuzzy. Individual differences in the feedback mechanism mean that some people in a modern environment respond more to the experience of reading than others and consequently become more short-sighted. In an environment empty of books such people would not be shortsighted.

Alternative Lives

Striking examples of interaction are found throughout the animal kingdom when genetically identical individuals develop in totally different ways, depending on environmental cues they received when they were young. After a fire on the high grassland plains of East Africa, for example, the young grasshoppers are black instead of being the normal pale yellowish-green. Something has switched the course of their development onto a different track. The grasshopper's color makes a big difference to the risk that it will be spotted and eaten by a bird, and the scorched grassland may remain black for many months after a fire. So matching its body color to the blackened background is important for its survival. The developmental mechanism for making this switch in body color is automatic and depends on the amount of light reflected from the ground (Rowell 1971). If the young grasshoppers are placed on black paper they are black when they molt to the next stage. But if they are placed on pale paper the molting grasshoppers are the normal green color. The grasshoppers actively select habitats with colors that match their own. If the color of the background changes they can also change their color at the next molt to match the background, but they are committed to a color once they reach adulthood.

Turtles, crocodiles, and some other reptiles commit themselves early in life to developing along one of two different developmental tracks and like grasshoppers, they do so in response to a feature of their environment. Each individual starts life with the capacity to become either a male or a female. The outcome depends on environmental temperature during the middle third of embryonic development (Yntema and Mrosovsky 1982). If the eggs from which they hatch are buried in sand below 30 °C, the young turtles become males. If, however, the eggs are incubated at above 30 °C they become females. Temperatures below 30 °C activate genes responsible for the production of male sex hormones and male sex hormone receptors. If the incubation temperature is above 30 °C, a different set of genes is activated, producing female hormones and receptors instead (Crews 1996). It so happens that in alligators the sex determination works the other way around, such that eggs incubated at higher temperatures produce males. (In humans and other mammals, by contrast, the sex of each individual is generally determined genetically at conception; if it inherits only one X sex chromosome, it becomes male.)

Each grasshopper and turtle starts life with the capacity to play two distinctly different developmental tunes—green or black, male or female. A particular feature of the environment then selects which of those tunes the individual will play during its life. And once committed, the individual cannot switch to the other tune. Once black as an adult, the grasshopper cannot subsequently change its color to green, just as a male turtle cannot transform itself into a female.

The broad pattern of an individual's social and sexual behavior may also be determined early in life, with the individual developing along one of two or more qualitatively different tracks. Many examples are found in the animal kingdom. The caste of a female social insect is determined by her nutrition early in life. The main egg producer of an ant colony, the queen, is part of a teeming nest in which some of her sisters care for her offspring, others forage, yet others clean or mend the nest, and finally other sisters specialize in guarding it. Locusts may or may not become migratory, depending on crowding; when the numbers living in a given area build up, their offspring develop musculature and behavior suitable for long flights and then the whole swarm moves off. Vole pups born in the autumn have much thicker coats than those born in spring; the cue to produce a thicker coat is provided by the mother before birth. The value of preparing in this way for colder weather is obvious.

The sexual behavior of some primates can also develop along two or more distinctly different tracks. An adult male gelada baboon, for example, will typically defend and breed with a harem of females. After a relatively brief but active reproductive life, he is displaced by another male and never breeds again. To position himself so that he can acquire and defend a harem, the male must grow rapidly at puberty. He develops the distinctive golden mane of a male in his prime and becomes almost twice the size of the females. However, when many such males are present in the social group, an adolescent male may adopt a distinctly different style of reproductive behavior. He does not develop a mane or undergo a growth spurt. Instead, he remains similar in appearance and size to the females. These small males hang around the big males' harems, sneakily mating with a female

when the harem-holder is not paying attention. Because the small, sneaky male never has to fight for females, he is likely to have a longer, if less intense, reproductive life. If he lasts long enough he may even do better in terms of siring offspring than a male who pursues the alternative route of growing large and holding a harem. These two different modes of breeding behavior represent two distinctly different developmental routes, and each male baboon must commit himself to one or other of them before puberty.

All of these examples illustrate a surprising aspect of development that has intriguing implications for humans. In each case, the individual animal starts its life with the capacity to develop in a number of distinctly different ways. Like a jukebox, the individual has the potential to play a number of different developmental tunes. But during the course of its life it plays only one tune. The particular developmental tune it does play is selected by a feature of the environment in which the individual is growing up—whether it be the color of the ground, the temperature of the sand, the type of food, or the presence of other males. Furthermore, the particular tune that is selected from the developmental jukebox is adapted to the conditions in which it is played.

Is it the case that people, like grasshoppers or baboons, are conceived with the capacity to play a number of qualitatively different developmental tunes—in other words, to live alternative lives? Each of us started life with the capacity to live many different lives, but each of us lives only one. In one sense individual humans are obviously bathed in the values of their own particular culture and become committed by their early experience to behaving in one of many possible ways. Differences in early linguistic experience, for example, have obvious and long-lasting effects. By the end of a typical high school education, a young American will probably know about fifty thousand different words. The words are different from those used by a Russian of the same age. In general, individual humans imbibe the particular characteristics of their culture by learning (often unwittingly) from older people. When environmental conditions select a particular developmental route in animals, the mechanisms involved are likely to be different; learning may not enter into the picture at all. Even so, is it possible that some aspects of human development are triggered by the environment, as though the individual were a jukebox? Was each of us conceived with the capacity to develop along a number of different tracks each of which is preadapted to the circumstances in which the individual finds itself? And does the environment select the particular developmental track that each of us follows?

A series of studies led by the epidemiologist David Barker, which assessed people across their entire lifespan from birth to death, has lent strength to the suggestion that human development may also involve environmental cues that prepare the individual for a particular sort of environment (Barker 1998). The work was based in part on a large sample of men born in the English county of Hertfordshire between 1911 and 1930. Those men who had had the lowest body weights at birth and at one year of age were most likely to die from cardiovascular disease later in life. The heaviest babies faced a subsequent risk of dying from cardiovascular disease that was only half the average for the group as a whole, whereas the risk for the smallest babies was 50 percent above average (in other words, three times greater than that for the largest babies). Individuals who had been small babies were also more likely to suffer from diseases such as diabetes and stroke in adulthood.

How could a link have arisen between an individual's birth weight and his physical health decades later? The evidence pointed to a connection with the mother's nutritional state: women with poor diets during pregnancy had smaller placentas, and forty years later their offspring had higher blood pressure (a risk factor for cardiovascular disease and stroke). But the links

with maternal nutrition went much further back than pregnancy. Measurements of the mothers' pelvises revealed that those who had a flat, bony pelvis tended to give birth to small babies. These small babies, after they had grown up, were much more likely as adults to die from stroke. The implication was that poor nutrition during their mother's childhood affected the growth of her pelvis which, in turn, curtailed the growth of her offspring during pregnancy, which, in turn, increased her offspring's risk of stroke and cardiovascular disease in adulthood.

Poor maternal physique and health are associated with reduced fetal growth, with consequences for the offspring's later health. The question arises, then, as to whether these connections make sense in adaptive terms. Could it be that, in bad conditions, the pregnant woman unwittingly signals to her unborn baby that the environment which her child is about enter is likely to be harsh? (Remember that we are thinking here about what might have been happening tens of thousands of years ago as these mechanisms were evolving in ancestral humans.) And perhaps this weather forecast from the mother's body results in her baby being born with adaptations, such as a small body and a modified metabolism, that help it to cope with a shortage of food. This hypothetical set of adaptations has been called the "thrifty phenotype" (Hales and Barker 1992; Hales, Desai, and Ozanne 1997). And perhaps these individuals with a thrifty phenotype, having small bodies and specialized metabolisms adapted to cope with meager diets, run into problems if instead they find themselves growing up in an affluent industrialized society to which they are poorly adapted. That, at least, is the hypothesis.

People who grow up in impoverished conditions tend to have a smaller body size, a lower metabolic rate, and a reduced level of behavioral activity (Waterlow 1990). These responses to early deprivation are generally regarded as pathological—just three of the many damaging consequences of poverty. But they could also be viewed as part of a package of characteristics that are appropriate to the conditions in which the individual grows up—in other words, adaptations to an environment that is chronically short on food, rather than merely the pathological byproducts of a bad diet. Having a lower metabolic rate, reduced activity, and a smaller body all help to reduce energy expenditure, which can be crucial when food is usually in short supply.

Now this conjecture might well be regarded as offensive. It could be seen as encouraging the rich to look complacently at their impoverished fellow human beings, by arguing that all is for the best in this best of all possible worlds (as Voltaire's Doctor Pangloss would have had it). Merely to assert that every human develops the body size, physiology, biochemistry, and behavior that is best suited to their station in life would indeed be banal. The point, however, is not that the rich and the poor have the same quality of life. Rather, it is that, if environmental conditions are bad and likely to remain bad, individuals exhibit adaptive developmental responses to those conditions. To put it simply, they are designed to make the best of a bad job.

Of course, many of the long-term effects on health of a low birth weight may simply be by-products of the social and economic conditions that stunted growth in the first place. Ignorance and shortage of money make the prevention and treatment of disease more difficult; overcrowding, bad working conditions, and poverty produce psychological stress and increase the risk of infection. People with little money have poorer diets, and adverse social or physical factors that foster depression and hopelessness increase the risks of disease. In industrialized nations the poor and unemployed have more illnesses and die sooner than the affluent. But social and economic conditions do not account for everything, because the connections between low birth weight and subsequent health are still found among babies born in affluent homes (Barker 1998).

Whether or not the thrifty phenotype hypothesis proves to be correct, everybody agrees that environmental conditions early in development have a significant impact on many other aspects of human biology, including size. People are getting bigger. For decades now, the average height of men and women in industrialized countries has been steadily increasing. Although some of the height differences between people are due to genetic differences, the general trend for average height to increase is almost certainly due primarily to improvements in nutrition and, to a lesser extent, health. Hence, successive generations of the same family have grown taller despite having a similar genetic makeup.

The environmental improvements that have led to this general increase in height have affected males and females somewhat differently. Men have been growing taller faster than women. For example, the average height of men in Britain has been increasing at a rate of just over one centimeter every ten years, whereas the average height of women has been increasing at about one third of that rate. In consequence, men are now relatively bigger than women than they were a century ago.

While the gap between the sexes has been widening, the average difference in height between social classes has remained roughly constant, with men from affluent professional homes being nearly 2 cm taller than men from manual backgrounds, and women from professional homes being 1.6 cm taller. In other countries the trends have been somewhat different. In Russia, where the improvements in nutrition have occurred more recently, the rate of increase in height lagged behind Britain but has been at almost three times the rates found in Britain in the last few decades. In the United States the trend toward ever taller offspring in successive generations, which started earlier than in Britain, has leveled off in recent years. These findings suggest an upper bound on the effect of nutrition on human height.

The Demise of Heritability

The examples of condition-dependent development do not pose any problems for evolutionary biologists, even though they should give pause to those who search for universals. From an adaptationist standpoint, the development of a phenotype appropriate to the circumstances in which the animal finds itself makes a great deal of sense. Nevertheless, the striking ways in which environmental factors can trigger one of a set of alternative responses pose serious difficulties for those behavior geneticists who seek to partition variation into genetic and environmental components. And worse is to come. The conventional analytical method that partitions behavioral variation into genetic and environmental components may be misleading in a different way. The two major contributors to variation may not combine even in nonlinear fashion to produce their overall effect. For example, the performances of adopted children in tests of cognitive ability are related to those of their adopting parents and their biological parents. Commonly in such studies, both types of parents have independent effects on the children (Mackintosh 1998). The effects of the genes (provided by the biological parents) and the effects of the environment (provided by the adopting parents) seem to add together. In the case of IQ scores, for example, each factor accounts for about 10 percent of the variation in the children's scores.

A common-sense view of what happens is that initially the cognitive abilities of the child are most strongly affected by its biological parents, but that later in development they are increasingly affected by the experiences the child has had with its adopting parents. However, the quality of the exchanges between the adopting parents and the child will depend on the match between their characteristics. A potentially able child who is adopted by dull people might be less stimulated and more frustrated than if he or she had been adopted by lively,

intelligent people. Conversely, adopting parents who are disappointed by the less able child might provide a less supportive environment than those whose expectations are satisfied by the responsiveness of an able child. Here again, the difference between the child and its adopting parents probably matters, but this time in the reverse direction. One study, for example, found that the bigger the absolute difference in IQ between the biological and adopting parents, the more the child was adversely affected (Bateson 1987a). The difference between the parents and child accounted for as much of the variation in the children as the direct influences of the biological and adopting parents. The consequences of the relationships between adopting parents and the children were not revealed by a simplistic analysis that assumes that what went in is directly related to what comes out. The appropriate analysis was not carried out until a plausible question was asked about the nature of the developmental process. I do not know why this should have happened but suspect the beauty of the statistical procedure called Analysis of Variance seemed to offer a sufficient explanation. The very language of "accounting for variation," common enough in statistics books, seemed to preempt thought about what might be happening during development. I will return to this point when I consider the types of model that may be used fruitfully in order to understand developmental process.

Attempts to partition phenotypic variation in behavioral characteristics may yield answers of a kind, but little sense of what happens as each individual grows up. The language of nature versus nurture, or genes versus environment, gives only a feeble insight into the processes. The best that can be said of the nature/nurture split is that it provides a framework for uncovering a few of the genetic and environmental ingredients that generate differences between people. At worst, it satisfies a demand for simplicity in ways that are fundamentally misleading.

Any scientific investigation of the origins of human behavioral differences eventually arrives at a conclusion that most nonscientists would probably have reached after only a few seconds' thought. Genes and the environment both matter. The more subtle question about how much each of them matters defies an easy answer; no simple formula can solve that conundrum. This then raises the need for a systems approach.

Metaphors and Models

The common image of a genetic blueprint for behavior fails because it is too static, too suggestive that adult organisms are merely expanded versions of the fertilized egg. In reality, developing organisms are dynamic systems that play an active role in their own development. Even when a particular gene or a particular experience is known to have a powerful effect on the development of behavior, biology has an uncanny way of finding alternative routes. If the normal developmental pathway to a particular form of adult behavior is impassable, another way may often be found. The individual may be able, through its behavior, to match its environment to suit its own characteristics. At the same time, playful activity increases the range of available choices and, at its most creative, enables the individual to control the environment in ways that would otherwise not be possible.

A low-tech cooking metaphor serves to shift the focus onto the multicausal and conditional nature of development. Using butter instead of margarine may make a cake taste different when all the other ingredients and cooking methods remain unchanged. But if other combinations of ingredients or other cooking methods are used, the distinctive difference between a cake made with butter and a cake made with margarine may vanish. Similarly, a baked cake cannot readily be disaggregated into its original raw ingredients and the various cooking processes, any more than a behavior

pattern or a psychological characteristic can be disaggregated into its genetic and environmental influences and the developmental processes that gave rise to it.

To use a different metaphor, development is not like a fixed musical score that specifies exactly how the performance starts, proceeds, and ends. It is more like a form of jazz in which musicians improvise and elaborate their musical ideas, building on what the others have just done. As new themes emerge, the performance acquires a life of its own, and may end up in a place none could have anticipated at the outset. Yet it emerges from within a fixed set of rules and the constraints imposed by the musical instruments.

It is clear, then, that because of the system in which they are embedded, no simple correspondence is found between individual genes and particular behavior patterns or psychological characteristics. Genes store information coding for the amino acid sequences of proteins; that is all. They do not code for parts of the nervous system and they certainly do not code for particular behavior patterns. Any one aspect of behavior is influenced by many genes, each of which may have a big or a small effect. Conversely, any one of many genes can have a major disruptive effect on a particular aspect of behavior. A disconnected wire can cause a car to break down, but this does not mean that the wire by itself is responsible for making the car move. Without a strong set of binding ideas, it is not easy to think about all aspects of the various strands of evidence, which often seem to point in opposite directions. Some theorists have argued that the seemingly simple and orderly characteristics of development (such as they are) are generated by dynamic processes of great complexity (Kauffman 1993). Many mathematical techniques, such as catastrophe theory and "chaos," have been developed to deal analytically with the complexities of dynamical systems. For all that, it is questionable whether the descriptive use of mathematics brings with it any explanatory power. Much more promising are those approaches that bind evidence across different levels of analysis.

Careful work on developmental processes such as imprinting and song-learning in birds have led to models that take account of both behavior and the underlying neural mechanisms. In the area in which I have worked extensively, the results of imprinting experiments depended greatly on the conditions that were used (Bateson 1966).

When many factors affect the outcome of a developmental process, what should be done about it? The chances are that all the different influences will not add together, and, if they do not, small changes in certain factors may sometimes make big differences to the outcome and large changes in others will have no effect whatsoever. For a long while it was thought that, in the case of filial imprinting, movement was critical to the young bird. A breakthrough came when a reanalysis of old data led to the conclusion that features in the jungle fowl, the ancestral form of the domestic fowl, were particularly attractive to chicks (Horn and McCabe 1984). The preference for aspects of naturalistic stimuli had been missed because, under laboratory conditions, the detectors take longer to develop in chicks than do the ones driven by an ambulance light. Even though the predisposition is less specific than at first it seemed, it looks as though such a head-neck feature detector, along with others responding to movement, color and contrast, feed into those bits of the brain that establish representations of the object to which the bird has been socialized (Horn 1991).

Imprinting involves another type of plasticity in the nervous system, namely connecting up the representation of the familiar object exclusively to the system controlling filial behavior and, much later in development, to the one controlling sexual behavior. One compelling strand of evidence is the result of taming. When a bird is well-imprinted and then exposed to another object, at first the bird withdraws showing every sign of great alarm. By degrees this alarm habituates and the bird becomes tame. However, tame birds do not express any social behavior toward the object, which is by now very familiar. They evidently recognize it, but that is all. It seems, therefore, that at least two stages are involved in imprinting. One involves recognition and one involves the control of social behavior by the representation of the familiar object. From this consideration emerged a three-stage model involving analysis, recognition, and execution. The first step involves detection of features in a stimulus presented to a young bird. Aspects of the stimulus which the bird is predisposed to find attractive are picked out by particular detectors at this level of processing. The second step involves comparison between what has already been experienced and the current input. Of course, before imprinting has taken place, no comparison is involved. Once it has occurred, recognition of what is familiar and what is novel is crucial. Finally, the third stage involves control of the various motor patterns involved in executing filial behavior. In the case of the tame bird, the assumption is that a representation is formed, but this representation has no way of gaining access to the executive system.

Darwinian Approaches to Development

I have long argued for the benefits of using a Darwinian standpoint when approaching the problems of behavioral development. Many biologists want to be told *why* the job needs to be done. In other words they want to be given a functional account or think about a characteristic in terms of design. Robert Hinde noted how much ethology has been helped by considering the adaptiveness of a behavior pattern, even when the primary concern is with mechanism (Hinde 1982). Why is it advantageous to bring in the functional argument? Animals live in a complex world and most biologists would argue that the degree of match between their behavior and the conditions in which they live makes a big difference to their survival and reproductive success.

Those who do not like Darwinian arguments about apparent natural design being brought into discussions of development see no value in them. If grasshoppers are green when the grass is green and black when the savanna has been blackened by fire, the obvious benefit to the individual of minimizing risk from predation is irrelevant to the question of how they come to match the color of their background. The appropriate developmental questions are about how the process works. They are right, but they miss the point. The design point frames the mechanistic argument. It leads to studies that might otherwise not have been done. To give one example from development, the functional approach provides a way of thinking about the difference in timing between sexual imprinting and filial imprinting. The suggestion is that an animal should not tune its reference point for mating preferences too early in development lest it obtains information about the juvenile appearance of its siblings that could not be used effectively when the time comes to choose a mate. On the other side it must not tune its mating preferences too late in development after the family group has broken up and it is likely to be exposed to non-kin. Indeed, the evidence suggests that birds delay sexual imprinting until their siblings have molted into adult plumage. In this way the bird is able use its experience of close kin so that it chooses a mate that is genetically a bit different from itself, but not too different. If the two types of imprinting are treated as part of the same general process, the difference seems to be of no importance and is quickly forgotten. However, with attention focused on the problem, we can attempt to analyze the mechanisms responsible for the difference in timing. The point is, then, that the functional approach can stimulate research on the processes of development.

The heuristic point about the mentally enabling role of functional explanations also relates also to the seeming conflict between selfish gene language and the system theories arising from studies of development. It is possible, I believe, to resolve the conflict between the developmental systems approach, which takes into account many influences, and the evolutionary selfish genes approach, which seems to suggest only one cause. However, we need to be very clear about the difficulties of translating one language in to the other and the attendant confusions that arise when translation occurs carelessly.

Dawkins suggested that the way to understand evolution is not in terms of the needs of species, groups or individuals, but in terms of the needs of genes (Dawkins 1976). Genes recombine in each generation to form temporary federations. The alliance forms an individual organism. By reproducing, individuals serve to perpetuate the genes which in the next generation recombine in some other kind of alliance. Genes are selfishly intent on replicating themselves by the best possible means. Dawkins was clearly and deliberately using a heuristic device when he attributed motives to genes. He obviously did not think that gene have intentions. It is easier for most of us to get our minds round a problem when we can think of a complex system in terms of the way they strive to reach a specific end state. This is not only true in biology. A great nineteenth-century physicist, William Rowan Hamilton, formulated a general and widely accepted teleological principle for use in mechanics. It is a powerful way of thinking about systems, the behavior of which is determined by many factors.

The language of intentions can, of course, be played many ways. When the ambient environmental temperature during development is crucial for the expression of a particular phenotype, changes in temperature by a few degrees may lead to a startling evolutionary change. It may lead to extinction—such as is predicted for turtles whose sex depends on temperature early in development and after global warming would all end up as females. Would not such cases give as much status to a necessary temperature value as to a necessary gene? The temperature value is also required for the expression of a particular set of phenotypes—balanced sex ratio in turtles before global warming. It is also stable (within limits) from one generation to the next. It may even be transmitted from one generation to the next if the survival machine makes a nest for its offspring. The bird is the nest's way of making another nest (Bateson 1978).

In concluding his discussion of alternative teleologies and my concern that he was giving too much status to the gene as programmer, Dawkins (1982) wrote amusingly:

> As is so often the case, an apparent disagreement turns out to be due to mutual misunderstanding. I thought Bateson was denying proper respect to the Immortal Replicator. Bateson thought that I was denying proper respect to the Great Nexus of complex causal factors interacting in development.[1]

Reflecting on this debate many years later, I think that more was at issue than different emphases and interests. Dawkins' response showed how easily we get snarled up in the language. The details of the evolutionary mechanism involving small changes in DNA had been mixed up with the intentions that were rhetorically attributed to genes. While Dawkins was quite justified, in my view, in writing about genes' intentions, he was wrong when he treated this language as readily translatable into the language of what genes actually do. The language of selfish genes does not easily translate in the causal language of population biologists even though the users are ostensibly talking about the same issue.

For population geneticists, a genetic difference is identified by means of a biochemical, physiological, structural, or behavioral difference between organisms (after other potential sources of difference have been excluded by appropriate procedures). Dawkins suggested that his move backward and forward between the language of gene intentions and the more orthodox language of genetic differences was acceptable because they are simply alternative ways of describing the same thing. To make his point, he described perception of the Necker cube. The front edges of the line drawing of the cube suddenly flip to the back as we look at them. Each perceived image of the cube is as real as the other. Dawkins suggests that, in similar ways, the teleological and mechanistic images of evolution translate backward and forward into the other. However, it doesn't make any sense to attribute motives to a comparison, as may be illustrated by a parable.

Let us consider the spread of a new brand of biscuit in supermarkets from the perspective of the recipe. While shoppers may compare biscuits and buy one brand, it is the recipe used for making desirable biscuits that survives and spreads in the long run. Therefore, the word in the recipe that makes the biscuit successful is selfish, because it serves to perpetuate itself. So far so good. But my story loses all coherence if I conclude by adding that the difference in the wording of recipes used for making successful and less successful is selfish.

It is worth developing the biscuits in a supermarket parable just a little further. What shoppers *really* do in supermarkets is to select a word in a faithfully reproduced recipe. Really? Words in recipes as the units of the shoppers' selection? It is an odd idea, since shoppers respond among other things to the outcome of the cooking process which gave rise to the biscuits. For very similar reasons many biologists, myself included, disliked the idea of genes being treated as the units of selection in Darwinian terms. After all, Darwin had used his metaphor of "natural selection" because he had been impressed by the ways in which plant and animal breeders selected the characteristics they sought to perpetuate. Of course, the gene selection idea grew up because it made sense of those cases in which the consequences of an act favored the survival of genetically related individuals rather than the actor. Dawkins (1982) helpfully advanced the argument when he drew a distinction between "replicators" and "vehicles."

To separate further the many different strands of thought that have been run together in the units of selection debate, it is worth making a three-way distinction that mirrors in part the mechanism Darwin introduced to explain the evolution of adaptations. Darwin suggested that three components of the mechanism are essential. First, competing biological entities must differ in their characteristics. (The entities have usually been individual organisms in conventional neo-Darwinian thinking, but they may be parts of organisms or assemblies of organisms.) Second, the entities must survive and/or reproduce themselves with differing degrees of success. Third, the entities must be more likely to share characteristics with their descendants or relatives than with unrelated entities.

The developmental processes creating the phenotypes of the entities have been the major concern of Developmental Systems Theory (DST) and, indeed, of this chapter. Darwin had nothing to say about how phenotypic variation is generated, and yet its existence is central to his evolutionary mechanism. The modern emphasis on developmental process has served to put empirical flesh on notions of what generates the variation in the raw material for differential survival and reproductive success. Once the phenotypes are created, DST has not much to say about differential survival and differential reproductive success. However, the necessary conditions for re-creating the characteristics of the successful entity in the next generation or for generating similar characteristics in kin such as siblings or cousins is once again the province of

DST. The conditions shared by related entities will commonly consist of genes but will include all those nongenetic factors that DST thinking has brought back on stage. The value of making the three-way distinction is that it separates out the first and third aspects of the Darwinian mechanism, which had been run together into the single concept of "replicator."

A confusion of teleological and causal explanation led critics and supporters alike to a non sequitur. Proponents argue that if genes are usefully regarded as selfish, it follows that they uniquely bring into being the phenotypic characters of the whole animal. Opponents argue that if it is valuable to treat development as a process involving feedback and many mutual actions between different agents, then the selfish gene language is inappropriate. Both arguments are mistaken, in my view. The developmental systems approach is not in conflict with the selfish gene approach to evolution.

The evolutionary process does not require a simple correspondence between genes and adaptive behavior. Darwinian evolution operates on individuals that have developed within a particular set of conditions. If those conditions are stable for many generations, then the changes that matter will arise from segregation of factors that give rise to individual differences. Individuals vary; some survive and reproduce more successfully than others because they possess a crucial characteristic; and close relatives are more likely to share that characteristic than unrelated individuals. Apparent design is produced, even when it is at the end of the long and complicated process of development. But the environment does not cease to be important for evolution just because it remains constant. Change the environment and the outcome of an individual's development may be utterly different. Indeed, if an individual does not inherit its parents' environment along with their genes, it may not be well adapted to the conditions in which it now finds itself.

Conclusion

Old styles of thought die hard. Even the much-used distinction between sex and gender has a strong whiff of the old genes/environment opposition. "Sex" is biology; but "gender" is part of culture, the acquired behavior deemed appropriate to the social role of that sex. Any fair-minded person listening to setpiece debates about behavioral development is likely to be left irritated by the claims and counterclaims. And well-meaning attempts to break out of the nature/nurture straitjacket have often resulted in an obscure and bewildering portrayal of development as a process of impenetrable complexity (what Salman Rushdie once described in another context as a P2C2E—a Process Too Complicated To Explain). Indeed, development seemed so unfathomably complex to eighteenth-century biologists that they believed that it must depend on supernatural guidance.

The processes involved in behavioral development do indeed look forbiddingly complicated on the surface. Some would argue that it is worse underneath and that such order as is found is generated by dynamical systems of great complexity. One approach to development has been to suggest that everything interacts with everything else. A challenge to such thinking is the evidence for the segregation of characteristics in closely related individuals. How is it that characteristics such as a big nose or a retiring disposition skip a generation? How is it that siblings are so different from each other at birth? How is rapid artificial selection for behavioral characteristics such as tameness possible? None of the evidence that leads to such questions implies any simple correspondence between an inherited factor and the development of a phenotypic characteristic. But the evidence does imply that fractionation and independent inheritance of some of the factors necessary for development happens all the time.

In contrast to an agenda that easily renders development a process too complicated to explain, I prefer to argue that simplicity and regularity may be found in the developmental processes that give rise to unique individuals. Confidence in that conclusion comes not from general principles but from the careful analysis of particular cases. The essence of development—change coupled with continuity—starts to make sense. It becomes possible to understand how the individual is so responsive to events at one stage and so unaffected by them at another.

Order underlies even those learning processes that make individuals different from each other. Knowing something of the underlying regularities in development does bring an understanding of what happens to the child as it grows up. The ways in which learning is structured, for instance, affect how the child makes use of environmental contingencies and how the child classifies perceptual experience. Yet predicting precisely how an individual child will develop in the future from knowledge of the developmental rules for learning is no easier than predicting the course of a chess game. The rules influence the course of a life, but they do not determine it. Like chess players, children are active agents. They influence their environment and are in turn affected by what they have done. Furthermore, children's responses to new conditions will, like chess players' responses, be refined or embellished as they gather experience. Sometimes normal development of a particular ability requires input from the environment at a particular time; what happens next depends on the character of that input. The upshot is that, despite their underlying regularities, developmental processes seldom proceed in straight lines. Big changes in the environment may have no effect whatsoever, whereas some small changes have big effects. The only way to unravel this is to understand the developmental processes.

Note

1   Dawkins 1982, p. 99.

References

Barker, D. J. P. (1998). *Mothers, Babies and Health in Later Life.* (2nd ed.). Edinburgh: Churchill Livingstone.

Bateson, P. P. G. (1966). The characteristics and context of imprinting. *Biological Reviews,* 41: 177–220.

Bateson, P. (1978). Review of *The Selfish Gene* by Richard Dawkins. *Animal Behaviour,* 26: 316–318.

Bateson, P. (1987a). Biological approaches to the study of behavioural development. *International Journal of Behavioral Development,* 10: 1–22.

Bateson, P. (1987b). Imprinting as a process of competitive exclusion. In J. P. Rauschecker and P. Marler (Eds.), *Imprinting and Cortical Plasticity,* pp. 151–168. New York: Wiley.

Cooper, R. M., & J. P. Zubek. (1958). Effects of enriched and restricted early environments on the learning ability of bright and dull rats. *Canadian Journal of Psychology,* 12: 159–164.

Crews, D. (1996). Temperature-dependent sex determination: The interplay of steroid hormones and temperature. *Zoological Science,* 13: 1–13.

Dawkins, R. (1976). *The Selfish Gene,* Oxford: Oxford University Press.

Dawkins, R. (1982). *The Extended Phenotype.* Oxford: Freeman.

Hales, C. N., & D. J. P. Barker. (1992). Type 2 (non-insulin-dependent) diabetes mellitus: The thrifty phenotype hypothesis. *Diabetologia,* 35: 595–601.

Hales, C. N., M. Desai, & S. E. Ozanne. (1997). The thrifty phenotype hypothesis: How does it look after 5 years? *Diabetic Medicine,* 14: 189–195.

Hinde, R. A. (1982). *Ethology.* Oxford: Oxford University Press.

Horn, G. (1991). Cerebral function and behaviour investigated through a study of filial imprinting. In P. Bateson (Ed.), *The Development and Integration of Behaviour,* pp. 121–148. Cambridge: Cambridge University Press.

Horn, G., and B. J. McCabe. (1984). Predispositions and preferences. Effects on imprinting of lesions to the chick brain. *Animal Behaviour,* 32: 288–292.

Lerner, R. M. (1998). *Handbook of Child Psychology,* vol 1. (5th ed.). New York: Wiley.

Mackintosh, N. J. (1998). *IQ and Human Intelligence.* Oxford: Oxford University Press.

Nesse, R. M., and G. C. Williams. (1994). *Evolution and Healing.* London: Weidenfeld & Nicolson.

Rowell, C. H. F. (1971). The variable coloration of the Acridoid grasshoppers. *Advances in Insect Physiology,* 8: 145–198.

Sarkar, S. (1996). Decoding "coding": Information and DNA. *Bioscience* 46: 857–864.

Waterlow. J. C. (1990). Mechanisms of adaptation to low energy intakes. In G. A. Harrison and J. C. Waterlow (Eds.), *Diet and Disease in Traditional and Developing Countries,* pp. 5–23. Cambridge: Cambridge University Press.

Yntema, C. L., and N. Mrosovsky. (1982). Critical periods and pivotal temperatures for sexual differentiation in loggerhead sea turtles. *Canadian Journal of Zoology,* 60: 1012–1016.

Zadnik, K. (1997). Myopia development in childhood. *Optometry and Vision Science,* 74: 603–608.

Chapter 13

Philip Kitcher

BATTLING THE UNDEAD
How (and How Not) to Resist Genetic Determinism[1]

"But wait," the exasperated reader cries, "everyone nowadays knows that development is a matter of interaction. You're beating a dead horse."

I reply, "I would like nothing better than to stop beating him, but every time I think I am free of him he kicks me and does rude things to the intellectual and political environment. He seems to be a phantom horse with a thousand incarnations, and he gets more and more subtle each time around. . . . What we need here, to switch metaphors in midstream, is the stake-in-the-heart move, and the heart is the notion that some influences are more equal than others.[2]

Nobody has done more to combat genetic determinism than Richard Lewontin, whose writings, from the original IQ controversy to present debates about the implications of human molecular genetics, diagnose errors that have seduced influential scholars and their readers into believing vulgar slogans about genes and destiny. Lewontin's reward for his decades of effort has often been the irritated response that what he claims is uncontroversial: once the intellectual poverty of a version of genetic determinism has been exposed, there is a rush to denial ("That is not what we meant; that is not what we meant at all"). Yet, within months or years, some new version of the view that human behavior is largely shaped by the

genes returns, inspiring a new rash of popular discussions and, in some instances, framing debates about social policy. It is small wonder, then, that people appalled by the sloppy thinking Lewontin has exposed yearn for the "stake-in-the-heart move."

Lewontin's own response to the continued reemergence of genetic determinism has been to deny the correctness of the interactionist credo, the conventional wisdom to which purveyors of determinist claims retreat in the face of criticism (see Levins and Lewontin 1985, Chapter 3 and Conclusion; Lewontin, Rose, and Kamin 1984, Chapter 10; Lewontin 1991, especially pp. 3–37). Although many of his best arguments consist in demonstrating how determinists have ignored interactions among genetic and nongenetic factors, Lewontin seems to believe that acceptance of these arguments is not enough, that we need to free ourselves from the grip of the Cartesian picture of the world as a machine, that we should recognize the interdependence between organism and environment, and that we should formulate a "dialectical biology." He is convinced that there has to be a fundamental error—an error that can be corrected only by reconceptualizing some parts of biology.

In my judgment, no such reconceptualization is needed, and Lewontin's positive proposals are in constant danger of relapsing into the obscurity that he rightly sees as affecting traditional forms of biological holism.[3,4] Genetic determinism persists not because of some subtle error in conventional ideas about the general character of biological causation but because biologists who are studying complicated traits in complex organisms are prone to misapply correct general views. Ironically, the existence of this tendency to error testifies to the social pressures on biological practice—pressures that Lewontin has been at some pains to point out. The search for the stake-in-the-heart rests on a misunderstanding of the problem and may even undermine the effectiveness of the more limited measures that Lewontin and others have crafted.

It is high time to back up assertion with argument. Let us begin more slowly by asking what the thesis of genetic determinism claims.

Here is a first version. To suppose that a particular trait in an organism is genetically determined is to maintain that there is some gene, or group of genes, such that any organism of that species developing from a zygote that possessed a certain form (set of forms) of that gene (or a certain set of forms of those genes) would come to have the trait in question, whatever the other properties of the zygote and whatever the sequence of environments through which the developing organism passed. Although this is a relatively simple way to articulate the idea that genetic causes take priority, it is of little use for reconstructing the debates about genetic determinism. Perhaps, with sufficient ingenuity, one can discover traits that are genetically determined in this sense, but any such traits will be causally "close" to the immediate biochemistry in which DNA is involved— they will not be the characteristics for which we wonder about the rival contributions of nature and nurture. Even if we apply the definition to a relatively uncontroversial exemplar, investigating whether it counts Huntington's disease (HD) as genetically determined, we encounter trouble. True enough, human beings who carry abnormally long CAG repeats at a particular locus near the tip of chromosome 4 undergo neural degeneration, typically between the ages of 30 and 50, and doctors know of no preventative treatment. Does this mean that no way is known of contriving an environment in which the terrible decay does not occur? Not really. Huntington's disease could be forestalled by giving those with the long repeats the opportunity to end their lives before the onset of the disease, and it is overwhelmingly probable that some people with such repeats have suffered accidental death early in life. Hence, strictly speaking, there are environments in which people who have abnormally long CAG repeats at the HD locus do not develop HD, and thus, according to the definition, HD would not count as genetically determined.

Of course, the existence of environments in which the expression of the HD phenotype is forestalled by early death is hardly comforting, and it would be reasonable to suggest that the account of genetic determinism ought to be refined in one of two obvious ways: (a) by replacing the demand that the trait be acquired in *all* environments with something weaker ("almost all") and (b) by restricting attention to complexes of causal factors that enable the organism to develop to the age at which the trait would normally first appear. But it seems more illuminating to make explicit the strategy that underlies the proposed definition. That strategy begins by isolating certain properties of organisms for exploration of their causal impact, regarding the phenotype as the product of contributions from particular kinds of DNA sequences, on the one hand, and from *everything else*, on the other. It goes on to inquire how the phenotype varies as the DNA sequences are held constant and as other factors (the cytoplasmic constitution of the zygote, the molecules passed across cell membranes, etc.) change. The graphical representation of this, the *norm of reaction* of the genotype, is a familiar concept in genetics, and the crudest sort of genetic determinism consists in claiming that the norm of reaction for the trait of interest is flat (see Figure 13.1).

162   Philip Kitcher

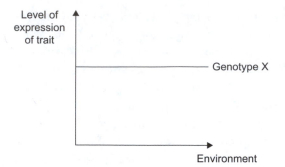

Figure 13.1 A graphical representation of the simplest type of genetic determinism. The level of expresson of the phenotypic trait of interest in individuals with the focal genotype ("Genotype X") remains constant no matter how the environment varies.

Just the kinds of difficulties that appeared in the HD example make doctrines of so simple a form implausible, but the pictorial style of representation suggests plenty of ways in which the genetic factors can be seen as playing important causal roles—perhaps the norm of reaction will be flat almost everywhere, perhaps it will vary only slightly, perhaps the norms of reactions for different genotypes will show a universal relation, perhaps the norm of reaction will be flat if we restrict ourselves to those complexes of other factors that we think of as healthy for the organism. (See Figure 13.2.) We might thus see genetic determination as a matter of degree, and, instead of quibbling about the proper definition of genetic determinism, investigate

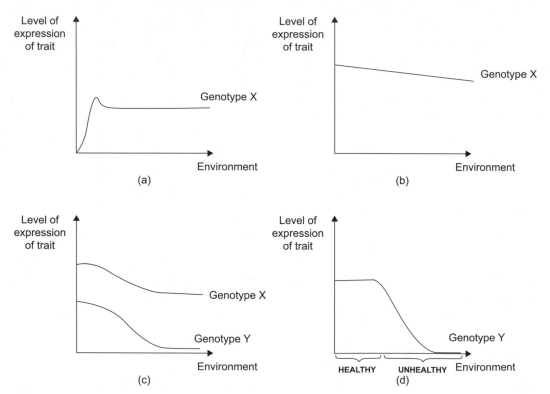

Figure 13.2 Some determinist themes. In (a), the level of expression of the trait is constant (for genotype X) in almost all environments; in (b), the level of expression is almost constant across all environments; (c), despite variation in level association with geneotypes X and Y, the level of expression for individuals with X is always greater than that for Y, no matter what the environment; in (d), there is considerable variation in the level of expression but only in environments that are unhealthy. These themes admit further refinements, combinations, and variations.

the shapes of the norms of reaction in the cases of interest to us.

One of the great insights of Lewontin's early discussions of these questions was his recognition of this as the real issue to which claims of genetic, determination were directed.[5] Moreover, Lewontin explained with admirable lucidity why the methods employed to establish those claims could not deliver such conclusions. Estimates of heritability do not reveal the contours of norms of reaction; cross-cultural surveys are only likely to do better if one can be confident that the entire space of nongenetic causal variables is covered.[6] If, as I believe, Lewontin was right in his diagnosis of the errors of popular behavior genetics (most evident in doctrines about the determination of IQ) and popular human sociobiology (manifested in conclusions about the ineradicability of sexual differences in behavior), then the besetting sin was the tendency to draw certain kinds of pictures on the basis of woefully inadequate evidence.

It should now be obvious how a weary critic of hasty generalizations about norms of reaction might go further. Perhaps the tendency to suppose that the relative invariance of a phenotypic trait, given a particular genotype across a manageable range of environments, indicates a flat norm of reaction might be scotched by denying the legitimacy of any such representation altogether. During the 1980s and 1990s, Lewontin and others (most prominently Susan Oyama, Paul Griffiths, and Russell Gray) began to argue that our entire view of genotype-phenotype relations needed to be changed, and that the framework within which I have been posing issues about genetic determination ought to be rebuilt.

Is the notion of a norm of reaction well defined? The writings of those who demand a new conception of nature and nurture—a "dialectical biology" (Lewontin) or "developmental systems theory" (Oyama, Griffiths, and Gray)—suggest several worries about the notion

and its relatives (such as the standard genetic idiom of a gene "for" such-and-such a trait). Organism and environment, it is said, are interdependent; there is "developmental noise" in the production of phenotypes; the singling out of genes as causal factors is an unwarranted abstraction from a complex causal situation wrongly giving priority to some determinants of the phenotype; the notion of a gene "for" a trait cannot be coherently reconstructed. These are important concerns, and I will take them up in order.

Lewontin has argued that an organism's environment should not be thought of as identifiable prior to the organism and its distinctive forms of behavior:

> Are the stones and the glass in my garden part of the environment of a bird? The grass is certainly part of the environment of a phoebe that gathers dry grass to make a nest. But the stone around which the grass is growing means nothing to the phoebe. On the other hand, the stone is part of the environment of a thrush that may come along with a garden snail and break the shell of the snail against the stone. Neither the grass nor the stone are part of the environment of a woodpecker that is living in a hole in a tree. That is, bits and pieces of the world outside of these organisms are made relevant to them by their own life activities.[7]

The facts reported here are uncontroversial, and the last sentence strikes me as completely correct. What exactly follows?

Lewontin uses these observations to oppose both the idea that we can think of organisms adapting to environments that are independent of them and the idea that we can think of the phenotype as dependent on causal interactions between genotype and environment. The latter conception is the principal concern here, although similar remarks apply to both types of criticism. Lewontin is moved by a principle about causes and causal dependence: C cannot be a causal factor in the production of P if C is dependent on P. Applying his conclusions about the dependence of environment on organism, he maintains that we cannot see the environment as a causal factor in the production of the phenotype, and thus the idea of a norm of reaction, with its partitioning of causal variables along different axes, is confused.

There are two related points to be made about this line of reasoning: first, it is not obvious what notion of dependence figures in the causal principle, and, second, it is not clear just one notion of environment is pertinent here. Consider the notion of dependence. In one very obvious sense, the stone in Lewontin's garden is independent of the presence of phoebe, thrush, and woodpecker—it sits there before the arrival of the birds, before the eruption of fledglings from the nest. So, if we understand "dependence" to mean that the existence of one thing is an effect of the presence of the other, then Lewontin's principle, although plausible, does not apply to the case at hand: there is no reason to think that the contents of the garden cannot play roles in the formation of phenotypes. On the other hand, if we understand "dependence" to mean that the causal relevance of one thing varies with the properties of the other, then the principle does apply to the relations between the birds and the garden. Whether grass, stones, or holes in trees are causally relevant to the development of the birds varies with the properties of the birds, as Lewontin's illustrations show. But now there is no great plausibility in the causal principle itself, for, elaborated, it says that if the causal relevance of C to P varies with the properties of the bearers of P, then C cannot be a causal factor in the production of P in *any* case, and this claim seems to verge on paradox.

The point can be clarified further by focusing on the other murky term in the argument, "environment." Biologists typically think of environments as those parts of the world outside the organism that are causally pertinent, and in

this, the *functional* environment, great tracts of nature are not part of the organism's environment. Lewontin's observations reveal very clearly that an organism's functional environment can depend on what the organism does. However, when we think about the development of an organism, we can pick out some potential causal factors—say the organism's DNA—and take the environment, the *total* environment, to be everything else. In Lewontin's phrase, the total environment is all "the bits and pieces of the world outside the organism" plus some more "bits and pieces"—to wit those inside the organism but not the DNA. The phenotype the organism acquires is determined together by the genotype (the DNA sequences) and the total environment, and, of course, a large part of the total environment will be causally irrelevant. Furthermore, it is quite correct to note that the functional environment, the bits and pieces that are pertinent, depends on (in the sense of varying with) the properties of the developing organism. But this is quite compatible with the causal analysis of phenotypes in terms of genotypes and total environments and with the attempt to draw norms of reactions that identify the causal contributions.

Yet there is an important point behind Lewontin's argument, one that becomes misfocused because of his eagerness to drive a stake into the heart of genetic determinism. To produce a picture indicating the shape of a norm of reaction is to advertise oneself as understanding how to order environments along the axis, and that is typically false advertising. In most instances, we only have the most rudimentary knowledge of how to identify the functional environment, and our ignorance affects the pictures and the conclusions drawn from them. Typically, we can divide the factors outside the DNA into three categories: those we can identify and know to be causally relevant, those we can identify and know not to be causally relevant, and those we either cannot pick out or whose relevance we do not know. (It is, of course, quite possible for us to realize that there is much about which we are likely to be ignorant.) Confronted with a claim about the genetic determination of human propensities to violent behavior (for example), modesty should urge us to think that the last category is quite large, and thus a demonstration that the norm of reaction for a genotype remains flat over a wide range of the nongenetic variables known to be relevant ought not to inspire much confidence that the result would survive a more detailed and fine-grained partitioning. Thus, the right point to make is that we should not leap to premature conclusions about the character of the functional environment, that we should recall the fragility of our representations of the nongenetic causal factors, and that, in consequence, even though the notion of a norm of reaction is perfectly well defined, even though norms of reaction are just what we are trying to discover, knowledge of such norms is very hard to come by. Lewontin has miscast the important methodological point about the difficulty of settling the questions of concern (the shapes of norms of reaction) as an incorrect conceptual point about the incoherence of the notion of a norm of reaction.

The second concern about interactionism focuses on the possibility of "developmental noise." Lewontin argues that even knowledge "of the genes of a developing organism and the complete sequence of its environments"[8] would not allow prediction of the phenotype. In support of this claim, he notes that fruitflies typically have different numbers of bristles at the left and right sides of their thorax, that the difference cannot be explained by a difference in genotype and is not traceable to differences in environment.

> Moreover, the tiny size of a developing fruitfly and the place it develops guarantee that both left and right sides have had the same humidity, the same oxygen, the same temperature. The differences between left and right

side are caused neither by genetic nor by environmental differences but by random variation in growth and division of cells during development: *developmental noise.*[9]

Once again, it is important to ask what is being counted as part of the environment and what standards are being used to assess identity of environment.

There are three main types of answer to the question Why do fruitflies have different numbers of bristles at the left and right sides of their thorax? One is to suggest that Lewontin has just counted environments as the same in too coarse a fashion. Perhaps the temperature on the left is the same as that on the right so long as we measure to two or three significant figures, but there are minute differences from side to side, and, at crucial stages of cell division, these differences make a difference. This answer would broadly accept Lewontin's conception of the environment but would eliminate the notion of developmental noise in terms of a more precise understanding of the environmental variables.

The second response would take advantage of the fact that, when interactionists undertake causal analysis of phenotypes in terms of the contributions of DNA and other factors, some of these other factors might be internal to the organism. One of the principal achievements of developmental biology in recent years has been the demonstration of how initial asymmetries in the cytoplasm interact with the DNA in the first stages of ontogeny to produce patterns in early embryos (worked out in greatest detail so far for *Drosophila*). It is quite possible that the differences in rates of cell division do account for the difference in bristle number and that these rate differences are remote effects of the inhomogeneity of the zygote. Although we could reasonably describe them as "random" in the sense that there is no uniform process that determines the distribution of molecules in the cytoplasm of the ovum—so that the initial state of the zygote is the result of contingencies of the formation of a particular egg—they are not *irreducibly* random. A fine-grained specification of the total environment of the DNA would provide a causal explanation of the asymmetry in bristle number. Thus, once again, the form of the phenotype can be viewed as fixed by the genotype and the environment provided that we conceive of the environment in the proper (total) fashion. There is no need to invoke developmental noise or to think that the notion of a norm of reaction breaks down here.

The last possibility is that even the initial distribution of molecules throughout the zygote together with the fine-grained structure of the sequence of environments through which the fly develops does not determine the bristle number. Perhaps the asymmetry is irreducibly random in that no further introduction of causal factors will account for it. I do not know if Lewontin has this possibility in mind, but the existence of fundamental indeterminacies in quantum physics makes it necessary to consider it. There are no well-established instances of quantum events playing a significant role in ontogeny, and many biologists and philosophers seem convinced that subatomic indeterminacies will wash out because of the enormous numbers of molecules that play a role in the development of an organism (the law of large numbers is often thought to be suggestive here). If irreducible randomness does not "percolate up" from the quantum level, then, of course, there is no challenge to the notion of a norm of reaction and no reason to think that subatomic indeterminacies are a source of developmental noise. But, even if some differences in phenotypes ultimately trace to random subatomic events, a simple revision would save the concept of a norm of reaction. Instead of thinking in terms of a single phenotype, fixed by the genotype and (total) environment, we would have to suppose that this congeries of factors determines a probability distribution of phenotypes: pictorial representations would thus illustrate expected values of phenotypes, and, given the elusiveness

of quantum effects at the phenotypic level, it would be entirely reasonable to suppose that the spread around the mean was very small.

I turn now to the third worry, the idea that singling out the genotype and considering its effects against background environmental conditions is misguided abstraction from a complex causal situation. No interactionist denies that many causal factors are involved in development (that, after all, is the point of interactionism). However, interactionists defend the legitimacy of a general strategy of causal analysis —the strategy of isolating some of the causal factors, holding them constant, and investigating how the effect varies when other factors are altered. Interactionists ought to support a principle of causal democracy: if the effect E is the product of factors in set S, then, for any $C \in S$, it is legitimate to investigate the dependence of E on C when the other factors in S are allowed to vary. Taking E to be a phenotypic trait, C to be a particular genotype, and S to be a large (probably mostly unknown) set of factors in the total environment (that is factors in the rest of nature outside the genotype), the democracy principle endorses the legitimacy of seeking norms of reaction for phenotypic traits. But it should already be clear that the democracy principle endorses lots of other ways of undertaking causal analysis. For example, we might consider a particular environmental factor and investigate what happens to the phenotype when we vary the genotype and other parts of the environment or we might pick out some mix of genotypic and (total) environmental factors, investigating how the phenotype varies with respect to the rest of the causal factors. The democracy principle accords no special privilege to the representations that foreground the role of genes.

But why, then, do we always end up discussing whether genotypes are all-powerful in development? Why does democracy in principle always translate into elitism in practice? As we shall see, the answers turn out to be complicated, but, for the present, the interactionist's claim is simply that we should not suppose that efforts to investigate the effects of some factors, while others are allowed to vary, are incoherent or illegitimate. Complex causal situations do not demand that we perform the impossible feat of considering everything at once; rather they challenge us to find ways of making these factors manageable. One defense of the prevalence of efforts to chart genotype–phenotype relations against the background of other variables would cite the epistemic benefits of such investigations: this is something we know how to do and that we can expect to prove informative. I will argue below that this cannot be the whole story.

For the moment, we can move on from the blanket charge that any kind of separation out of causal factors does violence to the causal complexities of development and turn to the last line of objection. Russell Gray (both writing on his own and in collaboration with Paul Griffiths) has provided the sharpest version of the charge that thinking in terms of genes "for" traits is a confusion. Alluding to an earlier attempt to suggest that talk of genes "for" traits always presupposes a relativization to "standard" genetic backgrounds and "standard" environments, Griffiths and Gray offer the following counter:

> Consider the DNA in an acorn. If this codes for anything, it is for an oak tree. But the vast majority of acorns simply rot. So "standard environment" cannot be interpreted statistically. The only interpretation of "standard" that will work is "such as to produce evolved developmental outcomes" or "of the sort possessed by successful ancestors." With this interpretation of "standard environment," however, we can talk with equal legitimacy of cytoplasmic or landscape features coding for traits in standard genetic backgrounds. No basis has been provided for privileging the genes over other developmental resources. (Griffiths and Gray 1994, p. 283).

There is much here with which I agree, although the last sentence contains an ambiguity that enables Griffiths and Gray to arrive at more exciting conclusions than those to which they are entitled.

An alternate way to reconstruct the everyday talk of genes "for" traits by developing the intuitive idea that "we can speak of genes for X if substitutions on a chromosome would lead, in the relevant environments, to a difference in the X-ishness of the phenotype."[10] The notion of environment we appealed to was that of *total* environment conceived as everything outside the locus (or loci) of interest, and we sketched accounts of standardness for the genetic background and for the part of the environment that does not consist of other parts of the DNA. With respect to the extraorganismal environment, we offered three theses: (1) there are alternative ways of explicating the notion of "standard conditions," (2) one of these ways is to count as standard those environments frequently encountered by organisms of the species under study, and (3) another is to count as standard only those environments that do not substantially reduce population mean fitness.[11]

Although (1) remains untouched, Griffiths and Gray have shown that (2) and (3) are problematic if the aim is to reconstruct standard genetic discourse. Botanists studying the oak genome want to identify some loci as affecting particular structures in the mature tree, but, for most acorns, genetic substitutions at the pertinent loci do not affect the form of the related structures because those acorns rot. In the accounts of standard environment offered in both (2) and (3), individuals with genetic differences at the loci do not manifest any phenotypic differences in the trait that is supposed to be influenced when they grow in standard environments because the most frequent environments, which also happen to be environments that do not reduce population mean fitness, are environments in which no mature tree grows.

Consider a locus "for" root proliferation. A botanist declares that the allele *A* is "for" root proliferation, meaning thereby that *AB* trees generate more roots than *BB* trees given standard complements of genes at other loci, standard distributions of molecules in the zygotes, and standard sequences of environments. Suppose now that we interpret "standard" in the fashion of (2) or (3). We have to acknowledge that, in most standard environments, the number of roots generated by an organism growing from an *AB* zygote is no greater than that generated by an organism growing from a *BB* zygote (both numbers are zero). However, the botanist could still claim that, for any standard environment, the number of roots generated by the organisms developing from *AB* zygotes is never less than the corresponding number for *BB* zygotes, and, in some standard environments, it is greater. So let the allele *A* be "for" root proliferation just in case in all standard (total) environments the number of roots generated by *AB* individuals is greater than or equal to the number of roots generated by *BB* individuals with the inequality holding strictly in some cases. Obvious challenge: surely, by luck, the sole oak tree growing in one environment might be *BB* whereas thousands of acorns around (some *BB*, some *AB*) rot; thus, in that environment, the inequality would be reversed. Response: once again, we have to be careful to individuate environments; at the fine-grained level, the environment encountered by the lucky acorn is different from that encountered by the unlucky ones, and, if an *AB* acorn had found itself in precisely that fortunate environment, then it would have generated more roots than its *BB* counterpart.

This strategy for reconstructing the "gene for X" locution allows us to retain the interpretation of "standard" as "statistically normal" by weakening the demand that genes "for" X promote X-ishness in every standard environment. Alternatively, we could decide that a standard environment is one that allows for the development of those features required for the

manifestation of the general (determinable) property of which the trait on which we are focusing is a particular (determinate) instance. So, in the case at hand, to talk about genes "for" root proliferation is to suggest that there are differences among individuals with various genotypes—*specifically individuals that have the capacity for producing roots (that is, trees)*. Environments that prevent the maturing organisms from manifesting the general property (exhibiting any form of the trait) are thus ruled out as nonstandard, but, in accordance with the pluralistic line offered in our thesis (1), that demarcation will vary with the kind of trait in which we are interested.

I conclude that talk of genes "for" traits can be coherently reconstructed (indeed along the lines that Sterelny and I originally suggested). However, Griffiths and Gray are right to note that a similar form of reconstruction would enable us to speak of "cytoplasmic or landscape features" for traits (here I drop their reference to "coding" since it is a rhetorical flourish irrelevant to the discussion). Indeed, the molecular developmental genetics of *Drosophila* has already begun to emphasize the causal role of proteins deposited by the mother in the cytoplasm of the ovum: to say that the *Bicoid* protein is "for" head–tail polarity is to note that variations in the forms or concentrations of that protein will lead zygotes with standard complements of genes, given environments standard in other respects, to develop variation with respect to the anterior and posterior structures. Moreover, we can speak of some environments as "stunting" the growth of plants of particular taxa, meaning that plants with standard complements of genes, grown in those environments, will be shorter than those grown in different environments. Far from being a *reductio* of the interactionist view, this point simply testifies to the democracy principle introduced above. Interactionists want to allow for various ways of analyzing the complex processes of development, *one* among which is the identification of norms of reaction for

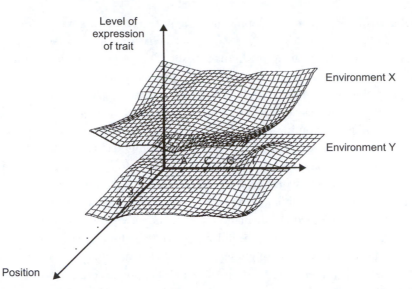

Figure 13.3 Graphical representation of a different style of causal analysis. In the plane of the two horizontal axes, we code genotypes at the locus of interest by specifying the nucleotide at each position. For a fixed environment, the variation of the level of expression of the trait, as the genotype varies, is represented by a surface in the space. (This can be thought of as a dual to the notion of norm of reaction.) For the example shown, the level of the trait for environment X is always greater than the level for environment Y.

genotypes, or the discovery of genes "for" traits. (See Figure 13.3.)

There is a standard temptation to think that all scientific disputes can be readily resolved into differences of principle. Finding that people who advance genetic determinist claims assent to interactionism, critics of genetic determinism want to find some substantive thesis that separates the two camps, and this accounts, I believe, for the repudiation of interactionism. At bottom, however, this dispute, like other significant debates in contemporary biology, is not quite like this. Instead of thinking of two groups of biologists who differ on general principles, we should view biological practice as supplying a toolkit that different people draw from in different ways. Faced with the complexities of ontogeny, biologists have some techniques of causal analysis—of the many forms sanctioned by the democracy principle. For reasons that will be probed shortly, the model of causal analysis that looks at the effects of a single genotype across varying environments is attractive when people are trying to fathom the causes of human behavior, but working out rigorous conclusions about the pertinent norms of reaction proves very difficult, and it is easy to leap to conclusions. Many of Lewontin's most pointed critiques expose the ease with which scholars have leaped to conclusions.

One moral we might draw is that we have a defective instrument, but that, I have been urging, is incorrect. There is nothing the matter with the type of model that has been applied. Rather, the trouble lies in the difficulty of the task and the tendency for the impetuous to bungle. Of course, we might do better if we had different tools—so maybe, after all, there is a case for moving beyond interactionism (not now dismissed as false or incoherent doctrine, but as a source of models too primitive for the important tasks of fathoming human ontogeny) toward "dialectical biology" or "developmental systems theory."

A different set of models for analyzing human development would be welcome, especially if they could be used to achieve insights into the causes of complex capacities and disabilities. Unfortunately, neither Lewontin's "dialectical biology" nor the "developmental systems theory" pioneered by Oyama offer anything that aspiring researchers can put to work. If we want to understand why people become addicted or resist addiction, have the sexual orientations they do, give way to violence or live peacefully (and I will consider, shortly, why we might want insight into these issues), then both versions of the transinteractionist approach to nature and nurture leave us helpless. In effect, they are primarily critiques of the past misuses of old tools and at best blueprints for new tools that we might develop. When problems of analyzing human behavior seem socially urgent, and when investigators believe that new advances in molecular genetics have given new scope to the old models, pleas for "dialectical biology" or "developmental systems theory" are likely to fall on deaf ears.

There is a profound irony here. Nobody has been more sensitive than Lewontin to the social pressures that shape biological research—especially in attempts to evaluate the contributions of nature and nurture. Oyama, too, clearly recognizes these pressures. Unless there are cogent reasons for thinking that past methods of analysis are fundamentally flawed (and I have argued that there are not) rather than simply misapplied in the episodes that Lewontin and Oyama view (rightly) as politically mischievous, then the social pressures to find answers will make fledgling ventures in transinteractionism seem vague and underdeveloped rivals to well-articulated techniques that promise resolution of important questions. Furthermore, the critics of conclusions about the important effects of genotype on phenotype will be seen as taking refuge in nebulous

appeals for a new general view of the causation of behavior and as driven to this predicament solely by their sense of outrage at the determinist claims.

Contemporary human genetics, including human behavior genetics, is full of promises largely because of the possibilities of using sequencing techniques to identify shared alleles (combinations of alleles) in different people. Instead of the dubious passages from heritability to conclusions about causation, genetic research can hope to discover norms of reaction more directly by finding large numbers of individuals who share a genotype and tracking the variation in phenotype across environment. Of course, our pervasive ignorance of the causally relevant features of the extraorganismic environment, to which I alluded earlier, should lead us to be tentative in evaluating the results, for we may well be overlooking some crucial environmental variable. Yet this is precisely the point on which the critique of genetic determinism should focus, and it would be unfortunate, perhaps even tragic, if we were to overlook it because the only way of opposing determinist theses was seen as the acceptance of some underdeveloped transinter actionist biology.

The confident behavior geneticist believes that new molecular techniques will enhance our understanding of socially important facets of human behavior. Sometimes the motivation for applying those techniques is impeccable. Researchers into addiction or alcoholism want to understand the causal pathways so that they can prevent human misery: in these areas, many investigations are continuous with attempts to fathom mechanisms behind diseases. They begin with genetic causes not because they are convinced that these are the most important (that the norms of reaction for certain "addictive" genotypes are virtually flat) but because they want to unravel the neurochemistry, and they see the investigation of genotypes as a thread that will lead them into the tangle. For they know how to sequence DNA, and, by finding allelic sequences that correlate with addiction, they may be able to see how abnormal proteins make a difference to certain reactions in the brain and thus understand the molecular details of the interactions between organism and environment that go differently in addicts and in others. There is no question of "privileging" the genes in this kind of inquiry but rather a pragmatic criterion for using a particular type of model and a readily comprehensible, even admirable, medical motivation.

At its best, research in behavior genetics is driven by a morally defensible motivation (that of alleviating human suffering). The investigator tries to understand the plight of the unfortunate by beginning with particular alleles and tracing how the associated phenotypes vary across environments because this is a readily applicable strategy. Yet the goal is to move from singling out certain loci as playing a causal role to identifying differences in the chemical reactions that occur in the formation of healthy and unhealthy phenotypes and from there to discovering what kinds of contributions the environment makes. For, at the end of the day, the goal is to bring relief by adjusting the input from the environment.

However, the reasons for entering on a program of genetic research are not always so easily defensible. Consider the much-disputed example of the genetics of violent behavior. There are good reasons to suspect that the environmental factors causally relevant to eruptions of violence are complex and varied, that there are fine-grained differences in environments that can have large effects, and that, in consequence, our attempts to construct the norms of reaction for "violence" genotypes will be highly fallible. Further, unless we are profoundly deceived, there are some readily identifiable features of the physical and social environment that have major impact: rates of crime are much higher in decaying inner cities, but I doubt that there is a "violence" allele that has the pleiotropic effect of sending its bearers into grim urban environments. Thus, there is an obvious form of causal analysis that could harness the techniques of molecular genetics and that would be sanctioned by the democracy principle enunciated above. Perhaps students of the causes of violent behavior should show how immersion in hostile environments generates greater levels of violence when genotypes vary, compared with sequestration in the leafy suburbs (see Figure 13.4). These students could expect to

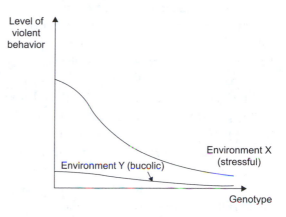

Figure 13.4 Representation of a pronounced environmental effect on tendencies to violence. The two axes for representing genotypes of Figure 13.3 have been condensed into one (surely more plausible than representing environmental variation on a single axis!), and the graphs show the variation in levels of violence for fixed environments as the genotype varies. The representation is purely hypothetical, but it is worth noting that the pronounced role of the environment is compatible with discoveries of "violence alleles"; individuals with genotypes near the origin who encounter stressful environments show much greater levels of violence than others—even those who share similar environments. This does not detract from the obvious fact that there is a very marked effect of environment.

show something important about the causes of violence and to support their conclusions with greater rigor than the hunters of "violence alleles." Yet, there has not been any notable impetus to do the work.

And, of course, we know why. In a society that consistently and callously turns its back on programs that might aid the unfortunate and that sees taxation as a form of robbery rather than a necessary means to social cooperation, the investigation I have outlined has no obvious point. (It might, after all, lead to campaigns for expensive new social programs.) Better, then, to take a different tack, to find out who the people are who are likely to become violent and do something about them in advance. Thus, a politically palatable solution would be to discover genotypes whose norms of reaction show a high propensity for violent behavior virtually invariant across environment. Perhaps there are a few such rare genotypes (the possibility should not be excluded), but the overwhelming likelihood is that we will mistakenly come to believe that they are far more frequent than they are (because of our massive ignorance about how to partition environments) and that these conclusions will reinforce the prevailing sense that social solutions are hopeless.

In fact, the motivations for the study are doubly illicit because they are blind both to the serious dangers of reaching erroneous conclusions and, when articulated, the practical policies are morally disreputable. What precisely is the "something" that is to be done to those who bear the "violent" genotypes? Are they to be branded as criminals, labeled from childhood up, even before they have done anything? Should they be forcibly restrained or treated with tranquilizing chemicals? It is precisely because the motivations for the investigation of the genetics of criminality are economic—after all, we could spend money and invest in jobs for inner city youths, clean up their environments, and make hope possible—that we know in advance that the solution has to be cheap. Hence, we cannot

anticipate that great moral niceties (always expensive) are likely to bulk large in the application of "discoveries" about "violence genotypes." Add the difficulty of discovering such genotypes (or, at least, common genotypes), and the potential for injustice is obvious.

Thus, there are two major questions that we ought to ask about proposals to unearth genes "for" complex human traits (including dispositions to forms of behavior that prove either personally or socially disruptive). First, is the investigation informed by the interactionist's commitment to explore the impact of some factors, while others vary, in a way that recognizes our ignorance about environmental causes and that pragmatically deploys the genetic techniques to remedy that ignorance? Second, does the information to be acquired lead to a social policy that is both applicable and morally defensible? As my pair of examples indicates, the answers will be quite different in different instances, and there is no shortcut for considering cases individually.

Some scientists bridle at the thought that my second question should ever figure in the evaluation of a program of scientific research, insisting that the business of science is to uncover the truth, however unpalatable, and that inquiry cannot be subordinated to moral critique. Lewontin has often been criticized for introducing extraneous "political" considerations into discussions of biological investigations, but, in my judgment, his recognition of the wider framework in which science is done is profoundly correct. Researchers cannot hide from themselves the fact that their findings will be applied, often by people who do not grasp the nuances of their positions, nor can they take refuge in the division of labor proposed by Tom Lehrer's brilliant song:

"When the rockets go up, who cares where they come down?
That's not my department," says Werner von Braun.

Many workers in contemporary human genetics, including the genetics of behavioral traits, are convinced that their inquiries will promote human well-being, although critical discussion of the ways in which genetical information can affect people's lives may sometimes undermine their confidence. Unless we have a scientifically informed and ethically sophisticated public discourse about possible programs of genetic research, we are likely either to lose important benefits or, more likely, by accepting the most extravagant promises at face value, mix in significant social harms with the improvements we seek.

Because he sees the latter possibility so clearly, Lewontin has come to advocate a "dialectical biology" that will move beyond interactionism. I have tried to argue that the critiques of interactionism are flawed, that they do not respond to the genuine problems of using biology to promote human good, and that there is no substitute for a detailed examination of the merits of individual cases. It is appropriate to close by noting that, in carrying out the much-needed piecemeal critique, there is no better paradigm than the writings of Richard Lewontin.

Notes

1 It's an honor and a pleasure to dedicate this chapter to Dick Lewontin who has inspired so many people in so many ways.

2 Oyama 1985, pp. 26–7.
3 For prominent examples, see Lewontin 1974, reprinted as Chapter 4 of Levins and Lewontin 1985; Lewontin, Rose and Kamin 1984, especially Chapters 5 and 9; and Lewontin 1991.
4 See Levins and Lewontin 1985, Chapter 3 and conclusion; Lewontin, Rose and Kamin 1984, Chapter 10; and Lewontin 1991, especially pp. 3–37.
5 Levins and Lewontin 1984, p. 114.
6 Lewontin, Rose and Kamin 1984, pp. 245–51.
7 Lewontin 1991, pp. 109–110.
8 Lewontin 1991, p. 26.
9 Lewontin 1991, p. 27.
10 Sterelny and Kitcher 1998, p. 348.
11 Sterelny and Kitcher 1998, p. 350.

References

Griffiths, P. E. and Gray, R. D. (1994) Developmental systems and evolutionary explanation. *Journal of Philosophy*, 91:277–304.

Levins, R. and Lewontin, R. C. (1985) *The Dialectical Biologist*. Cambridge, MA: Harvard University Press.

Lewontin, R. C. (1991) *Biology as Ideology*. New York: Harper.

Lewontin, R. C., Rose, S. E. and Kamin, L. (1984) *Not in Our Genes*. New York: Pantheon.

Oyama, S. (1985) *The Ontogeny of Information*. Cambridge, UK: Cambridge University Press.

Sterelny, K., and Kitcher, P. S. (1988). The return of the gene, *Journal of Philosophy* 85: 339–361.

PART II

Human Nature and Human Diversity

Topic 5 HUMAN UNIVERSALS, INDIVIDUAL VARIATION, AND CULTURAL VARIATION

THE BODIES, MINDS, AND BEHAVIORS of human beings vary tremendously. People tend to speak different languages in different countries, French in France, Russian in Russia, Portuguese in Brazil, etc. They eat differently in different places: dogs in Korea, snails in France, ant eggs (known as "ant caviar") and fried worms in tacos in some parts of Mexico, beaver in Latvia, etc. Religious and moral beliefs as well as values also vary across cultures. Naturally, variation does not only cluster along cultural lines. For instance, people vary across social classes: both in Brazil and in the USA, poorer, less educated people find it morally wrong to have sex with a dead chicken, while wealthier, more educated people find it just disgusting, but not morally wrong. Males and females also differ in various respects. And there is a tremendous amount of individual variation, a fact well documented by decades of personality psychology. Some people are more open to experience, less introvert, etc., than others. Add genetic variation to this phenotypic variation: There is a large amount of genetic variation across individuals, part of which is clustered along various population lines, part of which is found within each population.

This genotypic and phenotypic variation may seem to be in tension with the notion of a human nature. If humans really share a nature, why are they so different from one another? Donald Brown's well-known work on human universals challenges the apparent human diversity by looking for shared human habits, practices, and customs. For instance, he proposes incest taboos as a human universal, shared by all cultures across the globe. His aim is to establish a collection of such universals because on his view these universals are a window on human nature. John Tooby and Leda Cosmides's well-known essay also attempts to find shared traits among all of the apparent variation. Acknowledging the existence of large phenotypic and genetic differences, Tooby and Cosmides show that these are compatible with the existence of a human nature. They provide an influential but controversial argument for the claim that complex psychological adaptations have to be universal: If they were not, sexual recombination would disrupt the set of genes involved in the development of these complex adaptations. They also argue for the compatibility of genetic variation and human nature, holding that the part of the genome in which variation is found does not code for complex psychological adaptations; instead, these alleles code for proteins and have been selected to vary. (There are, naturally, other hypotheses about the nature of this genetic variation: Particularly, much of it could be neutral.) Finally, they propose a typology of the types of phenotypic variation.

The next essay in this section presents a mass of data on human variation that highlights the diversity of human psychology and should perhaps worry both Brown, and Cosmides and Tooby. Their data on variation in what have long been taken to be universal, hard-wired parts of our psychological make-up may prove a challenge to those holding out for human universals.

The next two essays in this section focus on the importance of culture in humans. Richerson and Boyd's essay, the first chapter of their book *Not by Genes Alone*, makes a compelling case that humans are a cultural species. It is part of human nature that we humans acquire much of our phenotype from people around us. They argue that evolutionary approaches to humans that neglect this fact are bound to fail to predict and explain part of human behavior and psychology.

Dan Fessler and Edouard Machery agree with Peter Richerson and Robert Boyd's main thesis—humans are a cultural species—and they focus on the consequences of this thesis for studying human mind and behavior. According to them, the most important consequence of Richerson and Boyd's thesis is that human nature includes various dispositions or mechanisms for extracting information from the social environment in which people live and grow up. Treating humans as a non-cultural species would lead us to overlook these fundamental characteristics of human nature.

Finally, Kim Sterelny presents a new approach to wedding our understanding of our widely varied human culture and the evolution of our uniquely human traits. Sterelny introduces his "evolved apprentice" view of human evolution, which emphasizes the feedback loops between humans and our constructed environments, for example our languages and all that comes with them.

Suggested Further Reading

Cavalli-Sforza, L. L., Menozzi, P. and Piazza, A. (1994) *The History and Geography of Human Genes*. Princeton, NJ: Princeton University Press.

Frazer, K. A., Murray, S. S., Schork, N. J. and Topol, E. J. (2009) Human genetic variation and its contribution to complex traits. *Nature Reviews Genetics*, 10: 241–251.

Haidt, J., Koller, S. and Dias, M. (1993) Affect, culture, and morality, or is it wrong to eat your dog? *Journal of Personality and Social Psychology*, 65: 613–628.

Hawks, J., Wang, E. T., Cochran, G. M., Harpending, H. C. and Moyzis, R. K. (2007) Recent acceleration of human adaptive evolution. *Proceedings of the National Academy of Sciences*, 104: 20753–20758.

Henrich, J. and McElreath, R. (2003) The evolution of cultural evolution. *Evolutionary Anthropology*, 12: 123–135.

Kitayama, S. and Cohen, D. (Eds.) (2007) *Handbook of Cultural Psychology*. New York: Guilford.

Levinson, S. C. (2003) *Space in Language and Cognition: Explorations in cognitive diversity*. Cambridge: Cambridge University Press.

Nisbett, R. E. (2003) *The Geography of Thought*. New York: Free Press.

Richerson, P. and Boyd, R. (2005) *Not by Genes Alone: How culture transformed human evolution*. Chicago, IL: The University of Chicago Press.

Sperber, D. (1996) *Explaining Culture: A naturalistic approach*. Cambridge, MA: Blackwell.

Sperber, D. and Hirschfeld, L. A. (2004) The cognitive foundations of cultural stability and diversity. *Trends in Cognitive Sciences,* 8: 40–46.

Tomasello, M., Kruger, A. C. and Ratner, H. H. (1993) Cultural learning. *Behavioral and Brain Sciences,* 16: 495–552.

Wilson, D. S. (1994) Adaptive genetic variation and human evolutionary psychology. *Ethology and Sociobiology,* 15: 219–235.

Chapter 14

Donald E. Brown

INCEST AVOIDANCE AND OTHER HUMAN UNIVERSALS

The apparent universality, or near-universality, of the incest taboo perennially fascinates anthropologists and has given rise to numerous speculations about its origin and function. The principal point of agreement is probably that incest is in some way harmful, so that avoiding it confers some benefit. What the harm, what the benefit, and how the taboo or avoidance comes about are points of contention.

Progress in understanding the whole issue has been retarded by several false starts and misconceptions (summarized in Fox 1980, Arens 1986). For example, there has been a tendency to conflate marriage rules with sexual regulations. While these concerns may impinge on one another—and might very well be equated in the folk categories of a given people[1]—there is no necessary connection between them: incest fundamentally concerns sex, only coincidentally may it concern marriage.

There was also an assumption that animals— unlike humans—do mate incestuously, so that the human prohibition of incest was a distinctively cultural marker of humanity's separation from the animal world. It is now known that incest is rare among animals in the wild (domestic animals, whose breeding patterns have been altered by human interference, are another matter). Between human incest avoidance and the patterns of behavior among other animals there may thus be a continuity that was previously denied.

As a corollary of the assumption that the incest taboo was a distinctively cultural invention—that would leave no obvious material remains in the archeological record—the actual origins of the taboo, being lost in antiquity, were not subject to empirical research. Indeed, most discussion of the incest taboo was little more than a sideline to other issues.

Another assumption now known to be wrong was that the incest taboo was universal. In a number of societies royalty were enjoined to commit incest (or, at any rate, to marry very close kin).[2] And in some societies there are no obvious incest taboos in the sense of rules (and sanctioned rules especially) against it, only a notion that no one would commit incest anyway.

Finally, the various relationships in which incest might occur—e.g., between brother and sister, or between father and daughter—tended to be all run together.

Here we focus on brother-sister incest, and a recent line of research conducted primarily by anthropologists to test an idea formulated in the last century—but long ignored—that it is human nature for brothers and sisters to avoid incest. This line of research moved an old anthropological subject out of the realm of speculation into the realm of concrete and comparative studies.

One of the leading controversies has turned fundamentally around an issue of human psychology: is incest tabooed because we naturally tend to commit it but shouldn't, or is it tabooed, somewhat paradoxically, because most humans don't want to do it? The former position was championed by Freud and others, who could see no reason why a taboo should exist for something we didn't want to do anyway. The later position was expounded late in the nineteenth century by a Finnish anthropologist, Edward Westermarck, who argued that there is "a remarkable lack of erotic feeling between persons who have been living closely together from childhood" (1922:192). Such persons, he noted, would typically be relatives. Incest avoidance, thus, was a natural tendency that resulted from childhood association. Westermarck's reply to the objection Freud raised was that incest was tabooed for the same reason bestiality and parricide are tabooed: not because we have a general tendency to commit them but because some individuals go awry in ways that shock general sentiments. The rules are for them.

Unlike most (if not all other) anthropologists, Westermarck was centrally concerned with the incest taboo and its implications, and he wrote voluminously on the matter over decades. He took a straightforward Darwinian view, that inbreeding was directly harmful. The avoidance that resulted from childhood association was an evolved human instinct. In spite of the extraordinary effort Westermarck put into understanding the incest taboo, his views were largely eclipsed by anthropology's opposition to biological reductionism in the period through World War II, because they "violat[ed] . . . every canon" of anthropology (Murdock 1932:209). But in the 1950s J. R. [Robin] Fox (1962) realized that social experiments conducted in Israel provided remarkable evidence bearing on the matter of incest avoidance between siblings. The ensuing revival of Westermarck's ideas led to most of the studies summarized below.

In Israeli kibbutzim, communal villages first founded early in this century, there was a deliberate attempt to break down the nuclear family. Boys and girls who were close in age to one another were raised together in peer groups (kvutza) of six to eight children; they shared common living quarters from a time shortly after they were born through adolescence. Under the tutelage of nurses and teachers rather than parents, the children shared an intimate association and underwent a socialization and education common to all. As small children they showed a typical sexual interest in each other, but as they matured this disappeared. Although they were free to marry one another, provided they were not in fact siblings, Spiro (1958) found not a single case of this happening nor even of sexual intercourse between children who had been raised together from childhood in the same peer group.

Fox (1962) saw that the kibbutz data supported Westermarck, but he thought that Freud was at least partly right too. In Fox's reformulation, the close and literally physical intimacy of children who are socialized together renders them sexually uninterested in each other after puberty. Among Freud's patients, however, most siblings were not raised with the physical intimacy that was common in the kibbutz, and so they grew up harboring sexual desires for each other.

According to Fox, societies that are kibbutz-like in their child-rearing patterns are likely to be relatively indifferent to incest; they disapprove but generally do not stringently punish it, and do not need to, because for most of the members it has no great interest. Societies with child-rearing patterns more similar to those of Freud's patients are more likely to have the taboo, and it is more likely to be stringent, because their members need the taboo to overcome real desires to commit incest. Fox's summary of the pattern is that "the intensity of heterosexual attraction between cosocialized children after puberty is inversely proportionate to the intensity of heterosexual activity between them before puberty" (1962:147). As illustrations, he shows that the Tallensi of Ghana, the Pondo of Southeast Africa, the Mountain Arapesh of New Guinea, the Tikopia, and a Chinese situation described below fit the *kibbutz* pattern, while the Chiracahua Apache and the Trobriand Islanders fit the pattern described by Freud.

A study based on three further Israeli communes indicated that the Westermarck effect, as Fox called it, was not confined to the commune Spiro had studied (Talmon 1964). Whether on the basis of Israeli or other data, most studies of incest avoidance from the mid-1960s onward have focused specifically on Westermarck's position, and Fox's defense of a modified Freudian position has received little attention.

A Chinese practice, described by Arthur Wolf (1966, 1968, 1970) and Wolf and Huang (1980), provided yet another natural experiment that supports Westermarck. In many areas of China there were until recently two forms of marriage, called "major" and "minor." In the minor form a young girl was adopted into the family of her future husband. The motivation for this kind of marriage came of course from parents. In Wolf's analysis, the strain between daughters-in-law and mothers-in-law was so serious among Chinese that it made viable the strategy of bringing the future daughter-in-law in as a very young child so that long before she became a bride she could adjust, and more readily subordinate herself, to her mother-in-law. The future husband and wife were unrelated—so there was no breaking of the incest taboo. But the boy and his future bride were raised under the conditions typical of brothers and sisters—in the intimacy of the family.

Wolf found, contrary to Freud and others who argue that familial intimacy is the breeding ground of sexual interests that must be thwarted by the incest taboo, and in support of Westermarck, that minor marriages were about 30 percent less fertile and were unhappier. Men in such marriages resorted to prostitutes, took mistresses, or sought extramarital affairs more frequently; their wives engaged in extramarital affairs more frequently; and such marriages more frequently resulted in separation or divorce. These objective indices buttressed Chinese statements to the effect that husband and wife in minor marriages found each other less romantically or erotically attractive. When various economic developments eroded parental ability to enforce minor-marriage arrangements, the couples who were to marry in this manner made other arrangements, spontaneously avoiding the minor marriages.

Wolf also drew attention to a study of sibling incest in Chicago (Weinberg 1963). It found that the only offenders who had contemplated marriage with each other were those who had been raised apart.

Wolf's conclusions have been criticized, generally by offering alternative interpretations of the same data. For example, it has been suggested that because the minor marriage is less prestigious, the bride in such a marriage will be treated poorly and hence make a poor wife, or the couple in such a marriage will be chagrined by the stigma of it and thus make a poor marriage. But Wolf and Huang (1980:173–175) point out that regular (major-marriage) brides are more mistreated when they move into their in-laws' household, and they show that couples brought together in a marriage that is clearly less prestigious than minor marriage—one in which the groom goes to live with the bride's family—have more fertile and more stable marriages than the minor marriages (1980:169, 185). Interestingly, Wolf and Huang (1980:285) report that their Chinese informants seemed unaware of the lesser fertility of minor marriages.

Further support for the Westermarck hypothesis comes from the Near East. Students of Arab societies have long been aware of a preference often found among those peoples for a man to marry his father's brother's daughter who, given the patrilineal nature of their kinship system, is a rather close relative by any sense of the term. Marriages that conform to this ideal are not in fact very common, though more common than in other parts of the world. Since brothers typically live in close social and spatial contact with each other in Arab societies, it follows that their children are likely to be close too and, hence, that the preference for them to marry appears to run counter to the Westermarck hypothesis. However, Justine McCabe (1983), who studied an Arab village in Lebanon, found that the evidence supports Westermarck.

In the village McCabe studied, "first cousins grew up in an association as close as that of siblings" (1983:58). She found that the relationship between a boy and his father's brother's daughter was essentially the same as between a boy and his sister: it rested on a constant and intimate interaction from birth (including sexual exploration when very young), and was characterized by "informality, candor, teasing, tattling, quarreling, laughing, joking" and the exchange of confidences (1983:59).

But marriages between patrilateral parallel cousins produced 23 percent fewer children during the first 25 years of marriage and were four times more likely to end in divorce than all other marriages. McCabe (1983:61) cites others scholars who, from early in this century, had noted signs of greater "sexual apathy" or "coolness" in patrilateral cousin marriages. As in the Chinese case, McCabe argues, it is parents or others, not the ones who actually marry, who prefer patrilateral parallel cousin marriages.

If the Westermarck effect is real, an important issue is the age limits within which it is created. Wolf and Huang (1980:185) offered some insight into the matter by noting that minor marriages in which the children were brought together before age 4 were two times more likely to end in divorce than minor marriages in which the children became acquainted at age 8 or later. Joseph Shepher (1983) has looked at the matter more closely. Born and raised in an Israeli commune himself, Shepher conducted the most thorough study of marriage in Israeli communes, getting data on 2769 married couples in 211 *kibbutzim*. Among them he found only 20 marriages between members of the same commune and only 14 that allegedly took place between persons who had been in the same peer group. But on contacting these 14 couples he found that all cases dissolved: there was not a single case of marriage between a boy and girl who had spent the first 6 years of their lives in the same peer group. In the one commune (his own) in which he could get reliable date on premarital sex he also found that none had occurred between persons raised from infancy in the same peer group. Boys and girls brought into the group at later ages sometimes did have an intense attraction to one of their group mates.

There was no attempt in the communes to stop the sexual experimentation of young children. There was no attempt to keep adolescents and young adults from dating or marrying their commune mates, though they were supposed to refrain from sex in general during high school. There was in fact some encouragement of intracommunal marriage.

Examining the pattern of entry and exist from peer groups, and the resulting pattern of attraction or sexual interest or uninterest among the relevant parties, Shepher concludes that a form of imprinting (or negative imprinting) occurred, that it was complete by the age of 6, and that it took about 4 years. He argues that this imprinting is a phylogenetic adaptation to reduce the harmful effects of inbreeding.

Certain lines of research conducted largely outside of anthropology also have a close bearing on the Westermarck hypothesis. They include studies of the physical or medical consequences of inbreeding among humans (as well as other animals), studies of evolved inbreeding avoidance mechanisms in nonhuman species, and studies of the social consequences of human incest.

Reviewing the scanty literature on the empirical consequences of inbreeding among humans, Shepher (1983) finds that full-sibling or parent-child incest results in about 17 percent child mortality and 25 percent child disability, for a combined result of about 42 percent nonviable offspring. The negative consequences decline rapidly for more distant inbreeding. If the figures Shepher cites are even approximately correct, mechanisms to avoid the costs of incest between close kin are quite expectable.

A third line of research, conducted mostly by psychologists and sociologists, and mostly in recent decades, concerns actual cases of human incest—a topic curiously neglected during most of the period in which the incest taboo has exercised the anthropological imagination. One of the most important consequences of these studies is their dismissal of the sociological or functionalist explanation of the incest taboo. In a line of thought that Arens (1986:29) traces back as far as Jeremy Bentham—but in more recent times through many distinguished anthropologists—it has often been argued that incestuous relations would confound the organization of the family, rendering it inefficient and thereby rendering society inefficient. As persuasive as this line of reasoning has been—in the absence of empirical tests—it now appears to be incorrect.

Bagley (1969: summarized in Arens 1986) analyzed 425 published cases of incest, finding 93 instances in which incest was the means that allowed the family to *maintain* its functional integrity. Typically, a father-daughter relationship replaced the father-mother relationship when the mother was either unable or unwilling to fulfill her role. Bagley (1969) describes this as "functional incest." Whatever the psychological costs may be to individuals, the study of actual cases of incest gives no obvious support to the assumption that society, or even the family, is necessarily threatened by incest (Arens 1986; see also Willner 1983 and La Fontaine 1988).

A recent study (Parker and Parker 1986) of incestuous relationships has a more direct bearing on the Westermarck hypothesis. Although the actual frequencies of the various forms of nuclear family incest—brother-sister, mother-son, and father-daughter—is a matter of

uncertainty, there is substantial agreement that father-daughter incest is much commoner than mother-son incest. Furthermore, the variant of stepfather-stepdaughter incest seems to be disproportionately common. There are a number of explanations for this, not all of them mutually exclusive. One of them has to do with imprinting: if some form of imprinting results in the inhibition of incestuous desires, on the average it would, as noted earlier, probably work best between mother and son, not so well between father and daughter, and even less well between stepfather and stepdaughter.

Parker and Parker (1986) tested this line of thought by comparing sexually abusive and nonabusive fathers with comparable backgrounds. Comparing fathers who had been present in the household during the first three years of their daughters' lives, the Parkers found that abusers had been "much less frequently involved in caring and nurturing activities" (1986:540). They also found that in general stepfathers or adoptive fathers were more likely to be abusive, apparently because such fathers were less likely to have an effective bonding (imprinting) experience. When biological fathers were compared to step- or adoptive fathers with similar degrees of early childhood contacts with their daughters, no significant differences in abuse were found (1986:541). These findings support the Westermarck hyphothesis and extend it beyond the brother-sister relationship that has been the principal focus of recent anthropological studies.

But in spite of the mounting evidence that supports the Westermarck hypothesis, and fails to support its rivals, such as the functionalist hyphothesis, the dust has not settled on all the issues involved. Ancient Egyptian materials, for example, pose a problem precisely where the evidence for the Westermarck effect seems strongest: inhibition of brother-sister incest. Keith Hopkins (1980) provides evidence that brother-sister marriages were actually common for a period in Egypt and, hence, that incest avoidance in general, not merely the taboo, may not in fact be universal.

About 44 years after Alexander the Great conquered Egypt in 332 B.C., a Greek king of Egypt divorced his wife and married his full sister (who was about 10 years older than he). While there may have been some Greek precedent for his action—half-sibling marriages were alleged to be possible in certain ancient Greek communities—he was also following an ancient Egyptian custom. Whatever the case, 7 of the next 11 Greek kings in Egypt married their sisters. There is some vague evidence that the custom was penetrating other parts of the populace. Egypt subsequently passed to Roman rule.

Beginning in A.D. 19–20 and lasting until 257–258, the Roman administrators of Egypt conducted periodic censuses of the Egyptian population. Some 270 actual household returns survives; 172 returns, listing 880 persons, are in good enough condition to be used. While not in any sense a random sample, they report households widely spread in time, space, and social class. Seventeen of the 113 marriages ongoing at the time of the censuses were definitely between brother and sister, another 6 may have been. Thus some 15 to 21 percent of the ongoing marriages reported in these returns were brother-sister marriages. Eleven or 12 marriages were between full siblings, 8 between half siblings; in 3 the kind of sibling relationship is uncertain. Given the probable demographic structure of the family under the conditions of the time, there was only about a 40 percent likelihood of any family having a brother and sister of marriageable age. Thus a third or more of those who could marry their sisters did so. This is a very high proportion and, if correct, it provides the only known case in which brother-sister marriages were common throughout a populace.

Other forms of documentation—such as wedding invitations, letters, and marriage contracts—routinely mention brother-sister marriage, which indicates not only that it occurred but that it was considered normal. Some letters indicate real affection between the sibling couples, although this line of evidence is weakened by the Egyptian use of the term "sister" as a euphemism or term of endearment for women who were not actually one's sister (Arens 1986:111–112).

The marriages were fertile, and no source indicates an awareness of harmful genetic consequences. But Hopkins does not indicate *how* fertile they were, and perhaps it should be asked whether the high rates of infant mortality in preindustrial societies might not tend to mask any mortality brought about by inbreeding (recall also that the Chinese seemed unaware of the lesser fertility of their minor marriages).

Hopkins is unable to find any reason peculiar to the Egyptian condition that may have induced parents to foist this kind of marriage on their children (though the late average age of first marriages—in their mid-twenties—does suggest parental involvement). Hopkins cites marriage contracts between brothers and sisters that specify dowry and/or separate property and hence suggest that sibling marriage was not a device to avoid marriage expenses or the division of family property.

Addressing the problem of how else to explain brother-sister marriage, Hopkins presents what can only be called a classically cultural explanation. He draws attention to the importance in Egyptian religion of Isis and Osiris, who were brother and sister, husband and wife; a romantic tradition of idealizing brother-sister love in story and poetry; and the evidence that the status of women was high and that they therefore exercised some autonomy in marriage and divorce. That love was a basis for marriage, and its cessation a basis for divorce, is well attested. Hence, Hopkins is left with the possibility that brothers and sisters married because they wanted to.

In A.D. 212–213 the Egyptians were made Roman citizens, for whom marriage with near-kin was prohibited. Sibling marriage disappeared.

Given the spottiness of the Egyptian data it is difficult to decide how much credence to give them. But a few points should be noted. Hopkins gives the ages of five sibling couples; they were separated in age by 7, 8, 4, 8, and 20 years. With one exception, then, these are not necessarily couples who were raised together as children or, at any rate, who were raised together in the manner that produces the Westermarck effect. It would be of interest to know more about child-rearing practices among Roman Egyptians.

Shepher's (1983) response to the Egyptian case was to dismiss it on the grounds that the data were few and that a single exception can carry little weight (he thereby reversed, by the way, the de facto opinion of many anthropologists that a single exception is all it takes to dismiss claims of universality). In this context, Shepher argued that unrestricted universals were not very likely to occur anyway—since nature operates by probability—so that a near-universal was the most to be expected.

Spiro (1982) summarizes other criticisms of the Westermarck hypothesis and adds his own. He notes, for example, an alternative interpretation of the *kibbutz* case. Spiro says it is not the child-rearing but rather the adolescent repression of sexuality that produces the strong tendency for boys and girls to go outside their peer group and *kibbutz* to find mates. In adolescence, children were still living together, but their childhood exploration of sexuality was to stop. They were strongly urged to forgo sex until education was complete. In Spiro's view, this adolescent frustration resulted in peer group members' lack of interest in one another—they responded, in effect, to a consciously stated taboo.

To support his argument, Spiro cites Kaffman (1977), a psychiatrist employed by the *kibbutz* movement, who says that liaisons between children raised in the same peer group do in fact now occur. Since infant socialization has not changed, but adolescent controls have been relaxed, it is adolescent conditions that are critical. Unfortunately, Kaffman gives no data. Shepher (1983) dismisses Kaffman's argument and notes that marriages between those who had been adolescent (but not childhood) peers did occur before; hence, adolescent repression of sexuality could not have been the crucial factor. (But note that such marriages weren't at all common. A defect in Shepher's contribution is that by narrowing imprinting to a 4-year period that must occur in the first 6 years of life he has made this a small part of what must be various controls on incest, since even individuals who were not reared in the same peer group but who were resident in the same commune seem to marry rather infrequently. The low rate of intra-*kibbutz* marriage in general must find some of its explanation in some other factors.)

Spiro also draws attention to two further considerations. One is the smallness of the peer groups, which makes finding a mate outside them statistically expectable. The other is that the boys and girls in the peer groups were the same age; since young girls tend to be interested in older boys, and older boys in younger girls, they therefore tend to seek mates outside the peer group.

What lessons, in conclusion, may be derived from the recent efforts to understand the incest taboo/avoidance? One is the sobering reflection that an alleged universal that has exercised the anthropological imagination for over 100 years is still not explained to everyone's satisfaction. It is not even certain that the phenomenon is a universal. The incest taboo clearly is not universal, though it surely is a statistical universal and might be a near-universal. On the other hand, incest avoidance may be universal.

Even more sobering has been the impact of biological considerations that for decades were all but banned from mainstream anthropological thought. The ethological discovery that humans are far from unique in avoiding incest has entirely reoriented the problem. The resuscitation of the Westermarck hypothesis has provided a successfully tested explanation for part of the phenomenon. In eliminating possible hypotheses, and in accumulating relevant data, then, there has been progress. This experience suggests that anthropologists might do well to look into other lines of thought that may have been neglected for no good reason.

Also important to notice in the incest-avoidance example is the clear attempt to explain the phenomenon by clarifying the ultimate (evolutionary) conditions that generate the mechanisms and by specifying the proximate mechanisms that generate the universal—infant (negative) imprinting, resulting in specified psychological states in the individual. Equally important has been the exploitation of natural experiments and the role that quantitative testing or analysis has played.

In the long run it may be that the Westermarck hypothesis will not stand up; certainly it is only a partial explanation that does not preclude other, complementary explanations. But the mode of explaining—involving ethological and evolutionary perspectives, a detailed specification of mechanisms and of individual motivation, a diligent search for natural experiments, and quantitative tests when possible—deserves emulation with other universals.

What do all people, all societies, all cultures, and all languages have in common? In the following pages I attempt to provide answers, in the form of a description of what I will call the Universal People (UP). Theirs is a description of every people or of people in general. Bear in mind the tentative nature of this chapter: as surely as it leaves out some universals it includes some that will prove in the long run not to be universal, and even more surely it divides up traits and complexes in ways that in time will give way to more accurate or meaningful divisions. At the end of the chapter I will discuss how it was put together and the ways in which it will change in the future.

Although humans are not unique in their possession of culture—patterns of doing and thinking that are passed on within and between generations by learning—they certainly are unique in the extent to which their thought and action are shaped by such patterns. The UP are aware of this uniqueness and posit a difference between their way—culture—and the way of nature.

A very significant portion of UP culture is embodied in their language, a system of communication without which their culture would necessarily be very much simpler. With language the UP think about and discuss both their internal states and the world external to each individual (this is not to deny that they also think without language—surely they do). With language, the UP organize, respond to, and manipulate the behavior of their fellows. UP language is of strategic importance for those who wish to study the UP. This is so because their language is, if not precisely a mirror of, then at least a window into, their culture and into their minds and actions. Their language is not a perfect mirror or window, for there are often discrepancies between what the UP say, think, and do. But we would be very hard pressed to understand many aspects of the UP without access to their thinking through their language. Because their language is not a simple reflex of the way the world is, we need to distinguish their (emic) conceptualization of it from objective (etic) conceptualizations of the world.

The UP's language allows them to think and speak in abstractions, and about things or processes not physically present. If one of them is proficient in the use of language—particularly if it is a male—it gains him prestige, in part because good speech allows him to more effectively manipulate, for better or worse, the behavior of his fellows. An important means of verbal manipulation among the UP is gossip.

In their conversations the UP manage in many ways to express more than their mere words indicate. For example, shifts in tone, timing, and other features of speech indicate that one person is or is not ready for another to take a turn at speaking. UP speech is used to misinform as well as inform. Even if an individual among the UP does not tell lies, he understands the concept and watches for it in others. For some UP do lie, and they dissimulate and mislead in other ways too. UP use of language includes ways to be funny and ways to insult.

UP speech is highly symbolic. Let me explain how this is different from animal communication. Many bird species vocalize a danger warning. The vocalization is substantially the same for the species from one location to another. Indeed, it is somewhat similar from one species to another. Humans have cries of fright and warning that are in some ways analogous to these bird calls, but between many, many members of our species our routine vocalizations are meaningless. This is so because speech sounds and the things they signify have very little intrinsic connection. Sound and sense, as a rule, are only arbitrarily associated. Equally arbitrary is the way units of speech that are equivalent to our words get strung together to make sentences. But in spite of this arbitrariness there are features of language at all basic levels—phonemic, grammatical, and semantic—that are found in all languages.

Thus UP phonemes—their basic speech sounds—include a contrast between vocalics (sounds produced in or channeled through the oral cavity) and nonvocalics (e.g., nasals). UP language has contrasts between vowels and contrasts between stops and nonstops (a stop, e.g., English p or b, stops the flow of air during speech). The phonemes of UP speech form a system of contrasts, and the number of their phonemes goes neither above 70 nor below 10.

In time, their language undergoes change. So it follows that the UP do not speak the language of their more remote ancestors, though it may be quite similar.

However much grammar varies from language to language, some things are always present. For example, UP language includes a series of contrasting terms that theoretically could be phrased in three different ways, but that are only phrased two ways. To illustrate, they could talk about the "good" and the "bad" (two contrasting terms, neither with a marker added to express negation); or they could talk about the "good" and the "not good" (i.e., not having the word "bad" at all but expressing its meaning with a marked version of its opposite, the marking in this case to negate), or they could talk about the "bad" and the "not bad" (i.e., not having the word "good," etc.). Logically, these alternatives are identical: each arrangement conveys the same information. Similar possibilities exist for "deep" and "shallow," "wide" and "narrow," etc. But in each case the third possibility never occurs as the obligatory or common way of talking. So the UP are never forced to express, for lack of an alternative, the ideas of "good," "wide," "deep," and so on as negated versions of their opposites.

By virtue of its grammar UP language conveys some information redundantly. In English, for example, both subject and verb indicate number, while in Spanish both noun and adjective indicate gender.

Two final points about UP grammar are that it contains nouns and verbs, and the possessive. The latter is used both for what have been called the "intimate" or "inalienable" possessions, i.e., to talk about their fingers, your hands, and her thoughts, and for "loose" or "alienable" possessions too, e.g., my axe.

The UP have special forms of speech for special occasions. Thus they have poetic or rhetorical standards deemed appropriate to speech in particular settings. They use narrative to explain how things came to be and to tell stories. Their language includes figurative speech: metaphor is particularly prominent, and metonymy (the use of a word for that with which it is associated, e.g., crown for king) is always included too. The UP can speak onomatopoeically (using words that imitate sound, like "bowwow"), and from time to time they do. They have poetry in which lines, demarcated by pauses, are about 3 seconds in duration. The poetic lines are characterized by the repetition of some structural, semantic, or auditory elements but by free variation too.

Most of the specific elementary units of meaning in UP language—units that are sometimes but not always equivalent to words—are not found in all the rest of the languages of the world. This does not prevent us from translating much of the UP speech into our own or any other particular language: centimeters and inches are not the same entities, but we can translate one to another quite precisely; people who lack a word for "chin" and thus call it the "end of the jaw" still make sense.

A few words or meanings cut across all cultural boundaries and hence form a part of UP language. I am not saying, of course, that the UP make the same speech sounds as we English speakers do for these words, but rather that the meanings for these terms are expressed by the UP in their terms. For example, the UP have terms for black and white (equivalent to dark and light when no other basic colors are encoded) and for face, hand, and so on.

Certain semantic components are found in UP language, even if the terms in which they are employed are not. For example, UP kin terminology includes terms that distinguish male from female (and thus indicate the semantic component of sex) and some generations from others. If not explicit, durational time is semantically implicit in their language, and they have units of time—such as days, months, seasons, and years. In various ways there is a temporal cyclicity or rhythmicity to UP lives. The UP can distinguish past, present, and future.

UP language also classifies parts of the body, inner states (such as emotions, sensations, or thoughts), behavioral propensities, flora, fauna, weather conditions, tools, space (by which they give directions), and many other definite topics, though each of them does not necessarily constitute an emically distinct lexical domain. The UP language refers to such semantic categories as motion, speed, location, dimension, and other physical properties; to giving (including analogous actions, such as lending); and to affecting things or people.

As is implied in their use of metaphor and metonymy, UP words (or word equivalents) are sometimes polysemous, having more than one meaning. Their antonyms and synonyms are numerous. The words or word equivalents that the UP use more frequently are generally shorter, while those they use less frequently are longer.

UP language contains both proper names and pronouns. The latter include at least three persons and two categories of number. Their language contains numerals, though they may be as few as "one, two, and many."

The UP have separate terms for kin categories that include mother and father. That is, whereas some peoples include father and father's brothers in a single kin category, and lump mother with her sisters—so that it is obligatory or normal to refer to each of one's parents with terms that lump them with others—it is not obligatory among the UP to refer to their actual parents in ways that lump mother with father.

UP kinship terms are partially or wholly translatable by reference to the relationships inherent in procreation: mother, father, son, daughter. The UP have an age terminology that includes age grades in a linear sequence similar to the sequence child, adolescent, adult, etc. Our first reflex is to think that it could not be otherwise, but it could: an elderly person can be "like a child"; an age classification that had a term indicating "dependent age" could break from the normal pattern of linearity.

The UP have a sex terminology that is fundamentally dualistic, even when it comprises three or four categories. When there are three, one is a combination of the two basic sexes (e.g., a hermaphrodite), or one is a crossover sex (e.g., a man acting as a woman). When there are four there are then two normal sexes and two crossover sexes.

Naming and taxonomy are fundamental to UP cognition. Prominent elements in UP taxonomy and other aspects of their speech and thought are binary discriminations, forming contrasting terms or semantic components (a number of which have already been mentioned— black and white, nature and culture, male and female, good and bad, etc.). But the UP also can order continua, so they can indicate not only contrasts but polar extremes with gradations between them. Thus there are middles between their opposites, or ranked orders in their classifications. The UP are able to express the measure of things and distances, though not necessarily with uniform units.

The UP employ such elementary logical notions as "not," "and," "same," "equivalent," and "opposite." They distinguish the general from the particular and parts from wholes. Unfortunately, the UP overestimate the objectivity of their mode of thought (it is particularly unobjective when they compare their in-group with out-groups).

The UP use what has been called "conjectural" reasoning to, for example, deduce from minute clues the identification, presence, and behavior of animals, or from miscellaneous symptoms the presence of a particular disease that cannot in itself be observed and is a wholly abstract conception.

Language is not the only means of symbolic communication employed by the UP. They employ gestures too, especially with their hands and arms. Some of their nonverbal communication is somewhat one-sided, in that the message is received consciously but may be sent more or less spontaneously. For example, the squeals of children, cries of fright, and the like all send messages that UP watch closely or listen to carefully, even though the sender did not consciously intend them to communicate. The UP do not merely listen and watch what is on the surface,

they interpret external behavior to grasp interior intention.

Communication with their faces is particularly complex among the UP, and some of their facial expressions are recognized everywhere. Thus UP faces show happiness, sadness, anger, fear, surprise, disgust, and contempt, in a manner entirely familiar from one society to another. When they smile while greeting persons it signifies friendly intentions. UP cry when they feel unhappiness or pain. A young woman acting coy or flirting with her eyes does it in a way you would recognize quite clearly. Although some facial communication is spontaneous, as noted earlier, the UP can mask, modify, and mimic otherwise spontaneous expressions. Whether by face, words, gesture, or otherwise, the UP can show affection as well as feel it.

The UP have a concept of the person in the psychological sense. They distinguish self from others, and they can see the self both as subject and object. They do not see the person as a wholly passive recipient or external action, nor do they see the self as wholly autonomous. To some degree, they see the person as responsible for his or her actions. They distinguish actions that are under control from those that are not. They understand the concept of intention. They know that people have a private inner life, have memories, make plans, choose between alternatives, and otherwise make decisions (not without ambivalent feeling sometimes). They know that people can feel pain and other emotions. They distinguish normal from abnormal mental states. The UP personality theory allows them to think of individuals departing from the pattern of behavior associated with whatever status(es) they occupy, and they can explain these departures in terms of the individual's character. The UP are spontaneously and intuitively able to, so to say, get in the minds of others to imagine how they are thinking and feeling.

In addition to the emotions that have already been mentioned, the UP are moved by sexual attraction: sometimes they are deeply disturbed by sexual jealousy. They also have childhood fears, including fear of loud noises and—particularly toward the end of the first year of life—of strangers (this is the apparent counterpart of a strong attachment to their caretaker at this time). The UP react emotionally—generally with fear—to snakes. With effort, the UP can overcome some of their fears. Because there is normally a man present to make a claim on a boy's mother, the Oedipus complex—in the sense of a little boy's possessiveness toward his mother and coolness toward her consort—is a part of male UP psychology.

The UP recognize individuals by their faces, and in this sense they most certainly have an implicit concept of the individual (however little they may explicitly conceptualize the individual apart from social statues). They recognize individuals in other ways too.

The UP are quintessential tool makers: not simply because they make tools—some other animals do too—but because they make so many, so many different kinds of them, and are so dependent upon them. Unlike the other animals, the UP use tools to make tools. They make cutters that improve upon what they can do with their teeth or by tearing with their hands. They make pounders that improve upon what they can do with their teeth, fists, feet, knees, shoulders, elbows, and head. They make containers that allow them to hold more things at one time, to hold them more comfortably or continuously, and to hold them when they otherwise couldn't as over a fire. Whether it be string, cord, sinew, vine, wire, or whatever, the UP have something to use to tie things together and make interlaced materials. They know and use the lever, Some of their tools are weapons, including the spear. The UP make many of their tools with such permanence that they can use them over and over again. They also make some of their tools in uniform patterns that are more or less arbitrary—thus we can often tell one people's tools from another's. Such patterns

persist beyond any one person's lifetime. Since tools are so closely related to human hands, we might note in passing that most people among the UP are right-handed.

The UP may not know how to make fire, but they know how to use it. They use fire to cook food but for other purposes too. Tools and fire do much to make them more comfortable and secure. The UP have other ways to make themselves feel better (or different). These include substances they can take to alter their moods or feelings: stimulants, narcotics, or intoxicants. These are in addition to what they take for mere sustenance.

The UP always have some form of shelter from the elements. Further ways in which they attend to their material needs will be discussed later.

The UP have distinct patterns of preparation for birth, for giving birth, and for postnatal care. They also have a more or less standard pattern and time for weaning infants.

The UP are not solitary dwellers. They live part of their lives, if not the whole of them, in groups. One of their most important groups is the family, but it is not the only group among them. One or more of the UP groups maintains a unity even though the members are dispersed.

The UP have groups defined by locality or claiming a certain territory, even if they happen to live almost their entire lives as wanderers upon the sea. They are materially, cognitively, and emotionally adjusted to the environment in which they normally live (particularly with respect to some of its flora and fauna). A sense of being a distinct people characterizes the UP, and they judge other people in their own terms.

The core of a normal UP family is composed of a mother and children. They biological mother is usually expected to be the social mother and usually is. On a more or less permanent basis there is usually a man (or men) involved, too, and he (or they) serve minimally to give the children a status in the community and/or to be a consort to the mother. Marriage, in the sense of a "person" having a publicly recognized right of a sexual access to a woman deemed eligible for childbearing, is institutionalized among the UP. While the person is almost always a male, it need not necessarily be a single individual, nor even a male.

The UP have a pattern of socialization: children aren't just left to grow up on their own. Senior kin are expected to contribute substantially to socialization. One of the ways children learn among the UP is by watching elders and copying them. The socialization of UP children includes toilet training. Through practice, children and adults perfect what they learn. The UP learn some things by trial and error.

One's own children and other close kin are distinguished from more distant relatives or nonrelatives among the UP, and the UP favor their close kin in various contexts.

UP families and the relationships of their family members to each other and to outsiders are affected by their sexual regulations, which sharply delimit, if not eliminate, mating between the genetically close kin. Mating between mother and son, in particular, is unthinkable or taboo. Sex is a topic of great interest to the UP, though there may be contexts in which they will not discuss it.

Some groups among the UP achieve some of their order by division into socially significant categories or subgroups on the basis of kinship, sex, and age. Since the UP have kinship, sex, and age statuses, it follows, of course, that they have statuses and roles and hence a social structure. But they have statuses beyond those of sex, age, and kinship categories. And while these are largely ascribed statuses, they have achieved statuses too. There are rules of succession to some of their statuses.

Although it may be only another way of saying that they have statuses and roles, the UP recognize social personhood: social identities, including collective identities, that are distinguishable from the individuals who bear them. The distinction between persons and individuals involves the entification of the former, i.e., the UP speak of statuses as though they were entities that can act and be acted upon, such as we do when we say, for example, that "the legislature" (a social entity) "punished the university" (another social entity).

Prestige is differentially distributed among the UP, and the members of UP society are not all economically equal. They acknowledge inequalities of various sorts, but we cannot specify whether they approve or disapprove.

The UP have a division of labor, minimally based on the sex and age statuses already mentioned. For example, their women have more direct child-care duties than do their men. Children are not expected to, and typically do not, engage in the same activities in the same way that adults do. Related to this division of labor, men and women and adults and children are seen by the UP as having different natures. Their men are in fact on the average more physically aggressive than women and are more likely to commit lethal violence than women are.

In the public political sphere men form the dominant element among the UP. Women and children are correspondingly submissive or acquiescent, particularly, again, in the public political sphere.

In addition to their division of labor, whereby different kinds of people do different things, the UP have customs of cooperative labor, in which people jointly undertake essentially similar tasks. They use reciprocal exchanges, whether of labor, or goods, or services, in a variety of settings. Reciprocity—including its negative or retaliatory forms—is an important element in the conduct of their lives. The UP also engage in trade, that is, in nonreciprocal exchanges of goods and services (i.e., one kind of good or service for another). Whether reciprocally or not, they give gifts to one another too. In certain contexts they share food.

Whether in the conduct of family life, of subsistence activities, or other matters, the UP attempt to predict and plan for the future. Some of their plans involve the maintenance or manipulation of social relations. In this context it is important to note that the UP possess "triangular awareness," the ability to think not only of their own relationships to others but of the relationships between others in relation to themselves. Without such an ability they would be unable to form their ubiquitous coalitions.

The UP have government, in the sense that they have public affairs and these affairs are regulated, and in the sense that decisions binding on a collectivity are made. Some of the regulation takes place in a framework of corporate statuses (statuses with orderly procedures for perpetuating membership in them).

The UP have leaders, though they may be ephemeral or situational. The UP admire, or profess to admire, generosity, and this is particularly desired in a leader. No leader of the UP ever has complete power lodged in himself alone. UP leaders go beyond the limits of UP reason and morality. Since the UP never have complete democracy, and never have complete autocracy, they always have a de facto oligarchy.

The UP have law, at least in the sense of rules of membership in perpetual social units and in the sense of rights and obligations attached to persons or other statuses. Among the UP's laws are those that in certain situations proscribe violence and rape. Their laws also proscribe murder—unjustified taking of human life (though they may justify taking lives in some contexts). They have sanctions for infractions, and these sanctions include removal of offenders from the social unit—whether by expulsion, incarceration, ostracism, or execution. They punish (or otherwise censure or condemn) certain acts that threaten the group or are alleged to do so.

Conflict is more familiar to the UP than they wish it were, and they have customary, though far from perfect, ways of dealing with it (their proscription of rape and other forms of violence, for example, does not eliminate them). They understand that wronged parties may seek redress. They employ consultation and mediation in some conflict cases.

Important conflicts are structured around in-group-out-group antagonisms that characterize the UP. These antagonisms both divide the UP as an ethnic group as well as set them off from other ethnic groups. An ethical dualism distinguishes the in-group from the out-group, so that, for example, cooperation is more expectable in the former than with the latter.

The UP distinguish right from wrong, and at least implicitly, as noted earlier, recognize responsibility and intentionality. They recognize and employ promises. Reciprocity, also mentioned earlier, is a key element in their mortality. So, too, is their ability to empathize. Envy is ubiquitous among the UP, and they have symbolic means for coping with its unfortunate consequences.

Etiquette and hospitality are among UP ideals. They have customary greetings and customs of visiting kin or others who dwell elsewhere. They have standardized, preferred, or typical times of day to eat, and they have occasions on which to feast. In other ways, too, they have normal daily routines of activities and are fundamentally diurnal.

They have standards of sexual modesty—even though they might customarily go about naked. People, adults in particular, do not normally copulate in public, nor do they relieve themselves without some attempt to do it modestly. Among their other taboos are taboos on certain utterances and certain kinds of food. On the other hand, there are some kinds of food—sweets in particular—that they relish.

The UP have religious or supernatural beliefs in that they believe in something beyond the visible and palpable. They anthropomorphize and (some if not all of them) believe things that are demonstrably false. They also practice magic, and their magic is designed to do such things as to sustain and increase life and to win the attention of the opposite sex. They have theories of fortune and misfortune. They have ideas about how to explain disease and death. They see a connection between sickness and death. They try to heal the sick and have medicines for this purpose. The UP practice divination. And they try to control the weather.

The UP have rituals, and these include rites of passage that demarcate the transfer of an individual from one status to another. They mourn their dead.

Their ideas include a worldview—an understanding or conception of the world about them and their place in it. In some ways their worldview is structured by features of their minds. For example, from early infancy they have the ability to identify items that they know by one sense with the same items perceived in another sense, and so they see the world as a unity, not as different worlds imposed by our different sense modalities. Their worldview is a part of their supernatural and mythological beliefs. They have folklore too. The UP dream and attempt to interpret their dreams.

However spiritual they may be, the UP are materialists also. As indicated by their language having the possessive for use on "loose property," the UP have concepts of property, distinguishing what belongs—minimal though it may be—to the individual, or group, from what belongs to others. They also have rules for the inheritance of property.

In addition to their use of speech in poetic or polished ways, the UP have further aesthetic standards. However little clothing they wear, they nonetheless adorn their bodies in one way or another, including a distinctive way of maintaining or shaping their hair. They have standards of sexual attractiveness (including, for example, signs of good health and a clear male preference for the signs of early nubility rather than those of the postmenopausal state). Their decorative art is not confined to the body alone, for the UP apply it to their artifacts too. In addition to their patterns of grooming for essentially aesthetic reasons, they also have patterns of hygienic care.

The UP know how to dance and have music. At least some of their dance (and at least some of their religious activity) is accompanied by music. They include melody, rhythm, repetition, redundancy, and variation in their music, which is always seen as an art, a creation. Their music includes vocals, and the vocals include words—i.e., a conjunction of music and poetry. The UP have children's music.

The UP, particularly their youngsters, play and playfight. Their play, besides being fun, provides training in skills that will be useful in adulthood.

The materials presented in this chapter—essentially a list of absolute universals—draws heavily from Murdock (1945), Tiger and Fox (1971) and Hockett (1973) and also from many other sources. In some cases I have added items to the list because my own experience or that of a colleague or student has convinced me that the items ought to be there even though appropriate references could not be found. In a few cases I have counted something as a universal even though that required setting aside ethnographic testimony. There are, for example, some reports of societies in which getting into other people's minds (empathizing, divining intent or inner feeling, and the like) is not done or even conceived as possible. My assumption is that these reports may be emically correct but not etically. For example, Selby (1974:106–107, 109) reports that the Zapotec, at least in some situations, do not think they can get into other people's minds, but he gives a clear case of this happening (1974:56). Similarly, to the Kaluli belief that "one cannot know what another thinks or feels," Ochs and Schieffelin (1984:290) comment that the Kaluli "obviously" do "interpret and assess one another's . . . internal states."

More important than uncertainties about the boundaries between universals and near-universals is the issue of adequate conceptualization or definition of particular universals. For example, the conceptualizations of marriage and the family that I presented are those that currently seem the most convincing to me; they have been differently conceived or defined in the past and may undergo further revision in the future.

In sum, a fuller and truer account of the UP would in various ways show the relationship between the universals. But then a fuller and truer account of the UP would list their conditional universals (and their interrelationships and hierarchies) and would also offer explanations of the universals and their interrelationships. Anthropology has scarcely begun to illuminate the architecture of human universals. It is time to get on with the task.

Notes

1 Following up the leads suggested by folk classifications might lead to an analysis of incest along with bestiality, irreverence, and sundry other topics. Whether to follow the leads suggested by folk classifications is a complication I will not treat here. But I should note that some anthropologists have recently explored incest from the viewpoint of child abuse, the category under which some forms of incest are classified in the West today (see especially Willner [1983] but also La Fontaine [1988]).

2 Marriages of royal brothers and sisters are well attested in the historical record, but evidence that this led to actual incest (i.e., reproduction) is extremely limited (Bixler 1982a, 1982b). Arens (1986:116) suggests that the motive of royal brother-sister marriages was not reproductive at all: such marriages merely took royal sisters out of the marriage market and thereby prevented them from bearing offspring who might rival the king. With their sisters safely married to themselves, nothing compelled kings to actually mate with them.

Bibliography

Arens, W. (1986). The Original Sin: Incest and its meaning. New York: Oxford University Press.

Fox, J. R. (1962). Sibling incest. British Journal of Sociology, 13: 128–150.

Hopkins, K. (1980). Brother-sister marriage in Roman Egypt. Comparative Studies in Society and History, 22: 303–354.

Kaffman, M. (1977). Sexual standards and behavior of the kibbutz adolescent. Orthopsychiatry 47: 207–216.

La Fontaine, J. S. (1988). Child sexual abuse and the incest taboo: Practical problems and theoretical issues. Man, 23: 1–18.

McCabe, J. (1983). FBD marriage: Further support for the Westermarck hypothesis of the incest taboo? American Anthropologist, 85: 50–69.

Murdock, G. P. (1932). The science of culture. American Anthropologist, 34: 200–215.

Murdock, G. P. (1945). The common denominator of cultures. In R. Linton (ed.), The Science of Man in the World Crisis (pp. 123–142). New York: Columbia University Press.

Ochs, E., & Schieffelin, B. B. (1984). Language acquisition and socialization: Three developmental stories and their implications. In R. A. Shweder and R. A. LeVine (eds.), Culture Theory: Essays on mind, self and emotion (pp. 276–320). Cambridge: Cambridge University Press.

Parker, H. A., & Parker, S. (1986). Father-daughter sexual abuse: An emerging perspective. American Journal of Orthopsychiatry, 56: 531–549.

Selby, Henry A. (1974). Zapotec Deviance: The convergence of folk and modern sociology. Austin: University of Texas Press.

Shepher, J. (1983). Incest: A biosocial view. New York: Academic Press.

Melford, S. (1958). Children of the Kibbutz. Cambridge, MA: Harvard University Press.

Melford, S. (1982). Oedipus in the Trobriands. Chicago, IL: University of Chicago Press.

Talmon, Y. (1964). Mate selection in collective settlements. American Sociological Review, 29: 491–508.

Tiger, L., & Fox, R. (1971). The Imperial Animal. New York: Holt, Rinehart & Winston.

Weinberg, K. S. (1963). Incest Behavior. New York: Citadel Press.

Westermarck, E. (1922). The History of Human Marriage, 5th edn, Vol. II. New York: Allerton.

Willner, D. (1983). Definition and violation: Incest and the incest taboos. Man, 18: 134–159.

Wolf, A. P. (1966). Childhood association, sexual attraction, and the incest taboo: A Chinese case. *American Anthropologist*, 68: 883–898.

Wolf, A. P. (1968). Adopt a daughter-in-law, marry a sister: A Chinese solution to the problem of the incest taboo. *American Anthropologist*, 70: 864–874.

Wolf, A. P. (1970). Childhood association and sexual attraction: A further test of the Westermarck hypothesis. *American Anthropologist*, 72: 503–515.

Wolf, A., & Huang C. S. (1980). *Marriage and Adoption in China, 1845–1945*. Stanford, CA: Stanford University Press.

Chapter 15

Joseph Henrich, Steven J. Heine and Ara Norenzayan

THE WEIRDEST PEOPLE IN THE WORLD?

Introduction

In the tropical forests of New Guinea, the Etoro believe that for a boy to achieve manhood he must ingest the semen of his elders. This is accomplished through ritualized rites of passage that require young male initiates to fellate a senior member. In contrast, the nearby Kaluli maintain that male initiation is only properly done by ritually delivering the semen through the initiate's anus, not his mouth. The Etoro revile these Kaluli practices, finding them disgusting. To become a man in these societies, and eventually take a wife, every boy undergoes these initiations. Such boy-inseminating practices, which are enmeshed in rich systems of meaning and imbued with local cultural values, were not uncommon among the traditional societies of Melanesia and Aboriginal Australia, as well as in Ancient Greece and Tokugawa Japan.

Such in-depth studies of seemingly "exotic" societies, historically the province of anthropology, are crucial for understanding human behavioral and psychological variation. However, this chapter is not about these peoples. It is about a truly unusual group: people from Western, Educated, Industrialized, Rich, and Democratic (WEIRD) societies. In particular, it is about the Western, and more specifically American, undergraduates who form the bulk of the database in the experimental branches of psychology, cognitive science, and economics, as well as allied fields (hereafter collectively labeled the "behavioral sciences"). Given that scientific knowledge about human psychology is largely based on findings from this subpopulation, we ask just how representative are these typical subjects in light of the available comparative database. How justified are researchers in assuming a species-level generality for their findings? Here, we review the evidence regarding how WEIRD people compare with other populations.

We pursued this question by constructing an empirical review of studies involving large-scale comparative experimentation on important psychological or behavioral variables. Although such larger-scale studies are highly informative, they are rather rare, especially when compared to the frequency of species-generalizing claims. When such comparative projects were absent, we relied on large assemblies of studies comparing two or three populations, and, when available, on meta-analyses.

We also do not address societal-level behavioral universals, or claims thereof, related to phenomena such as dancing, fire making, cooking, kinship systems, body adornment, play, trade, and grammar, for two reasons. First, at this surface level alone, such phenomena do not make specific claims about universal underlying psychological or motivational processes. Second, systematic, quantitative, comparative data based on individual-level measures are typically lacking for these domains.

Our examination of the representativeness of WEIRD subjects is necessarily restricted to the rather limited database currently available. We have organized our presentation into a series of telescoping contrasts showing, at each level of contrast, how WEIRD people measure up relative to the available reference populations. Our first contrast compares people from modern industrialized societies with those from small-scale societies. Our second telescoping stage contrasts people from Western societies with those from non-Western industrialized societies. Next, we contrast Americans with people from other Western societies. Finally, we contrast university-educated Americans with non-university-educated Americans, or university students with non-student adults, depending on the available data. At each level we discuss behavioral and psychological phenomena for which there are available comparative data, and we assess how WEIRD people compare with other samples.

We emphasize that our presentation of telescoping contrasts is only a rhetorical approach guided by the nature of the available data. It should not be taken as capturing any unidimensional continuum, or suggesting any single theoretical explanation for the variation. Throughout this article we take no position regarding the substantive origins of the observed differences between populations. While many of the differences are probably cultural in nature in that they were socially transmitted, other differences are likely environmental and represent some form of non-cultural phenotypic plasticity, which may be developmental or facultative, as well as either adaptive or maladaptive. Other population differences could arise from genetic variation, as observed for lactose processing. Regardless of the reasons underlying these population differences, our concern is whether researchers can reasonably generalize from WEIRD samples to humanity at large.

Many radical versions of interpretivism and cultural relativity deny any shared commonalities in human psychologies across populations. To the contrary, we expect humans from all societies to share, and probably share substantially, basic aspects of cognition, motivation, and behavior. As researchers who see great value in applying evolutionary thinking to psychology and behavior, we have little doubt that if a full accounting were taken across all domains among peoples past and present, the number of similarities would indeed be large, as much ethnographic work suggests—ultimately, of course, this is an empirical question. Thus, our thesis is not that humans share few basic psychological properties or processes; rather, we question our current ability to distinguish these reliably developing aspects of human psychology from more developmentally, culturally, or environmentally contingent aspects of our psychology given the disproportionate reliance on WEIRD subjects. Our aim here, then, is to inspire efforts to place knowledge of such universal features of psychology on a firmer footing by empirically addressing, rather than a priori dismissing or ignoring, questions of population variability.

Background

Before commencing with our telescoping contrasts, we first discuss two observations regarding the existing literature: (1) The database in the behavioral sciences is drawn from an extremely narrow slice of human diversity; and (2) behavioral scientists routinely assume, at least implicitly, that their findings from this narrow slice generalize to the species.

The Behavioral Sciences Database is Narrow

Who are the people studied in behavioral science research? A recent analysis of the top journals in six sub-disciplines of psychology from 2003 to 2007 revealed that 68% of subjects came from the United States, and a full 96% of subjects were from Western industrialized countries, specifically those in North America and Europe, as well as Australia and Israel. The make-up of these samples appears to largely reflect the country of residence of the authors, as 73% of first authors were at American universities, and 99% were at universities in Western countries. This means that 96% of psychological samples come from countries with only 12% of the world's population.

Even within the West, however, the typical sampling method for experimental studies is far from representative. In the *Journal of Personality and Social Psychology*, the premier journal in social psychology—the subdiscipline of psychology that should (arguably) be the most attentive to questions about the subjects' backgrounds—67% of the American samples (and 80% of the samples from other countries) were composed solely of undergraduates in psychology courses. In other words, a randomly selected American undergraduate is more than 4,000 times more likely to be a research participant than is a randomly selected person from outside of the West. Furthermore, this tendency to rely on undergraduate samples has not decreased over time. Such studies are therefore sampling from a rather limited subpopulation within each country.

It is possible that the dominance of American authors in psychology publications just reflects that American universities have the resources to attract the best international researchers, and that similar tendencies exist in other fields. However, psychology is a distinct outlier here: 70% of all psychology citations come from the United States—a larger percentage than any of the other 19 sciences that were compared in one extensive international survey (see May 1997). In chemistry, by contrast, the percentage of citations that come from the United States is only 37%. It seems problematic that the discipline in which there are the strongest theoretical reasons to anticipate population-level variation is precisely the discipline in which the American bias for research is most extreme.

Beyond psychology and cognitive science, the subject pools of experimental economics and decision science are not much more diverse—still largely dominated by Westerners, and specifically Western undergraduates. However, to give credit where it is due, the nascent field of experimental economics has begun taking steps to address the problem of narrow samples.

In sum, the available database does not reflect the full breadth of human diversity. Rather, we have largely been studying the nature of WEIRD people, a certainly narrow and potentially peculiar subpopulation.

Researchers often Assume their Findings are Universal

Sampling from a thin slice of humanity would be less problematic if researchers confined their interpretations to the populations from which they sampled. However, despite their narrow samples, behavioral scientists often are interested in drawing inferences about the *human* mind and *human* behavior. This inferential step is rarely challenged or defended—despite the lack of any general effort to assess how well results from WEIRD samples generalize to the species. This lack of epistemic vigilance underscores the prevalent, though implicit, assumption that the findings one derives from a particular sample will generalize broadly; one adult human sample is pretty much the same as the next.

Leading scientific journals and university textbooks routinely publish research findings claiming to generalize to "humans" or "people" based on research done entirely with WEIRD undergraduates. In top journals such as *Nature* and *Science*, researchers frequently extend their findings from undergraduates to the species—often declaring this generalization in their titles. These contributions typically lack even a cautionary footnote about these inferential extensions.

In psychology, much of this generalization is implicit. A typical article does not claim to be discussing "humans" but will rather simply describe a decision bias, psychological process, set of correlations, and so on, without addressing issues of generalizability, although findings are often linked to "people." Commonly, there is no demographic information about the participants, aside from their age and gender. In recent years there is a trend to qualify some findings with disclaimers such as "at least within Western culture," though there remains a robust tendency to generalize to the species. Arnett (2008) notes that psychologists would surely bristle if journals were renamed to more accurately reflect the nature of their samples (e.g., *Journal of Personality and Social Psychology of American Undergraduate Psychology Students*). They would bristle, presumably, because they believe that their findings generalize much beyond this sample. Of course, there are important exceptions to this general tendency, as some researchers have assembled a broad database to provide evidence for universality (Buss 1989; Daly & Wilson 1988; Ekman 1999; Elfenbein & Ambady 2002; Kenrick & Keefe 1992a; Tracy & Matsumoto 2008).

When is it safe to generalize from a narrow sample to the species? First, if one had good empirical reasons to believe that little variability existed across diverse populations in a particular domain, it would be reasonable to tentatively infer universal processes from a single subpopulation. Second, one could make an argument that as long as one's samples were drawn from near the center of the human distribution, then it would not be overly problematic to generalize across the distribution more broadly—at least the inferred pattern would be in the vicinity of the central tendency of our species. In the following, with these assumptions in mind, we review the evidence for the representativeness of findings from WEIRD people.

Contrast 1: Industrialized Societies Versus Small-Scale Societies

Our theoretical perspective, which is informed by evolutionary thinking, leads us to suspect that many aspects of people's psychological repertoire are universal. However, the current empirical foundations for our suspicions are rather weak because the database of comparative studies that include small-scale societies is scant, despite the obvious importance of such societies in understanding both the evolutionary history of our species and the potential impact of diverse environments on our psychology. Here we first discuss the evidence for differences between populations drawn from industrialized and small-scale societies in some seemingly basic psychological domains, and follow this with research indicating universal patterns across this divide.

Visual Perception

Many readers may suspect that tasks involving "low-level" or "basic" cognitive processes such as vision will not vary much across the human spectrum (Fodor 1983). However, in the 1960s an interdisciplinary team of anthropologists and psychologists systematically gathered data on the susceptibility of both children and adults from a wide range of human societies to five "standard illusions" (Segall et al. 1966). Here we highlight the comparative findings on the famed Müller-Lyer illusion, because of this illusion's importance in textbooks, and its prominent role as Fodor's indisputable example of "cognitive impenetrability" in debates about the modularity of cognition. Note, however, that population-level variability in illusion susceptibility is not limited to the Müller-Lyer illusion; it was also found for the Sander-Parallelogram and both Horizontal-Vertical illusions.

Segall et al. (1966) manipulated the length of the two lines in the Müller-Lyer illusion (Figure 15.1) and estimated the magnitude of the illusion by determining the approximate point at which the two lines were perceived as being of the same length. Figure 15.2 shows the results from 16 societies, including 14 small-scale societies. The vertical axis gives the "point of subjective equality" (PSE), which measures

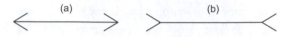

Figure 15.1 The Müller-Lyer illusion. The lines labeled "a" and "b" are the same length. Many subject perceive line "b" as longer than line "a".

the extent to which segment "a" must be longer than segment "b" before the two segments are judged equal in length. PSE measures the strength of the illusion.

The results show substantial differences among populations, with American undergraduates anchoring the extreme end of the distribution, followed by the South African-European sample from Johannesburg. On average, the undergraduates required that line "a" be about a fifth longer than line "b" before the two segments were perceived as equal. At the other end, the San foragers of the Kalahari were unaffected by the so-called illusion (it is not an illusion for them). While the San's PSE value cannot

be distinguished from zero, the American undergraduates' PSE value is significantly different from all the other societies studied.

As discussed by Segall et al., these findings suggest that visual exposure during ontogeny to factors such as the "carpentered corners" of modern environments may favor certain optical calibrations and visual habits that create and perpetuate this illusion. That is, the visual system ontogenetically adapts to the presence of recurrent features in the local visual environment. Because elements such as carpentered corners are products of particular cultural evolutionary trajectories, and were not part of most environments for most of human history, the Müller-Lyer illusion is a kind of culturally evolved by-product.

These findings highlight three important considerations. First, this work suggests that even a process as apparently basic as visual perception can show substantial variation across populations. If visual perception can vary, what kind of psychological processes can we be sure

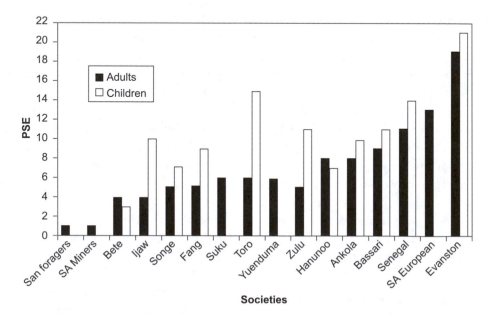

Figure 15.2 Müller-Lyer results for Segall et al's (1966) cross-cultural project. PSE (point of subjective equality) is the percentage that segment "a" must be longer than "b" before subjects preceived the segments as equal in length. Children were sampled in the 5-to-11 age range.

will not vary? It is not merely that the strength of the illusory effect varies across populations—the effect cannot be detected in two populations. Second, both American undergraduates and children are at the extreme end of the distribution, showing significant differences from all other populations studied; whereas, many of the other populations cannot be distinguished from one another. Since children already show large population-level differences, it is not obvious that developmental work can substitute for research across diverse human populations. Children likely have different developmental trajectories in different societies. Finally, this provides an example of how population-level variation can be useful for illuminating the nature of a psychological process, which would not be as evident in the absence of comparative work.

Fairness and Cooperation in Economic Decision-Making

By the mid-1990s, researchers were arguing that a set of robust experimental findings from behavioral economics were evidence for a set of evolved universal motivations (Fehr & Gächter 1998; Hoffman et al. 1998). Foremost among these experiments, the Ultimatum Game provides a pair of anonymous subjects with a sum of real money for a one-shot interaction. One of the pair—the proposer—can offer a portion of this sum to the second subject, the responder. Responders must decide whether to accept or reject the offer. If a responder accepts, she gets the amount of the offer and the proposer takes the remainder; if she rejects, both players get zero. If subjects are motivated purely by self-interest, responders should always accept any positive offer; knowing this, a self-interested proposer should offer the smallest non-zero amount. Among subjects from industrialized populations—mostly undergraduates from the United States, Europe, and Asia—proposers typically offer an amount between 40% and 50% of

the total, with a modal offer of 50% (Camerer 2003). Offers below about 30% are often rejected.

With this seemingly robust empirical finding in their sights, Nowak et al. (2000) constructed an evolutionary analysis of the Ultimatum Game. When they modeled the Ultimatum Game exactly as played, they did not get results matching the undergraduate findings. However, if they added reputational information, such that players could know what their partners did with others on previous rounds of play, the analysis predicted offers and rejections in the range of typical undergraduate responses. They concluded that the Ultimatum Game reveals humans' species-specific evolved capacity for fair and punishing behavior in situations with substantial reputational influence. But, since the Ultimatum Game is typically played one-shot without reputational information, Nowak et al. argued that people make fair offers and reject unfair offers because their motivations evolved in a world where such interactions were not fitness relevant—thus, we are not evolved to fully incorporate the possibility of non-reputational action in our decision-making, at least in such artificial experimental contexts.

Recent comparative work has dramatically altered this initial picture. Two unified projects (which we call Phase 1 and Phase 2) have deployed the Ultimatum Game and other related experimental tools across thousands of subjects randomly sampled from 23 small-scale human societies, including foragers, horticulturalists, pastoralists, and subsistence farmers, drawn from Africa, Amazonia, Oceania, Siberia, and New Guinea (Henrich et al. 2005a; 2006; 2010). Three different experimental measures show that people in industrialized societies consistently occupy the extreme end of the human distribution. Notably, people in some of the smallest-scale societies, where real life is principally face-to-face, behaved in a manner reminiscent of Nowak et al.'s analysis *before* they added the reputational information. That is, these populations made low offers and did not reject.

To concisely present these diverse empirical findings, we show results only from the Ultimatum and Dictator Games in Phase II. The Dictator Game is the same as the Ultimatum Game except that the second player cannot reject the offer. If subjects are motivated purely by self-interest, they would offer zero in the Dictator Game. Thus, Dictator Game offers yield a measure of "fairness" (equal divisions) among two anonymous people. By contrast, Ultimatum Game offers yield a measure of fairness combined with an assessment of the likelihood of rejection (punishment). Rejections of offers in the Ultimatum Game provide a measure of people's willingness to punish unfairness.

Using aggregate measures, Figure 15.3 shows that the behavior of the U.S. adult (non-student) sample occupies the extreme end of the distribution in each case. For Dictator Game offers, Figure 15.3A shows that the U.S. sample has the highest mean offer, followed by the Sanquianga from Colombia, who are renowned for their prosociality (Kraul 2008). The U.S. offers are nearly double that of the Hadza, foragers from Tanzania, and the Tsimane, forager-horticulturalists from the Bolivian Amazon. Figure 15.3B shows that for Ultimatum Game offers, the United States has the second highest mean offer, behind the Sursurunga from Papua New Guinea. On the punishment side in the Ultimatum Game, Figure 15.3C shows the income-maximizing offers (IMO) for each population, which is a measure of the population's willingness to punish inequitable offers. IMO is the offer that an income-maximizing proposer would make if he knew the probability of rejection for each of the possible offer amounts. The U.S. sample is tied with the Sursurunga. These two groups have an IMO five times higher than 70% of the other societies. While none of these measures indicates that people from industrialized societies are entirely unique vis-à-vis other populations, they do

show that people from industrialized societies consistently occupy the extreme end of the human distribution.

Analyses of these data show that a population's degree of market integration and its participation in a world religion both independently predict higher offers, and account for much of the variation between populations. Community size positively predicts greater punishment (Henrich et al. 2010). The authors suggest that norms and institutions for exchange in ephemeral interactions culturally coevolved with markets and expanding larger-scale sedentary populations. In some cases, at least in their most efficient forms, neither markets nor large populations were feasible before such norms and institutions emerged. That is, it may be that what behavioral economists have been measuring among undergraduates in such games is a specific set of social norms, culturally evolved for dealing with money and strangers, that have emerged since the origins of agriculture and the rise of complex societies.

Suppose that Nowak and his coauthors were Tsimane, and that the numerous empirical findings they had on hand were all from Tsimane villages. If this were the case, presumably these researchers would have simulated the Ultimatum Game and found that there was *no need to add* reputation to their model. This unadorned evolutionary solution would have worked fine until they realized that the Tsimane are not representative of humanity. According to the above data, the Tsimane are about as representative of the species as are Americans, but at the opposite end of the spectrum. If the database of the behavioral sciences consisted entirely of Tsimane subjects, researchers would likely be quite concerned about generalizability.

Folkbiological Reasoning

Recent work in small-scale societies suggests that *some* of the central conclusions regarding the development and operation of human

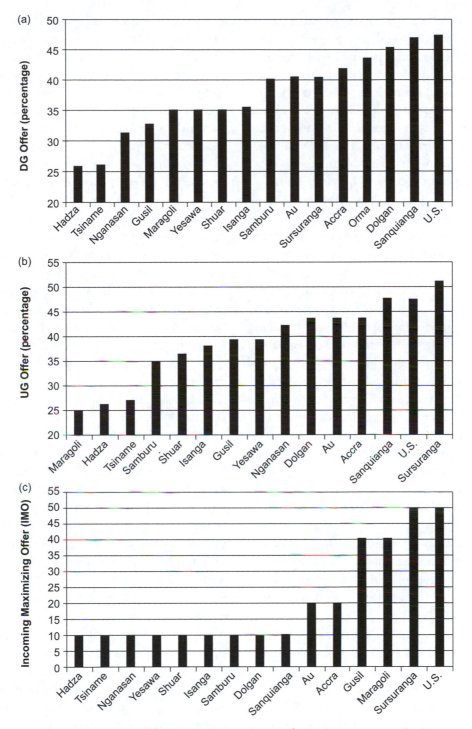

Figure 15.3 Behavioral measures of fairness and punishment from the Dictator and Ultimatum Games for 15 societies (Phase II). Figures 15.3A and 15.3B show mean offers for each society in the Dictator and Ultimatum Games, respectively. Figure 15.3C gives the income-maximizing offer (IMO) for each society.

folkbiological categorization, reasoning, and induction are limited to urban subpopulations of non-experts in industrialized societies. Although much more work needs to be done, it appears that typical subjects (children of WEIRD parents) develop their folkbiological reasoning in a culturally and experientially impoverished environment, by contrast to those of small-scale societies (and of our evolutionary past), distorting both the species-typical pattern of cognitive development and the patterns of reasoning in WEIRD adults.

Cognitive scientists using (as subjects) children drawn from U.S. urban centers—often those surrounding universities—have constructed an influential, though actively debated, developmental theory in which folkbiological reasoning emerges from folkpsychological reasoning. Before age 7, urban children reason about biological phenomena by analogy to, and by extension from, humans. Between ages 7 and 10, urban children undergo a conceptual shift to the adult pattern of viewing humans as one animal among many. These conclusions are underpinned by three robust findings from urban children: (1) Inferential projections of properties from humans are stronger than projections from other living kinds; (2) inferences from humans to mammals emerge as stronger than inferences from mammals to humans; and (3) children's inferences violate their own similarity judgments by, for example, providing stronger inference from humans to bugs than from bugs to bees (Carey 1985; 1995).

However, when the folkbiological reasoning of children in rural Native American communities in Wisconsin and Yukatek Maya communities in Mexico was investigated (Atran et al. 2001; Ross et al. 2003; Waxman & Medin 2007) none of these three empirical patterns emerged. Among the American urban children, the human category appears to be incorporated into folkbiological induction relatively late compared to these other populations. The results indicate that some background knowledge of the relevant species is crucial for the application and induction across a hierarchical taxonomy. In rural environments, both exposure to and interest in the natural world is commonplace, unavoidable, and an inevitable part of the enculturation process. This suggests that the anthropocentric patterns seen in U.S. urban children result from insufficient cultural input and a lack of exposure to the natural world. The only real animal that most urban children know much about is *Homo sapiens*, so it is not surprising that this species dominates their inferential patterns. Since such urban environments are highly "unnatural" from the perspective of human evolutionary history, any conclusions drawn from subjects reared in such informationally impoverished environments must remain rather tentative. Indeed, studying the cognitive development of folkbiology in urban children would seem the equivalent of studying "normal" physical growth in malnourished children.

This deficiency of input likely underpins the fact that the basic-level folkbiological categories for WEIRD adults are life-form categories (e.g., bird, fish, and mammal), and these are also the first categories learned by WEIRD children—for example, if one says "What's that?" (pointing at a maple tree), their common answer is "tree." However, in all small-scale societies studied, the generic species (e.g., maple, crow, trout, and fox) is the basic-level category and the first learned by children.

Impoverished interactions with the natural world may also distort assessments of the typicality of natural kinds in categorization. The standard conclusion from American undergraduate samples has been that goodness of example, or typicality, is driven by similarity relations. A robin is a typical bird because this species shares many of the perceptual features that are commonly found in the category BIRD. In the absence of close familiarity with natural kinds, this is the default strategy of American undergraduates, and psychology has assumed it is the universal pattern. However, in samples which interact with the natural world regularly, such as Itza Maya villagers, typicality is based not on similarity but on knowledge of cultural ideals, reflecting the symbolic or material significance of the species in that culture. For the Itza, the wild turkey is a typical bird because of its rich cultural significance, even though it is in no way most similar to other birds. The same pattern holds for similarity effects in inductive reasoning—WEIRD people make strong inferences from computations of similarity, whereas populations with greater familiarity with the natural world, despite their capacity for similarity-based inductions, prefer to make strong inferences from folkbiological knowledge that takes into account ecological context and relationships among species (Atran et al. 2005). In general, research suggests that *what* people think about can affect *how* they think (Bang et al. 2007). To the extent that there is population-level variability in the content of folkbiological beliefs, such variability affects cognitive processing in this domain as well.

So far we have emphasized differences in folkbiological cognition uncovered by comparative research. This same work has also uncovered reliably developing aspects of human folkbiological cognition that do not vary, such as categorizing plants and animals in a hierarchical taxonomy, or that the generic species level has the strongest inductive potential, despite the fact that this level is not always the basic level across populations, as discussed above. Our goal in emphasizing the differences here is to show (1) how peculiar industrialized (urban, in this case) samples are, given the unprecedented environment they grow up in; and (2) how difficult it is to conclude a priori what aspects will be reliably developing and robust across diverse slices of humanity if research is largely conducted with WEIRD samples.

Spatial Cognition

Human societies vary in their linguistic tools for, and cultural practices associated with, representing and communicating (1) directions in physical space, (2) the color spectrum, and (3) integer amounts. There is some evidence that each of these differences in cultural content may influence some aspects of nonlinguistic cognitive processes. Here we focus on spatial cognition, for which the evidence is most provocative. As above, it appears that industrialized societies are at the extreme end of the continuum in spatial cognition. Human populations show differences in how they think about spatial orientation and deal with directions, and these differences may be influenced by linguistically based spatial reference systems.

Speakers of English and other Indo-European languages favor the use of an egocentric (relative) system to represent the location of objects – that is, relative to the self (e.g., "the man is on the right side of the flagpole"). In contrast, many if not most languages favor an allocentric frame, which comes in two flavors. Some allocentric languages such as Guugu Yimithirr (an Australian language) and Tzeltal (a Mayan language) favor a geocentric system in which absolute reference is based on cardinal directions ("the man is west of the house"). The other allocentric frame is an object-centered (intrinsic) approach that locates objects in space, relative to some coordinate system anchored to the object ("the man is behind the house"). When languages possess systems for encoding all of these spatial reference frames, they often privilege one at the expense of the others. However, the fact that some languages lack one or more of the reference systems suggests that the accretion of all three systems into most contemporary languages may be a product of long-term cumulative cultural evolution.

In data on spatial reference systems from 20 languages drawn from diverse societies—including foragers, horticulturalists, agriculturalists, and industrialized populations—only three languages relied on egocentric frames as their single preferred system of reference. All three were from industrialized populations: Japanese, English, and Dutch (Majid et al. 2004).

The presence of, or emphasis on, different reference systems may influence nonlinguistic spatial reasoning. In one study, Dutch and Tzeltal speakers were seated at a table and shown an arrow pointing either to the right (north) or the left (south). They were then rotated 180 degrees to a second table where they saw two arrows: one pointing to the left (north) and the other one pointing to the right (south). Participants were asked which arrow on the second table was like the one they saw before. Consistent with the spatial-marking system of their languages, Dutch speakers chose the relative solution, whereas the Tzeltal speakers chose the absolute solution. Several other comparative experiments testing spatial memory and reasoning are consistent with this pattern, although lively debates about interpretation persist (Levinson et al. 2002; Li & Gleitman 2002).

Extending the above exploration, Haun and colleagues (Haun et al. 2006a; 2006b) examined performance on a spatial reasoning task similar to the one described above, using children and adults from different societies and great apes. In the first step, Dutch-speaking adults and 8-year-olds (speakers of an egocentric language) showed the typical egocentric bias, whereas Hai//om-speaking adults and 8-year-olds (a Namibian foraging population who speak an allocentric language) showed a typical allocentric bias. In the second step, 4-year-old German-speaking children, gorillas, orangutans, chimpanzees, and bonobos were tested on a simplified version of the same task. All showed a marked preference for allocentric reasoning. These results suggest that children share with other great apes an innate preference for allocentric spatial reasoning, but that this bias can be overridden by input from language and cultural routines.

If one were to work on spatial cognition exclusively with WEIRD subjects (say, using subjects from the United States and Europe),

one might conclude that children start off with an allocentric bias but naturally shift to an egocentric bias with maturation. The problem with this conclusion is that it would not apply to many human populations, and it may be the consequence of studying subjects from peculiar cultural environments. The next telescoping contrast highlights some additional evidence suggesting that WEIRD people may even be unusual in their egocentric bias vis-à-vis most other industrialized populations.

Summary

Although there are several domains in which the data from small-scale societies appear similar to that from industrialized societies, comparative projects involving visual illusions, social motivations (fairness), folkbiological cognition, and spatial cognition all show industrialized populations as outliers. Given all this, it seems problematic to generalize from industrialized populations to humans more broadly, in the absence of supportive empirical evidence.

Contrast 2: Western Versus Non-Western Societies

For our second contrast, we review evidence comparing Western with non-Western populations. Here we examine three of the most studied domains: social decision making (fairness, cooperation, and punishment), independent versus interdependent self-concepts (and associated motivations), and moral reasoning. We also briefly return to spatial cognition.

Anti-social Punishment and Cooperation

In the previous contrast, we reviewed social decision-making experiments showing that industrialized populations occupy the extreme end of the behavioral distribution vis-à-vis a broad swath of smaller-scale societies. Here we

show that even among industrialized populations, Westerners are again clumped at the
extreme end of the behavioral distribution.
Notably, the behaviors measured in the experiments discussed below are strongly correlated
with the strength of formal institutions, norms
of civic cooperation, and Gross Domestic
Product (GDP) per capita.

In 2002, Fehr and Gächter published their
classic paper, "Altruistic Punishment in
Humans," in *Nature*, based on Public Goods
Games with and without punishment, conducted
with undergraduates at the University of Zurich.
The paper demonstrated that adding the possibility of punishment to a cooperative dilemma
dramatically altered the outcome, from a gradual
slide towards little cooperation (and rampant
free-riding), to a steady increase towards stable
cooperation. Enough subjects were willing to
punish non-cooperators at a cost to themselves
to shift the balance from free-riding to cooperation. In stable groups this cooperation-
punishment combination dramatically increases
long-run gains (Gächter et al. 2008).

To examine the generalizability of these
results, which many took to be a feature of our
species, Herrmann, Thoni, and Gächter
conducted systematic comparable experiments
among undergraduates from a diverse swath of
industrialized populations (Herrmann et al.
2008). In these Public Goods Games, subjects
played with the same four partners for 10 rounds
and could contribute during each round to a
group project. All contributions to the group
project were multiplied by 1.6 and distributed
equally among all partners. Players could also
pay to punish other players by taking money
away from them.

In addition to finding population-level differences in the subjects' initial willingness to cooperate, Gächter's team unearthed in about half of
these samples a phenomenon that is not observed
beyond a trivial degree among typical undergraduate subjects (see our Figure 15.4): Many
subjects engaged in anti-social punishment; that

is, they paid to reduce the earnings of "overly"
cooperative individuals (those who contributed
more than the punisher did). The effect of this
behavior on levels of cooperation was dramatic,
completely compensating for the cooperation-
inducing effects of punishment in the Zurich
experiment. Possibilities for altruistic punishment do not generate high levels of cooperation
in these populations. Meanwhile, participants
from a number of Western countries, such as
the United States, the United Kingdom, and
Australia, behaved like the original Zurich
students. Thus, it appears that the Zurich sample
works well for generalizing to the patterns of
other Western samples (as well as the Chinese
sample), but such findings cannot be readily
extended beyond this.

Independent and Interdependent Self-concepts

Much psychological research has explored the
nature of people's self-concepts. Self-concepts
are important, as they organize the information
that people have about themselves, direct
attention to information that is perceived to be
relevant, shape motivations, influence how
people appraise situations that influence their
emotional experiences, and guide their choices
of relationship partners. Markus and Kitayama
(1991) posited that self-concepts can take on a
continuum of forms stretching between two
poles, termed independent and interdependent
self-views, which relate to the individualism-
collectivism construct (Triandis 1989, 1994).
Do people conceive of themselves primarily as
self-contained individuals, understanding themselves as autonomous agents who consist largely
of component parts, such as attitudes, personality traits, and abilities? Or do they conceive of
themselves as interpersonal beings intertwined
with one another in social webs, with incum-
bent role-based obligations towards others
within those networks? The extent to which
people perceive themselves in ways similar to
these independent or interdependent poles has

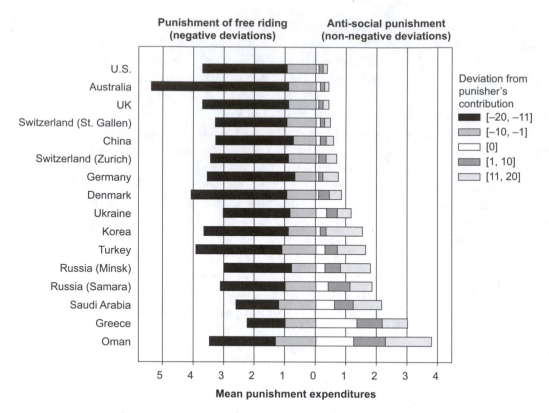

Figure 15.4 Mean punishment expenditures from each sample for a given deviation from the punisher's contribution to the public good. The deviations of the punished subject's contribution from the punisher's contribution are grouped into five intervals, where [−20, −11] indicates that the punished subjects contributed between 11 and 20 less than the punishing subject; [0] indicates that the punished subject contributed exactly the same amount as the punishing subject; and [1,10] ([11,20]) indicates that the punished subject contributed between 1 and 10 (11 and 20) more than the punishing subject. Adapted from Herrmann et al. (2008).

significant consequences for a variety of emotions, cognitions, and motivations.

Much research has underscored how Westerners have more independent views of self than non-Westerners. For example, research using the Twenty Statements Test (Kuhn & McPartland 1954) reveals that people from Western populations (e.g., Australians, Americans, Canadians, Swedes) are far more likely to understand their selves in terms of internal psychological characteristics, such as their personality traits and attitudes, and are less likely to understand them in terms of roles and relationships, than are people from non-Western populations, such as Native Americans, Cook Islanders, Maasai and Samburu (both African pastoralists), Malaysians, and East Asians.

There are numerous psychological patterns associated with self-concepts. For example, people with independent self-concepts are more likely to demonstrate (1) positively biased views of themselves; (2) a heightened valuation of personal choice; and (3) an increased motivation to "stand out" rather than to "fit in." Each of these represents a significant research enterprise, and we discuss them in turn.

Positive Self-views

The most widely endorsed assumption regarding the self is that people are motivated to view themselves positively. Roger Brown (1986) famously declared this motivation to maintain high self-esteem an "urge so deeply human, we can hardly imagine its absence" (1986 p. 534). The strength of this motivation has been perhaps most clearly documented by assessing the ways that people go about exaggerating their self-views by engaging in self-serving biases, in which people view themselves more positively than objective benchmarks would justify. For example, in one study, 94% of American professors rated themselves as better than the average American professor (Cross 1977). However, meta-analyses reveal that these self-serving biases tend to be more pronounced in Western populations than in non-Western ones. Indeed, in some cultural contexts, most notably East Asian ones, evidence for self-serving biases tends to be null, or in some cases, shows significant reversals, with East Asians demonstrating self-effacing biases (Heine & Hamamura 2007). At best, the sharp self-enhancing biases of Westerners are less pronounced in much of the rest of the world, although self-enhancement has long been discussed as if it were a fundamental aspect of human psychology.

Personal Choice

Psychology has long been fascinated with how people assert agency by making choices and has explored the efforts that people go through to ensure that their actions feel freely chosen and that their choices are sensible. However, there is considerable variation across populations in the extent to which people value choice and in the range of behaviors over which they feel that they are making choices. For example, one study found that European-American children preferred working on a task, worked on it longer, and performed better on it, if they had made some superficial choices regarding the task than if others made the same choices for them. In contrast, Asian-American children were equally motivated by the task if a trusted other made the same choices for them (Iyengar & Lepper 1999). Another two sets of studies found that Indians

were slower at making choices, were less likely to make choices consistent with their personal preferences, and were less likely to view their actions as expressions of choice, than were Americans (Savani et al. 2008). Likewise, the extent to which people feel that they have much choice in their lives varies across populations. Surveys conducted at bank branches in Argentina, Brazil, Mexico, the Philippines, Singapore, Taiwan, and the United States found that Americans were more likely to perceive having more choice at their jobs than were subjects from the other countries (Iyengar & DeVoe 2003). Another survey administered in more than 40 countries found, in general, that feelings of free choice in one's life were considerably higher in Western nations (e.g., Finland, the United States, and Northern Ireland) than in various non-Western nations (e.g., Turkey, Japan, and Belarus: Inglehart et al. 1998). This research reveals that perceptions of choice are experienced less often, and are a lesser concern, among those from non-Western populations.

Motivations to Conform

Many studies have explored whether motivations to conform are similar across populations by employing a standard experimental procedure (Asch 1951, 1952). In these studies, which were initially conducted with Americans, participants first hear a number of confederates making a perceptual judgment that is obviously incorrect, and then participants are given the opportunity to state their own judgment. A majority of American participants were found to go along with the majority's incorrect judgment at least once. This research sparked much interest, apparently because Westerners typically feel that they are acting on their own independent resolve and are not conforming. A meta-analysis of studies performed in 17 societies (Bond & Smith 1996), including subjects from Oceania, the Middle East, South America, Africa, South America, East Asia, Europe, and the United States, found that motivations for conformity are weaker in Western societies than elsewhere.

Other research converges with this conclusion. For example, Kim and Markus (1999) found that Koreans preferred objects that were more common, whereas Americans showed a greater preference for objects that were more unusual.

Moral Reasoning

A central concern in the developmental literature has been the way people acquire the cognitive foundations of moral reasoning. The most influential approach to the development of moral reasoning has been Kohlberg's (1971, 1976, 1981), in which people's abilities to reason morally are seen to hinge on cognitive abilities that develop over maturation. Kohlberg proposed that people progressed through the same three levels: (1) Children start out at a pre-conventional level, viewing right and wrong as based on internal standards regarding the physical or hedonistic consequences of actions; (2) then they progress to a conventional level, where morality is based on external standards, such as that which maintains the social order of their group; and finally (3) some progress further to a post-conventional level, where they no longer rely on external standards for evaluating right and wrong, but instead do so on the basis of abstract ethical principles regarding justice and individual rights—the moral code inherent in most Western constitutions.

While all of Kohlberg's levels are commonly found in WEIRD populations, much subsequent research has revealed scant evidence for post-conventional moral reasoning in other populations. One meta-analysis carried out with data from 27 countries found consistent evidence for post-conventional moral reasoning in all the Western urbanized samples, yet found no evidence for this type of reasoning in small-scale societies (Snarey 1985). Furthermore, it is not just that formal education is necessary to achieve Kohlberg's post-conventional level. Some highly educated non-Western populations do not show this post-conventional reasoning. At Kuwait University, for example, faculty members scored lower on Kohlberg's schemes than the typical norms for Western adults, and the elder faculty there scored no higher than the younger ones, contrary to Western patterns (Al-Shehab 2002; Miller et al. 1990).

Research in moral psychology indicates that typical Western subjects rely principally on justice- and harm/care-based principles in judging morality. However, recent work indicates that non-Western adults and Western religious conservatives rely on a wider range of moral principles than these two dimensions of morality. Shweder et al. (1997) proposed that in addition to a dominant justice-based morality, which they termed an "ethic of autonomy," there are two other ethics that are commonly found outside the West: an ethic of community, in which morality derives from the fulfillment of interpersonal obligations that are tied to an individual's role within the social order, and an ethic of divinity, in which people are perceived to be bearers of something holy or god-like, and have moral obligations to not act in ways that are degrading to or incommensurate with that holiness. The ethic of divinity requires that people treat their bodies as temples, not as playgrounds, and so personal choices that seem to harm nobody else (e.g., about food, sex, and hygiene) are sometimes moralized (for a further elaboration of moral foundations, see Haidt & Graham 2007). In sum, the high-socioeconomic status (SES), secular Western populations that have been the primary target of study thus far, appear unusual in a global context, based on their peculiarly narrow reliance, relative to the rest of humanity, on a single foundation for moral reasoning (based on justice, individual rights, and the avoidance of harm to others).

Other Potential Differences

There are many other psychological phenomena in which Western samples differ from non-Western ones; however, at present there are insufficient data in these domains derived from diverse populations to assess where Westerners reside in the human spectrum. For example, compared with Westerners, some non-Westerners (1) have less dynamic social networks, in which people work to avoid negative interactions among their existing networks rather than seeking new relations (Adams 2005); (2) prefer lower to higher arousal-positive affective states (Tsai 2007); (3) are less egocentric when they try to take the perspective of others (Cohen et al. 2007; Wu & Keysar 2007); (4) have weaker motivations for consistency (Kanagawa et al. 2001; Suh 2002); (5) are less prone to "social-loafing" (i.e., reducing efforts on group tasks when individual contributions are not being monitored) (Earley 1993); (6) associate fewer benefits with a person's physical attractiveness (Anderson et al. 2008); and (7) have more pronounced motivations to avoid negative outcomes relative to their motivations to approach positive outcomes (Elliot et al. 2001; Lee et al. 2000).

With reference to the spatial reasoning patterns discussed earlier, emerging evidence suggests that a geocentric bias (i.e., a landscape- or earth-fixed spatial coordinate system) may be much more widespread than previously thought—indeed, it may be the common pattern outside of the West, even among non-Western speakers of languages which make regular use of egocentric linguistic markers. Comparative research contrasting children and adults in Geneva with samples in Indonesia, Nepal, and rural and urban India have found the typical geocentric reasoning pattern in all of these populations, except for the Geneva samples (Dasen et al. 2006). Although many of these population-level differences are pronounced, more research is needed before we can assess whether the geocentric pattern is common across a broader swath of humanity.

Summary

Although robust patterns have emerged among people from industrialized societies, Westerners emerge as unusual—frequent global outliers—on several key dimensions. The experiments reviewed are numerous, arise from different disciplines, use diverse methods, and are often part of systematically comparable data sets created by unified projects. Many of these differences are not merely differences in the magnitude of effects but often show qualitative differences, involving effect reversals or novel phenomena such as allocentric spatial reasoning and antisocial punishment.

References

Adams, G. (2005). The cultural grounding of personal relationships: Enemyship on West African worlds. *Journal of Personality and Social Psychology*, 88: 948–68.

Al-Shehab, A. J. (2002). A cross-sectional examination of levels of moral reasoning in a sample of Kuwait University faculty members. *Social Behavior and Personality*, 30: 813–820.

Anderson, S. L., Adams, G. & Plaut, V. C. (2008). The cultural grounding of personal relationship: The importance of attractiveness in everyday life. *Journal of Personality and Social Psychology*, 95: 352–368.

Arnett, J. (2008). The neglected 95%: Why American psychology needs to become less American. *American Psychologist*, 63(7): 602–14.

Asch, S. E. (1951). Effects of group pressure upon the modification and distortion of judgments. In H. Guetzkow, Ed. *Groups, Leadership and Men*, (pp. 177–90). Carnegie.

Asch, S. E. (1952). Group forces in the modification and distortion of judgments. In *Social Psychology* (pp. 450–501). Prentice Hall.

Atran, S., Medin, D. L., Lynch, E., Vapnarsky, V., Ucan, E. E., Sousa, P. (2001). Folkbiology doesn't come from folkpsychology: Evidence from Yukatek Maya in cross-cultural perspective. *Journal of Cognition and Culture*, 1(1): 3–42.

Atran, S., Medin, D. L., & Ross, N. (2005). The cultural mind: Environmental decision making and, cultural modeling within and across populations. *Psychological Review*, 112(4): 744–76.

Bang, M., Medin, D. L., & Atran, S. (2007). Cultural mosaics and mental models of nature. *Proceedings of the National Academy of Sciences USA*, 104: 13868–74.

Bond, R., & Smith, P. B. (1996). Culture and conformity: A meta-analysis of studies using Asch's (1952b, 1956) line judgment task. *Psychological Bulletin* 119(1): 111–137.

Brown, R. (1986) *Social psychology*, 2nd edition. Free Press.

Buss, D. M. (1989). Sex-differences in human mate preferences: Evolutionary hypothesis tested in 37 cultures. *Behavioral and Brain Sciences*, 12(1): 1–14.

Camerer, C. (2003). *Behavior Game Theory: Experiments in strategic interaction*. Princeton, NJ: Princeton University Press.

Carey, S. (1985). *Conceptual Change in Childhood*. Combridge, MA: MIT Press.

Carey, S. (1995). On the origins of causal understanding. In D. Sperber, D. Premack & A. Premack, (Eds.), *Causal Cognition* (pp. 268–302). Oxford University Press.

Cohen, D., Hoshino-Browne, E., & Leung, A. (2007). Culture and the structure of personal experience: Insider and outsider phenomenologies of the self and social world. In M. P. Zanna (Ed.), *Advances in Experimental Social Psychology*, vol. 39, (pp. 1–67). Academic Press.

Cross, P. (1977). Not can but will college teaching be improved. *New Directions for Higher Education*, 17: 1–15.

Daly, M., & Wilson, M. (1988). *Homicide*. Aldine de Gruyter.

Dasen, P. R., Mishra, R. C., Niraula, S., & Wassmann, J. (2006). Développement du langage et de la cognition spatiale géocentrique. *Enfance*, 58: 146–58.

Earley, P. C. (1993) East meets West meets Mideast: Further explorations of collectivistic and individualistic work groups. *Academy of Management Journal* 36: 319–348.

Ekman, P. (1999). Facial expressions. In T. Dalgleish and T. Power, (Eds.), *The Handbook of Cognition and Emotion*, (pp. 301–20.) Wiley.

Elfenbein, H. A., Ambady, N. (2002). On the universality and cultural specificity of emotion recognition: A meta-analysis. *Psychological Bulletin*, 128: 203–235.

Elliot, I. T., Chirkov, V. I., Kim, Y., Sheldon, K. M. (2001) A cross-cultural analysis of avoidance (relative to approach) personal goals. *Psychological Science* 12: 505–510.

Fehr, E., and Gächter, S. (1998). Reciprocity and economics: The economic implications of Homo reciprocans. *European Economic Review*, 42(3–5): 845–859.

Fehr, E., and Gächter, S. (2002). Altruistic punishment in humans. *Nature*, 415: 137–140.

Fodor, J. A. (1983). *The Modularity of Mind: An essay on faculty psychology*. Cambridge, MA: MIT Press.

Gachter, S., Renner, E., & Sefton, M. (2008). The long-run benefits of punishment. *Science*, 322(5907): 1510.

Haidt, J., & Graham, J. (2007). When morality opposes justice: Conservatives have moral intuitions that liberals may not recognize. *Social Justice Research*, 20: 98–116.

Haun, D. B. M., Call, J., Janzen, G., & Levinson, S. C. (2006a). Evolutionary psychology of spatial representations in the hominidae. *Current Biology*, 16(17): 1736–1740.

Haun, D. B. M., Rapold, C. J., Call, J., Janzen, G., & Levinson, S. C. (2006b) Cognitive cladistics and cultural override in hominid spatial cognition. *Proceedings of the National Academy of Sciences USA*, 103(46): 17568–73.

Heine, S. J. and Hamamura, T. (2007) In search of East Asian self-enhancement. *Personality and Social Psychology Review* 11: 1–24.

Henrich, J., Boyd, R., Bowles, S., Camerer, C. F., Fehr, E., Gintis, H., McElreath, R., Alvard, M., Barr, A., Ensminger, J., Henrich, N. S., Hill, K., Gil-White, F., Gurven, M., Marlowe, F. W., Patton, J. Q., & Tracer, D. (2005a). "Economic man" in cross-cultural perspective: Behavioral experiments in 15 small-scale societies. *Behavioral and Brain Sciences*, 28(6): 795–815; discussion 815–55.

Henrich, J., McElreath, R., Ensminger, J., Barr, A., Barrett, C., Bolyanatz, A., Cardenas, J. C., Gurven, M., Gwako, E., Henrich, N., Lesorogol, C., Marlowe, F., Tracer, D., & Ziker, J. (2006). Costly punishment across human societies. *Science*, 312(5868): 1767–1770.

Herrmann, B., Thoni, C., & Gächter, S. (2008) Antisocial punishment across societies. *Science* 319(5868): 1362–1367.

Hoffman, E., McCabe, K., & Smith, V. (1998). Behavioral foundations of reciprocity: Experimental economics and evolutionary psychology. *Economic Inquiry* 36: 335–52.

Inglehart, R., Basanez, M., & Moreno, A. (1998) *Human Values and Beliefs: A cross-cultural sourcebook*. University of Michigan Press.

Iyengar, S. S., & DeVoe, S. E. (2003). Rethinking the value of choice: Considering cultural mediators of intrinsic motivation. In: V. Murphy-Berman and J. J. Berman (Eds.), *Nebraska Symposium on Motivation: vol. 49. Cross-cultural differences in perspectives on the self*, ed. (pp. 129–74). University of Nebraska Press.

Iyengar, S. S., & Lepper, M. R. (1999). Rethinking the value of choice: A cultural perspective on intrinsic motivation. *Journal of Personality and Social Psychology*, 76: 349–366.

Kanagawa, C., Cross, S. E., & Markus, H. R. (2001). "Who am I?": The cultural psychology of the conceptual self. *Personality and Social Psychology Bulletin*, 27: 90–103.

Kenrick, D. T., & Keefe, R. C. (1992). Age preferences in mates reflect sex-differences in reproductive strategies. *Behavioral and Brain Sciences* 15(1): 75–133.

Kim, H., & Markus, H. R. (1999). Deviance or uniqueness, harmony or conformity? A cultural analysis. *Journal of Personality and Social Psychology*, 77: 785–800.

Kohlberg, L. (1971) From is to ought: How to commit the naturalistic fallacy and get away with it in the study of moral development. In: L. Mischel (Ed.), *Cognitive Development and Epistemology*, (pp. 151–284) Academic Press.

Kohlberg, L. (1976) Moral stages and moralization. In T. Lickona, (Ed.), *Moral Development and Behavior: Theory, research and social issues* (pp. 31–53). Holt, Rinehart and Winston.

Kohlberg, L. (1981) *The philosophy of Moral Development*. Harper & Row.

Kraul, C. (2008). Environmental pollution and encroaching narco have taken their toll on Narino's state's Afro-Columbians. The community's unique culture, and altruism, is in peril. *Los Angeles Times*, April 14, 2008, p. 1.

Kuhn, M. H., & McPartland, T. (1954). An empirical investigation of self-attitudes. *American Sociological Review* 19:68–76.

Lee, A. Y., Aaker, J. L. & Gardner, W. L. (2000) The pleasures and pains of distinct self-construals: The role of interdependence in regulatory focus. *Journal of Personality and Social Psychology*, 78: 1122–1134.

Levinson, S. C., Kita, S., Haun, D., & Rasch, B. H. (2002). Returning the tables: Language affects spatial reasoning. *Cognition* 84: 155–188.

Li, P. & Gleitman, L. (2002). Turning the tables: Language and spatial reasoning. *Cognition* 83: 265–294.

Majid, A., Bowerman, M., Kita, S., Haun, D. B. M., & Levinson, S. C. (2004). Can language restructure cognition? The case for space. *Trends in Cognitive Sciences*, 8(3): 108–114.

Markus, H. R., & Kitayama, S. (1991). Culture and the self: Implications for cognition, emotion, and motivation. *Psychological Review*, 98: 224–253.

May, R. M. (1997). The scientific wealth of nations. *Science*, 275: 793–796.

Miller, J. G., Bersoff, D. M., & Harwood, R. L. (1990). Perceptions of social responsibilities in India and the United States: Moral imperatives or personal decisions? *Journal of Personality and Social Psychology*, 58: 33–47.

Nowak, M. A., Page, K. M., & Sigmund, K. (2000). Fairness versus reason in the Ultimatum Game. *Science*, 289(5485):1773–1775.

Ross, N., Medin, D. L., Coley, J. D., & Atran, S. (2003). Cultural and experiential differences in the development of folkbiological induction. *Cognitive Development*, 18(1): 25–47.

Savani, K., Markus, H. R., & Conner, A. L. (2008). Let your preference be your guide? Preferences and choices are more tightly linked for North Americans than for Indians. *Journal of Personality and Social Psychology*, 95: 861–876.

Savani, K., Markus, H. R., Naidu, N. V. R., Kumar, S., & Berlia, N. (in press). What counts as choice? Americans are more likely than Indians to construe actions as choices. *Psychological Science*.

Segall, M. H., Campbell, D. T., & Herskovits, M. J. (1966). *The Influence of Culture on Visual Perception*. Bobbs-Merril.

Shweder, R. A., Much, N. C., Mahapatra, M., & Park, L. (1997). The "big three" of morality (autonomy, community, divinity) and the "big three" explanations of suffering. In: A. M. Brandt & P. Rozin, *Morality and Health*, (Eds.), (pp. 119–169). Routledge.

Snarey, J. R. (1985) The cross-cultural universality of social-moral development: A critical review of Kohlbergian research. *Psychological Bulletin*, 97(2): 202–232.

Suh, E. M. (2002) Culture, identity consistency, and subjective well-being. *Journal of Personality and Social Psychology*, 83: 1378–1319.

Tracy, J. L., & Matsumoto, D. (2008). The spontaneous expression of pride and shame: Evidence for biologically innate nonverbal displays. *Proceedings of the National Academy of Sciences USA*, 105(33): 11655–11660.

Triandis, H. C. (1989). The self and social-behavior in differing cultural contexts. *Psychological Review*, 96(3): 506–520.

Triandis, H. C. (1994) *Culture and Social Behavior*. McGraw-Hill.

Waxman, S., & Medin, D. L. (2007). Experience and cultural models matter: Placing firm limits on childhood anthropocentrism. *Human Development*, 50(1): 23–30.

Wu, S., & Keysar, B. (2007). Cultural effects on perspective taking. *Psychological Science* 18: 600–606.

Chapter 16

John Tooby and Leda Cosmides

ON THE UNIVERSALITY OF HUMAN NATURE AND THE UNIQUENESS OF THE INDIVIDUAL
The Role of Genetics and Adaptation

Personality psychology has two distinct traditions the search for a universal human nature, and the search for an explanation of individual differences in psychological traits (Buss, 1984). These two traditions have developed in parallel, but cohabit in the same field uneasily because the conceptual relations between them are cloudy and often seem contradictory. Paradoxically, theories of human nature make claims about a universal human psychology, whereas personality research into individual differences depends on the existence of stable, interesting differences between individuals, and correspondingly tends to ignore, deny, or minimize universals. Of course, one half of the reconciliation between the two is a straightforward commonplace of psychological thinking. A human nature composed of uniform psychological mechanisms may produce individual differences as a result of different individual experiences. It is the existence of genetic differences between individuals that poses problems. It renders the study of the causation of individual differences difficult, and, more importantly, it calls into question the very idea of a universal human nature. Indeed, some behavior geneticists are forceful about challenging the value of characterizing a shared human nature, given their estimation of the magnitude of genetic differences. For this reason, they tend to focus on variation rather than on universality. "The questions that most often confront scientists studying human behavior are those dealing with differences among people. And genetics, the study of variation of organisms, is uniquely qualified to aid us in analyzing these individual differences" (Plomin, DeFries, & McClearn, 1980, p. 11).

The tension between the two traditions in personality psychology has had its direct analog in evolutionary biology (Buss, 1984). Theories of and claims about species-typical behavioral adaptations appear to conflict with the discovery, through molecular genetic techniques, of vast reservoirs of genetic variability (Hubby & Lewontin, 1966, reviewed in Ayala, 1976 and Nevo, 1978; Lewontin & Hubby, 1966). Systematists find species to be clearly and recognizably characterizable by species-specific, species-typical physical and behavioral traits, and yet on genetic grounds, each individual is a unique combination of genes (with their associated traits), and varies in tens of thousands of ways from its conspecifics. Is the concept of the psychic unity of humankind, of a single, universal human nature, insupportable in the light of what is known about human and nonhuman genetics? Can the uniqueness of the individual be reconciled with the claim of a universal human nature?

We believe that evolutionary biology provides the conceptual framework that allows this reconciliation. Both the psychological universals that constitute human nature and the genetic differences that contribute to individual variation are the product of the evolutionary process, and personality psychology must therefore be made consistent with the principles of evolutionary biology. This means that every personality phenomenon is, from an evolutionary perspective, analyzable as either (*a*) an adaptation, (*b*) an incidental by-product of an adaptation, (*c*) the product of noise in the system, or (*d*) some combination of these. Standards for recognizing these three varieties of evolutionary outcome will allow one to discover new, adaptively patterned personality traits and to place previous findings in evolutionary perspective. In this chapter, we attempt to sketch out some of these standards. In the process, we will argue that (*a*) some personality differences may be the expression of different, environmentally triggered adaptive strategies, (*b*) different adaptive personality strategies cannot, in principle, be coded for by suites of genes that differ from person to person, and (*c*) most *heritable* personality differences are *not* the expression of different adaptive strategies. They are either mutationally driven genetic noise, or else an incidental by-product of an adaptation that has nothing to do with personality per se—pathogen-driven selection for biochemical diversity (Tooby & Cosmides, 1988).

Evolutionary Foundations

An Evolutionary Perspective on Nature and Nurture

The Environment as the Product of Evolution

An evolutionary perspective is not a form of "genetic determinism," if by that one means the idea that genes determine everything, immune from environmental influence. Anyone with a biological education acknowledges that the phenotype is the result of the interaction between genes and environment, and all aspects of the phenotype are equally codetermined by this interaction. Developmental programs (i.e., the regulatory processes that control development) are directed by the genes, but they require and depend upon an entire range of properties of the environment being reliably and stably present in order to successfully produce a healthy individual. If either the genes or the environment are sufficiently changed, the result will change. Thus, as with all interactions, the product cannot be analyzed into separate genetically determined, as opposed to environmentally determined, components.

However, because of the nature of the evolutionary process that creates this interaction, "genes" and "environment" exist in a highly structured relationship that is very different from popular conceptions of separate but parallel genetic and environmental "influences." Many social scientists have labored under the false impression that only certain things are under the "control" of the genes, that evolutionary approaches are relevant only to those traits under such "control," and that the greater the environmental influence or control, the less evolutionary analyses apply. In place of evolutionary analyses of those things purportedly under genetic control, they conduct atheoretical or nonevolutionary explorations of those traits under (what they believe to be) "environmental" control. This kind of erroneous thinking is associated with the idea that genes are "biological," whereas "the environment" is nonbiological, the "social environment" is thought to be the opposite of "biological determination." But a close examination of how natural selection actually drives evolutionary processes leads to a very different view of how "genes" and the "environment" are related. Evolution acts *through* genes, but it acts on the *relationship* between the genes and the environment. The "environment" is as much a part of the process of evolutionary inheritance as are the "genes," and equally as "biological" and evolved. No organism reacts to every aspect of the environment. Instead, the developmental programs rely on and interact with only certain defined subsets of properties of the environment, while others are ignored. For example, different diets transform a female ant into a worker or a queen, but there is no diet that will transform her into a dog, and guitar music or religious exhortation does not affect her growth. Over evolutionary time, genetic variation in developmental programs (with selective retention of advantageous variants) explores the properties of the environment, discovering those that are useful sources of information in the task of regulating development and behavior, and rendering those features of the environment that are unreliable or disruptive irrelevant to development. Across generations, this process of exploration of alternative gene-environment relations operates by varying developmental programs with respect to (a) what kinds of inputs from the environment they accept or are sensitive to, and (b) how they shape phenotypic outcomes in response to these inputs. "The environment" of an animal—in the sense of which features of the world it depends on or uses as inputs—is just as much the creation of the evolutionary process as the genes are. Thus, the evolutionary process can be said to store information necessary for development in both the environment and the genes, in that it shapes the relationship of the two so that both are necessary participants in the ontogenetic construction of adaptations. Both are "biologically determined," if such a phrase has any meaning.

Environmentalism Depends on Nativism

"The environment," per se, is powerless to act on the psyche of an animal, except in ways specified by the developmental programs and psychological mechanisms that already happen to exist in that animal at a given time. These procedures take environmental information as input and generate behavior or psychological change as output. The actual relationship between environment and behavior is created solely and entirely by the nature and design of the information-processing mechanisms that happen to exist in the animal, and in principle, information-processing mechanisms could be "designed" to create a causal relationship between any imaginable environmental input and any imaginable behavioral output. The smell of excrement may be repulsive to us, but it is attractive to dung flies. Aside from a few gross effects, such as gravity, the relationship between the environment and the behavior of the organism is not a matter of physical necessity, but is decided by the structure of the organism's psychological mechanisms.

The information-processing procedures that exist in an organism at a given time are either (a) genetically specified, that is, innate, or (b) the product of other, prior procedures. In the event they are the product of other, prior procedures, such prior procedures must themselves be either innate or the product of still other, even more antecedent procedures. After ruling out infinite regression as a tenable theory of the origins of psychological structure, one must necessarily conclude that the psyche of an organism at any point in time is the product of its innate procedures, plus the changes—including any constructed procedures and their effects—created by those innate procedures operating on a sequence of environmental inputs. Therefore, innate procedures must exist, are the necessary foundation of any full model of the psychology of any organism, and are always *necessarily entailed* by any environmentalist claim. Environmentalist theories depend on prior nativist theories, and therefore environmentalism and nativism are not opposed, but are instead interdependent doctrines.

Thus, valid environmentalism inescapably posits innately regulated psychological mechanisms. Any environmentalist claim about the influence of a given part of the environment entails a claim about an innately specified relationship between the environment and the hypothesized psychological output. Consider, for example, the claim that girls learn gender-appropriate behavior by watching their parents.

This entails the claims that (a) girls have innate mechanisms specialized for learning gender-appropriate behavior (otherwise, why wouldn't a girl be just as likely to imitate her father?), (b) these mechanisms compute the frequency with which each parent performs various behaviors, and, for each behavior, compare the mother's tally to the father's, and (c) these mechanisms cause girls to imitate behaviors that their mothers perform more frequently than their fathers, and to avoid the behaviors that their fathers perform more frequently than their mothers. Rather than escaping claims of innateness, this "socialization hypothesis" tacitly posits some rather sophisticated and specialized innate machinery linking informational input to behavioral output.

Every coherent psychological theory has at its foundation innate mechanisms or procedures, either explicitly recognized or tacitly entailed. To say such procedures are innate means that they are specified in the organism's genetic endowment, that is, in how genetically based programs regulate the mechanisms governing development. This genetically specified, innate foundation of the psyche is the product of the evolutionary process, and is the means through which the evolutionary process organizes the psychology of the animal over generations. Evolutionary biology is relevant to psychology because it studies the evolutionary processes responsible for shaping the innate foundations of psychological mechanisms, just as it does for physiological mechanisms.

Manifest Variability and Innate Universals: What is Human Nature?

Genetics had enormous difficulty making progress as a science until geneticists drew the distinction between genotype and phenotype, that is, between the inherited basis of a trait and its observable expression. This distinction allowed them to move beyond the bewildering complexity of surface characteristics to an underlying level of clear principles that explained the surface variability. We believe a similar distinction will be

equally useful for an evolutionarily informed personality psychology. We will refer to this as the distinction between an individual's innate psychology and his or her manifest psychology and behavior. If one believes in a universal human nature, as we do, one observes variable manifest psychologies, traits, or behaviors between individuals and across cultures, and views them as the product of a common, underlying evolved innate psychology, operating under different circumstances (see, e.g., Daly, Wilson, & Weghorst, 1982). The mapping between the innate and the manifest operates according to principles of expression that are specified in innate psychological mechanisms or in innate developmental programs that shape psychological characteristics, these expressions can differ between individuals when different environmental inputs are operated on by the same procedures to produce different manifest outputs (Cosmides & Tooby, 1987; Tooby & Cosmides, 1989). This set of universal innate psychological mechanisms and developmental programs constitutes human nature. Individual differences that arise from exposing the same human nature to different environmental inputs relate the study of individual differences to human nature in a straightforward way. Those researchers who are interested in applying an evolutionary perspective to individual differences can investigate the adaptive design of these universal mechanisms by seeing whether different manifest outputs are adaptively tuned to their corresponding environmental input. Does the algorithm which relates input to output show evidence of complex adaptive design?

Evolution Produces Adaptive Organization and a Residue of Nonadaptive Disorder

Reconceptualizing psychology from an evolutionary perspective requires the careful use of concepts developed in evolutionary biology, of which the most important is adaptation. Evolutionary biology explains the characteristics of living processes primarily through relating their organization to adaptive requirements. If evolution has anything to contribute to personality psychology, it will be through investigating which personality phenomena are adaptations and which are not. To address this issue, one needs clear standards for recognizing adaptations. An adaptation is a characteristic of the phenotype developmentally manufactured according to instructions contained in its genetic specification or basis, whose genetic basis became established and organized in the population because the characteristic systematically interacted with stable features of the environment in a way that promoted the reproduction of the individual bearing the characteristic, or the reproduction of the relatives of that individual (Dawkins, 1982; Hamilton, 1964; Williams, 1966). Adaptations are mechanisms or systems of properties "designed" by natural selection to solve the specific biological problems posed by the physical, ecological, and social environments encountered by the ancestors of a species during the course of its evolution. The evolutionary biologist's definition of adaptive function is subtly but profoundly different from either common-sense notions of function or many psychologists' notions of function. The promotion of the reproduction of the individual and/or his or her relatives is a very different standard of functional operation from such intuitively reasonable standards as happiness, social harmony, success, welfare, well-being, adjustment, long life, health, goal realization, and self-actualization, although in many circumstances and at many levels of explanation they may correspond. Nevertheless, in seeking an explanation for the organization of our innate (i.e., evolved, genetically specified) psychological mechanisms and developmental programs, it is the biological definition of function and adaptation that tracks the forces that have shaped us.

To properly account for psychological phenomena in evolutionary terms, one must recognize that evolution produces both adaptations and nonadaptive aspects of the phenotype,

and distinguish between them carefully (Williams, 1966). Although natural selection is the single major organizing process in evolution, promoting adaptive coordination between organism and environment, evolutionary outcomes are shaped, however weakly, by many other processes, many of which disrupt such coordination (e.g., mutation, recombination, genetic hitchhiking, antagonistic pleiotropy, engineering constraints, antagonistic coevolution).

The outcomes from evolution break down into three basic categories (a) adaptations (often, though not always, complex and polygenically specified), (b) concomitants of adaptation, and (c) random effects. Adaptations are the result of coordination brought about by selection as a feedback process, they are recognizable by "evidence of special design"—that is, by a highly nonrandom coordination between properties of the phenotype and the environment, which mesh to promote fitness (genetic propagation). Concomitants of adaptation are those properties of the phenotype which do not contribute to adaptation per se, but which are tied to properties that are, and so are incorporated into the organism's design, they are incidental by-products of adaptation. Bone happens to be white, but was selected not for its color but for its rigidity. Such concomitant aspects will tend to be selectively neutral, in comparison to the functional advantages conferred by the adaptive aspect of the concomitant system. Similarly, there are an infinite number of personality traits one can define and measure, but evolutionarily analyzable order will tend to be found only in those causally related to adaptive function. Finally, entropic effects of many types act to introduce disorder into the "design" of organisms. They are recognizable by the lack of coordination between phenotype and environment that they produce, and by their variability. Examples of such entropic processes include mutation, environmental change, and rare circumstances.

In analyzing personality phenomena from an evolutionary perspective, adaptations will tend to be recognizable because of the functional coordination of psychological characteristics or behavior. Complex organization which systematically leads to adaptive outcomes constitutes evidence of "special design" (Dawkins, 1986; Symons, 1987; Williams, 1966). Moreover, complex architecture or articulation of parts per se suggests (though does not prove) that the properties were organized by natural selection, since random entropie effects are unlikely to construct complex systems of covariation by chance. Uniformity without adaptive patterning or apparent functional significance (e.g., all bones are white, all blood is red) suggests the characteristics in question are incidental concomitants of adaptation. Finally, unstructured variation will tend to be the result of entropic processes, and will often be adaptively neutral. Entropic processes will also cause maladaptation, either through disruption of developmental organization or through a mismatch between the organism and the environment.

By applying these standards one can determine whether a personality trait is the product of an adaptation, a concomitant of adaptation, or noise.

Constraints on Organic Design

Many Psychological Adaptations Will be Complex

Few would deny that humans successfully perform a wide array of tasks, including many that are functionally similar to what other animals do finding mates, having offspring, helping relatives, seeing objects, identifying food, and so on. Described in terms of their goals, such activities can seem transparently simple. Introspectively, we experience many of them (e.g., seeing objects) as effortless. But when one tries to discover sets of procedures that will actually implement such goals, their real complexity, intricacy, and difficulty become oppressively clear (see, e.g., Marr, 1982 on

vision). The history of artificial intelligence has largely been the history of discovering how complex information-processing procedures must be if they are to perform even very simple tasks (e.g., moving around half a dozen blocks in a small area). Work in cognitive science and artificial intelligence has shown that mechanisms capable of solving even supposedly simple real-world cognitive tasks must contain very complex "innate" prespecified procedures or information, matched narrowly to the structural features of the domains within which they are designed to operate (Boden, 1977; Marr, 1982; Minsky, 1986, on the "frame problem," see Brown, 1987; Fodor, 1983).

Expectations derived from evolutionary biology reinforce the conclusion that many psychological mechanisms will be complex and function-specific. Our ancestors had to be able to solve a large number of different adaptive problems, and any attempt to specify procedurally how to solve such problems demonstrates that many of them, at least, are both intricate and dependent for their solution upon mechanisms that differ in structure from one another. For example, successful cooperation requires the coordinated operation of a surprising number of information-processing procedures that are function-specific (Cosmides, 1985, 1989; Cosmides & Tooby, 1989), other adaptive problems (e.g., avoiding poisonous foods, dealing with threats) are solved by other mechanisms.

At the heart of Darwin's theory of the origin of adaptations is the following precept. The more important the adaptive problem, the more intensely selection should have specialized and improved the performance of the mechanism for solving it. Consequently natural selection tends to produce functionally distinct adaptive specializations—a heart to pump blood, a liver to detoxify poisons, and so on. This insight led Chomsky (1980) to argue that the innate information-processing mechanisms of the human mind should include a number of functionally distinct cognitive adaptive specializations. Just as the human body is composed of many complex, functionally distinct physiological organs, he argued, one can expect the human mind to be composed of many complex, functionally distinct "mental organs." Indeed, we have argued elsewhere that a psyche that contained nothing but general-purpose information-processing procedures could not, in principle, generate adaptive behavior, and therefore is an evolutionary impossibility (Cosmides & Tooby, 1987).

Thus, the lessons for psychology from artificial intelligence and evolutionary biology are twofold. First, most or all innate psychological mechanisms will be highly complex in their procedures and design. Second, this complexity will usually be structured in function-specific ways. Our ancestors would not have been able to solve the large array of adaptive information-processing problems necessary for survival and reproduction without a large array of complex, function-specific information-processing mechanisms (Barkow, 1989; Cosmides & Tooby, 1987; Rozin, 1976; Symons, 1987; Tooby & DeVore, 1987).

Complex Adaptations are Monomorphic within an Integrated Functional Design

Viewed from a biological perspective, organisms are complexly designed systems. In fact, there is no nonliving system, natural or artificial, that rivals the complexity of organic design (Dawkins, 1986). Moreover, biological complexity is not a random collection of unconnected properties, but rather an intricate and articulated set of interdependently organized parts that function together in an adaptive mesh to promote fitness.

It is this interdependence among subcomponents that requires a monomorphism of integrated functional design. In any specific system of interdependent parts, each part must present a uniform, regular, and predictable set of properties to the system, so that the other parts can interact with it in a predictable and organized fashion. Any automobile engine can be brought to a halt by significantly altering the design properties of almost any of its parts. Of course, the function of the system can be used to divide the properties of its parts into two sets: those properties whose variation does affect the functional operation of the system, and those whose variation does not (e.g., the color of the radiator hose). We will term the first functional variation, and the second, superficial variation.

The structure of functional interdependence shapes what kinds of variation the system can tolerate. Incremental functional variation is easy to tolerate. If a part or subassembly varies in a way that improves or degrades performance somewhat without disrupting the operation of the rest of the system, such variation can be introduced, tolerated, and evaluated through its effect on comparative performance. On the other hand, a radical change in the design of a part will bring the rest of the system to a halt unless compensatory design changes are simultaneously made in the other parts, in order to preserve their functional integration. For this reason, when a human engineer makes a major change in the design of a computer or car, the "variation" introduced into the design is usually coordinated variation. A change in one part is linked in tandem to a suite of associated compensatory changes, simultaneously introduced in other parts.

Variation, then, can be classified as (a) *superficial variation*, within design tolerance limits, not changing the functional operation of the system significantly, (b) *limited functional variation* deriving from incremental changes in a single part or a small number of parts, which either improves or degrades the functional performance of the system, (c) *disruptive variation*, where the changes introduced violate the functional integrity of the system, causing it to fail, or (d) *radical but coordinated functional variation*, where entire sets of parts vary simultaneously between discrete alternatives, so that each set is functionally integrated. Such variation corresponds to discretely different designs, different models of a car, or different species, or different morphs (e.g., male and female) within a species.

Neo-Darwinism is an account of how functional integration in biological systems can arise through selective retention of a superior functional variant—superior in the sense that the variation modifies the functioning of the system in ways that promote the variant's own propagation. Because the generation of variation through mutation is believed to be a random process, elementary probability indicates that coordinated functional variation $((d)$, as defined above) will come into existence by chance mutation very rarely or never, and therefore such "hopeful monsters" will play only a minor role in evolution. Despite some recent modest challenges to this view (Gould & Eldredge, 1972), both theory and evidence indicate that evolution by natural selection generally proceeds by using the second type of variation—incremental functional variation of limited magnitude, which does not require coordinated, compensatory changes in the rest of the system (Dawkins, 1986). Such evolution takes place within the context of an existing integrated monomorphic design, so that variation within a design either is superficial rather than functional, or consists of incremental random steps away from existing designs of each subcomponent. (Although typological thinking has been properly replaced by populational thinking [Mayr, 1982], the nature of complex adaptations constrains how variation operates within sexually reproducing species.[1])

Human Physiology is Monomorphic within an Integrated Functional Design

This line of analysis is confirmed by commonplace biological observation. The architecture of human physiology, which is better understood and easier to observe than psychological functioning, nicely illustrates these constraints on organic design.

As any biological anthropologist can attest, the "architecture" or physiological design of humans is both distinctively species-specific and species-typical. When one examines the organs, with their complex design and interlocking architecture, one finds (within a sex, and to a large extent between sexes) monomorphism of design. Virtually everyone has two lungs, one neck, a stomach, a pancreas, a tongue, two irises, 10 fingers, blood, hemoglobin, insulin, and so on. And, although there is a great deal of superficial variation—no two stomachs are exactly the same size or shape, for example (Cosmides, 1974; Williams, 1958, 1967)—each organ system has the same basic design. The locations and connections between organs are topologically the same, and the internal tissue structures and physiological processes have a uniformity of structure and functional regulation. One has to descend to specific enzymatic pathways before design differences—as opposed to quantitative variation—start showing up. Individual proteins may indeed differ due to genetic differences between individuals, but genetically specified, coordinated functional variation in biochemical pathways between individuals of the same sex and age is very rare.

There are no substantive reasons to suspect that the kinds of evolutionary forces that shaped our innate psychological mechanisms are fundamentally different from those that shaped our innate physiology. Indeed, Chomsky's arguments on the necessity for innate, modular, complex design in human linguistic cognition are well-known, and have been aptly termed "the new organology" (Chomsky, 1980; Marshall, 1980; see also Marr, 1982). Of course there can be individual variation in cognitive programs, just as there is individual variation in the size and shape of stomachs. This can be true of any structure or process in a sexually recombining species, and such genetic variation constitutes the basis for inherited psychological differences. But even relatively simple cognitive programs or "mental organs" must contain a large number of interdependent processing steps, limiting the nature of the variation that can exist without violating the functional integrity of psychological adaptation. Thus, personality variation is not likely to consist of an alternative, wholly different, coordinated design that differs "from the ground up." On the basis of population genetics considerations described below, we find implausible the notion that different humans have fundamentally different and competing cognitive programs, resting on wholly different genetic bases.

The Paradox of Design Monomorphism in a World of Genetic Polymorphism

Obviously, there is a natural tension between complex functional interdependence in a system and the existence of a large amount of variability in its components. For living systems, design is controlled by the genetic programs that regulate development. If the design of organisms is truly monomorphic, the genes underlying the design should also be monomorphic. Why, then, does there appear to be substantial genetic polymorphism[2] within populations?

This mystery is deepened by the fact that almost all complex organisms reproduce sexually, that is, when reproduction occurs, genes from two parents are randomly recombined to form genetically differentiated, genetically unique offspring. Sexual reproduction, through recombining genes, introduces potentially disruptive variation into a functional design that in the parental generation was functionally integrated enough to reproduce. For this and other reasons, the function of sexual recombination has been obscure, and it has been the subject of intense interest in the evolutionary community (Bell, 1982; Maynard Smith, 1978; Williams, 1975). The alternative, asexual reproduction (i.e., cloning), seems much saner from an evolutionary and from an engineering point of view. In asexual reproduction, each offspring has exactly the same genetic programs as its parent, keeping the integrated design of the parent wholly intact. Moreover, asexual reproduction offers efficient evolutionary progress as well. Functional variants can be effectively

incorporated through mutation and selection (for discussion of these issues see Bell, 1982; Maynard Smith, 1978; Williams, 1975). Traditional claims that sex has been favored because it accelerated evolutionary progress have not withstood recent critical scrutiny (Maynard Smith, 1978; Williams, 1975).

The role of genetic polymorphism and the adaptive significance of sexual reproduction are linked questions (Tooby, 1982). Indeed, they are two sides of the same coin. If all individuals were alike genetically, recombining their genes would be pointless, just as exchanging identical parts on a mass production line does not change the functional end product. Why swap identical parts? The more genetic polymorphism there is, the more sexual recombination produces genetically differentiated offspring. Both interact to produce unique and genetically differentiated individuals, a system that potentially disrupts functionally integrated monomorphic design.

This is all the more puzzling because sex is clearly an adaptation. The high cost and coordinated complexity of the physiological and psychological systems that are necessary if sexual reproduction is to occur are evidence of special design, the hallmark of adaptation (Williams, 1966, 1975).

Sexual Reproduction and Genetic Variation: Evolved Defenses against Pathogens?

Recent developments in evolutionary biology may hold the answer to the linked questions of the adaptive significance of sex and the role of genetic polymorphism. These developments may have significant implications for the study of human nature and individual differences as well. Over the last decade, a growing number of researchers (Bell & Maynard Smith, 1987; Hamilton, 1980; Hamilton & Zuk, 1982; Jaenike, 1978; Rice, 1983; Tooby, 1982) have argued that the selection pressures created by parasites acting on the genetic systems of host populations have the properties required to explain why almost all higher organisms reproduce sexually. Indeed, there is a great deal of ecological and experimental evidence supporting the theory that pathogens selected for the evolution of sex (Hamilton & Zuk, 1982; Kelley, Antonovics, & Schmitt, 1988; Rice, 1983; Tooby, 1982 and others). As Tooby (1982) and Rice (1983) have pointed out, this hypothesis also answers the interlocking question. Why have so many different alleles at so many different loci in a population? The argument is summarized briefly below (see Tooby, 1982, for details, evidence, and supporting references).

Large, complex, long-lived organisms constitute ecological environments for immense numbers of short-lived, rapidly evolving parasites—disease-causing microorganisms. For this reason, parasites and hosts are locked in an antagonistic coevolutionary race. The hosts are selected to evolve defenses against these parasites, and the pathogens are selected to evolve around those defenses. In this evolutionary race, the pathogens have one crucial advantage. They have a shorter generation time than host species, often by a factor of millions, and, other things being equal, can evolve around host defenses faster than host species can evolve new defenses or countermeasures. During an individual host's lifetime, a particular pathogen species may have nearly one million generations in which to adapt to the host's particular physiology, proteins, and biochemistry. Once a pathogen species has "cracked" that host's defenses, by evolving around them, it has simultaneously cracked the defenses of all genetically identical individuals. For an asexually reproducing individual, this means all of its offspring and kin. According to this theory, there are almost no long-lived asexual animal lineages because they fall prey to rapidly evolving diseases.

On the other hand, sexual reproduction is the act of reproducing individuals with a unique new genotype a never-before-encountered set of genes. By mixing genes with those of another individual through sexual recombination, an organism can protect its offspring from the pathogens that have adapted to its biochemistry and physiology during its lifetime. Instead of being perfectly adapted to an individual's offspring, they will have to "start from scratch" with each new offspring. Sexual reproducers foil the decisive evolutionary advantage pathogens have with their rapid generation times by genetically differentiating between parent and offspring, and among siblings, so that each new individual constitutes a unique habitat that must be independently adapted to. Long-lived organisms can survive in a world of rapidly evolving parasitic antagonists because they reproduce sexually.

Among other things, genes code for the proteins which participate in every physiological process. These proteins form the microenvironment of the pathogen (Damian, 1964, 1979). As mentioned earlier, if all individuals were alike genetically, then recombining their genes through sexual reproduction would be pointless, as exchanging identical parts does not change the end product. Alternative alleles at a locus code for alternative proteins. Thus, the more alternative alleles exist at more loci—i.e., the more genetic polymorphism there is—the more sexual recombination produces genetically differentiated offspring, thereby complexifying the series of habitats faced by pathogens. Most pathogens will be adapted to proteins and protein combinations that are common in a population, making individuals with rare alleles less susceptible to parasitism, thereby promoting their fitness. If parasitism is a major selection pressure, then such frequency-dependent selection will be extremely widespread across loci, with incremental advantages accruing to each additional polymorphic locus that varies the host phenotype for a pathogen. This process will build up in populations immense reservoirs of genetic diversity coding for biochemical diversity (Clarke, 1979; Tooby, 1982).

In other words, the existence of multiple alternative alleles at a large proportion of loci is a prediction of the pathogenic theory of the evolution of sex. Indeed, there is considerable evidence that selection has driven the accumulation of allozymic diversity in populations. It is far greater than can be accounted for by random processes acting on selectively neutral alleles (Brues, 1954, 1963; Lewontin, 1974; Nevo, 1978; Tooby, 1982). In short, pathogens supply an intense selection pressure for sexual over asexual reproducers, and are an intense and general source of frequency-dependent selection for protein polymorphism.

Monomorphic Design out of Polymorphic Materials

The pathogen theory suggests that the evolution of multicellular organisms has depended on simultaneously satisfying two conflicting, almost mutually exclusive, demands (a) that a species' complex adaptations be monomorphic in their design properties, and (b) that those properties that parasites target and depend upon be polymorphic. What makes the satisfaction of these conflicting demands possible is that parasites decompose the properties of the host's phenotype differently from the way that the demand for "functional design" does. To make this clear, imagine three tract houses, all identical in layout, but made of different materials wood, brick, and stone. The termites that eat the wood cannot migrate next door to eat the brick or stone. The ants that dig through the brick mortar cannot digest wood or stone, and so on. For the human occupants, the layouts are identical, but for the insects, the materials the houses are built from make them different. Protein polymorphism appears to function similarly within the context of physiological design. The organ system and within-organ functional design are relatively uniform, with each component presenting a regular and predictable set of functional properties to the system. But to find "design diversity" or qualitative diversity as opposed to quantitative diversity (e.g., size,

rate), one must descend to the level of protein structure. This is because the biochemical microenvironment that a pathogen inhabits is a function of protein structure. To reproduce, pathogens use the enzymes, substrates, and biochemical pathways they are exposed to, rather than, necessarily, the ultimate functional product of such pathways.

In other words, the resolution of this conflict is to produce variation which is significant from the point of view of the pathogen's life cycle, but superficial from the point of view of the ultimate functional design of an organ system. Selection can create protein variation that thwarts pathogenic function, while not disrupting the functioning of the organism too radically.

Pathogens Mix Human Genetic Diversity, Making Individuals Different, but Ethnic Groups Similar

People find it easy to believe that there are profoundly different types of humans (e.g., Block, 1971; Block & Ozer, 1982; Jung, 1921). Indeed, people in many cultures have historically harbored the belief that there were important "blood differences" between themselves and whatever other ethnic groups they knew of, and that these others constituted different types of human beings. Are ethnic groups differentiated in a fundamental way because of significant and substantial genetic differences, so that each ethnic group has a set of genes shared by members of the group, but not shared by others? In terms of ethnic differences, one could imagine (as many folk beliefs have it) that neighbors from the same group are very similar "hereditarily," "of one blood," but that members from different groups or different races are very different. Even according to standard biological reasoning, such a result would be easy to account for. People do, after all, mate locally, and given genetic drift and selection to local circumstances, one could easily imagine local gene pools that are internally homoge-neous, but very different from each other (Gould, 1985).

The measures provided by modern molecular genetics have shown that there is no basis for such a belief. Leaving aside the genetic mono-morphism at the sequence level (in excess of 99.99%), and at the protein level (60% to 75%), the examination of the distribution of genetic variation that exists among humans leads to a surprising result. Members of any one human group do not all share fixed combinations of genes that members of other groups lack, or even share single genes that members of other groups entirely lack. Human groups do not differ substantially in the types of genes found, but instead only in the relative proportions of those alleles. Eighty-five percent of human genetic variation is within-group variation, 8% is between tribes or nations within a "race," and only 7% is between "races" (for discussion and references, see Gould, 1985; Lewontin, 1982; Lewontin, Rose, & Kamin, 1984; Nei, 1987). What this means is that the average genetic difference between one Peruvian farmer and his neighbor, or one Bornean horticulturist and her best friend, or one Swiss villager and his neighbor, is 12 times greater than the difference between the "average genotype" of the Swiss population and the "average genotype" of the Peruvian population (i.e., the within-group variance is 12 times greater than the between-group variance). Indeed, as Lewontin, Rose, and Kamin put it (1984 p. 127). "The remarkable feature of human evolution and history has been the very small degree of divergence between geographical populations as compared with the genetic variation among individuals." This result, contrary to what ideas of local selection or genetic drift might lead one to believe, is consistent with the pathogenic theory. People catch diseases from their neighbors, so it is important to be genetically different from them, such selection attracts and recruits genetic vari-ants from outside the local group, promoting

local within-group diversity and reducing inter-group diversity (Tooby, 1982). There is no struc-tured genetic substrate separating human groups discretely into different kinds. Although there is a sea of genetic diversity (measured at the protein level), it is a well-mixed sea.

On the Nonheritability of Inherited Human Nature: Panspecific Versus Idiotypic Nativism

The tale of the Tower of Babel cautions that common enterprises may be defeated if the languages used by those attempting to cooperate are too different. Certainly, cooperation between ethology, behavioral ecology, comparative psychology, behavior genetics, cognitive science, and social and personality psychology has been seriously damaged by the use of the same terms to mean different things. Although researchers are generally (although not always) careful and precise in their usage within their own disci-pline, when terms and results get exported to neighboring fields meanings frequently become inadvertently shifted, leading to persistent misunderstandings. For example, the terms "genetic" and "heritable" have come to mean very different things to geneticists and psychologists. This has caused many researchers to erroneously believe that in order to show that a trait is an evolved adaptation, one must demon-strate that it has a high heritability. These prob-lems reflect a larger confusion within the social sciences that has resulted from the failure to distinguish consistently between what we will call idiotypic nativism—the study of which genetic differences cause which individual differ-ences—and panspecific nativism—the study of the innate developmental and psychological mecha-nisms that all humans share.

In any species, there are features of the genetic system that vary between individuals, and there are features that are species-typical and shared by all normal members of the species. Because differences are easier to investigate, control for, and experimentally manipulate, the bulk of experimental genetics (and behavior genetics) is about within-species genetic differences.

In behavior genetics texts, phrases such as "genetic effects," "genetic influences on behavior," the "genetic hypothesis about behavior," "the role of heredity," "the influence of genetic factors," and "the action of the genes" are used to refer to how genetic differences between individuals affect behavioral differences between individuals—idiotypic nativism. The fact that genetics methods, of necessity, have focused primarily on differences has led to the widespread misimpression among many psychologists that evolutionary, "biological," or nativist approaches all attempt to explain phenomena solely or primarily through reference to genetic differences.

However, the single most important fact to realize about these studies of differences is that they bypass entirely the question of what all humans have in common, how the genetic inheritance that all humans share produces (in conjunction with existing human environments) the human nature we all share, including our complex psychological adaptations. Because the elaborate functional design of individuals is largely monomorphic, our adaptations do not vary in their architecture from individual to individual (except quantitatively). Thus, they are not "genetic" in the carefully delimited sense in which behavior geneticists use the term—that is, caused by genetic differences between individuals. They are, however, genetic, hereditary, or inherited in the sense that nongeneticists use these terms. Their structured design has its characteristic form because of the information in our DNA, which we all share by virtue of the fact that we are human and not members of another species. This is all that evolutionists mean by "genetic" when they are making claims about evolved adaptations in human psychology. For this reason, scientists tend to study complex adaptations using assumptions and concepts drawn from a panspecific nativist orientation.

Confusion also arises from the diversity of ways psychologists interpret the significance of the heritable differences uncovered by behavior geneticists. For selection to produce evolutionary change, traits responsible for differences in fitness must be heritable. For this reason, population geneticists, in modeling selection, are interested in heritable differences (Fisher, 1930/1958). Because of this, the assertion is often made that evolutionary claims about traits cannot be valid unless the trait in question can be shown to be heritable, that is, to vary between individuals because of genetic differences among individuals (Lewontin, Rose, & Kamin, 1984). However, this belief results from a confusion between the input to the evolutionary process and its output. Nonadaptively organized, randomly generated, heritable variation is the raw material selection uses to produce evolutionary change, but the output of the evolutionary process is not variation, rather it is monomorphic adaptive design at the genetic level. Although heritable variation is necessary for selection to act, natural selection is a process that *eliminates* variation (Fisher, 1930/1958). (Despite widespread belief to the contrary, even stabilizing selection eventually eliminates genetic variation.) Barring balanced polymorphism, the longer selection acts, the more heritable variation is used up. The better variant becomes more common, until it is fixed in the gene pool and thus becomes a universal part of the species' genetic endowment. At that point in the process, the trait has a *zero* heritability. But no sensible person would claim that when it became universal it ceased to have a genetic basis.

For example, there is virtually no variation in leg number. We all have two legs at birth. Therefore, the trait "having two legs" has a zero heritability in the human population (Loehlin & Nichols, 1976). Yet no one would deny that leg number is specified in the genome. Leg number, the presence of a prefrontal cortex, hemoglobin, the capacity for language, an immune system—all these things have zero heritability, are adaptations, have a genetic basis, and are the product of the evolutionary process. Their lack of heritability supports, rather than undermines, the presumption that they are innately specified adaptations.

In fact, not only is heritability not required to establish adaptation, heritable variation in a trait generally signals a *lack* of adaptive significance. The longer selection has operated on a trait and the more intensely it has operated, the less heritable variation is left. Consequently, those traits that have high heritabilities will generally be those traits that are not adaptations (Crawford & Anderson, 1989), although they may interact in interesting ways with adaptations. Therefore, behavior geneticists tend to be studying phenomena that are not themselves adaptations (however interesting they may be for other reasons), but the raw material out of which future adaptations may someday be made. Those interested in studying complex psychological adaptations should be most interested in design features that are inherited, but not heritable.

To fully appreciate this point, one must keep in mind the distinction between studying heritable variation in a design and studying the design against which variation is measured. This distinction is important because mutation and pathogen-driven diversifying selection inject heritable differences into nearly every aspect of our species-typical design. Let us assume, for example, that all humans have a complex psychological mechanism regulating aggression (which we believe to be true), but that pathogen pressure has created heritable variation in that mechanism's threshold of activation. As a result, some people would have a "shorter fuse" than others, and this difference would be heritable. Nevertheless, this would not mean that the complex "aggression" mechanism is not an adaptation. It is (by hypothesis) universal, and therefore has zero heritability. It would mean, however, that the *variations* in the exact level at

which the threshold of activation is set are probably not adaptations. Similarly, stomachs vary in size, shape, and acidity, yet stomachs are still adaptations. Those features of the system that can be described in terms of uniform design are likely to be adaptations, whereas the heritable variations in the system are not. The task is to extract a description of the mechanism from the noisy variation in such a way that uniformity of design appears and heritability localizes in nonessential parts of the design. Comparing the relative heritability of various candidate design features can help one accomplish this.

The one exception to the rule that selection uses up heritable variation is the case of balanced polymorphism. For example, if alternative variants become more fit the rarer they are, the evolutionary result is often a stable balance of heritable alternatives in the population. A typical instance is variation in appearance in prey species. When predators form a search image of the most common color pattern of their prey, prey with rare color patterns are less frequently eaten, and this selection pressure creates stable diversity in prey color, similarly, as discussed above, the fact that parasites adapt to the most common proteins of their hosts selects for biochemical diversity between hosts. Such frequency-dependent selection leads to a situation where heritable differences subserving adaptive functions may stably persist in the population indefinitely. As Maynard Smith (1982) and others have shown using game theoretic techniques, this kind of reasoning may also apply at the phenotypic level to many kinds of social strategies (e.g., cooperators and defectors in an iterated prisoner's dilemma, or "hawks" and "doves" in a series of aggressive encounters). As will be argued below, however, these phenotypic alternatives are unlikely to be specified through suites of genetic differences, because sexual recombination breaks apart the functional coordination of the component parts. Therefore, although alternative social strategies may well exist, they are probably not an explanation for much of the heritable variation in psychological traits.

Implications for Personality Psychology

Clearly, environmental and genetic variation makes humans behave differently from one another, and one can arbitrarily lump or divide humans into as few or as many kinds and categories as one pleases, depending on one's purpose. In applying an evolutionary perspective to personality psychology, however, there are several obvious questions of interest. (a) Because differences must be located within the encompassing framework of universal human psychological architecture, the initial question is, what is the adaptive organization of our universally shared psychological mechanisms (i.e., what is human nature)? (b) Which individual differences covary, and which do not? (c) Do those individual differences that covary divide humans into different personality types, and if so, are these "types" adaptively organized behavioral strategies, with clear-cut evolutionary functions? (d) Do those individual differences that do not covary—that are randomly distributed with respect to one another—have any adaptive function? (e) Is there an evolutionary explanation for why some individual differences are cross-situationally stable, while others are situationally evoked? Answering these questions constitutes an entire research program, but certain tentative conclusions can be drawn about the probable relationship of individual differences, behavioral strategies, and personality types.

Morphs, Personality Types, and Strategies: Are there Discrete Kinds of Humans?

Although integrated adaptive design requires functional monomorphism, such monomorphism is necessary only within discrete kinds, or "morphs." All automobile engines of a given brand and model are monomorphic in design, but different models can and do have entire suites of design differences. They display *coordinated* functional variation.

Different species certainly correspond to different designs or "models," and these different phenotypic designs are the product of systematic design differences in the species' genetic endowments. Sometimes, however, evolution produces discrete alternative "models" *within* a species different "morphs." Morphs are alternative designs that differ from one another in substantial, discrete, and adaptively coordinated ways. Different morphs are the incarnation of different adaptive strategies. For example, males and females constitute different morphs of the same species. The two sexes are distinguished by entire suites of coordinated differences, and this distinguishing variation is discrete. An individual has the necessary physiological traits either of a female or of a male, but not a mixture of the two (except in pathological individuals).

The biological world contains numerous examples of multiple morphs within a species. Within many social insect species, for example, females are divided into different "castes"—"soldiers," "workers," and "queens"—whose morphology and behavior differ from each other in such substantial, discrete, and coordinated ways that they sometimes look and act like completely different species (Oster & Wilson, 1978; Wilson, 1971). All animal species contain different juvenile and adult morphs, which, depending on the species, may be nearly identical or as startlingly different as caterpillar and butterfly, tadpole and frog.

One need not think of morphs as differing only in gross physical morphology. Two individuals of a species whose behavioral strategies differ in substantial, discrete, and coordinated ways—i.e., two individuals who differ in "personality"—might also be considered different morphs. For example, recent game theoretical and ecological work has shown that alternative adaptive behavioral strategies, such as "hawks" and "doves" (individuals who escalate violent conflicts and individuals who retreat from them), can stably coexist within a species (Maynard Smith, 1982; Maynard Smith & Price, 1973). Using the theory of evolutionarily stable strategies (ESS), one can determine whether such alternative "personality types" can coexist in a population, or whether one personality will be selected for over another, until it becomes a universal, species-typical trait.

If there are discrete personality "morphs" in humans, they are obviously far more modest than the striking physiological difference between workers and queens in the social insects, or between males and females in most species. It is not the *amount* of variation between individuals that determines whether they constitute different morphs, but the *organization* of this variation. To sustain the claim that different personality types constitute discrete morphs, the traits must show, through the complex coordination of their parts, evidence of adaptive design.

Are there Discrete Human Personality Morphs?

This question is central to personality psychology and needs to be addressed at two levels, the phenotypic and the genetic.

At the phenotypic level, human males and human females clearly qualify as different morphs, and the study of sex differences is the study of their coordinated design differences. Also, if one samples within-sex human design at sufficiently separated points during development, from zygote to embryo to puberty to senescence, age can provide another example of coordinated design change in humans. Aside from these two dimensions, however, which manifest themselves in humans in dramatic physiological ways, there is no evidence for discrete, physiologically differentiated human morphs. As discussed above, despite persistent folk beliefs, there is overwhelming genetic evidence that different ethnic groups are not discretely differentiated, and do not constitute

"types." If any genuine kinds of human type exist in addition to age-sex categories, they are clearly far more modest than adult-child or male-female differences. Since other physiologically recognizable "types" have not been found among humans, if there are any additional discrete types still to be discovered, they will be psychologically, rather than morphologically, differentiated types.

Have personality psychologists, by finding organized systems of personality variation, found alternative adaptive strategies in humans? A related question is, are the heritable components of personality differences likely to be adaptations? Although the first question is difficult to answer with confidence at this time, below we develop standards of evidence for addressing it. The answer to the second question, we will argue, will usually be "no," although some kinds of selection pressures may account for some such variation.

The possibility that the various personality variables currently under investigation constitute alternative adaptive strategies is difficult to assess in the abstract. Nevertheless, evolutionary principles provide standards of evidence that personality psychologists can use in exploring this question. The first criterion is whether the personality trait under discussion represents a single quantitative variable, or whether an entire range of variables covaries in an organized, coordinated fashion. If it is a single quantitative trait involving heritable variation, it is less likely to be an adaptive strategy, since most strategies require finely sculptured performances beyond the power of a single gene or an additive quantitative genetic system to specify. The second criterion is, do the variables covary in a way that makes adaptive sense? If they do, this adds plausibility. For example, does "large and strong" covary with "aggressive," and "small and weak" covary with "restrained"? Evidence of *special design* is the primary criterion for imputing adaptation. It is not sufficient to show that a trait sometimes provides a benefit, one must show that its parts function together in a way that suggests that they were specially designed to solve that adaptive problem efficiently (Williams, 1966).

Finding that two alternative strategies are heritable—that they are coded for by genes that differ from person to person—is *not* a criterion of adaptation. From the point of view of natural selection it does not matter whether an alternative strategy is activated in an individual by a gene, an environmental cue, or a cognitive assessment of the situation. All that matters is that the innate mechanism is designed such that the right alternative is activated under the right circumstances. In the next section we argue that environmental cues or situational assessments are usually the best way to accomplish this, and therefore most alternative adaptive strategies will *not* show up as heritably determined. Because alternative strategies can also be switched on or off by a single gene difference— a genetic "switch"—one cannot rule out the possibility that some alternative strategies may show adaptively patterned heritable variation. We argue, however, that alternative, coordinated adaptive strategies cannot, in principle, be coded for by *suites* of genes that differ from person to person. Our argument is based on a consideration of the structure of coordinated variation at the genetic level. (And, of course, mutation pressure and selection for biochemical individuality are expected to inject some measure of nonadaptively patterned heritable variation into all systems.)

One Genetic Architecture: Multiple Phenotypic Designs

Different species, of course, constitute different integrated designs at the phenotypic level. This difference across species between integrated designs is caused by systematic coordinated genetic differences between species. Different species are different designs because of different suites of genes. The genetic and the phenotypic levels reflect each other. Contrary to intuition,

however, the coordinated variation between different morphs within a species does not reflect coordinated variation at the genetic level between morphs. Different morphs do not owe their different designs to alternative underlying suites of genes present in some individuals and absent in others. This is true even though, in an engineering sense, it would be an effective way to specify different designs. The obvious way to create, for example, a female, would be to have all the genetic information necessary to specify the development of a female linked into a single unrecombining genetic unit, and have it transmitted only to females. Nevertheless, this is not how genetic systems actually operate. Alternative morphs within a species must be genetically "engineered" in another manner, without recourse to alternative heritable genetic bases.

This surprising fact derives from the evolutionary genetics of sexual recombination. Sexual recombination efficiently and systematically tears apart linked genetic associations, and does so throughout the genome, so that genes do not form functionally organized superunits, for all practical purposes genes are eventually atomized, and they are thrown together in random, effectively unlinked permutations by the process of sexual reproduction. Species are species by virtue of the fact that the individuals that compose them interbreed. The result of this interbreeding is that genes circulate in continuously changing combinations over generations. This means that genes that are in one kind of individual appear in subsequent generations in other kinds of individuals. All of the genes in women have been, in previous generations, in both men and women. All of the genes in men (with the exception of the Y chromosome, a genetic "switch", see below) have been in women and men. All of the genes in infants have been in adults. In social insects, all of the genes in workers have been in queens. The differences between men and women, fetuses and adults, workers and queens, and so on, are not primarily genetic (in the sense that they have different genes). With the exception of genetic switches such as the Y chromosome, they have the same genes. Different functional subsets of genes are activated and inactivated in different morphs, but are present in all individuals.

Complex adaptations, such as organs, require a great deal of genetic specification—far more than could be provided for by any single gene. Single genes are insufficient to specify all of the different regulatory steps necessary to build such complex systems. Instead, complex adaptations are constructed by developmental programs, which in turn are regulated by genetic programs. These genetic programs comprise hundreds or thousands of genes, operating within a fixed developmental background created by the rest of the genome (Gilbert, 1985). For example, human females have an enormously intricate system of interlocking tissues which allow reproduction. The uterus, fallopian tubes, hormonal receptors in the preoptic area of the hypothalamus, a system of milk secretion, and so on, require the coordinated action of thousands of separate genes (Gilbert, 1985). Even organisms as simple as bacteria depend on coordinate gene expression in gene sets numbering more than 50 (Youngman et. al., 1985). If all of the genes that acted to specify female organ systems existed only in females, and all of the genes that acted to specify male organ systems existed only in males, what kind of offspring would they produce when they mated? Sexual reproduction randomly selects half of the genes from each parent and combines them to produce genetically different offspring. Consequently, sexual reproduction would take some of the genes responsible for male organ systems and mix them with some of the genes responsible for female organ systems, to produce a series of children that were pathological because they were randomly intermediate individuals, each would have some of the traits necessary to be male, some necessary to be female, but without all of the necessary features to be either successfully. Genes recombine in an uncoordinated way,

and complex design requires coordination among its functional parts.

If there is a complex series of interdependent adaptations required to produce a sex, a behavioral strategy, or a personality type, there is only one way to insure the necessary coordination. All of the parts of the genetic programs necessary to build the integrated design must be present when needed in every individual of a given type. The only way that the 50 genes, or 100 genes, or 1,000 genes that may be required to assemble all of the features defining a given type can rely on each other's mutual presence is if they are all present in every individual. If they are present in everyone, then they can be activated as alternative developmental programs.

For this reason, different coordinated designs, psychological or physiological, cannot be the direct product of suites of genetic differences. Different genetic programs (corresponding to subsets of genes) are activated in one morph or another, but are present in all individuals. In short, the conclusion from evolutionary genetics is that different species have different designs because of different genes, but that within a species, different designs emerge from the same genes (excepting genetic "switches").

What Design? Genetic "switches" Versus Environmental Cues

If the genetic programs that regulate the development of alternative designs are universal, what determines which design an individual has? There are several methods of determination, of which the simplest are genetic "switches" and environmental cues. Which is used depends on the specific system under discussion. In humans, for example, sex determination is controlled by a genetic switch, the presence or absence of a single gene, the H-Y antigen on the Y chromosome (for a review of sex-determining mechanisms, see Bull, 1983). It is important to realize that although this design difference, male or female, is triggered by a single gene, this gene does not contain the information necessary for building the alternative designs, it acts only as a switch, in a binary fashion, activating one of two extensive functionally integrated genetic subsystems, both of which are simultaneously present in all humans. As an alternative system, in many vertebrates such as silverside fish and alligators, sex is determined via an environmental cue, usually temperature during incubation (Bull, 1983), rather than a genetic switch. This cue acts as the switch that shunts development onto the male or female path, activating male or female genetic programs.

In general, environmental cues or assessments are a better way of determining what morph to become. A genetic switch determines an individual's future at conception, so that individual has one set of adaptations and not another regardless of how suited they might be to the local situation. A far more effective system, in general, is to determine what to be as a response to what environment one finds oneself in, for example, be aggressive in those environments where one is victimized for passiveness and peaceful in those environments where one is penalized for aggressive behavior. An individual can better tailor its morphology and behavior to its local environment by relying on environmental cues, or by assessing the relationship between itself and its environment. For this reason, genetic personality determination, as an adaptation, is expected to be rare, although it cannot be ruled out.

Determination of adaptive strategy by genetic switches seems to be favored only when the decision of what type to be must be made early in development, irreversibly, in order to develop physiological specializations during embryological differentiation. In mammals, for example, sex determination takes place early, without environmental cuing, because physiological differentiation must take place early in development, prior to any reliable sampling of the environment. The cost of using genetic switches is that the individual is subsequently committed to

pursuing that strategy, even if it finds itself in situations where that strategy is radically inappropriate. It is possible that strategies that require extensive periods of learning might also require early and irreversible commitment, in a way that parallels commitment to embryological specialization. Given the payoffs of making one's behavior appropriate to one's situation, however, one expects that alternative psychological specializations are chosen, whenever possible, through cues or assessments of one's situation. This should prove true regardless of the amount of irreversible commitment required in pursuing a behavioral strategy. The major requirement for the evolution of such a system is the existence of reliable cues that at present indicate (if strategies can be rapidly adopted or discarded) or reliably predict (if strategies must be prepared for) the kind of situation the individual faces. Lacking reliable cues, genetic switches whose frequency in the population has been adjusted by recent selection remain the only alternative.

Categories of Genetic Differences and their Relationship to Individual Differences

The relationship between genetic differences and phenotypic differences turns out to be a surprising one. Adaptively coordinated individual differences will not generally be coded for by extensive systems of genetic differences, but instead will be universal human potentialities, activated (perhaps irreversibly) by situational assessments, by environmental cues, or by the minimal genetic input of a genetic switch.

On the other hand, uncoordinated phenotypic variation commonly will be created by randomly distributed genetic differences between individuals. (By uncoordinated variation, we mean individual differences that do not covary in an adaptively coordinated way with the presence or absence of other individual differences.) This variation breaks down into three components (a) differences that are adaptive (the smallest category), (b) differences that are maladaptive, and (c) differences that are effectively neutral (the largest category).

Adaptive Differences

Uncoordinated phenotypic variation can be adaptive when the phenotypic feature making it adaptive is simple enough to be specified by a single gene for example, lactose metabolization (selected for in milk-drinking cultures), and the sickle cell gene (inhibiting malaria). Some adaptive variation is due to favorable mutations, which are in the process of spreading through the population. These are rare, yet do appear with regularity. These generally consist of single-step additions to the genetic programs that underlie physiological and psychological mechanisms. Given estimated rates of evolution, however, only a small fraction of existing genetic variation consists of favorable genes displacing unfavorable genes. Additionally, frequency-dependent selection can give rise to stably maintained uncoordinated variation, where all of the alternative alleles are fit (Lewontin, 1974). Hamilton (1987) has argued that the diversity of niches in human social life may select for genetic diversity in psychological traits, a process that invokes frequency-dependent selection. Finally, local ecological, cultural, and social circumstances, if they persist long enough, may select for genes that are locally adaptive but not generally adaptive (e.g., the genes for lactose metabolism and malaria inhibition cited above). It is unlikely that local optima for metabolic rate, or mean arousal, or threshold for anger are everywhere exactly the same, and so selectively driven quantitative deviations between populations are a possibility (although such processes are very slow, require conditions that are stable for long periods, and depend upon relative genetic isolation). Given the wealth of genetic polymorphism, which injects minor amplifications, inhibitions, and modifications throughout our psychological and physiological mechanisms, it would be surprising if there were not at least some local adaptations and

frequency-dependent adaptations. As we have argued, however, the major constraint on the emergence of genetic differences as adaptations arises from recombination. Adaptations require that all their parts be present, and so cannot be coded for by a series of genes at different loci that are present in some individuals in the population and not in others. The destructive power of recombination is proportional to the number of different loci involved. An adaptation wholly coded for by a single gene can survive this filter without any problem, single genes that quantitatively modulate mechanisms or processes can as well, and, in addition, may collectively add up into systems of quantitative genetic variation. As a result, arguments that genetic differences are adaptations depend on the proposed adaptation being coded for on a single gene (or at most a few genes), or being a quantitative modifier of an existing process. Complex adaptations resting on genetic diversity cannot survive the destructive filter of recombination, and so cannot be a significant factor explaining human genetic diversity.

Maladaptive Differences

Much uncoordinated phenotypic variation is maladaptive minor modifications that degrade the performance of an integrated functional design (e.g., flat feet, malocclusion, astigmatism, dyslexia), or modifications so major that the integrity of the entire system is disrupted (e.g., phenylketonuria). These deleterious alleles, which appear through mutation pressure and are on their way to being eliminated, are present in every individual (Cavalli-Sforza & Bodmer, 1971; Nei, 1987).

Neutral Differences

Finally, a huge reservoir of genetic variability exists that creates psychological differences that are expected to be neutral, on balance, neither consistently adaptive nor consistently maladaptive. This will be either because the genetic differences have no selectively important phenotypic consequences (Kimura, 1983), or because pathogens select for allelic diversity (Clarke, 1976, 1979; Rice, 1983; Tooby, 1982), which carries along as an incidental concomitant psychological variation. Pathogens select for protein diversity, introducing the maximum tolerable quantitative variation and noise into the human system. The less a psychological or physiological characteristic is under intense natural selection, the more variation can be tolerated as a way of defeating pathogens. Where design constraints are relaxed, variation will differentially accumulate. Consequently, one expects to find that heritable diversity is inversely proportional to adaptive importance.

Therefore, each human of a given sex and age should be, in *overall potential functional architecture*, nearly the same as every other individual of the same sex and age, with variation generally confined to generally nonadaptive random fluctuations around this monomorphic design, or in those parts of the functional architecture that have been developmentally activated. Below the level of functional architecture, however, there is a sea of uncoordinated protein variation. Given the intricate design complexity of the nervous system (as well as of other organ systems), this protein variation gives rise to a wealth of quantitative variation in nearly every manifest feature of the psyche. Tastes, reflexes, perceptual abilities, talents, deficits, thresholds of activation, motor skills, verbal skills, activity level, abilities to remember different kinds of things, and so on—all vary from individual to individual in a quantitative way (see, e.g., Kalmus, 1967; McKusick, 1971). The nearest comparison might be to imagine what would happen if everyone were initially identical, but had 10,000 microscopic lesions, as well as a few larger lesions, placed randomly in each brain. The microscopic lesions correspond to the sea of genetic diversity that causes subtle individual differences, the larger lesions correspond to the disruptive mutations or combinations that regularly crop up, that push the system outside of the envelope of quantitative variation and into occasional violations of adaptive design.

The Differential Activation of Mental Organs Creates Adaptively Coordinated Personality Traits

The differential activation of mental organs can give rise to personality traits that are *adaptively coordinated*. To see how this can happen, we will consider a concrete example: A mental organ that evolved to solve the adaptive problems posed by sexual infidelity. We will treat such a mental organ as hypothetical, although we believe work done by Symons (1979), Daly and Wilson and colleagues (Daly & Wilson, 1988, Daly et. al., 1982), and Buss (1988) have provided strong evidence that such a mental organ exists.

Males and females tend to suffer fitness costs (though in somewhat different ways) if their sexual partners engage in relations outside the established (or hoped for) relationship. It would therefore be reasonable to expect the human mind to contain a mental organ designed to increase fitness by producing behaviors that encourage fidelity, penalize "cheating," and interfere with sexual competitors. Suppose then, that the human mind contains a mental organ specialized for seeking out and processing information about potential infidelity. When activated, this mental organ produces the coordinated set of thought patterns, behavior patterns, physiological responses, and phenomenal feelings that we would recognize as "sexual jealousy."

Evolutionary analyses tell us that this mental organ should differ somewhat between males and females, because their reproductive strategies differ (Daly et. al., 1982, Symons, 1979). Whether one has the male or female form of this mental organ is determined by the same genetic switch that determines one's sex: The H-Y antigen.

If one constructs a personality scale that probes adaptively relevant questions about sexual jealousy, one would therefore expect to find two discrete, functionally coordinated adaptive personality types one for males and one for females. These two "personality morphs" should share many common features, because the adaptive problems they evolved to solve are similar. But because infidelity poses somewhat different problems for males and females, there will also be qualitative differences between the cognitive programs that compose each morph. These qualitative differences should lead to quantitative differences on many of the dimensions assessed in the personality scale. For example, catching a partner either kissing or giving expensive gifts to a sexual competitor should make both men and women very jealous, but the kissing may bother men more and the gifts may bother women more. Jealous men might be more likely than jealous women to compete for their lover's attention by making it known that they have received a job promotion, whereas women might be more likely than men to compete by enhancing their physical attractiveness (Buss, 1988). Nevertheless, the fact that one finds quantitative differences on any single dimension does not mean that the differences between men and women will be merely quantitative. The various dimensions should cluster into distinctive configurations that show the coordinated adaptive patterning predicted by evolutionary theory. Thus, when comparing the male and female morphs of the mental organ governing sexual jealousy, one expects to find differences in kind, and not just of degree.

All normal men will have the male morph of this mental organ, and all normal women will have the female morph. The probability that any given individual will lack this mental organ entirely is very low—comparable to the probability that one might lack any other organ, such as a pancreas or a spleen. Thus, this mental organ will exist latently in every individual. This does not mean, however, that every individual will have experienced sexual jealousy. An individual whose mental organ has never been activated will have never experienced sexual jealousy.

The mental organ contains specialized situation-recognition procedures, which seek out and evaluate evidence suggesting infidelity. Situational cues indicating that an infidelity is likely to take place will set these detectors off, strongly activating the mental organ. When it is activated, the person will experience an episode of sexual jealousy.

Insofar as they are transitory, however, these situationally evoked episodes of sexual jealousy fall outside the realm of trait psychology. They are "states," not "traits." Can a universal, situationally activated mental organ lead to stable, within-sex, individual differences?

Enduring individual differences are the focus of trait psychology. Many psychological mechanisms, however, are only temporarily activated to deal with passing situations. Most psychological phenomena will be of this kind. The psyche is there to produce behavior that is responsive to the environment, and so sensitivity to environmental change is a ubiquitous feature of psychological adaptation. The idea that there could be individual differences that remain stable, despite changes in one's situation, superficially conflicts with the idea that adaptive behavior should be governed by the demands of the situation one is in. But universal mental organs can give rise to enduring individual differences when conditions that differentially activate or modulate them endure, or when the activation of a mental organ is irrevocable. This process can give rise to adaptively coordinated differences between individuals of the same sex.

Nonadaptive Stable Individual Differences

Although the functional architecture of a mental organ may be uniform from person to person, quantitative features in that architecture will tend to vary as a result of mutation or pathogen-driven selection for biochemical diversity. Nonadaptive, random fluctuations in the monomorphic design of a mental organ can give rise to heritable individual differences in nearly every manifest feature of human psychology. Obviously, this quantitative variation can lead to stable individual differences in simple, single-variable attributes, such as phoneme articulation, intensity of a specific reflex, or the ability to taste a chemical. It can also lead to stable individual differences in the adaptively patterned output of a complex psychological program.

Latent psychological programs are activated through exposure to cues that have proven evolutionarily reliable. The co-occurrence of other people expressing fear in the presence of snakes indicates the possibility of a venomous bite, and provides cues for the activation of a snake phobia (Seligman, 1971, Seligman & Hager, 1972). Researchers studying identical twins have found evidence for such heritable variation in fears and phobias (Rose & Ditto, 1983). But random variation in quantitative features of that program can give rise to individual differences in the required strength, number, or lack of ambiguity of the diagnostic cues that must be present before the latent program is activated. Such differences would affect the program's threshold of activation. Similarly, there can be random quantitative variation in how strongly a program is activated, or in how long its activation endures. This variation can also lead to certain kinds of psychopathology, such as those due to the activation of mechanisms under inappropriate circumstances or in inappropriate intensities. For example, the sexual jealousy mental organ is so easily and strongly activated in some individuals that they display morbid, obsessive jealousy (Shepard, 1961).

Variation in quantitative factors can create the spurious appearance that some people have a mechanism that others lack. Exposed to identical conditions, one person may develop a snake phobia while another does not, simply because there is quantitative variation between individuals in the threshold of activation of the human universal snake phobia mechanism. Described in terms of manifest expression, some individuals will have the trait "afraid of snakes," while others will not, described in terms of innate mental organs, however, all individuals will have the snake phobia mechanism, which through differential experience or heritable differences in threshold will be activated in some individuals and not others.

Under what circumstances should we expect to find these kinds of random, nonadaptive individual differences? Variation tends to occur wherever uniformity is not imposed by selection, and selection acts to impose its organizing influence in proportion to how significantly a feature impacts fitness. People display more diversity in their preferences for hat color or in their beliefs about gods and spirits than in their desire to continue breathing, their attraction to sex, or their desire to avoid pain (Sperber, 1984). Consequently, the more irrelevant a dimension of human psychology is to Pleistocene adaptation, the more likely that dimension is to accumulate and manifest individual differences. For this reason, many categories of individual differences may show no adaptive patterning whatsoever.

Reactive Heritability: Adaptive Responses to One's Genetic Endowment

It is plausible to suppose that larger, stronger, defter, less fearful individuals will prevail more often in fights. It seems equally plausible to suppose that size, strength, motor coordination, and physical courage vary across individuals, presumably as a result of genetic differences, environmental differences, and their interaction. If, as seems likely, the human mind contains mechanisms that regulate behavior according to the rule, "Be aggressive when aggression is likely to be a successful method for attaining goals," then larger, stronger, more coordinated individuals will resort to aggression or aggressive intimidation more often than individuals who are smaller, weaker, and less coordinated. Such a psychological mechanism may be absolutely invariant, showing no variation in its structure attributable to genetic differences, and yet its individual output, the trait "aggressiveness," may show considerable heritability, because the variables that the psychological mechanism assesses include individual traits that show heritable differences.

Evolutionary biology leads to the expectation that adaptively designed psychological mechanisms will generally be monomorphic in structure. The expression of such uniform mechanisms will show heritable differences, however, whenever there are heritable differences in the variables that these psychological mechanisms assess. A reaction to a heritable difference gives "reactive heritability" to the performance of a mechanism that itself has zero heritability.

One fruitful source of personality research is attempting to identify important variables that psychological mechanisms can be expected to adaptively assess. Functional analyses derived from evolutionary framings of adaptation allow a straightforward identification of many such variables: sexual attractiveness, health, age, gender, whether one is in an established spousal relationship, whether one has children, whether one lives in an environment that threatens one with violence, control over socially desired resources or "wealth," aggressive formidability, amount of familial or social support, social status, and so on. Honing in on personality characteristics and personal situations which, for practical reasons, must be functionally accommodated, gives a rationale in personality psychology for treating some traits and variables as causally prior to others. Some variables may be assessed for only limited purposes, but others may be important and may be assessed by a multitude of different psychological mechanisms. Where this is the case, coordination among personality traits will emerge as the

result of their all being partially determined in response to assessment of the same input variable. Being male, large, and muscular may have a large number of systematic consequences on one's personality. Physical action may be more attractive, in small group situations, people may be more attentive, women may treat such men differentially, other males of the same age and approximate status may be more threatened, or more interested in recruiting such men as coalition members, and so on.

Conclusion

Human psychological characteristics appear in three forms (a) universal functional design, (b) unstructured variation, and (c) organized systems of covariation. The mapping of universal functional architecture is clearly worth doing, and depends upon the evolutionary definition of adaptive problems (Buss, 1984; Cosmides & Tooby, 1987; Daly & Wilson, 1988; Symons, 1987). Below this level of functional uniformity exist psychological phenomena that show unstructured variation, much of it genetic in origin.

Structured systems of coordinated individual differences are a major focus of personality psychology (Cattell, 1957). In fact, one of the major findings of personality psychology is that there appear to be a restricted number of independent personality dimensions or superfactors (at least five) that constitute significant systems of covariation among personality traits (e.g., McCrae & Costa, 1987). Covariation, if genuine, must be explained, and an evolutionary orientation suggests that there are three alternative ways such systems can be accounted for:

1   *Condition-responsive adaptive strategies* Systems of covariation among personality traits may constitute adaptive responses by uniform, innate, psychological mechanisms to given individual characteristics and circumstances, processed as "input conditions." Assessments of the same input variables by multiple mechanisms

will coordinate adaptive outputs. To the extent such assessed input variables are shaped by heritable differences, such covarying systems of personality traits may display "reactive heritability." This seems to be the most plausible explanation for adaptively covarying systems of personality traits. An evolutionarily logical relationship among the traits (e.g., strong with aggressive) is the hallmark of condition-responsive adaptive strategies.

2 *Frequency-dependent adaptive strategies* Covariant systems may constitute alternative frequency-dependent behavioral strategies, a construct in personality psychology that would correspond to evolutionarily stable polymorphic strategies in evolutionary biology. If a frequency-dependent strategy requires systematic modifications in many different mechanisms at once to implement or facilitate the strategy, such a result could show up on personality measures (e.g., hawk, dove). Because of the requirement for functional organization among the psychological mechanisms, heritability should play only a small role in the creation of such systems, for example as a system of simple genetic switches, or as an initial biasing factor that makes the choice of one developmental path more likely than another. A better design would be to use a system of environmental cues, designed to detect local rarity or "undersubscription" of the strategy (and one's own ability to pursue the strategy successfully). Adaptive coordination among the component traits should be apparent in such situations.

3 *Nonadaptive developmental amplification* Covariation may be the result of the impact of the same neurophysiological peculiarity on different mental organs. Psychological mechanisms are implemented neurologically, and different mechanisms may share neurophysiological resources or respond to the same trigger. Anything that influences some aspect of a widely distributed neurophysiological process may create covariation among the output of different psychological mechanisms. For example, endorphins participate in many kinds of psychological

processes. A mutation in receptor or endorphin structure may have very widespread effects. Moreover, these systems of covariation may even appear to have an adaptive logic, because evolution has often shaped neurological mechanisms so that those that are usually functionally activated together are potentiated by the same chemical signal (e.g., norepinephrine, serotonin, testosterone). Modifications in the production of such chemical signals may lead to systems of covariation in which the components are related to each other in adaptively nonarbitrary ways that appear coordinated (e.g., higher testosterone may be related to increase in muscle mass, faster metabolic rate, lower threshold of violence, greater suspiciousness, heightened competitiveness, etc.). What will be lacking is an adaptive logic in a relationship between the environment and the individual differences. Heritable variation is expected to play a prominent role in such systems of personality variation. It seems likely that much of what personality psychologists recognize as temporally and cross-situationally stable individual differences will be of this kind.

Obviously, all three processes may interact to produce a patterned outcome.

Few personality measures have been generated because the investigator was interested in discovering evolved adaptations. So throughout, we have generated standards of evidence for assessing whether or not personality traits that have already been discovered are adaptively patterned. Nevertheless, implicit in the evolutionary perspective we have been advocating is an alternative approach to personality psychology.

An evolutionary approach would focus on the adaptive coordination of traits from the beginning. First, one would identify what adaptive problems the human mind must be able to solve. Then one would generate measures that reveal what kind of mechanisms we have for solving them, and whether these mechanisms assess other traits in determining what strategy to use. Thus, the search for adaptive coordination would guide the process from beginning to end. It should be pointed out that this approach not only allows one to discover stable individual differences, it also provides a window into the structure of universal human nature.

By proceeding in this way, adaptive problem by adaptive problem, one should be able to construct measures that will eventually reveal the organized structure of the human personality.

Notes

1 Such a view reconciles the populational thinking necessary for understanding how evolutionary change proceeds (Mayr, 1982) with an understanding of how complex adaptations (i.e., adaptations with interdependent parts) can emerge, operate, and evolve within populations over time (Fisher 1930/1958).

2 Genetic polymorphism refers to the existence, within a population, of two or more alternative alleles (genes) for a given trait (or more exactly, at a given locus). It may also be used to refer to genetic variation in the aggregate, without reference to a specific trait.

References

Ayala, F. J. (Ed.) (1976). *Molecular evolution*. Sunderland, MA: Sinauer.

Barkow, J. (1989). *Darwin sex and status: Biological approaches to mind and culture*. Toronto University of Toronto Press.

Bell, G. (1982). *The Masterpiece of Nature: The evolution and genetics of sexuality*. Berkeley, CA: University of California Press.

Bell, G. and Maynard Smith, J. (1987). Short-term selection for recombination among mutually antagonistic species. *Nature*, 328; 66–68.

Block, J. (1971). *Lives Through Time*. Berkeley, CA: Bancroft.

Block, J., and Ozer, D. J. (1982). Two types of psychologists: Remarks on the Mendelsohn Weiss and Feimer contribution. *Journal of Personality and Social Psychology*, 42: 1171–1181.

Boden, M. (1977). *Artificial Intelligence and Natural Man*. New York: Basic Books.

Brown, F. M. (1987). *The Frame Problem in Artificial Intelligence*. Los Altos, CA: Morgan Kaufmann.

Brues, A. M. (1954). Selection and polymorphism in the ABO blood groups. *American Journal of Physical Anthropology*, 12: 559–597.

Brues, A. M. (1963). Stochastic tests of selection in the ABO blood groups. *American Journal of Physical Anthropology*, 21: 287–299.

Bull, J. J. (1983). *The Evolution of Sex Determining Mechanisms*. Menlo Park, CA: Benjamin/Cummings.

Buss, D. M. (1984). Evolutionary biology and personality psychology: Toward a conception of human nature and individual differences. *American Psychologist*, 39: 1135–1147.

Buss, D. M. (1988). The evolution of human intrasexual competition: Tactics of mate attraction. *Journal of Personality and Social Psychology*, 54: 616–628.

Cattell, R. B. (1957). *Personality and Motivation Structure and Measurement*. New York: World Book.

Cavalli-Sforza, L. L. & Bodmer, W. F. (1971). *The Genetics of Human Populations*. San Francisco, CA: Freeman.

Chomsky, N. (1980). *Rules and Representations*. New York: Columbia University Press.

Clarke, B. (1976). The ecological genetics of host-parasite relationships. In A. E. R. Taylor and R. Muller (Eds.), *Genetic Aspects of Host-parasite Relationships* (pp. 87–103). Oxford: Blackwell.

Clarke, B. (1979). The evolution of genetic diversity. *Proceedings of the Royal Society, London B*, 205: 453–474.

Cosmides, G. J. (1974). Human variability—and safer more effective pharmacotherapy. *Orthopaedic Review*, 3: 7–12.

Cosmides, L. (1985). *Deduction or Darwinian algorithms: An explanation of the "elusive" content effect on the Wason selection task*. Unpublished doctoral dissertation Harvard University.

Cosmides, L. (1989). The logic of social exchange: Has natural selection shaped how humans reason? Studies with the Wason selection task. *Cognition*, 31: 187–276.

Cosmides, L. & Tooby, J. (1987). From evolution to behavior: Evolutionary psychology as the missing link. In J. Dupre (Ed.), *The Latest on the Best: Essays on evolution and optimality* (pp. 277–306). Cambridge: MIT Press.

Cosmides, L. & Tooby, J. (1989). Evolutionary psychology and the generation of culture, part II: Case study A computational theory of social exchange. *Ethology and Sociobiology*, 10: 51–97.

Crawford, C. B. & Anderson, J. L. (1989). Sociobiology: An environmentalist discipline? *American Psychologist*, 44: 1449–1459.

Daly, M. & Wilson, M. (1988). *Homicide*. New York Aldine.

Daly, M. Wilson, M., & Weghorst, S. J. (1982). Male sexual jealousy. *Ethology and Sociobiology*, 3: 11–27.

Damian, R. T. (1964). Molecular mimicry: Antigen sharing by parasite and host and its consequences. *American Naturalist*, 98: 129–149.

Damian, R. T. (1979). Molecular mimicry in biological adaptation. In B. B. Nickol (Ed.), *Host-parasite Interfaces at Population Individual and Molecular Levels* (pp. 103–126). New York: Academic Press.

Dawkins, R. (1982). *The Extended Phenotype: The gene as the unit of selection*. San Francisco, CA: Freeman.

Dawkins, R. (1986). *The Blind Watchmaker: Why the evidence of evolution reveals a universe without design*. New York: Norton.

Draper, P. & Harpending, H. (1987). Parent investment and the child's environment. In J. Lancaster, J. Altmann, A. Rossi & L. Sherrod (Eds.), *Parenting across the Life Span: Biosocial dimensions* (pp 207–235). New York: Aldine.

Fisher, R. A. (1958). *The Genetical Theory of Natural Selection* (2nd rev. ed.). New York: Dover (Original work published 1930).

Fodor, J. A. (1983). *The Modularity of Mind*. Cambridge: MIT Press.

Gilbert, S. F. (1985). *Developmental Biology*. Sunderland, MA: Sinauer.

Gould, S. J. (1985). Human equality is a contingent fact of history. In *The Flamingo's Smile: Reflections in natural history* (pp. 185–198). New York: Norton.

Gould, S. J., & Eldredge, N. (1972). Punctuated equilibria: The tempo and mode of evolution reconsidered. *Paleobiology*, 3: 115–151.

Hamilton, W. D. (1964). The genetical evolution of social behaviour. *Journal of Theoretical Biology*, 7: 1–52.

Hamilton, W. D. (1980). Sex versus non-sex versus parasite. *Oikos*, 35: 282–290.

Hamilton, W. D. (1987). Discriminating nepotism: Expectable, common overlooked. In D. J. C. Fletcher & C. D. Michener (Eds.), *Kin Recognition in Animals* (pp. 417–437) New York: Wiley & Sons.

Hamilton W. D., & Zuk, M. (1982). Heritable true fitness and bright birds: A role for parasites? *Science*, 218: 384–387.

Hubby, J. L., & Lewontin, R. C. (1966). A molecular approach to the study of genic heterozygosity in natural populations I: The number of alleles at different loci in *Drosophila pseudoobscura*. Genetics, 54: 577–594.

Jaenike, J. (1978). An hypothesis to account for the maintenance of sex within populations. *Evolutionary Theory*. 3: 191–194.

Jung, C. G. (1921). *Psychological Types*. New York. Harcourt Brace.

Kalmus, H. (1967). Sense perception and behavior. In J. N. Spuhler (Ed:), *Genetic Diversity in Human Behavior*. (pp. 73–87). Chicago Aldine.

Kelley, S. E., Antonovics, J., & Schmitt, J. (1988). A test of the short-term advantage of sexual reproduction. *Nature*, 331: 714–716.

Kimura, M. (1983). *The Neutral Theory of Molecular Evolution*. Cambridge: Cambridge University Press.

Lewontin, R. C. (1974). *The Genetic Basis of Evolutionary Change*. New York: Columbia University Press.

Lewontin, R. C. (1982). *Human Diversity*. New York: Scientific American Library.

Lewontin R. C., & Hubby, J. L. (1966). A molecular approach to the study of genic heterozygosity in natural populations II: Amount of variation and degree of heterozygosity in natural populations of *Drosophila pseudoobscura*. Genetics, 54: 595–609.

Lewontin R. C. Rose, S. & Kamin, L. J. (1984). *Not in our Genes: Biology, ideology and human nature*. New York: Pantheon.

Loehlin, J. C., & Nichols, R. C. (1976). *Heredity environment and personality*. Austin: University of Texas Press.

Marr, D. (1982). *Vision A computational investigation into the human representation and processing of visual information*. San Francisco: Freeman.

Marshall, J. C. (1980). The new organology. *Behavioral and Brain Sciences*, 3: 23–25.

Maynard Smith, J. (1978). *The evolution of sex*. Cambridge: Cambridge University Press.

Maynard Smith, J. (1982). *Evolution and the Theory of Games*. Cambridge: Cambridge University Press.

Maynard Smith, J., & Price, G. R. (1973). The logic of animal conflict. *Nature*, London, 246: 15–18.

Mayr, E. (1982). *The Growth of Biological Thought*. Cambridge: Harvard University Press.

McCrae, R. R., & Costa, P.T., Jr. (1987). Validation of the five-factor model of personality across instruments and observers. *Journal of Personality and Social Psychology*, 52: 81–90.

McKusick, V. (1971). *Mendelian Inheritance in Man*. Baltimore: Johns Hopkins University Press.

Minsky, M. (1986). *The Society of Mind*. New York: Simon & Schuster.

Nei, M. (1987). *Molecular Evolutionary Genetics*. New York: Columbia University Press.

Nevo, E. (1978). Genetic variation in natural populations: Patterns and theory. *Theoretical Population Biology*, 13: 121–177.

Oster, G. F., & Wilson, E. O. (1978). *Caste and Ecology in the Social Insects*. Princeton: Princeton University Press.

Plomin, R., DeFries, J. C., & McClearn, G. E. (1980). *Behavioral Genetics: A primer*. San Francisco: W. H. Freeman.

Rice, W. R. (1983). Parent-offspring pathogen transmission: A selective agent promoting sexual reproduction. *American Naturalist*, 121: 187–203.

Rose, R. J., & Ditto, W. D. (1983). A developmental-genetic analysis of common fears from early adolescence to early adulthood. *Child Development*, 54: 361–368.

Rozin, P. (1976). The evolution of intelligence and access to the cognitive unconscious. In J. M. Sprague & A. N. Epstein (Eds.), *Progress in Psychobiology and Physiological Psychology* (Vol. 6, pp. 245–280). New York: Academic Press.

Seligman, M. E. P. (1971). Phobias and preparedness. *Behavior Therapy*, 2: 307–320.

Seligman, M. E. P., & Hager, J. L. (1972). *Biological Boundaries of Learning*. New York: Appleton-Century-Crofts.

Shepard, M. (1961). Morbid jealousy: Some clinical and social aspects of a psychiatric syndrome. *Journal of Mental Science*, 107: 687–753.

Sperber, D. (1984). Anthropology and psychology: Towards an epidemiology of representations. *Man*, n. s., 20: 73–89.

Symons, D. (1979). *The Evolution of Human Sexuality*. Oxford: Oxford University Press.

Symons, D. (1987). If we're all Darwinians, what's the fuss about? In C. B. Crawford, M. F. Smith, & D. L. Krebs (Eds.), *Sociobiology and Psychology* (pp. 121–146) Hillsdale, NJ: Lawrence Erlbaum.

Tooby, J. (1982). Pathogens, polymorphism and the evolution of sex. *Journal of Theoretical Biology*, 97: 557–576.

Tooby, J., & Cosmides, L. (1988). On reconciling individuality with complex adaptive design: Can non-universal mental organs evolve? *Institute for Evolutionary Studies Technical Report 88–4*.

Tooby, J., & Cosmides, L. (1989). Evolutionary psychology and the generation of culture, Part I: Theoretical considerations. *Ethology and Sociobiology*, 10: 29–49.

Tooby, J., & DeVore, I (1987). The reconstruction of hominid behavioral evolution through strategic modeling. In W. G. Kinzey (Ed.), *The Evolution of Human Behavior; Primate models*. (pp. 183–237) New York: State University of New York Press.

Williams, G. C. (1966). *Adaptation and Natural Selection: A critique of some current evolutionary thought*. Princeton. Princeton University Press.

Williams, G. C. (1975). *Sex and evolution*. Princeton Princeton University Press.

Williams, R. J. (1958). *Biochemical Individuality: The basis for the genetotrophic concept*. New York: Wiley.

Williams, R. J. (1967). *You are Extraordinary*. New York: Random House.

Wilson, E. O. (1971). *The Insect Societies*. Cambridge: Harvard University Press.

Youngman, P., Zuber, P., Perkins, J. B., Sandman, K., Igo, M., & Losick, R. (1985). New ways to study developmental genes in spore-forming bacteria. *Science*, 228: 285–291.

Chapter 17

Daniel M. T. Fessler and Edouard Machery

CULTURE AND COGNITION

Humans are unique among animals for both the diverse complexity of our cognition and our reliance on culture, the socially-transmitted representations and practices that shape experience and behavior. Adopting an evolutionary psychological approach, in this essay we consider four different facets of the relationship between cognition and culture. We begin with a discussion of two well-established research traditions, the investigation of features of mind that are universal despite cultural diversity, and the examination of features of mind that vary across cultures. We then turn to two topics that have only recently begun to receive attention, the cognitive mechanisms that underlie the acquisition of cultural information, and the effects of features of cognition on culture. Throughout, our goal is not to provide comprehensive reviews so much as to frame these issues in such a way as to spur further research.

Psychological Universals

Psychological universals can be defined as those traits, processes, dispositions, or functions that recur across cultures, with at least a subset of each population (e.g., individuals of a specific gender or at a specific developmental stage) exhibiting the trait. The search for psychological universals has a long tradition, as illustrated by Darwin's (1872) investigation of universal emotions, behaviorists' search for universal laws of learning (Hull, 1943), and the Chomskian approach to language and cognition (e.g., Chomsky, 1986). This tradition has been in part motivated by the desire to establish the "psychic unity" of humanity.

Generatively Entrenched Homologies

Because cultures vary tremendously with respect to their ecology, social organization, scale, and technology, and because cultural variables affect cognitive development, one might wonder why psychological universals exist at all. The answer is simple for those traits the development or acquisition of which reflects universal properties of physical or social environments, e.g., the belief that water is wet, or the distinction between males and females. The answer is not so straightforward for other psychological universals, because cultural variables could plausibly affect their development. One might argue that such universals are the product of evolution by natural selection, and that natural selection tends to select for species-typical traits (Tooby & Cosmides, 1992). However, this would be a mistake on two counts. First, much recent research emphasizes that natural selection has favored particular forms of phenotypic plasticity in humans, including the capacity to adapt to, and exploit, parochial cultural information. Second, one cannot presume that natural selection generates homogeneity. In most species, many traits are adaptive polymorphisms, either as a result of frequency-dependent selection or as an adaptive response to environmental variation in the species' range.

So, where do psychological universals come from? Some traits may be psychological universals because they are homologies—features possessed by humans and their relatives by virtue of common descent—that are generatively entrenched. A trait is generatively entrenched if its development is a necessary condition for the development of other traits (Wimsatt, 1986). Most modifications of a generatively entrenched trait are selected against because they prevent the development of these other traits. If a psychological trait in humans is homologous to traits in other species, then, given the general absence of culture outside of our own lineage, it follows that the trait originally evolved in a species that had little (if any) capacity for culture. If this trait became generatively entrenched, then natural selection had little scope to act on its development, which remained insensitive to cultural variables.

The approximate numerical sense provides a clear example of a generatively entrenched homology. Research in the USA and in Europe has established that children and adults possess an approximate number sense (Hauser & Spelke, 2004; Piazza & Dehaene, 2004), being able to approximate the cardinality of sets of visually presented objects or of sequences of sounds without counting, to compare the cardinality of different sets or sequences, and to approximate the results of adding several sets of objects. The accuracy of people's numerical evaluation obeys Weber's law: the mean evaluation is identical to the cardinality of the target set, and the evaluation's standard deviation linearly increases as a function of the cardinality of the target set. Because evaluation is thus increasingly noisy, the accuracy of the numerical comparison between sets or sequences increases as a function of the distance between the cardinality of the sets or

sequences to be compared. These are the signature properties of an analogical encoding of the cardinality of sets or sequences.

Recent studies by Pica, Lemer, Izard, and Dehaene (2004) and Gordon (2004) provide strong evidence that this approximate number sense is a psychological universal. Pica et al. studied approximate estimation, comparison, and addition among the Mundurukú, a small-scale society in Brazilian Amazonia having limited contact with non-indigenous people. Most Mundurukú have not received any formal education. Their language has words for only the numbers 1 to 5; above 5, the Mundurukú rely on locutions signifying "some" or "many." Strikingly, the numbers 3, 4, and 5 are also used to refer to approximate quantities. For instance, in Pica et al.'s experiments, the word for 4 was used for sets of 4 and 5 objects, and the word for 5 was used for sets of 5 to 9 objects. In spite of the differences between the Mundurukú counting system and that in European (and other) languages, and in spite of the many other differences between the respective cultures, the Mundurukú's approximate number sense is identical to Europeans'. Their performances in estimation, comparison, and addition tasks show the signature properties of the analogical system assumed to encode the cardinality of sets or of sequences. Gordon (2004) found similar results with the hunter-gatherer Pirahã tribe in the Lowland Amazonia region of Brazil. Most strikingly, the language spoken by the Pirahã has words for only 1, 2, and 3. Nonetheless, their performances in tasks tapping into their approximate number sense were very close to Europeans' and Americans', providing further evidence for the universality of the approximate number sense.

The approximate number sense, evident in cultures as diverse as small-scale hunter-horticulturalist societies and modern, technologically complex societies, is also present in numerous animal species (Hauser & Spelke, 2004). Thus, in line with our discussion of the origins of psychological universals, the approximate number sense is plausibly a generatively entrenched homology.

Canalized Traits

Not all psychological universals are generatively entrenched homologies. A number of uniquely human psychological traits are also universal because their development has been canalized during the evolution of human cognition. Natural selection selects against development pathways that rely on specific environmental inputs when these environmental inputs vary, when variation in these environmental inputs cause the development of variable traits, and when there is a single optimally adaptive variant (Waddington, 1940). When this happens, natural selection buffers the development of the relevant traits against environmental variation by selecting for developmental pathways that do not depend on these environmental inputs. This phenomenon, known as canalization, likely explains the origins of some psychological universals. Note that, in contrast to the explanation of the evolution of psychological universals examined above, this second account can explain the universality of psychological traits that are not homologies.

Research on so-called folk theories provides some of the best evidence for such universals (Sperber & Hirschfeld, 2004; Boyer & Barrett, 2005). Folk theories are domain-specific, often implicit bodies of information that people use to reason. Although many folk theories vary across cultures, in some domains, folk theories have a universal core; folk biology and folk psychology are two such cases.

Some aspects of folk biology vary across cultures: in some cultures people have much more extensive biological knowledge than in others, and some reasoning strategies about the biological domain are found only in some cultures. Despite such heterogeneity, across cultures, people classify animals and plants in a similar way (Berlin, Breedlove, & Raven, 1973; Berlin, 1992; Atran, 1990, 1998). Plants and animals are organized into hierarchically organized taxonomies of kinds that include (at least) three levels: a "generic species" category (e.g., dogs and cedars), a superordinate category of biological domains (e.g., animals and plants), and a subordinate category of species varieties (e.g., particular breeds or strains). At any level, membership in a kind is exclusive. For instance, no animal is both a dog and a cat or a fish and a mammal.

From a cognitive perspective, the generic species level is of particular importance. Atran and colleagues have shown that while Itza' Maya's biological knowledge is much more extensive than American undergraduates', both Itza' Maya and American undergraduates avoid generalizing biological properties to the members of categories whose level is above the generic-species level (Coley, Medin, & Atran, 1997). Furthermore, in a range of diverse cultures, membership in generic species is associated with "psychological essentialism" (Medin & Ortony, 1989; Gelman, 2003): people believe that membership in a biological kind is associated with the possession of a causal essence— that is, some property or set of properties that define membership in the kind and cause the members of this kind to possess the kind-typical properties independently of their rearing environment. An essentialist disposition has been found among American children and adults (Keil, 1989; Gelman & Wellman, 1991), Yucatek adults (Atran, Medin, Lynch, Vapnarsky, et al., 2001), Brazilian adults (Sousa, Atran, & Medin, 2002), and among children and adults from Madagascar (Astuti, Solomon, & Carey, 2004).

Cross-cultural Psychological Diversity

An entirely different approach to the relations between culture and cognition focuses on differences across cultures. Many differences are best described as ethnographic: because across cultures, people live in different social and physical environments, and different cultural framings thereof, and have correspondingly different experiences, their beliefs, concepts, and desires—in brief, the contents of their minds—will often similarly vary. However, looking beyond such differences, scholars have explored the effects of cultural variation on cognitive processes, personality, and perception (for an extensive review, see Kitayama & Cohen, 2007). The search for cross-cultural differences is deemed successful to the extent that the differences across cultures are marked and are explained by relevant differences among these cultures.

The search for cross-cultural psychological differences has a long history. Particularly, numerous scholars have addressed the role of linguistic differences in producing psychological differences. The anthropologist Edward Sapir and the linguist Benjamin Whorf famously proposed that the syntax and the vocabulary of different languages promote irreducibly different patterns of thought—what is known as the Sapir-Whorf hypothesis (Whorf, 1956). Similarly, Soviet psychologists, particularly Lev Vygotsky and Alexander Luria, argued that languages as well as social activities (e.g., counting routines) constitute tools that allow children to develop symbolic thinking (Vygotsky, 1986).

Proximal Origins of Cross-cultural Differences: Extended Cognition

Traditionally, psychologists and anthropologists searching for cross-cultural differences have given little thought to the evolutionary origins of this diversity, assuming that evolutionary considerations were only relevant for universal traits, or that evolution was only relevant in so far as it produced an undifferentiated "capacity for culture." As discussed in the next two sections, recent theories and findings belie these assumptions. Here, we successively focus on two

proximal causes of cross-cultural psychological diversity.

First, while cognitive science has tended to be methodologically solipsist, neglecting the social and physical environment in which cognition takes place, an influential approach, termed "extended cognition," now insists that social practices, such as counting routines and formal education, as well as physical artifacts dramatically modify (or, in some formulations of this idea, are constitutive of) people's cognitive processes (e.g., Hutchins, 1995; Clark, 1997). Because practices and artifacts vary tremendously across cultures, their effect on the mind is a potent source of cross-cultural diversity.

Language is one of the social practices that can potentially cause cognition to differ substantially across cultures. Since the 1990s, a flurry of cross-cultural work in linguistics and psychology has revived interest in the Sapir-Whorf hypothesis (for reviews, see Gentner & Goldin-Meadow, 2003; Gleitman & Papafragou, 2005; Chiu, Leung, & Kwan, 2007). We consider in turn the research on spatial orientation and the more decisive research on color perception.

Levinson and colleagues have shown that languages encode spatial orientation in a variety of ways (Levinson, 2003; Pederson, Danzinger, Wilkins, Levinson, et al., 1998). They identify three main ways of describing the location of objects. Speakers who use an intrinsic frame of reference locate objects by describing the relations between these objects (the spoon is besides the plate). Speakers who use a relative frame of reference locate objects by describing the position of these objects in relation to themselves and others (the knife is on my/your right). Speakers who use an absolute frame of reference locate objects by using cardinal directions (the knife is west of the plate).

Levinson and colleagues have argued that these linguistic differences affect people's spatial reasoning. In the rotation experiment (Pederson et al., 1998), subjects are shown an array of objects displayed on a table in front of them.

Then, they are asked to turn by 180°. They are then given the objects and asked to recreate the original array on a new table. If speakers of a language with a predominantly relative frame reference also reason relatively, they should preserve the orientation of the objects with respect to their own body: the object that was on the subject's left on the first table should be on her left on the second table, and so on. If speakers of a language with a predominantly absolute frame reference reason absolutely, they should preserve the absolute orientation of objects, thereby changing the orientation of the objects with respect to their own body: the object that was on the subject's left on the first table should now be on her right on the second table. As predicted, Dutch and Japanese subjects, whose languages use a relative frame of reference, preserved the relative orientation of the objects, while Mayans, whose language uses an absolute frame of reference, preserved the absolute orientation of objects. Levinson and colleagues take this and other findings to support the Sapir-Whorf hypothesis.

This finding has, however, been criticized (Gallistel, 2002; Li & Gleitman, 2002). Li and Gleitman (2002) have shown that when a salient object is present in their physical environments, American subjects can be primed to replicate the first array in an absolute manner. Since subjects who replicated the array of objects in a relative manner and those who replicated it in an absolute manner speak the same language (English), it would seem that the linguistic differences between Teztlan and Dutch (or Japanese) do not explain Pederson et al.'s original findings (but see Levinson, Kita, Haun, & Rasch, 2002). Li and Gleitman propose that the task description of the rotation experiment, "Make it the same," is ambiguous, because there are two different ways to reproduce the original array of objects. Subjects use the fact that their language relies predominantly on a relative or on absolute frame of reference to disambiguate the task. Thus, Levinson and colleagues' work does not

show an effect of language on thought, but rather an effect of language on the interpretation of a linguistic expression. Furthermore, Li, Abarbanell, and Papafragou (2005) have shown that Teztlan speakers are not only able to use a relative frame of reference to solve spatial problems, but are better at doing it than at using an absolute frame of reference—in clear contrast to the Sapir-Whorf hypothesis.

This is not to say that the Sapir-Whorf hypothesis is unsupported by recent research, as shown by the research on color. The color lexicon varies tremendously across languages (Berlin & Kay, 1969). While English has 11 basic color terms, the Dani, a hunter-horticulturalist society in Papua New Guinea, use only two, one for light colors and one for dark colors. Color vocabulary is not entirely arbitrary, however (Kay & Regier, 2006). Focal colors constrain languages' color vocabulary: Regier, Kay, and Cook (2005) found that the best examples of color terms for 110 languages from non-industrialized societies cluster around the focal colors. Furthermore, colors tend to be grouped by similarity. Finally, Kay and Regier (2007) have shown that the boundaries between color terms are not arbitrary, but rather map closely across languages.

Because color vocabulary varies across languages, one might wonder whether people's perception and memory of colors vary across linguistic communities. Heider (1972) and Heider and Olivier (1972) have answered negatively to this question, as the Dani's limited color vocabulary seems to have limited effect on their color perception and memory. Heider and Olivier showed Dani and American subjects a color patch. After a 30-second interval, subjects were shown an array of similar color patches and were asked to identify the original patch in this array. The pattern of color recognition was very similar between the two groups. Particularly, in both groups, focal colors were recognized more easily (that is, less confused with other colors) than non-focal colors.

This body of evidence against the Sapir-Whorf hypothesis has been challenged in recent years (Davidoff, Davies, & Roberson, 1999; Roberson, Davies, & Davidoff, 2000; Roberson, Davidoff, Davies, & Shapiro, 2005; see also Lucy & Schweder, 1979; Kay & Kempton, 1984). Davidoff and colleagues (1999; Roberson et al., 2000) have focused on color perception among the Berinmo in Papua New Guinea, who have only five basic color terms. They failed to replicate Heider and Olivier's (1972) experiments. In contrast to Americans, the Berinmo were not more accurate at recognizing focal colors than non-focal colors. Furthermore, when Davidoff and colleagues compared the Berinmo's pattern of color confusion with their pattern of color naming and with the American pattern of color confusion, they found that the Berinmo pattern of color confusion was more similar to the Berinmo pattern of color naming than to the American pattern of color confusion. In line with the Sapir-Whorf hypothesis, this suggests that the Berinmo's color vocabulary affects their color memory.

Proximal Origins of Cross-cultural Differences: Effects of Environmental Differences

A second approach to the proximal origins of cross-cultural differences notes that people typically have various processes and strategies for fulfilling a given psychological function (for instance, categorizing, reasoning inductively, making decisions under uncertainty, etc.). In any given environment, these strategies do not equally well fulfill their functions. For instance, the different types of spatial orientation do not work equally well in all environments. As a result, people can learn to rely on the processes and strategies that are most efficient in their environments. It is therefore important that social and physical environments vary across cultures. Indeed, culturally transmitted norms directly shape people's social environments, and cultural practices can powerfully modify

people's physical environments. Culture is thus a source of diversity in social and physical environments; hence, across cultures, people might come to learn to rely on different processes and strategies, because these are the best ways to fulfill the relevant functions in the environments they inhabit.

It is important to note that the two proximal causes we have considered lead to two different forms of cross-cultural psychological diversity. The idea that artifacts and social practices dramatically modify or are constitutive of people's cognitive processes implies that particular cognitive processes (and other psychological traits) might exist in some cultures, but not in others. In contrast, the idea that people learn to rely on the strategies and processes that are most efficient in their environment suggests that the same processes (and other psychological traits) are present (if only in nascent form) in all cultures, but are differently employed.

Recent work on cultural differences in attention and reasoning provides a good example of the second type of cross-cultural psychological diversity. Nisbett and colleagues distinguish two cognitive styles (Nisbett, Peng, Choi, & Norenzayan, 2001; Nisbett, 2003; Norenzayan, Choi, & Peng, 2007). The analytic cognitive style involves detaching focal objects from their context (field independence), focusing on the properties of objects in contrast to relations between objects, relying on rules to classify and reason, and appealing to causal explanation. By contrast, the holistic cognitive style involves paying attention to the context (field dependence), focusing on the relations between objects, and relying on similarity to classify and reason. Nisbett and colleagues have gathered an impressive body of evidence showing that Westerners exhibit an analytic cognitive style, while East Asians display a holistic cognitive style.

Westerners' attention abstracts objects from their context, while East Asians' attention relates them to their context. In the rod-and-frame test, subjects are shown a rod inside a frame and are asked to adjust the rod to a vertical position. People are considered field-dependent to the extent that their judgment is affected by the verticality of the frame. Ji, Peng, and Nisbett (2000) found that Chinese subjects are more field-dependent than American subjects. These different patterns of attention affect Westerners' and East Asians' perception (for review, see Nisbett & Miyamoto, 2005). Using an eye-tracking method, Chua, Boland, and Nisbett (2005) have shown that Chinese and American students have different patterns of visual exploration of a scene, Americans focusing on the main object of the scene, and Chinese paying greater attention to the background. They propose that the differences between Westerners' and East Asians' attentional patterns might result from the differences between the visual scenes that are characteristic of the two cultures.

Westerners and East Asians also reason differently in a large number of contexts. According to Norenzayan, Smith, Kim, and Nisbett (2002), when asked to assess the similarity between a target object and members of two different categories, East Asians rely on the family resemblance of the target object to the members of each category, while Euro-American look for properties that are necessary and sufficient for belonging to one of the categories. Furthermore, although East Asians are perfectly able to reason according to the rules of propositional logic, they are less disposed than Westerners to do so.

The Cognitive Mechanisms Underlying Culture Acquisition

As exemplified by the work reviewed above, a substantial body of research now documents the extent to which cultural information can play an influential, at times even determinative, role in cognitive processes. Missing from much of this literature, however, are ultimate explanations as to why the human mind is so reliant on, or plastic with respect to, cultural information. Some scholars content themselves with the generalization that because much of human social, economic, and even biological life is structured by culture, the general propensity to think in the same manner as those around one evolved because it facilitates coexistence. Congruent with the "extended cognition" perspective described earlier, others argue that human cultures themselves owe their existence to the effectiveness with which cultural concepts, ways of thinking, and artifacts extend basic human information-processing capacities, thereby bootstrapping our innate potential to a higher level of behavioral complexity. Without contesting either of these generalizations, a nascent school of thought adopts a more explicitly mechanistic evolutionary perspective on the relationship between culture and cognition. This perspective begins with the long-recognized observation that, to a much greater extent than is true of other species, humans depend on cultural information to cope with the challenges posed by their physical and social worlds. The adaptive significance of cultural information suggests that natural selection can be expected to have crafted the human mind so as to maximally exploit this resource. We suggest that the evolved mental mechanisms that serve this goal fall into two general categories, reflecting differences in the degree of specificity of the types of information that they acquire (see also Boyer, 1998 and Henrich & McElreath, 2003 for relevant discussions). We turn first to mechanisms dedicated to the acquisition of specific bodies of knowledge.

Domain-specific Cultural Information Acquisition Mechanisms

Two principal obstacles confronting learners who seek to benefit from others' knowledge are the richness of the informational environment and the incompleteness of the discernable information therein. First, human behavior is enormously complex, varying across contexts and persons, while linguistic utterances convey information ranging from the trivial to the life-saving. If, as is often tacitly presumed, learners were indiscriminate sponges, then (a) learners would often fail to understand how to apply what they have learned, and (b) learners would fail to properly prioritize their acquisition efforts, often resulting in both precocity in domains irrelevant to the learner and retardation in relevant domains. Second, much social learning involves the problem of the poverty of the stimulus, as many actions and utterances explicitly present only fractional portions of the information that motivates them (Boyer, 1998). We suggest that, for many domains of learning, natural selection has addressed both of these problems by endowing the mind with inborn mechanisms, possessing considerable content, that serve to structure the acquisition of cultural information. Such a system can address the prioritization problem via variable motivational valence, as the attentional resources that various mechanisms command in pandemonium-style competition can be calibrated by natural selection to reflect the relative importance of acquiring cultural information in the respective domains: to foreshadow the discussion that follows, acquiring cultural information about dangerous animals likely has recurrently had a greater impact on children's survival than has learning to perform adult rituals, and, correspondingly, natural selection appears to have crafted the mind such that children find the former much more interesting than the latter. Likewise, by adjusting the developmental timing of such mechanisms, natural selection can ensure that learners acquire the cultural information that is most relevant to the fitness challenges characteristic of their current stage of life (for example, we postulate that young children are more interested in dangerous animals than they are in courtship behaviors). Finally, as has been argued extensively for the case of language acquisition, innate content can help to overcome the poverty of the stimulus problem, as such structure can serve as a foundation that

narrows the possible referents or implications of statements and actions.

We believe that investigations aimed at uncovering what we term *domain-specific cultural information acquisition mechanisms* can shed considerable light on how, when, and why knowledge is acquired from others. In designing such investigations, it is important to recognize that, for any given learning domain, three factors can be expected to constitute necessary conditions for the evolution of a domain-specific cultural information acquisition mechanism. First, the domain must have been of substantial and relatively uniform importance to biological fitness across the diverse socioecological circumstances that characterized ancestral human populations, as this will have provided the steady selection pressure necessary for the evolution of a complex adaptation. Second, the domain needs to involve content that will have varied significantly across said circumstances as, on the one hand, this precludes the evolution of extensive innate knowledge, and, on the other hand, this maximally exploits culture's ability to effectively compile information of parochial relevance. Lastly, the domain must be one in which individual learning through trial-and-error or direct observation would have been either very costly or impossible much of the time under ancestral circumstances.

To illustrate the above three factors, consider Barrett's (2005) proposal that a dedicated mechanism or set of mechanisms facilitates learning about dangerous animals. Dangerous animals were a persistent threat to ancestral humans. A few classes of dangerous animals will have been ubiquitous, sharing key perceptual features across disparate environments. For example, poisonous snakes are found in most of the ecosystems inhabited by humans. While snakes vary in their morphological details, all snakes share the same basic body plan. This combination of a significant and recurrent source of selection pressure and uniform perceptual features allowed for the evolution of a template-driven learning mechanism that requires only minimal input to produce a fear of snakes, a homologous trait shared with other primates (Öhman & Mineka, 2003). Notably, however, in contrast to the case of snakes, many dangerous animals are either confined to discrete geographical areas, do not exhibit categorically-distinguishing features, or both. As a consequence, natural selection cannot construct a learning mechanism with the same type of content as that responsible for the fear of snakes—at most, selection can assign innate salience to cues, such as large sharp teeth, that are imperfectly associated with dangerousness. Nevertheless, because cultures can be relied upon to contain information about the identity and attributes of, and strategies for dealing with, locally dangerous animals, natural selection could construct a mechanism dedicated to acquiring this kind of information from others. Importantly, fulfilling the third criterion listed above, learning about dangerous animals from other actors is almost always vastly cheaper than learning through trial and error.

With regard to the informational challenges, described earlier, that confront the human learner, Barrett (2005) suggests that what we would term a *dangerous-animal domain-specific cultural information acquisition mechanism* likely contains conceptual primitives ("animal," "dangerous") that (a) are rapidly mapped onto local lexical terms, (b) have high salience (leading to enhanced attending to, and retention of, any co-occurring information), (c) assist in solving problems of reference and inference (e.g., the learner presumes that statements concerning dangerousness refer to whole species rather than individual instances, that dangerousness will loom large in others' minds as well, allowing for inference as to the topic being discussed, etc.) and (d) structure the manner in which information is organized and stored (e.g., the learner constructs a danger-based taxonomy of animals, etc.). This mechanism may also be linked to other mechanisms that govern defensive

strategies (e.g., freeze, hide, flee, seek arboreal refuge, etc.) such that learning consists of reinforcing one of a number of preexisting potential responses. Next, because the threat posed by dangerous animals begins early in life (and, all else being equal, is often inversely proportional to an individual's size), this mechanism can be expected to begin operating early in development. Finally, children are expected to not only preferentially attend to and retain cultural information about dangerous animals, but, moreover, to actively pursue such information (e.g., more frequently asking questions regarding dangerous than non-dangerous animals, allocating time to social contexts in which information regarding dangerous animals is likely to be available, etc.).

The above discussion is intended to be illustrative, not exhaustive; other domains in which domain-specific cultural information acquisition mechanisms likely operate include navigation, fire building (Fessler, 2006), disease avoidance, gathering, hunting (Barrett, 2005), courtship and mateship, and, perhaps most importantly, morality (Haidt & Joseph, 2004). Moreover, research aimed at mapping domain-specific cultural information acquisition mechanisms will likely overlap somewhat with, and should drawn on, existing work on psychological universals of the type discussed in Section 1. For example, the postulated dangerous-animal domain-specific cultural information acquisition mechanism is likely either part of, or linked to, broader mechanisms responsible for learning about living things; these mechanisms likely contain considerable innate content, generating the universality of core features of folk biology described earlier. Our goal here, however, is not simply to expand the scope of the search for psychological universals, but rather to direct attention to the means whereby cultural information is acquired.

We hope that, by considering the three criteria of universal ancestral fitness relevance, parochial content variation, and high-cost individual learning, scholars will identify numerous areas in which domain-specific cultural information acquisition mechanisms likely exist, and will then test predictions that ensue. However, even if this enterprise proves successful, it will necessarily capture only a portion of the domains for which cultural learning is important. This is because much of the information that must be acquired to succeed in any given society is parochial in both content and type. For example, although it is true that public performance is universally an avenue for achieving prestige, nevertheless, the nature of such performance is so variable across cultures (and even across roles within a culture) as to likely have made it impossible for natural selection to have provided substantial foundations for the acquisition of the relevant information (e.g., while the category "performance" may be a conceptual primitive, it probably does not subsume more specific concepts, and thus lacks a rich structure that can serve as a scaffold for learning).

Domain-general Cultural Information Acquisition Mechanisms

Our species' reliance on cultural information that is parochial in both content and type suggests that natural selection may have favored the evolution of *domain-general cultural information acquisition mechanisms*. At least two classes of such postulated mechanisms are relevant to the present discussion; both address the problems of the complexity and opacity of cultural information and related behavior discussed earlier. First, selection may have favored the evolution of mechanisms dedicated to the complementary tasks of pedagogy and the receipt of pedagogy. Second, whether the agent serving as the source of cultural information is an active pedagog or a passive target of imitation, in a crowded social world, learners must select whom to attend to as a source of cultural information, a task that may be subserved by evolved mechanisms.

Csibra and Gergely (2006) argue that much cultural information transfer is achieved through a goal-directed social process of teaching and learning contingent on ostension, reference, and relevance. Ostension denotes the act of indicating that one's current actions are communicative efforts, thereby differentiating such behavior from the stream of potentially-observable actions. Reference addresses the need to constrain the topic of the communication from the class of all possible topics. Both ostension and reference can be enacted by either the pedagog (who strives to indicate "now I am *teaching* about X") or the learner (who strives to indicate "I *need information* about X"). Csibra and Gergely argue that specific cues, and the cognitive mechanisms that process them, have evolved to facilitate, respectively, ostension (e.g., eye contact, eyebrow flashing, and turn-taking contingency by both parties; motherese by pedagogs interacting with infants) and reference (e.g., gaze directing/gaze-direction detection; pointing). Relevance, a feature of the inferential process engaged in by the learner once a teaching/learning interaction has been established, involves the presumption that actions lacking an ulterior explanation are designed to convey information in light of the learner's state of knowledge.

To date, the work of Gergely, Csibra, and colleagues has focused primarily on adult/infant interactions. However, ostension, reference, and relevance ought to characterize all teaching/learning interactions, the only principal modification being that bidirectional linguistic communication expands the channels available for ostension and reference. A more substantial difference, however, between infant learners and older learners is that infants have a vastly smaller range of potential pedagogs from which to choose. Older learners therefore face the problem of selecting the targets from whom they hope to learn. This is true both with regard to pedagogical interactions and with regard to imitating a passive (non-teaching) model (while noting that the cognitive mechanisms underlying imitation are deserving of attention from students of the evolved psychology of culture acquisition, we leave this topic for another day). However, the selection criteria differ for the two types of targets. Because pedagogs scale their communication to the competence of the learner, learners can usefully solicit pedagogy from individuals who possess vastly superior skills. In contrast, because cultural information is complex and opaque, in the case of imitation without pedagogy, learners must select targets that are closer to their own current competence, else much of the model's behavior will be subject to misinterpretation.

Differences between the two types of learning are reduced somewhat when the issue of social structure is considered, as the distribution of cultural information over roles is such that individuals will often benefit from seeking to learn from others whose position in the social structure is not too distant from their own, since similar roles entail similar resources, opportunities, and obligations (for seminal empirical work, see Harris, 1995). Lastly, the task of target selection is complicated by the bidirectionality of the interaction: even imitation in the absence of pedagogy often has a bidirectional component, as the target must tolerate the presence of the learner. Henrich and Gil-White (2001) argue that, in exchange for access, learners grant higher status to individuals whom they wish to imitate; market forces then influence individual choices, with less-desired targets willing to grant more access. In contrast to Csibra and Gergely (2006), who argue that the costs to the pedagog are such that pedagogy can be expected to be primarily kin-based (as kin have an interest in the welfare of their relatives), we suggest that the same market model applies to pedagogy: in both cases, the costs that accompany being targeted by a learner can be outweighed by the elevated prestige and power that flows from social support. The learner must thus trade off the value of the knowledge possessed by the target (skill, success, etc.) against the costs of access, keeping in mind that other learners are also competing for access.

The task of selecting targets from whom to learn is characterized by both sufficient importance and sufficient overarching uniformity as to suggest that evolution has created domain-general cultural information acquisition mechanisms for this purpose. We thus expect that actors will be adept at identifying others who possess the optimal combination of superiority and role-relevant knowledge; that observation of such individuals will be more acute, and subsequent information better retained; that ostensive cues will be both displayed toward and sought from such individuals; and that learners will be quite good at optimizing the access/cost ratio in a fluid market.

An alternative strategy to selecting a single individual as the focus of learning is to adopt the prevailing pattern of behavior in the local group. Because a single individual's success may be the product of many factors, raising the dual problems that (a) it may be unclear which aspects should be acquired by the learner, and (b) some of these factors may not be acquirable through learning, the conformist strategy will often prove profitable (Boyd & Richerson, 1985; Henrich & Boyd, 1998). Note, however, that this is not so much a method of learning as it is a method of deciding which of a number of variants of behavior to adopt. This is because at least some understanding of those variants (and hence some learning) must precede this decision; presumably, this process must be iterated, with the actor coming to recognize finer distinctions among variants as her command of the relevant information increases. Accordingly, many of the same cognitive learning processes must underlie both information acquisition strategies that target particular individuals as sources and conformist strategies that survey larger numbers of individuals. There are also some parallels as regards the task demands of target selection, since the relevance of behavior common across a set of prospective models is in part contingent on their degree of similarity to the learner: behavior that is common among individuals who occupy positions in the social structure similar to the learner's will generally be most relevant to, and hence should be most salient to, the learner. We can thus expect some form of a domain-general cultural information acquisition mechanism to combine information about the respective behaviors of actors with information about their relative social structural similarity to the learner in order to efficiently promote conformist acquisition. Lastly, the conformist strategy is less complex than individually-focused learning in regard to calculating cost/benefit ratio in target selection: because the goal is to acquire the most common variant of behavior, there is no shortage of potential models; hence it is a buyers' market, and the learner should be unwilling to pay much for access to prospective models.

The Effects of Cognition on Culture

Thus far, we have explored the extent to which cultural information shapes cognition, and examined how the acquisition of cultural information may be underlain by evolved psychological mechanisms of varying degrees of domain specificity. This may give the impression that cultural information is a static feature of the environment. However, because culture exists in the minds of individuals, the relationship between culture and cognition is bidirectional, and thus dynamic. Specifically, because culture is instantiated through processes of the transmission, retention, and application of information, the composition of culture is subject to the influence of actors' minds, as information that is more likely to be transmitted, retained, and applied will come to predominate, while information for which this is less true will become rarer, and may disappear entirely.[1]

Design Features of Mental Mechanisms can Influence Cultural evolution

Anthropologists have long recognized that some ideas are "good to think" (Lévi-Strauss, 1962), meaning that they interdigitate with the mind in ways that make them attractive. Originally, this notion was developed with regard to the manner in which the affordances of real-world objects and entities (e.g., animals) facilitate symbolic distinctions that usefully organize human social life. Such nebulous intuitions were later more rigorously reconceptualized by cognitive anthropologists, who observed, for example, that folk taxonomies tend to be structured in ways that complement features of short-term memory.[2] More generally, the relative learnability (ease of acquisition, retention, and use) of cultural information can be expected to influence its persistence and spread. With regard to information acquired via domain-general cultural information acquisition mechanisms, learnability will in part be a function of the way that information is organized (as in the case of folk taxonomies), and will in part be a function of features of social transmission (e.g., ceteris paribus, because of the costs of pedagogy, ideas that can be acquired through imitation alone will spread faster than those that require pedagogy). With regard to information acquired via domain-specific cultural information acquisition mechanisms, learnability will in part be a function of the extent to which ideas contact the evolved content of the respective mechanisms (see also Boyer, 1998). For example, Sperber and Hirschfeld (2004) and Barrett (2005) note that the special salience of information regarding dangerous animals is such that ideas concerning dangerous animals are more likely to spread and persist over time, even to the extent that erroneous information about actual creatures (e.g., the belief that wolves often prey on humans, see Sperber & Hirschfeld, 2004) and fantastical notions about nonexistent creatures (Sasquatch, the Loch Ness Monster, see Barrett,

2005) become widely accepted (for a pressing contemporary example, see Lombrozo, Shtulman, and Weisberg [2006] on the obstacles to learnability of evolutionary theory). Similarly, using both experimental and naturalistic data, Heath, Bell, and Sternberg (2001) have shown that the likelihood that urban legends will be transmitted, and will persist, is in part contingent on the degree to which they elicit disgust. Given that disgust is prototypically elicited by cues associated with pathogen transmission (Curtis & Biran, 2001), this pattern is parsimoniously understood as the result of the operation of a domain-specific cultural information acquisition mechanism dedicated to the acquisition of knowledge relevant to disease avoidance.

A general principle that can be expected to apply to many of the mechanisms postulated thus far is that of error management (Haselton & Buss, 2000): natural selection will have built biases into information processing systems such that, when these mechanisms err, they do so "on the safe side," making the mistake that, under ancestral conditions, would have been the least costly of the possible errors. One consequence of this is that, as illustrated by the above examples, domain-specific cultural information acquisition mechanisms that address possible hazards will lead to credulity, as actors will accept without evidence, and will not seek to test, socially-transmitted information; aggregated over many individuals, the result will often be a proliferation of wholly imaginary dangers. Consistent with this perspective, preliminary evidence from an extensive evaluation of ethnographic materials suggests that, around the globe, supernatural beliefs tend to depict a world filled with anxiety-provoking dangerous agents and processes (Fessler, Pisor, & Navarrete, n.d.). At a more general level still, the content of beliefs that describe hazards in the world will influence the likelihood that those beliefs will persist over time. For example, many proscriptive beliefs include notions of supernatural sanctions. We can expect that the most successful proscriptions will involve sanctions that either (a) are vague, referring to a wide class of possible events (e.g., misfortune, etc.), or (b) though specific, nonetheless refer to a negative event that is relatively common, and for which the objective causes are not readily evident (e.g., infant death in small-scale societies). Given the issue of credulity mentioned earlier, proscriptions enforced by vague supernatural sanctions will be likely to persist because bad things eventually happen to everyone; hence, when a taboo is violated, it is inevitable that sooner or later events will unfold that can be interpreted as evidence of the veracity of the belief. Likewise, proscriptions enforced by more specific sanctions will be likely to persist if the events described therein happen with sufficient frequency that, eventually, they will occur in the lives of rule-breakers.

Misfirings of Other Mental Mechanisms can Influence Cultural Evolution

In addition to the question of how design features of domain-specific cultural information acquisition mechanisms and domain-general cultural information acquisition mechanisms influence cultural evolution, a growing literature seeks to explain widespread cultural traits in terms of the accidental misfiring of evolved cognitive mechanisms that are not dedicated to the acquisition of cultural information per se. This approach arguably began with Westermarck (1891), who hypothesized that incest taboos result from the accidental triggering by third-party behavior of mechanisms that evolved to reduce inbreeding among close kin. More recently, Boyer (2001) argues that beliefs in supernatural agents are more likely to persist if they are minimally counterintuitive, meaning that the agents possess nearly all, but not all, of the properties expected by mechanisms that serve to detect agents and predict their actions; Fessler and Navarrete (2003) suggest that the centrality of meat in food taboos is an accident of the salience of meat as a stimulus in toxin-detection and pathogen-avoidance mechanisms; and Boyer and Lienard (2006) argue that the combination of constraints on working memory, the operation of mechanisms devoted to avoiding hazards, and the parsing of actions generates a non-functional attraction to ritualized behavior. While we feel that efforts such as these are to be encouraged, such hypotheses are necessarily developed on an ad hoc basis, in contrast to the bottom-up predictive potential of a dedicated effort to explore the nature, and consequences for cultural content and evolution, of mechanisms dedicated to the acquisition of cultural information.

Conclusion

There are many ways to study the relations between culture and cognition. In this chapter, we have discussed two traditional approaches in psychology and anthropology: searching for psychological universals and for cross-cultural psychological differences. Furthermore, we have attempted to describe what we take to be two of the most exciting contemporary approaches to studying these relations: looking for domain-specific and domain-general cultural information acquisition mechanisms, and identifying the influences of the structure of our minds on how information is retained and transmitted.

Notes

1 Sperber 1996, Chapter 5.
2 O'Andrade 1995, pp. 42–43.

References

Astuti, R., Solomon, G. A., & Carey, S. (2004). *Constraints of Conceptual Development: A case study of the acquisition of folkbiological and folksociological knowledge in Madagascar*. Oxford: Blackwell Publishing.

Atran, S. (1990). *Cognitive Foundations of Natural History: Towards an anthropology of science*. Cambridge: Cambridge University Press.

Atran, S., Medin, D. L., Lynch, E., Vapnarsky, V., Ucan Ek'., & Sousa, P. (2001). Folkbiology doesn't come from folkpsychology: Evidence from Yukatec Maya in cross-cultural perspective. *Journal of Cognition and Culture*, 1: 3–42.

Barrett, H. C. (2005). Adaptations to predators and prey. In D. M. Buss (Ed.), *The Handbook of Evolutionary Psychology* (pp. 200–223). New York: Wiley.

Berlin, B. (1992). *Ethnobiological Classification*. Princeton, NJ: Princeton University Press.

Berlin, B., & Kay, P. (1969). *Basic Color Terms: Their universality and evolution*. Berkeley, CA: University of California Press.

Berlin, B., Breedlove, D., & Raven, P. (1973). General principles of classification and nomenclature in folk biology. *American Anthropologist*, 74: 214–42.

Boyd, R., & Richerson, P. (1985). *Culture and the Evolutionary Process*. Chicago, IL: University of Chicago Press.

Boyer, P. (1998). Cognitive tracks of cultural inheritance: How evolved intuitive ontology governs cultural transmission. *American Anthropologist*, 100: 876–89.

Boyer, P. (2001). *Religion Explained: The Evolutionary Origins of Religious Thought*. New York: Basic Books.

Boyer, P., & Barrett, H. C. (2005). Domain specificity and intuitive ontology. In D. M. Buss (Ed.), *Handbook of Evolutionary Psychology* (pp. 96–188). New York: Wiley.

Boyer, P., & Lienard, P. (2006). Why ritualized behavior? Precaution systems and action parsing in developmental, pathological and cultural rituals. *Behavioral and Brain Sciences*, 29(6): 595–650.

Chiu, C.-Y., Leung, A. K.-Y., & Kwan, L. (2007). Language, cognition, and culture: The Whorfian hypothesis and beyond. In S. Kitayama and D. Cohen (Eds.), *Handbook of Cultural Psychology* (pp. 668–90). New York: Guilford.

Chomsky, N. (1986). *Knowledge of Language: Its nature, origin, and use*. New York: Praeger.

Chua, H. F., Boland, J. E. and Nisbett, R. E. (2005). Cultural variation in eye movements during scene perception. *Proceedings of the National Academy of Sciences, USA*, 102: 12629–33

Clark, A. (1997). *Being There: Putting brain, body, and world together again*. Cambridge, MA: MIT Press.

Coley, J. D., Medin, D. L., & Atran, S. (1997). Does rank have its privilege? Inductive inferences within folkbiological taxonomies. *Cognition*, 63: 73–112.

Csibra, G., & Gergely, G. (2006). Social learning and social cognition: The case for pedagogy. In Y. Munakata and M. H. Johnson (Eds.), *Processes of Change in Brain and Cognitive Development: Attention and performance XXI* (pp. 249–274). Oxford: Oxford University Press.

Curtis, V., & Biran, A. (2001). Dirt, disgust, and disease: is hygiene in our genes?, *Perspectives in Biology and Medicine*, 44: 17–31.

D'Andrade, R. (1995). *The Development of Cognitive Anthropology*. Cambridge: Cambridge University Press.

Darwin, C. (1872). *The Expressions of Emotions in Man and Animals*, 1st ed. New York: Philosophical Library.

Davidoff, J., Davies, I., & Roberson, D. (1999). Colour categories in a stone-age tribe. *Nature*, 398: 203–4.

Fessler, D. M. T. (2006). A burning desire: Steps toward an evolutionary psychology of fire learning. *Journal of Cognition and Culture*, 6(3–4): 429–51.

Fessler, D. M. T., Pisor, A.C., & Navarrete, C. D. (n.d.). The spirits are not your friends: Biased credulity and the cultural fitness of beliefs. Manuscript in preparation.

Fessler, D. M. T., & Navarrete, C. D. (2003). Meat is good to taboo: Dietary proscriptions as a product of the interaction of psychological mechanisms and social processes. *Journal of Cognition and Culture*, 3(1): 321–22.

Gallistel, C. R. (2002). Language and spatial frames of reference. *Trends in Cognitive Sciences*, 6: 321–22.

Gelman, S. A. (2003). *The Essential Child: Origins of essentialism in everyday thought*. New York: Oxford University Press.

Gelman, S. A., & Wellman, H. M. (1991). Insides and essences: early understandings of the nonobvious. *Cognition*, 38: 213–44.

Gentner, D., & Goldin-Meadow, S. (2003) *Language in Mind: Advances in the study of language and thought*. Cambridge, MA: MIT Press.

Gleitman, L., & Papafragou, A. (Papafragou, A.). Language and thought. In K. H. Morrison and R. Morrison (Ed.), *Cambridge Handbook of Thinking and Reasoning* (pp. 633–61). Cambridge: Cambridge University Press.

Gordon, P. (2004). Numerical cognition without words: Evidence from Amazonia. *Science*, 306: 496–99.

Haidt, J., & Joseph, C. (2004). Intuitive ethics: How innately prepared intuitions generate culturally variable virtues. *Daedalus*, 133: 55–66

Harris, J. R. (1995) Where is the child's environment? A group socialization theory of development. *Psychological Review*, 102(3): 458–89.

Haselton, M., & Buss, D. M. (2000). Error management theory: A new perspective on biases in cross-sex mind reading. *Journal of Personality and Social Psychology*, 78(1): 81–91.

Hauser, M. D., & Spelke, E. S. (2004). Evolutionary and developmental foundations of human knowledge: a case study of mathematics. In M. Gazzaniga (Ed.), *The Cognitive Neurosciences*, 3rd ed. (pp. 853–64). Cambridge, MA: MIT Press.

Heath, C., Bell, C, & Sternberg, E. (2001). Emotional selection in memes: The case of urban legends. *Journal of Personality and Social Psychology*, 81(6): 1028–41.

Heider, E. R. (1972). Universals in color naming and memory. *Journal of Experimental Psychology*, 93: 10–20.

Heider, E. R., & Oliver, C. C. (1972). The structure of the color space in naming and memory for two languages. *Cognitive Psychology*, 3: 337–54.

Henrich, J. & Boyd, R. (1998). The evolution of conformist transmissionand between-group differences. *Evolution and Human Behavior*, 19: 215–42.

Henrich, J., & Gil-White, F. J. (2001). The evolution of prestige: Freely conferred status as a mechanism for enhancing the benefits of cultural transmission. *Evolution and Human Behavior*, 22: 165–96.

Henrich, J., & McElreath, R. (2003). The evolution of cultural evolution. *Evolutionary Anthropology*, 12(3): 123–35.

Hull, C. L. (1943). *Principles of Behavior*. New York: Appleton-Century-Crofts.

Hutchins, E. (1995). *Cognition in the Wild*. Cambridge, MA: The MIT Press.

Ji, L., Peng, K., & Nisbett, R. E. (2000). Culture, control, and perception of relationships in the environment. *Journal of Personality and Social Psychology*, 78: 943–55.

Kay, P., & Kempton, W. (1984). What is the Sapir-Whorf hypothesis?, *American Anthropologist*, 86: 65–79.

Kay, P., & Regier, T. (2006). Language, thought and color: recent developments. *Trends in Cognitive Sciences*, 10(2): 51–54.

Kay, P., & Regier, T. (2007). Color naming universals: The case of Berinmo. *Cognition*, 102: 289–98.

Keil, F. (1989). *Concepts, Kinds, and Cognitive Development.* Cambridge, MA: MIT Press.

Kitayama, S., & Cohen, D., (Eds.), (2007). *Handbook of Cultural Psychology.* New York: Guilford Publications.

Levinson, S. C. (2003). *Space in Language and Cognition: Explorations in cognitive diversity.* Cambridge: Cambridge University Press.

Levinson, S. C., Kita, S., Haun, D. B. M., & Rasch, B. H. (2002). Returning the tables: Language affects spatial reasoning. *Cognition,* 84: 155–88.

Lévi-Strauss, C. (1962). *Totemism,* R. Needham, trans. Chicago, IL: University of Chicago Press.

Li, P. & Gleitman, L. (2002). Turning the tables: Language and spatial reasoning. *Cognition,* 83: 265–94.

Li, P., Abarbanell, L., & Papafragou, A. (2005). Spatial reasoning skills in Tenejapan Mayans. *Proceedings from the 27th Annual Meeting of the Cognitive Science Society.* Hillsdale, NJ: Erlbaum.

Lombrozo, T., Shtulman, A., & Weisberg, M. (2006). The Intelligent Design controversy: Lessons from psychology and education. *Trends in Cognitive Sciences,* 10(2): 56–57.

Lucy, J. A., & Shweder, R. A. (1979). Whorf and his critics: Linguistic and nonlinguistic influences on color memory. *American Anthropologist,* 81: 581–615.

Medin, D. L., & Ortony, A. (1989). Psychological essentialism. In S. Vosniadou and A. Ortony (Eds.), *Similarity and Anological Reasoning* (pp. 179–95). New York: Cambridge University Press.

Nisbett, R. E. (2003). *The Geography of Thought.* New York: Free Press.

Nisbett, R. E., & Miyamoto, Y. (2005). The influence of culture: Holistic versus analytic perception. *Trends in Cognitive Sciences,* 9(10): 467–73.

Nisbett, R. E., Peng, K., Choi, I., & Norenzayan, A. (2001). Culture and systems of thought: Holistic vs. analytic cognition. *Psychological Review,* 108: 291–310.

Norenzayan, A., Choi, I., & Peng, K. (2007). Cognition and perception. In S. Kitayama and D. Cohen (Eds.), *Handbook of Cultural Psychology* (pp. 569–94). New York: Guilford Publications.

Norenzayan, A., Smith, E. E., Kim, B., & Nisbett, R. E. (2002). Cultural preferences for formal versus intuitive reasoning. *Cognitive Science,* 26: 653–84.

Öhman, A., & Mineka, S. (2003). The malicious serpent: Snakes as a prototypical stimulus for an evolved module of fear. *Current Directions in Psychological Science,* 12(1): 5–9.

Pederson, E., Danziger, E., Wilkins, D., Levinson, S., Kita, S., & Senft, G. (1998). Semantic topology and spatial conceptualization. *Language,* 74(3): 557–89.

Piazza, M., & Dehaene, S. (2004). From number neurons to mental arithmetic: The cognitive neuroscience of number sense. In M. Gazzaniga (Ed.), *The Cognitive Neurosciences,* 3rd ed. (pp. 865–76). Cambridge, MA: MIT Press.

Pica, P., Lemer, C., Izard, V., & Dehaene, S. (2004). Exact and approximate arithmetic in an Amazonian Indigene group. *Science,* 306: 499–503.

Regier, T., Kay, P., & Cook, R. S. (2005). Focal colors are universal after all. *Proceedings of the National Academy of Sciences,* 102(23): 8386–91.

Roberson, D., Davies, I., & Davidoff, J. (2000). Color categories are not universal: Replications and new evidence from a stone-age culture. *Journal of Experimental Psychology: General,* 129: 369–98.

Roberson, D., Davidoff, J., Davies, I., & Shapiro, L. (2005). Color categories in Himba: Evidence for the cultural relativity hypothesis. *Cognitive Psychology,* 50: 378–411.

Sousa, P., Atran, S., & Medin, D. L. (2002). Essentialism and folkbiology: Further evidence from Brazil. *Journal of Cognition and Culture,* 2: 195–223.

Sperber, D. (1996). *Explaining Culture: A naturalistic approach.* Cambridge, MA: Blackwell.

Sperber, D., & Hirschfeld, L. A. (2004) The cognitive foundations of cultural stability and diversity. *Trends in Cognitive Sciences,* 8(1): 40–46.

Tooby, J., & Cosmides, L. (1992). The psychological foundations of culture. In J.H. Barkow, L. Cosmides, and J. Tooby (Eds.), *The Adapted Mind: Evolutionary Psychology and the Generation of Culture* (pp. 19–136). New York: Oxford University Press.

Vygotsky, L. S. (1986). *Thought and Language.* Cambridge, MA: MIT Press.

Waddington, C. H. (1940). *Organisers and Genes.* Cambridge: Cambridge University Press.

Westermarck, E. (1891). *The History of Human Marriage.* New York: Macmillan and Co.

Whorf, B. L. (1956). *Language, Thought, and Reality.* Cambridge, MA: MIT Press.

Wimsatt, W. C. (1986). Developmental constraints, generative entrenchment, and the innate-acquired distinction. In W. Bechtel (Ed.), *Integrating Scientific Disciplines.* (pp. 185–208). Dordrecht: Martinus-Nijhoff.

Chapter 18

P. J. Richerson and R. Boyd

NOT BY GENES ALONE
How Culture Transformed Human Action

The American South has long been more violent than the North. Colorful descriptions of duels, feuds, bushwhackings, and lynchings features prominently in visitors' accounts, newspaper articles, and autobiographies from the eighteenth century onward. Statistics bear out these impressions. For example, over the period 1865–1915, the homicide rate in the South was ten times the current rate for the whole United States, and twice the rate in our most violent cities. Modern homicide statistics tell the same story.

In their book, *Culture of Honor*, psychologists Richard Nisbett and Dov Cohen argue that the South is more violent than the North because southern people have culturally acquired beliefs about personal honor that are different from their northern counterparts.[1] Southerners, they argue, believe more strongly than Northerners that a person's reputation is important and worth defending even at great cost. As a consequence, arguments and confrontations that lead to harsh words or minor scuffles in Amherst or Ann Arbor often escalate to lethal violence in Asheville or Austin.

What else could explain these differences? Some feature of the southern environment, such as its greater warmth, could explain why Southerners are more violent. Such hypotheses are plausible, and Nisbett and Cohen are at pains to test them. Northerners and Southerners might differ genetically, but this hypothesis is not very plausible. The settlers of the North and South came mostly from the British Isles and adjacent areas of northwestern Europe.[2] Human populations are quite well mixed on this scale.

Nisbett and Cohen support their hypothesis with an impressive range of evidence. Let's start with statistical patterns of violence. In the rural and small-town South, murder rates are elevated for arguments among friends and acquaintances, but not for killings committed in the course of other felonies. In other words, in the South men are more likely than Northerners to kill an acquaintance when an argument breaks out in a bar, but they are no more likely to kill the guy behind the counter when they knock off a liquor store. Thus, Southerners seem to be more violent than other Americans only in situations that involve personal honor. Competing hypotheses don't do so well: neither white per-capita income nor hot climate nor history of slavery explain this variation in homicide.

Differences in what people say about violence also support the "culture of honor" hypothesis. For example, Nisbett and Cohen asked people to read vignettes in which a man's honor was challenged—sometimes trivially (for example, by insults to his wife), and in other cases seriously (for example, by stealing his wife). Southern respondents were more likely than Northerners to say that violent responses were justified in all cases, and that one would "not be much of a man" unless he responded violently to insults. In the case of more serious affronts, southern respondents were almost twice as likely to say that shooting the perpetrator was justified.

Interestingly, this difference in behavior is not just talk; it can also be observed under the controlled conditions of the psychology laboratory. Working at the University of Michigan, Nisbett and Cohen recruited participants from northern and southern backgrounds, ostensibly to participate in an experiment on perception. As part of the procedure, an experimenter's confederate bumped some participants and muttered "Asshole!" at them. This insult had very different effects on southern and northern participants, as revealed by the next part of the experiment. Sometime after being bumped, participants encountered another confederate walking toward them down the middle of a narrow hall, setting up a little game of chicken. This confederate, a six-foot, three-inch, 250-pound linebacker on the UM football squad, was much bigger and stronger than any participant, and had been instructed to keep walking until either the participant stepped aside and let him pass or a collision was imminent. Northerners stepped aside when the confederate was six feet away, whether or not they had been insulted. Southerners who had not been insulted stepped aside when they were nine feet away from the confederate, while previously insulted Southerners continued walking until they were just three feet away. Polite, but prepared to be violent, uninsulted Southerners take more care, presumably because they attribute a sense of honor to the football player and are careful not to test it. When their own honor is challenged, however, they are willing to challenge someone at considerable risk to their own safety. These behavioral differences have physiological correlates. In a similar confederate-insulter experiment, Nisbett and Cohen measured levels of two hormones, cortisol and testosterone, in participants before and after they had been insulted. Physiologists know that cortisol levels increase in response to

stress, and testosterone levels rise in preparation for violence. Insulted Southerners showed much bigger jumps in cortisol and testosterone than insulted Northerners.

Nisbett and Cohen argue that the difference in beliefs between northern and southern people can be understood in terms of their cultural and economic histories. Scots-Irish livestock herders were the main settlers of the South, while English, German, and Dutch peasant farmers populated the North. States historically have had considerable difficulty imposing the rule of law in the sparsely settled regions where herding is the dominant occupation, and livestock are easy to steal. Hence in herding societies a culture of honor often arises out of necessity as men seek to cultivate reputations for willingly resorting to violence as a deterrent to theft and other predatory behavior. Of course, bad men may also subscribe to the same code, the better to intimidate their victims. As this arms race escalates, arguments over trivial acts can rapidly get out of hand if a man thinks his honor is at stake. This account is supported by the fact that Southern white homicide rates are unusually high in poor regions with low population density and a historically weak presence of state institutions, not in the richer, more densely settled, historically slave-plantation districts. In such an environment the Scots-Irish honor system remained adaptive until recent times.

This fascinating study illustrates the two main points we want to make in this book.

Culture is crucial for understanding human behavior. People acquire beliefs and values from the people around them, and you can't explain human behavior without taking this reality into account. Murder is more common in the South than in the North. If Nisbett and Cohen are right, this difference can't be explained in terms of contemporary economics, climate, or any other external factor. Their explanation is that people in the South have acquired a complex set of beliefs and attitudes about personal honor that make them more polite, but also more quick to take offense than people in the North. This complex persists because the beliefs of one generation are learned by the next. This is not an isolated example. We will present several other similar well-studied examples demonstrating that culture plays an important role in human behavior. These are only the tip of the iceberg— a complete scholarly rehearsal of the evidence would try the patience of all but the most dedicated reader. Culturally acquired ideas are crucially important for explaining a wide range of human behavior—opinions, beliefs, and attitudes, habits of thought, language, artistic styles, tools and technology, and social rules and political institutions.

Culture is part of biology. An insult that has trivial effects in a Northerner sets off a cascade of physiological changes in a southern male that prepare him to harm the insulter and cope with the likelihood that the insulter is prepared to retaliate violently. This example is merely one strand in a skein of connections that enmesh culturally acquired information in other aspects of human biology. Much evidence suggests that we have an evolved psychology that shapes what we learn and how we think, and that this in turn influences the kind of beliefs and attitudes that spread and persist. Theories that ignore these connections cannot adequately account for much of human behavior. At the same time, culture and cultural change cannot be understood solely in terms of innate psychology. Culture affects the success and survival of individuals and groups; as a result, some cultural variants spread and others diminish, leading to evolutionary processes that are every bit as real and important as those that shape genetic variation. These culturally evolved environments then affect which genes are favored by natural selection. Over the evolutionary long haul, culture has shaped our innate psychology as much as the other way around.

Few who have thought much about the problem would dispute either of these claims *in principle*. Beliefs and practices that we learn from

one another are clearly important, and like all human behavior, culture must in some way be rooted in human biology. However, *in practice* most social scientists ignore at least one of them. Some scholars, including most economists, many psychologists, and many social scientists influenced by evolutionary biology, place little emphasis on culture as a cause of human behavior. Others, especially anthropologists, sociologists, and historians, stress the importance of culture and institutions in shaping human affairs, but usually fail to consider their connection to biology. The success of all these disciplines suggests that many questions can be answered by ignoring culture or its connection to biology. However, the most fundamental questions of how humans came to be the kind of animal we are can *only* be answered by a theory in which culture has its proper role *and* in which it is intimately intertwined with other aspects of human biology. In this book we outline such a theory.

Culture Can't be Understood Without Population Thinking

Eminent biologist Ernst Mayr has argued that "population thinking" was Charles Darwin's key contribution to biology.[3] Before Darwin, people thought of species as essential, unchanging types, like geometric figures and chemical elements. Darwin saw that species were populations of organisms that carried a variable pool of inherited information through time. To explain the properties of a species, biologists had to understand how the day-to-day events in the lives of individuals shape this pool of information, causing some variant members of the species to persist and spread, and others to diminish. Darwin famously argued that when individuals carrying some variants were more likely to survive or have more offspring, these would spread through a process of natural selection. Less famously, he also thought that beneficial behaviors and morphologies acquired during an individual's lifetime were transmitted to the offspring, and that this process, which he called the "inherited effects of use and disuse," also shaped which variants were present. We now know that the latter process is unimportant in organic evolution, and that many processes Darwin never dreamed of are important in molding populations, including mutation, segregation, recombination, genetic drift, gene conversion, and meiotic drive. Nonetheless, modern biology is fundamentally Darwinian, because its explanations of evolution are rooted in population thinking: and if through some miracle of cloning Darwin were to be resurrected from his grave in Westminister Abbey, we think that he would be quite happy with the state of the science he launched.

Population thinking is the core of the theory of culture we defend in this book. First of all, let's be clear about what we mean by *culture*:

> *Culture is information capable of affecting individuals' behaviour that they acquire from other members of their species through teaching, imitation, and other forms of social transmission.*

By *information* we mean any kind of mental state, conscious or not, that is acquired or modified by social learning and affects behavior. We will use everyday words like *idea, knowledge, belief, value, skill* and *attitude* to describe this information, but we do not mean that such socially acquired information is always consciously available, or that it necessarily corresponds to folk-psychological categories. Our definition is rooted in the conviction that most cultural variation is caused by information stored in human brains— information that got into those brains by learning from others. People in culturally distinct groups behave differently, mostly because they have acquired different skills, beliefs, and values, and these differences persist because the people of one generation acquire their beliefs and attitudes from those around them. Hence Southerners are more likely to kill than

Northerners because they hold different attitudes about personal honor. The same is true of many other aspects of culture. Different populations exhibit persistent variation in language, social customs, moral systems, practical skills and devices, and art. These and all the other dimensions of culture exist because people possess different socially acquired skills, beliefs, or values.

Population thinking is the key to building a causal account of cultural evolution. We are largely what our genes and our culture make us. In the same way that evolutionary theory explains why some genes persist and spread, a sensible theory of cultural evolution will have to explain why some beliefs and attitudes spread and persist while others disappear. The processes that cause such cultural change arise in the everyday lives of individuals as people acquire and use cultural information. Some moral values are more appealing and thus more likely to spread from one individual to another. These will tend to persist, while less attractive alternatives tend to disappear. Some skills are easy to learn accurately, while others are more difficult and are likely to be altered as we learn them. Some beliefs make people more likely to be imitated, because the people who hold those beliefs are more likely to survive or more likely to achieve social prominence. Such beliefs will tend to spread, while beliefs that lead to early death or social stigma will disappear. In the short run, a population-level theory of culture has to explain the net effect of such processes on the distribution of beliefs and values in a population during the previous generation. Over the longer run, the theory explains how these processes, repeated generation after generation, account for observed patterns of cultural variation. The heart of this book is an account of how the population-level consequences of imitation and teaching work.

Taking a population approach does not imply that cultural evolution is closely analogous to genetic evolution. For example, population thinking that does not require cultural information takes the form of *memes*, discrete, faithfully replicating, genelike bits of information. A range of models are consistent with the facts of cultural variation as they are presently understood, including models in which cultural information is not discrete and is never replicated. The same goes for the processes that give rise to cultural change. Natural selection—like processes are sometimes important, but processes that have no analog in genetic evolution also play important roles. Culture is interesting and important because its evolutionary behavior is distinctly different from that of genes. For example, we will argue that the human cultural system arose as an adaptation, because it can evolve fancy adaptations to changing environments rather more swiftly than is possible by genes alone. Culture would never have evolved unless it could do things that genes can't!

Population Thinking Makes it Easy to Link Cultural and Genetic Evolution

Many social scientists have treated culture as a "superorganic" phenomenon. As one of the founders of modern anthropology, A. L. Kroeber, put it,

[P]articular manifestations of culture find their primary significance in other cultural manifestations, and can be most fully understood in terms of these manifestations; whereas they cannot be specifically explained from the generic organic endowment of the human personality even though cultural phenomena must always conform to the frame of this endowment.[4]

Social scientists in Kroeber's tradition have long dismissed the need to incorporate biology in any serious way into their study of human behavior. Humans cannot fly by flapping their arms or breathe underwater, but outside of such obvious constraints, biology has little to do with culture. On this view, biology is important, of course, because we need bodies and brains to have culture. But biology just furnishes the blank slate on which culture and personal experience write.[5]

Superorganicism is wrong because it ignores the rich interconnections between culture and other aspects of our behavior and anatomy. Culture is as much a part of human biology as walking upright. Culture causes people to do many weird and wonderful things. Nonetheless, the equipment in human brains, the hormone-producing glands, and the nature of our bodies plays fundamental role in how we learn and why we prefer some ideas to others. Culture is taught by motivated human teachers, acquired by motivated learners, and stored and manipulated in human brains. Culture is an evolving product of populations of human brains, brains that have been shaped by natural selection to learn and manage culture. Culture-making brains are the product of more than two million years of more or less gradual increases in brain size and cultural complexity. During this period, culture must have increased the reproductive success of our ancestors: otherwise, the features of our brain that make culture possible would not have evolved. The operational products of this evolution are innate predispositions and organic constraints that influence the ideas that we find attractive, the skills that we can learn, the emotions that we can experience, and the very way we see the world. To take an exceedingly simple example, why are the doorways of houses in many cultures usually a little above head high? Because the human skull, for obvious adaptive reasons, is rather well endowed with pain sensors. Those who emphasize the role that organic evolution plays in explaining human behavior are surely correct to emphasize that a plethora of such innate adaptations strongly affect how culture evolves, although we still know little about the details. Why did Southerners need a *culture* of honor? Perhaps because on average, human males are *neither* innately sufficiently sensitive to insults *nor* sufficiently ready to respond violently to them in an environment where self-help violence is the chief means of protecting one's livelihood.

Thinking about culture as something that is acquired, stored, and transmitted by a population of *individuals* enables us to explore interactions between culture and other aspects of human biology. Individual psychologies determine which ideas are likely to be easy to learn and remember and which kinds of people are likely to be imitated. Of course, individuals do not behave in isolation. Individual psychologies may interact in interesting and complex ways, and we have to be careful to make sure that such structure finds its way into our theories. Individuals are also the main locus of generic variation within the human species; to a first approximation, selection has acted over time to increase the fitness of individuals. A population-based theory of cultural change tells us how the details of individual psychology affect what kinds of skills, beliefs, and values that individuals acquire. In concept, modeling the evolution of the innate psychological machinery that gives rise to social learning is easy—you just allow individual psychology to be genetically variable. Individuals with different psychologies will acquire different beliefs and values that will lead to different fitness outcomes. Of course, many complications can arise, so making such theory can be very hard work indeed. This is, however, straightforward scientific labor—when you use population thinking to conceptualize culture, intriguing questions appear where paradoxes and confusion once reigned.

Culture Changes the Nature of Human Evolution in Fundamental Ways

Although we do not doubt that culture is deeply intertwined with other aspects of human biology, we also believe that the evolution of culture has led to fundamental changes in the

way that our species responds to natural selection. Over the last forty years or so, behavioral evolutionists have developed a rich theory predicting how natural selection will shape social behavior under various conditions. This theory explains a great deal about different aspects of behavior—mating and parenting, signaling, and cooperation—and has been fairly successful in explaining the differences between species throughout the animal kingdom. In the 1970s a group of scientists, then called human sociobiologists, created an intense controversy by applying the same body of theory to humans.[6] Two contemporary research traditions have grown out of this work: human behavioral ecology and evolutionary psychology. Human behavioral ecologists typically use evolutionary theory to understand contemporary human behavior. Evolutionary psychologists use it to generate hypotheses about the evolved structure of human psychology. While both traditions have been quite successful, their application of evolutionary theory to humans is still the cause of much debate.

Some of the opposition to evolutionary approaches to human behavior comes from thinking about these issues in terms of nature versus nurture. Biology is about nature; culture is about nurture. Some things, like whether you have sickle-cell anemia, are determined by genes—nature. Other things, like whether you speak English or Chinese, are determined by the environment—nurture. Evolutionary biology, many opponents of evolutionary explanations believe, can explain genetically determined behaviors, but not behaviors that are learned or are the result of contact with the environment. Since most human behavior is learned, they conclude evolutionary theory has little to contribute toward shaping or understanding it.

Although this way of thinking is common, it is deeply mistaken. To ask whether behavior is determined by genes or environment does not make sense. *Every* bit of the behavior (or physiology or morphology, for that matter) or every single organism living on the face of the earth results from the interaction of genetic information stored in the developing organism and the properties of its environment. To think of genes like blueprints that specify the adult properties of the organisms—one gene says you are tall, the other short—is wrong. A much better analogy is that genes are like a recipe, but one in which the ingredients, cooking temperature, and so on are set by the environment. Different traits *do* vary in how sensitive they are to environmental differences. Some traits aren't much affected by the normal range of environment—humans develop five fingers on each hand in almost all environments[7]—while others are highly sensitive—genetically similar people may end up with very different body sizes depending on nutrition and health during their childhood. Asking whether observed *differences* are due to genetic differences, differences in the environment, or some combination of these factors is sensible. However, the answer you get will tell you nothing about whether the traits in question are adaptations shaped by natural selection.

The reason is that natural selection shapes the way that developmental processes respond to environmental variation. Environment plays only a *proximate* role. Differences in the environment may cause genetically identical individuals to behave differently, and in this sense environmental differences are immediate causes of behavior. However, if we want to know why the organism develops one way in one environment and a different way in a different environment, we have to find out how natural selection has shaped the developmental process of the organism so that it responds to the environment as it does. Or, as biologists put it, the *ultimate* determinant of behavior is natural selection on genes. Learning and other developmental processes that cause individuals to respond differently to different environments implement structures built into the genes. In the natural

world, proximate causes are typically physiological. Birds migrate toward the equator when days shorten because their brain converts changes in day length to hormonal signals that activate migratory behavior. Ultimate causes are evolutionary. Migration is an evolved strategy to exploit the favorable season at higher latitude while passing the harsh winter in less demanding habitats. Selection has shaped the reaction of the brain to day length and all the downstream physiological and behavioral machinery in order to motivate geese to fly from the Yukon River delta to central California before Arctic winter weather arrives.

While evolutionary social scientists reject the naïve idea that genes and environment can be independent causes, many accept that culture can be lumped with other environmental influences. They think that the psychological mechanisms that govern the acquisition of culture are just another form of behavioral plasticity whose structure can be understood in terms of natural selection acting on genes.[8] As a result, many in the evolutionary social science community rejected the idea that culture makes any *fundamental* difference in the way that evolutionary thinking should be applied to humans. Because the psychological machinery that molds human culture was shaped by natural selection, so, at least in ancestral environments, the machinery *must have* led to fitness-enhancing behavior. If it goes wrong in modern environments, culture is not the culprit but the fact that our evolved, formerly adaptive psychology "misfires" these days. While the sort of adaptationist thinking inherent is this approach has many famous critics, we are not among their number.

Instead, our concern is that lumping culture with other environmental influences leads people to ignore the novel evolutionary processes that are created by culture. Selection shapes individual learning mechanisms so that interaction with the environment produces adaptive behavior. For example, many plants contain toxic substances. Selection makes these chemicals taste bitter to herbivores so that they learn not to consume the toxic plants species. Culture adds something quite new and different to this scenario. Like other animals, humans normally use bitter taste as a signal that a plant is inedible. However, some bitter plant compounds (like salicylic acid in willow bark) have medicinal values, so we also learn from others that we can override the aversive bitter taste of certain plants when we have the need to cure an ailment. The genes making the plant taste bitter don't change at all, but the behavior of a whole population can change anyway as the belief in the bitter plant's medicinal value spread. We take our medicine in spite of its bitter taste, not because our sensory physiology has evolved to make it less bitter, but because the idea that it has therapeutic value has spread through the population. In the distant past, some inquisitive and observant healer discovered the curative properties of a bitter plant. Then a number of processes that we describe in this book might cause this belief to increase in frequency, despite its horrible taste. You can't understand this process by asking how individuals interact with their environment. Instead, you have to understand how a population of individuals interact with their environments *and* each other over time.

Thus, culture is neither nature nor nurture, but some of both. It combines inheritance and learning in a way that cannot be parsed into genes or environment. This fact has two important consequences for human evolution, consequences to which we now turn.

Culture is a Necessary Part of the Design Problem for Human Psychology

One of the key steps in an adaptationist analysis of human behavior is to decide on the design problem that natural selection had to solve. Most students of human evolution begin by asking, how should evolution have shaped the psychology of a group-living, foraging homicide? From

there, they ask how the evolved psychology will shape human culture. The implicit evolutionary scenario seems to be that Pleistocene hominids were just extra-smart chimpanzees, clever social animals in which learning from each other played a negligible role until the evolution of our brain was complete, at which point the souped-up chimpanzee was able to take up culture. First we got human nature by genetic evolution; *then* culture arose as an evolutionary byproduct.

This way of thinking neglects the inevitable feedback between the nature of human psychology and the kind of social information that this psychology should be designed to process. For us to take bitter medicine, our psychology must have evolved both to learn from others and to let this culturally acquired information override aversive stimuli. Culture is adaptive because the behavior of other individuals is a rich source of information about which behaviors are adaptive and which are not. We all know that plagiarism is often easier than the hard work of writing something by ourselves; imitating the behavior of others can be adaptive for the same reason. The trick is that once culture becomes important, the nature of the behavior that is available to imitate is itself strongly affected by the psychology that shapes how we learn from others. To take an extreme example, if everyone relied completely on imitation, behavior would become decoupled from the environment. With any environmental change, imitation would no longer be adaptive. To understand the evolution of the psychology that underlies culture, we must take this population-level feedback into account. We want to know how evolving psychology shapes the ideas and behaviors that can be acquired from others, and how natural selection shapes how we think and learn in an environment featuring direct information from personal experience *and* the potential to use the behavior of others at a lower cost but perhaps greater risk of error.

This kind of reasoning leads to conclusions quite different from other evolutionary theories of human behavior. Under the right conditions, selection can favor a psychology that causes most people most of the time to adopt behaviors "just" because the people around them are using those behaviors. The last 800,000 years or so have seen especially large, rapid fluctuations in world climate; the world average temperature sometimes changed more than 10 degrees Celsius in a century, leading to massive shifts in ecosystem structure. A group of hominids living in a habitat something like contemporary Madrid could find themselves in a habitat like Scandinavia one hundred years later. You might think that such rapid and extreme environmental changes would put a premium on individual learning over imitation. Odd as it may seem, in many kinds of variable environments, the best strategy is to rely mostly on imitation, not your own individual learning. Some individuals may discover ways to cope with the new situation, and if the not-so-smart and not-so-lucky can imitate them, then the lucky or clever of the next generation can add other tricks. In this way the ability to imitate can generate the cumulative cultural evolution of new adaptations at blinding speed compared with organic evolution. A population of purely individual learners would be stuck with what little they can learn by themselves; they can't bootstrap a whole new adaptation based on cumulatively improving cultural traditions. This design for human behavior depends on people adopting beliefs and technologies *largely* because other people in their group share those beliefs or use these technologies. When lots of imitation is mixed with a little bit of individual learning, *populations* can adapt in ways that outreach the abilities of any individual genius.

Thinking about the population properties of culture helps us understand the psychology of social learning. For example, we will see that selection can favor a psychology that causes people to conform to the majority behavior even though this mechanism sometimes prevents populations from adapting to a change in the environment. Evolution also favors a psychology that makes people more prone to imitate prestigious individuals and individuals who are like themselves even though this habit can easily result in maladaptive fads. These psychological mechanisms in turn give rise to important patterns of behavior, like the symbolic marking of social groups that would not evolve unless their culture had certain population level consequences.

Culture is an Ultimate Cause of Human Behavior

If the only processes shaping culture arose from our innate evolved psychology, then culture would be a strictly proximate cause of human behavior. Understanding how natural selection gave rise to our psychology would be more complicated than for other forms of behavioral plasticity, but in the end we could, at least in principle, reduce human culture to the actions of evolution by natural selection to increase genetic fitness.

However, not all of the processes shaping culture *do* arise from our innate psychology—culture itself is subject to natural selection. Much as a child resembles her parents, people resemble those from whom they have acquired ideas, values, and skills. Culturally acquired ideas, values, and skills affect what happens to people during their lives—whether they are successful, how many children they have, and how long they live. These events in turn affect whether their behavior will be culturally transmitted to the next generation. If successful people are more likely to be imitated, then those traits that lead to becoming successful will be favored. Even more obviously, if living people are more likely to be imitated than the dead, then ideas, values, and skills that promote survival will tend to spread. Consequently, a culture of honor arises, at least in part, because in lawless societies, men who are not aggressive in protecting their herds and their families tend to fall victim to tough, ruthless predators. If these advantages to a culture of honor have disappeared in the modern South, the higher death rate of those who cling to the custom will eventually extinguish it.

Such selective processes can often favor quite different behaviors from those favored by selection on genes. For example, beliefs and values that lead to prestige and economic success in modern societies may also reduce fertility. Such beliefs spread because the prestigious are more likely to be imitated, even though this lowers genetic fitness. Opening our minds to ideas in the environment allows rapid adaptation, but it also leads to the evolution of pathological cultural maladaptations. Our psychology has a delicately balanced set of mechanisms designed to exclude harmful ideas in the environment yet not attack the beneficial ones.

Natural selection acting on culture is an ultimate cause of human behavior, just like natural selection acting on genes. Consider the following example. Much cultural variation exists at the group level. Different human groups have different norms and values, and the cultural transmission of these traits can cause such differences to persist for long periods of time. Now, the norms and values that predominate in a group plausibly affect the probability that the group is successful, whether it survives, and whether it expands. For the purposes of illustration, suppose that groups having norms that promote group solidarity are more likely to survive than groups lacking this sentiment. This creates a selective process that leads to the spread of solidarity. Of course, this process may be opposed by an evolved innate psychology that biases what we learn from others, making us more prone to imitate and invent selfish or nepotistic beliefs rather than ones favoring group solidarity, like patriotism. The long-run evolutionary outcome would then depend on the balance of the processes favoring and disfavoring patriotism. Again for the sake of illustration, let us suppose that net effect of these opposing processes causes patriotic beliefs to predominate. In this case, the population behaves patriotically *because* such behavior promotes group survival, in exactly the same way that the sickle-cell gene is common in malarial areas *because* it promotes individual survival. Human culture participates in ultimate causation.

Cultural scientists, we believe, should not fear a reunion with biology. Culture is a brawny phenomenon and is in no real danger of being "reduced" to genes. Of course genetic elements of our evolved psychology shape culture—how could it be otherwise? But at the same time, natural selection acting on cultural variation shaped the environments in which our psychology evolved (and is evolving). The coevolutionary dynamic makes genes as susceptible to cultural influence as vice versa. We argue that the phenomenon of group selection on cultural variation described above could have produced institutions encouraging more cooperation with distantly related people than would be favored by our original evolved psychology. These cooperators would have discriminated against individuals who carried genes that made them too belligerent to conform to the new cooperative norms. Then the cultural rules could expand cooperation a bit further, generating selection for still more-docile genes. Eventually, innate elements of human social psychology became tolerably well adapted to promote living in tribes, not just families.

Culture Makes us Odd

Thinking about cultural evolution at the population level leads to a picture of a powerful adaptive system that is necessarily accompanied by some exotic side effects. Some of our evolutionist friends take a dim view of this motion, seeing it as giving aid and comfort to those who would deny the relevance of evolution to human affairs. We prefer to think that population-based theories of cultural evolution strengthen the Darwinian's grasp on the human species by providing a picture of the engine that powered the furious pace of human evolution over the last few hundred thousand years. Our ape cousins still live in the same tropical forests in the same small social groups, and eat the same fruits, nuts, and bits of meal as our common ancestors did. By the late Pleistocene (say, 20,000 years ago), human foragers already occupied a much wider geographical and ecological range than any other species, using a remarkable range of subsistence systems and social arrangements. Over the last ten millennia we have exploded to become the earth's dominant organism by dint of deploying ever more-sophisticated technology and ever more-sophisticated social systems. The human species is a spectacular evolutionary anomaly, so we ought to expect that the evolutionary system behind it is pretty anomalous as well. Our quest is for the evolutionary motors that drove our divergence from our ancestors, and we believe that the best place to hunt is among the anomalies of cultural evolution. This does not mean that gene-based evolutionary reasoning is worthless. To the contrary, human sociobiologists and their successors have explained a lot about human behavior even though most work ignores the novelties introduced by cultural adaptation. However, there is still much to explain, and we think that the population properties of culture are an essential ingredient of a satisfactory theory of human behavior.

The Path Not Taken

In the preface to the second edition of the *Descent of Man* in 1874, Darwin noted that he

[took the] opportunity of remarking that my critics frequently assume that I attribute all changes of corporeal structure and mental power exclusively to the natural selection of such variations as are often called spontaneous; whereas, even in the first edition of the *Origin of Species* I distinctly stated that great

weight must be attributed to the inherited effects of use and disuse, with respect both to the body and mind.[9]

From the biologists' point of view, Darwin's belief in the inheritance of acquired variation was his greatest error. Darwin thought "inherited habits," by which he meant something very close to human culture, were important in a wide variety of species. In a sense he was correct—simple forms of social learning are widespread in the animal kingdom.[10] However, Darwin imagined that even honeybees had humanlike imitative capacities, whereas the best modern evidence, as we shall see, suggests that all other animals, including our closest ape relatives, have rudimentary capacities for culture compared with ourselves.

Darwin's intuitions about "inherited habits" no doubt came from his observation that humans had such things, combined with his desire to minimize the gap between humans and other animals. He is sometimes said to have biologized human culture, but he is more accurately accused of culturizing biology.[11] Darwin had a sophisticated, if erroneous, picture of the distribution of the inherited effects of use and disuse across traits. He thought that behavior was more susceptible to the inheritance of acquired variation and that anatomy was much more conservative in this regard, so he could account for the fact that human behavior was much more variable from place to place than were human bodies. As "On the Races of Man," chapter 7 of the *Descent*, shows, Darwin was not seduced into thinking that the huge behavioral differences he and other pioneering anthropologists observed among humans could be accounted for by differences in conservative—we would say today genetic—characters. Rather, he attributed them to the more labile characters that we would today label cultural.

We thus have an interesting historical paradox: Darwin's theory was a better starting point for humans than any other species, and required a major pruning to adjust to the rise of genetics. Nevertheless, the *Descent* had no lasting influence on the social sciences that emerged at the turn of the twentieth century.[12] Darwin was pigeonholed as a biologist, and sociology, economics and history all eventually wrote biology out of their disciplines. Anthropology relegated his theory to a subdiscipline, biological anthropology, behind the superorganic firewall. Since the midtwentieth century, many social scientists have treated Darwinian initiatives as politically tainted threats. If anything, the gulf between the social and natural sciences continues to widen as some anthropologists, sociologists, and historians adopt methods and philosophical commitments that seem to natural scientists to abandon the basic norms of science entirely.

Notes

1 Nisbett and Cohen 1996.
2 Nisbett and Cohen's analysis is restricted to European Southerners.
3 Mayr 1982, 45–47.
4 Kroeber 1948, 62.
5 This idea goes back to the pioneers of sociology and anthropology at the turn of the twentieth century. Ingold 1986, 223, discusses three different senses of "superorganic" used by social scientists over the years, about which he summarizes, "the superorganic has become a banner of convenience under which have paraded anthropological and sociological philosophies of the most diverse kinds."
6 Alexander 1974, 1979; Wilson 1975; Symons 1979; Chagnon and Irons 1979; and Barash 1977. See Segerstrale 2000 for a history of the controversy.
7 Roughly 0.05% of live births in the United States show some form of hand or arm reduction, and some fraction of these cases may be due to exposure to environmental factors (Centers for Disease Control 1993). About 0.2% of live births have more than five digits on either the hands or feet. Many cases of polydactyly seem to be caused by rare mutant alleles.

8 Richard Alexander 1979, 75–81, is quite clear on this point. Evolutionary thinkers disagree about the specificity of these psychological mechanisms. Human behavioral ecologists tend to hold that the psychological mechanisms are what cause humans to act, to a decent first approximation, as general-purpose genetic fitness maximizers. Culture, as defined here, has a strictly secondary role, and for most practical purposes it can be neglected (Smith, Borgerhoff Mulder, and Hill 2001). Many evolutionary psychologists are nativists who believe that the mind has a large collection of rather narrowly specialized, gene-based, content-rich algorithms that can solve a series of narrow problems that had confronted Pleistocene foragers. Contemporary environments have changed so radically that it is vain to hope that behavior will be fitness maximizing today. Evolution is too slow to have readapted the human mind significantly in the last few thousand years (Tooby and Cosmides 1992).
9 Darwin 1874.
10 Galef 1996.
11 Alland 1985; Richerson 1988.
12 Hodgson 2004; Richards 1987; Richerson and Boyd 2001a.

References

Alexander, R. D. (1974). The evolution of social behavior. *Annual Review of Ecology and Systematics*, 5: 325–383.
Alexander, R. D. (1979). *Darwinism and Human Affairs*. Seattle, WA: University of Washington Press.
Barash, D. (1977) *Sociobiology and Behavior*. New York: Elsevier.
Darwin, C. (1874). *The Descent of Man and Selection in Relation to Sex*, 2nd edn, 2 vols. New York: American Home Library.
Ingold, T. (1986). *Evolution and Social Life*. Cambridge: Cambridge University Press.
Kroeber, A. L. (1948). *Anthropology: Race, language, culture, psychology, pre-history*. New edn. New York: Harcourt, Brace & World.
Mayr, E. (1982). *The Growth of Biological Thought: Diversity, evolution, and inheritance*. Cambridge MA: Harvard University Press.

Nisbett, R.E., & Cohen, D. (1996). *Culture of Honor: The psychology of violence in the South*. Boulder, CO: Westview Press.

Segerstråle, U. (2000). *Defenders of the Truth: The battle for science in the sociobiology debate and beyond*. New York: Oxford University Press.

Smith, E. A., Borgerhoff Mulder, M., & Hill, K. (2001). Controversies in the evolutionary social sciences: A guide for the perplexed. *Trends in Ecology & Evolution*, 16, 128–135.

Symons, D. (1979). *The Evolution of Human Sexuality*. New York: Oxford University Press.

Tooby, J., & Cosmides, L. (1992). The psychological foundations of culture. In J. Barkow, L. Cosmides, and J. Tooby (Eds.), *The Adapted Mind: Evolutionary psychology and the generation of culture* (pp. 1–159). New York: Oxford University Press.

Wilson, E. O. (1975). *Sociobiology: The new synthesis*. Cambridge, MA: Harvard University Press.

Chapter 19

Kim Sterelny

THE INFORMATIONAL COMMONWEALTH

The Rise of the Hominins

The hominin lineage diverged from that of the chimps between six and seven million years ago. The fossil records left by the two lineages are quite different. For a large, terrestrial mammal, the hominin fossil record is very rich: it is possible to publish coffee-table books of hominin fossils (Tattersall, 2008). In contrast, there are almost no chimp fossils (McBrearty & Jablonski, 2005). In part, that difference reflects differences in luck and in investigative effort. But in part, it reflects a real difference in the evolutionary, ecological, and demographic history of the two lineages. The more numerous; the more widely dispersed in space, the more varied the habitats, the more likely it is that the occasional fossil will form and survive. Hominins began as a minor player in a very rich East African fauna, but even the early hominins, the Australopithecines, speciated into a number of forms with different ecological preferences, and the later species dispersed across much of the old world. As far as we can tell, the chimp lineage has retained, to a fair approximation, its ancestral distribution and its habitat preferences.

The hominin geographic and ecological expansion was coupled to, and coevolved with, a behavioral and social revolution. One obvious example is the massive expansion of tool use and technical capacity in our lineage. Beginning about 2.5 million years ago, we became obligate

technovores, with the pace of innovation picking up over the last 200,000 years. Technical skill expanded from a high base. While we are clearly more dependent on technology and on skilled physical processing than the great apes,[1] the great apes are also skilled technicians. Richard Byrne (in particular) has emphasized the fact that great apes are "extractive foragers." They exploit their environment with intelligence and skill. Common chimps (and orang-utans) use a range of simple tools, but even when they are not using tools, great apes often depend on complex, quite precise procedures to harvest resources: Byrne's stock example is that of gorillas stripping and folding nettles, thus making them palatable (Byrne, 1995, 2004). So in this respect, hominin evolution built on an already impressive great ape baseline.

In other respects, our divergence from great ape norms is still more extreme; in particular, in the cooperative aspects of our social lives. There is some cooperation between chimps in the struggle for resources (males sometimes form coalitions); but not much (Wrangham, 1999). Indeed, one apparent form of cooperation, collectively hunting monkeys, may turn out not to be a form of cooperation after all (Tomasello, 2008). In contrast, human cooperation is extensive and probably ancient. There is a clear archaeological signal that humans have hunted large game for 400,000 years; almost certainly, very much longer (Stiner, 2002; Jones, 2007; Foley &

Gamble, 2009). Humans became hunters long before the invention of high-velocity projectile weapons—there were, for example, no bows until perhaps 30,000 years ago (Marlowe, 2005), so success with reasonable safety depended on efficient cooperation and coordination. Again in contrast to the chimps, humans cooperated in sharing information, not just in securing resources and guarding against danger. Chimps communicate to direct other chimps, rather than to share information. Chimps gesture, but they do not point indicatively, and they find it difficult to learn to exploit human indicative pointing (Tomasello, 2008, 2009; Warneken, forthcoming). Chimps learn socially, as a side effect of others using information in their daily life. There are almost no reports of intentional teaching amongst the great apes. Humans do share information, and while there are profound uncertainties in dating the origins of language, teaching, and other forms of informational cooperation, there is good reason to think that some forms of informational cooperation are ancient. The use of fire, and the exploitation of sophisticated, and apparently highly conserved, stone-working techniques date to 800,000 years ago, perhaps still deeper in time (Stout, 2011). Hunting large game without undue risk depends on good information about the target and the environment, not just coordination in the encounter itself. So ancient humans combined sophisticated technique with ecological expertise, and we can reasonably conjecture that this form of life depended on the more skilled actively informing the less skilled; not just on their passive tolerance of onlookers. A life dependent on cooperation depends as well on the evolution of new cognitive capacities: on communication and social navigation. Agents need to coordinate, communicate, anticipate others' actions and reactions, to minimize and manage conflict, to negotiate the division of jointly produced resources.

Kristin Hawkes, Sarah Hrdy and others have emphasized the fact that humans also cooperated reproductively (O'Connell et al. 1999; Hawkes & Bird, 2002; Hawkes, 2003; Hrdy, 2005, 2009). Mothers rely on others: female kin, fathers, siblings, elder children, friends. Perhaps by the evolution of *Homo erectus*, perhaps 1.7 million years ago, women would have needed aid at birth, and their babies and infants were probably as helpless as young *sapiens*, though probably not for as long. So they probably needed aid feeding, carrying, or creching these infants. In short, as Sarah Hrdy emphasizes, our sex lives and family organization became increasingly peculiar. There is much variation in the historical record, but (as a rule) human males recognize their own paternity and invest resources in their offspring, often in the context of a semi-stable, quasi-monogamous relationship with the mother. But they do so (and did so) in a fission–fusion social world, with social groups fragmenting into small foraging parties before fusing again at night (Foley & Gamble, 2009). Male investment does not combine easily with a fission–fusion social organization, for it is difficult for males to be confident of paternity. Thus male chimps and bonobos (who also live in fission–fusion social environments) do not invest in their offspring.

In summary, then, over the last 3–4 million years, the hominin lineage has dispersed broadly over space and habitat type; speciated quite richly; expanded demographically. Hominin bodies changed as well: hands, limbs, and bodies adapted to new demands; teeth, jaws, gut and brain adapted to a changed diet. Almost certainly, this spread across ecological and geographic space was in part an effect of the behavioral and cognitive revolution in the species, as humans became more socially skilled, as they acquired new adaptations for communication; as they acquired a much expanded set of technical and ecological skills. Many accounts of human evolution depend on the idea that there was a critical adaptive breakthrough in our lineage, and that the ecological and geographic spread of the hominins, and their unique cognitive and behavioral profile, derive from that key innovation. Language, reproductive cooperation, and cooking have all been mooted as the key innovation in question (Deacon, 1997; Hrdy, 2009; Wrangham, 2009). I am unpersuaded by any of these ideas: human uniqueness is not the result of a big breakthrough, but of feedback. For the hominin expansion across the globe, and the environmental and social variability that accompanied it, also selected for increased capacities to learn, communicate and coordinate. Expansion is cause as well as effect. Human environments became less stereotyped and more complex, in part as a result of humans' own activities. Humans interact with their physical, biological, social and technical environment; we molded our world as well as responding to it. These feedback loops explain the rapidity of the hominin divergence from the chimp lineages.

Thus I am skeptical about all "key innovation" pictures of the rise of the hominins. I shall outline a conceptual model—the apprentice learning model—of the hominin career that differs from more standard ones in three ways. First: there is no key innovation. In my view, the Australopithecines began to diverge from their great ape relatives in a number of respects, and that divergence intensified and accelerated through positive feedback. The characteristic rapid, extensive hominin phenotypic divergence is the result of positive feedback between many factors, rather than being the consequence of a single, revolutionary innovation. One of those factors, though, is enhanced social learning, and I offer a model of that expansion, together with its causes and consequences. Second: the model situates agents in their immediate environment. For it focuses not just on intrinsic features of hominin cognition (still less on genetically canalized features), but on their local social and physical environment. In company with Andy Clark, Dan Dennett, and their allies, I argue that hominin cognitive and behavioral capacities depend critically on environmental support (Dennett, 2000; Clark, 2008; Chemero, 2009;

Menary, 2010; Sterelny, 2010). The hominin career depends on assembling and stabilizing environments (especially developmental environments) that support technical and social capacities, not just on the evolution of genes that help build the right wetware. Third, the picture is dynamic. Much of standard evolutionary psychology has aimed at identifying the end product of human cognitive evolution; indeed, they have been especially interested in identifying specific cognitive adaptations, and mapping their operations: language, metareprsentation, theory of mind, naive physics, moral and religious cognition (Povinelli et al., 2000; Hauser, 2006; Johnson & Bering, 2006; Mercier & Sperber, 2011). They have been less interested in developing "lineage explanations" (Calcott, 2008a): explanations of the incremental construction of these adaptations. In contrast, I aim to outline a lineage explanation of the incremental evolution of the distinctive, hominin forms of social learning.

The Informational Commonwealth

While I doubt that there is a single key innovation that explains human uniqueness, there is no doubt that the flow of information (and misinformation) across social networks and between generations is one of the most distinctive features of human life. Most obviously, we use language, a unique communication system that allows agents to extensively share information about the elsewhere and the elsewhen. Almost as unusually, we teach others at some cost in time and trouble. We teach skills, norms, and factual information, and this is a feature not just of advanced western societies, but of small-scale, traditional societies as well (Csibra & Gergely, 2011; Hewlett et al., 2011).[2] Indeed, it is likely that at least for the last 250,000 years, and perhaps for the last 800,000 years, core hominin technical competences were so demanding that their reliable transmission relied on teaching (Stout, 2002; Ambrose, 2010). Teaching is not unique to our lineage, but it is distinctive: it evolves only under special conditions (Thornton & Raihani, 2008), and there is very little evidence of teaching in other primates.

We exploit our capacity to communicate with remarkably avidity. We have empathetic, prosocial emotions, and are often willing to share, but for the most part, sharing needs to be taught and to be reinforced by norms against selfishness. Forager societies are typically very co-operative and egalitarian, but this does not *just happen*. Thus Hewlett et al. (2011: 1175) write that

> !Kung value sharing very highly, and from the time their infants are six months of age mothers and other adults frequently say "Na" meaning "Give" when a bit of food is in the infant's hand and on the way to its mouth. The criterion is that they should inhibit the very strong impulse to eat and reliably turn the morsel over to the adult making the demand.

Information-sharing does not need to be explicitly taught in this way. We share information far more readily, and with less temptation to retain the data for ourselves alone, than we do any other resource. Very few of us suffer personal disaster, or even serious inconvenience, because we succumb to an irresistible temptation to be excessively generous in giving away material possessions. Many of us suffer from needless social friction, because we cannot resist the temptation to donate information, in the form of gossip and unwanted advice. This is a remarkable feature of our motivational world. For information is a precious resource. Discovery requires time and effort; sometimes risk, as well. It is true that an agent does not lose that investment and information by sharing it with the less well informed. But he (or she) does lose the leverage—the relative advantage—that an informational edge, sometimes dearly bought, provides. Yet most of us positively relish passing on gossip and advice, even when it is true. Of

course, people do keep secrets, reserving for themselves and their allies strategically important information, technology, skill. There are legal institutions designed to defend "intellectual property".

Even so, we are surely far closer to a communism of information than of goods. How did this informational commons, partial though it is, evolve in our lineage, and how has it shaped our minds? A satisfactory evolutionary account must satisfy four conditions. First, and obviously, it must be incremental. As with other complex adaptations, it must be built by small, successive improvements (Dawkins, 1996). Second, it should avoid tacit circularity. Human cognition and social life has many features that have evolved as a consequence of the increasing profile of cooperation, coordination and communication in our lineage. We cannot assume, for example, that agents with sophisticated theory of mind capacities, or with a prosocial emotional profile, are present at early stages of this trajectory. This is particularly important in explaining the stability of co-operation given the potential risks of defection and deception. Early hominins probably did not come equipped with sophisticated capacities to detect deception,[3] or with a prosocial willingness to punish it at net cost to themselves. In short, we must estimate the cognitive and social baseline conservatively.[4] Third, estimates of the selective advantage offered by early forms of information flow must be robust over variation in ecology and demography. Early hominin environments were probably quite variable, as a consequence of external disturbance, mobility, and hominins' effects on their own circumstances (Potts, 1996; Klein & Edgar, 2002). Finally, the selective advantage of information flow should accrue to individuals. Group selection has probably been an important factor in human evolution, and perhaps especially in the evolution of cooperation (Bowles & Gintis, 2011). But the conditions which make group selection powerful prevail partially as a result of the evolution of information sharing, for information sharing and enhanced cultural learning tend to decrease variation within a group, and increase it between groups. So at least in the early stages of the elaboration of information sharing, the benefits must accrue to the individuals sharing information, not (or not just) to the groups to which they belong.

In Sterelny (2011a), I present a conceptual model satisfying these conditions: a model I outline in the next section. That model relies on three background ideas: *environmental scaffolding, genetic accommodation,* and *hybrid learning.* First, scaffolding. Eva Jablonka has pointed out that a fortunate innovation can be stabilized by the changes in behavior and environment that that very innovation brings about (Avital & Jablonka, 2000; Jablonka & Lamb, 2005). She shows that stable, cross-generational behavioral traditions need not depend on language, imitation, or other sophisticated adaptations for social learning. Trial and error can suffice, if (i) a fortunate innovation in one generation results in a significant and persistent change in the innovating agent's way of life, and (ii) juveniles routinely accompany their parents. For a side effect of the adult change in lifeway is a change in the learning environment of the young. For example, the world a young chimp explores by trial and error depends on the foraging choices of her mother. So if a mother chimp learns to use stones to crack open nuts, and if nuts are an important and re-appearing resource, her infant will explore a local environment rich in nuts, nut fragments, discarded hammers and the like. If the exposure to the new environment is repeated and prolonged, the infant will have many opportunities to stumble on the nature of nuts and the use of hammers.

The example is not fanciful: Tennie et al. (2009) note that chimp termite fishing exposes young chimps to termites, mounds and the paraphernalia of termite fishing, and that this eases their learning journey. A very lucky break at the innovating generation can become a routine outcome for the next. Even rudimentary

adaptations for social learning would make relearning such a skill even more likely: if, for example, infants were interested in their mothers' activities, and were more likely to play with objects she touches, the chances of a happy accident go up. Chimp social learning capacities are still not well mapped (Whiten et al., 2009), but they are more than rudimentary (and the same is likely to be true of the last common human/chimp ancestor). The point, however, is the transformation of the fluke into the routine does not *depend* on adaptations for social learning, for the environment can scaffold trial and error learning, biasing its direction. Avital and Jablonka detail a number of examples in which behavioral traditions appear to have established just through innovations being stabilized by trial and error in the changed environment (perhaps the most convincing involves rat exploitation of pine cones).

I shall suggest that environmental scaffolding played a central role in explaining the stability of early hominin capacities. In particular, hominin technical capacities—most obviously those involved in stone working—were reliably acquired only because young hominins developed their foraging skills in an environment seeded with raw materials, stone tools, and partially made tools. Stone tools became central to the success of hominins (perhaps between 2.5 and 2 million years ago), and so the young were *repeatedly* in environments in which they were made and used. Their learning environments were inadvertently enriched with information about stone technology.

Second, genetic accommodation. Jablonka's examples of stabilizing innovations show that new capacities do not have to wait for lucky genetic changes: they can appear and establish through the exploitation of pre-exiting phenotypic plasticity, often in conjunction with environmental changes. It is most unlikely that chimps are specifically adapted for nut-cracking or termite fishing (Laland & Galef, 2009). The earliest hominin regular stone tool makers were probably not adapted to make stone tools. There were new phenotypes but not new genotypes. However, as West-Eberhard points out, if the new phenotype—the new behavioral tradition—is persistent and important, we would expect genetic accommodation (West-Eberhard, 2003). Over time, there will be selection for genes which accelerate the acquisition of the skill; genes which accentuate or enhance the skill; genes which reduce the cost of acquisition, perhaps by increasing the efficiency through which the less skilled can learn from the more skilled.[5] Change which begins as an expression of phenotypic plasticity becomes genuinely evolutionary, as genetic accommodation kicks in. Moreover, the process can iterate: once the new lifeway establishes and spreads, further innovation through learning can trigger further genetic accommodation.

Third: these traditions stabilize through hybrid learning. Much of the theoretical and experimental work on social learning is on pure social learning: for example, on how accurately a mimic-model imitation link preserves information, or on the environmental conditions which select in favor of an agent copying another rather than finding out something for himself. But stabilized skill traditions depend on hybrid learning. Trial and error is critical: chimps learn to exploit termites and nuts, and (I conjecture) hominins learned to make simple tools by doing, not by looking. They learn by interaction with the learning target. But they do not learn on their own, by themselves. They learn because others already know. Their learning environment is enriched because others in their local group (in particular, their mothers) are knowledgeable. The apprentice learning model identifies many roots through which social inputs support and enhance learning by doing.

The Apprentice Learning Model

By two million years ago, and perhaps much earlier (McPherron et al., 2010), technical competence, including the manufacture and use of tools, had became an essential feature of the hominin lifeway. The Oldowan industry, dating to perhaps 2.6 million years ago, is direct evidence of dependence on technology, for it is unlikely that we would find material traces of stone tool use if using tools were a marginal, peripheral activity of ancient hominins (Toth & Schick, 2009). But there is indirect evidence as well. In his case for ancient cooking, Richard Wrangham argues that both *habilis* and *erectus* show evidence of a revolutionary change in diet, allowing brains to expand while teeth, gut and jaws shrank (Wrangham, 2009). Erectines (somewhat later, at perhaps 1.7 million years ago) had bodies our size, and they show some signs of a change in life history from great ape to sapiens patterns: longer lives, larger bodies, longer periods of juvenile dependence (Hill & Kaplan, 1999; Mace, 2000; Kennedy, 2003). In short, changes in hominin lifeways resulted in improved access to resources and increased life expectancy. In explaining this transformation, there are continuing debates about the relative importance of (i) meat and marrow (by some changing combination of adventitious scrounging; bully-scavenging; hunting), (ii) adding value to food through early forms of cooking and food preparation, and (iii) exploiting the underground storage organs of plants (O'Connell et al., 1999).

I suspect all three of these resource-amplifying activities were important, though probably their relative importance varied across time and place. But for this argument, I can be neutral on these questions. For these are all skilled, tool-dependent forms of foraging. For hominins as distinct from great apes, tools and tool use became mandatory rather than optional. Fire and the controlled application of heat to food is itself a challenging technology. Marrow and meat were exploited using stone tools, and in their recent review of the Oldowan, Toth and Schick point out that even the most ancient stone technologies "demonstrate remarkable skill and control in flaking stone."[6] Likewise, underground storage organs are protected mechanically and chemically. To harvest them, hominins needed field skills to recognize the right plants; digging sticks to extract the organ, and then, usually, they needed to process these corms and tubers to make the starch edible. In many cases, these plant storage organs are protected from herbivores by poisons which must be leeched out or neutralized by some combination of grating or pounding followed by soaking and cooking.

If this picture of our deep history is right, over the last two million years (and perhaps longer) hominins evolved into cooperative foragers, but foragers that depended on sophisticated technology, technique, and a detailed picture of their local patch and its resources. Human life came to depend on collective, coordinated action at a time. But it also came to depend on informational cooperation across time. Our ecological expansion was the result of combining the benefits of cooperation with those of expertise (Sterelny, 2007). By 100,000 years ago, technology and technique had become very sophisticated: humans used a wide range of materials in their technology; exploited an increasing range of resources (a pattern that was to become even more marked); and had spread to much of the old world. But well before then, by the Middle Stone Age (beginning around 250,000 years ago), no hominin could assemble by individual learning all the informational resources needed for a successful life.[7]

Craft apprenticeship is a good model of skill and expertise transmission in forager societies. Apprentice learning is hybrid learning: as apprentices learn, they combine information from the social world with information from the physical–biological environment. Apprentices learn by doing. But they do so in an environment seeded with informational resources; with raw materials; partially processed materials; physical templates, tools. There is social information too. Obviously, in the modern context, there is explicit, institutionalized teaching. Explicit teaching is probably less important in traditional cultures,[8] but the less adept can observe, and ask for advice from the more skilled. They also can listen in to experts talking to one another; eavesdropping helps in acquiring local lore. Moreover, experts indirectly drive apprentice learning by structuring their trial-and-error experiences. By assigning tasks to apprentices, they decompose the overall expertise into subskills, and order their acquisition, so that each step prepares the next. This is in the interests of the expert, as it maximizes the value of the apprentices who work with them; it is in the interests of the apprentice, because it increases the efficiency of their learning. Thus the acquisition of craft skills depends on individual cognitive adaptations for social learning. But it also depends on these adaptively structured learning environments.

The same is true of the acquisition of forager expertise, and in my view, this mode of social learning has deep roots in hominin history. Forager skill sets are fine-tuned at a generation and reliably transmitted across generations through learning by doing, but learning by doing in an environment that is organized to support learning. The apprentice learning model has five virtues. First: it lends itself to an incremental account of the evolution of social learning. Second, apprentice learning is known to be a powerful mode of learning: craft apprentices master and learn to use a lot of information with high fidelity. Likewise, foragers are experts: their way of life depends on their mastery of subtle skills and much information. So the model is adequate for its explanatory target. Third, it is ethnographically plausible. Fourth, it fits the archaeological record. Fifth, it fits a coevolutionary, feedback-driven explanation of human uniqueness.

Incremental Evolution

Apprentice learning is a form of hybrid learning that can be assembled incrementally. First, as noted, rudimentary but reliable skill transmission does not presuppose the presence of adaptations for social learning. But once established, skill transmission then brings with it selection for cognitive and social changes that increase the reliability or reduce the cost of learning. The process of genetic assimilation is likely to begin. An important aspect of the apprentice learning model is that these initial changes can be very simple indeed: they can begin as motivational changes; adults becoming more tolerant of inquisitive juveniles; juveniles becoming more interested in adult activities.

Moreover, great apes certainly have some social learning capacities: they can learn by emulation; probably, they have some capacity to learn by imitation (Whiten et al., 2009).[9] These capacities, too, could initially be upgraded by changes in motivation: by directing greater attention to what others are doing; by becoming more persistent, less distracted. At some stage in this process, more radical changes evolved in our lineage; new capacities to communicate, and to anticipate the consequences of communication. Humans teach and practice, and these are sophisticated skills (Csibra & Gergely, 2006, 2011). Good teaching requires the expert to understand what the less expert does and does not know. But it also requires them to understand their own expertise: to represent their own skill. To coach batting, it is not enough to be a fine batsman. The coach needs to identify and diagnose errors in technique; to be able to decompose a skill into components which can be demonstrated separately, usually in an exaggerated and slowed down form. It is very difficult indeed to learn a complex skill just from observation of fluent performance; fluency conceals structure. Likewise, those acquiring skills often practice. This involves a motivational change: exercising a capacity without the stimulus of anticipated material reward. But often it involves other changes as well. Rehearsal too needs a skill to be decomposed into components which can be practiced separately. In turn, that

will require agents to assess their practice by comparing their performance to an inner template. Think, for example, of ghost practice: rehearsing your batting swing and foot movements in front of the mirror, but without a ball; sometimes even without a bat.

Thus the evolution of social learning involved the evolution of new capacities in communication and theory of mind. These new capacities increase the bandwidth of skill transmission through hybrid learning. Initially, the skills in question were physical skills involving the manufacture and use of artifacts. But once these new communicative capacities are in play, expert-organized and supervised learning by doing has a much wider scope. Until recently, many professional skills were learned through an apprentice system. Accountants and lawyers joined practices as juniors, initially working long hours at menial, routine activities while gradually having their skill base expanded. Obviously, language is part of this mix. But the human advance in communication involved much more than language. In particular, the evolution trajectory here involves not just the incremental evolution of human minds increasingly adapted for social learning; it involved the evolution of a social context of active, organized information sharing.

So the apprentice learning model shows how intergenerational transmission can evolve gradually: through gradual increases in fidelity, the breadth of information transmitted, and through small changes in the cognitive and emotional profiles of the agents in question. Nor does this picture make tendentious assumptions about fitness. The reliable transmission of skill can begin as a side effect of adult activity, without adult teaching, or adaptations for social learning in the young. This happens when an innovation becomes central to adult economic activity, and so as a side effect transforms the local environment that juveniles explore, positively biasing learning probabilities. In this early phase, while adults are not adapted to teach their offspring, social learning is adaptive for both. There is no conflict of interest here: juvenile fitness is increased through the reliable acquisition of an important skill at no cost to the parents. The selective environment becomes more complex in the later stages of the evolution of social skill transmission, as it becomes less strictly vertical, and as the skills become so complex that active teaching is required. Once skills are both complex and essential, there will be selection of skilled adults to teach their children (Thornton & Raihani, 2008). Often, though, information will flow obliquely to less closely related individuals in the next generation. But even in oblique flow contexts, selection will often favor information-sharing rather than information-masking.[10] The ethnographic evidence suggests that there is social reward for highly skilled experts (Henrich & Gill-White, 2001). Moreover, craft production often depends not just on highly skilled inputs but on laborious but less skilled work: grinding ochre into powder to make a glue; collecting and carrying heavy raw materials to work sites (Stout, 2002; Wadley, 2010). The inexpert can and do pay in labor for advice and instruction from the expert. So the apprentice learning model makes no strange assumptions about fitness: even in the later phases of the evolution of skill transmission, we do not have to suppose that experts are acting altruistically in sharing their expertise.

Power

I have just defended at some length the idea that the apprentice learning model shows how cross-generation social learning can evolve incrementally. Much less needs to be said about power. We know from the paleoarchaeological record that the reliable cross-generation transmission of large amounts of information is an ancient feature of sapiens social life. The ancient humans that migrated out of Africa around 70,000 years ago were experts on their local environment, and were masters of technical skills that take

years to acquire (Foley & Lahr, 2003; Ambrose, 2010; Stout, 2011). The reliable transmission of natural history information, local lore, and artisan skills did not require literacy, or the educational institutions of sedentary society. Given our evolved cognitive capacities, apprentice learning is clearly a reliable way of structuring the learning environment, ensuring high fidelity transmission of demanding skills. Until recently, almost all technical skill depended on this way of organizing learning. To the extent that skill acquisition in forager societies was similar to this mode of hybrid learning, we can explain the high-volume, high-fidelity social learning visible in the archaeological record.

Ethnographic Plausibility

Forager children typically grow up with a lot of freedom, but in environments richly seeded with educational resources. Villages often keep a large range of semi-wild pets, and this gives children the opportunity to learn the animals' calls, behaviors, tracks, and scats. They practice foraging skills, but in ways guided by adult judgment. So, for example, in many forager societies, older children contribute to the family economy, but they do so using equipment appropriate to their size, strength, skill level, and local ecology. Their parents provide fishing lines or spears, nets, baskets, and the like. They learn by doing, but in ways influenced by their parents' judgments about their capacities (Bock, 2005). In their study of Congo Basin foragers, Barry Hewlett and his colleagues note that parents provide children with effective but miniaturized tools (axes, digging sticks, baskets and the like) and encouraged and advised on their use.[11] Play, likewise, is educational and structured by adult intervention; forager children's toys are often hunting toys.

In general, then, forager children learn by doing, but in ways made safer or more efficient by adult activities. That is only a rough similarity with apprentice learning; often, though, the parallels are much closer. In some cultures, hunting skill is passed on through explicit apprenticeships. More generally, the ethnographic literature often describes craft skill transmission (particularly weaving traditions) as a form of apprentice learning.[12] Perhaps the most striking example is Dietrich Stout's (2002) study of stone adze-making in Irian Jaya. The social and informational organization of adze-making, as he pictures it, is strikingly akin to a medieval craft guild. The apprenticeship system is quite formal. There is a master adze-maker. Apprentices have to be accepted by a recognized master, and apprentices (while usually being relatives of their master) have to show commitment by doing scut work until accepted, and once accepted, their produce belongs to their master until their own mastery is recognized. It usually takes about five years until an apprentice is accepted as an acknowledged master, so the commitment is serious. There is a genuine, difficult skill to be mastered: apprentice-made adzes are smaller, because controlling appropriate proportions becomes increasingly difficult as the size of the stone "blank" increases. There is no formal teaching. But much of the initial selection of raw material and initial processing is done in public, and discussed in public, with a good deal of public advice and aid from the more skilled to the less skilled.[13] As with the formal, institutionalized systems of apprentice guilds, adze-makers have developed a complex technical vocabulary of stone-working. Their jargon includes specialist terms for types of stone, hammerstone shapes, impact zones for knapping, and the type and angle of strikes. The similarities here are close, striking, and informative.

Archaeological Record

Overall, the archaeological record shows an increasing trend in technical competence, from perhaps 3.5 mya. There is direct testimony from the remains of the artifacts themselves and of their products. There is indirect evidence from the effects of technical competence on the bodies of humans (the signals of better diet and reduced mortality); from their expanding geographic and ecological distribution; and, perhaps, from their increasing ecological impact on biological communities. By itself, increasing technical competence is not evidence for the apprentice learning model.[14] We would expect to see such an increase if there was continued positive selection for technical competence and if as a consequence, hominins gradually became more technically adept as a result of evolutionary change in their intrinsic psychology. For example, we might expect to see competence increase, if an innate intuitive physics model gradually evolved and elaborated.

The apprentice learning model differs from an increasing-intelligence model in claiming that technical competence rests as much on stable features of the social and learning environment as it does on intrinsic psychology. The idea that skill depends on an organized environment, not just an adapted mind, is supported by a salient and pervasive feature of the record. In the long run there has been a revolution in technical competence. But there is no smoothly increasing curve of skill. Rather, in the first three million years or so of this period, there is little obvious change. Oldowan tools date from 2.6 million years ago (though as we have seen, there is indirect evidence from cut marks on bone almost a million years earlier). These were supplemented by Acheulian handaxes from about 1.7 million years ago; controlled fire from about 800 kya. It was not until the Middle Stone Age beginning in Africa perhaps 300 kya (or a little less), that the toolkit began to obviously expand. That expansion does not become rapid until perhaps 100 kya (Foley & Lahr, 2003). This change does not correlate well with hominin species turn over. The handaxe may have been an *erectus* innovation, but these early technologies were almost certainly used by a number of hominin species, presumably with differing intrinsic psychologies.

So, depending on the connection between speciation and change in cognitive profile, the pattern of technical advance may not fit an intelligence-driven model. More importantly, from the Middle Stone Age, there were reversals in technical competence. Innovations were made, adopted, spread, disappeared. We see this pattern in the record of *sapiens'* immediate ancestors, but even more, we see it in the record of ancient *sapiens*. There are reversals as well as increases (Brumm & Moore, 2005; Conard, 2006; Hiscock & O'Conner, 2006; Conard, 2007; O'Connell & Allen, 2007). This pattern fits poorly with the idea that the technical proficiency of ancient cultures is an expression of their individual technical intelligence. It fits much better with the idea that the technical proficiency of ancient cultures is an expression of the interaction of individual technical intelligence with social environment and local demography. Destabilization of the social environment that supports intergenerational skill transmission can result in cultural deskilling. I have argued elsewhere that such deskilling was probably the immediate cause of Neanderthal extinction: unfavorable environmental changes stressed the social arrangements that made their skill sets stable (Sterelny, 2011a). Local demography is important too: larger populations spread risk, making crucial skills less likely to be lost by unlucky accident, and larger populations support skill by making specialization and the division of labor possible (Henrich, 2004; Powell et al., 2009). In short, an interactionist model of competence fits the archaeological record far better than one which sees competence as a simple reflection of individual capacity.

Feedback and Coevolutionary Loops

There is widespread agreement that hominin cognitive, social and behavioral evolution has been extraordinarily rapid, and that these changes are not plausibly explained as a response to external disturbance. For, if that were the case, we would expect similarly rapid and extensive changes in other lineages. Since we do not, the consensus is that the driver of hominin evolution is a positive feedback loop; our lineage has experienced a form of runaway selection. Moreover, there is a popular candidate for that loop; it is the problem of managing cooperation. I think this basic idea is right, but I do not agree with the way it has usually been elaborated; namely, as the challenge of managing defection.[15] Cooperation, the idea runs, is profitable but risky. The potential benefits of cooperation are great, so we are selected to cooperate. The potential risks of being ripped-off are pressing, so we are under selection to be vigilant cooperators, carefully evaluating the acts of our partners (and preparing to seize the chance to cheat, if we can do so safely). So there is selection for increased intelligence, for increased skill in playing social chess. But as the intelligence of individuals in the population increases, the scrutiny problem becomes more difficult, selecting for still greater intelligence, and so on.

In my view, this way of developing the thought that cooperation is challenging overlooks the cognitive challenge of getting cooperation to work, and overstates the problem of identifying defectors (Calcott, 2008b). In small, repeatedly interacting communities (a village, a hunting band, a ship's crew, a lab group) everyone knows who is reliable and who is not to be trusted. The problem of successful coordination, though, really is challenging. Cooperative foraging depends on synthesizing social, ecological and technical information. So successful social foraging—especially in high-risk environments—depends on each partner having a well-tuned sense of the skills and intentions of the others. It depends on communication and planning. But it also depends on rich, accurate local knowledge; on a detailed grip of the natural history of target species; on locally made technology used with great expertise.

Since no generation acquires these informational resources from scratch, the cognitive capital on which successful foraging depends is acquired by cross-generation information pooling. One generation inherits informational resources which are modified (as conditions change and through innovation) and then transmitted to the next for further modification. Thus high-volume, high-fidelity, intergenerational cultural learning coevolves with social foraging through positive feedback: Adult foraging was more profitable because hominins had plenty of time, opportunity and support to learn crucial skills; because it was very profitable, they could afford to support semi-dependent adolescents through their long apprenticeship. As the fidelity of social learning improves, social foraging becomes more effective, for technology and technique improve across the generations. As social foraging becomes more profitable, adults can more effectively support the next generation while they acquire skills and information. Reproductive cooperation is part of this mix too. Alloparental care makes social learning more reliable, by giving children access to more of the group's informational resources, as they are cared for by aunts, grandparents, siblings, friends, near-adult girls practicing, fathers (Burkart et al., 2009). Reproductive cooperation adds redundancy to the system and redundancy adds reliability. The more opportunities a child has to learn the better, especially if the skills they must acquire are challenging.

In summary, while there were no Palaeolithic craft guilds anticipating those of Medieval Europe, skill transmission in formal apprenticeships and skill transmission in traditional society had essentially the same structure. They both depend on socially organized and adapted learning environments fusing the power of trial and error learning with that of cultural transmission. In concert with minds adapted for teaching and learning, these environments made possible the transmission of high-fidelity, high-volume information across the generations. That in turn made possible the reliable acquisition of the social and technical competences on which human life depended. In general, evolutionary approaches to psychology emphasize the idea that human minds are evolved learning machines. But in contrast to nativist versions of evolutionary psychology, on the apprentice model, our minds are adapted to evolutionarily salient channels, sources and contexts of learning (and teaching), as much as (or more than) our minds are evolved to learn about specific factual domains. It is for this reason that humans manage remarkably well in evolutionarily novel environments. Even during our history as foragers, humans experienced very different physical and biological environments, and as a consequence different social environments too. But over the last 10,000 years, we have come to live in utterly different physical environments (built environments), biological environments (farms, then urban landscapes), and social environments (from the vast increases in size and social differentiation). The environments in which humans live after the establishment of farming are extraordinarily different from those in which our lineage mostly evolved. The last ten thousands years has seen some "shock of the new," some adaptive lag, as our historically tuned responses failed to deliver adaptive responses to new challenges. That is no surprise. Much more remarkable is how rare these maladaptive failures have been. Individually and collectively, we have coped extraordinarily well with testing, novel problems: that is why so many of us are here. Any evolutionary theory of human nature and cognition must explain our adaptive resilience in the face of novel environmental challenges, and the apprentice learning model passes that test.

Notes

1 Indeed, our hands and arms show clear marks of selection for manual skills (Ambrose, 2001).
2 There is some ethnographic skepticism about the importance of teaching in traditional societies, but

this seems to be a consequence of a narrow, institutionalized conception of teaching.

3   See Dan Sperber and his colleagues for a nuanced theory of these mechanisms and their evolution: Sperber, 2001; Sperber et al., 2010; Mercier and Sperber, 2011.

4   For such conservative estimates of great ape baselines, see Tomasello, 2008; Warneken and Tomasello, 2009; Warneken, forthcoming.

5   The notorious Baldwin Effect is one, but only one, form of genetic accommodation.

6   Toth and Schick 2009, p. 293.

7   In fact, actively supported social learning has probably been essential for at least 800,000 years. There is clear evidence of the control of fire that long (Alperson-Afil et al., 2007), and it has been persuasively argued that late Acheulian technology was too sophisticated to acquire without active help from experts (Stout, 2002, 2011).

8   Though there is certainly some: see (MacDonald, 2007; Csibra and Gergely, 2011; Hewlett et al., 2011).

9   Emulation is learning about resources and dangers from other agents; I notice that nuts have food in them by seeing you open them, but I do not learn by watching you how to open them; if I learn technique by watching you, this is imitation.

10   If agents forage cooperatively in small, intimate groups, it would be very difficult to mask special skills, and doing so would offer few advantages; a skill is profitable only if it can be exercised.

11   Hewlett et al., 2011, 1174–1175.

12   Tehrani and Riede, 2008, pp. 321–322.

13   Stout, 2002, p. 702.

14   Some archaeologists think that we can, in some cases, tell from the tools themselves that teaching and social learning must have been important. Summarizing this line of argument, Stout, 2001 and Tehrani and Riede, 2008) both suggest that when the skill itself is complex and difficult, its transmission must depend on something like an apprenticeship system of skill transmission. While this argument is plausible, it can hardly be decisive.

15   This idea has usually been discussed as the social intelligence hypothesis or the Machiavellian intelligence hypothesis. See for example Humphrey, 1976; Byrne and Whiten, 1988; Whiten and Byrne, 1997; Dunbar, 1998.

References

Alperson-Afil, N., D. Richter, et al. (2007). Phantom hearths and the use of fire at Gesher Benot Ya'Aqov, Israel. PaleoAnthropology, 3: 1–15.

Ambrose, S. (2001). Paleolithic technology and human evolution. Science, 291: 1748–1753.

Ambrose, S. (2010). Coevolution of composite-tool technology, constructive memory, and language. Current Anthropology, 51: S135–S147.

Avital, E., & Jablonka, E. (2000). Animal Traditions: Behavioural inheritance in evolution. Cambridge: Cambridge University Press.

Bock, J. (2005). What Makes a Competent Adult Forager? In B. S. Hewlett and M. E. Lamb (Eds.), Hunter Gatherer Childhoods: Evolutionary, developmental and cultural perspectives (pp. 109–128). New York: Aldine.

Bowles, S., & Gintis, H. (2011). A Cooperative Species: Human reciprocity and its evolution. Princeton, NJ: Princeton University Press.

Brumm, A., & Moore, M. (2005). Symbolic revolutions and the Australian archaeological record. Cambridge Archaeological Journal, 15: 157–175.

Burkart, J., Hrdy, S. B., et al. (2009). Cooperative breeding and human cognitive evolution. Evolutionary Anthropology, 18: 175–186.

Byrne, R. (1995). The Thinking Ape: Evolutionary origins of intelligence. Oxford: Oxford University Press.

Byrne, R. (2004). The manual skills and cognition that lie behind hominid tool use. In A. Russon and D. R. Begun (Eds.), Evolutionary Origins of Great Ape Intelligence (pp. 31–44). Cambridge: Cambridge University Press.

Byrne, R., & Whiten, A. (Eds.) (1988). Machiavellian Intelligence. Oxford: Oxford University Press.

Calcott, B. (2008). Lineage explanations: Explaining how biological mechanisms change. British Journal for the Philosophy of Science, 60: 51–78.

Calcott, B. (2008). The other cooperation problem: Generating benefit. Biology and Philosophy, 23: 179–203.

Chemero, A. (2009). Radical Embodied Cognitive Science. Cambridge, MA: MIT Press.

Clark, A. (2008). Supersizing the Mind: Embodiment, action, and cognitive extension. Oxford: Oxford University Press.

Conard, N. (2006). An overview of the patterns of behavioural change in Africa and Eurasia during the Middle and Late Pleistocene. In F. d'Errico and

L. Blackwell (Eds.), *From Tools to Symbols from Early Hominids to Humans* (pp. 294–332). Johannesburg: Wits University Press.

Conard, N. (2007). Cultural evolution in Africa and Eurasia during the Middle and Late Pleistocene. In W. Henke and I. Tattersall (Eds.), *Handbook of Paleoanthropology* (pp. 2001–2037). Berlin: Springer-Verlag.

Csibra, G., & Gergely, G. (2006). Social learning and social cognition: The case for pedagogy. In M. H. Johnson and Y. Munakata (Eds.), *Processes of Change in Brain and Cognitive Development*. Oxford: Oxford University Press.

Csibra, G., & Gergely, G. (2011). Natural pedagogy as evolutionary adaptation. *Philosophical Transactions of the Royal Society B*, 366: 1149–1157.

Dawkins, R. (1996). *Climbing Mount Improbable*. New York: W.W. Norton.

Deacon, T. (1997). *The Symbolic Species: The co-evolution of language and the brain*. New York: W.W Norton.

Dennett, D. C. (2000). Making tools for thinking. In D. Sperber (Ed.), *Metarepresentation: A multidisciplinary perspective* (pp. 17–29). Oxford: Oxford University Press.

Dunbar, R. (1998). The social brain hypothesis. *Evolutionary Anthropology*, 6: 178–190.

Foley, R., & Gamble, C. (2009). The ecology of social transitions in human evolution. *Philosophical Transactions of the Royal Society B*, 364: 3267–3279.

Foley, R., & Lahr, M. M. (2003). On stony ground: Lithic technology, human evolution and the emergence of culture. *Evolutionary Anthropology*, 12: 109–122.

Hauser, M. (2006). *Moral Minds: How nature designed our universal sense of right and wrong*. New York: HarperCollins.

Hawkes, K. (2003). Grandmothers and the evolution of human longevity. *American Journal of Human Biology*, 15: 380–400.

Hawkes, K., & Bird, R. (2002). Showing off, handicap signaling and the evolution of men's work. *Evolutionary Anthropology*, 11: 58–67.

Henrich, J. (2004). Demography and cultural evolution: Why adaptive cultural processes produced maladaptive losses in Tasmania. *American Antiquity*, 69: 197–221.

Henrich, J., & Gil-White, F. (2001). The evolution of prestige: Freely conferred deference as a mechanism for enhancing the benefits of cultural transmission. *Evolution and Human Behavior*, 22: 165–196.

Hewlett, B., H. Fouts, et al. (2011). Social learning among Congo Basin hunter-gatherers. *Philosophical Transactions of the Royal Society B*, 366: 1168–1178.

Hill, K., & Kaplan, H. (1999). Life history traits in humans: Theory and empirical studies. *Annual Review of Anthropology*, 28: 397–430.

Hiscock, P., & O'Conner, S. (2006). An Australian perspective on modern behaviour and artefact assemblages. *Before Farming*, 2.

Hrdy, S. B. (2005). Evolutionary context of development: The cooperative breeding model. In C. S. Carter, L. Ahnert, K. E. Grossman et al. *Attachment and Bonding: A new synthesis* (pp. 9–32). Cambridge, MA: MIT Press.

Hrdy, S. B. (2009). *Mothers and Others: The evolutionary origins of mutual understanding*. Cambridge, MA: Harvard University Press.

Humphrey, N. (1976). The social function of intellect. In P. P. G. Bateson and R. A. Hinde (Eds.), *Growing Points in Ethology* (pp. 303–317). Cambridge: Cambridge University Press.

Jablonka, E., & Lamb, M. (2005). *Evolution in Four Dimensions*. Cambridge, MA: MIT Press.

Johnson, D. D. P., & Bering, J. M. (2006). Hand of God, mind of man: Punishment and cognition in the evolution of cooperation. *Evolutionary Psychology*, 4: 219–233.

Jones, M. (2007). *Feast: Why humans share food*. Oxford: Oxford University Press.

Kennedy, G. (2003). Palaeolithic grandmothers? Life history theory and early homo. *Journal of the Royal Anthropological Institute*, 8: 549–572.

Klein, R., & Edgar, B. (2002). *The Dawn of Human Culture*. New York: Wiley.

Laland, K., & Galef, B. (Eds.) (2009). *The Question of Animal Culture*. Cambridge, MA: Harvard University Press.

MacDonald, K. (2007). Cross-cultural comparison of learning in human hunting: Implications for life history evolution. *Human Nature*, 18: 386–402.

Mace, R. (2000). The evolutionary ecology of human life history. *Animal Behaviour*, 59: 1–10.

Marlowe, F. W. (2005). Hunter-gatherers and human evolution. *Evolutionary Anthropology*, 14: 54–67.

McBrearty, S., & Jablonski, N. (2005). First fossil chimpanzee. *Nature*, 437: 105–108.

McPherron, S., Z. Alemseged, et al. (2010). Evidence for stone-tool-assisted consumption of animal tissues before 3.39 million years ago at Dikika, Ethiopia. *Nature*, 466: 857–860.

Menary, R. (Ed.) (2010). *The Extended Mind*. Cambridge, MA: MIT Press.

Mercier, H., & Sperber, D. (2011). Why do humans reason? Arguments for an argumentative theory. *Behavioral and Brain Sciences*, 34: 57–111.

O'Connell, J. F., & Allen, J. (2007). Pre-LGM Sahul (Pleistocene Australia-New Guinea) and the archaeology of early modern humans. In P. Mellars, K. Boyle, O. Bar-Yosef and C. Stringer (Eds.), *Rethinking the Human Revolution* (pp. 395–410). Cambridge: McDonald Institute for Archaeological Research.

O'Connell, J. F., K. Hawkes, et al. (1999). Grandmothering and the evolution of *Homo erectus*. *Journal of Human Evolution*, 36: 461–485.

Potts, R. (1996). *Humanity's Descent: The consequences of ecological instability*. New York: Avon.

Povinelli, D., with, et al. (2000). *Folk Physics for Apes: The chimpanzee's theory of how the world works*. Oxford: Oxford University Press.

Powell, A., S. Shennan, et al. (2009). Late Pleistocene demography and the appearance of modern human behavior. *Science*, 324: 298–1301.

Sperber, D. (2001). An evolutionary perspective on testimony and argumentation. *Philosophical Topics*, 29: 401–413.

Sperber, D., F. Clément, et al. (2010). Epistemic vigilance. *Mind and Language*, 25: 359–393.

Sterelny, K. (2007). Social intelligence, human intelligence and niche construction. *Proceedings of the Royal Society, London (series B)*, 362: 719–730.

Sterelny, K. (2010). Minds: Extended or scaffolded? *Phenomenology and the Cognitive Science*, 9: 465–481.

Sterelny, K. (2011). *The Evolved Apprentice*. Cambridge, MA: MIT Press.

Sterelny, K. (2011). From hominins to humans: How sapiens became behaviourally modern. *Philosophical Transactions of the Royal Society, London, B*, 366: 809–822.

Stiner, M. C. (2002). Carnivory, coevolution, and the geographic spread of the genus homo. *Journal of Archaeological Research*, 10: 1–63.

Stout, D. (2002). Skill and cognition in stone tool production: An ethnographic case study from Irian Jaya. *Current Anthropology*, 43: 693–722.

Stout, D. (2011). Stone toolmaking and the evolution of human culture and cognition. *Philosophical Transactions of the Royal Society, series B*, 366: 1050–1059.

Tattersall, I. (2008). *The Fossil Trail: How we know what we think we know about human evolution*. Oxford: Oxford University Press.

Tennie, C., J. Call, et al. (2009). Ratcheting up the ratchet: On the evolution of cumulative culture. *Philosophical Transactions of the Royal Society, London, B*, 364: 2405–2415.

Thornton, A., & Raihani, N. J. (2008). The evolution of teaching. *Animal Behaviour*, 75: 1823–1836.

Tomasello, M. (2008). *Origins of Human Communication*. Cambridge, MA: MIT Press.

Tomasello, M. (2009). *Why We Cooperate*. Cambridge, MA: MIT Press.

Toth, N., & Schick, K. (2009). The Oldowan: The tool making of early hominins and chimpanzees compared. *Annual Review of Anthropology*, 38: 289–305.

Wadley, L. (2010). Compound-adhesive manufacture as a behavioural proxy for complex cognition in the Middle Stone Age. *Current Anthropology*, 51: S111–S119.

Warneken, F. (forthcoming). The origins of human cooperation from a developmental and comparative perspective. In G. Hatfield (Ed.), *The Evolution of Mind*. Philadelphia, PA: University of Pennsylvania Press.

Warneken, F., & Tomasello, M. (2009). Varieties of altruism in children and chimpanzees. *Trends in Cognitive Science*, 13: 397–402.

West-Eberhard, M. J. (2003). *Developmental Plasticity and Evolution*. Oxford: Oxford University Press.

Whiten, A., & Byrne, R. (Eds.) (1997). *Machiavellian Intelligence II: Extensions and evaluations*. Cambridge: Cambridge University Press.

Whiten, A., N. McGuigan, et al. (2009). Emulation, imitation, over-imitation and the scope of culture for child and chimpanzee. *Philosophical Transactions of the Royal Society, series B*, 364: 2417–2428.

Wrangham, R. (1999). Evolution of coalitionary killing. *Yearbook of Physical Anthropology*, 42: 1–30.

Wrangham, R. (2009). *Catching Fire: How cooking made us human*. London: Profile Books.

Topic 6 SOCIAL CONSTRUCTION

HUMANS DIVIDE INTO KINDS: children, teenagers, adults, and old people; French, German, Chinese, Korean, Mexican, South-Africans, etc.; Tutsis, Hutus, Corsicans, Texans, Quebecquois, etc.; men and women; blacks, whites, Latinos, etc.; blue collars and white collars; psychopaths, depressed individuals, melancholics, people with Koro (who are afraid that their genitals will retract into their body), etc.; pregnant teenagers, obese people, anorexics, etc. Such classifications help each of us organize the human diversity we are regularly confronted with. They are also often part and parcel of scientific (or, sometimes, pseudo-scientific) efforts to understand humans.

But what is the nature of these kinds? According to social constructionists, many (if not all) of these kinds are the products of particular historical trajectories, social circumstances, and cultural contexts: They are socially constructed. To give a single example, according to historian Philippe Aries, children as a group did not exist during the Middle Ages. Of course, there were young individuals, but these did not form a class with a distinctive set of characteristics. Rather, children were simply small adults, meant to do what adults do and interact with adults. Childhood was invented or constructed during the late-sixteenth and early-seventeenth century, an invention that was made possible by a growing recognition that people's moral sense had to be educated.

Social constructionists often hold that the existence of a particular kind (children, pregnant teenagers, blacks, etc.) requires that this kind be recognized by others: No children without people having a concept of children. As a result, they often run together (some would say confuse) the claims that a particular kind (children) was invented at a particular time and place and the claim that a concept of this kind (the concept of children) was invented at this time and place, and they often take evidence for the latter claim to be evidence for the former claim. Thus, much of the evidence for Aries's provocative thesis comes from the lack of pictorial representations of and discourse about children before the late-sixteenth century—thus from the absence of a concept of childhood.

Social constructionism is not a very clear idea, and unfortunately presentations of this approach are often murky. Ian Hacking's essay is a well-known effort to clarify an important form of social constructionism, which focuses on the kinds that are the objects of investigation in social sciences such as sociology, psychiatry, and psychology—what he calls "human kinds." Members of these kinds are aware of being classified by scientists, and, because these kinds have a moral significance (consider, e.g., pregnant teenagers or hooligans), they modify their behavior in response to scientists' claims about them, sometimes confirming these claims, sometimes invalidating them—a phenomenon Hacking calls a "looping effect." As a result of these interactions, the kinds themselves, with their distinctive sets of properties, are constructed.

Social constructionism has been particularly influential among historians, particularly those whose historical work is influenced by social justice concerns. Frances McCrea's article on the treatment of menopause by means of estrogen from the 1950s to the 1970s illustrates this approach. One of her most striking claims is that menopause as a pathological condition requiring treatment is a "construction" and that menopause was so constructed to fulfill some sexist prejudices about women and to satisfy the economic interests of pharmaceutical companies.

One may have the impression that social constructionism is incompatible with the approach to human nature illustrated by many essays in the first section (Human Nature and Evolution) of this volume. Just like many constructionists, Hacking seems to think so. However, Ronald Mallon and Stephen Stich show that the two approaches are perfectly compatible. There is room for social constructionism and for an evolutionary, scientific approach to human characteristics.

Suggested Further Reading

Aries, P. (1965) *Centuries of Childhood: A social history of family life*. New York: Vintage.

Berger, P. L. and Luckmann, T. (1966) *The Social Construction of Reality: A treatise in the sociology of knowledge*. Garden City, NY: Anchor Books.

Bloor, D. (1976) *Knowledge and Social Imagery*. Boston, MA: Routledge.

Foucault, M. (1967) *Madness and Civilization: A history of insanity in the age of reason*. London: Tavistock Publications.

Foucault, M. (1978) *The History of Sexuality, Volume I, An Introduction*. New York: Pantheon.

Gergen, K. J. (1985) The social constructionist movement in modern psychology. *American Psychologist*, 40: 266–275.

Gergen, K. J. and Davis, K. E. (1985) *The Social Construction of the Person*. New York: Springer-Verlag.

Hacking, I. (1986) Making up people. In T. C. Heller, M. Sosna and D. E. Wellbery (Eds.), *Reconstructing Individualism: Autonomy, individuality, and the self in Western thought* (pp. 222–236). Stanford, CA: Stanford University Press.

Hacking, I. (1991) The making and molding of child abuse. *Critical Inquiry*, 17: 253–288.

Hacking, I. (1995) *Rewriting the Soul: Multiple personality and the sciences of memory*. Princeton, NJ: Princeton University Press.

Hacking, I. (1998) *Mad Travelers: Reflections on the reality of transient mental illnesses*. Charlottesville, VA: University of Virginia Press.

Hacking, I. (1999) *The Social Construction of What?* Cambridge, MA: Harvard University Press.

Harré, R. (Ed.) (1986) *The Social Construction of Emotions*. Oxford: Basil Blackwell.

Haslanger, S. (1995) Ontology and social construction. *Philosophical Topics*, 23: 95–125.

Laqueur, T. W. (1990) *Making Sex: Body and gender from the Greeks to Freud.* Cambridge, MA: Harvard University Press.

Latour, B. and Woolgar, S. (1979) *Laboratory Life: The social construction of scientific facts.* Princeton, NJ: Princeton University Press.

Lutz, C. (1988) *Unnatural Emotions: Everyday sentiments on a Micronesian atoll and their challenge to Western theory.* Chicago, IL: University of Chicago Press.

Lutz, C. and White, G. (1986) The anthropology of emotions. *Annual Review of Anthropology,* 15: 405–436.

Machery, E. and Faucher, L. (2005) Social construction and the concept of race. *Philosophy of Science,* 72: 1208–1219.

Mallon, R. (2007) A field guide to social constructionism. *Philosophy Compass,* 2: 93–108.

Pickering, A. (1984) *Constructing Quarks: A sociological history of particle physics.* Edinburgh: Edinburgh University Press.

Chapter 20

Frances B. McCrea

THE POLITICS OF MENOPAUSE
The "Discovery" of a Deficiency Disease

In the 1960s the medical profession in the United States hailed the contraceptive pill as the "great liberator" of women, and estrogens in general as the fountain of youth and beauty. Prominent gynecologists "discovered" that menopause was a "deficiency disease," but promised women that estrogen replacement therapy would let them avoid menopause completely and keep them "feminine forever." Yet within a few years, U.S. feminists in the vanguard of an organized women's health movement defined the health care system, including estrogen treatment, as a serious social problem. The male-dominated medical profession was accused of reflecting and perpetuating the social ideology of women as sex objects and reproductive organs. Treating women with dangerous drugs was defined as exploitation and an insidious form of social control.

These issues raised several questions: How did such diametrically opposed definitions evolve? How, under what conditions, and by whom does a certain behavior become defined as deviant or sick? In what context does a putative condition become defined as a social problem?

I believe that definitions of health and illness are socially constructed and that these definitions are inherently political. "Deviant behaviors that were once defined as immoral, sinful or criminal," according to Conrad and Schneider "have now been given new medical meanings" which are "profoundly political in nature" and have "real political consequences" (Conrad and Schneider, 1980, p. 1). Indeed "in many cases these medical treatments have become a new form of social control."

I interpret the definition of menopause from this framework. During the 19th century, Victorian physicians viewed menopause as a sign of sin and decay; with the advent of Freudian psychology in the early 20th century, it was viewed as a neurosis; and as synthetic estrogens became readily available in the 1960s, physicians treated menopause as a deficiency disease (McCrea, 1981). Perhaps more important than these differences, however, are four themes which pervade the medical definitions of menopause. These are: (1) women's potential and function are biologically destined; (2) women's worth is determined by fecundity and attractiveness; (3) rejection of the feminine role will bring physical and emotional havoc; (4) aging women are useless and repulsive.

In this chapter I first analyze the rise of the disease definition of menopause and show that this definition reflects and helps create the prevailing ageism and sexism of our times. Then I show how the disease definition has been challenged from inside the medical community. Finally I examine how feminists outside the medical community have also challenged the disease model, claiming that menopause is normal and relatively unproblematic.

Menopause as Disease

The roots of the disease definition of menopause can be traced back to the synthesis of estrogens. The earliest interest in these hormones grew out of efforts to find a cure for male impotence (Buxton, 1944; Page, 1977). In 1889, Charles Édouard Brown-Sequard, a French physiologist, reported to the Société de Biologie in Paris that he experienced renewed vigor and rejuvenation after injecting himself with extracts from animal testicles. Four years later another French scientist, Regis de Bordeaux, used an ovarian extract injection to treat a female patient for menopausal "insanity." And in 1896 a German physician, Theodore Landau, used desiccated ovaries to treat menopausal symptoms at the Landau Clinic in Berlin. In the late 1920s, Edgar Allen and Edward Doisey isolated and crystallized theelin (later known as estrone) from the urine of pregnant women. In 1932 Samual Geist and Frank Spielman described in the *American Journal of Obstetrics and Gynecology* their efforts to treat menopausal women with theelin. Such treatments, however, were expensive and supplies of the drug limited, since it was derived from human sources. These problems were solved in 1936 when Russell Marker and Thomas Oakwood developed a synthetic form of estrogen known as diethylstilbesteral (DES). This cheap and potent hormone substance could be made readily available to a large number of women and paved the way for the development of the contraceptive pill. The last step in the development of hormone therapy occurred in 1943 when James Goodall developed an estrogen extract from the urine of pregnant mares. Termed conjugated equine estrogen and manufactured by Ayerst under the brand name Premarin, it was only about half as potent as synthetic estrogen, but it created fewer unpleasant side effects.

By the early 1960s exogenous estrogen (that is, estrogen originating outside the human body) was widely available in the United States,

and was inexpensive and easy to administer. It was used to treat various conditions of aging. But if estrogens were to become the cure, what was to be the disease?

> [Medicine] is active in seeking out illness. . . . One of the greatest ambitions of the physician is to discover and describe a "new" disease or syndrome and to be immortalized by having his name used to identify the disease. Medicine, then, is oriented to seeking out and finding illness, which is to say that it seeks to create social meanings of illness where that meaning or interpretation was lacking before. And insofar as illness is defined as something bad—to be eradicated or contained—medicine plays the role of what Becker called the "moral entrepreneur." (Freidson, 1970, p. 252)

The moral entrepreneur who, during the 1960s, led the crusade to redefine menopause as a disease was the prominent Brooklyn gynecologist Robert A. Wilson. As founder and head of the Wilson Foundation, established in New York in 1963 to promote estrogens and supported by $1.3 million in grants from the pharmaceutical industry (Mintz and Cohn, 1977), Wilson's writings were crucial to the acceptance of menopause as a "deficiency disease" and the large-scale routine administration of Estrogen Replacement Therapy (ERT). He claimed that menopause was a hormone deficiency disease similar to diabetes and thyroid dysfunction. In an article published in the *Journal of the American Medical Association*, Wilson (1962) claimed that estrogen prevented breast and genital cancer and other problems of aging. Even though his methodology was weak, this article launched a campaign to promote estrogens for the prevention of menopause and age-related diseases.

A year later, writing with his wife Thelma in the *Journal of the American Geriatrics Society*, Wilson and Wilson (1963) advocated that women be given estrogens from "puberty to grave." Crucial to the popular acceptance of the disease model of menopause was Robert Wilson's widely read book *Feminine Forever* (1966a), which claimed that menopause is a malfunction threatening the "feminine essence." In an article summarizing his book, Wilson described menopausal women as "living decay"(1966b, p. 70) but said ERT could save them from being "condemned to witness the death of their womanhood" (1966b, p. 66). He further proclaimed that menopause and aging could be allayed with ERT and listed 26 physiological and psychological symptoms that the "youth pill" could avert—including hot flashes, osteoporosis (thinning of bone mass), vaginal atrophy (thinning of vaginal walls), sagging and shrinking breasts, wrinkles, absent-mindedness, irritability, frigidity, depression, alcoholism, and even suicide.

Wilson also was aware of the physician's potential and even mandate for social control. The first paragraph of a chapter titled "Menopause—The Loss of Womanhood and Good Health" states:

> . . . I would like to launch into the subject of menopause by discussing its *effect on men*. Menopause covers such a wide range of physical and emotional symptoms that the implications are by no means confined to the woman. *Her husband, her family, and her entire relationship to the outside world* are affected almost as strongly as her own body. Only in this broader context can the problem of the menopause—as well as the benefits of hormonal cure—be properly appreciated (1966a, p. 92, emphasis added).

Wilson gives an example of how he helped a distressed husband who came to him for help with the following complaint:

> She is driving me nuts. She won't fix meals. She lets me get no sleep. She picks on me all the time. She makes up lies about me. She hits the bottle all day. And we used to be happily married (1966a, p. 93).

This man's wife, Wilson says, responded well to "intensive" estrogen treatment and in no time resumed her wifely duties (1966a, p. 94).

From Wilson's own words it is obvious that the disease label is not neutral. This label, like any disease label, decreases the status and the autonomy of the patient while increasing the status and power of the physician. When seen as part of a political process,

> knowledge and skill are claimed by a group to advance its interests. True or false the knowledge, disinterested or interested the motive, claims of knowledge function as ideologies. . . . insofar as claims to knowledge and skill are essential elements in a political process . . . it is highly unlikely that they can remain neutrally descriptive (Freidson, 1971, p. 30).

By individualizing the problems of menopause, the physician turns attention away from any social structural interpretation of women's conditions. The locus of the solution then becomes the doctor–patient interaction in which the physician is active, instrumental, and authoritative while the patient is passive and dependent. The inherent authority of physicians is institutionalized in ways that minimize reliance on explanation and persuasion. This clinical mentality is "intrinsically imperialistic, claiming more for the profession's knowledge and skill, and a broader jurisdiction than in fact can be justified by demonstrable effectiveness" (Freidson, 1971, p. 3). Such imperialism is independent of the particular motivation of the physician. Not only could it function as "crude self-interest," but also as "a natural outcome of the deep commitment to the value of his work developed by the thoroughly socialized professional" (Freidson, 1971, p. 31).

A number of prominent U.S. physicians supported Wilson's claims. Robert Greenblatt (1974), former president of the American Geriatrics Society, claimed that about 75 percent of menopausal women are acutely estrogen-deficient and advocated ERT for them, even if

296 Frances B. McCrea

they were without symptoms. Another crusader for ERT, Helen Jern, a gynecologist at the New York Infirmary, wrote a book of case studies proclaiming the miraculous recoveries made by elderly women placed on ERT:

I know the remarkably beneficial effect of estrogen as energizer, tranquilizer and anti-depressant. I know that it stimulates and maintains mental capacity, memory, and concentration, restores zest for living, and gives a youthful appearance. . . . Hormone therapy, once begun, should be continued throughout a woman's lifetime. It is my firm belief that many female inmates of nursing homes and mental institutions could be restored to full physical and mental health through adequate hormone therapy (Jern, 1973, p. 156).

Throughout the late 1960s and early 1970s, Wilson's book was excerpted widely in traditional women's journals, and over 300 articles promoting estrogens appeared in popular magazines (Johnson, 1977). During the same period an aggressive advertising campaign, capitalizing on the disease label, was launched by the U.S. pharmaceutical industry. ERT products were widely advertised in medical literature and promotional material as amelioratives for a variety of psychological, as well as somatic, problems. One advertisement depicted a seated woman clutching an airline ticket, with her impatient husband standing behind her glancing at his watch. The copy read:

Bon Voyage? Suddenly she'd rather not go. She's waited thirty years for this trip. Now she doesn't have the "bounce." She has headaches, hot flashes, and she feels tired and nervous all the time. And for no reason she cries (Seaman and Seaman, 1977, p. 281).

Such advertisements paid off: between 1963 and 1973 dollar sales in the United States for estrogen replacements quadrupled (U.S. Bureau of the Census, 1975). As one Harvard researcher stated, "few medical interventions have had as widespread application as exogenous estrogen treatment in post-menopausal women" (Weinstein, 1980). By 1975, with prescriptions at an all-time high of 26.7 million (Wolfe, 1979), estrogens had become the fifth most frequently prescribed drug in the United States (Hoover et al., 1976). A 1975 survey in the Seattle–Tacoma area of Washington State revealed that 51 percent of all post-menopausal women had used estrogens for at least three months, with a median duration of over 10 years (Weiss et al., 1976).

Indeed, 1975 was a watershed year for estrogen therapy: sales were at an all-time high and physicians routinely used estrogens to treat a wide variety of purported menopausal symptoms. Yet within a few years this trend changed as estrogen therapy came under attack from inside and outside the medical community.

Medical Controversy

Researchers had suspected an association between estrogens and cancer since the 1890s (Johnson, 1977). Experimental animal studies, conducted in the 1930s and 1940s, claimed that estrogenic and progestinic substances were carcinogenic (Cook and Dodds, 1933; Gardner, 1944; Perry and Ginzton, 1937). Novak and Yui (1936) warned that estrogen therapy might cause a pathological buildup of endometrial tissue.

Most investigators trace the roots of the ERT controversy back to 1947. In that year Dr. Saul Gusberg, then a young cancer researcher at the Memorial Sloane-Kettering Hospital and Columbia University in New York City, made a histologic link between hyperplasia (proliferation of the cells) and adenocarcinoma in the female endometrium (lining of the uterus). After finding a significant increase in endometrial cancer among estrogen users, Gusberg wrote:

Another human experiment has been set up in recent years by the widespread administration of estrogens to post-menopausal women. The relatively low cost of stilbestrol [synthetic estrogen] and the ease of administration have made its general use promiscuous (1974, p. 910).

Why was more attention not paid to these early warnings? In addition to the low cost and ease of administering estrogens mentioned by Gusberg, most scientists judged these early cancer studies to be scientifically unsound: those based on animal studies were dismissed as not applicable to humans. Perhaps most importantly, physicians found estrogens to be remarkably effective in alleviating vasomotor disturbances (hot flashes) and vaginal atrophy (Page, 1977, p. 54). In his book *The Ageless Woman*, Sherwin Kaufman described menopausal symptoms as the result of hormone deficiency, and lamented:

> Many women are obviously in need of estrogen replacements but are so afraid of "hormones" that it requires a good deal of explanation to persuade them that estrogen does not cause cancer and may, on the contrary, make them feel much better (1967, p. 61).

Kaufman regretted that some of his colleagues also share this unwarranted fear of cancer:

> Some doctors prescribe estrogens reluctantly. . . . Historically, and too often hysterically, estrogens have been endowed with malignant potentialities. Paradoxically, it has been pointed out that even conservative physicians may not hesitate to give sedatives or tranquilizers, yet they stop at the suggestion of estrogen replacement therapy. This is baffling to a good many doctors (1967, p. 67).

The ERT controversy erupted in 1975 when two epidemiological studies, by research teams from Washington University (Smith et al., 1975) and The Kaiser-Permanente Medical Center in Los Angeles (Ziel and Finkle, 1975), found a link between post-menopausal estrogen therapy and endometrial cancer. The two studies were written independently of each other and published side by side in the prestigious *New England Journal of Medicine*. By 1980, nine more studies, all done in the United States, concluded that women on ERT were four to 20 times more likely to develop endometrial cancer than non-users (Ziel, 1980). Moreover, the risk of cancer purportedly increased with the duration and dose of estrogens. Indeed, according to Gusberg, endometrial cancer has "superseded cervical cancer as the most common malignant tumor of the female reproductive tract" (1980, p. 729).

At a 1979 Consensus Development Conference on Estrogen Use and Post-Menopausal Women, sponsored by the National Institute on Aging, researchers unanimously concluded that ERT substantially increases the risk of endometrial cancer.[1] The final report of the conference concluded that ERT is only effective in the treatment of hot flashes and vaginal atrophy, and, if used at all, should be administered on a cyclical basis (three weeks of estrogen, one week off), at the lowest dose for the shortest possible time.[2] Any candidate for post-menopausal estrogen, the report recommended, "should be given as much information as possible about both the benefits and risks and then, with her physician, reach an individualized decision regarding whether to receive estrogens" (Gastel et al., 1979, p. 2).

Not only has the treatment of menopause come under criticism, the disease label has also been challenged by medical researchers. Saul Gusberg, who first warned of the ERT-cancer link, called the deficiency disease label for menopause "nonsense," adding "People are beginning to be more sensible about this, and realize that not a great trauma has happened to the average woman going through the menopause" (Reitz, 1977, p. 197.3). Research presented at the Consensus Development Conference in 1979 claimed that although ovarian production of estrogen declines after the menopause, older women need less estrogen. Moreover, production of the hormone by the adrenal glands partially compensates diminished ovarian production for most women (Ziel and Finkle, 1976). Furthermore, only 10 to 20 percent of women experience severe or incapacitating symptoms, and even those are generally temporary and decline over time (Gastel et al., 1979; McKinley and Jeffreys, 1974).

Researchers have also criticized the disease model on ideological grounds. Ziel and Finkle, two well-known cancer researchers, argued that the disease model was based on a traditional view of women's role:

> Because they desire the preservation of cosmetic youth and the unflagging libido of the patients, physicians have championed estrogen replacement therapy in the hope of attaining a maximal quality of life for their patients (1976, p. 737).

The female patient, in turn, "is readily deluded by her wish to preserve her figure and her physician's implication that estrogen promises eternal youth" (1976, p. 739).

Despite a strong consensus in the research community that ERT increases the risk of endometrial cancer, practicing physicians continued to prescribe the drug. As one San Francisco gynecologist stated after the 1975 cancer studies were published:

> I think of the menopause as a deficiency disease like diabetes. Most women develop some symptoms whether they are aware of them or not, so I prescribe estrogens for virtually all menopausal women for an indefinite period. (quoted in Brody, 1975, p. 55).

Even though U.S. prescriptions for ERT have steadily declined since the 1975 cancer studies, some 16 million were written in 1978 (Wolfe, 1979). Indeed, a 1978 Detroit-area survey showed that two-thirds of all women who saw their physicians about menopausal complaints received estrogens and 50 percent received

tranquilizers (Dosey and Dosey, 1980). In fact, a 1978 drug analysis by the U.S. Food and Drug Administration (FDA) concluded that menopausal estrogens, even after a major decline, were still "grossly overused" (Burke et al., 1978). My analysis of 1979 estrogen replacement prescriptions revealed that 31 percent were still written for such vague diagnostic categories as "symptoms of senility," "special conditions without sickness," and "mental problems"—in violation of FDA specifications.[3]

Other measures of physicians' endorsement of ERT are authoritative references which describe menopause as a morbid condition for which estrogen therapy is indicated. For example, *The Merck Manual* (Berkow, 1980), a book of diagnosis and therapy widely used by physicians, lists menopause under "Ovarian Dysfunction." Modell's (1980) *Drugs of Choice* lists it under "Diseases of the Endocrine system." Both sources advocate estrogens for treatment. *Drugs of Choice* states that "objective studies" evaluating the risks and benefits are "not currently available" (Modell, 1980, p. 54).

U.S. physicians have viewed the use of ERT as a political issue, and their endorsement of the therapy as an exercise of professional control. Editorials in the *Journal of the American Medical Association* have been critical of outside interference in the doctor-patient relationship. A 1979 editorial criticized the FDA Commissioner for mandating a "biased" warning: "In doing so he has officially expressed his distrust of the medical profession" (Landau, 1979, p. 47). A 1980 editorial castigated the FDA for creating unnecessary "public anxiety." Contradicting almost all the then-current U.S. research, the editorial concluded that "Estrogens already rank among the safest of all pharmaceuticals"(Meier and Landau, 1980, p. 1658).

Menopause as Normal

In the late 1960s and early 1970s, U.S. feminists began to challenge medical authority by questioning the legitimacy of the disease model of menopause. They argued that menopause is not a disease or sickness but a natural process of aging, through which most women pass with minimum difficulty.[4] The medical problems that do arise can be effectively treated or even prevented by adequate nutrition and exercise combined with vitamin supplements. According to feminists, the menstrual and menopausal myths are a form of social control. If women are perceived as physically and emotionally handicapped by menstruation and menopause, they cannot and may not compete with men. The health care system legitimates sexism, under the guise of science, by depicting women's physical and mental capabilities as dependent on their reproductive organs.

Schur calls these struggles over collective definitions "stigma" contests, wherein subordinate groups reject their deviant label (1980, p. 6). Although economic, legal, and political power are often involved in stigma contests, "what is essentially at stake in such situations is the power of moral standing or acceptability." Thus, stigma contests are always partly symbolic, since prestige and status are important issues (Gusfield, 1966; 1967). Stigmatized individuals must rectify a "spoiled identity" (Goffman, 1963) through collective efforts. In the United States, feminists have tried to neutralize stigma by claiming that menopause is a normal experience of normal women.

On these ideological grounds, feminists have opposed the routine use of ERT. For example, an article, published in *Ms.* in 1972, before strong medical evidence against ERT was uncovered, maintained that menopause was not a traumatic experience for most women. Because menopause freed women from the risk of pregnancy, it was viewed as a sexually liberating event. ERT, seen as an attempt to keep women "feminine forever," was thus viewed as a male exploitation, relegating women to the status of sex objects (Solomon, 1972). Four years later, offering a feminist interpretation of the menstrual and menopausal taboo, Delaney et al. stated that "the main fault of *Feminine Forever* lies not in the medicine but in the moralizing" (1976, p. 184).

After medical evidence became available to strengthen the ideological arguments, feminist criticism became widespread. In *Women and the Crisis in Sex Hormones* (Seaman and Seaman, 1977), the ERT controversy received a 70-page analysis titled "Promise Her Anything But Give Her . . . Cancer." These authors warned against the increasing medicalization of normal female functions:

Pregnancy or non-pregnancy are hardly diseases; and neither is menopause. The latter is a normal developmental state wherein reproductive capacity is winding down; the temporary hot flashes some women experience may be compared to the high-to-low voice register changes adolescent boys evidence when their reproductive capacity is gearing up. We no longer castrate young boys to preserve their male sopranos, nor should we treat hot flashes with a cancer-and-cholesterol pill (Seaman and Seaman, 1977, p. xi).

In a collection of feminist critiques, Grossman and Bart, two social scientists, make a similar claim in a chapter entitled "Taking Men Out of Menopause":

. . . [the] actions of the medical and pharmaceutical groups dramatize the sexism and general inhumanity of the male-dominated, profit oriented U.S. medical system. A "deficiency disease" was invented to serve a drug that could "cure" it, despite the suspicion that the drug caused cancer in women. That the suspicion has been voiced for so many years before anyone would investigate it is yet another example of how unimportant the well-being of women is to men who control research and drug companies who fund much of it (1979, p. 167).

The 1981 edition of *The Ms. Guide to a Woman's Health* warns women that "Estrogen replacement therapy (ERT) is a dangerously overused treatment. Avoid it if at all possible" (Cooke and Dworkin, 1981, p. 310).

Though most of the criticism has been voiced by younger feminists, some older women have also opposed ERT. Reitz referred to ERT as "The No. 1 Middle-Age Con" and proclaimed:

> I accept that I'm a healthy woman whose body is changing. No matter how many articles and books I read that tell me I'm suffering from a deficiency disease, I say I don't believe it. I have never felt more in control of my life than I do now and I feel neither deficient nor diseased. I think that people who are promoting this idea—that something is wrong with me because I am 50—have something to gain or are irresponsible or stupid (Reitz, 1977, p. 181).

Health-related associations and consumer groups have also joined feminists in their opposition to ERT. *Consumer Reports* (1976), the official publication of Consumers Union, published a lengthy article warning women of the risks; Citizens Health, Ralph Nader's organization, opposes (and regularly testifies against) ERT (Wolfe, 1979). Smaller groups such as Coalition For the Medical Rights of Women (Brown, 1978), and National Action Forum for Older Women (1979), have all warned women of the risks of ERT and advocated alternate treatment (diet, exercise, and vitamin supplements) for menopause. Menopause workshops and self-help groups have sprung up across the United States (Page, 1977).

After the 1975 cancer studies several feminist and consumer groups, including the National Women's Health Network and Consumers Union, began to pressure the FDA to warn consumers of the dangers of ERT. On July 22, 1977, after two years of public hearings, the FDA issued a ruling that a "patient package insert" (PPI), warning of the risk of cancer and other dangers, be included with every estrogen

and progesterine prescription. On October 5, 1977, in an effort to block this regulation, the Pharmaceutical Manufacturing Association—together with the American College of Obstetricians and Gynecologists, the National Association of Chain Drug Stores, the American Society of Internal Medicine, and various state and county medical societies—responded by filing a civil suit in the Wilmington, Delaware, Federal District Court against the FDA. The plaintiffs charged that the FDA lacked statutory authority to require the patient package insert warning, and that such a requirement was an unconstitutional interference with the practice of medicine. They also asserted that such a regulation is "arbitrary, capricious [and] an abuse of discretion" (*Pharmaceutical Manufacturers Association v. Food and Drug Administration*, 1980).

To represent the interests of women patients, the National Women's Health Network, Consumers Union, Consumers Federation of America, and Women's Equity Action League filed as interveners in the lawsuit in support of the FDA. Three years later, in 1980, Federal District Judge Walter K. Stapleton upheld the FDA decision, giving estrogen replacements the distinction of being one of only four classes of drugs which require such patient package inserts in the United States (*Pharmaceutical Manufacturers Association v. Food and Drug Administration*, 1980). Regulation, however, does not mean compliance, and the feminist victory appears more symbolic than instrumental. A 1979 FDA survey of 271 drug stores in 20 U.S. cities revealed that only 39 percent of all ERT prescriptions were accompanied by the required insert (Morris et al., 1980). Moreover, under the administration of President Ronald Reagan, the FDA has suspended all proposed PPI regulations and is reconsidering existing ones (National Women's Health Network, 1981).

Conclusion

In this article I have characterized the medical–feminist struggle over the collective definition of menopause as a stigma contest. Feminists have attempted to show that menopause is not an event that limits women's psychological or physical capacities, but a natural part of aging. Physicians have tried to explain the problems of middle-aged women through a medical model. In so viewing the life course, including menopause, physicians have tended to see problems experienced during menopause as either "all in the head" or the result of a deficiency disease, to be treated with tranquilizers or hormones.

The aging woman has a particularly vulnerable status in our society. She is no longer the object of adoration and romanticism that youthful women frequently are. Menopause usually comes at a time when children leave home, and husbands frequently seek younger sexual partners. Physical changes taking place in her body might be compounded, and negatively interpreted, by the loss of status and primary social role. Clearly, such women are vulnerable to the promise of a "youth" pill which purports to allay the aging process. Yet to blame all the problems that aging women experience on menopause is a classic case of blaming the victim. The medical model individualizes the problem, and deflects responsibility from the social structure which assigns aging women to a maligned and precarious status.

The vulnerable status of women makes fertile ground for medical imperialism. A health care system, based on fee-for-service, is conducive to defining more and more life events as illnesses. A disease definition of menopause has served the interests of both the medical profession and the pharmaceutical industry. Until these structural arrangements change, the hormone deficiency definition of menopause, or some equivalent to it, is likely to prevail.

Feminists, particularly those in the women's health movement (Ruzek, 1979) have exposed the sexism in women's health care. Publications such as *Our Bodies, Ourselves* (Boston Women's Health Collective, 1976) offered a new definition of women's role in health care. No longer

passive consumers of male-dominated medicine, women asserted the right to control their own bodies. Feminists in the health movement have begun to demystify menopause and have made it a topic for discussion. By making their stigma contest part of a broad-based social movement, feminists have been able to define women's health care as a social problem (Mauss, 1975).

Yet in their efforts to fight off the stigma of menopause, some feminists have inadvertently contributed to ageism. Most criticisms have been voiced by younger feminists who have not gone through menopause. Their main focus has been on the medicalization of childbirth and menstruation, and they have extrapolated their analysis to menopause without adequate appreciation of the problems of aging women. By emphasizing the natural and unproblematic nature of menopause, they have overlooked the minority of women who do need medical attention. Such women might feel shame or guilt for suffering through what others claim is normal or unproblematic (Posner, 1979).

Moreover, most feminist studies of menopause have ignored structural factors, restricting their analyses to ideological and social psychological issues. Most feminists in the health movement see women's oppression rooted in arguments of biological inferiority. Feminists have tried to settle the nature-nurture debate by showing that differences in socialization, not biology, account for women's inferior status. In their attempt to overthrow the dictum "biology is destiny," feminists have argued that menstruation, childbirth, and menopause are natural events and, in most cases, do not warrant medical intervention. They charge that myths surrounding these events function as social control. In so doing, feminists have attempted to substitute a new ideology (biology is irrelevant) for an old one (biology is destiny).

The women's health movement, largely middle-class, has approached the problems of women's health care from a point most visible

to the middle-class consumer: the private office of the gynecologist or psychiatrist. Focusing on doctor-patient interaction, they have advocated self-help outside the established health care system. Admirable though these actions are, they are not sufficient to change the collective status of women. Nor will the call by radical feminists for self-help, alternative health care accomplish this goal; it only takes the struggle to the margins of the established order (Fee, 1975).

Neither ideological nor social-psychological analyses challenge the private health care system or the economic and social infrastructure which support it. What is needed are studies which elucidate the structural affinities between the economics of health care and the status of women. Such scholarship might point the way toward more meaningful change.

Notes

1 Other U.S. studies claimed that ERT increased the risk of breast cancer, atherosclerosis, myocardial infarction, pulmonary emboli, thrombophlebitis, gall bladder disease, and diabetes (Gastel et al., 1979).

2 In Great Britain researchers are skeptical of the cancer link. They claim that sequential therapy (the addition of progestin for the last five to 13 days of a 20-to-30-day course of estrogen) would eliminate the potential risk of cancer. U.S. researchers claim that sequential treatment may not prevent endometrial cancer (Ziel, 1980: 451) and the dangers associated with progestins have not been fully evaluated (Gastel et al., 1979). British researchers also promote ERT for the prevention of osteoporosis (loss of bone mass), but U.S. researchers contend more research is needed on osteoporosis and, at this time, the established cancer risk outweighs the potential benefit of the treatment. For a discussion of the cancer and osteoporosis debates, see McCrea and Markle (1984).

3 The FDA has found menopausal estrogens effective only for the treatment of vasomotor symptoms and atrophic vaginitis, and probably effective for estrogen deficiency-induced osteoporosis, and

only when used in conjunction with other important therapeutic measures such as diet, calcium, physiotherapy, and good general health-promoting measures. Furthermore, the FDA states that estrogens are not effective for nervous symptoms or depression and should not be used to treat such conditions (Physicians Desk Reference, 1982:641).

4 Althouth the majority of U.S. feminists, particularly those in the women's health movement, have defined menopause as unproblematic, there are notable exceptions. For example, Posner (1979: 189) charges that feminists have been led into the ideological trap of denying their own hormones. Lock (1982) argues that physicians ought pay more attention to physiology, and not dismiss women's medical complaints as psychological. British feminists also want more medical services made available in the treatment of menstruation and menopause (McCrea and Markle, 1984; Sayers, 1982).

References

Berkow, R. (1980) The Merck Manual of Diagnosis and Therapy, 13th edn. Rahway, NJ: Merck and Company.

Boston Women's Health Collective (1976) Our Bodies, Ourselves. New York: Simon and Schuster.

Brody, J. (1975) Physicians' views unchanged on use of estrogen therapy. New York Times, December 5: 55.

Brown, S. (1978). The second forty years. Second Opinion, 1: 1–10.

Burke, L., Crosby, D., & Lao, C. (1978) Estrogen prescribing in menopause. Paper presented at the annual meeting of the American Public Health Association, Washington, D.C., November 2, 1977. Updated June 23, 1978.

Buxton, C. L. (1944) Medical therapy during the menopause. The Journal of Endocrinology, 12: 591–596.

Conrad, P., & Schneider, J. W. (1980) Deviance and Medicalization: From badness to sickness. St. Louis, MO: Mosby.

Consumer Reports (1976) Estrogen therapy: The dangerous road to Shangri La. Consumer Reports, 5: 642–645.

Cook, J. W. and Dodds, E. C. (1933) Sex hormones on cancer-producing compounds. Nature, 131: 205.

Cooke, C., & Dworkin, S. (1981) The Ms. Guide to a Woman's Health. New York: Berkeley Publishing.

Delaney, J., Lupton, M., & Toth, E. (1976) *The Curse*. New York: E. P. Dutton and Co.

Dosey, M., & Dosey, M. (1980) The climacteric women. *Patient Counseling and Health Education*, 2(First Quarter): 14–21.

Fee, E. (1975) Women and health care: A comparison of theories. *International Journal of Health Services*, 5: 397–415.

Freidson, E. (1970) *Profession of Medicine*. New York: Harper and Row.

Freidson, E. (1971) *The Professions and Their Prospects*. Beverly Hills, CA: Sage.

Gardner, W. U. (1944) Tumors in experimental animals receiving steroid hormones. *Surgery*, 16: 8.

Gastel, B., Coroni-Huntley, J., & Brody, J. (1979) Estrogen use and post-menopausal women: A basis for informed decisions. Summary Conclusion, National Institute on Aging Consensus Development Conference. Bethesda, Maryland, September 13–14.

Geist, S. H., & Spielman, F. (1932) Therapeutic value of theelin in menopause. *American Journal of Obstetrics and Gynecology*, 23: 701.

Goffman, E. (1963) *Stigma*. Englewood Cliffs, NJ: Prentice Hall.

Greenblatt, R. (1974) *The Menopausal Syndrome*. New York: Medcom Press.

Grossman, M., & Bart, P. (1979) Taking men out of menopause. In R. Hubbard, M. S. Henifin and B. Fried (Eds.), *Women Looking at Biology Looking at Women* (pp. 163–184). Boston: G. K. Hall and Co.

Gusberg, S. (1947) Precursors of corpus carcinoma estrogens and adenomatous hyperplasia. *American Journal of Obstetrics and Gynecology*, 54: 905–926.

Gusberg, S. (1980) Current concepts in cancer. *New England Journal of Medicine*, 302: 729–731.

Gusfield, J. (1966) *Symbolic Crusade*. Urbana, IL: University of Illinois Press.

Gusfield, J. (1967) Moral passage: The symbolic process in public designations of deviance. *Social Problems*, 15: 175–188.

Hoover, R., Gray, L., Cole, P. and MacMahon, B. (1976) Menopausal estrogens and breast cancer. *New England Journal of Medicine*, 295: 401–405.

Jern, H. (1973) *Hormone Therapy of the Menopause and Aging*. Springfield, IL: Charles C. Thomas Publishers.

Johnson, A. (1977) The risks of sex hormones as drugs. *Women and Health*, 1: 8–11.

Kaufman, S. (1967) *The Ageless Woman*. Englewood Cliffs, NJ: Prentice-Hall.

Landau, R. (1979) What you should know about estrogens. *Journal of the American Medical Association*, 241: 47–51.

Lock, M. (1982) Models and practice in medicine: Menopause as syndrome or life transition? *Culture, Medicine and Psychiatry*, 6: 261–280.

McCrea, F. (1981) The medicalization of normalcy? Changing definitions of menopause. Paper presented at the International Interdisciplinary Congress on Women, Haifa, Israel, December 28–January 1, 1982.

McCrea, F., & Markle, G. Estrogen replacement therapy in the United States and Great Britain: Different answers to the press same questions? *Social Studies of Science*.

McKinley, S. M., & Jeffreys, M. (1974) The menopausal syndrome. *British Journal of Preventive and Social Medicine*, 28: 108–115.

Mauss, A. (1975) *Social Problems as Social Movements*. Philadelphia, PA: J. B. Lippincott.

Meier, P. and Landau, R. (1980) Estrogen replacement therapy. *Journal of the American Medical Association*, 243: 1658.

Mintz, M. and Cohn, V. (1977) Hawking the estrogen fix. *The Progressive*, 41: 24–25.

Modell, W. (1980) *Drugs of Choice, 1980–1981*. St. Louis, MO: Mosby.

Morris, L., Meyers, A., Gibbs, P. and Lao, C. (1981) Estrogen PPIs: A survey. *American Pharmacy*, 20(June): 318–322.

National Action Forum for Older Women (1979) *Forum. Newsletter of the National Action Forum for Older Women*, 2(2): 8.

Novak, E., & Yui, E. (1936) Relation of endometrial hyperplasia to adenocarcinoma of the uterus. *American Journal of Obstetrics and Gynecology*, 321: 596–674.

Page, J. (1977) *The Other Awkward Age: Menopause*. Berkeley, CA: Ten Speed Press.

Perry, I. H., & Ginzton, L. L. (1937) The development of tumors in female mice treated with 1:2:5:6 dibenzanthracone and theelin. *American Journal of Cancer*, 29: 680.

Physicians' Desk Reference (1982) *Physicians' Desk Reference*, 36th edn. Oradell, NJ: Medical Economics Company, Inc.

Posner, J. (1979) It's all in your head: Feminist and medical models of menopause (strange bedfellows). Sex Roles, 5: 179–190.

Reitz, R. (1977) Menopause: A Positive Approach. Radnor, PA: Chilton Book Co.

Ruzek, S. B. (1979) The Women's Health Movement. New York: Praeger.

Sayers, J. (1982) Biological Politics. London: Tavistock Publications, Ltd.

Schur, E. (1980) The Politics of Deviance. Englewood Cliffs, NJ: Prenctice Hall.

Seaman, B., & Seaman, G. (1977) Women and the Crisis in Sex Hormones. New York: Rawson Association Publishers, Inc.

Smith, D. D., Ross, P., Thompson Donovan, J. and Herrmann, W. L. (1975) Association of exogenous estrogen and endometrial carcinoma. New England Journal of Medicine, 293: 1164–1167.

Solomon, J. (1972) Menopause: A rite of passage. Ms., (December) 1: 16–18.

U.S. Bureau of the Census (1975) Pharmaceutical Preparations, Except Biologicals. Current Industrial Reports, Series Ma-28G(73)-1. Washington, DC: U.S. Government Printing Office.

Weinstein, M. (1980) Estrogen use in post-menopausal women-costs, risks and benefits. New England Journal of Medicine, 303: 308–316.

Weiss, N. S., Szekely, D., & Austin, D. F. (1976) Increasing incidence of endometrial cancer in the United States. New England Journal of Medicine, 294: 1259–1262.

Wilson, R. (1962) Roles of estrogen and progesterine in breast and genital cancer. Journal of the American Medical Association, 182: 327–331.

Wilson, R. (1966a) Feminine Forever. New York: M. Evans.

Wilson, R. (1966b) A key to staying young. Look, (January): 68–73.

Wilson, R. and Wilson, T. (1963) The fate of nontreated post-menopausal woman: A plea for the maintenance of adequate estrogen from puberty to the grave. Journal of the American Geriatrics Society, 11: 347–361.

Wolfe, S. (1979) Women in Science and Technology Equal Opportunity Act, 1979. Testimony before the Committee on Labor and Human Resources, Subcommittee on Health and Scientific Research. 96th Congress, 1st session. Washington, DC: U.S. Government Printing Office.

Ziel, H. K. (1980) The negative side of long-term post-menopausal estrogen therapy. In L. Lasagna (Ed.), Controversies in Therapeutics (pp. 450–452). Philadelphia, PA: W. B. Saunders.

Ziel, H. K., & Finkle, W. D. (1975) Increased risks of endometrial carcinoma among users of conjugated estrogens. New England Journal of Medicine, 293: 1167–1170.

Ziel, H. K., and Finkle, W. D. (1976) Association of estrone with the development of endometrial carcinoma. American Journal of Obstetrics and Gynecology, 134: 735–740.

Case Cited

Pharmaceutical Manufacturers Association v. Food and Drug Administration, 484 F. Supp. 1179, 1980.

Chapter 21

Ian Hacking

THE LOOPING EFFECTS OF HUMAN KINDS

What are Human Kinds?

"**H**uman kinds" is such an ugly turn of phrase that, as Auguste Comte said of *sociologie*, no one else would ever want to use it. I do not intend to pick out a definite and clearly bounded class of classifications. I mean to indicate kinds of people, their behaviour, their condition, kinds of action, kinds of temperament or tendency, kinds of emotion, and kinds of experience. I use the term "human kinds" to emphasize kinds—the systems of classification—rather than people and their feelings. Although I intend human kinds to include kinds of behaviour, act, or temperament, it is kinds of people that concern me. That is, kinds of behaviour, act, or temperament are what I call human kinds if we take them to characterize kinds of people.

However, I do not mean any kinds of people. I choose the label "human kinds" for its inhumane ring, and mean the kinds that are studied in the marginal, insecure, but enormously powerful human and social sciences. An operational definition of an insecure science is: a science whose leaders say they are in quest of a paradigm, or have just found a paradigm. Insecurity is consistent with immense power.

By human kinds I mean kinds about which we would like to have systematic, general, and accurate knowledge; classifications that could be used to formulate general truths about people; generalizations sufficiently strong that they seem like laws about people, their actions, or their sentiments. We want laws precise enough to predict what individuals will do, or how they will respond to attempts to help them or to modify their behaviour. The model is that of the natural sciences. Only one kind of causality is deemed relevant: efficient causation. One event brings about another, although the causal laws may be only probabilistic laws of tendency.

The term "human kind" is patterned after the philosopher's "natural kind", and so I have to make some disclaimers. It is hard to believe that a philosopher could be so mealy-mouthed about natural kinds. I have no doubt that nature has kinds which we distinguish. Some seem fairly cosmic: quarks, probably genes, possibly cystic fibrosis. Others are mundane: mud, the common cold, headlands, sunsets. The common cold is as real as cystic fibrosis, and sunsets are as real as quarks. More law-like regularities are known about mud than quarks—known to youths who play football, parents who do the family laundry, and to mud engineers on oil rig sites. The regularities about mud do not have profound consequences for theoreticians. That does not make mud any the less a natural kind of stuff.

Nelson Goodman has used the happy phrase "relevant kinds" in which he includes "such artificial kinds as musical works, psychological experiments and types of machinery". As far as I am concerned, natural kinds are relevant kinds that we find in nature. Are the varieties of plants and animals that we owe to horticulturalists and stock breeders "natural" by now? For me, plutonium is a natural kind, even though humans made it. There are many distinctions to be made among the natural kinds, including historical ones. Psycholinguists debate whether children innately distinguish the artefactual from the natural, or the mechanical from the living. On a quite different level there is undoubtedly a sense in which some kinds are more cosmic (the word is Quine's) than others. Perhaps nature and its laws are such that some kinds are more truly fundamental than others. Graceless philosophers repeat Plato's words out of context and talk of carving nature at her joints. Does nature have ultimate joints? For present purposes I am indifferent to all such questions—metaphysical, psycholinguistic, or historical. This is because they do not matter to the distinctions that I do wish to notice between human kinds and natural kinds.

Since I am so tolerant about natural kinds, should I not count human kinds among the natural kinds? For a certain convenience I shall restrict human kinds to kinds that are, at least at first sight, peculiar to people in a social setting. I do not deny that people are natural or that human societies are part of nature. For convenience, I follow the custom of calling something natural only when it is not peculiar to people in their communities. A great many types of attributes of people apply in the world at large or at least to other living beings: mass, longevity, distribution of digestive organs, the pancreatic enzymes such as amylopsin, trypsin, and steapsin, or the structure of the genome. Many items that occur in the scientific study of human beings present no significant contrast with other kinds that we find in nature. There is a proper tension here, because one thrust of research into human kinds is to biologize them. Drunkards form a human kind; according to one school of thought, apparently favoured by the editor of *Science*, alcoholism is carried by a gene. Five years

ago I copied from a doctor's office the statement. "We have learned more about this illness in the past five years than in the past five hundred years and it is now evident that alcoholism and other drug additions are truly psychosocial biogenetic diseases". Suicide is a kind of human behaviour; it was proposed late in 1990 that it too has a genetic component. These are instances not so much of what Imre Lakatos called research programmes as of what Gerald Holton called themata. Holton gives atomism in its successive manifestations (Leucippus, Lucretius, Boyle, Dalton, and onwards) as an example of a thema. Equally old and powerful is the idea that we acquire knowledge of humanity by replacing human kinds by physiological or mechanical or neuroelectrical or biochemical ones.

There are many more tensions—some in the philosophy of the natural and some in the methodology of the biological. Yet I think that there is little difficulty in picking out characteristic human kinds. When I speak of human kinds, I mean (i) kinds that are relevant to some of us, (ii) kinds that primarily sort people, their actions, and behaviour, and (iii) kinds that are studied in the human and social sciences, i.e. kinds about which we hope to have knowledge. I add (iv) that kinds of people are paramount; I want to include kinds of human behaviour, action, tendency, etc. only when they are projected to form the idea of a kind of person. Homosexuality provides us with a perhaps all too familiar example. It is quite widely asserted that, although same-sex acts are common in most human societies, the idea of "the homosexual" as a kind of person came into being only late in the nineteenth century as homosexual behaviour became an object of scientific scrutiny. If this were correct, then homosexual behaviour would be what I am calling here a "human kind" only late in the nineteenth century, even though there has been plenty of pederasty, for example, at all times and places, for only at that time was this kind of behaviour taken as an indication of a kind of person.

In important personal relationships we seldom think or feel directly in terms of human kinds. In friendship, love, and animosity we care about all that is particular, unusual, intimate, and circumstantial, all that is glimpsed or shared or felt glancingly—in short, all that is caught in the nuance of the novel rather than the classifications of the scientist. One person is trusting, another gentle, a third selfish and arrogant. One, who although forgetful is responsive and enthusiastic, has a friend who is an insensitive busybody. We know a great deal about such kinds of people, but we do not profess scientific knowledge about them. We neither make surveys that count their proportions in a given population, nor subject them to factor analysis. Yet these are the kinds that matter to us—the kinds we use to organize our thoughts about our companions, friends, and loved ones, not to mention those whom we try to avoid. Since they also matter to employers, teachers, and the military, psychologists devise tests that use questions often recalling these familiar traits. The results are tabulated or summarized to form "profiles" or "personal inventories" that then become human kinds. They are digests of what matters in intimacy, but they acquire the abstraction of the sciences or impersonal management.

Yet human kinds are not so irrelevant to us as people. Straightforward and well-established human kinds studied in the social sciences *do* affect intensely personal concerns. If you see someone whom you love (or see yourself) as of a kind, that may change your entire set of perceptions. Human kinds usually present themselves as scientific and hence as value-free, but they have often been brought into being by judgements of good and evil. Sociology of the numerical sort began by measuring the incidence of behaviour such as suicide. Durkheim's classic and originating work *Suicide* could draw upon 80 years of studies. Suicide was tabulated because it was a Bad Act, perhaps the very worst, beyond the possibility of repentance and even forgiveness. A body of knowledge about suicide changed beliefs about what kind of deed it was, and hence its moral evaluation: "an attempted suicide is a cry for help". Your attitude to a friend who attempts suicide will be different from that which your great-grandparents would have had. Suicides in novels today are not what they were at the time of young Werther or Heinrich Kleist, partly because science has made suicide into a human kind.

Human kinds are of many categories. I use the word "category" in an old fashioned way, which is also the colloquial way. A category is a tree of classifications, or else the most general classification at the top of such a tree. Many authorities, ranging from cognitive scientists to psycholinguists, now use "category" as a synonym for "class" as in George Lakoff's title, *Women, fire and dangerous things: What categories show about the human mind*. Women-fire-and-dangerous-things is a class, or kind, distinguished by an Australian people, but Lakoff calls it a category. I do not. Race, gender, native language, nationality, type of employment, and age cohort are all what I call categories. The experts most versed in these categories work out of census bureaux, institutions whose modern form is coeval with quantitative social science. Indeed I willingly extend my grouping, human kinds, to include any of the kinds enumerated by the census, or at least those kinds when endowed with their social connotations. Say, to abbreviate too much, that gender is the social meaning of sex—the category of sex not being peculiar to human beings, but the category of gender being peculiar to humans in a society. I follow tradition surprisingly closely in all this. Philosophers took "natural kind" as a term of art after J. S. Mill. As soon as he had introduced his idea of a *real Kind*, he asked whether the sexes and races were real Kinds. (He hoped not. His programme was anti-sexist and anti-racist). These two human categories, race and gender, have been obsessively discussed of late. Our thoughts about them are so redolent of ideology that I shall leave them on one side. Conclusions about human kinds are indeed relevant to those categories, but we would be misled about human kinds if we followed Mill and used race and gender as our core examples. The very relationship between science, and race or gender, is unclear. I have defined human kinds as the objects of the insecure sciences, as the kinds about which we would like to have knowledge. I took for granted that those sciences are modelled on natural science, particularly in their conception of causality. That was what Mill was talking about. However, there is a strong present prejudice against making race the object of science. A few forthright spokesmen like Michael Dummett make plain that we do not want the knowledge that we might find out. The more familiar pusillanimous complaint is that race science is bad science. In the case of gender, many outspoken feminists claim knowledge, but reject a knowledge patterned on causal natural science. These important issues would take us aside from my main topic.

I have mentioned kinds "with their social meaning"—an obscure phrase. To illustrate, take teen-age pregnancy. That is as determinate a classification as could be. You are teen-aged, female, pregnant, and (unwritten premise) unmarried. There is a rigorous definition, then, with succinct chronological, physiological and legal clauses. If we make "teen-age" precise and adapt "unmarried", then this concept can be applied in many cultures unlike our own. However, it became a relevant kind only at a certain moment in American history. After 1967 it was the subject of interminable sociological study and debate. Recently the cultural meaning of the term has switched sufficiently that a euphemism has been introduced by sociologists: early parenting. Teen-age pregnancy—the word, and also the idea with a certain set of implications—reared its ugly head in the white American suburbs of the 1960s. Early parenting connotes black urban ghettos of the 1990s. Thus far we have an idea and no knowledge, but once the idea was in motion experts arrived to

determine a knowledge and to transform it. The classification "teen-age pregnancy" or "early parenting" is completely grounded in nature, but is a human kind—and is the subject of social science—only in a certain social context. There is a similarity to—and a difference from another human kind of person—the adolescent. Adolescence cannot be fully grounded in nature. Even if we define it as beginning with first menarche/ejaculation, there is nothing in nature beyond a social context that signals its end. Anna Freud said that we owe the discovery of adolescence to psychoanalysis. Historians of developmental psychology locate its discovery elsewhere. Nevertheless there is a remarkable agreement that whatever grander social changes made adolescence possible, the adolescent exists as a kind of person thanks to the social sciences. The first major work on adolescence was the two volume treatise by G. Stanley Hall (1904), the man who is commonly called the founder of American experimental psychology. He called it *Adolescence: its psychology and its relations to physiology, anthropology, sociology, sex, crime, religion and education.* You might think that this title is exhaustive, but it is not quite. After over 1200 pages we reach a long final chapter, "Ethnic psychology and pedagogy, or adolescent races and their treatment". We find that one third of the human race are "adolescents of adult size".

Those were the bad old days, of course. To fix ideas further, I shall take two up-to-date human kinds and a recently proposed causal law that connects them. Child abuse is a kind of human behaviour. It breaks up into several kinds, including sexual abuse, physical abuse, neglect, and, a current topic of fierce controversy in North America, sadistic cult abuse (read Satanic rituals). Child abuse is a kind that has been remarkably malleable. It has connections with cruelty to children, a classic kind of behaviour brought to the fore in Europe and America about 120 years ago. But the present classification, child abuse, began exactly 30 years ago with battered baby syndrome, took incest and sexual abuse under its wing 18 years ago, and picked up cruel ritual cult abuse 5 years ago. The recent trajectory is primarily American with European classifications following loosely in step (Hacking 1991, 1992c).

Child abuse certainly fits my rough and ready criteria for being a human kind.

1   In many quarters today, it is a highly relevant kind.
2   It is peculiar to people, even when we draw some analogies to some sorts of primate behaviour.
3   It is a kind of behaviour about which we would like to have knowledge, for example to prevent child abuse and to help abused children.
4   We have an inclination to project the kind of behaviour to the person, i.e., we think that there are child abusers, that abusive parents may be a type of parent.

We can make an even stronger statement about child abuse. The Center for Advanced Study in the Behavioral Sciences at Stanford University liked, and perhaps still likes, to use the epithet "cutting edge" for work conducted under its auspices. An operational definition of a cutting-edge human kind would be: there is at least one professional society of experts dedicated to studying it; there are regular conferences, one of which is major and a number of which are more specialized; there is at least one recently established professional journal to which the authorities contribute (and which helps define who the authorities are). We have the International Society for the Prevention of Child Abuse and Neglect, a great many conferences, and the journal *Child Abuse and Neglect*, among others. Child abuse is a cutting-edge human kind.

Child abusers are all too common. A much rarer kind of person is the one suffering from what is now called multiple personality disorder (Hacking 1992). These people used to be very rare indeed, and they usually suffered from two,

or perhaps three or four, alternative personalities; one personality was usually amnesic for another. There has been an epidemic of multiple personalities in North America, starting in the early 1970s; the 9th International Conference on the topic was attended by 800 professionals (psychiatrists, psychologists, social workers), many of whom have case loads of over 40 multiples a year. The face of multiplicity has changed a great deal in the past 20 years. It is now commonplace for clinicians to have patients with 25 alter personalities. This whole discourse takes place under a larger rubric of "dissociative behaviour". Dissociation was first named by Pierre Janet during the French wave of multiples that started in Bordeaux in 1875, but has been retrieved only recently. In the inner circles of dissociation experts, Janet is revered while Freud is cast out.

Many psychiatrists, particularly those with a medical/biochemical/neurological approach to mental illness, are dubious or even cynical about multiple personality. They argue that multiples are a cultural artefact. Now, if I had said (as so many philosophers do say) that human kinds must in some sense be indubitably "real", and perhaps even cross-culturally cosmic, I should have been obliged to discuss this opposition. Instead, I made some disclaimers not only about the human but also about the natural. I do believe that some psychiatrists, the media, a wing of the women's movement, concern about sexual abuse of children, and much else have brought about the present prevalence of multiple personality disorder. That does not make the malady any less real. It is a condition with associated behaviour that afflicts a significant number of people who at present are crying out for help. It is a human kind, and a cutting-edge human kind to boot. There is the International Society for the Study of Multiple Personality and Dissociation. There is an annual international conference and many regional conferences. The journal *Dissociation* is about to enter its fifth year of publication.

I stated that we want knowledge about human kinds. There has been a remarkable breakthrough in thinking about multiple personality. The cause of this disorder is now known to people who work in the field. Multiple personality is the consequence of repeated trauma early in childhood, almost always involving sexual abuse. This fact is so accepted among workers in the field that many regard it as almost definitional. This causal knowledge is deeply incorporated into theories of the disorder. The various alters represent dissociated ways of coping with particular experienced trauma. This in turn has had a great impact on methods of treatment, which now focus on abreaction of the trauma through the voices of the various alters which may in time become co-conscious, collaborative, and finally integrated. Thanks to media exposure, particularly on afternoon television talk shows that appeal to lower-class women who empathize with the oppressed and the bizarre, this scientific knowledge is very widely disseminated in the USA. The details are the property of experts, but the general structure is remarkably common knowledge.

My example is sensational but serves to fix ideas. Despite its role in social rhetoric and politics of numerous stripes, child abuse was first presented and is still intended to be a "scientific" concept. Of course, there are demarcation disputes. Which science? Medicine, psychiatry, sociology, psychology, social work, jurisprudence, or self-help? Whatever the standpoint, there are plenty of authorities firmly convinced that there are important truths about child abuse, for example "most abusers were abused as children". Research and experiment should reveal them. We hope that cause and effect are relevant, that we can find predictors of future abuse, that we can explain it, that we can prevent it, and that we can determine its consequences and counteract them. For example, it is held that abusive mothers have often not bonded adequately to their children, and that premature babies in incubators are at risk of inadequate bonding. This causal hypothesis leads authorities to establish elaborate bonding rituals in maternity hospitals.

It might be thought that child abuse is such a complex concept that questions of developmental psychology or the theory of cognition could not arise. We are considering how a social organization makes and moulds an idea, not about concept acquisition in children. Quite the contrary. Many American jurisdictions introduced early training to enable children to recognize and report incipient abuse. Two years ago California rescinded these laws, on the basis of declarations by expert witnesses, based on Piagetian grounds, that children could not understand these ideas. There is now a back-backlash contesting this cognitive claim.

On the score of being scientific, a different type of issue emerges. Perhaps we fail to help children (some say) because all our endeavours assume that we are dealing with a scientific kind? This worry has been expressed in terms of the "medicalization" of child abuse. Child abuse is not for the doctors, even if paediatricians did first sound the alert with battered baby syndrome. Thus far, the complaint is only about the type of expert, not about the very possibility of expertise. In general, the anti-experts usually claim that they are the true experts: the social workers defy the police, the psychologists confront the judiciary, etc. Multiple personality is a case of yet another type of concern about scientism. Some critics contend that there is no such thing as multiple personality disorder (I have heard it called "the UFO of psychiatry") and that multiple behaviour results from interaction with doctors or, more recently, from sensationalist reports in the media. Nevertheless the debate is left to experts. This or that group claims to have knowledge about what really ails the troubled patients and how they could be treated better.

Thus what I call human kinds begin in the hands of scientists of various stripes. Human kinds live there for a while. A while? My example of the homosexual foreshadows something to be discussed later. People of the kind may rise up against the experts. The known may overpower the knowers.

I have stated that *we* want laws precise enough to predict what individuals will do. Or *we* want to know how people of a kind will respond to attempts to help them or to modify their behaviour. I have stated "we" would like all this, typically in order to help "them". I made these statements because that is what the social sciences have been up to since their inception. The search for human kinds that conform to psychological or social laws is inextricably intertwined with prediction and reform. These aims can be perverted, but they have generally been well-intentioned when seen from the vantage point of the reformers. Groups of experts now collaborate and say that together they are members of the "helping professions": social workers, therapists, parole officers, policemen, judges, psychiatrists, teachers, "Ph.D. psychologists", paediatricians. They try to distinguish kinds of people or behaviour that are deviant. They invite more theoretical and foundational studies on which to base their practical work. Sociologists and statisticians form and test lawlike conjectures about people of those kinds. Such knowledge enables the front line to interfere and intervene so as to help more effectively and predictably. Or so the sciences present themselves: cynics suspect that there is no knowledge to be had, and that these forms of knowledge legitimate the use of power.

Why are my examples so unattractive? I seem to have in mind a rather shady bunch of kinds, marginal human kinds, kinds about which we claim or hope to have systematic knowledge, kinds that are, loosely, topics for actual or prospective sciences. But not real social science! I could develop the argument that what I call human kinds are at the historical root of sociology—the science of normality and deviance. Even if I am correct, should not "human kinds" by now serve as the generic name for the classifications

used in the social sciences—the *sciences humaines*, or perhaps even *Geisteswissenschaften*? What then of the classifications made in anthropology, linguistics, economics, and history? Why lay such emphasis on the sciences of deviancy, social pathology, healing, and control?

I shall evade the question (and the historical or archaeological response) by saying that I am choosing my own type of causal understanding to think about. I fix on a certain type of practical causality. By human kinds I mean kinds of people and their behaviour which (it is hoped) can enter into practical laws—laws that if we knew them we would use to change present conditions, and predict what would ensue. We want the right classification—the correct sorting of child abuse or teen-age pregnancy—so that confronted by abusive parents or pregnant teenagers we can embark on a course of action that will change them for the better and will prevent others from joining their ranks. We do not want to know the "structure" of teen-age pregnancy in the fascinating but abstract way in which we want to know the structure of kinship among a certain people, or the structure of the modal auxiliaries in their language. We want principles according to which we can interfere, intervene, help, and improve. The closest comparison within the social sciences would be with economics. The applied economists say that they want to make things better, but their kinds are not usually what I call human kinds. Most of them are at least one remove from individual people and their actions. The bank rate and the money supply depend upon what some people do, but they are not kinds of people.

I have been trying to make vivid the concept of a human kind. There is one last general point to make. Which comes first, the classification or the causal connections between kinds? There are two coarse pictures of concept formation. In one, people first make certain distinctions and then learn the properties and causal relationships between distinguished classes. In another, causal relationships are recognized between individuals, and these relationships are used to distinguish classes. I believe that my fellow philosophers are the chief sinners in cleaving to one or other of these extreme pictures. Whatever conclusion be urged about infant cognition, it is plain that in later life recognition and expectation are of a piece. Or, to put it linguistically, to acquire and use a name for any kind is, among other things, to be willing to make generalizations and form expectations about things of that kind. We should take for granted that guessing at causes goes hand in hand with increasingly precise definition.

To take two examples which are unfavourable to this theme, suicide and teen-age pregnancy have been with us always, and with many another society. Hence one might have the picture of first there being the kind of human behaviour or condition, and then the knowledge. That is not the case. The kind and the knowledge grow together. At the beginning of the nineteenth century people were still debating the noble suicide of Cato the Elder, but soon suicide was to be defined as "a kind of madness" with numerous subkinds, all tended over by the right sort of medical man. Suicides were sorted by their conjectured causes. When we turn to child abuse, it sounds as if it were a classification of behaviour preceding any knowledge. But this is not the case. It emerged in 1961–1962 in company with a quite specific body of knowledge—paediatric X-rays (which showed unexpected healed fractures of babies' arms and legs). The technology of the rapidly declining profession of infant radiology was revived to define "battered baby syndrome", and doctors asserted in powerful public statements that they were in control of the treatment and prevention of abusive behaviour. Cause, classification, and intervention were of a piece.

What's so Special about Human Kinds?

My phrase "human kind" is patterned after "natural kind". Evidently I think that human kinds are importantly different from natural kinds. In this section I shall do three things.

1   I shall sympathetically state the idea to which I am opposed: that human kinds are, at worst, messy natural kinds.

2   I shall make plain that I am not arguing anything remotely like either a *Verstehen* or a constructionist position. Yes, I think that the human differs from the natural, but not because what I call human kinds are to be understood hermeneutically rather than explained by causal principles. Yes, I think that the human differs from the natural, but not because human kinds are social constructions while natural kinds are discovered in nature.

3   I shall state the difference between natural and human kinds that interests me. I do not argue that it is the only difference. Perhaps the *Verstehen* and the construction distinctions are both right, but they are not mine. They are deep. Mine is shallow.

Natural and Human

The modern phrase "natural kind" resonates with antique controversies. Does nature have kinds, or are they of our making? If nature has kinds, do those kinds themselves have natures (essences)? Whatever stance we take on these issues, another arises. Given the aspirations of those sciences that investigate human kinds, will not something be a "real", or at any rate a useful human kind, only if it is a natural kind?

The positivist version of this idea proceeds roughly as follows. If we want to obtain knowledge about people and their behaviour, we have to make correct distinctions. Only if we sort correctly will we be able to formulate descriptive law-like statements. But that fact is not peculiar to the human sciences. In any science we must discover what the natural kinds are. That involves rigorous exploration, experimentation, conjecture, and refutation. As we hone our causal hypotheses, we sharpen our classifications, and approach closer and closer to the kinds that are found in nature. The chief difference between natural and human kinds is that the human kinds often make sense only within a certain social context. But even there we constantly strive to go behind the phenomena. Where once we had descriptive criminology, now we have genes for violence and we are working on the genetic component of suicide.

The positivist supposes that the idea of a natural kind is clear and timeless. Here is a historicist version of the view that the human must be the natural. The idea of a natural kind (it is proposed) is not timeless but has evolved during the history of Western science. Long before the advent of the natural sciences, kinds played a major role in the development of early technological civilizations. Sowing and reaping, breeding and baking, mining and melting have all needed an ability to pick out the right kinds. The kinds of animals, vegetables, and minerals that came to be named, cultivated, and created are the very kinds that philosophers came to call natural kinds. Some features of them have been invaluable as we have learned how to alter, improve, control, or guard against nature. The different theories about these kinds, whether in Aristotle, Locke, Mill, or Hilary Putnam, are owl-of-Minerva state of the art. That is, they effectively correspond to the level of technological expertise and scientific mastery current at the time that they were proposed. Each author thought that he was giving a timeless account of universals, or sorts (Locke), or real Kinds (Mill), or kind terms (Putnam). But each obediently represented a particular state of mastery of the non-human world, so that when we read these authors, we read a précis that could have been headed "natural kinds as we know them today". The chief source of the differences among these canonical writings is that they represent different stages in the growth of Western knowledge. The concept "natural kind" (by whatever name) is not impugned. We are reminded only that this idea is (like everything else) historical and evolving.

The history of human kinds will prove (continues the historicist) to be similar and indeed part of the story. We find attention to suicide, incest, cruelty to children, and even teen-age pregnancy in many places and times. Some scholars urge that demonic possession, trance states, and shamanism are "the same kind of condition" as multiple personality disorder, perhaps even deploying distinct sites in the brain. Human kinds require a fairly specific social organization for their existence. Teen-age pregnancy cannot exist until unmarried teen-age girls form a distinct group who are not supposed to be pregnant. The idea of juvenile delinquency depends partly on the family, on views of dependency, and on how age cohorts are structured. Nevertheless, there may be some human kinds that are of more general application than others.

We have (the historicist concludes) slowly come to a correct understanding of the idea of a law of nature—we have passed from Aristotelian essences through positivist instrumentalism, and to some extent back again to universal laws of causation and symmetry. In much the same way we will come to a correct understanding of laws of human beings. We could only do so, perhaps, when our idea of law had passed from the deterministic to the probabilistic, when we had created a new type of science geared to normalcy and deviation from the norm, when (just as essences gave way to law-like natural kinds) the idea of human nature had been displaced by the idea of normal people (Hacking 1990). The right laws about human beings have been slow in coming, and we have only just begun to come to grips with human kinds that will prove to be useful. But human kinds will in the end be a subclass of natural kinds. That will not leave things the same. The inclusion of human kinds within natural kinds will be one further step in the evolution of our causal understanding of nature.

You will have expected, from my early profession of indifference to any particular theory about natural kinds, that I do not want to conduct a stale argument with the positivist view, that all good human science is natural science, and that all good human kinds will be made into natural kinds. I take issue with the far more sensitive historicist view. It is the right view about philosophies of natural kinds, but it is wrong about the end of the story.

Understanding, Construction

I am liable to be misunderstood. I shall be thought to be arguing for old theses, not for a new one. I have to make plain that whatever cleavage may result from my analysis, it is not one that has been much discussed. I do not argue for or imply either of two extremely important-sounding theses. I do not contend that the natural sciences want explanation while the human sciences demand understanding. I do not urge that human kinds are constructed while natural kinds are not.

The *Verstehen* dispute has partly to do with methodology, a subject that I abhor. There is an immense body of argument to the effect that quite distinct methods befit the natural and the human sciences, the one aiming at explanation and the other at understanding. I believe that there are some deep insights on the *Verstehen* side of the argument, but here they are irrelevant. That is because I have defined human kinds as finding their place in bodies of knowledge patterned after the efficient causation of the natural sciences. I am not about to say that human kinds are a horrible mistake—the error of striving for control rather than understanding.

We do not have the choice not to use human kinds, and human kinds (as I have defined the idea) are causal and instrumental. We are stuck with human kinds that demand causal analysis rather than *Verstehen* or meanings. They are part of what we mean by knowledge about people. It may be a pleasant romantic fantasy to think of abandoning or replacing the instrumental human sciences, but that is not possible. They are not just part of our system of knowledge; they are part of what we take knowledge to be. They are also our system of government, our way of organizing ourselves; they have become the great stabilizers of the Western post-manufacturing welfare state that thrives on service industries. The methodology of making "studies" to detect law-like regularities and tendencies is not just our way of finding out what's what; "studies" generate consensus, acceptance, and intervention. Although the conscious aims of the social sciences are knowledge and helping, the function served is that of preserving and adapting the status quo.

I now turn to the other way in which I might be understood. I do not claim that human kinds are somehow constructed while natural kinds are somehow given. Here I try to take absolutely no view on the constructionist controversies that swirl around us. I cannot exactly take no notice, because I have found that the anti-constructionist ("realist", for short) says that all good human kinds are (real) natural kinds, while the social constructionist says that everything is social and so the natural is social.

I take courage from the fact that the most compelling social constructionist arguments about kinds are about high class "high tech" natural kinds. I think of Latour's first book (with Steven Woolgar), *Laboratory life: the (social) construction of a scientific fact*—the word "social" was in the 1979 edition but deleted from the 1986 edition on the ground that everything is social. The book is about the discovery to the chemical structure of a tripeptide important to the hypothalamus, to metabolism, and to maturation. Or I think of Andy Pickering's *Constructing quarks*. These authors contend, among many other things, that it is misleading to talk of scientific discoveries. The facts in question were constructed by a microsociological process, and in an important sense did not exist before the incidents described.

My strategy is willingly to swerve to the left and side with the constructionists. Yes, facts are socially constructed, and so are the kinds about which there are facts. But within the domain of social constructions, I can still claim that there is an important difference between quarks and tripeptides on the one hand, and what I call human kinds on the other. Hearing an uproar to my right I then turn to the realists and willingly agree that multiple personality disorder and adolescence are just as real as electricity and sulphuric acid; Anna Freud claims the discovery of adolescence for psychoanalysis, and the discovery of the phenomenon of dissociation is claimed for Pierre Janet. Who am I to resist such claims to fame, except on petty points that perhaps somebody else made the discovery?

Hence for present purposes I operate as if there were no vital contradiction between realism and constructionism. Teen-age pregnancy is as "real" as could be, with rigorous defining characteristics. It is also aptly described as socially constructed as a human kind at a certain point in American history. Likewise, children were abused before "child abuse". The history of the concept in the past three decades displays social making and moulding if anything could. This example has the fortuitous advantage that some of the more vociferous social constructionists, who urge that almost anything is a social construction, say (without noticing the switch) exactly the opposite about child abuse. It is, they rightly say, a real evil that the family and the state covered up. Our discovery of the prevalence of child abuse is a powerful step forward in Western awareness, they say. I agree. Child abuse is a real evil, and it was so before being socially constructed as a human kind. Neither reality nor construction should be in question.

I do not mean to imply that no construction–realism issues are important for human kinds. They do matter, but only in a specific context. Their significance is independent of inflated all-purpose general philosophical themes. The most

carefully worked-out example, i.e. what has been called the social constructionist controversy about homosexuality, has mattered deeply to the people who were classified. It was important to one party to maintain that "the homosexual" as a "kind of person" is a social construct, chiefly of psychiatry and jurisprudence. It was important for others to insist that some people in every era have been sexually and emotionally attracted chiefly to people of their own sex. There are endless variants on these themes. Stein (1992) (in an essay in his collection *Forms of desire*) has made the appropriate conceptual distinctions, and thereby established several ways in which essentialist and constructionist attitudes are not only compatible but also mutually supporting.

Looping

How then may natural kinds differ from what I call human kinds? I do accept, but wish to downplay, one fundamental difference. Human kinds are laden with values. Caked mud and polarized electrons may be good or bad depending on what you want to do with them, but child abuse is bad and multiple personality is a disorder to be healed.

It is the shibboleth of science that it is value-neutral. Throughout the history of the social sciences there has been a strident insistence on the distinction between fact and value. That is a give-away, for the natural sciences have seldom had to insist upon this distinction. On the contrary, elderly natural scientists regularly regret that there are not more values to be found in the natural sciences. Should we not argue that we are moving closer to the mind of God, and therefore to the Good? In social science things go differently. There is the clarion call for facts, facts, and more facts. Only with facts, and generalizations inferred therefrom, can the social scientist serve the apparatus of our civilization. The social sciences deliver the raw facts and we, the people, are then able to make rational choices depending on the facts and our values.

There has been much cynical backbiting about the valiant claim to value neutrality. It is said that the professed knowledge serves certain interests, and so is value-laden. That is controversial, and I have little use for what has been called interest theory—the sweeping attribution of interests to all sorts of knowledge. Instead, I dwell on the less controversial observation that the classes I call human kinds are themselves laden with value. In sociology they have typically been classes of deviants, to which have been opposed normal children, normal behaviour, normal development, normal reactions, and normal feelings, and the deviations are usually bad. Of course, normal distributions in statistics have two tails, idiots on one side of normal intelligence, and geniuses on the other, with (as Francis Galton put it) mediocrity in between. Value-free? I am not implying that there need be evaluation in the causal laws about characteristic human kinds. The discoveries need serve no interest and the facts discovered may be value-free. I am drawing attention to the presuppositions of enquiries: we investigate human kinds that are loaded with values.

There is a regular attempt to strip human kinds of their moral content by biologizing or medicalizing them. Child abusers are not bad; they are sick and need help! Their crimes are not their fault. They were abused as children, and that is why they abuse their own children. We must not make pregnant teen-age girls feel guilty. The world would be a better place if there were no single parents/child abusers/suicides/multiple personalities/vagrants/prostitutes/juvenile delinquents/recidivists/bulimics/alcoholics/homosexuals/paedophiles/chronic unemployed/homeless/runaways, etc. But let us not blame them, let us medicalize them. This fits well with the metaphysical thrust that I mentioned earlier, that somehow causal connections between kinds are more intelligible if they operate at a biological rather than a psychological or social level.

I do not propose to discuss the intense moral content of human kinds. I am not interested in the moral overtones of human kinds as a way of challenging the fact-value distinction, or as a way of challenging sociology's claim to be above (or underneath) the level of evaluation. I mention it because it is relevant to another difference between the human and the natural. Human kinds are kinds that people may want to be or not to be, not in order to attain some end but because the human kinds have intrinsic moral value.

If N is a natural kind and Z is N, it makes no direct difference to Z, if it is called N. It makes no direct difference to either mud or a mud puddle to call it "mud". It makes no direct difference to thyrotropin-releasing hormone or to a bottle of TRH to call it TRH. Of course seeing that the Z is N, we may do something to it in order to melt it or mould it, cook it or drown it, breed it or barter it. If there is mud on my child's T-shirt I use ordinary detergent to remove it, not the enzyme-activated product that I would use for a grass stain or blood. Because a particular liquid is a thyrotropin-releasing factor, an experimenter may see what happens if it is injected into sex-starved frogs or sleeping alligators, or given in megadoses to suicidal women (true stories all). But calling Z N, or seeing that Z is N, does not, in itself, make any difference to Z.

If H is a human kind and A is a person, then calling A H may make us treat A differently, just as calling Z N may make us do something to Z. We may reward or jail, instruct or abduct. But it also makes a difference to A to know that A is an H, precisely because there is so often a moral connotation to a human kind. Perhaps A does not want to be H! Thinking of me as an H changes how I think of me. Well, perhaps I could do things a little differently from now on. Not just to escape opprobrium (I have survived unscathed so far) but because I do not want to be that kind of person. Even if it does not make a difference to A it makes a difference to how people feel about A—how they relate to A—so that A's social ambience changes. I discuss this second-hand effect below in connection with children who cannot in any direct sense understand how they are classified and treated, for example autistic children.

It is a common theme in the theory of human action that to perform an intentional act is to do something "under a description". As human kinds are made and moulded, the field of descriptions changes and so do the actions that I can perform, i.e. the field of human kinds affects the field of possible intentional actions. Yet intentional action falls short of the mark. There are more possible ways to see oneself, more roles to adopt. I do not believe that multiple personalities intentionally choose their disorder, or that they are trained by their therapists. However, if this way of being were not available at the moment, hardly anyone would be that way. It is a way for troubled people to express their difficulties; the role is one of many that awaits, and some are chosen for it, often by a new way of describing their own past.

Human kinds have (what could be presented as) an even more amazing power than that of opening possibilities for future action. They enable us to redescribe our past to the extent that people can come to experience new pasts. A striking number of adults come to see themselves as having been abused as children. There has recently been a fashion of saying that we define ourselves by our biographies, by our personal narratives. Well, if there are new story lines, there can be new stories. To take an extreme example, some people come to see themselves as incest survivors, which in turn changes their lives and their relationships to their families. This is no mere matter of recovering forgotten trauma; it is a matter of there being new descriptions available, connected in law-like ways to other new descriptions, explanations, and expectations. One of the more powerful words in this group of examples is "trauma" itself,

naming a relatively new kind of human experience. The word used to denote physical wounds, injuries, or lesions, but now it denotes a kind of mental event in the lives of people—the psychic wound, forgotten but ever active. We did not know that we had them until recently—or, more paradoxical but more true, they were not a possible kind of experience to have had. But surely trauma, in its present sense of psychic wound, has been a permanent fixture in human life? Only in the past century has it been a human kind, i.e. a kind of experience about which scientific knowledge is claimed. Only recently has it become a self-evident link between rape, infant seduction, shell-shock, and being held hostage by terrorists, as in Judith Herman's powerful study, *Trauma and recovery* (1992).

Thus one way in which some human kinds differ from some kinds of thing is that classifying people works on people, changes them, and can even change their past. The process does not stop there. The people of a kind themselves are changed. Hence "we", the experts, are forced to rethink our classifications. Moreover, causal relationships between kinds are changed. Sometimes they are confirmed to the point of becoming essential definitional connections. It becomes part of the *essence* of multiple personality that it is caused by repeated childhood trauma. This is not because we have found out more about the natural disorder, but because people who see themselves as having this human disorder now find in themselves memories of trauma, often traumas of a kind that they could not even have conceptualized 20 years ago. (This can be illustrated by astonishing empirical facts, for example hundreds of people with memories of grotesque sadistic ritual cult abuse appeared in American clinics 6 years ago; much of what they remember under these descriptions they could not have thought of 12 years ago).

To create new ways of classifying people is also to change how, we can think of ourselves, to change our sense of self-worth, even how we remember our own past. This in turn generates a looping effect, because people of the kind behave differently and so are different. That is to say the kind changes, and so there is new causal knowledge to be gained and perhaps, old causal knowledge to be jettisoned.

Here I should both acknowledge labelling theory and distance myself from it. It was once argued that calling a person a juvenile delinquent (etc.), and institutionally confirming that label, made the person adopt certain stereotypical patterns of behaviour. When a youth was labelled as J, he assumed more and more of the characteristic features of J. That is a claim about labelling *individuals*. I am sure that there is some truth in it for some individuals. I go two steps further. I assert that there are changes in individuals of that kind, which means that the kind itself becomes different (possibly confirmed in its stereotype but, as I go on to urge, quite the opposite may happen). Next, because the kind changes, there is new knowledge to be had about the kind. But that new knowledge in turn becomes part of what is to be known about members of the kind, who change again. This is what I call the looping effect for human kinds.

The greater the moral connotations of a human kind, the greater the potential for the looping effect. Although I shall not develop the theme here, we find similar effects in the relatively value-neutral kinds counted by the national census and similar government agencies. These effects have been investigated with remarkable results by a number of researchers such as Desrosières (1993). That is a piece of self-reflection in itself—the bureau that includes the French census looking at what past censuses have done to the very people who have been enumerated. Each decade the census draws up a new classification of the population, a classification that then becomes experienced as the structure of the society for the next decade or more. Similarly, Americans know that "Hispanic" is an ethnic kind invented by the Bureau of the Census, with some effect on many people who

now think of themselves as Hispanic and with rather more effect on their non-Hispanic neighbours, but see below in the discussion of administrative and self-ascriptive kinds.

Responses of people to attempts to be understood or altered are different from the responses of things. This trite fact is at the core of one difference between the natural and human sciences, and it works at the level of kinds. There is a looping or feedback effect involving the introduction of classifications of people. New sorting and theorizing induces changes in self-conception and in behaviour of the people classified. Those changes demand revisions of the classification and theories, the causal connections, and the expectations. Kinds are modified, revised classifications are formed, and the classified change again, loop upon loop.

More Kinds

Two distinct objections arise. First, it will be objected that I choose some examples that may be favourable to the looping-effect thesis, and that even in those cases the evidence is skimpy. I cannot reply to that objection here because I require detailed observation, history, and to some extent "archaeology" (in the sense of Michel Foucault). I list some of my recent homework in the references at the end of this chapter.

Secondly, it will be objected that my thesis rests on special pleading, on an all too judicious choice of examples. I sympathize completely. My reply is slightly circuitous. The objection may suggest that there are really core, "prototypical", kinds studied in the human and social sciences, and that these are different in many respects from my overly sensational and problematic examples. In my opinion there are many more types of human kinds than I have discussed—thus far I agree with the objection—but I do not think that there is any core. Therefore I shall suggest a number of types of kinds in the region of the social and human sciences. I should have liked to provide a taxonomy of these, but I do not believe that there is a structure to be had. Hence I offer only a motley collection governed by very rough headings such as second-order kind, biologized kinds, inaccessible kinds, administrative kinds, and self-ascriptive kinds. These are neither exhaustive nor mutually exclusive. I intend to diminish the appeal of any one fixed idea of what human kinds are like by drawing attention to many facets of human kinds that people tend not to think about. I want to transform the second objection from "You have missed the most central examples of human kinds" into Wittgenstein's warning, "You have too slender a diet of examples". My response is to agree, and then to vary the diet.

Second-order Kinds

For well over a hundred years the most powerful second-order kind used in connection with people has been normalcy. We owe to Georges Canguilhem the recognition of the normal as a key organizing concept for medicine. Michel Foucault took over the idea when he described the nineteenth-century clinic as a site that focused not on health but on normalcy. Normal–pathological cast its net far beyond the medical domain. Auguste Comte readily adapted it to the political sphere. It was given a statistician's formulation by Adolphe Quetelet, Francis Galton, and Karl Pearson (who in the 1890s renamed the Gaussian bell-shaped curve "the normal distribution").

I call normalcy second-order for much the same reason that one might (after Kant) call existence a second-order predicate or (after Frege) call number a second-order concept. Nothing is just two (or for that matter one): there are two apples or two heroes or two sources of infection. You have to say two *what*. Likewise nothing is just normal. You have to say normal *what*: a normal child, normal idiosyncrasies, normal speech patterns, or normal development. Normalcy provides a remarkable all-purpose vehicle for characterizing new human kinds as deviations from the norm.

Typically, the human kinds that involve normalcy are defined in terms of abnormality. The *Journal of Abnormal Psychology*, founded in 1906, was once a cutting-edge organization of kinds. It was in the business of carving out human kinds with, as it happens, a particular emphasis on multiple personality. "Ortho", which is Greek for normal, is also for kind-forming. The American Orthopsychiatric Association was formed in 1924 by the child guidance clinicians; the *Journal of Orthopsychiatry* followed soon after. It may sound as if the object of study was the normal, but this was not the case. The aims were to recognize, classify, guide, and heal deviant children. They were to be transformed so that they could develop as normally as possible.

Normalcy is not restricted to the human. Its origin is in physiology (normal and pathological physiology), and it readily adapts to much that is biological and beyond. We can have abnormal quasi-stellar objects—even pathological ones. The adjectives are not used to indicate that the quasar is sick, but that there is something quite out of the ordinary about it which astrophysics and cosmology cannot quite understand yet.

The normal can be anywhere, but its home is human. The idea of the normal is partly responsible for the moral overtones of so many human kinds. Deep in the root of the words, the Latin "norm" and the Greek "ortho" bridge the fact–value distinction. Any human kind explained in terms of deviation from the normal is partly descriptive—the kind differs from the usual. However, it is also partly evaluative: the kind differs from what is right; it is worse, or in the case of Galton's deviation from mediocrity, possibly better.

Biologized Kinds

I have mentioned the thrust of human kinds towards the biological. Biological is my shorthand for biochemical, neurological, electrical, mechanical, or whatever is the preferred model of efficient causation in a given scientific community or era. This thrust is one of the more powerful themata in scientific thought. Its very success has made us swell with optimism. We have an immense confidence in its potential and plenty of proven examples. I have no quarrel with biological research programmes into human behaviour. However, I do want to note that biologizing human kinds does not thereby make them immune to looping effects.

One effect is obvious. At present we tend to hold that we are not responsible for our biological attributes, except such as we can change by regimens, namely abstinence and spiritual or physical exercises. Of course biology is not a foolproof excuse; Susan Sontag has written about how people are made to feel as morally involved in their cancers as others once were in their tuberculosis. Then the claim is that the disease is not purely biological, but also has a psychic component. The disorders of women have been particularly ambivalent in this respect. However, by and large, biology is exculpating.

Thus alcoholism has plausibly been regarded as a moral failing. It is regarded as such by the most successful widespread programme to counteract it, namely Alcoholics Anonymous. It evolved a form of meeting patterned on both chapel and confessional, in which resort is made to a higher power "as each individual understands that term". The alternative view, favoured by many treatment programmes patterned after hospitalization, is biological, biochemical and even genetic. In this view the alcoholic has a disease for which he is not responsible, and is required to follow a regimen chiefly in the way in which someone with high blood pressure follows a regimen. The scientific (biological) knowledge about alcoholics produces a different kind of person. Results about this are masked because both the scientist and the moralist compete for control over all alcoholics, as a kind, and will not acknowledge that the persons

under their sway tend to have projections, expectations, and (probabilistic) law-like regularities different from those of the other lot. Sometimes this comes out at a straightforward level. Thus the Alcohol Research Foundation in my city, a very powerful medical institution, claims to have identified a class of alcoholics who can return to very moderate social drinking; Alcoholics Anonymous denies that there is such a human kind.

Until recently, i.e. until the surge of self-ascriptive kinds discussed below, Alcoholics Anonymous and kindred anti-addiction groups have been anomalously moralistic. Few others have fought the demoralizing impact of biologization. We are exposed to enthusiastic programmes every day. Partly because they tend to be programmes rather than conclusions, they are involved in the looping dynamics of human kinds. Today (as I write) happens to be 13 November 1992. This morning's *New York Times* has on the front page an article headed "Study cites biology's role in violent behavior". It begins:

> In a sharp departure from traditional criminology, the [U.S.] National Research Council has found that biological and genetic factors should be considered along with environmental factors such as poverty in efforts to understand the causes of violence.

In case we are in doubt as to the authority of the National Research Council, the next sentence reminds us that the Council is "the research arm of the [U.S.] National Academy of Sciences". One of the general messages is that "instead of relying on more prisons and longer sentences, America needs more flexible more pragmatic and less ideological approaches". After all, if the violence is partly genetic and biological, people are not usefully put in penitentiaries and reformatories to repent and reform. Is this a "sharp departure from traditional criminology"? What is described is in outline similar to the criminal anthropology of Cesare Lombroso and many others. It flourished a century ago; its heyday in Italy was 1875–1895. Those are Bad Guys, refuted to the point of ridicule in many a wise volume, of which Gould's (1981) *The mismeasure of man* is the best known. Yet the programme of the criminal anthropologists was parallel to that of the most recent report of the National Research Council, right down to its mixture of biology, inheritance, prison reform, and exculpation.

Violence is not a human kind according to my criteria (i)–(iv). However, criminology is a social science. Institutionally, it is descended from criminal anthropology, i.e. the first criminology departments had Lombrosian aspirations. "Criminal", like "suicide", has been used by professionals as a grouping of human kinds. The concluding sentence of the *New York Times* story reads:

> "The most significant accomplishment of the [National Research Council] panel is the integration of biological and social science data to develop a new conceptual framework", said Klaus Miczek, a professor of psychology at Tufts University and director of the psychopharmacological laboratory.

A 'new conceptual framework" is in part a new sorting, a new taxonomy, a new array of human kinds, or a reorganization of old ones.

Reorganization is critical. Very seldom do we devise a wholly new human kind. Rather, as in all our endeavours, we build on old ones. Child abuse inherits a good deal from cruelty to children. What we do not notice is the extraordinary amount of not merely making and moulding of kinds that occurs, but also of what is best described as wandering. The wandering is partly the result of the way in which a human kind, once biologized, reacts to the way in which the people who fall under the kinds themselves react to being treated in the way that science dictates.

Inaccessible Kinds

I have laid great emphasis on the ways in which people of a kind can become self-conscious about that kind. What about human kinds in which the people classified cannot take in how they are classified? Call those inaccessible kinds. Human beings who cannot understand, such as infants, provide obvious examples. There cannot be self-conscious feedback. However, there can be looping that involves a larger human unit, for example the family. I was brought up by a generation of parents who accepted, as scientific knowledge about infants, that babies must be nursed at set times, regardless of how much they might fuss and scream for more food. Current science holds that the psyches of my age cohort are irrevocably damaged.

The dictionary defines **autism** as "abnormal self-absorption, usually affecting children, characterized by lack of response to people and actions and limited ability to communicate; children suffering from autism often do not learn to speak". We seem to owe the word to Bleuler's description of the self-absorption and "separation of thought from logic and reality" in schizophrenics, an idea proposed in his profoundly influential book of 1911, *Dementia praecox oder die Gruppe der Schizophrenien*. We now apply the term primarily to children, or to adults who were autistic children and remain abnormal.

By my criteria, "the autistic child" is a human kind. It became a cutting-edge kind in the 1970s. *The Journal of Autism and Childhood Schizophrenia* was founded in 1971, and was renamed the *Journal of Autism and Developmental Disorders* in 1979. We are strongly inclined to say that autistic children form a definite class that could, in principle, have been picked out in many populations at many times. We say this because we take it to result from a biological rather than a social deficit. In fact, autism was first characterized by Leo Kanner on the basis of children he noticed in 1938. He thought that they would previously have been called born-deaf or feeble-minded.

He described them in print (Kanner 1943) in *The nervous child*, a cutting-edge journal then entering its second year of publication.

The criteria for identification, let alone theories about what autism "is", have changed a good deal since 1938. The optimistic scientific view is that we are establishing a better and better understanding of autism, refining our definition of this natural kind of behaviour and discovering its cause and its essence. The outside observer may be less sanguine. I think that no one now doubts that many children, diagnosed as autistic, are suffering from some distinct biological (biochemical or neurological) impairment. This must, we feel, be a human kind (or several kinds) that will yield to biology! At the time of writing there is no known brain pathology, and various optimistic correlates (PET scans etc.) do not seem to replicate. We should also note that autism is regularly defined in contrast with the "normal" development of a child.

Kanner reported 11 children who were "self-absorbed" almost from birth. They adopted abnormal postures when picked up. They did not connect a part of another person's body with the person. Normal children, when annoyed by an interruption, look at the face of the intruder; Kanner's children struck out at the foreign hand or other body part that was disturbing them. The children had remarkable rote memory. They did not learn to communicate, but many echoed what other people said. There was an obsessive desire to keep everything "the same", and every arrangement of objects or pattern of behaviour was obsessively repeated. There were serious feeding problems; whereas children with lack of affect tend to overeat when given the chance, Kanner's children ate little and stayed away from anything living, but were fascinated by objects. Their toys of choice were inanimate, or sometimes mechanical, rather than cuddly. They had a rigorous compulsion to preserve objects in "the same" geometrical arrangements.

Kanner's children, drawn from a Johns Hopkins clinic, had very successful workaholic parents. Autism was soon taken to be an innate inability to relate to people, exacerbated by parents who were not very good at that either. In those days children at public schools in North America had their report cards graded according to their ability to "relate to" children of their own age and to "relate to" their teachers. Low grades in relationships had heavy loads of guilt laid on them, as I can assure you from personal experience as a 7-year-old in 1943 in the backwoods of a Canadian province a long way from the heartland of such doctrines.

Kanner came to emphasize lack of relatedness and wrote of parents who reared their children in "emotional refrigerators". By 1955 this was understood as the primary cause of autism: it was the parents' fault. Parents of these abnormal children were advised to undergo years of intensive therapy. Over 20 years later Bruno Bettelheim (1967) was still urging exactly that concept of autism. Notice the moral shift. Kanner's children would once have been dismissed as stupid, feeble-minded (therefore feeble, bad), or deaf (therefore dumb, stupid). Now they are liberated. It is not their fault. The parents are emotional refrigerators and that, the whole period 1938–1967, is *bad*.

Autism moved around a good deal. Authors ceased to mention the unusual postures of infants. Feeding had virtually disappeared as a stated problem by 1955 (but see ICD-10 in 1992). After that the disorder was increasingly described as "psychobiological". The 1968 *Diagnostic and statistical manual* (DSM-II) did not distinguish autism from a kind of schizophrenia. Here there was a certain loyalty to Bleuler, but also a strong resistance to recognizing autistic children as a distinct kind at all. Note the change in title, mentioned above, in the premier journal for autism: from *Autism and Childhood Schizophrenia* (1971) to *Autism and Developmental Disorders* (1979). That was the decade in which autism was separated from schizophrenia, for example by epidemiology: 75 per cent of autistic children are male and the onset is in early childhood; the disproportion is not nearly so great for schizo-phrenia and the onset is in adolescence. This is an example of the characteristic self-sealing argument we find in debates about human kinds. On the basis of our diagnoses, we find measur-able (here chronological) differences between two populations; therefore our distinctions and diagnoses are sound. By 1980 the *Diagnostic and statistical manual* (DSM-III) gave a separate defini-tion of "infantile autism" that was nevertheless rejected by people working with these children. The definition in the 1987 DSM-III(R) is more acceptable but is much altered in the proposals for the next edition.

A standard survey article (Sevin et al. 1991) lists five fairly distinct systems for diagnosing autism. There is much emphasis on social prob-lems, lack of play with other children, lack of imaginative play with objects, lack of empathy, and inability to perceive other people's emotions. Half the children do not develop useful speech. The clinical descriptions are rather different from those of non-parents who have to work closely with autistic children. Workers with sufficient time and a small case-load often develop close emotional bonds; the more commonly overworked and underpaid staff quickly lapse into discussions of how hard it is to "handle" these children. We have a kind, doubtless biological, that nevertherless has been wandering. An authoritative article by Steffenburg and Gillberg states that:

> It is high time that autism be regarded as an administrative rather than specific disease label. Autism, like mental retardation, is not a disease, but an umbrella term, covering a variety of disease entities with certain common behavioural features (1989 p. 75)

This remark can usefully contribute to the typology of human kinds; autism is an *administra-tive* kind about which I say a little more below.

Under what sciences should autism be inves-tigated? One contender is cognitive science.

Premack and Woodruff (1978) introduced criteria for saying that "an individual has a theory of mind". They meant "that the individual imputes mental states to himself and others" (1978 p. 515). Philosophers commenting on the paper (Jonathan Bennett, Daniel Dennett, and Gilbert Harman) all referred to an idea apparently first described by Lewis (1969). Two subjects observe a state of affairs. One leaves and the state of affairs is changed; the other sees this. Does the second subject subse-quently act as if the other still believes (falsely) that the old state of affairs obtains? For example children are shown a sweet package and shown that it does contain sweets. Some children leave and a plastic alligator is put in the sweet box in front of remaining children; do these expect the other children, on returning, to be surprised by the contents of the package? If so, they impute beliefs to others and have the kernel of a theory of mind.

In the early 1980s numerous experiments in developmental psychology were published to discover the point at which young children acquired a theory of mind, attributing belief systems to others (Wimmer and Perner 1983; Perner and Wimmer 1985; Perner et al. 1989). The definitive application to autistic children was made by Baron-Cohen et al. (1985). Children with Down's syndrome and autism were compared. The researchers found striking contrasts in the experimental ability to impute beliefs to others: "our results strongly support the hypothesis that autistic children as a group fail to employ a theory of mind". These conclu-sions have been corroborated a number of times by more sophisticated experiments. There turns out to be a residual class of autistic children (one in five) who do "impute intentionality". Children in this class tend to be better at language in general. That fits well with Paul Grice's idea, elaborated by Sperber and Wilson (1986) and by Dennett (1987), that linguistic communica-tion demands attributions of intentions. This research has stabilized in a body of thinking represented in the papers collected by Baron-Cohen et al. (1991).

However, cognitive scientists do not own autism outright. From the antipodes comes a rehabilitation worker, Rosemary Crossley, who started "facilitated communication" about 20 years ago. She had begun with cerebral palsy patients, helping them to have control over their movements. The facilitator holds the hand, shoulder, or finger of an autistic person who presses keys on a keyboard—primarily, it is said, to stop the autist from repeatedly pressing the same key (controlling the fixation on "sameness"). The result is vastly more ability to express understanding of other people than cognitive science allows for. But was not this all the work of the facilitator choosing the keys? (The Supreme Court of Victoria ruled that it was not, siding with a cerebral palsy victim who, working with a facilitator, had communicated a desire to be deinstitutionalized.) The procedure has stood up to fairly rigorous testing to exclude overenthusiastic facilitation. The facilitator is blind to events observed by the autist and then reported by the keyboard. The method has been exported from Australia with a vengeance: for highbrow professional audiences, in the *Harvard Educational Review* (Biklen 1991); for middlebrow audiences where I live, in a five-part series run by the Canadian Broadcasting Corporation in 1991, and in more popular media. It has had a great impact on pressure and self-help activist groups such as (again where I live) the Autism Society of Canada. Not for them the theory that autistic children lack a theory of mind. They lack facilitators. There are all sorts of forces at work. For example, Crossley's star autist is taking a university degree. Autistic children are not stupid, not retarded, and not feeble-minded, but suffer from an unknown disadvantage. There is no stigma attached to autism, and so there is much urgency to have children with difficulties classified as autistic. The cognitive science approach is disliked, for if there were children who did not think that other people have minds, they

themselves would thereby be inhuman. But is there not a truth of the matter? Is there not a real kind (or kinds) of children out there that in the end we will know something about? That is by no means clear to me. The looping effect works on the kind and its auxiliaries—family and remedial workers—and of course on the success stories who simply deny the no-theory-of-mind approach.

Administrative Kinds

It was suggested that autism is an "administrative" entity. When we reflect on the origins of the social sciences, this becomes a rather compelling concept. Obviously it fits census classifications. Naturally an administrative kind can have quite unexpected effects, as when "Hispanic" becomes a tool of political unity. Another example is "Lithuanian language", in part a product of emigrés in Pittsburgh and the US Census (Petersen 1986). The idea of an administrative kind equally fits many social kinds if, as I claim, the social sciences arose together with the bureaucratic imperative to distinguish, enumerate, control, and improve deviants. In the beginning and in the end the deviants would be an administrative problem. In our day the "administrative" tag is used negatively by those who want a biological kind of which there is biological knowledge. Thus the urge to say both that autism is administrative and that there are several kinds of disorder which we shall find out about. Exactly the same thing has been said about child abuse. The idea of an administrative kind reminds us that there may be rivalry between administrators, battles for territory. Those have been very evident in the child abuse field from the beginning, and at present there is plenty of more muted dispute about who owns autism.

The idea of an administrative kind enables us to bring together a number of different types of objections to my looping thesis. Of course, it will be said, there may be looping effects on administrative kinds. The administered react to their administration! Administrative kinds probably cover a number of different natural kinds, for which there is no feedback effect, and which have real causal, perhaps biological, relationships between them. Except on the point of brevity, I will not be accused of understating the force of this objection. What I deny is that there is a sharp distinction, within the human kinds, between what is given by nature and what is administrative. I deny this in part because of characteristics that I take to be essential to the social sciences and the kinds with which they deal. Doubtless, we shall debate this. Having set the terms of a debate, I wish to conclude with a further, and very recent, feature of human kinds.

Self-ascriptive Kinds

Human kinds, I claim, are the product of a particular vision of the sciences of Man. They were formed on two axes. The one is that of the natural sciences. After 1815 the moral sciences were to be patterned on the quantitative natural sciences—sciences that themselves took a notable leap forward as new types of physical phenomena were made the target of measurement. In particular, their conception of causality was made identical to that of the physical sciences, a move abetted by the positivist movement from the 1820s which interpreted causation as regularity. Their other axis was bureaucratic-statistical, which allowed both the counting and tabulation of kinds of people—the analysis of statistical regularity as cause.

Within these two axes there is knowledge and the known. "We" know about "them". There are plenty of looping effects, but the known are passive and do not take charge of knowledge of themselves. The second half of the twentieth century has seen the introduction of a radically new axis. Gay liberation provides the classic example.

I have mentioned one official story about homosexuality—that the homosexual as a kind of person emerges in medico-forensic discouse late in the nineteenth century, with instant dispersion. (A colleague in Montreal, an emigré Chinese psychiatrist, noted in a paper that although there were numerous stories and colourful terms in Chinese literature, there was no word meaning "homosexual" until 1887 or 1888. I had to tell him that was about 2 months or one boat trip after it was confirmed in Europe.) To simplify overly much, the label "homosexual" was a term in its original sites applied by the knowers to the known. However, it was quickly taken up by the known, and gay liberation was the natural upshot. One of the first features of gay liberation was gay pride and coming out of the closet. It became a moral imperative for people of the kind to identify themselves, to ascribe a chosen kind-term to themselves. That way they also became the knowers, even if not the only people authorized to have knowledge.

There are plenty of obvious relations to other categories, such as race and gender, black pride and women's liberation. That is only the beginning. A very general process of self-ascription of kinds has arisen, which I believe will go on affecting human kinds in ways that we cannot foresee. It is no accident that the USA is in the forefront of this movement (just as post-revolutionary post-empire bureaucratized France was the original site of human kinds). There are two reasons. One is the far greater role of rights in American social consciousness than is found anywhere else. People of a human kind demand their rights, or people associated with that kind demand rights for members of that kind. The other is that the USA is a uniquely democratic society (with most of the properties that Plato abhorred in the *demos*) which is also predicated on freedom of speech and information flow. (Do not misunderstand me, I am not praising or envying; my own national ethos sides with Plato on such matters.)

There has been a bizarre proliferation of self-help groups of late. Their core feature has been self-ascription; their rhetoric is that of taking control of themselves. New categories emerge. One of the most powerful has been that of the "handicapped". This is, like so many matters pertaining to the human, an administrative category. It groups a subclass of those who do not have "normal" abilities in this or that respect. The label originated during the Second World War, with procedures enabling people with various kinds of disabilities to work in understaffed industries. There were many jobs that people with different disadvantages could perform perfectly well. Subsequently, interest groups arose urging the rights of people with a variety of handicaps. The old pejorative labels—cripples, dumb, retarded, feebleminded—were replaced. People gladly took the new labels on themselves and became members of pressure groups—or else their friends or family members did it for them.

There is little end to this process of self-ascription, or even ascription and then rejection: witness the current rejection of Hispanic by some of those for whom the term was invented, and replacement by Latino and other self-avowed subgroups. I have mentioned autistic support societies which include activist groups, self-help groups for families with autistic children, and groups whose direct members are autistic individuals in several age groups. A decade ago I injudiciously made a point sharply by contrasting multiple personality and homosexuality as human kinds. There would, I said, never be any split bars for people with multiple personality disorder. Well there are now multiple personality social groups, and I am told that there is indeed a multiple personality bar in Denver. Self-help groups tend to remoralize a human kind. Some are even patterned after Alcoholics Anonymous, developing their own twelve-step variations.

This is the right place to conclude a discussion introducing the looping effects of human kinds. We are experiencing a wholly new type of looping effect, when so many of the kinds claim rights to their own knowledges.

References

American Psychiatric Association (1987). *Diagnostic and Statistical Manual III* (Revised). American Psychiatric Association, Washington, DC.

Baron-Cohen S., Leslie, A. M. and Frith, U. (1985). Does the autistic child have a "theory of mind"? *Cognition*, 21: 37–46.

Baron-Cohen, S., Tager-Flusberg, H., Cohen, D. and Volmar, F. (Eds.) (1991). *Understanding Other Minds: perspectives from autism*. Oxford University Press.

Bettelheim, B. (1967). *The Empty Fortress: Infantile autism and the birth of the self*. MacMillan, London.

Biklen, D. (1990). Communication unbound: autism and praxis. *Harvard Educational Review*, 60: 291–314.

Desrosières, A. (1993). *La Politique des grands nombres*. Découverte, Paris.

Dennett, D. C. (1987). *The Intentional Stance*. Cambridge, MA: MIT Press.

Gould, S. J. (1981). *The Mismeasure of Man*, New York: Norton.

Hacking, I. (1990). The normal state. *The Taming of Chance*, (pp. 160–9, see also pp. 178 ff). Cambridge University Press.

Hacking, I. (1991). The making and molding of child abuse. *Critical Inquiry*, 17: 235–58.

Hacking, I. (1992). Multiple personality disorder and its hosts. *History of the Human Sciences*, 5(2): 3–31.

Hacking, I. (1992c). World-making by kind-making: child abuse for example. In M. Douglas and D. Hull (Eds.), *How Classification Works*. (pp. 180–238). Edinburgh University Press.

Hall, G. (1904). *Adolescence. Its psychology and its relation to physiology, anthropology, sociology, sex, crime, religion and education*. New York: Appleton.

Herman, J. L. (1992). *Trauma and Recovery*, New York: Basic Books.

Kanner, L. (1943). Autistic disturbances of affective contact. *Nervous Child*, 2: 217–50.

Lewis, D. (1969). *Convention: A philosophical study*. Cambridge, MA: Harvard University Press.

Perner, J., & Wimmer, H. (1985). "John thinks that Mary thinks that . . ." Attributions of second-order beliefs by 5- and 10-year old children. *Journal of Experimental Child Psychology*, 9: 315–60.

Perner, J., Leekham, S. R. and Wimmer, H. (1989). Exploration of the autistic child's theory of mind: knowledge, belief and communication. *Child Development*, 60: 689–700.

Petersen, W. (1986). Politics and the measurement of ethnicity. In W. Alonso and P. Starr (Eds.), *The Politics of Numbers* pp. 187–233. New York: Sage.

Premack, D. and Woodruff, G. (1978). Does the chimpanzee have a theory of mind? *Behavioral and Brain Sciences*, 4: 515–26.

Sevin, J. A., Matson, J. L., Coe, D. A., Fee, V. E., & Sevin, B. M. (1991). A comparison of three commonly used autism scales. *Journal of Autism and Developmental Disorders*, 21: 417–32.

Sperber, D. and Wilson, D. (1986). *Relevance: Communication and cognition.* Oxford: Blackwell.

Steffenburg, S., & Gillberg, C. (1989). The etiology of autism. In C. Gillberg (Eds.), *Diagnosis and Treatment of Autism* (ed C. Gillberg). New York: Plenum.

Stein, E. (1992). The essentials of constructionism and the construction of essentialism. In E. Stein, (Eds.), *Forms of Desire* (pp. 295–325). New York: Routledge.

Wimmer, H., & Perner, J. (1983). Beliefs about beliefs: representation and constraining function of wrong beliefs in young children's understanding of deception. *Cognition*, 13: 103–28.

World Health Organization (1992). *The ICD-10 Classification of Mental and Behavioural Disorders. Clinical descriptions and diagnostic guidelines.* Geneva: World Health Organization.

Chapter 22

Ron Mallon and Stephen P. Stich

THE ODD COUPLE
The Compatibility of Social Construction and Evolutionary Psychology

Introduction

By all appearances there is a battle raging for the soul of the social sciences. On one side, and in some disciplines the prevailing establishment, are social constructionists and other advocates of what John Tooby and Leda Cosmides have dubbed the Standard Social Science Model (SSSM).[1] Social constructionists emphasize the enormous diversity of social and psychological phenomena to be found in cultures around the world and throughout history, and much of the research in this tradition has been devoted to describing that diversity—in emotions, moral and religious beliefs, sexual behavior, kinship systems, theories about nature, and much else besides.[2] Advocates of the SSSM are heirs to the empiricist conception of the mind as a blank tablet which experience writes upon. And while no serious social constructionist would deny that our innate mental endowment imposes *some* constraints on what we can learn and what we can do, they believe that most of these constraints are weak and uninteresting. Thus when it comes to explaining the diversity of psychological phenomena like emotions, beliefs, and preferences, differences in the surrounding culture loom large. Those cultural differences are in turn explained by differences in history and in local conditions.

On the other side are evolutionary psychologists who advocate a distinctly rationalist-inspired conception of the mind.[3] According to evolutionary psychologists, human minds have a rich, species-typical cognitive architecture composed of functionally distinct systems—"mental organs" as Steven Pinker has called them—that have been shaped by natural selection over millions of years. Many of these mental organs embody complex, domain-specific algorithms and theories (or stores of information) which play a major role in shaping and constraining beliefs, preferences, emotional reactions, sexual behavior, and interpersonal relationships. This evolved psychology also plays a major role in shaping and constraining social institutions. In studying social and psychological phenomena, evolutionary psychologists focus on commonalties rather than differences, and in explaining these commonalties they emphasize the contributions of innate, information-rich mental mechanisms that were selected to be adaptive in the sorts of environments in which humans evolved.

Advocates of the SSSM have little sympathy with this quest for cross-cultural patterns and universal features of human psychology. The highly influential anthropologist, Clifford Geertz, apparently doubts that there are any substantive universals to be found. "There is," he writes, "a logical conflict between asserting that, say, 'religion', 'marriage', or 'property' are empirical universals and giving them very much in the way of specific content, for to say that they are empirical universals is to say that they have the same content, and to say they have the same content is to fly in the face of the undeniable fact that they do not."[4]

Evolutionary psychologists are not much moved by this sort of skepticism, however. On their view the demand for exceptionless universals sets the standard too high. According to Tooby and Cosmides,

> Whenever it is suggested that something is "innate" or "biological," the SSSM-oriented anthropologist or sociologist rifles through the ethnographic literature to find a report of a culture where the behavior (or whatever) varies. ... Upon finding an instance of reported variation, the item is moved from the category of "innate," "biological," "genetically determined," or "hardwired" to the category of "learned," "cultural," or "socially constructed." ... Because almost everything human is variable in one respect or another, nearly everything has been subtracted from the "biologically determined" column and moved to the "socially determined" column. The leftover residue of "human nature," after this process of subtraction has been completed, is weak tea indeed.[5]

On the face of it, the dispute between social constructionists and evolutionary psychologists has two major and interrelated components. First, there is an empirical disagreement about the extent to which all normal humans share innate, informationally-rich mental mechanisms that strongly constrain our psychology and our social interactions and institutions. Second, there is a strategic or methodological disagreement—a disagreement about the best way to make progress in understanding psychological and social phenomena. Evolutionary psychologists urge that we focus on what people have in common, while social constructionists think that it is more important to attend to the many ways in which people differ. We do not

deny that there are real and important disagreements on both of these points. But it is our contention, and one of the central theses of this paper, that there is a third, much less obvious issue dividing social constructionists and evolutionary psychologists. This disagreement is not an empirical dispute about the nature of the human mind nor is it a methodological dispute about the best way of studying minds and social phenomena. Rather, it is a *semantic* disagreement (or perhaps it is better described as a *philosophical* disagreement—we've never been very clear about how much of semantics counts as philosophy). What is at issue is the *meaning* and *reference* of many ordinary terms for mental states, and for other psychological and social phenomena—terms like "anger", "disgust", "gender", and "homosexuality".

We think it is crucially important to bring this covert component of the dispute out into the open. When we have a clear view of the role that this third component of the dispute is playing, it will also become clear that this philosophical dispute can easily be bracketed and set aside. Evolutionary psychologists could easily accept the semantic assumptions made by social constructionists—if only for argument's sake—without changing in the least the claims they want to make about minds, evolution, and social interactions. Moreover, and this is the other central thesis of this paper, once the philosophical dispute has been set aside, the remaining empirical and methodological disagreements between social constructionists and evolutionary psychologists look much less serious. When the fog that the philosophical dispute engenders has been cleared, social constructionists and evolutionary psychologists look less like adversaries and more like natural partners.

In this paper our focus will be on the dispute between evolutionary psychology and social constructionist approaches to the emotions, though we think that much of what we say is more generally applicable. The emotions are a crucial case, both because they play a central role in discussions of other social and psychological phenomena like violence, sexual behavior, religious practices, and moral beliefs, and also because there has been extensive research on the emotions within both an evolutionary psychology paradigm and a social constructionist paradigm. In fact, when reading this literature, it is easy to get the feeling that each side considers the emotions one of its success stories.

Here is how we will proceed. In Section 2, we will give a brief overview of the social constructionist approach by sketching a few details from Catherine Lutz's (1988) widely admired study of the emotions of the Ifaluk, inhabitants of a Micronesian atoll. In Section 3, we will provide a quick review of work on emotions in the evolutionary psychology tradition and set out a model of the psychological mechanisms underlying the emotions drawn from recent work in that tradition. Though there are lots of disagreements over how the details are to be filled in, there is a growing consensus among evolutionary psychologists on the broad outlines of the sort of model we will describe. At the core of this model is an innate, evolved system for triggering and sequencing emotional responses, present in all normal humans. Another important feature of the model is that it allows for quite extensive cross-cultural variation both in the circumstances that provoke various emotions and in the patterns of behavior that the emotions produce. Since this sort of variation is a central theme in social constructionist accounts of the emotions, one might well wonder whether social constructionists and evolutionary psychologists have anything left to disagree about.

The answer, as we will demonstrate in Section 4, is *yes*. For while evolutionary psychologists agree that emotions can be provoked by different situations in different cultures, and that they can give rise to quite different patterns of behavior, they maintain that the emotions themselves are cross-cultural universals. Fear, anger, sadness, and other emotions can be found in all

cultures. And this is a claim that many social constructionists vigorously dispute. Must social constructionists then reject the sort of nativistic, evolutionary psychological model of the emotions set out in Section 3? Here, we think, the answer in no. For, as we will argue in Section 5, social constructionists can maintain that emotions like fear and anger are not cross-cultural universals and *still* accept the evolutionary psychologists' account of the mechanisms underlying the emotions, provided that they accept what we will call a *thick description* account of the meaning and reference of ordinary language emotion terms. And, it is our contention that, either explicitly or tacitly, most social constructionists do indeed assume that a thick description account is correct. But we will also note that the thick description account of meaning and reference is not the only game in town. There are numerous alternative accounts of meaning and reference to choose from, some of which will not sustain the social constructionists' claim that emotions are culturally-local.

In Section 6, we will begin by asking which account of the meaning and reference of emotion terms is correct, and go on to suggest that no one really knows and that the question itself may not be clear enough to *have* a determinate answer. But we will also argue that *it really doesn't matter* which side is right since it is easy to see how this dispute can be bracketed and set aside. Moreover, and this is the essential point, once we set aside this dispute over the reference of emotion terms, it is far from clear that any deep disagreements between social constructionist and evolutionary psychological accounts remain. The philosophically motivated controversy about universality is little more than a distraction which obscures the fact that the findings and theories produced on both sides of the divide, far from being in competition with one another, are actually complementary. Many people will find our conclusion quite startling since it is widely believed that the battle between social constructionists and evolutionary psychologists is driven by radically different views about the nature of minds, social institutions and human kinds. If we are right, there is relatively little fundamental disagreement about any of these matters. What drives the dispute is a covert philosophical disagreement whose resolution is of little moment to those on either side.

The Social Constructionist Approach to the Emotions

When studying the emotions, as when studying other social and psychological phenomena, social constructionists are primarily concerned to describe the rich, multifaceted, culturally-local network in which the phenomena are embedded. Since many social constructionists concerned with the emotions are anthropologists, problems of translation are a major concern. Thus their inquiry often begins by focusing on the *words* for emotions that are used in the culture they are studying and the problem of how those words should be translated. In order to accomplish this task, social constructionists pay careful attention to a number of interrelated aspects of emotion discourse and behavior in the target culture, including:

i) the often very complex circumstances in which people in that culture claim that they or others experience the emotions picked out by various emotion words

ii) the pattern of inferences that are drawn when someone is believed to be experiencing the emotion

iii) the patterns of interaction that exist (and/or that people in the culture *believe* to exist) among the emotions and also among emotions and other mental states and among emotions and various sorts of behavior; some of these interactions will be within a single person while others involve two or more people

iv) the ways in which both emotions and discourse about emotions interact with the moral, political and economic lives of the people in the culture.

When done well, the detailed "ethnopsychological" accounts that result from studies of this sort—"thick descriptions" as Geertz would call them—can be fascinating. Part of what makes them so interesting is that many of the patterns described are wonderfully exotic, differing in surprising and unexpected ways from the patterns of interaction in which our own emotions and emotion language are embedded.

To see how all this works in practice, let us briefly review Lutz's account of the emotion that the Ifaluk people call "*song*". *Song* is an emotion akin to the one that we call "anger", though in contrast with anger, there is a strong moral component to *song*. In order to count as being or feeling *song*, an Ifaluk must be *justifiably* angry at another person who has engaged in morally inappropriate behavior. The Ifaluk have an array of other terms for types of anger that do not involve this moral dimension: "*tipmochmoch*" for the irritability that often accompanies sickness, "*lingeringer*" for anger that builds up slowly when one is confronted with a series of minor annoyances, etc.[6] But they have no generic term that picks out all and only these various sorts of anger.[7]

There are various sorts of moral transgression that can provoke *song*. Lutz's account of these reasons or triggering conditions for the emotion make it clear how the emotion is woven into the fabric of Ifaluk society, and also how very different that society is from ours. One important category of events that can provoke *song* is the violation of a taboo, and among the Ifaluk taboos are not in short supply. There are taboos that apply only to women (they are forbidden to enter the canoe houses or to work in the taro gardens when they are menstruating) and others that apply only to men (they are not to enter birth houses). Other taboos apply to everyone.

Violation of these taboos provokes *song* among the chiefs who may impose fines or other punishments. On a less public level, *song*[8] is often provoked when people fail to live up to their obligation to share or when they are lazy, loud, or disrespectful.[9] From a Western perspective, one of the stranger features of *song* is that it can be provoked by a sort of excited happiness that the Ifaluk call "*ker*". "Happiness/excitement," Lutz reports, "is an emotion people see as pleasant but amoral. It is often, in fact, immoral because someone who is happy/excited is more likely to be unafraid of other people. While this lack of fear may lead them to laugh and talk with other people, it may also make them misbehave or walk around showing off".[10]

Just as the circumstances that can provoke *song* are different from those that can provoke anger in our culture, so too is the pattern of behavior that a *song* person may display. In the West, anger often leads to physical confrontation and sometimes to violence. But among the Ifaluk, according to Lutz, "it is expected that those who are justifiably angry [*song*] will *not* physically aggress against another. And in fact, interpersonal violence is virtually nonexistent on the island."[11] Some of the behavior that the Ifaluk exhibit when they are *song* is familiar enough. They may refuse to speak or eat with the offending party or produce a facial expression indicative of disapproval. But other *song*-induced behavior is rather more exotic. People often react to *song* by gossiping about the offending person so that he or she may learn indirectly that someone claims to be justifiably angry with them.[12] In extreme cases they may threaten to burn down the offending person's house[13] or fast or threaten suicide.[14]

When people learn that they are the object of another person's *song*, the typical reaction is to experience the emotion that the Ifaluk call "*metagu*" which Lutz characterizes as a sort of fear or anxiety. *Metagu* can be brought on by circumstances other than the *song* of another—strange situations is one that Lutz

mentions[15]—but the term is not used for the sort of fear produced by sudden and unexpected events like the falling of a coconut nearby,[16] nor is it used for the fearful emotion produced by events like the erratic behavior of a drunk.[17] When offenders experience *metagu*, it leads them to behave more calmly and appropriately and it also often leads them to take some corrective action like apologizing, paying a fine levied by the chiefs, or sending some object of value to the aggrieved parties or their families. This causes those experiencing *song* to "forget their justifiable anger".[18]

As noted earlier, the Ifaluk concept of *song*, in contrast with the Western notion of anger, is intrinsically tied to moral concerns. One *cannot* be *song* unless one's anger is justified. And, according to the prevailing moral views, if two people are involved in a dispute, only one can *really* be *song*, regardless of what the other person may think about the emotion he or she is experiencing.[19] Not surprisingly, "daily negotiations over who is *song* and over the proper reasons for that anger lie at the heart of the politics of everyday life".[20] It would, of course, be quite bizarre for two people in our culture to assume that only one could be genuinely angry with the other and to argue about which one it was. In this way, our conception of anger seems quite different from the Ifaluk conception of *song*. Nor is it clear that we have *any* notion that corresponds all that closely to *song*, since even our notion of justifiable anger can be and often is applicable to *both* parties to a dispute. *Metagu* also has a role to play in the moral and political life of the Ifaluk community, since people who describe themselves as *metagu* declare themselves to be harmless and in accord with the moral code of the island.[21]

What we have presented in this section is only a fragment of the complex cultural web into which the emotional life of the Ifaluk is woven. Our goal has been to illustrate the social constructionist approach to the study of emotion and to provide a few examples of the sort of culturally-local facts that play a central role in the ethnopsychological descriptions of those who adopt this approach.

The Evolutionary Psychology Account of the Emotions

The account of the emotions on which we believe contemporary evolutionary psychologists are converging had its beginnings in Charles Darwin's *The Expression of the Emotions in Man and Animals* (1872 [1998]). Darwin pioneered a technique in which subjects are shown photographs of emotionally expressive faces and asked to identify the emotion that the person is experiencing. Using this test Darwin demonstrated that people are capable of identifying emotions from facial displays with considerable reliability. However, Darwin used the technique only on English test subjects. To learn about other cultures, he relied on an extensive correspondence with missionaries, traders, and others. Unfortunately, the questionnaires he used included some rather leading questions, rendering his cross-cultural findings suspect.

In part because of these methodological problems, Darwin's work on facial expressions made relatively little impact until, in the late 1960s and early 1970s, a number of researchers, including Paul Ekman, Wallace Friesen, and Carol Izard began using Darwin's experimental strategy with subjects from non-Western cultures. The results of this work have become quite famous and have made a major impact on subsequent research on the emotions. In one series of experiments, members of the preliterate Fore language group in Papua New Guinea, who had rarely if ever seen Western faces before Ekman and his colleagues arrived, succeeded in picking out photos of Western faces that expressed the emotions involved in various emotionally charged stories. The Fore were also asked to show how their own faces would look if the events in the stories happened to them. American university students who were shown

video tapes of the faces that the Fore produced were comparably successful matching the faces with the intended emotion (Ekman and Friesen 1971). These results, along with much other cross-cultural work on the facial expression of emotion, have convinced many investigators that there do indeed exist *universal* facial expressions for some emotions including happiness, sadness, anger, fear, and disgust. In later work Ekman and others have also accumulated evidence indicating that some of these emotions are accompanied by characteristic patterns of autonomic nervous system activity (Ekman, Levenson, and Friesen 1983; Levenson 1992).

To explain these findings, Ekman and his colleagues posited the existence of *affect programs* associated with each emotion. Affect programs can be thought of as universal and largely automated or involuntary suites of coordinated emotional responses that are subserved by evolved, innate mental and physiological mechanisms present in all normal members of the species.

While the immediate consequences of the initiation of an affect program are taken to be universal, Ekman and his colleagues recognized early on that behaviors further along in the causal stream may be strongly influenced by culture. One of the most dramatic examples of this was Ekman's demonstration that when Japanese subjects were shown unpleasant films in the presence of an authority figure they would begin the muscle contractions required to produce the facial expressions of negative emotions, but then immediately mask these expressions with a polite smile. American subjects, by contrast, made no attempt to mask the expression of negative emotions, nor did Japanese subjects when they viewed the distressing films alone. Ekman and his colleagues explained these findings by positing the existence of culturally-local "display rules" which can override or radically alter the pattern of emotional expression after an affect program has begun to unfold (Ekman 1972). In

334 Ron Mallon and Stephen P. Stich

subsequent work, other researchers in the evolutionary psychology tradition have expanded and elaborated upon this idea, positing display rules and other sorts of culturally-local mental representations that affect not only facial expressions but also tone of voice, posture, self reports about one's emotional experience, and other cognitive and behavioral patterns that follow after the initiation of an affect program (Hochschild 1979; Mesquita and Frijda 1992; Levenson 1994).

What is it that initiates or "triggers" an affect program? What gets it going? In the mid-1970s Ekman proposed that the system of affect programs was linked to an innate "appraisal mechanism" which selectively attends to those stimuli (external or internal) that are the occasion for one or another emotion. Once it is triggered by appropriate stimuli, the appraisal mechanism operates automatically and initiates the appropriate affect program. It is not clear whether Ekman ever thought that there are some stimuli which the appraisal mechanism is built to respond to directly, without the mediation of other cognitive states and processes. But by the mid-1990s he had come to believe that just about all the activity of the appraisal mechanism was affected by culturally-local factors.[22]

Similar proposals have been developed by a number of other researchers. Robert Levenson has offered the "biocultural model" of the emotions, depicted in Figure 22.1, which "reflects a confluence between innate and learned influences".[23] The "innate hardwired" parts of the model—corresponding roughly to Ekman's appraisal and affect program mechanisms—are in the center of the diagram, between the black panels. Those panels are "the primary loci of cultural influences" and can include local knowledge and belief, local values, and display rules of various sorts.

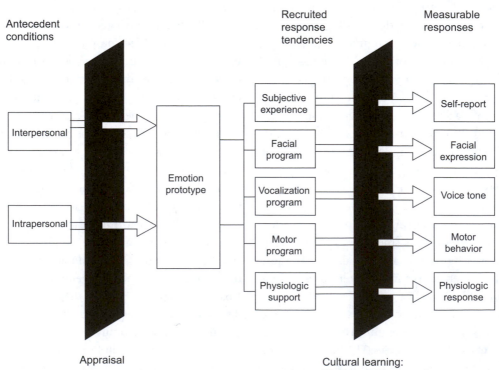

Figure 22.1 Levenson's biocultural model (1994, 126).

While those who study emotion in the evolutionary psychology tradition disagree, often quite vigorously, about lots of the details, we think that most of them would concede that a model like Levenson's is on the right track—that *something* along those lines will be needed to explain both the innate and universal aspects of the emotions and the enormous cultural variability in the circumstances that elicit emotions and in the behavioral and cognitive consequences that emotions produce.

The Debate Over Universality

From what we have said so far about social constructionist and evolutionary psychological approaches to the emotions, the reader might well wonder where evolutionary psychologists and social constructionists *disagree*? There is no obvious logical incompatibility in the two accounts that we have presented. Quite the opposite. An evolutionary psychologist might well take on board much of Lutz's detailed ethnopsychology as an illustration of one of the ways in which the black panels in Levenson's model can be filled in. Lutz describes local knowledge, beliefs, and values among the Ifaluk that determine such things as what sorts of behavior is offensive and how one is expected to behave when angered by an offense of that sort, or what sorts of situations are dangerous and how best to deal with that kind danger, and so on. And this is just the sort of information needed for "appraisal" of the situation and for determining a culturally appropriate response. Social constructionists, for their part, could embrace a model like Levenson's as providing a framework for a theory about the psychological mechanisms underlying many of the phenomena that Lutz and other anthropologists have described, a framework that would explain how innate mechanisms interact with culturally-local beliefs and values. But if the two research programs fit together so nicely, why does it often seem that the two sides are at war? What is all the fighting about?

The answer, or at least one important part of the answer, is that evolutionary psychologists and social constructionists are inclined to make very different claims about the *universality* of emotions. For theorists like Ekman, the psychological mechanisms between the black panels in Levenson's diagram are innate adaptations, present in all normal humans. Moreover, when the appraisal system (whose innate components are housed in the box labeled "Emotion prototype" in Levenson's model) determines that the abstract conditions (or the "core relational theme") appropriate to fear or anger or sadness have been satisfied, *fear or anger or sadness ensues*. Since situations that satisfy the abstract conditions are present in all cultures (though these situations may be quite different in different cultures), people in all cultures will experience these emotions. Indeed, since evolutionary psychologists maintain that some of the mechanisms in models like Levenson's are homologous to mechanisms in other species, they are not at all uncomfortable about attributing some emotions to members of other species.

Social constructionists, for the most part, will have none of this. For them, emotions are culturally-local phenomena, and thus people in very different cultures typically have very different emotions. *Song* and *metagu* are Ifaluk emotions which outsiders do not experience. *Amae* is a Japanese emotion that is unknown (or at least unrecognized) in the West.[24] And *accidie* is an emotion that once was widespread in the West but now has disappeared.[25] Moreover, it is not just exotic emotions like *metagu* or *amae* that social constructionists have claimed to be culturally-local. They make much the same claim for emotions that are commonplace in our own culture. So, for example, Jean Briggs (1970) claims that anger is unknown among the Inuit, and Averill agrees that "anger *as a specific emotion*" is not "universal across all cultures".[26] Robert Levy (1984) suggests that sadness is unknown amongst Tahitians. And, perhaps most radically of all, Richard Shweder (1994) maintains not only that there are no universal emotions, but also that there may well be some cultures in which there are no emotions at all!

The Philosophical Origin of the Dispute

What is going on here? How could researchers whose theories appear to complement each other so nicely disagree so sharply about the universality of emotions? Since they have no fundamental disagreements about the psychological mechanisms underlying the emotions[27] or about the important role that culturally-local beliefs, preferences, and values play in people's emotional lives, why are they at loggerheads about the cultural locality of emotions? The answer, we maintain, or at least one very important part of the answer, is that social constructionists and evolutionary psychologists have a deep though largely hidden *philosophical* disagreement—a disagreement about the meaning and the reference of the emotion terms that ordinary folk use, words like "anger", "*metagu*", "fear", and "*song*". To make the point, we will begin by sketching one version of what is perhaps the most widely held view, among philosophers, about the meaning and reference of terms about mental states. We will then argue that if one held this view one might agree that Levenson's model (or something very like it) was the correct account of the psychological mechanisms underlying the emotions, *and still insist that emotions are culturally-local.*

The account of the meaning of mental state terms that we will present is a version of what is sometimes called *analytic functionalism*, though for reasons that will soon be obvious, we prefer to call it *the description theory*. Views like it have been endorsed by many philosophers, most notably David Lewis. As we view the description theory, it makes three interrelated claims. The first is that the mental state terms of ordinary language can be treated as *theoretical* terms. The second is that

theoretical terms are implicitly defined by the theory in which they are embedded. Building on a strategy first proposed by Ramsey, Lewis showed how the implicit definition that a theory provides for its theoretical terms can be turned into an explicit definition in the form of a *definite description* of the theoretical entities being defined.[28] There is an important sense in which the implicit definitions provided by a theory are *holistic* since the theory implicitly defines *all* its theoretical terms in one fell swoop, and in the definite descriptions that explicitly define each theoretical term, the entire theory plays a role in determining the content of the description. The third claim of the description theory is that the theory which implicitly defines ordinary mental state terms is commonsense (or "folk") psychology, which Lewis characterizes as our "extensive, shared understanding of how we work mentally"—an understanding that "is common knowledge among us".[29] On Lewis's view, our commonsense psychological theory implicitly defines *all* of our ordinary language mental state terms, including terms for the basic propositional attitudes (like "belief" and "desire"), terms for qualitative states (like "pain"), and terms for the emotions. If Lewis's description theory, or something close to it, is the correct theory about the meaning of ordinary mental state terms, then a culture's folk psychological theory implicitly defines their emotion terms, and to fully understand the meaning of one ordinary language emotion term in a culture requires knowing the meanings of all the others.

The ethnopsychological accounts provided by researchers like Lutz are intended *inter alia* to describe part of the folk psychology of the culture being studied. The beliefs about the causes, effects, and moral implications of emotions that Lutz reports are common knowledge (or at least common *belief*) among the Ifaluk. But how much of this belief structure are we to count as part of the Ifaluk's commonsense *psychology*, and thus as contributing to the meaning of their emotion terms? Lewis offers little guidance here, and opinions may differ. Those who would include within the purview of commonsense psychology only a relatively small part of an ethnopsychology like the one Lutz offers adopt what we propose to call an *austere* account of folk psychology, while those who would include much more of a Lutz-style ethnopsychology within folk psychology advocate what we shall call an *opulent* view of folk psychology.[30] This terminology can be extended, in an obvious way, to apply to description theories of meaning as well. An *opulent description theory* is one that maintains that a great deal of ethnopsychology contributes to the meaning of mental state terms, while an *austere description theory* holds that only a much smaller part of ethnopsychology is relevant to the meaning of these terms.

So much for the *meaning* of mental state terms. Now what about their *reference?* To what things in the world do these terms refer? Since the explicit definitions of mental state terms, on a theory like Lewis's, take the form of definite descriptions, the most obvious proposal is that the terms refer to those things in the world that satisfy the descriptions—the things the descriptions are true of. But, as Lewis noted long ago,[31] this would be a rather extreme doctrine, since if any aspect of a folk psychological theory turned out to be mistaken, then *all* the mental state terms that the theory implicitly defined would end up referring to nothing at all. The remedy, Lewis proposed, is to require that the referents of mental state terms *more or less* satisfy the descriptions provided by folk theory. But how much is that, exactly? The answer, of course, is that Lewis's proposal is vague, and different theorists may wish to diminish the vagueness by insisting on a more or less stringent standard. On what we will call the *high accuracy* end of the spectrum are those who insist that a mental state term refers to a state only if *most* of what folk psychology says about states of that kind is true of the state in question. On the *low accuracy* end of

the spectrum are those who will allow much more error in folk psychology before concluding that the terms of folk psychology do not refer. One final bit of terminology: We shall use the term *thick description theory* for accounts that combine an *opulent* description theory of the meaning of mental state terms with a *high accuracy* theory of reference for those terms.

What does all of this have to do with the dispute between social constructionists and evolutionary psychologists? To see the connection, let's assume that a theorist has adopted a thick description theory for the meaning and reference of emotion terms. What might such a theorist conclude about the universality or cultural locality of emotions? Lutz and her fellow ethnopsychologists tell us a great deal about the common knowledge about mental states that people in a culture share. Among the Ifaluk, for example, it is common knowledge that if a man comes into the birthing house, or if a woman works in the taro gardens when she is menstruating, it will provoke *song* in those who know about it. And it is common knowledge that when one realizes one is the object of someone's *song*, one typically experiences *metagu*. On an opulent description theory, these and many other similar claims are part of the folk psychological knowledge of the Ifaluk and thus they contribute to the meaning of "*song*" and "*metagu*". Moreover, on a thick description account of reference, which requires high accuracy, most of these claims must be true of a mental state if it is to count as an instance of *song* or *metagu*. But, of course, in our culture there is no mental state that satisfies (or comes close to satisfying) the thick description that Lutz provides for *song* and *metagu*. If we learn that someone we know has worked in a taro garden while menstruating, it provokes no emotion at all. So there is no mental state in our culture that counts as an instance of *song. Song* does not exist here.

Much the same applies in the opposite direction. It is common knowledge in our culture that if someone burns the national flag, shouts racial epithets, reaches out and touches a stranger, or gives someone "the finger," it is likely to provoke anger in those around him, and that that anger will often lead to a heated exchange of words and occasionally to physical confrontation and violence. On an opulent account, these and many similar commonly-known facts are part of our folk psychological theory and thus part of the meaning of our term "anger". For a thick description theorist, most of them must be true of a mental state if that state is to count as an instance of anger. But situations like these would not provoke any emotion among the Ifaluk, and (if Lutz is right) no mental state there is likely to lead to violence. So, if one accepts a thick description account of the reference of emotion terms, it follows that among the Ifaluk, *anger does not exist*.

It is important to note that the argument leading to these conclusions is quite independent of any views one might have about the psychological mechanisms underlying the emotions. All that matters is that emotion terms get their meaning from the relevant folk psychological theory, that folk theories are construed opulently and differ substantially in different cultures, and that most of what the folk theory says about a state must be true if the state is to count as an instance of the emotion in question.

What we have argued so far is that if one accepted a thick description account of the meaning and reference of emotion terms, then in light of the facts that Lutz and others report one should conclude that the emotions denoted by commonsense emotion terms are culturally-local. But is this what leads social constructionists to this conclusion? Do *they* accept a thick description theory? Here, we must admit, the answer is less than clear cut. The social constructionist anthropologists and psychologists who study the emotions rarely set out and defend their semantic views in any systematic way, nor do they pay careful attention to the distinctions

between meaning and reference or use and mention that are so central to philosophical discussion. Still, we think there is good reason to suspect that something somewhere in the vicinity of the thick description theory is indeed playing an important role in the thinking of many social constructionists. Consider, for example, the following passage from Shweder:

> Across languages, the range of implications, suggestions, and connotations of psychological state terms do not easily map, at least not *lexically*; and to adequately understand the meaning of the terms in either language is to understand a good deal about different local systems of values and particular ways of life. Under such circumstances of hazardous lexical mapping, any strong claim about the distribution around the world of the "emotions," as we define them, is bound to be controversial.[32]

Since Shweder thinks that understanding the meaning of psychological state terms requires understanding a good deal about local values and ways of life, and since he takes this to be relevant to the distribution of the emotions themselves, we don't think it is too much of a stretch to see something like a thick description theory hovering in the wings.

Similar ideas about meaning can be found in Lutz:

> Emotion words are treated here as coalescences of complex ethnotheoretical ideas about the nature of self and social interaction. . . . To understand the meaning of an emotion word is to be able to envisage (and perhaps to find oneself able to participate in) a complicated scene with actors, actions, interpersonal relationships in a particular state of repair, moral points of view, facial expressions, personal and social goals, and sequences of events.[33]

Here again we think it is plausible to think that if Lutz were to recast these ideas in the vocabulary favored by analytic philosophers, the result would bear more than a passing resemblance to the thick description theory.

Now what about those on the other side—the evolutionary psychologists who champion a "biosocial" model—what account of meaning and reference do they accept? It is impossible to give a positive answer to this question, since the evolutionary psychologists who study emotions say little about semantics. However, it is possible to give a negative answer. Since theorists in this tradition insist that emotions like fear and anger are to be found in *all* human cultures and probably in many other species as well, and since they recognize that there are significant cross-cultural differences in the situations which provoke these emotions and the behaviors they lead to, they *cannot* accept a thick description account of the reference of emotion terms. For "fear" and "anger" are terms in English and, as we saw earlier, the thick description theory entails that if a mental state does not share most of the causes and effects of anger that are commonly known among English speakers, then that state does not count as an instance of anger. Also, though the point is less important for our purposes, since evolutionary psychologists sometimes claim that there are terms synonymous with English emotion terms in languages whose speakers have folk psychological theories that are significantly different from ours, they cannot accept an opulent description theory of the meaning of emotion terms. Being unable to accept thick description theories of meaning and reference is hardly a major embarrassment for evolutionary psychologists, since those theories are far from the only games in town. And among the alternatives available, there are some—most notably *causal/historical* theories of reference (Putnam 1975, Devitt and Sterelny 1987)—that would enable evolutionary psychologists to say what they want to say about the universality

of emotions while not in the least contesting that Lutz and others have demonstrated that ethnopsychologies differ quite substantially from one culture to another.

Who's Right, and Why It Doesn't Matter

What we have argued in the previous section is that the dispute between social constructionists and evolutionary psychologists over the universality of the emotions *could be* generated by a philosophical (or semantic) disagreement about the meaning and reference of ordinary language emotion terms. We also suggested, albeit more tentatively, that this philosophical disagreement is largely responsible for the dispute, though the point has gone almost entirely unnoticed by partisans on both sides. If we are correct, then the next obvious question to ask is: Who's right? Does the thick description theory give the correct account of the meaning and reference of commonsense mental state terms, or is the correct account to be found among one of the competing theories on which an emotion term may refer to a mental state even if much of what the relevant folk psychological theory claims about the state is not true? These are questions that are being hotly debated in the philosophical literature, and we will not even try to answer them here.[34] Indeed, one of us has argued at some length that there is an important sense in which the questions *cannot* be answered until those debating them get a lot clearer than they are now on what facts a theory of reference must answer to and thus what counts as getting a theory of reference right.[35]

This might sound like bad news, since if we cannot determine who's right about reference we cannot settle the debate about the universality of the emotions. But we are inclined to be rather more optimistic since, for two rather different reasons, it *really doesn't much matter who's right.* The first reason why it really doesn't matter is that if the debate about the universality of the emotions is indeed driven by disagreements about meaning and reference, then the debate is largely isolated from the rich bodies of empirical and theoretical work done by social constructionists and evolutionary psychologists. As we saw earlier, the social constructionist argument for the cultural locality of the emotions is *entirely independent* of any claims about the psychological mechanisms underlying the emotions. Thus a social constructionist who accepts a thick description theory of meaning and reference could perfectly well remain agnostic about, *or even endorse*, a model like Levenson's and *still* conclude that the emotions are culturally-local. All that's needed is the premise that ethnopsychologies vary significantly from culture to culture. And this, as we have seen, is not a premise that evolutionary psychologists are in the least inclined to dispute.

Quite the opposite; biosocial models like Levenson's are built to accommodate such diversity. But this is no impediment at all to evolutionary psychologists who want to insist on the universality of emotions. For they can simply adopt an account of meaning and reference on which an emotion term in English can refer to mental states in some other culture even if the ethnopsychology in that culture is significantly different from our own. If we are correct, it is the implicit adoption of a thick description theory on one side and an implicit rejection of it on the other which has given rise to the widespread perception that there is a substantial empirical dispute. On our view, this gives rise to the situation depicted in Figure 22.2.

The second reason why we think it doesn't much matter who's right is that, even on the contested issue of universality, no matter who is

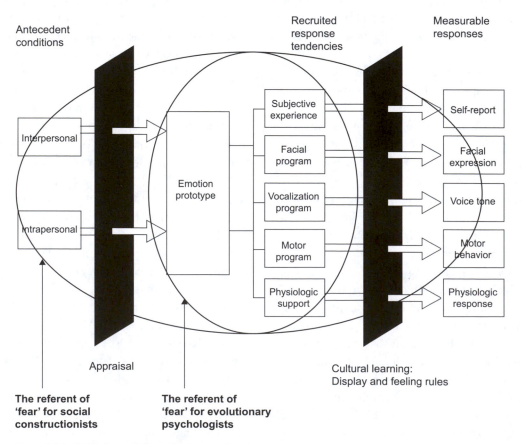

Figure 22.2 Will the *real* fear please stand up?

right about meaning and reference each side could perfectly well say what it wants to say, with the help of a bit of technical terminology. So, for example, if it turns out that a thick description theory gives the correct account of the reference of ordinary language emotion terms, then evolutionary psychologists must concede that fear and other emotions are not universal. Rather, there is a whole family of distinct emotions which are subserved by the same innate emotion prototype and affect program that subserve fear in us. But if we introduce a technical term to refer to *all* of these emotions—*core-fear*, perhaps—then the evolutionary psychologists who have conceded that fear is *not* universal can go on to claim that core-fear *is* universal. And that, surely, is all they ever wanted to claim.

Once it is seen how the debate over the universality of the emotions is rooted in a dispute about the meaning and reference of emotion terms, and how little it matters who is right in *that* dispute, it may be much easier for evolutionary psychologists and social constructionists to stop seeing each other as adversaries and start seeing each other as natural allies in the attempt to understand the emotions. We believe it is time for this odd couple to stop the philosophical quarreling and to recognize how compatible their theories are and how nicely they complement each other.

Notes

1 Throughout we use "social constructionist" as a label for those who advocate important parts of the Standard Social Science Model. This can be misleading in three different ways. First, social constructionism is sometimes identified (usually pejoratively) with a set of radical metaphysical theses that call into question the mind independence of reality or the possibility of knowing it (e.g., Pinker 1997, 57). We use "social constructionism" for the more limited and prima facie more plausible view that particular features of human psychology or social life are culturally

caused and local in character. A second source of confusion is that "social constructionist" as we use it includes theorists who do not characterize themselves as social constructionists, but nonetheless endorse the cultural locality of a given phenomenon. Finally, "social constructionism" thus characterized picks out only one portion of the more extensive doctrine Tooby and Cosmides call the Standard Social Sciences Model (1992, 31–32). Closely enough, then, all SSSM advocates are social constructionists in our sense, though not all social constructionists need endorse every aspect of SSSM as characterized by Tooby and Cosmides. Still, we take it that the examples of social constructionists we discuss and the doctrines they hold are paradigmatic examples of SSSM advocates.

2 See, e.g., Lutz 1988, Kessler and McKenna 1977, Oberoi 1994, Shweder 1985.

3 We use the term "evolutionary psychologist" expansively to include a variety of naturalistic psychological approaches of the sort sketched below. The term has recently been used proprietarily to refer to evolutionary approaches of the sort favored by John Tooby, Leda Cosmides and Steven Pinker (Tooby and Cosmides 1992, Pinker 1997). This latter group is distinguished by its commitment to the thesis of "massive modularity": the claim that a great many (perhaps even all) mental processes, including core cognitive processes, are subserved by domain-specific mechanisms.

4 Geertz 1973, p. 39.

5 Tooby and Cosmides 1992, p. 43.

6 Lutz 1998, p. 157.

7 Lutz personal communication.

8 Lutz 1998, p. 160.

9 Lutz 1998, p. 165.

10 Lutz 1998, p. 167.

11 Lutz 1998, p. 176.

12 Lutz 1998, p. 175.

13 Lutz 1998, p. 171.

14 Lutz 1998, p. 174.

15 Lutz 1998, p. 186.

16 Lutz 1998, p. 202.

17 Lutz 1998, p. 203.

18 Lutz 1998, p. 175.

19 Lutz 1998, p. 173.

20 Lutz 1998, p. 170.

21 Lutz 1998, pp. 201–202.

22 Ekman 1994, p. 16.

23 Levenson 1994, p. 125.

24 Harré maintains that "The Japanese . . . create and sustain an emotion, *amae*, quite distinct from anything found in the adult repertoire of Western cultures" (1986, 10). The Japanese psychiatrist Doi characterizes amae as "a sense of helplessness and the desire to be loved." (Quoted in Morsbach and Tyler 1986, 290.)

25 Harré and Finlay-Jones 1986, p. 27 Harré writes: "I offer accidie as an example of an obsolete emotion, since I think modern people do not associate any specific emotion with laziness or procrastination in the carrying out of tasks that duty demands . . . The basic idea of accidie was boredom, dejection or even disgust with fulfilling one's religious duty" (221).

26 Averill 1994, p. 143.

27 Indeed, social constructionists rarely say anything at all about the psychological and physiological mechanisms that subserve emotions, though they do not deny the existence of such mechanisms (see, e.g., Lutz 1988, 210).

28 For further details, see Lewis 1970, 1972, or Stich 1996, 74ff.

29 Lewis 1994, p. 416.

30 The terms "opulent" and "austere" are borrowed from Horgan and Graham 1990, though the meanings we have assigned them are not quite the ones that Horgan and Graham propose.

31 Lewis 1972, 210ff.

32 Shweder 1994, pp. 33–34, italics and quote marks in the original.

33 Lutz 1998, p. 10.

34 For example, Braddon-Mitchell and Jackson 1996, Lycan 1988, Griffiths 1997, Recanati 1993.

35 Stich 1996, Chapter 1.

References

Averill, James (1994), "It's a Small World But a Large Stage", in Ekman and Davidson 1994, 143–5.

Braddon-Mitchell, David and Frank Jackson (1996), *The Philosophy of Mind and Cognition*. Oxford: Blackwell.

Briggs, Jean L. (1970), *Never in Anger: Portrait of an Eskimo Family*. Cambridge, MA: Harvard University Press.

Darwin, Charles (1872 [1998]), *The Expression of the Emotions in Man and Animals*. Paul Ekman (ed.). New York: Oxford University Press.

Devitt, Michael and Kim Sterelny (1987), *Language and Reality*. Cambridge, MA: MIT Press.

Ekman, Paul (1972), "Universals and Cultural Differences in Facial Expressions of Emotion", in James K. Cole (ed.), *Nebraska Symposium on Motivation 1971, vol 4*. Lincoln: University of Nebraska Press, 207–283.

——. (1994), "All Emotions Are Basic", in Ekman and Davidson 1994, 15–19.

Ekman, Paul and Richard J. Davidson (eds.) (1994), *The Nature of Emotion: Fundamental Questions*. New York: Oxford University Press.

Ekman, Paul and Wallace Friesen (1971), "Constants Across Cultures in the Face and Emotion", *Journal of Personality and Social Psychology* 17: 124–129.

Ekman, Paul, R. Levenson, and Wallace Friesen (1983), Autonomic Nervous System Activity Distinguished Between Emotions", *Science* 221: 1208–1210.

Geertz, Clifford (1973), "Thick Description: Toward an Interpretive Theory of Culture", in *The Interpretation of Cultures: Selected Essays*. New York: Basic Books, 3–32.

Griffiths, Paul E. (1997), *What Emotions Really Are*. Chicago: University of Chicago Press.

Harré, Rom (1986), "An Outline of the Social Construcionist Viewpoint", in Rom Harré (ed.), *The Social Construction of Emotions*. New York: Basil Blackwell, 2–14.

Harré, Rom and Robert Finlay-Jones (1986), "Emotion Talk Across Times: Accidie and Melancholy in the Psychological Context", in Rom Harré (ed.), *The Social Construction of Emotions*. New York: Basil Blackwell, 220–227.

Hochschild, A. (1979), "Emotion Work, Feeling Rules and Social Structure", *American Journal of Sociology* 85: 551–575.

Horgan, Terence and George Graham (1990). "In Defense of Southern Fundamentalism", *Philosophical Studies* 62: 107–134.

Kessler, Suzanne J. and Wendy McKenna (1977), *Gender: An Ethnomethodological Approach*. Chicago: University of Chicago Press.

Levenson, Robert (1992), "Autonomic Nervous System Differences Among the Emotions", *Psychological Science* 3" 23–27.

——. (1994), "Human Emotion: A Functional View", in Ekman and Davidson 1994, 123–130.

Levy, Robert (1984), "The Emotions in Comparative Perspective", in Klaus Scherer and Paul Ekman (eds.), *Approaches to Emotion*. Hillsdale, NJ: Lawrence Erlbaum.

Lewis, David (1970), "How to Define Theoretical Terms", *Journal of Philosophy* 67: 427–446.

——. (1972), "Psychophysical and Theoretical Identifications", *Australasian Journal of Philosophy* 50: 249–258.

——. (1994), "Reduction of Mind", in S. Guttenplan (ed.), *A Companion to the Philosophy of Mind*. Oxford: Blackwell, 412–431.

Lutz, Catherine (1988), *Unnatural Emotions: Everyday Sentiments on a Micronesian Atoll and Their Challenge to Western Theory*. Chicago: University of Chicago Press.

Lycan, William (1988), *Judgement and Justification*. Cambridge: Cambridge University Press.

Mesquita, B. and N. Frijda (1992), "Cultural Variations in Emotions: A Review", *Psychological Bulletin* 112: 179–204.

Morsbach, H. and W. J. Tyler (1986), "A Japanese Emotion, *Amae*", in Rom Harré (ed.), *The Social Construction of Emotions*. New York: Basil Blackwell, 289–307.

Oberoi, Harjot (1994), *The Construction of Religious Boundaries: Culture, Identity, and Diversity in the Sikh Tradition*. Chicago: University of Chicago Press.

Pinker, Steven (1997), *How the Mind Works*. New York: W. W. Norton and Co.

Putnam, H. (1975). The meaning of "meaning". In H. Putnam, *Mind, Language and Reality: Philosophical Papers*, vol.2 (pp.215–271. Cambridge: Cambridge University Press.

Recanati, François (1993), *Direct Reference: From Language to Thought*. Cambridge, MA: Basil Blackwell.

Shweder, Richard (1985), "The Social Construction of the Person: How Is It Possible?", in K. Gergen and K. Davis (eds.), *The Social Construction of the Person*. New York: Springer-Verlag, 41–69.

——. (1994), " 'You're Not Sick, You're Just in Love': Emotion as an Interpretive System", in Ekman and Davidson 1994, 32–44.

Stich, Stephen (1996), *Deconstructing the Mind*. New York: Oxford University Press.

Tooby, John and Leda Cosmides (1992), "The Psychological Foundations of Culture", in Jerome Barkow, Leda Cosmides, and John Tooby (eds.), *The Adapted Mind*. New York: Oxford University Press, 19–136.

Topic 7 HUMAN GENETIC DIVERSITY

WHILE AT FIRST GLANCE the chapters in this section seem only to invoke highly technical arguments about proper research approaches in genetics and the proper application of statistical concepts, a careful read reveals another aspect of the debate about human nature. E. O. Wilson argued that understanding human nature would ultimately be a matter of mining the genetic basis of our traits, and understanding variation in our genetic make-up is crucial to understanding the way in which genes contribute to our make-up. One type of genetic variation has proved tremendously useful to forensic scientists. At certain loci on our genome, there is a great deal of variation between individuals, so much so that an individual can be picked out from a genetic test performed on a sample of blood with a very high degree of certainty. Although this type of variation can rule out the innocent or implicate the guilty, it does not tell us much about how we are made up or what traits we have. Specific patterns in genetic variation provide evidence to population geneticists that a gene is currently under selection or not. If genes are being acted upon by selection, there may be differences in those genes—and their associated traits—in different geographic regions or populations. Finally, if variation in certain of our genes is widespread and knows no racial or geographical boundary, then that variation is not a useful guide to dividing us up into racial groups.

Here we present a dispute over the measurement of human variation and its implications for understanding human evolution and variation in human traits. Evolutionary biologist Richard Lewontin proposes and defends a view that became orthodoxy among evolutionary biologists for many years: There is more genetic variation within human groups than between them. The view has implications for whether or not race is biological (see Topic 9) and for whether or not genetic determinism is correct (see Topic 4). In a recent response to Lewontin, statistician and geneticist A. W. F. Edwards argued that while Lewontin made no error in his estimation of the difference between in-group and between-group variation, he erred in concluding from his estimation that studies of genetic variation had no relevance to racial classification. At around the same time, Nathan Rosenberg and his colleagues published results that, while they agreed more or less with Lewontin on the issue of the distribution of variation, indicated that genetics could still be used to distinguish between the relevant human groups, including races. If correct, this finding indicates that genetic diversity can be counted among the ways in which humans from different populations differ. Importantly, however, this is still far from the claim that there are genes for specific racial traits.

Suggested Further Reading

Bamshad, M., Wooding, S., Salisbury, B. A. and Stephens, J. C. (2004) Deconstructing the relationship between genetics and race. *Nature Genetics*, 5: 598–609.

Brown, R. A. and Armelagos, G. J. (2001) Apportionment of racial diversity: A review. *Evolutionary Anthropology*, 10: 34–40.

Cochran, G. and Harpending, H. (2009) *The 10,000 Year Explosion: How civilization accelerated human evolution*. New York: Basic Books.

Frazer, K. A., Murray, S. S., Schork, N. J. and Topol, E. J. (2009) Human genetic variation and its contribution to complex traits. *Nature Reviews Genetics*, 10: 241–251.

Hawks, J., Wang, E. T., Cochran, G. M., Harpending, H. C. and Moyzis, R. K. (2007) Recent acceleration of human adaptive evolution. *Proceedings of the National Academy of Sciences of the United States of America*, 104: 20753–20758.

Koenig, B. A., Lee, S. S.-J. and Richardson, S. S. (2008) *Revisiting Race in a Genomic Age*. New Brunswick, NJ: Rutgers University Press.

Krimsky, S. and Sloan, K. (2011) *Race and the Genetic Revolution: Science, myth, and culture*. New York: Columbia University Press.

Laland, K. N., Odling-Smee, J. and Myles, S. (2010) How culture shaped the human genome: Bringing genetics and the human sciences together. *Nature Reviews Genetics*, 11: 137–149.

Lao, O., Lu, T. T., Nothnagel, M., Junge, O., Freitag-Wolf, S., Caliebe, A., Balascakova, M., Bertranpetit, J., Bindoff, L. A. and Comas, D. (2008) Correlation between genetic and geographic structure in Europe. *Current Biology*, 18: 1241–1248.

Long J. C. and Kittles, R. A. (2003) Human genetic diversity and the nonexistence of biological races. *Human Biology*, 75: 449–471.

Long, J. C., Li, J. and Healy, M. E. (2009) Human DNA sequences: More variation and less race. *American Journal of Physical Anthropology*, 139: 23–34.

Patrinos, A. (Ed.) (2004) Special issue of *Nature Genetics* "Genetics for the human race", 36, 11.

Novembre, J., Johnson, T., Bryc, K., Kutalik, Z., Boyko, A. R., Auton, A., Indap, A., King, K. S., Bergmann, S., Nelson, M. R., *et al.* (2008) Genes mirror geography within Europe. *Nature*, 456: 98–101.

Serre, D. and Pääbo, S. (2004) Evidence for gradients of human genetic diversity within and among continents. *Genome Research*, 14: 1679–1685.

Witherspoon, D. J., Wooding, S., Rogers, A. R., Marchani, E. E., Watkins, W. S., Batzer, M. A. and Jorde, L. B. (2007) Genetic similarities within and between human populations. *Genetics*, 176: 351–335.

Chapter 23

R. C. Lewontin

THE APPORTIONMENT OF HUMAN DIVERSITY

Introduction

It has always been obvious that organisms vary, even to those pre-Darwinian idealists who saw most individual variation as distorted shadows of an ideal. It has been equally apparent, even to those post-Darwinians for whom variation between individuals is the central fact of evolutionary dynamics, that variation is nodal, that individuals fall in clusters in the space of phenotypic description, and that those clusters, which we call demes, or races, or species, are the outcome of an evolutionary process acting on the individual variation. What has changed during the evolution of scientific thought, and is still changing, is our perception of the relative importance and extent of intragroup as opposed to intergroup variation. These changes have been in part a reflection of the uncovering of new biological facts, but only in part. They have also reflected general sociopolitical biases derived from human social experience and carried over into "scientific" realms. I have discussed elsewhere (Lewontin, 1968) long-term trends in evolutionary doctrine as a reflection of long-term changes in socioeconomic relations, but even in the present era of Darwinism there is considerable diversity of opinion about the amount or importance of intragroup variation as opposed to the variation between races and species. Muller, for example (1950), maintained that for sexually reproducing species, man in particular, there was very little genetic variation within populations and that most men were homozygous for wild-type genes at virtually all their loci. On such a view, the obvious genetical differences in morphological and physiological characters between races are a major component of the total variation within the species. Dobzhansky, on the other hand (1954) has held the opposite view, that heterozygosity is the rule in sexually reproducing species, and this view carries with it the concomitant that population and racial variations are likely to be less significant in the total species variation.

As long as no objective quantification of genetic variation could be given, the problem of the relative degree of variation within and between groups remained subjective and necessarily was biased in the direction of attaching a great significance to variations between groups. This bias necessarily flows from the process of classification itself, since it is an expression of the perception of group differences. The erection of racial classification in man based upon certain manifest morphological traits gives tremendous emphasis to those characters to which human perceptions are most finely tuned (nose, lip and eye shapes, skin color, hair form and quantity), precisely because they are the characters that men ordinarily use to distinguish individuals. Men will then be keenly aware of group differences in such characters and will place strong emphasis on their importance in classification. The problem is even more pronounced in the classification of other organisms. All wild mice look alike because we are deprived of our usual visual cues, so small inter-group differences in pelage color are seized upon for subspecific identification. Again this tends to emphasize between-group variation in contrast to individual variation.

In the last five years there has been a revolution in our assessment of inherited variation, as a result of the application of molecular biological techniques to population problems. Chiefly by use of protein electrophoresis, but also by immunological techniques, it has become possible to assess directly and objectively the genetic variation among individuals on a locus by locus basis. The techniques do not depend upon any *a priori* judgments about the significance of the variation, nor upon whether the variation is between individuals or between groups, nor do they depend upon how much or how little variation is actually present (Hubby and Lewontin, 1965). As a result, the original question of how much variation there is within populations has now been resolved. In a variety of species including Drosophila, mice, birds, plants, and man, it is the rule, rather than the exception, that there is genetic variation between individuals within populations. For example, Prakash et al. (1969) found 42% of a random sample of loci to be segregating in populations of D. *pseudoobscura*, producing an average heterozygosity per locus per individual of 12%. A study of a number of populations of Mus *musculus* by Selander and Yang (1969) gave almost identical results. Two analyses for man, one on enzymes by Harris (1970) and one on blood groups by Lewontin (1967), give respective estimates of 30% and 36% for polymorphic loci within populations, and 6% and 16% for heterozygosity per gene per individual.

The existence of these objective techniques for the assessment of genetic variation, and their widespread application in recent years to large numbers of populations, in conjunction with older information on the distribution of human blood group genes, makes it possible to estimate, from a random sample of genetic loci, the degree of variation within and between human populations and races, and so to put the comparative differentiation within and between groups on a firm quantitative basis.

The Genes

Of the 35 or so blood group systems in man, 15 are known to be segregating with an alternative form in frequency greater than 1% in some human populations. Of these, 9 systems have been characterized in enough populations to make them useful for our purposes. They are listed in Table 23.1 together with the extremes of gene frequency known over the whole range of human populations. I use the concept of "system" rather than "gene" here since it is uncertain whether the MNS system is a single locus with four alleles (as I treat it here) or two closely linked loci with two alleles each. The same ambiguity exists for the Rhesus group, which, again, I treat as a single locus with multiple alleles. For the Rh system, there are many more alleles known than the six listed, but most studies have not had available the full range of antisera, especially anti-Du, anti-e and anti-d, so that the six classes used here include some confounding of subclasses. All the blood group data upon which the present calculations have been made are taken from Mourant (1954), Mourant et al. (1958), and Boyd (1950).

A second group of loci that have more recently been surveyed are serum proteins and red blood cell enzymes (Table 23.1). In contrast to the blood groups, which are detected by immune differences, the serum proteins and RBC enzymes are studied by electrophoretic techniques, different alleles producing proteins with altered electrophoretic mobility. A full discussion of these methods is given by Harris

Table 23.1 Human Genes or "Systems" Included in this Study and Extremes of Allele Frequency in Known Populations

Locus		Allele	Frequency Range	Extreme Populations
Haptoglobin	(Hp)	Hp^1	.09–.92	Tamils-Lacondon
Lipoprotein	(Ag)	Ag^x	.23–.74	Italy-India
Lipoprotein	(Lp)	Lp^a	.009–.267	Labrador-Germany
	(Xm)	Xm^a	.260–.335	Easter Is.-U.S. Blacks
Red Cell Acid Phosphatase	(APh)	p^a	.09–.67	Tristan da Cunha-Athabascan
		p^b	.33–.91	Athabascan-Tristan da Cunha
		p^c	0–.08	Many
6-phosphogluconate dehydrogenase	(6PGD)	PGD^A	.753–1.000	Bhutan-Yucatan
Phosphoglucomutase	(PGM_1)	PGM_1	.430–.938	Habbana Jews-Yanomama
Adenylate kinase	(AK)	AK^2	0–.130	Africans, Amerinds-Pakistanis
Kid d	(Jk)	JK^a	.310–1.000	Chinese-Dyaks, Eskimo
Duffy	(Fy)	Fy^a	.061–1.000	Bantu-Chenchu, Eskimo
Lewis	(Le)	Le^b	.298–.667	Lapps-Kapinga
Kell	(K)	K	0–.063	Many-Chenchu
Lutheran	(Lu)	Lu^a	0–.086	Many-Brazilian Amerinds
P		P	.179–.838	Chinese-West Africans
MNS		MS	0–.317	Oceanians-Bloods
		Ms	.192–.747	Papuans-Malays
		NS	0–.213	Borneo, Eskimo-Chenchu
		Ns	.051–.645	Navaho-Palauans
Rh		CDe	0–.960	Luo-Papuans
		Cde	0–.166	Many-Chenchu
		cDE	0–.308	Luo, Dyak-Japanese
		cdE	0–.174	Many-Ainu
		cDe	0–.865	Many-Luo
		cde	0–.456	Many-Basques
ABO		I^A	.007–.583	Toba-Bloods
		I^B	0–.297	Amerinds, Austr. Abo.-Toda
		i	.509–.993	Oraon-Toba

(1970), who was the first to use it for population genetic purposes in man; and by Giblett (1969), who also gives extensive information on the distribution of alleles in different human populations. It is from this latter source that the data for this paper are taken.

The Samples

The amount of world survey work carried out for the different genes obviously varies considerably. For Xm only four populations are reported: a Norwegian, a U.S. white, a U.S. black, and an Easter Island sample; while for the ABO system literally hundreds of populations in all regions of the world had been sampled by the time Mourant's 1954 compilation was made. In the case of the better known blood groups such as ABO, Rh, and MNS, there is an *embarras de richesse*, and some small sample of population is included in the present calculation. Since our object is to look at the distribution of genic diversity throughout the species, I have tried to include what would appear to be *a priori* representatives of the range of human diversity. But how does one do that? Do the French, the Danes, and the Spaniards, say, cover the same range of density as the Ewe, Batutsi, and Luo? How many different European nationalities should be included as compared with how many African peoples or Indian tribes? There is, morever, the problem of weighting. The population of Japan is vastly larger than the Yanomama tribes of the Orinoco. Should each population be given equal weight, or should some attempt be made to weight each by the proportion of the total species population that it represents? Such weighting would clearly decrease any total measure of human diversity since it would reduce effectively to zero the contribution of all of the small, isolated and usually genetically divergent groups. It would also decrease the proportion of all human diversity calculated to be between populations, for the same reason. In this paper I have chosen to count each population included as being of equal value and to include, as much as possible, equal numbers of African peoples, European nationalities, Oceanian populations, Asian peoples, and American Indian tribes. Both of these choices will maximize both the total human diversity and the proportion of it that is calculated betweeen populations as opposed to within populations. This bias should be born in mind when interpreting the results.

A second methodological problem arises over the question of racial classification. In addition to estimating the within-and between-population diversity components, I attempt to break down the between-population components into a fraction within and between "races." Despite the objective problems of classification of human population into races, anthropological, genetical, and social practice continues to do so. Racial classification is an attempt to codify what appear to be obvious nodalities in the distribution of human morphological and cultural traits. The difficulty, however, is that despite the undoubted existence of such nodes in the taxonomic space, populations are sprinkled between the nodes so that boundary lines must be arbitrary. No one would confuse a Papuan aboriginal with any South American Indian, yet no one can give an objective criterion for where a dividing line should be drawn in the continuum from South American Indians through Polynesians, Micronesians, Melanesians, to Papuans. The attempts of Boyd (1950) and Mourant (1954) to use blood group data and other genetic information for racial classification illustrate that, no matter what the form of the data, the method of classification remains the same. Obvious and well differentiated stereotypes are set up representing well-differentiated population groups. Thus, the inhabitants of Europe speaking Indo-European languages, the indigenes of sub-Saharan Africa, the aborigines of North and South America, and the peoples of mainland East and Southeast Asia, become the modal groups for Caucasian, Negroid, Amerind, and Mongoloid races. Then by the use of linguistic, morphological, historical, and cultural information, all those not yet included are assorted by affinity into these original classes or, in the case of particularly divergent groups like the Australian aborigines, set up as separate races or subraces. In such a scheme, some populations always create difficulties. Are the Lapps Caucasians or do they belong with the Turkic peoples of Central Asia to the Mongoloid race? Linguistically they are Asians; morphologically they are ambiguous; they have the ABO and Lutheran blood group frequencies typical of Europeans but their Duffy, Lewis, Haptoglobin, and Adenylate-kinase gene frequencies are Asian. Their MNS blood group is clearly non-Asian but also is a very poor fit to European frequencies. Similar great difficulties exist for Hindi-speaking Indians and Urdu-speaking Pakistanis. They are, genetically, the mixture of Aryans, Persians, Arabs, and Dravidians that history tells us they should be.

For the purpose of this paper there are two alternatives. Racial classification could be done entirely from evidence external to the data used here (i.e., linguistic, historical, cultural, and morphological). This convention would then decrease the calculated diversity between races and increase the within-race, between-population component, since it would lump together, in one race, groups that are genetically divergent. The alternative would be to use internal evidence only and establish the racial lines that maximize the similarity of the populations with races. The difficulty of such a procedure is that it has no end. The between-race component would be maximized if every population were made a separate race! Even a reasonable application of this method would require that Indians and Arabs each be made separate races and that Oceania be divided into a number of such groups. I have chosen a conservative path and have used mostly the classical racial groupings with a few switches based on obvious total genetic divergence. Thus, the question I am asking is, "How much of human diversity between populations is accounted for by more or less conventional racial classification?" Table 23.2 shows the racial classification used in this chapter. I have made seven such "races" adding South Asian aborigines and Oceanians to the usual four races, also segregating off the Australian aborigines with the Papuan aborigines. Not all the populations listed under each race are sampled for every gene, but the racial classification was, of course, consistent over all genes.

The Measure of Diversity

The basic data are the frequencies of alternative alleles at various loci (or supergenes) in different populations. The problem is to use these data to characterize diversity. One ordinarily thinks of some sort of analysis of variance for this purpose, an analysis that would break down genetic variance into a component within population, between populations, and between races. A moment's reflection, however, will reveal that this is an inappropriate technique for dealing with allelic frequencies since, when there are more than two alleles at one locus, there is no single well-ordered variable whose variance can be calculated. If there are two alleles at a locus, say A_1 and A_2, they can be assigned random variable values, say 0 and 1, respectively, and the variance of the numerical random variable could be analyzed within and between populations. If there are three alleles, however, this trick will not work, for if we assigned random variable values, say 0, 1, and 2 to three alleles A_1, A_2 and A_3, we would get the absurd result that a population with equal proportions of A_1 and A_3 would have a greater variance than are those with equal proportions of A_1 and A_2, and A_2 or A_3.

Any measure of diversity ought to have the following characteristics: (1) It should be a minimum (conveniently, 0) when there is only a single allele present so that the locus in question shows no variation. (2) For a fixed number of alleles, it should be maximum when all are equal in frequency—this corresponds to our intuitive notion that the diversity is much less, for a given number of alternative kinds, when one of the kinds is very rare. (3) The diversity ought to increase somehow as the number of different alleles in the population increases. Specifically, if all alleles are equally frequent, then a population with ten alleles is obviously more diverse in any ordinary sense than a population with two alleles. (4) The diversity measure ought to be a *convex function* of frequencies of alleles; that is, a collection of individuals made by pooling two populations ought always to be more diverse than the average of their separate diversities, unless the two populations are identical in *composition*. It is the identity of *composition*, not of diversity which matters here. Hence, a population with alleles A_1 and A_2 in a 0.70:0.30 ratio, and a population with A_1 and A_2 in a 0.30:0.70 ratio ought to have identical diversity values, but a collection of individuals from both populations ought to have a higher diversity.

There are two measures that immediately suggest themselves as qualifying under the four requirements. One is simply the proportion of

Table 23.2 Inclusive List of All Populations Used For Any Gene in this Study by the Racial Classification Used in this Study

---

Caucasians

Arabs, Armenians, Austrians, Basques, Belgians, Bulgarians, Czechs, Danes, Dutch, Egyptians, English, Estonians, Finns, French, Georgians, Germans, Greeks, Gypsies, Hungarians, Icelanders, Indians (Hindi speaking), Italians, Irani, Norwegians, Oriental Jews, Pakistani (Urdu-speakers), Poles, Portuguese, Russians, Spaniards, Swedes, Swiss, Syrians, Tristan da Cunhans, Welsh

Black Africans

Abyssianians (Amharas), Bantu, Barundi, Batutsi, Bushmen, Congolese, Ewe, Fulani, Gambians, Ghanaians, Hobe, Hottentot, Hututu, Ibo, Iraqi, Kenyans, Kikuyu, Liberians, Luo, Madagascans, Mozambiquans, Msutu, Nigerians, Pygmies, Sengalese, Shona, Somalis, Sudanese, Tanganyikans, Tutsi, Ugandans, U.S. Blacks, "West Africans," Xosa, Zulu

Mongoloids

Ainu, Bhutanese, Bogobos, Bruneians, Buriats, Chinese, Dyaks, Filipinos, Ghashgai, Indonesians, Japanese, Javanese, Kirghiz, Koreans, Lapps, Malayans, Senoy, Siamese, Taiwanese, Tatars, Thais, Turks

South Asian Aborigines

Andamanese, Badagas, Chenchu, Irula, Marathas, Naiars, Oraons, Onge, Tamils, Todas

Amerinds

Alacaluf, Aleuts, Apache, Atacameños, "Athabascans", Ayamara, Bororo, Blackfeet, Bloods, "Brazilian Indians," Chippewa, Caingang, Choco, Coushatta, Cuna, Diegueños, Eskimo, Flathead, Huasteco, Huichol, Ica, Kwakiutl, Labradors, Lacandon, Mapuche, Maya, "Mexican Indians," Navaho, Nez Percé, Paez, Pehuenches, Pueblo, Quechua, Seminole, Shoshone, Toba, Utes, "Venezuelan Indians," Xavante, Yanomama

Oceanians

Admiralty Islanders, Caroline Islanders, Easter Islanders, Ellice Islanders, Fijians, Gilbertese, Guamians, Hawaiians, Kapingas, Maori, Marshallese, Melanauans, "Melanesians," "Micronesians," New Britons, New Caledonians, New Hebrideans, Palauans, Papuans, "Polynesians," Saipanese, Samoans, Solomon Islanders, Tongans, Trukese, Yapese

Australian Aborigines

---

heterozygotes that would be produced in a random mating population or assemblage. If the frequency at the ith allele at a locus is p_i then

$$h = \sum_{i,j=1}^{n} p_i\, p_j \qquad i \neq j \qquad (1)$$

is the herterozygosity, and it can be verified that h, so defined, satisfies requirements (1) to (4) above.

A second measure, which bears a strong resemblance numerically to h, is the Shannon information measure

$$H = - \sum_{i=1}^{n} p_i\, \ln_2 p_i. \qquad (2)$$

This latter measure is widely used to characterize species diversity in community ecology,

and since I am performing a kind of taxonomic analysis here, I will use H. The calculation of H is somewhat eased by published tables of $p\ln_2 p$ (Dolanský and Dolanský, 1952). In line with our requirements for a diversity measure,

$$H = 0 \qquad p_k = 1$$
$$\text{if}$$
$$p_i = 0 \quad i = 1,2,\dots,k-1,\,k+1,\dots,n$$
$$H_{max} = \ln_2 n \quad \text{if} \quad p_i = \frac{1}{n} \text{ for all i.}$$

H has been calculated at three levels for gene frequencies. For each gene, H has been calculated for each population. This within-population value is designated H_0 and its average over populations within a race is designated H_{pop}. Second, for each gene, H has been calculated on the *average gene frequency* over all populations within a race. This value, designated as H_{race}, is greater than the average H_0 for the race, H_{pop}, by virtue of the convexity of the measure H. The difference between H_{race} and H_{pop} is the added diversity that arises from considering the collection of all populations within a race. It is the between-population, within-race component of diversity.

Third, H is calculated on the average gene frequencies at a locus over all the populations in the species. This value, $H_{species}$, is the total species diversity at that locus and will be greater than the average H_{race} over all races. The difference between $H_{species}$ and $\bar{H}_{race}$ is a measure of the added diversity from the factor of race. It is the between-race component of diversity.

The calculation of H_{pop}, $\bar{H}_{pop}$, H_{race}, $\bar{H}_{race}$, and $H_{species}$ involves some convention on how each population shall be weighted. I have already indicated that each population in the sample is given equal weight, so that H_{pop} is the unweighted average of all H_0 within a race, and H_{race} is calculated on the unweighted average gene frequency within each race. $\bar{H}_{pop}$ and $\bar{H}_{race}$ are averaged over all races weighted by the number of populations studied in each race, and $H_{species}$ is likewise calculated on the average gene frequency of the whole species counting each population once. These latter conventions are necessary to be constant with H_0 and H_{pop}, and to make the total diversity add up. The effect of these conventions is to overestimate the total human diversity, $H_{species}$ since small populations are given equal weight with large ones in the calculation of the average gene frequency, $\bar{P}_{species}$ of each allele. These conventions also overestimate the proportion of the total diversity that is between populations and races as opposed to within populations since it gives too much weight to small isolated populations and to less numerous races like the Amerinds and Australian aborigines, both of which have gene frequencies that differ markedly from the rest of the species.

The Results

Table 23.3 shows the results in detail for the 17 genes included in the study. For each gene the number of populations in each race, N, the gene frequency p for each race, the value of H_{race} based on each gene frequency $\bar{p}$, the average within-population H_{pop} for each race separately, and the ratio H_{pop}/H_{race} for each race separately, are given. Where there are only two alleles at a locus known, one of them is arbitrarily chosen for $\bar{p}$, which contains all the information. Where more than two alleles are known, separate $\bar{p}_i$ are given for each allele. Separate race components have not been calculated for lipoprotein Ag, lipoprotein Lp, and protein Xm, because too few populations were available. The last three columns show the value of $H_{species}$ calculated on grand average gene frequency of the species, $\bar{H}_{race}$ and $\bar{H}_{pop}$ average over all races and populations.

There are several interesting details. Where aboriginals, Amerinds, and Oceanians have been studied, they are usually the groups with the lowest H_{race}. Particularly striking examples are the very low diversities for Amerinds in 6PGD, Ak, and ABO; for aborigines in Lutheran, MNS, and ABO; and for Oceanians in Duffy, Kell, and Rh. The only cases where one of the three large races is low in diversity are the Africans for Duffy and the Mongoloids for Lutheran. Since H_{race} measures also the heterozygosity within the race, the low diversities in Aborigines, Amerinds, and Oceanians suggest an effect of genetic isolation and small breeding size for these races. Such effects must apply to the race as a whole, however, and not simply to the breeding structure of each population within it. If a race consists of many small isolated populations, the homozygosity within each population should be high, so that H_{pop} should be low for the race; but different alleles would be randomly fixed in different populations, so that H_{race} would not be especially low. The effect of subdivision of a race into many small populations would be a small ratio, H_{pop}/H_{race}. The only striking example of

Table 23.3 Gene Frequencies and Diversity Components for 17 Genes in 7 Races. See Text for Detailed Explanation

	Caucasians	African	Mongoloid	S. Asian Aborigines	Amerinds	Oceanians	Australian Aborigines	Total	$\bar{H}_{species}$	$\bar{H}_{race}$	$\bar{H}_{pop}$
Haptoglobin											
N	25	21	12	6	21	15	1	101			
$\bar{p}$	.354	.563	.303	.157	.581	.565	.200		.456		
H_{race}	.938	.989	.885	.627	.981	.988	.722		.994	.938	
H_{pop}	.912	.934	.873	.586	.900	.913	.722				.888
H_{pop}/H_{race}	.972	.944	.986	.935	.917	.924	—				
Lipoprotein Ag											
N	4	0	3	0	0	0	0	7			
$\bar{p}$	—	—	—	—	—	—	—		.453		
H_{race}	—	—	—	—	—	—	—		.994	.829	
H_{pop}	—	—	—	—	—	—	—				.600
Lipoprotein Lp											
N	5	2	0	0	2	1	0	10			
$\bar{p}$	—	—	—	—	—	—	—		.162		
H_{race}	—	—	—	—	—	—	—		.639	—	
H_{pop}	—	—	—	—	—	—	—				
Xm											
N	2	1	0	0	0	1	0	4			
$\bar{p}$	—	—	—	—	—	—	—		.290		
H_{race}	—	—	—	—	—	—	—		.869	—	
H_{pop}	—	—	—	—	—	—	—				.866
Red Cell Ap H											
N	7	3	4	0	7	3	0	24			
$\bar{p}_1$	.276	.203	.310	—	.376	.280	—		.302		
$\bar{p}_2$	.693	.767	.685	—	.621	.713	—		.683		
$\bar{p}_3$	.031	.015	.005	—	.003	.007	—		.014		
$\bar{p}_4$	.000	.015	.000	—	.000	.000	—		.001		
H_{race}	1.035	.942	.936	—	.983	.912	—		.989	.977	
H_{pop}	.973	.919	.912	—	.878	.886	—				.917

	Pop 1	Pop 2	Pop 3	Pop 4	Pop 5	Pop 6	Total
H_{pop}/H_{race} (cont.)	.940	.975	.974		.893	.971	
6PGD							
N	5	4	5	0	3	0	17
$\bar{p}$	.961	.914	.905	—	.999	—	.940
H_{race}	.238	.423	.453	—	.011	—	.327
H_{pop}	.231	.410	.411	—	.007	—	.305
H_{pop}/H_{race}	.971	.969	.907	—	.636	—	.286
PGM							
N	6	4	4	0	7	0	21
$\bar{p}$	.690	.785	.769	—	.863	—	.781
H_{race}	.893	.751	.780	—	.576	—	.758
H_{pop}	.842	.750	.751	—	.564	—	.739
H_{pop}/H_{race}	.942	.999	.963	—	.979	—	.714
Adenylate kinase							
N	9	6	4	0	2	0	21
$\bar{p}$	.056	.003	.016	—	0	—	.028
H_{race}	.311	.029	.095	—	0	—	.184
H_{pop}	.297	.028	.004	—	0	—	.160
H_{pop}/H_{race}	.955	.966	.042	—	—	—	.156
Kidd							
N	2	2	2	0	4	0	10
$\bar{p}$	.520	.757	.655	—	.615	—	.411
H_{race}	.999	.800	.930	—	.961	—	.977
H_{pop}	.999	.798	.446	—	.688	—	.930
H_{pop}/H_{race}	1.000	.998	.480	—	.716	—	.724
Duffy							
N	7	2	4	4	5	3	25
$\bar{p}$	.410	.072	.784	.715	.826	1.000	6.45
H_{race}	.977	.373	.753	.862	.667	—	.938
H_{pop}	.835	.370	.680	.671	.586	—	.695
H_{pop}/H_{race}	.854	.992	.903	.778	.879	—	.597
Lewis							
N	5	0	6	0	0	5	16
$\bar{p}$	.459	—	.432	—	—	.483	.456
H_{race}	.995	—	.987	—	—	.999	.994
H_{pop}	.994	—	.935	—	—	.956	.993 / .960

(Continued overleaf)

Table 23.3 Continued

	Caucasians	African	Mongoloid	S. Asian Aborigines	Amerinds	Oceanians	Australian Aborigines	Total	$\bar{H}_{species}$	$\bar{H}_{race}$	$\bar{H}_{pop}$
H_{pop}/H_{race}	.999	—	.947	—	—	.957	—				
Kell											
N	9	4	5	0	0	1	0	19			
$\bar{p}$	.040	.016	.025	—	—	0	—		.029		
H_{race}	.242	.118	.169	—	—	0	—		.189	.184	
H_{pop}	.240	.101	.135	—	—	0	—				.170
H_{pop}/H_{race}	.992	.856	.799	—	—	—	—				
Lutheran											
N	5	4	3	4	4	0	2	22			
$\bar{p}$	.028	.027	.011	0	.051	—	0		.022		
H_{race}	.184	.179	.087	0	.291	—	0		.153	.139	
H_{pop}	.177	.166	.081	0	.137	—	0				.106
H_{pop}/H_{race}	.962	.927	.931	—	.471	—	—				
P											
N	18	4	5	6	4	4	0	41			
$\bar{p}$	.533	.693	.433	.388	.431	.572	—		.509		
H_{race}	.997	.890	.987	.963	.986	.985	—		1.000	.978	
H_{pop}	.980	.812	.934	.931	.971	.969	—				.949
H_{pop}/H_{race}	.983	.912	.946	.967	.985	.984	—				
MNS											
N	13	12	6	6	5	4	2	48			
$\bar{p}_1$	.246	.140	.072	.188	.227	.002	.009		.158		
$\bar{p}_2$	.320	.434	.554	.456	.585	.356	.224		.420		
$\bar{p}_3$	.084	.060	.090	.080	.041	.057	.052		.070		
$\bar{p}_4$	.350	.366	.284	.306	.147	.585	.715		.353		
H_{race}	1.854	1.695	1.574	1.785	1.609	1.236	1.112		1.746	1.663	
H_{pop}	1.819	1.648	1.443	1.611	1.465	1.181	1.045				1.591
H_{pop}/H_{race}	.981	.972	.917	.903	.911	.956	.940				

Rh

N	16	13	9	3	9	10	1	61
$\bar{p}_1$	.469	.096	.766	.813	.506	.831	.585	.518
$\bar{p}_2$	.019	.024	.001	.055	.029	.001	.129	.020
$\bar{p}_3$	.097	.075	.137	.088	.392	.123	.201	.148
$\bar{p}_4$	.006	.004	.035	0	.009	0	0	.009
$\bar{p}_5$	.060	.608	.049	.020	.018	.045	.085	.166
$\bar{p}_6$	.342	.192	.016	.023	.035	0	0	.139
H_{race}	1.763	1.659	1.175	1.020	1.509	.805	1.600	1.900
H_{pop}	1.679	1.537	.994	.855	1.307	.716	1.600	1.420
H_{pop}/H_{race}	.952	.926	.846	.838	.866	.899	—	1.281

ABO

N	22	11	10	6	10	10	1	70
$\bar{p}_1$	.258	.154	.216	.174	.226	.247	.306	.223
$\bar{p}_2$	.117	.134	.200	.187	.009	.092	0	.117
$\bar{p}_3$	.625	.712	.583	.639	.765	.661	.694	.660
H_{race}	1.290	1.154	1.396	1.304	.842	1.210	.889	1.241
H_{pop}	1.276	1.132	1.334	1.219	.667	1.141	.889	1.204
H_{pop}/H_{race}	.989	.981	.956	.935	.792	.943	—	1.126

such a small ratio is for Lutheran in the Amerinds. There is a general tendency for Oceanian and Amerind ratios to be smaller than for the three main races, and Caucasians tend to have the highest ratios, but much of this difference arises from arbitrarily classifying certain populations together in one race. Allowing for this uncertainty, we must conlude that there is no internal evidence that sparse aboriginal populations are more genetically isolated from their neighbors than are more continuously distributed large races.

The lower H_{race} values for the aboriginal populations must reflect something about their early history rather than their general breeding structure. It is generally assumed that both the Amerinds and Australian aborigines became isolated, as groups, rather early and stemmed from a small number of respective ancestors. The genetic evidence of low H_{race} strongly supports this view. The Oceanians are more of a surprise since there appears to be more genetic homogeneity within the group than might have been expected from the variety of physical types.

Table 23.4 summarizes the results of Table 23.3 in a form relevant to the main problem I have posed. The first column gives the value of $H_{species}$ for each gene. The next three columns show how this total diversity is apportioned to within-population, between-population, and between-race components, calculated as follows from Table 23.3:

$$\text{Within populations} = \frac{H_{pop}}{H_{species}}$$

$$\text{Between populations in races} = \frac{H_{race} - H_{pop}}{H_{species}}$$

$$\text{Between races} = \frac{H_{species} - H_{race}}{H_{species}}$$

The results are quite remarkable. The mean proportion of the total species diversity that is

Table 23.4 Proportion of Genetic Diversity Accounted for Within and Between Populations and Races

Gene	Total $H_{species}$	Proportion		
		Within Populations	Within Races Between Populations	Between Races
Hp	.994	.893	.051	.056
Ag	.994	.834	–	–
Lp	.639	.939	–	–
Xm	.869	.997	–	–
Ap	.989	.927	.062	.011
6PGD	.327	.875	.058	.067
PGM	.758	.942	.033	.025
Ak	.184	.848	.021	.131
Kidd	.977	.741	.211	.048
Duffy	.938	.636	.105	.259
Lewis	.994	.966	.032	.002
Kell	.189	.901	.073	.026
Lutheran	.153	.694	.214	.092
P	1.000	.949	.029	.022
MNS	1.746	.911	.041	.048
Rh	1.900	.674	.073	.253
ABO	1.241	.907	.063	.030
Mean		.854	.083	.063

contained within populations is 85.4%, with a maximum of 99.7% for the Xm gene, and a minimum of 63.6% for Duffy. Less than 15% of all human genetic diversity is accounted for by differences between human groups! Moreover, the difference between populations within a race accounts for an additional 8.3%, so that only 6.3% is accounted for by racial classification.

This allocation of 85% of human genetic diversity to individual variation within populations is sensitive to the sample of populations considered. As we have several times pointed out, our sample is heavily weighted with "primitive" peoples with small populations, so that their H_0 values count much too heavily compared with their proportion in the total human population. Scanning Table 23.3 we see that, more often than not, the H_{pop} values are lower for South Asian aborigines, Australian aborigines, Oceanians, and Amerinds than for the three large racial groups. Moreover, the total human diversity, $H_{species}$, is inflated because of the over-weighting of these small groups, which tend to have gene frequencies that deviate from the large races. Thus the fraction of diversity within populations is doubly underestimated since the numerator of that fraction is underestimated and the denominator overestimated.

When we consider the remaining diversity, not explained by within-population effects, the allocation to within-race and between-race effects is sensitive to our racial representations. On the one hand the over-representation of aborigines and Oceanians tends to give too much weight to diversity between races. On the other hand, the racial component is underestimated by certain arbitrary lumpings of divergent populations in one race. For example, if the Hindi and Urdu speaking peoples were separated out as a race, and if the Melanesian peoples of the South Asian seas were not lumped with the Oceanians, then the racial component of diversity would be increased. Of course, by assigning each population to separate races we would carry this procedure to the *reductio ad absurdum*. A *post facto* assignment, based on gene frequencies, would also increase the racial component, but if this were carried out objectively it would lump certain Africans with Lapps! Clearly, if we are to assess the meaning of racial classifications in genetic terms, we must concern ourselves with the usual racial divisions. All things considered, then, the 6.3% of human diversity assignable to race is about right, or a slight overestimate considering that H_{pop} is overestimated.

It is clear that our perception of relatively large differences between human races and subgroups, as compared to the variation within these groups, is indeed a biased perception and that, based on randonly chosen genetic differences, human races and populations are remarkably similar to each other, with the largest part by far of human variation being accounted for by the differences between individuals.

Human racial classifcation is of no social value and is positively destructive of social and human relations. Since such racial classification is now seen to be of virtually no genetic or taxonomic significance either, no justification can be offered for its continuance.

References

Boyd, W. C. (1950). *Genetics and the Races of Man*. Boston: D. C. Heath and Co.

Dolanský, L., & M. P. Dolanský. (1952). *Table of log_2 1/P, p·log_2 1/p, and p·log_2 1/p + (1−p); log_2 1/(1−p)*. Technical Report 227, Research Laboratory of Electronics. Cambridge Massachusetts Institute of Technology

Dobzhansky, T. (1954). A review of some fundamental concepts and problems of population genetics. *Sympos. Quant. Biol.*, 20: 1–15.

Giblett, E. R. (1969). *Genetic Markers in Human Blood*. Oxford and Edinburgh: Blackwell.

Harris, H. (1970). *The Principles of Human Biochemical Genetics*. Amsterdam: North Holland Publishing Co.

Hubby, J. L., & R. C. Lewontin. (1965). A molecular approach to the study of genetic heterozygosity in natural population. *Genetics*, 54: 77–609.

Lewontin, R. C. (1967). An estimate of the average heterozygosity in man. *Amer. J. Hum. Genet.* 19: 681–685.

Lewontin, R. (1968). The concept of evolution. *The International Encyclopedia of the Social Sciences*, 5: 202–209.

Mourant, A. E. (1954). *The Distribution of the Human Blood Groups*. Oxford: Blackwell.

Mourant, A. E., A. C. Kope , and K. Domaniewska-Sobczak. (1958). *The ABO Blood Groups*. Oxford: Blackwell.

Muller, H. J. (1950). Our load of mutations, *Amer. J. Human. Gent.*, 2: 111–176.

Prakash, S., R. C. Lewontin, & J. L. Hubby. (1969). A molecular approach to the study of genic heterozygosity in natural populations. IV. Patterns of genic variation in central, marginal and isolated populations of *Drosophila pseudoobscura*. *Genetics*, 61: 841–858.

Selander, R. K., & S. Y. Yang. (1969). Protein polymorphism and genic heterozygosity in a wild population of the house mouse (*Mus musculus*). *Genetics*, 63: 563–667.

Chapter 24

A. W. F. Edwards

HUMAN GENETIC DIVERSITY
Lewontin's Fallacy

When a large number of individuals [of any kind of organism] are measured in respect of physical dimensions, weight, colour, density, etc., it is possible to describe with some accuracy the population of which our experience may be regarded as a sample. By this means it may be possible to distinguish it from other populations differing in their genetic origin, or in environmental circumstances. Thus local races may be very different as populations, although individuals may overlap in all characters. Fisher (1925).

It is clear that our perception of relatively large differences between human races and subgroups, as compared to the variation within these groups, is indeed a biased perception and that, based on randomly chosen genetic differences, human races and populations are remarkably similar to each other, with the largest part by far of human variation being accounted for by the differences between individuals. Human racial classification is of no social value and is positively destructive of social and human relations. Since such racial classification is now seen to be of virtually no genetic or taxonomic significance either, no justification can be offered for its continuance. Lewontin (1972)

The study of genetic variations in *Homo sapiens* shows that there is more genetic variation within populations than between populations. This means that two random individuals from any one group are almost as different as any two random individuals from the entire world. Although it may be easy to observe distinct external differences between groups of people, it is more difficult to distinguish such groups genetically, since most genetic variation is found within all groups. *Nature* (2001)

Introduction

In popular articles that play down the genetical differences among human populations it is often stated, usually without any reference, that about 85% of the total genetical variation is due to individual differences within populations and only 15% to differences between populations or ethnic groups. It has therefore been suggested that the division of *Homo sapiens* into these groups is not justified by the genetic data. People the world over are much more similar genetically than appearances might suggest.

Thus an article in *New Scientist* (Ananthaswamy, 2002) reported that in 1972 Richard Lewontin of Harvard University "found that nearly 85 per cent of humanity's genetic diversity occurs among individuals within a single population." "In other words, two individuals are different because they are individuals, not because they belong to different races." In 2001, the *Human*

Genome edition of Nature came with a compact disc containing a similar statement, quoted above.

Such statements seem all to trace back to a 1972 paper by Lewontin in the annual review Evolutionary Biology. Lewontin analysed data from 17 polymorphic loci, including the major blood-groups, and 7 "races" (Caucasian, African, Mongoloid, S. Asian Aborigines, Amerinds, Oceanians, Australian Aborigines). The gene frequencies were given for the 7 races but not for the individual populations comprising them, although the final analysis did quote the within-population variability.

> The results are quite remarkable. The mean proportion of the total species diversity that is contained within populations is 85.4%. ... Less than 15% of all human genetic diversity is accounted for by differences between human groups! Moreover, the difference between populations within a race accounts for an additional 8.3%, so that only 6.3% is accounted for by racial classification.

Lewontin (1972) concluded "Since . . . racial classification is now seen to be of virtually no genetic or taxonomic significance . . ., no justification can be offered for its continuance."

Lewontin included similar remarks in his 1974 book The Genetic Basis of Evolutionary Change

> The taxonomic division of the human species into races places a completely disproportionate emphasis on a very small fraction of the total of human diversity. That scientists as well as nonscientists nevertheless continue to emphasize these genetically minor differences and find new "scientific" justifications for doing so is an indication of the power of socioeconomically based ideology over the supposed objectivity of knowledge.

The Fallacy

These conclusions are based on the old statistical fallacy of analysing data on the assumption that it contains no information beyond that revealed on a locus-by-locus analysis, and then drawing conclusions solely on the results of such an analysis. The "taxonomic significance" of genetic data in fact often arises from correlations amongst the different loci, for it is these that may contain the information which enables a stable classification to be uncovered.

Cavalli-Sforza and Piazza (1975) coined the word "treeness" to describe the extent to which a tree-like structure was hidden amongst the correlations in gene-frequency data. Lewontin's superficial analysis ignores this aspect of the structure of the data and leads inevitably to the conclusion that the data do not possess such structure. The argument is circular. A contrasting analysis to Lewontin's, using very similar data, was presented by Cavalli-Sforza and Edwards (1965) at the 1963 International Congress of Genetics. Making no prior assumptions about the form of the tree, they derived a convincing evolutionary tree for the 15 populations that they studied. Lewontin (1972, 1974), though he participated in the Congress, did not refer to this analysis.

The statistical problem has been understood at least since the discussions surrounding Pearson's "coefficient of racial likeness" (Pearson, 1926) in the 1920s. It is mentioned in all editions of Fisher's Statistical Methods for Research Workers from 1925. A useful review is that by Gower in a 1972 conference volume The Assessment of Population Affinities in Man. As he pointed out, "the human mind distinguishes between different groups because there are correlated characters within the postulated groups."

The original discussions involved anthropometric data, but the fallacy may equally be exposed using modern genetic terminology. Consider two haploid populations each of size n. In population 1 the frequency of a gene, say "+" as opposed to "−", at a single diallelic locus is p and in population 2 it is q, where $p + q = 1$. (The symmetry is deliberate.) Each population manifests simple binomial variability, and the overall variability is augmented by the difference in the means. The natural way to analyse this variability is the analysis of variance, from which it will be found that the ratio of the within-population sum of squares to the total sum of squares is simply 4pq. Taking $p = 0.3$ and $q = 0.7$, this ratio is 0.84; 84% of the variability is within-population, corresponding closely to Lewontin's figure. The probability of misclassifying an individual based on his gene is p, in this case 0.3. The genes at a single locus are hardly informative about the population to which their bearer belongs.

Now suppose there are k similar loci, all with gene frequency p in population 1 and q in population 2. The ratio of the within-to-total variability is still 84% at each locus. The total number of "+" genes in an individual will be binomial with mean kp in population 1 and kq in population 2, with variance kpq in both cases. Continuing with the former gene frequencies and taking k = 100 loci (say), the mean numbers are 30 and 70 respectively, with variances 21 and thus standard deviations of 4.58. With a difference between the means of 40 and a common standard deviation of less than

4.6, there is virtually no overlap between the distributions, and the probability of misclassification is infinitesimal, simply on the basis of counting the number of "+" genes. Figure 24.1 shows how the probability falls off for up to 20 loci.

One way of looking at this result is to appreciate that the total number of "+" genes is like the first principal component in a principal component analysis (Box 24.1). For this component the between-population sum of squares is very much greater than the within-population sum of squares. For the other components the reverse will hold, so that overall the between-population sum of squares is only a small proportion (in this example 16%) of the total. But this must not beguile one into thinking that the two populations are not separable, which they clearly are.

Each additional locus contributes equally to the within-population and between-population sums of squares, whose proportions therefore remain unchanged but, at the same time, it contributes information about classification which is cumulative over loci because their gene frequencies are correlated.

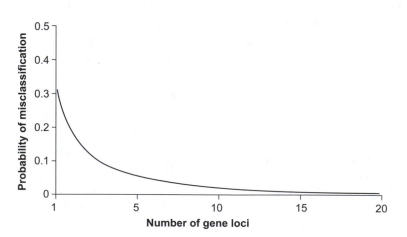

Figure 24.1 Graph showing how the probability of misclassification falls off as the number of gene loci increases, for the first example given in the text. The proportion of the variability within groups remains at 84% as in Lewontin's data, but the probability of misclassification rapidly becomes negligible.

Box 24.1   Principal component analysis

Principal Component Analysis (PCA) is a way of teasing out the more important information in multivariate data, where the high dimensionality renders simple graphical presentation impossible. The procedure can easily be understood even with just two variates, though its use might then be unnecessary. Taking an example from anthropometry where PCA originated, we might have data on the lengths and breadths of a number of human skulls. Each skull can be represented by a point in a diagram whose two axes are length and breadth. Since length and breadth will almost certainly be associated to some extent, the points will tend to be spread out preferentially in a certain direction, stretching from short length and breadth (a small skull) to long length and breadth (a large skull).

PCA defines this direction precisely as that of the line for which the sum of the squares of the perpendicular distances from the points to the line is a minimum. This line passes through the centre of gravity of the points, and a simple application of Pythagoras's Theorem shows that the one-dimensional array of the points defined by the feet of the perpendiculars from the points to the line then has the maximum possible sum of squares. In other words, the variability of the data has been partitioned into two components, one of which, along this line, is known as the (First) Principal Component because it encapsulates as much of the variability as can be represented in one dimension. The Second Component, at right angles to the First, encapsulates the remainder, which is, of course, a minimum.

These two components can be used as replacement axes on the graph. Sometimes the First Component will have an obvious meaning, as would be the case with the skulls, where it is clear that it corresponds in a general way to "size". Similarly the Second Component corresponds in some sense to "shape", because a skull whose data-point is far from the line of the First Component will either be longer and narrower than the norm, or shorter and broader.

The procedure generalises to any number of variates, and the successive First, Second, Third, ... Components are then mutually-orthogonal directions partitioning the total variability into ever-decreasing amounts. A graph of the first two components will represent as much of the information as is possible using only two dimensions.

Classification

It might be supposed, though it would be wrong, that this example is prejudiced by the assumptions that membership of the two populations is known in advance and that, at each locus, it is the same population that has the higher frequency of the "+" gene. In fact the only advantage of the latter simplifying assumption was that it made it obvious that the total number of "+" genes is the best discriminant between the two populations.

To dispel these concerns, consider the same example but with "+" and "−" interchanged at each locus with probability ½, and suppose that there is no prior information as to which population each individual belongs. Clearly, the total number of "+" genes an individual contains is no longer a discriminant, for the expected number is now the same in each group. A cluster analysis will be necessary in order to uncover the groups, and a convenient criterion is again based on the analysis of variance as in the method introduced by Edwards and Cavalli-Sforza

(1965). Here the preferred division into two clusters maximises the between-clusters sum of squares or, what is the same thing, minimises the sum of the within-clusters sums of squares.

As pointed out by these authors, it is extremely easy to compute these sums for binary data, for all the information is contained in the half-matrix of pairwise distances between the individuals, and at each locus this distance is simply 0 for a match and 1 for a mismatch of the genes. Since interchanging "+" and "−" makes no difference to the numbers of matches and mismatches, it is clear that the random changes introduced above are irrelevant. Continuing the symmetrical example, the probability of a match is $p^2 + q^2$ if the two individuals are from the same population and $2pq$ if they are from different populations. With k loci, therefore, the distance between two individuals from the same population will be binomial with mean $k(p^2 + q^2)$ and variance $k(p^2 + q^2)(1 - p^2 - q^2)$ and if from different populations binomial with mean $2kpq$ and variance $2kpq(1-2pq)$. These variances are, of course, the same.

Taking $p = 0.3$, $q = 0.7$ and $k = 100$ as before, the means are 58 and 42 respectively, a difference of 16, the variances are 24.36 and the standard deviations both 4.936. The means are thus more than 3 standard deviations apart (3.2415). The entries of the half-matrix of pairwise distances will therefore divide into two groups with very little overlap, and it will be possible to identify the two clusters with a risk of misclassification which tends to zero as the number of loci increases.

By analogy with the above example, it is likely that a count of the four DNA base frequencies in homologous tracts of a genome would prove quite a powerful statistical discriminant for classifying people into population groups.

Conclusion

There is nothing wrong with Lewontin's statistical analysis of variation, only with the belief that it is relevant to classification. It is not true that "racial classification is . . . of virtually no genetic or taxonomic significance". It is not true, as *Nature* claimed, that "two random individuals from any one group are almost as different as any two random individuals from the entire world", and it is not true, as the *New Scientist* claimed, that "two individuals are different because they are individuals, not because they belong to different races" and that "you can't predict someone's race by their genes". Such statements might only be true if all the characters studied were independent, which they are not.

Lewontin used his analysis of variation to mount an unjustified assault on classification, which he deplored for social reasons. It was he who wrote "Indeed the whole history of the problem of genetic variation is a vivid illustration of the role that deeply embedded ideological assumptions play in determining scientific 'truth' and the direction of scientific inquiry" (Lewontin, 1974). In a 1970 article *Race and intelligence* Lewontin had earlier written

> I shall try, in this article, to display Professor Jensen's argument, to show how the structure of his argument is designed to make his point and to reveal what appear to be deeply embedded assumptions derived from a particular world view, leading him to erroneous conclusions.

A proper analysis of human data reveals a substantial amount of information about genetic differences. What use, if any, one makes of it is quite another matter. But it is a dangerous mistake to premise the moral equality of human beings on biological similarity because dissimilarity, once revealed, then becomes an argument for moral inequality. One is reminded of Fisher's (1956) remark in *Statistical Methods and Scientific Inference* "that the best causes tend to attract to their support the worst arguments, which seems to be equally true in the intellectual and in the moral sense."

Epilogue

This article could, and perhaps should, have been written soon after 1974. Since then many advances have been made in both gene technology and statistical computing that have facilitated the study of population differences from genetic data. The magisterial book of Cavalli-Sforza, Menozzi and Piazza (1994) took the human story up to 1994, and since then many studies have amply confirmed the validity of the approach. Very recent studies (Pritchard, Stephens and Donnelly, 2000; Rosenberg, Pritchard, Webes, Cann, Kidd, Zhivotovsky and Feldman, 2002) have treated *individuals* in the same way that Cavalli-Sforza and Edwards treated *populations* in 1963, namely by subjecting their genetic information to a cluster analysis thus revealing genetic affinities that have unsurprising geographic, linguistic and cultural parallels. As the authors of the most extensive of these (Rosenberg et al. 2002) comment, "it was only in the accumulation of small allele-frequency differences across many loci that population structure was identified."

References

Ananthaswamy, A. (2002). Under the skin. *New Scientist*, 174: 34–37.

Cavalli-Sforza, L. L., & Piazza, A. (1975). Analysis of evolution: evolutionary rates, independence and treeness. *Theor Pop Biol*, 8: 127–165.

Cavalli-Sforza, L. L., & Edwards, A. W. F. (1965). Analysis of human evolution. In *Proceedings of the 11th International Congress on Genetics, The Hague 1963, Genetics Today 3* (pp. 923–933). Oxford: Pergamon.

Cavalli-Sforza, L. L., Menozzi, P., & Piazza, A. (1994). *The History and Geography of Human Genes*. Princeton, NJ: Princeton University Press.

Edwards, A. W. F., & Cavalli-Sforza, L. L. (1965). A method for cluster analysis. *Biometrics*, 21: 362–375.

Fisher, R. A. (1925). *Statistical Methods for Research Workers*. Edinburgh: Oliver and Boyd.

Fisher, R. A. (1956). *Statistical Methods and Scientific Inference*. Edinburgh: Oliver and Boyd.

Gower J. C. Measures of taxonomic distance and their analysis. In J. S. Weiner and J. Huizinga (Eds.), *The Assessment of Population Affinities in Man* (pp. 1–25). Oxford: Clarendon

Lewontin, R. C. (1970). Race and intelligence. *Bulletin of the Atomic Scientists*, March: 2–8.

Lewontin, R. C. (1972). The apportionment of human diversity. In T. Dobzhansky, M. K. Hecht and W. C. Steere (Eds.), *Evolutionary Biology 6* (pp. 381–398). New York: Appleton-Century-Crofts.

Lewontin, R. C. (1974). *The Genetic Basis of Evolutionary Change*. New York: Columbia University Press.

Nature (2001). The Human Genome Edition.

Pearson, K. (1926). On the coefficient of racial likeness. *Biometrika*, 18: 105–117.

Pritchard, J. K., Stephens, M., & Donnelly, P. (2000). Inference of population structure using multilocus genotype data. *Genetics* 155: 945–959.

Rosenberg, N. A., Pritchard, J. K., Weber, J. L., Cann, H. M., Kidd, K. K., Zhivotovsky, L. A., & Feldman, M. W. (2002). Genetic structure of human populations. *Science*, 298: 2381–2385.

Chapter 25

Noah A. Rosenberg, Jonathan K. Pritchard, James L. Weber, Howard M. Cann, Kenneth K. Kidd, Lev A. Zhivotovsky and Marcus W. Feldman

GENETIC STRUCTURE OF HUMAN POPULATIONS

Most studies of human variation begin by sampling from predefined "populations." These populations are usually defined on the basis of culture or geography and might not reflect underlying genetic relationships (Foster and Sharp, 2002). Because knowledge about genetic structure of modern human populations can aid in inference of human evolutionary history, we used the HGDP-CEPH Human Genome Diversity Cell Line Panel (Cann et al., 2002) to test the correspondence of predefined groups with those inferred from individual multilocus genotypes.

The average proportion of genetic differences between individuals from different human populations only slightly exceeds that between unrelated individuals from a single population (Lewontin, 1972; Latter, 1980; Barbujani, Magagni, Minch and Cavalli-Sforza, 1997). That is, the within-population component of genetic variation, estimated here as 93 to 95% (Table 25.1), accounts for most of human genetic diversity. Perhaps as a result of differences in sampling schemes, our estimate is higher than previous estimates from studies of comparable geographic coverage (Lewontin, 1972; Latter, 1980; Barbujani et al., 1997; Romauldi et al., 2002), one of which also used microsatellite markers (Barbujani et al. 1997). This overall similarity of human populations is also evident in the geographically widespread nature of most alleles. Of 4199 alleles present more than once in the sample, 46.7% appeared in all major regions represented: Africa, Europe, the Middle East, Central/South Asia, East Asia, Oceania, and America. Only 7.4% of these 4199 alleles were exclusive to one region; region-specific alleles were usually rare, with a median relative frequency of 1.0% in their region of occurrence.

Despite small among-population variance components and the rarity of "private" alleles, analysis of multilocus genotypes allows inference of genetic ancestry without relying on information about sampling locations of individuals (Bowcock et al., 1994; Mountain and Cavalli-Sforza, 1997; Pritchard, Stephens and Donnelly, 2000). We applied a model-based clustering algorithm that, loosely speaking, identifies subgroups that have distinctive allele frequencies. This procedure, implemented in the computer program *structure* (Pritchard et al., 2000), places individuals into K clusters, where K is chosen in advance but can be varied across independent runs of the algorithm. Individuals can have membership in multiple clusters, with membership coefficients summing to 1 across clusters.

In the worldwide sample, individuals from the same predefined population nearly always shared similar membership coefficients in inferred clusters. At $K = 2$ the clusters were anchored by Africa and America, regions separated by a relatively large genetic distance.

Table 25.1 Analysis of molecular variance (AMOVA). Eurasia, which encompasses Europe, the Middle East, and Central/South Asia, is treated as one region in the five-region AMOVA but is subdivided in the seven-region design. The World-B97 sample mimics a previous study

Sample	Number of regions	Number of populations	Variance components and 95% confidence intervals (%)		
			Within populations	Among populations within regions	Among regions
World	1	52	94.6 (94.3, 94.8)	5.4 (5.2, 5.7)	
World	5	52	93.2 (92.9, 93.5)	2.5 (2.4, 2.6)	4.3 (4.0, 4.7)
World	7	52	94.1 (93.8, 94.3)	2.4 (2.3, 2.5)	3.6 (3.3, 3.9)
World-B97	5	14	89.8 (89.3, 90.2)	5.0 (4.8, 5.3)	5.2 (4.7, 5.7)
Africa	1	6	96.9 (96.7, 97.1)	3.1 (2.9, 3.3)	
Eurasia	1	21	98.5 (98.4, 98.6)	1.5 (1.4, 1.6)	
Eurasia	3	21	98.3 (98.2, 98.4)	1.2 (1.1, 1.3)	0.5 (0.4, 0.6)
Europe	1	8	99.3 (99.1, 99.4)	0.7 (0.6, 0.9)	
Middle East	1	4	98.7 (98.6, 98.8)	1.3 (1.2, 1.4)	
Central/South Asia	1	9	98.6 (98.5, 98.8)	1.4 (1.2, 1.5)	
East Asia	1	18	98.7 (98.6, 98.9)	1.3 (1.1, 1.4)	
Oceania	1	2	93.6 (92.8, 94.3)	6.4 (5.7, 7.2)	
America	1	5	88.4 (87.7, 89.0)	11.6 (11.0, 12.3)	

Each increase in K split one of the clusters obtained with the previous value. At K = 5, clusters corresponded largely to major geographic regions. However, the next cluster at K = 6 did not match a major region but consisted largely of individuals of the isolated Kalash group, who speak an Indo-European language and live in northwest Pakistan. In several populations, individuals had partial membership in multiple clusters, with similar membership coefficients for most individuals. These populations might reflect continuous gradations in allele frequencies across regions or admixture of neighboring groups. Unlike other populations from Pakistan, Kalash showed no membership in East Asia at K = 5, consistent with their suggested European or Middle Eastern origin (Qamar et al., 2002).

In America and Oceania, regions with low heterozygosity, inferred clusters corresponded closely to predefined populations. These regions had the largest among-population variance components, and they required the fewest loci to obtain the clusters observed with the full data. Inferred clusters for Africa and the Middle East were also consistent across runs but did not all correspond to predefined groups. For the other samples, among-population variance components were below 2%, and independent structure runs were less consistent. For K ≥ 3, similarity coefficients for pairs of runs were typically moderate (0.1 to 0.85), rather than large (0.85 to 1.0). However, various patterns were observed across runs.

In East Asia, Yakut, whose language is Altaic, and Japanese, whose language is often classified as Altaic, were usually identified as distinctive. Other speakers of Altaic languages, including Daur, Hezhen, Mongola, Oroqen, and Xibo, all from northern China, shared a greater degree of membership with Japanese and Yakut than with more southerly groups from other language families, such as Cambodian, Dai, Han, Miao,

Naxi, She, Tujia, and Yi. However, Tu, who speak an Altaic language and live in north-central China, largely grouped with the southern populations. Lahu, who speak a Sino-Tibetan language and were the least heterozygous population in the region, frequently separated despite their proximity with other groups sampled from southern China (Du and Yip, 1996).

Eurasia frequently separated into its component regions, along with Kalash. Adygei, from the Caucasus, shared membership in Europe and Central/South Asia. Within Central/South Asia, Burusho of northern Pakistan, a linguistic isolate, largely separated from other groups, although less clearly than the genetic isolate, Kalash. Perhaps as a result of shared Mongol ancestry (Qamar et al., 2002; Du and Yip, 1996), Hazara of Pakistan and Uygur of northwestern China, whose languages are Indo-European and Altaic, respectively, clustered together. For Balochi, Makrani, Pathan, and Sindhi, all of whose languages are Indo-European, and less so for Dravidian-speaking Brahui, multiple clusters were found, with individuals from many populations having membership in each cluster.

Europe, with the smallest among-population variance component (0.7%), was the most difficult region in which to detect population structure. The highest-likelihood run for K = 3 found no structure; in other runs, Basque and Sardinian were identified as distinctive. Russians variously grouped with Adygei and Orcadians; Russian-Orcadian similarity might derive from shared Viking contributions (Haywood, 1995). French, Italians, and Tuscans showed mixed membership in clusters that contained other populations.

Because genetic drift occurs rapidly in small populations, particularly in those that are also isolated, these groups quickly accumulate distinctive allele frequencies. Thus, *structure* efficiently detects isolated and relatively homogeneous groups, even if the times since their divergences or exchanges with other groups are short (Rosenberg et al., 2001). This

phenomenon may explain the inferred distinctiveness of groups with low heterozygosity, such as Lahu and American groups, and those that are small and isolated, such as Kalash. Groups with larger sample sizes are also more easily separated; thus, the difficulty of clustering in East Asia was exacerbated by small sample sizes. Because sampling was population-based, the sample likely produced clusters that were more distinct than would have been found in a sample with random worldwide representation. However, world-level boundaries between major clusters mostly corresponded to major physical barriers (oceans, Himalayas, Sahara).

The amount of among-group variation affects the number of loci required to produce clusters similar to those obtained with the full data. For the Middle East, with an among-population variance component of 1.3%, nearly all the loci were required to achieve a similarity of 0.8 to the clustering on the basis of full data, and use of more loci would likely produce more consistent clustering. For Oceania and Africa, only ~200 loci were needed; for the world sample, ~150 were needed, and ~100 were sufficient for America. Fewer loci would probably suffice for larger samples (Rosenberg et al., 2001); conversely, accuracy decreased considerably when only half the sample was used. The number of loci required would also decrease if extremely informative markers, such as those with particularly high heterozygosity, were genotyped (Rosenberg et al., 2001). The loci here form a panel intended for use primarily in individuals of European descent (Weber and Broman, 2001). Although 10 of the loci had heterozygosity less than 0.5 in East Asia, none had similarly low European heterozygosities; thus, inference of subclusters using "random" markers might be more difficult than observed here, especially in Europe. However, the effect of excluding markers with low European heterozygosity is likely minimal, because generally high microsatellite heterozygosities ensure that relatively few loci are discarded on these grounds

(Rogers and Jorde, 1996). The fact that regional heterozygosities here follow the same relative order as and have nearly equal values to those of loci that were ascertained in a geographically diverse panel (Bowcock et al., 1994) provides further evidence that the ascertainment effect on heterozygosity estimates and on statistics derived from these estimates, such as genetic variance components (Urbanek and Goldman, 1996), is small.

Genetic clusters often corresponded closely to predefined regional or population groups or to collections of geographically and linguistically similar populations. Among exceptions, linguistic similarity did not provide a general explanation for genetic groupings of populations that were relatively distant geographically, such as Hazara and Uygur or Tu and populations from southern China. Our finer clustering results compared with other multilocus studies derive from our use of more data. General correspondence between regional affiliation and genetic ancestry has been reported (Bowcock et al., 1994; Mountain and Cavalli-Sforza, 1997; Pritchard et al., 2000), with clearer correspondence in studies that used more loci (Mountain and Cavalli-Sforza, 1997) than in those that used fewer loci (Romauldi et al., 2002; Wilson et al., 2001); we have further identified correspondence between genetic structure and population affiliation in regions with among-population variance components larger than 2 to 3%.

The structure of human populations is relevant in various epidemiological contexts. As a result of variation in frequencies of both genetic and nongenetic risk factors, rates of disease and of such phenotypes as adverse drug response vary across populations (Wilson et al., 2001; Risch, Burchard, Ziv and Tang, 2002). Further, information about a patient's population of origin might provide healthcare practitioners with information about risk when direct causes of disease are unknown (Risch et al., 2002). Recent articles have considered whether it is preferable to use self-reported population ancestry or genetically inferred ancestry in such situations (Wilson et al., 2001; Risch et al., 2002; Thomas and Witte, 2002). We have found that predefined labels were highly informative about membership in genetic clusters, even for intermediate populations, in which most individuals had similar membership coefficients across clusters. Sizable variation in ancestry within predefined populations was detected only rarely, such as among geographically proximate Middle Eastern groups.

Thus, for many applications in epidemiology, as well as for assessing individual disease risks, self-reported population ancestry likely provides a suitable proxy for genetic ancestry. Self-reported ancestry can be obtained less intrusively than genetic ancestry, and if self-reported ancestry subdivides a genetic cluster into multiple groups, it may provide useful information about unknown environmental risk factors (Risch et al., 2002; Wacholder, Rothman and Caporaso, 2002). One exception to these general comments may arise in recently admixed populations, in which genetic ancestry varies substantially among individuals; this variation might correlate with risk as a result of genetic or cultural factors (Thomas and Witte, 2002). In some contexts, however, use of genetic clusters is more appropriate than use of self-reported ancestry. In genetic case-control association studies, false positives can be obtained if disease risk is correlated with genetic ancestry (Thomas and Witte, 2002; Pritchard and Donnelly, 2001). Basing analyses on self-reported ancestry reduces the proportion of false positives considerably (Wacholder, Rothman and Caporaso, 2002). However, association studies are usually analyzed by significance testing, in which slight differences in genetic ancestry between cases and controls can produce statistically significant false-positive associations in large samples. Thus, errors incurred by using self-reported rather than genetic ancestry might cause serious problems in large studies that will be required for identifying susceptibility loci with small effects (Pritchard and Donnelly, 2001). Genetic clustering is also more appropriate for some types of population genetic studies, because unrecognized genetic structure can produce false positives in statistical tests for population growth or natural selection (Ptak and Przeworski, 2002).

The challenge of genetic studies of human history is to use the small amount of genetic differentiation among populations to infer the history of human migrations. Because most alleles are widespread, genetic differences among human populations derive mainly from gradations in allele frequencies rather than from distinctive "diagnostic" genotypes. Indeed, it was only in the accumulation of small allele-frequency differences across many loci that population structure was identified. Patterns of modern human population structure discussed here can be used to guide construction of historical models of migration and admixture that will be useful in inferential studies of human genetic history.

References

Barbujani, G., Magagni, A., Minch, E., & Cavalli-Sforza, L. L. (1997). An apportionment of human DNA diversity. *Proceedings of the National Academy of Sciences of the U.S.A.*, 94: 4516–4519.

Bowcock, A. M., Ruiz-Linares, A., Tomfohrde, J., Minch, E., Kidd, J. R., & Cavalli-Sforza, L. L. (1994). High resolution of human evolutionary trees with polymorphic microsatellites. *Nature*, 368: 455–457.

Brown, R. A., & Armelagos, G. J. (2001). Apportionment of racial diversity: a review. *Evolutionary Anthropology* 10: 34–40.

Calafell, F., Shuster, A., Speed, W. C., Kidd, J. R., Kidd, K. K. (1998). Short tandem repeat polymorphism evolution in humans. *European Journal of Human Genetics*, 6: 38–49.

Cann, H. M., de Toma, C., Cazes, L., Legrand, M. F., Morel, V., Piouffre, L., Bodmer, J., Bodmer, W. F., Bonne-Tamir, B., Cambon-Thomsen, A., Chen, Z., Chu, J., Carcassi, C., Contu, L., Du, R., Excoffier, L., Ferrara, G. B., Friedlaender, J. S., Groot, H., Gurwitz, D., Jenkins, T., Herrera, R. J., Huang, X., Kidd, J., Kidd, K. K., Langaney, A., Lin, A. A., Mehdi, S. Q., Parham, P., Piazza, A., Pistillo, M. P., Qian, Y., Shu, Q., Xu, J., Zhu, S., Weber, J. L., Greely, H. T., Feldman, M. W., Thomas, G., Dausset, J., & Cavalli-Sforza, L. L. (2002) A human genome diversity cell line panel. *Science*, 296: 261–262.

Foster, M. W., & Sharp, R. R. (2002). Race, ethnicity, and genomics: social classifications as proxies of biological heterogeneity. *Genome Research*, 12: 844–850.

Jin, L., & Chakraborty, R. (1995). Population structure, stepwise mutations, heterozygote deficiency and their implications in DNA forensics. *Heredity*, 74: 274–285.

Jorde, L. B., Watkins, W. S., Bamshad, M. J., Dixon, M. E., Ricker, C. E., Seielstad, M. T., & Batzer, M. A. (2000). The distribution of human genetic diversity: a comparison of mitochondrial, autosomal, and Y-chromosome data. *American Journal of Human Genetics*, 66: 979–988.

Latter, B. D. H. (1980). Genetic differences within and between populations of the major human subgroups. *American Naturalist*, 116: 220–237.

Lewontin, R. C. (1972). The apportionment of human diversity. *Evolutionary Biology*, 6: 381–398.

Mountain, J. L., & Cavalli-Sforza, L. L. (1997). Multilocus genotypes, a tree of individuals, and human evolutionary history. *American Journal of Human Genetics*, 61: 705–718.

Pritchard, J. K., & Donnelly, P. (2001). Case–Control studies of association in structured or admixed populations. *Theoretical Population Biology*, 60: 227–237.

Pritchard, J. K., Stephens, M., & Donnelly, P. (2000). Inference of population structure using multilocus genotype data. *Genetics*, 155: 945–959.

Ptak, S. E., & Przeworski, M. (2002). Evidence for population growth in humans is confounded by fine-scale population structure. *Trends in Genetics*, 18: 559–563.

Qamar, R., Ayub, Q., Mohyuddin, A., Helgason, A., Mazhar, K., Mansoor, A., Zerjal, T., Tyler-Smith, C., & Mehdi, S. Q. (2002). Y-chromosomal DNA variation in Pakistan. *American Journal of Human Genetics*, 70: 1107–1124.

Risch, N., Burchard, E., Ziv, E., & Tang, H. (2002). Categorization of humans in biomedical research: genes, race and disease. *Genome Biology*, 3, comment2007.1.

Rogers, A. R., & Jorde, L. B. (1996). Ascertainment bias in estimates of average heterozygosity. *American Journal of Human Genetics*, 58: 1033–1041.

Romualdi, C., Balding, D., Nasidze, I. S., Risch, G., Robichaux, M., Sherry, S. T., Stoneking, M., Batzer, M. A., & Barbujani, G. (2002). Patterns of human diversity, within and among continents, inferred from biallelic DNA polymorphisms. *Genome Research*, 12: 602–612.

Rosenberg, N. A., Burke, T., Elo, K. Feldman, M. W., Freidlin, P. J., Groenen, M. A. M., Hillel, J., Mäki-Tanila, A., Tixier-Boichard, M., Vignal, A., Wimmers, K., & Weigend, S. (2001) Empirical evaluation of genetic clustering methods using multilocus genotypes from 20 chicken breeds. *Genetics*, 159: 699–613.

Thomas, D. C., & Witte, J. S. (2002). Point: population stratification: a problem for case–control studies of candidate-gene associations? *Cancer, Epidemiology, Biomarkers & Prevention*, 11: 505–512.

Urbanek, M., Goldman, D., & Long, J. C. (1996). The apportionment of dinucleotide repeat diversity in Native Americans and Europeans: a new approach to measuring gene identity reveals asymmetric patterns of divergence. *Molecular Biology and Evolution*, 13: 943–953.

Wacholder, S., Rothman, N., & Caporaso, N. (2002). Counterpoint: Bias from population stratification is not a major threat to the validity of conclusions from epidemiological studies of common polymorphisms and cancer. *Cancer, Epidemiology, Biomarkers & Prevention* 11: 513–520.

Weber, J. L., & Broman, K. W. (2001). Genotyping for human whole-genome scans: past, present, and future. *Advances in Genetics*, 42: 77–96.

Wilson, J. F., Weale, M. E., Smith, A. C., Gratrix, F., Fletcher, B., Thomas, M. G., Bradman, N., & Goldstein, D.B. (2001). Population genetic structure of variable drug response. *Nature Genetics*, 29: 265–269.

Topic 8 RACES

IN PAST CENTURIES, PEOPLE HAVE often grappled with human diversity by partitioning humans into different groups believed to be importantly different from one another. Thus, following the lead of eighteenth-century natural scientists and Enlightenment thinkers such as Cuvier, Buffon, Blumenbach, Voltaire, and Kant, nineteenth-century biologists and anthropologists attempted to classify humans into distinct races—roughly, groups of humans identified on the basis of distinctive superficial phenotypic properties (skin color, hairstyle, facial features, etc.) and believed to share some important psychological and behavioral properties in virtue of a common ancestry. In addition, races were often (though not always) ranked, with white Europeans unsurprisingly coming out as the superior race! While this pseudo-scientific tradition was deeply influenced by the sciences and social values of the nineteenth century, it is also probably deeply rooted in a universal tendency of the human mind.

In part as a response to the genocide committed by the Nazis, the UNESCO released a statement by leading sociologists and anthropologists (including Levi-Strauss and Montagu) criticizing the folk notion of race, and insisting that "the scientific investigations of recent years fully support the dictum of Confucius (551–478 BC):'Men's natures are alike; it is their habits that carry them far apart'" and stating that "for all practical social purposes 'race' is not so much a biological phenomenon as a social myth"—a position often called "racial skepticism." In the second half of the century, anthropologists and biologists piled on arguments and empirical evidence in support of this racial skepticism, showing, e.g., that there is substantially more genetic diversity within racial groups than between them (see Topic 8). In addition, the work of those few scientists, such as Jensen, Rushton, and Herrnstein, who persisted in looking for psychological and behavioral differences between races was strongly and convincingly criticized.

However, one may wonder whether recent progress in biology does not cast some doubts on the scientific consensus underwriting racial skepticism. Some research in genetics and molecular biology (Topic 8) divides humans into distinct groups on the basis of their genes, while various companies sell kits meant to determine people's "ethnic background." Some geneticists, such as Rosenberg, have gone as far as to claim that their findings provide some support for the legitimacy of the folk concept of race. Meanwhile, pharmaceutical companies are busy developing drugs targeted to particular racial groups, such as the famous Bidil, a drug marketed for African Americans with heart problems. But do these scientific and technological discoveries really legitimize the concept of race? Focusing on the research in genealogy, Deborah Bolnick answers negatively, criticizing this research for illegitimately suggesting that races have a biological reality.

One may wonder whether the widespread racial skepticism entails that there are no races? Sally Haslanger examines this question in detail, and distinguishes various ways to tackle it. On the basis of considerations drawn from the philosophy of language, she argues that races are real, but that, far from being biological kinds, they are social groups. Races are not like species; rather, they are more like social classes.

The topics discussed in these two essays echo the discussions of other essays in this volume. Bolnick's essay discusses the implications for the concept of race of the recent research in genetics already discussed in Topic 7. Haslanger's essay touches upon the nature of kinds and the possibility that some of them are socially constructed (see Topic 6), and she draws a comparison between race and gender (see Topics 9 and 11).

Suggested Further Reading

American Association of Physical Anthropologists. (1996) Statement on biological aspects of race. *American Journal of Physical Anthropology*, 101: 569–570.

Andreasen, R. O. (2000) Race: biological reality or social construct? *Philosophy of Science*, 67: S653–S666.

Appiah, K. A. (1995) The uncompleted argument: Du Bois and the illusion of race. In L. A. Bell and D. Blumenfeld (Eds.), *Overcoming Racism and Sexism* (pp. 59–78). Lanham, MD: Rowman and Littlefield.

Appiah, K. A. (1996) Race, culture, identity: Misunderstood connections. In K. A. Appiah and A. Gutmann (Eds.), *Color Conscious: The political morality of race* (pp. 30–105). Princeton, NJ: Princeton University Press.

Brown, R. A. and Armelagos, G. J. (2001) Apportionment of racial diversity: A review. *Evolutionary Anthropology*, 10: 34–40.

Fredrickson, G. M. (2003) *Racism: A short history*. Princeton, NJ: Princeton University Press.

Gossett, T. (1963) *Race: The history of an idea in America*. Dallas, TX: SMU Press.

Gould, S. J. (1981) *The Mismeasure of Man*. New York: W. W. Norton.

Haslanger, S. (2000) Gender and race: (What) are they? (What) do we want them to be? *Noûs*, 34: 31–55.

Herrnstein, R. J. and Murray, C. (1994) *Bell Curve: Intelligence and class structure in american Life*. New York: Free Press.

Hirschfeld, L. A. (1996) *Race in Making: Cognition, culture, and the child's construction of human kinds*. Cambridge, MA: MIT Press.

Isaac, B. H. (2004) *The Invention of Racism in Classical Antiquity*. Princeton, NJ: Princeton University Press.

Kelly, D., Machery, E. and Mallon, R. (2010) Race and racial cognition. In J. M. Doris and the Moral Psychology Research Group (Eds.), *The Moral Psychology Handbook* (pp. 463–472). Oxford: Oxford University Press.

Kitcher, P. (1999) Race, ethnicity, biology, culture. In L. Harris (Ed.), *Racism* (pp. 87–120). New York: Humanity Books.

Lewontin, R. C. (1972) The apportionment of human diversity. *Evolutionary Biology*, 6: 381–398.

Machery, E. and Faucher, L. (2005) Social construction and the concept of race. *Philosophy of Science*, 72: 1208–1219.

Machery, E. and Faucher, L. (2005) Why do we think racially? In H. Cohen and C. Lefebvre (Eds.), *Handbook of Categorization in Cognitive Science* (pp. 1009–1033). Amsterdam: Elsevier.

Mallon, R. (2004) Passing, traveling and reality: Social constructionism and the metaphysics of race. *Noûs*, 38: 644–673.

Montagu, A. (1942) *Man's Most Dangerous Myth: The fallacy of race*. New York: Columbia University Press.

Omi, M. and Winant, H. (1994) *Racial Formation in the United States: From the 1960s to the 1990s*. New York: Routledge.

Rosenberg, N. A., Pritchard, J. K., Weber, J. L., Cann, H. M., Kidd, K. K. Zhivotovsky, L. A., & Feldman, M. W. (2002) Genetic structure of human populations. *Science*, 298 (5602): 2381–2385.

Sesardic, N. (2010) A social destruction of a biological concept. *Biology and Philosophy*, 25: 143–162.

Tattersall, I. and DeSalle, R. (2011) *Race? Debunking a scientific myth*. College Station, TX: Texas A&M University Press.

Chapter 26

Sally Haslanger
A SOCIAL CONSTRUCTIONIST ANALYSIS OF RACE

In the contemporary world the term "race" is used widely both in American popular culture and in a variety of academic disciplines, and its meanings evolve in different ways in response to the pressures in each. This chapter brings philosophical analysis to bear on the debate among geneticists, humanists, and social scientists over the meaning of the term "race" in a genomic age—a debate that extends beyond our immediate disciplines and into the public domain. What are the genuine disagreements and what are only apparent disagreements due to the use of different vocabularies? Why does it matter which of the positions we accept? What sort of evidence is relevant to adjudicating the claims? How should we go about resolving the controversy? In answering these questions, I develop a realist, social constructionist account of race. I recommend this as an account that does justice to the meanings of "race" in many ordinary contexts and also as an account that serves widely shared antiracist goals.

I argue that in debates over the meaning of "race" in a genomic age we are better served by shifting from the metaphysical/scientific question, Is race real? to the political question, What concept of race should we employ in order to achieve the antiracist goals we share? To answer this question, I contend that we must also look at the semantics of the term "race" in public— specifically nonscientific—discourse, for this popular notion of race is what we use to frame

our identities and political commitments. Anyone using the term "race" in public life should be aware of its ordinary meanings; and if we want to change or refine the concept of race, we should be aware of where we are starting from as well as the normative basis for where we want to go.

Race Eliminativism, Race Constructionism, and Race Naturalism

Questions of what the term "race" means and whether race is *real* have become tied up with different political goals and strategies for achieving them. Race *eliminativists* maintain that talk of races is no better than talk of witches or ghosts, and in order to achieve racial justice we should stop participating in a fiction that underwrites racism.[1] Race *constructionists* argue that races are real, but that they are social rather than natural groups; on the constructionist view, racial justice requires us to recognize the mechanisms of racial formation so that we can undo their damage.[2] Present-day race *naturalists* agree with the eliminativists and constructionists that races are not what they were once thought to be—they are not groups with a common racial essence that explains a broad range of psychological and moral features of the group's members—but they disagree with both other views in maintaining that the human species can be divided on the basis of natural (biological, genetic, physical) features into a small set of groups that correspond to the ordinary racial divisions,[3] *and* that this natural division is socially and politically important for the purposes of achieving racial justice, for example, by enabling us to address racially divergent medical needs.[4]

Although the choice between these approaches to race may seem to some as "just semantics" (in the pejorative sense), the debate plays a role in framing and evaluating social policy. For example, consider the FDA approval of BiDil, a drug to treat heart failure, for Black patients. Eliminativists, naturalists, and constructionists will have very different approaches to this decision. For example, if, as the eliminativist argues, race is not real, then the approval of BiDil for Blacks is as (un)justified as the approval of BiDil for witches. The category *Black*, on the eliminativist view, is a fiction projected onto the world, and the FDA has done social harm by reinforcing the illusion that the category is scientifically grounded. In contrast, a race naturalist could support the FDA's action—or if not in the particular case of BiDil, in a similar sort of case—arguing that racial categories map biological categories that may have significant health consequences and should not be ignored in developing new medicines. On the naturalist's view, it is as politically important for the FDA to address the biological implications of race differences as it is to address the biological implications of any other genetic differences that have medical implications; in fact, to ignore the real differences between the races would be a form of injustice. The constructionist would disagree with the naturalist that there are natural differences between the races that warrant different medical treatment, but could allow that the social differences race makes must be taken into account in deciding a course of treatment or the approval of a drug. Although disagreeing with the eliminativist's rejection of race, the constructionist would be sympathetic with the eliminativist's worry that the FDA has reinforced a pernicious belief in the natural basis for racial categories. But how should we adjudicate these different positions?

Natural and Social Kinds

Some are tempted to view the debate between eliminativists, constructionists, and naturalists as (primarily) a metaphysical/scientific debate about the reality of race. On this construal, the question is whether races are natural kinds. Eliminativists and naturalists agree that races, if *they exist*, are natural kinds. Naturalists hold that races are a natural division of human beings, i.e., a division which rests entirely on natural properties of things; eliminativists deny it. Constructionists reject the claim that races are natural kinds, i.e., they allow that races are kinds, but hold that the division rests at least partly on social properties (being viewed and treated in a certain way, functioning in a certain social role, etc.) of the things in question. This requires understanding social kinds as just as fully real as natural kinds (see Table 26.1). There are semantic issues: What does "race" mean? Is it part of the *meaning* of "race" that races are natural kinds? There are scientific/metaphysical issues: Is race real? Do races exist? And there are moral/political issues: How should we, as a nation, address the problem of racial injustice?

Following Aristotle, the term "kind" is sometimes used to capture the classification of objects in terms of their *essence*. On this view, objects—genuine objects as opposed to heaps or weird scattered bits and parts of things—are distinctive because they have an essence. The rose bush in my garden is an object because of its

Table 26.1 Sources of Disagreement

	Eliminativism	Constructivism	Naturalism
Is race a natural category?	Yes	No	Yes
Is race real?	No	Yes	Yes

rose-essence; the scattering of petals, leaves, dirt, pebbles, gum wrappers, and fertilizer under it is not an object because it has no essence. The essence of the individual is (roughly) that set of properties without which the object cannot exist and which serves in some important way in explanations of the object's characteristic behavior.

Are *races* Aristotelian *kinds*? Traditional racialists would probably think they are:[5] Whites and Blacks have different natures that explain their characteristic behaviors, and this nature is essential to who they are. However, this view is not credible at this point in time. It would be implausible to claim that an individual could not have existed as a member of a different race. In fact, people can travel from the United States to Brazil and function socially as a member of a different race; and features as superficial as skin color, hair texture, and eye shape are clearly not essential (they, too, can be changed with chemicals and surgery). If one thinks that one has one's entire genetic makeup necessarily (something with even a slight difference from your genetic makeup wouldn't be you), then there might be a case to be made for the claim that one could not have been a member of a different race. But essences are supposed to be rich explanatory resources for explaining the characteristic behavior of the individual, and there is no support for the idea that there are racial essences of this sort.

Locke has a different account of kinds than Aristotle. For Locke, kinds are highly unified, but not by virtue of the essences of their members. So, e.g., red things constitute a kind (their unity consists in their all being red), even though redness is seldom an essential property of the things that have it. On a Lockean view, the main contrast to consider is between "real" kinds and "nominal" kinds. Real kinds are those types unified by properties that play a fundamental role in the causal structure of the world and, ideally, in our explanations. Nominal kinds are types unified by properties that happen to be

useful or interesting to us. Whether there are real kinds corresponding to (and underlying) the nominal kinds we pick out is an open question. On this view *concepts* or *properties* (and, contra Aristotle, not individuals) have essences.

Are races Lockean kinds? Can we give necessary and sufficient conditions for being a member of a particular race? This question actually opens a long debate between realists and nominalists that (fortunately!) we don't need to get into about whether one can *ever* give necessary and sufficient conditions for membership in a kind. If our goal is to do justice to our pretheoretical judgments about membership in a given race, then there are reasons to doubt whether races are definable in the sense required. However, if we stipulate a definition, either as a nominal essence to pick out a group of things we are interested in, or in postulating explanatory categories as part of a theoretical project, then the definition will give the Lockean essence of the kind.

Note that on both the Lockean and Aristotelian accounts, kinds or types may be either social or natural. Types are *natural* if the properties that constitute their unity are natural, and *social* if the properties are social. It is notoriously difficult to characterize the distinction between natural and social properties (and relations), but for our purposes we could take natural properties of things to be those studied by the natural sciences and the social properties to be those studied by the social sciences. So the set of quarks is a natural type; the set of adoptive families is a social type. Plausibly, there is *some* degree of unity in the members of a race, e.g., one could list a cluster of physical, historical, and sociological properties associated with each race such that members of the race share a weighted subset of those properties. If for a category to be real is just for it to pick out a set with some loose connection amongst the members, then there is a sense in which, on any non-empty construal of race, races are real. It takes very little to be an objective type in this sense.

Can "Facts" Settle the Matter?

Some may find it tempting to respond that to resolve this issue, we just need to look at the facts: either there are races or there aren't; either races are social or they aren't. One significant problem with this approach is that we can determine whether there "really are" races only if the term "race" has a specified meaning; and what it means—at least for the purposes at hand—is part of the question. Consider a different example. Suppose we ask, What percentage of the U.S. population is on welfare? Well, it depends on what you mean by "welfare." Do we include only those who receive TANF (Temporary Assistance for Needy Families, the successor to "welfare as we know it")? Or do we include those who receive social security benefits? What about "corporate welfare" in the form of tax breaks? We ask, Is race real? Well, it depends on what you mean by "race."

This is not to say that the controversy will dissipate if we only would make clear our stipulated definitions. If I maintain that 99% of the U.S. population is on welfare, then presumably I am using a non-mainstream definition of "welfare." For me to justify my claim it would not be sufficient to say that given my meanings, I've uttered a truth, if my meaning of "welfare" is idiosyncratic and beside the point. But it may be that what I say is true and especially useful in the context of the debate in which I engage. In such a case the task of justification would be to show that my definition of "welfare" better tracks what is important for the purposes at hand.[6]

The reason why the facts don't settle the issue is that simply establishing that there is a fact of the matter about something doesn't establish that it is a significant or relevant fact for the purposes at hand. Suppose I say that I'm going to use the term "White" for all and only those who have blonde hair. Whites, then, are a natural kind. Turn now to the public context in which we are discussing, say, affirmative action. If I argue that non-Whites should be given preferential treatment because of historical injustice, my claim sounds familiar, but the category I am using is not the most apt for considering the justice of affirmative action. The fact that "White," as I defined the term, captures a real kind, even combined with the truth that (some) non-Whites have been treated unjustly, does not usefully further the debate because I have chosen categories for addressing the problem that are ill-suited to the task.[7] Truth alone does not set us free; there are too many irrelevant and misleading truths. The choice of truths must—at the very least—be insightful and judicious.

Lessons from Philosophy of Language

So it would seem that the next step in our inquiry should be to adjudicate what the term "race" means. There need not be only one meaning for the term. But for the purposes of engaging in discussion concerning matters of biological research on race, it would be useful to have a shared understanding of race. And to achieve this, we should have a sense of what the folk concept of race is. This is not because I believe that we should honor the folk concept as the true meaning, but because in any context where communication is fraught, it is useful to understand the competing meanings at issue. If there is a socially dominant understanding of race, then even if we want to recommend a change in the concept, we should know what it is.

This suggests that we must not simply resolve semantic disagreements in order to make headway in the debate. We must look more closely at our purposes and how we might achieve them: should we as biologists, social scientists, scholars, citizens, and as people who care about social justice frame our dialogue—our narratives of explanation, justification, and justice—in terms of race? And if so, then what concept of race should we employ? These questions can be broken down further:

- Is there currently a single or dominant public meaning (or folk concept) of "race"? If so, what is it (or what are the contenders)?

- In the quest for social justice, e.g., in debating health policy, do we need the concept of race? For what purposes? If so, can we make do with the folk concept or should we modify the concept?

- If the folk concept of race is not an adequate tool to help achieve social justice (if, perhaps, it is even a barrier), then how should we proceed?

In what follows, I will suggest that an answer to the first question, in particular, is not straight-forward; and yet if we are going to speak mean-ingfully in a public context, then we need to recognize the force and implications of our words in that context. In science it is common-place to define or redefine terms in whatever way suits the theory at hand (e.g., "atom," "mass," "energy," "cell,"), without much concern with the ordinary meanings these terms have or the political import of stipulating new meanings. But semantic authority cannot be granted to the biologist in considering a term like "race" that plays such a major role in our self-understandings and political life.

In undertaking conceptual analysis of, say, Fness (in our case, Fness might be "Blackness," "Whiteness," "Asianness," or the broader cate-gory, "race"), it is typically assumed that it is enough to ask competent users of English under what conditions someone is F. After all, if competent speakers know the meaning of their terms, then all that is needed is linguistic compe-tence to analyze them. However, this stance is not plausible if one takes into account argu-ments in philosophy of language over the past 30 years that call into question the assumption that competent users of a term have full knowl-edge of what the term means. This assumption in particular is challenged by the tradition of semantic externalism. Externalists maintain that

the content of what we think and mean is determined not simply by what we think or intend, but at least in part by facts about our social and natural environment. For example, one can be competent in using the term "water" without knowing that water is H_2O; one can use the term "elm" meaningfully even if one cannot tell the difference between a beech and an elm. When I say, "Elm trees are deciduous" I say something meaningful and true, even though I couldn't identify an elm or give any clear description of one. The externalist holds that these sorts of cases point to two features of language that the traditional picture ignored: reference magnetism and the division of linguistic labor. These ideas can be expressed very roughly as follows:

Reference magnetism:[8] type-terms (such as general nouns) pick out a type, whether or not we can state the essence of the type, by virtue of the fact that their meaning is determined by a selection of paradigms together with an implicit extension of one's reference to things of the same type as the paradigms. For example, the marketing department and the R&D department of a toy manufacturer have a meeting. R&D has produced a new "squishy, stretchy substance that can transform into almost anything," and they present a sample. The marketing director points to it and says, "Let's call the stuff 'Floam.' " Bingo. "Floam" now refers to a whole kind of stuff, some of which has not yet been produced, and the ingredients of which are totally mysterious. Which stuff? Presumably, "floam" refers to the most unified objective type of which the sample is a paradigm instance. This example is artificial, but the phenomenon of reference magnetism is ubiquitous.

Division of linguistic labor:[9] the meaning of a term used by a speaker is determined at least in part by the linguistic usage in his or her community, including, if necessary, expert usage. For example, before the invention of chemistry, people used the term "water" to refer to H_2O because the kind H_2O was a "reference magnet" for their term. However, in cases where one cannot even produce a paradigm, e.g., when I can't tell the difference between a beech and an elm, my use of the term "elm" gets its meaning not from *my* paradigms, but from the linguistic labor of others in my community, including botanists. The division of linguistic labor may also play an important role if I have idiosyncratic paradigms. The idea is that what I mean in using a term such as "elm" or "arthritis" is not just a matter of what is in my head, but is determined by a process that involves others in my language community.

Most commonly, externalist analyses have been employed to provide *naturalistic* accounts of knowledge, mind, etc.; these seek to discover the *natural* (non-*social*) kind within which the selected paradigms fall. But it is possible to pursue an externalist approach within a social domain as long as one allows that there are social kinds or types, such as "democracy" and "genocide," or ethical terms such as "responsibility" and "autonomy."

Of course, an externalist analysis of a social term cannot be done in a mechanical way and may require sophisticated social theory both to select the paradigms and analyze their commonality. It may take sophisticated social theory to determine what "parent" or "Black" means. In an externalist project, intuitions about the conditions for applying the concept should be considered secondary to what the cases in fact have in common: as we learn more about the paradigms, we learn more about our concepts.

Is Race a Fiction?

If we are externalists about meaning, which is the approach I am recommending, then the eliminativist about race is in a very weak position. We can all confidently identify members of

different races. Martin Luther King, Nelson Mandela, Malcolm X, Toni Morrison, Oprah Winfrey, W.E.B. DuBois, Kofi Annan, Thabo Mbeki (insert here your choice of various friends and relatives) are Black. George Bush, Arnold Schwarzenegger, Margaret Thatcher, Golda Meir, Bertrand Russell, Vincent Van Gogh (insert here your choice of various friends and relatives) are White. Similar lists can be constructed for Asians, Latino/as, and other groups usually considered races. But if this is the case, then the terms "Black" and "White" pick out the best fitting and most unified objective type of which the members of the list are paradigms—even if I can't describe the type or my beliefs about what the paradigms have in common are false. What that type is is not yet clear. But given how weak the constraints on an objective type are, undoubtedly there is one. The term "race" then, picks out the more generic type or category of which "Black," "White," etc. are subtypes.

I believe that these considerations about meaning show that eliminativism is the wrong approach to understand the public or folk meaning of "race." It is compatible with this that we should work to change the public meaning of "race" in keeping with the eliminativist strategy so that it becomes clear that the racial terms are vacuous. In other words, eliminativism may still be a goal for which to aim. But as things stand now, race is something we *see* in the faces and bodies of others; we are surrounded by cases that function to us as paradigms and ground our meanings. The eliminativist's suggestion that "our" concept of race is vacuous is not supported by the observation that we tend to think of races as natural kinds because the meaning of "race" isn't determined simply by what we think races are. So the eliminativist project needs to be rethought.

Race as a Social Kind

Recent work in race genetics and biology leads me to believe that there are no very unified natural types that are good candidates for the reference of race terms, where the reference of these terms is fixed by generally acceptable paradigms of each race.[10] What "we" in public discourse call race is not a natural or genetic category. Rather, the ordinary term "race" picks out a social type, i.e., the objective type that attracts our reference is unified by social features rather than natural ones. Let me sketch one suggestion along these lines.

Feminists define "man" and "woman" as *genders* rather than sexes (male and female). The slogan for understanding gender is this: gender is the social meaning of sex. It is a virtue, I believe, of this account of gender that, depending on context, one's sex may have a very different meaning and it may position one in very different kinds of hierarchies. The variation will clearly occur from culture to culture (and subculture to subculture); so, e.g., to be a Chinese woman of the 1790s, a Brazilian woman of the 1890s, or an American woman of the 1990s may involve very different social relations and very different kinds of oppression. Yet on the analysis suggested, these groups count as women insofar as their subordinate positions are marked and justified by reference to (female) sex.

With this strategy of defining gender in mind, let's consider whether it will help in giving some content to the social category of race. The feminist approach recommends this: don't look for an analysis that assumes that the category's meaning is always and everywhere the same; rather, consider how members of the group are *socially positioned* and what *physical markers* serve as a supposed basis for such treatment.

I use the term "color" to refer to the (contextually variable) physical markers of race, just as the term "sex" refers to the (contextually variable) physical markers of gender. "Color" is more than just skin tone: racial markers may include eye, nose, and lip shape, hair texture, physique, etc. Virtually any cluster of physical traits that are assumed to be inherited from those who occupy a specific geographical region or regions can count as "color." (Although the term "people of color" is used to refer to non-Whites, the markers of "Whiteness" also count as "color.") Borrowing the slogan used before, we can say then that race is the social meaning of the "colored," i.e., geographically marked, body (see Figure 26.1).

To develop this briefly, consider the following account. A group is *racialized* (in context C) if and only if (by definition) its members are (or would be) socially positioned as subordinate or privileged along some dimension (economic, political, legal, social, etc.) (in C), and the group is "marked" as a target for this treatment by observed or imagined bodily features presumed to be evidence of ancestral links to a certain geographical region.

In other words, races are those groups demarcated by the geographical associations accompanying perceived body type when those associations take on evaluative significance concerning how members of the group should be viewed and treated. Given this definition, we can say that S is of the White (Black, Asian, etc.) race (in C) if and only if (by definition) Whites (Blacks, Asians, etc.) are a racialized group (in C) and S is a member.

Note that on this view, whether a group is racialized, and so how and whether an individual is raced, will depend on context. For example, Blacks, Whites, Asians, and Native Americans are currently racialized in the United

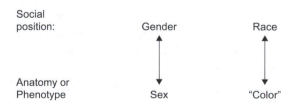
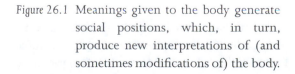

Figure 26.1 Meanings given to the body generate social positions, which, in turn, produce new interpretations of (and sometimes modifications of) the body.

States insofar as these are all groups defined in terms of physical features associated with places of origin and membership in the group functions as a basis for evaluation. However, some groups are not currently racialized in the United States but have been so in the past and possibly could be again (and in other contexts are), e.g., the Italians, the Germans, the Irish.

I offer the constructionist analysis of "race" just sketched as one that captures our ordinary use of the term. The social constructionist analysis of race presents the strongest conceptual framework and consensus point for cross-disciplinary and public discussions around race and genetics research. I believe it also provides important resources in politically addressing the problem of racial injustice; specifically, it gives us a way of capturing those groups that have suffered injustice due to assumptions about "color." These are groups that matter if we are going to achieve social justice. Moreover, we already use racial terms in ways that seem to track these groups (or groups very close to them). So by adopting the constructionist account we can proceed politically without recommending a semantic revolution as well.

Conclusion

I have argued that the debate between eliminativists, constructionists, and naturalists about race should be understood as not simply about whether races are real or whether they are natural kinds, but about how we should understand race and employ racial concepts in our public discourse. I have argued that the debate cannot be settled simply by considering "the facts" of genetics, but requires close attention to the language of "race" and "kind" as well as contemporary racial politics. With this reframing of the question, I have argued that our ordinary concept of race is of a social kind and for a particular analysis of race that highlights social hierarchy. Given the history of racial injustice and the need to address this history, it is important for us to attend publicly to those who have suffered from what we might call *color hierarchy*. Since we have reason to track racial injustice, and since the naturalist and eliminativist accounts do not come close to matching our ordinary term for "race," constructionism about race is currently the best candidate of the three views considered. My conclusions are qualified, however. I do not argue that my account of race captures *the meaning of "race"* (or what we should mean by "race") for all time and in all contexts; it would be foolhardy for anyone to attempt that. More specifically, it would reveal a misunderstanding of how language, as a collective social practice, works.

Notes

1 Appiah, 1996; Zack, 2002.
2 Omi and Winant, 1994; Mills, 1997; Haslanger, 2000.
3 Kitcher, 1999; Andreason, 2000; Rosenberg et al., 2002; Mountain & Risch, 2004.
4 Risch, Burchard, Ziv, & Tang., 2002; cf. Lee, Mountain, & Koenig, 2001.
5 Appiah, 1993, chap. 2.
6 Anderson, 1995.
7 See Anderson, 1995.
8 Putnam, 1973, 1975; Kripke, 1980.
9 Putnam, 1975, Burge, 1979.
10 See Feldman and Lewontin, 2008; Bolnick, 2008.

References

Anderson, E. S. (1995). Knowledge, human interests, and objectivity in feminist epistemology. *Philosophical Topics*, 23: 27–58.

Andreason, R. (2000). Race: Biological reality or social construct? *Philosophy of Science*, 67 (supplementary volume): S653–666.

Appiah, K. A. (1993). *In my Father's House*. New York: Oxford University Press.

Appiah, K. A. (1996). Race, culture, identity: Misunderstood connections. In K. A. Appiah and A. Gutmann (Eds.), *Color Conscious: The political morality of race* (pp. 30–105). Princeton J: Princeton University Press.

Bolnick, D. A. (2008). Individual ancestry inference and the reification of race as a biological phenomenon. In B. A. Koenig, S. S.-J. Lee, & S. S. Richardson (Eds.), *Revisiting Race in a Genomic Age* (pp. 70–85). New Brunswick, NJ: Rutgers University Press.

Burge, T. (1979). Individualism and the mental. *Midwest Studies in Philosophy*, 4: 73–121.

Burge, T. (1986). Intellectual norms and foundations of mind. *Journal of Philosophy*, 83: 697–720.

Delphy, C. (1984/1970). *Close to Home: A materialist analysis of women's oppression* (D. Leonard, Trans.). Amherst: University of Massachusetts Press.

Feldman, M. W., & Lewontin, R. C. (2008). Race, ancestry, and medicine. In B. A. Koenig, S. S.-J. Lee, & S. S. Richardson (Eds.), *Revisiting Race in a Genomic Age* (pp. 89–101). New Brunswick, NJ: Rutgers University Press.

Hartmann, H. (1981). The unhappy marriage of Marxism and feminism: Towards a more progressive union. In Lydia Sargent (Ed.), *Women and Revolution* (pp. 1–42). Cambridge, MA: South End Press.

Haslanger, S. (1995). Ontology and social construction. *Philosophical Topics*, 23 (2): 95–125.

Haslanger, S. (2000). Gender and race: (What) are they? (What) do we want them to be? *Noûs*, 34: 31–55.

Haslanger, S. (2003). Social construction: The "debunking" project. In Frederick F. Schmitt (Ed.), *Socializing Metaphysics: The nature of social reality* (pp. 301–325). Lanham, MD: Rowman and Littlefield.

Kitcher, P. (1999). Race, ethnicity, biology, culture. In L. Harris (Ed.), *Racism* (pp. 87–117). New York: Humanity Books.

Kripke, S. (1980). *Naming and Necessity*. Cambridge, MA: Harvard University Press.

Lee, S. S.-J., Mountain, J., & Koenig, B. (2001). The meanings of "race" in the new genomics: Implications for health disparities research. *Yale Journal of Health Policy, Law and Ethics*, 1: 33–75.

MacKinnon, C. (1987). *Feminism Unmodified*. Cambridge, MA: Harvard University Press.

Mills, C. (1997). *The Racial Contract*. Ithaca, NY: Cornell University Press.

Mountain, J. L., & Risch, N. (2004). Assessing genetic contributions to phenotypic differences among "racial" and "ethnic" groups. *Nature Genetics*, 36 (II Suppl) S48–53.

Omi, M., & Winant, H. (1994). Racial formation. In M. Omi and H. Winant, *Racial formation in the United States* (pp. 53–76). New York: Routledge.

Putnam, H. (1973). Meaning and reference. *The Journal of Philosophy*, 70: 699–711.

Putnam, H. (1975). The meaning of "meaning." In H. Putnam, *Mind, Language, and Reality*. Vol. 2 of *Philosophical Papers* (pp. 215–271). Cambridge, MA: Cambridge University Press.

Risch, N., Burchard, E., Ziv, E., & Tang, H. (2002). Categorization of humans in biomedical research: Genes, race, and disease. *Genome Biology*, 3: 2007.1–2007.12.

Rosenberg, N. A., Pritchard, J. K., Weber, J. L., Cann, H. M., Kidd, K. K., Zhivotovsky, L. A., et al. (2002). Genetic structure of human populations. *Science*, 298: 2381–2385.

Scott, J. (1996). Gender: A useful category of historical analysis. In J. Scott (Ed.), *Feminism and History* (pp. 152–180). Oxford: Oxford University Press.

Wittig, M. (1992). *The Straight Mind and Other Essays*. Boston: Beacon Press.

Zack, N. (2002). *Philosophy of Science and Race*. New York: Routledge.

Chapter 27

Deborah A. Bolnick

INDIVIDUAL ANCESTRY INFERENCE AND THE REIFICATION OF RACE AS A BIOLOGICAL PHENOMENON

Anthropological ideas about the pattern of human diversity shifted drastically during the 20th century. Prior to World War II, *Homo sapiens* was generally perceived as a polytypic species with biologically distinct subgroups, or races (Stepan, 1982; Marks, 1995). This biological differentiation was thought to be the result of long periods of independent evolution when each race was largely isolated from the others. Anthropologists gradually moved away from such typological thinking during the latter half of the 20th century, in part because new genetic data did not support this paradigm. Instead, genetic research suggested that humans could not be neatly divided into a few discrete, isolated races (Brown & Armelagos, 2001; Kittles & Weiss, 2003). Studies of human biological diversity therefore began to focus less on classification and more on the actual patterns of variation among populations, as well as on the evolutionary processes that shaped those patterns.

With this shift away from typological thought has come an increased interest in *individuals* and what genetics can tell us about the unique identity and history of each person. As part of this trend, anthropologists and geneticists have recently begun to explore how genomic data can be used to infer an individual's "ancestry." I will consider the meaning of this term in more detail later in this chapter, but "ancestry" is generally used to refer to the geographic region

or regions where one's biological ancestors lived (Jorde & Wooding, 2004; Race, Ethnicity, and Genetics Working Group, 2005).

Several methods have been developed for inferring an individual's ancestry from genetic data (Rannala & Mountain, 1997; McKeigue, Carpenter, Parra, & Shriver, 2000; Pritchard, Stephens, & Donnelly, 2000), and these methods are starting to be used in a variety of contexts. For example, individual ancestry inference has important biomedical applications because ancestry may influence disease susceptibility and drug response (Wilson et al., 2001; Risch, Burchard, Ziv, & Tang, 2002; Helgadottir et al., 2005; Tate & Goldstein, 2008). Individual ancestry inference can also aid forensic investigations by determining the genetic heritage of DNA left at a crime scene, which can then be used to narrow the pool of potential suspects (Frudakis et al., 2003; Shriver, Frudakis, & Budowle, 2005). Finally, these methods are also of great interest to members of the general public who want to reconstruct their personal genealogical histories (Elliott & Brodwin, 2002; Bolnick, 2003; TallBear, 2005; Greely, 2008; Shriver & Kittles, 2008; TallBear, 2008).

Although this body of work emphasizes the *individual* as the crucial unit of analysis, individual ancestry inference is closely tied to our understanding of human *groups* and the distribution of genetic variation among them. Inferring an individual's genetic ancestry entails deciding that his or her DNA was inherited from a certain group or groups, and that cannot be accomplished unless one first distinguishes groups that differ genetically in some way. Thus, even such individually oriented genetic research has implications for our understanding of race and the pattern of human biological diversity.

In this chapter, I begin with an overview of our current understanding of the pattern of human biodiversity. I then examine two widely cited studies that use the *structure* program (Pritchard et al., 2000) to infer individual ancestry (Rosenberg et al., 2002; Bamshad et al., 2003) and discuss what these studies imply about the relationship between human genetic structure and traditional notions of race.

The Distribution of Human Genetic Variation

Our current understanding of human genetic structure is based on hundreds of studies that have been conducted over the past few decades. Both mitochondrial DNA and nuclear loci have been surveyed using many different types of markers (Tishkoff & Verrelli, 2003). While the specific findings of each study have varied, two general patterns have consistently emerged.

First, African populations exhibit greater genetic diversity and less linkage disequilibrium than non-African populations (Tishkoff & Williams, 2002; Kittles & Weiss, 2003).[1] This pattern reflects the evolutionary and demographic history of our species. Because *Homo sapiens* evolved in Africa before dispersing throughout the rest of the world (Klein, 1999), African populations are older and have had more time to accumulate genetic differences through mutation. Similarly, the greater age of African populations helps to explain the lower levels of linkage disequilibrium in Africa since linkage disequilibrium decreases over time due to recombination (Kittles & Weiss, 2003). Differences between African and non-African populations also reflect a genetic bottleneck that

occurred when humans dispersed out of Africa. The individuals who left Africa carried only a subset of the genetic variants found in the ancestral African population. Consequently, non-Africans are less genetically diverse and exhibit increased linkage disequilibrium compared to Africans (Bamshad, Wooding, Salisbury, & Stephens, 2004; Tishkoff & Kidd, 2004).

The second pattern that has emerged from many genetic studies is that human variation is clinally distributed (see Figure 27.1). Allele frequencies change gradually across geographic space, with few sharp discontinuities (Barbujani, 2005). Populations are most genetically similar to others that are found nearby, and genetic similarity is inversely correlated with geographic distance (Relethford, 2004; Ramachandran et al., 2005).

There are several reasons for this pattern. First, it reflects localized gene flow and isolation by distance (Cavalli-Sforza, Menozzi, & Piazza, 1994; Relethford, 2004). In other words, because geographic distance limits migration, individuals tend to mate with those who live nearby and geographically close populations tend to exchange more genes than geographically distant ones (Wright, 1943; Malécot, 1969). Restricted gene flow therefore contributes to the observed

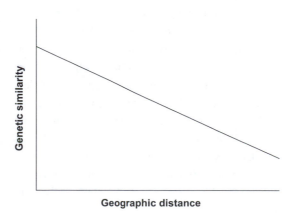

Figure 27.1 The relationship between genetic similarity and geographic distance under a pattern of clinal variation.

pattern of decreasing genetic similarity with increasing geographic distance.

The clinal pattern of human genetic variation also reflects successive founder effects that occurred as humans migrated out of Africa to populate the rest of the world (Relethford, 2004; Prugnolle, Manica & Balloux, 2005; Ramachandran et al., 2005). Prugnolle et al., (2005) and Ramachandran et al. (2005) suggest that this form of genetic drift played a particularly important role in shaping the patterns of variation among human populations. According to their analyses, serial founder effects explain 76–85% of the observed variation (Prugnolle et al., 2005; Ramachandran et al., 2005).

Finally, clinal variation at some loci reflects selection in response to environmental gradients. Clines due to selection vary from locus to locus (i.e., allele frequencies at one locus change faster than those at another locus over the same geographic distance). Since many loci show similar patterns of allele frequency change across human populations, the overall pattern of genetic variation in our species reflects selection less than serial founder effects and restricted gene flow with isolation by distance (Relethford, 2004).

Because of the patterns of human genetic variation described here, many anthropologists argue that traditional notions of race misrepresent human biological diversity and the evolutionary history of our species. While traditional notions of race are extremely variable—no consensus has ever been reached regarding the number or composition of human races, for example—most describe racial groups as equivalent, biologically distinct units. However, the patterns described above suggest that this is not the case. From a genetic perspective, non-Africans are essentially a subset of Africans (Quintana-Murci et al., 1999; Underhill et al., 2000; Kidd, Pakstis, Speed, & Kidd, 2004). No discrete boundaries separate humans into a few genetically distinct groups, and the members of each racial group are highly variable (Brown & Armelagos, 2001). Consequently, human racial groups do not appear to be distinct genetic groups.

Individual Ancestry Inference, Race, and Genetic Structure

Several recent studies of individual ancestry seem to challenge this understanding of the distribution of human genetic variation. These new studies instead suggest genetic differentiation among what are essentially races based on continental ancestry. For example, Rosenberg et al., "identified six main genetic clusters, five of which correspond to major geographic regions".[2] Since the five "major geographic regions" comprise Africa, Eurasia, East Asia, Oceania, and America, these results have been interpreted as showing that racial divisions based on continental ancestry are biologically significant (Burchard et al., 2003; Mountain & Risch, 2004). Similarly, Bamshad et al. (2003) identified three genetic clusters that correspond to Africa, Europe, and Asia. These studies have been widely cited as verifying traditional ideas about race and the pattern of human biological diversity (Wade, 2002; Seebach, 2003).[3]

The conclusions of both the Rosenberg et al. (2002) and Bamshad et al. (2003) studies were based on the Bayesian computer program *structure* (Pritchard et al., 2000). To understand the results of these two studies and what they imply about the structure of the human gene pool, it is important to first understand how this computer program works.

The *structure* program implements a model-based clustering method to infer population structure from multilocus genotype data and then allocates individuals into populations. It can be used to estimate the number of genetic clusters or populations present in a given data set as well as the population of origin of each individual. The populations are expected to be in Hardy-Weinberg equilibrium. Pritchard et al. (2000) assume a model in which a number

(K) of populations exist, each of which is characterized by a set of allele frequencies.

A data set of multilocus genotypes (X) is therefore viewed as being made up of individuals sampled from K separate populations (see Figure 27.2). When running the *structure* program, the user defines K in advance. *Structure* then assigns individuals probabilistically to K populations with the goal of maximizing Hardy-Weinberg equilibrium in each population. In other words, for any given value of K, *structure* searches for the most probable way to divide the sampled individuals into that pre-defined number of clusters based on their genotypes. If an individual's genotype suggests that he or she has ancestry from more than one population, *structure* can assign the individual jointly to two or more populations and estimate the proportion of ancestry from each. The analysis can (and should) be performed for multiple different values of K.

Thus, the fact that *structure* identifies a particular number of clusters is insignificant: it does so simply because the user told it to do so. What is more important is that *structure* provides a way to determine the value of K that is most appropriate for the data set in question (i.e., the most likely number of clusters or populations represented). The "best" value of K is the one that maximizes the probability of observing that set of data. Structure calculates the probability of the data given each value of K submitted (i.e., Pr $[X|K]$), and the inferred value for K is the one associated with the highest Pr $(X|K)$.

However, it is not entirely straightforward to determine the true number of genetic clusters in a given data set for three reasons. First, because it is computationally difficult to estimate Pr $(X|K)$, *structure* provides only an approximation. Pritchard et al. note that "the assumptions underlying [this approximation] are dubious at best, and we do not claim (or believe) that our procedure provides a quantitatively accurate estimate of the posterior distribution of K. We see it merely as an *ad hoc* guide to which models are most consistent with the data, with the main justification being that it seems to give sensible answers in practice."[4] Thus, because *structure*'s estimates of Pr $(X|K)$ may or may not be accurate, the value of K estimated as maximizing the probability of the data may not actually do so.

Second, if a data set is complex, different runs of *structure* may produce substantially different results. In these cases, the composition of genetic clusters varies among runs using the same pre-defined value for K. A simplistic illustration of this situation would be a case where the analysis of four individuals (A, B, C, and D) using $K = 2$ yielded clusters (A, B) and (C, D) in run 1, but clusters (A, C) and (B, D) in run 2. Pritchard and Wen (2004) suggest that this mostly occurs with data sets containing a large number of genetic clusters ($K > 5$) and is either because the program did not run long enough (i.e., *structure* did not have enough time to determine the optimal clustering of individuals) or because there are several highly probable ways to divide the sampled individuals into that number of

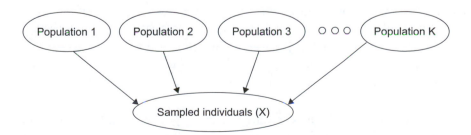

Figure 27.2 The population model assumed by the *structure* program.

clusters. If the latter is the case, it may not be possible to determine a single optimal clustering scheme. Furthermore, the different ways to divide individuals into a particular number of clusters may each yield a different Pr $(X|K)$. For example, in the above illustration with $K = 2$, the clustering scheme in run 1 might be associated with a high Pr $(X|K)$, whereas the clustering scheme in run 2 might be associated with a low Pr $(X|K)$. Consequently, it is not always clear which of the probabilities associated with a given K should be used when determining the "best" value for K.

Third, the underlying model used in the *structure* program is not appropriate for all data sets. In particular, Pritchard and Wen (2004) note that the *structure* model is not well suited to data shaped by restricted gene flow with isolation by distance. If *structure* is used to analyze such data, they warn that "the inferred value of K . . . can be rather arbitrary."[5] Thus, although the *structure* program can estimate the number and composition of genetic clusters present in a given data set, such estimates must be interpreted carefully.

Rosenberg et al.'s (2002) Study of Human Genetic Structure

Rosenberg et al. (2002) used the *structure* program to analyze genotypic variation at 377 autosomal microsatellite loci in 1,056 individuals from around the world (the HGDP-CEPH Human Genome Diversity Cell Line Panel). The abstract of their article mentioned the identification of 6 main genetic clusters (Africa, Eurasia, East Asia, Oceania, America, and the Kalash of Pakistan), but Rosenberg et al. actually presented results for multiple values of K (2–6) in the body of the paper. They also analyzed the data set using values of K > 6 (up to K = 20; N. Rosenberg, personal communication), but they did not publish those results because *structure* identified multiple ways to divide the sampled individuals into K clusters

when K > 6. For example, in 10 replicates, *structure* found 9 different ways to divide the sampled individuals into 14 clusters and 10 different ways to divide them into 20 clusters (N. Rosenberg, personal communication). The different clustering schemes in these replicates were fairly similar, but they often yielded very different Pr $(X|K)$, making it difficult to interpret the results for a given value of K when K > 6. Rosenberg et al. (2002) therefore published the results for K < 7 for the worldwide sample, as well as further analyses using regional subsets of the entire data set.

Thus, the fact that *structure* identified 6 genetic clusters is not significant in and of itself—the program also identified 2, 5, 10, and 20 genetic clusters using the same set of data. As noted above, *structure* will identify as many clusters as the user tells it to identify. While it may be interesting that 5 of the 6 clusters identified with K = 6 correspond to major geographic regions, such clustering does not necessarily provide a better representation of human genetic differentiation than the clustering observed when K is set to 4, 9, 12, or any other number. Only by evaluating the probability of the observed data given each value of K (i.e., Pr $[X|K]$) is it possible to determine the number of genetic clusters *most likely* represented in this data set.

Rosenberg et al. (2002) did not report the *most likely* number of genetic clusters, nor did they publish the probabilities of the observed data given each value of K. Since some of the larger values of K were associated with several different Pr $(X|K)$ across runs, and since Rosenberg et al. wanted to present results that could be easily replicated, they felt that it was more informative to show the robust results for multiple small K than to focus on a larger value of K that was associated with variable clustering schemes and both high and low probabilities. In other words, no single value of K clearly maximized the probability of the observed data. Probabilities increased sharply from K = 1 to K = 4 but were fairly similar for values of K ranging from 4 to 20. The probability of the observed data was higher for $K = 6$ than for smaller values of K, but not as high as for some replicates with larger values of K. The highest Pr $(X|K)$ was associated with a particular replicate of $K = 16$, but that value of K was also associated with very low probabilities when the individuals were grouped into 16 clusters in other ways. Consequently, it is uncertain what number of genetic clusters *best* fits this data set, but there is no clear evidence that $K = 6$ is the best estimate.

Thus, the Rosenberg et al. study does not challenge our current understanding of human genetic structure as much as some have suggested. Indeed, the fact that it was not possible to determine a single best value for K is exactly what we would expect given the clinal variation and pattern of isolation by distance found in our species. In addition, as Tishkoff and Kidd (2004) have noted, individuals from areas near the borders of the five "major geographic regions" exhibited ancestry from multiple genetic clusters. These results suggest a gradient of change between geographic regions, not discrete boundaries.

So why has so much emphasis been placed on the results of the analysis using $K = 6$? Despite the fact that Rosenberg et al. presented no evidence that $K = 6$ represented the *most likely* number of genetic clusters in their data set, virtually all references to this study in both the scientific literature and the popular press mention the identification of either 5 or 6 genetic clusters (for examples, see Wade, 2002; Seebach, 2003; Bamshad et al., 2004; Tishkoff & Kidd, 2004; Barbujani, 2005; and Tate & Goldstein, 2008). I would suggest that these particular results have been emphasized simply because they fit the general notion in our society that continental groupings are biologically significant. This notion is a legacy of traditional racial thought and seems to persist even when not clearly supported by biological data.

Bamshad et al.'s (2003) Study of Population Structure and Group Membership

Bamshad et al. (2003) analyzed 100 *Alu* insertion polymorphisms in 565 individuals from sub-Saharan Africa, East Asia, Europe, and India, as well as 60 microsatellites in 206 of the individuals from sub-Saharan Africa, Europe, and East Asia. Like Rosenberg et al., they used the *structure* program to help determine the number of genetic clusters present in their data set. Bamshad et al. (2003) first analyzed only the samples from sub-Saharan Africa, East Asia, and Europe and ran *structure* using values of K between 1 and 6. When all of the individuals from these three regions were included in the analysis, they found that $K = 4$ maximized the probability of observing that set of data (Pr $[X|K = 4] = 1$). The sampled individuals likely represented four genetic clusters, comprising (1) East Asians, (2) Europeans, (3) sub-Saharan Africans except for the Mbuti and three other individuals, and (4) the Mbuti and three other sub-Saharan Africans. This division of sub-Saharan Africans into two genetic clusters is consistent with other evidence of greater genetic diversity and greater genetic structure among Africans.

Bamshad et al. also conducted this analysis excluding the Mbuti samples. In this case, *structure* found that $K = 3$ best fit the observed data (Pr $[X|K = 3] = 1$), indicating three genetic clusters of individuals (sub-Saharan Africans, Europeans, and East Asians). Bamshad et al. set K equal to 3 for most subsequent analyses even though those analyses used the complete data set (including the Mbuti), which most likely contained four genetic clusters. Given this, Bamshad et al. may have taken other (unnamed) factors into consideration when deciding upon the number of genetic clusters present in their data. They did note that "K provides only a rough guide for determining which models may be consistent with the data" because estimates of K depend on the number of

392 Deborah A. Bolnick

individuals per population, the number of loci studied, and the amount of differentiation between populations.[6]

Bamshad et al. (2003) also investigated whether genetic data could be used to correctly infer an individual's ancestry. They used *structure* to assign individuals to genetic clusters and to estimate the proportion of an individual's ancestry from each genetic cluster. An individual "was considered assigned 'correctly' if the cluster with the greatest proportion of ancestry was the same as the continent of origin of the sample."[7] Thus, Bamshad et al. assumed that continental groupings were important from the start, which perhaps explains why they chose K = 3 as the best estimate of human genetic structure.

Using the 100 *Alu* markers and 60 microsatellites, *structure* was able to identify the correct continent of origin for 99% of the individuals from sub-Saharan Africa, Europe, and East Asia. These results demonstrate that substantial genetic differentiation exists among the populations sampled, but they do not necessarily indicate substantial genetic differentiation among continental groupings. As Bamshad et al. note, these analyses included individuals from only a few widely separated regions of Africa, Asia, and Europe. The observed genetic differentiation may therefore reflect the large geographic distances between sampled populations rather than continental divisions per se.

Additional analyses using samples from areas closer to the continental holders support this hypothesis. When Bamshad et al. (2003) included samples from India in a data set with the European and East Asian samples, *structure* found that the optimal number of genetic clusters (K) was one. In other words, when a more representative geographic sample was analyzed, continental groupings no longer appeared to be genetically distinct. Accordingly, Bamshad et al. concluded that "the inclusion of [geographically intermediate] samples demonstrates geographic continuity in the distribution of genetic

variation and thus undermines traditional concepts of race."[8]

The *structure* analysis in this study therefore supports our current understanding of human genetic structure. It indicates greater genetic diversity and greater genetic structure among Africans as well as little genetic differentiation among continental groupings *when a representative geographic sample is analyzed*. The results using the expanded Eurasian sample are also consistent with previous evidence that human genetic variation is clinally distributed with few sharp discontinuities.

Despite these results, Bamshad et al.'s (2003) study has been cited as showing that groups defined by continental ancestor or race are genetically differentiated (Mountain & Risch, 2004). This interpretation likely reflects the way that Bamshad et al. (2003) presented their results, rather than the results themselves. First, as noted above, they emphasized the significance of the three continental groupings even though *structure* identified four genetic clusters in the complete data set of sub-Saharan Africans, East Asians, and Europeans. Second, while Bamshad et al. (2003) recognized that the inclusion of samples from India demonstrated the continuous distribution of genetic variation in Eurasia, they excluded those samples from most analyses. As a result, many of the reported analyses implied continental discontinuities even though the more complete data set showed that such discontinuities do not exist.

Third, *structure* found that the European, Indian, and East Asian data set most likely contained a single genetic cluster, but Bamshad et al. focused primarily on an analysis of that data set using K = 3. In the text of their paper, Bamshad et al. wrote:

If we assumed that three clusters were present (i.e., K = 3), as suggested by proxy information (i.e., place of origin), three groups were distinguished. Correct assignment of samples to their place of origin was 97% for samples from East Asia, 94% for samples from Europe, and 87% for samples from southern India.[9]

The article abstract also made no mention of the optimal clustering scheme (K = 1), but instead stated that "less accurate assignment (87%) to the appropriate genetic cluster was possible for a historically admixed sample from southern India."[10]

Of course, as noted earlier, *structure* will identify as many groups as the program user tells it to identity, so it is not surprising—or significant—that *structure* distinguished three groups when Bamshad et al. set K equal to 3. Nor is it clear how to interpret the results of this analysis since it is statistically unlikely that three genetic clusters really exist in this data set. Bamshad et al.'s (2003) presentation of this analysis obscures these issues and makes it seem as if the three racial/ethnic groups (Europeans, East Asians, and Indians) are more genetically distinct than they really are.

Finally, Bamshad et al.'s description of the Indian population as "historically admixed"[11] reinforces traditional racial views of human variation and human evolutionary history. Previous studies have shown that the genetic makeup of the Indian population reflects gene flow from European and Asian sources (Bamshad et al., 2001; Majumder, 2001), but Bamshad et al.'s (2003) description suggests that such gene flow occurred only in historical times. Racial studies of the early 20th century presented a similar picture of Eurasian history. For example, Hooton (1931, 1939) suggested that populations resembling multiple races (such as Indians) formed only recently due to gene flow between the primary races, which were isolated from one another during prehistoric times. There is no evidence that a significant barrier to Eurasian gene flow existed in the more distant past, though, and other studies indicate migration and gene flow throughout Eurasia at many points in human history (Templeton, 2002; Basu et al., 2003). Thus, the way that Bamshad et al. (2003) describe their research reinforces traditional racial views of human variation even though the data do not necessarily support such views.

Ancestry and Race

Given the descriptions and interpretations of the studies by Rosenberg et al. and Bamshad et al., the relationship between ancestry and race should be examined more carefully. In recent years, ancestry has been widely promoted as an objective, scientific alternative to race. The term "ancestry" is often used without being clearly defined, but it generally refers to the geographic region or regions where one's biological ancestors lived (Collins, 2004; Jorde & Wooding, 2004; Shriver et al., 2004; Race, Ethnicity, and Genetics Working Group, 2005). Because of this focus, ancestry is seen as being more specific and objective than race, which is highly charged and encompasses geographic origins, political history socioeconomic status, culture, skin color, and other perceived physical, behavioral, and genetic characteristics. Jorde and Wooding also argue that ancestry is "a more subtle and complex description of an individual's genetic makeup than is race."[12] An individual can have ancestry from multiple geographic regions, and the concept of ancestry is flexible enough that those regions could be local (e.g., southwestern Nigeria) or much broader (e.g., all of Africa).

However, other aspects of ancestry are more problematic. Just as the term is rarely defined, there has been little discussion of the size of geographic regions, how they should be defined, or why specific geographic divisions are more relevant than others for studies of human genetic variation. Nor is it always clear what time frame should be considered when determining an individual's ancestry. For example, my grandparents lived in the United States, but my great-great-grandparents lived in Eastern Europe. My more distant ancestors, like those of all humans, lived in Africa. The time depth of interest depends on the question or hypothesis being addressed, but this issue is often discussed only briefly, if at all.

Furthermore, ancestry is not that different from race in practice. Like race, ancestry is sometimes defined politically or culturally. In individual ancestry studies, the ancestral regions are almost always continents (Risch et al., 2002; Mountain & Risch, 2004; The Unexamined "Caucasian," 2004). Since the contemporary Euro-American definition of race is based on continental geography, anthropologists and human geneticists use the term "ancestry" much as the general public uses the term "race." Indeed, some scientists explicitly define ancestry as an individual's racial group or the race of his or her ancestors (Risch et al., 2002; Frudakis et al., 2003).

Because an individual can have ancestry from multiple geographic regions, ancestry does differ from conceptions of race based on the one-drop rule, which allow an individual to belong to only a single race. However, contemporary understandings of race accept the existance of "mixed-race" individuals, as evidenced by the large number of Americans who checked the box associated with the Other category on the last U.S. census. Thus, while ancestry has the potential to be a more subtle, objective, and scientific alternative to race, it currently appears to be quite similar to race in practice.

Conclusion

Recent studies of individual ancestry have been cited as verifying traditional ideas about race, but these studies do not present new data suggesting that racial groups are genetically distinct. Rather, the data and *structure* analyses reported in the Rosenberg et al. (2002) and Bamshad et al. (2003) studies are consistent with our current understanding of human genetic structure. However, the results of these studies have been described and interpreted in ways that both reflect and reinforce traditional racial views of human biological diversity and the evolutionary history of our species. The disconnect between the results and the interpretations of these studies is unfortunate since they are playing an important role in the reification of race as a biological phenomenon.

Notes

1 Linkage disequilibrium (LD) refers to (a) the nonrandom association of alleles at different sites and (b) the length of a chromosomal segment that is inherited without recombination from a common ancestor (Kittles & Weiss, 2003; Tishkoff & Kidd, 2004).
2 Rosenberg et al. 2002, p. 2381.
3 Other studies have been cited as proving the same point, but I do not discuss those studies in this chapter since they are based on different methods of analysis than the Rosenberg et al. (2002) and Bamshad et al. (2003) studies. For example, Frudakis et al. (2003) used a linear classification method and Shriver et al. (2004) used a tree-based method. DNA Print's Ancestry by DNA test, which also suggest the validity of race as a biological phenomenon (Bolnick, 2003), is based on an admixture-mapping approach (R. Malhi, personal communication).
4 Pritchard et al. 2000, p. 949.
5 Pritchard and Wen 2004, p. 14.
6 Bamshad et al. 2003, p. 579.
7 Bamshad et al. 2003, p. 579.
8 Bamshad et al. 2003, p. 587.
9 Bamshad et al. 2003, p. 584.
10 Bamshad et al. 2003, p. 578.
11 Bamshad et al. 2003, p. 578.
12 Jorde and Wooding 2004, S 30.

References

Bamshad, M. (2005). Genetic influences on health: Does race matter? *Journal of the American Medical Association*, 294: 937–946.

Bamshad, M., Kivisild, T., Watkins, W. S., Dixon, M. E., Ricker, C. E., Rao, B. B., et al. (2001). Genetic evidence on the origins of Indian caste populations. *Genome Research*, 11: 994–1004.

Bamshad, M., Wooding, S., Salisbury, B. A., & Stephens, J. C. (2004). Deconstructing the relationship between genetics and race. *Nature Reviews Genetics*, 5: 598–609.

Bamshad, M. J., Wooding. S., Watkins, W. S., Ostler, C. T., Batzer, M. A., & Jorde, L. B. (2003). Human population structure and inference of group membership. *American Journal of Human Genetics*, 72: 578–589.

Barbujani, G. (2005). Human race: Classifying people vs. understanding diversity. *Current Genomics*, 6: 215–226.

Basu, A. Mukherjee, N., Roy, S. Sengupta. S., Benerjee, S., Chakraborty, M., et. al. (2003). Ethnic india: A genomic view, with special reference to peopling and structure. *Genome Research*, 13: 2277–2290.

Bolnick, D. A. (2003). "Showing who they really are": Commercial ventures in genetic genealogy. Paper presented at the American Anthropological Association Annual Meeting. November, Chicago, IL.

Brown, R., & Armelagos, G. J. (2001). Apportionment of racial diversity: A review. *Evolutionary Anthropology*, 10: 34–40.

Burchard, E. G., Ziv. E., Coyle, N., Gomes, S. L., Tang. H., Karter, A. J., et al. (2003). The importance of race and ethnic background in biomedical research and clinical practice. *New England Journal of Medicine*, 348: 1170–1175.

Cavalli-Sforza, L. L., Menozzi, P., & Piazza, A. (1994). *History and Geography of Human Genes*. Princeton, NJ: Princeton University Press.

Collins, F. S. (2004). What we do and don't know about "race," "ethnicity," genetics, and health at the dawn of the genome era. *Nature Genetics*, 36: S13–S15.

Elliott, C., & Brodwin, P. (2002). Identity and genetic ancestry tracing. *British Medical Journal*, 325: 1469–1471.

Frudakis. T., Venkateswarlu, K., Thomas, M. J., Gaskin, Z., Ginjupalli, S., Guntari, S., et al. (2003). A classifier for the SNP-based inference of ancestry. *Journal of Forensic Sciences*, 48: 771–778.

Greely, H. T. (2008). Genetic genealogy: Genetics meets the marketplace. In B. A. Koenig, S. S.-J. Lee, & S. S. Richardson (Eds.), *Revisiting Race in a Genomic Age* (pp. 215–234). New Brunswick. NJ: Rutgers University Press.

Helgadottir, A., Menolescu, A., Helgason, A., Thorleifsson, G. Thorsteindottir, U., Gudbjartsson, D. F., et al. (2005). A variant of the gene encoding leukotriene A4 hydrolase confers ethnicity-specific risk of myocardial infarction. *Nature Genetics*, 38: 68–74.

Hooton, E. (1931). *Up from the Ape*. New York: Macmillan Company.

Hooton, E. (1939). *Twilight of Man*. New York: G. P. Putnam's Sons.

Jorde, L. B., & Wooding, S. P. (2004). Genetic variation, classification, and "race." *Nature Genetics*, 36: S28–S33.

Kidd, K. K., Pakstis, A. J., Speed, W. C., & Kidd, J. R. (2004). Understanding human DNA sequence variation. *Journal of Heredity*, 95: 406–420.

Kittles, R. A., & Weiss, K. M. (2003). Race, ancestry, and genes: Implications for defining disease risk. *Annual Review of Genomics and Human Genetics*, 4: 33–67.

Klein, R. G. (1999). *The Human Career: Human biological and cultural origins* (2nd ed.). Chicago, IL: University of Chicago Press.

Majumder, P. P. (2001). Ethnic populations of India as seen from an evolutionary perspective. *Journal of Biosciences*, 26: 533–545.

Malécot, G. (1969). *The Mathematics of Heredity*. San Francisco: W. H. Freeman.

Marks, J. (1995). *Human Biodiversity: Genes, race, and history*. New York: Aldine de Gruyter.

McKeigue, P. M., Carpenter, J., Parra, E. J., & Shriver, M. D. (2000) Estimation of admixture and detection of linkage in admixed populations by a Bayesian approach: Application to African-American populations. *Annals of Human Genetics*, 64: 171–186.

Mountain, J., & Cavalli-Sforza L. L. (1997). Multilocus genotypes, a tree of individuals, and human evolutionary history. *American Journal of Human Genetics*, 61: 705–718.

Mountain, J. L., & Risch, N. (2004). Assessing genetic contributions to phenotypic differences among "racial" and "ethnic" groups. *Nature Genetics*, 36: S48–S53.

Pritchard, J. K., Stephens, M., & Donnelly, P. (2000). Inference of population structure using multilocus genotype data. *Genetics*, 155: 945–959.

Pritchard, J. K., & Wen, W. (2004). *Documentation for Structure Software: Version 2*. Chicago, IL.

Prugnolle, F., Manica, A., & Balloux, F. (2005). Geography predicts neutral genetic diversity of human populations. *Current Biology*, 15: R159–R160.

Quintana-Murci, L., Semino, O., Bandelt, H.-J., Passarino, G., McElreavey, K., & Santachiara-Benerecetti, A. S. (1999). Genetic evidence of an early exit of *Homo sapiens* from Africa through Eastern Africa. *Nature Genetics*, 23: 437–441.

Race, Ethnicity, and Genetics Working Group. (2005). The use of racial, ethnic, and ancestral categories in human genetics research. *American Journal of Human Genetics*, 77: 519–532.

Ramachandran, S., Deshpande, O., Roseman, C. C., Rosenberg, N. A., Feldman, M. W., & Cavalli-Sforza, L. L. (2005). Support from the relationship of genetic and geographic distance in human populations for a serial founder effect originating in Africa. *Proceedings of the National Academy of the sciences USA*, 102: 15942–15947.

Rannala, B., & Mountain, J. L. (1997). Detecting immigration by using multilocus genotypes. *Proceedings of the National Academy of the Sciences USA*, 94: 9197–9201.

Relethford, J. H. (2004). Global patterns of isolation by distance based on genetic and morphological data. *Human Biology*, 76: 499–513.

Risch, N., Burchard, E., Ziv, E., & Tang, H. (2002). Categorization of humans in biomedical research: Genes, race, and disease. *Genome Biology*, 3: 1–12.

Rosenberg, N. A., Pritchard, J. K., Weber, J. L., Cann, H. M., Kidd, K. K., Zhivotovsky, L. A., et al. (2002). Genetic structure of human populations. *Science*, 298: 2381–2385.

Seebach, L. (2003, May 8). Biology and race: A clearer link; new genetic research establishes firmer basis for connection, *Rocky Mountain News*, p. 58A.

Shriver, M., Frudakis, T., & Budowle, B. (2005). Getting the science and the ethics right in forensic genetics. *Nature Genetics*, 37: 440–450.

Shriver, M. D., Kennedy, G. C., Parra, E. J., Lawson, H. A., Sonpar, V., Hnang, J., et al. (2004). The genomic distribution of population substructure in four populations using 8,525 autosomal SNPs. *Human Genomics*, 1: 274–286.

Shriver, M. D., & Kittles, R. A. (2008). Genetic ancestry and the search for personalized genetic histories. In B. A. Koenig, S. S.-J. Lee, & S. S. Richardson (Eds.), *Revisiting Race in a Genomic Age* (pp. 201–214). New Brunswick, NJ: Rutgers University Press.

Stepan, N. L. (1082). *The Idea of Race in Science*. Hamden, CT: Archon Books.

TallBear, K. (2005). Native American DNA: Narratives of origin and race. Ph.D. Dissertation. University of California at Santa Cruz.

TallBear, K. (2008). Native-American-DNA.com: In search of Native American race and tribe. In B. A. Koenig, S. S.-J. Lee, & S. S. Richardson (Eds.), *Revisiting Race in a Genomic Age* (pp. 235–252). New Brunswick, NJ: Rutgers University Press.

Tate, S. K., & Goldstein, D. B. (2008). Will tommorow's medicines work for everyone? In B. A. Koenig, S. S.-J. Lee, & S. S. Richardson (Eds.), *Revisiting Race in a Genomic Age* (pp. 102–128). New Brunswick, NJ: Rutgers University Press.

Templeton, A, (2002). Out of Africa again and again. *Nature*, 416: 45–51.

Tishkoff, S. A., & Kidd, K. K. (2004). Implications of biogeography of human populations for "race" and medicine. *Nature Genetics*, 36: S21–S27.

Tishkoff, S. A., & Verrelli, B. C. (2003). Patterns of human genetic diversity: Implications for human evolutionary history and disease. *Annual Review of Genomics and Human Genetics*, 4: 293–340.

Tishkoff, S. A., & Williams, S. M. (2002). Genetic analysis of African populations: Human evolution and complex disease. *Nature Reviews Genetics*, 3: 611–621.

Underhill, P. A., Shen, P., Lin, A. A., Jin, L., Passarino, G., Yang, W. H., et al. (2000). Y chromosome sequence variation and the history of human populations. *Nature Genetics*, 26: 358–361.

The Unexamined "Caucasian." (2004) *Nature Genetics*, 36: 541.

Wade, N. (2002, December 20). Gene study identifies five main human populations, linking them to geography. *New York Times*, p. A37.

Wilson, J. F., Weale, M. E., Smith, A. C., Gratrix, F., Fletcher, B. Thomas, M. G., et al. (2001). Population genetic structure of variable drug response. *Nature Genetics*, 29: 265–269.

Wright, S. (1943). Isolation by distance. *Genetics*, 28: 114–138.

Topic 9 SEX

A S DALE SPENDER'S QUIP, "Man, like the other mammals, breastfeeds his young," illustrates, anthropologists, biologists, philosophers, and psychologists may project their sexist biases when theorizing about human nature. In the Western philosophical tradition, human nature and the nature of "Man" were taken to be one and the same. After Darwin, humans are understood as a product of evolution, and evolutionary theory also provides ways of understanding the evolution of sex and the contributions of the sexes to our evolution. Darwin's own discussion of the sexes includes a liberal sprinkling of cultural bias, and the resulting theory of sexual selection and its role in evolutionary change perpetuated some of this bias via the language used: "choosey" and "coy" females strive to attract the most "resourceful" males. Presenting an evolutionary account of sex, sexual activity, and sexual reproduction without any indication of gender biases remains a challenge.

Still, the study of sex and sexual reproduction is central to the development of a coherent notion of human nature. The essays in this section include a clear defense of the status quo in evolutionary thinking, an outright rejection of the applicability of evolutionary thought to human sex and gender, and the introduction of ways in which we may understand the evolution of same-sex behavior.

Donald Symons first rehearses Darwin's view of our reproductive choices: Choosey females with more investment risk in successful reproduction select between males on the basis of their resources. Symons then goes on to present evolutionary approaches to a host of issues relating to sex, including sexual choice, sexual arousal, parent offspring conflict, sex differences, and the role of attractiveness in mate selection. He introduces work on these topics from evolutionary anthropology, sociobiology as well as evolutionary psychology, his own preferred perspective. His own position is that the underlying psychological mechanisms guiding human mate choice are "adaptations to maximize reproductive success." Others in evolutionary anthropology and evolutionary psychology are critical of much work on the evolution of sexual choice but their aims are to reform this work, rather than to overthrow it. In contrast, John Dupré is highly skeptical of work on sex and gender in evolutionary anthropology, evolutionary psychology, and sociobiology. Dupré argues that evolutionary anthropology, evolutionary psychology and related fields can shed *no* light on variation in sexual practices across cultures, fail to account for the diversity of sexual proclivities, including homosexuality, and do not even provide the beginnings of an account of the interaction of sexual and other motivations. Nathan Bailey and Marlene Zuk provide the beginnings of a reply to Dupré, specifically with respect to homosexuality. They present work on the evolution of same-sex behavior and argue that evolutionary explanations *can* be given for the origin and persistence of same-sex behavior and the impacts that such behavior has when viewed as a selective force on other traits.

Suggested Further Reading

Buss, D. M. (1989) Sex differences in human mate preferences: Evolutionary hypotheses tested in 37 cultures. *Behavioral and Brain Sciences*, 12: 1–49.

Buss, D. M. (2003) *The Evolution of Desire: Strategies of human mating*, revised edn. New York: Basic Books.

Buss, D. M. and Schmitt, D. P. (1993) Sexual strategies theory: An evolutionary perspective on human mating. *Psychological Review*, 100: 204–232.

Campbell, A. (2002) *A Mind of Her Own: The evolutionary psychology of women*. Oxford: Oxford University Press.

Cashdan, E. (1993) Attracting mates: effects of paternal investment on mate attraction strategies. *Ethnology and Sociobiology*, 14: 1–23.

Darwin, C. (1874/1998) *The Descent of Man*. New York: Prometheus Books.

Gangestad, S. W. and Simpson, J. A. (2000) On the evolutionary psychology of human mating: Trade-offs and strategic pluralism. *Behavioral and Brain Sciences*, 23: 573–587.

Hamer, D. (1995) *Science of Desire: The gay gene and the biology of behavior*. New York: Simon and Schuster.

Hrdy, S. (1999) *Mother Nature*. New York: Ballantine.

Rice, G., Anderson, C., Neil Risch, N. and Ebers, G. Male homosexuality: Absence of linkage to microsatellite markers at *Xq28*. *Science* 284(5414): 665–667.

Scheib, J. E., Gangestad, S. W. and Thornhill, R. (1999) Facial attractiveness, symmetry, and cues of good genes. *Proceedings of the Royal Society of London B*, 266: 1318–1321.

Sommer, V and Vasey, P. L. (Eds.) (2011) *Homosexual Behaviour in Animals: An evolutionary perspective*. Cambridge: Cambridge University Press.

Symons, D. (1979) *The Evolution of Human Sexuality*. Oxford: Oxford University Press.

Wilson, E. O. (1979) *On Human Nature*. Cambridge, MA: Harvard University Press.

Chapter 28

Donald Symons

THE EVOLUTION OF HUMAN SEXUALITY
Sexual Choice

. . . many men are goats and can't help committing adultery when they get a chance; whereas there are numbers of men who, by temperament, can keep their purity and let an opportunity go by if the woman lacks in attractiveness.

MARK TWAIN

Selection can be expected to favor humans who prefer to copulate with and to marry the fittest members of the opposite sex, and since human female parental investment may typically exceed male investment, females might be expected to be choosier than males. By and large, these expectations probably are fulfilled, but the matter is more involved than it may at first appear. Crook (1972) argues that among preliterate peoples, and by inference among our Pleistocene ancestors, the constraints of marriage rules and restrictions leave little room for mate selection based on personal choice. Indeed, the fact that marriages normally are negotiated by elder kinsmen narrows the scope for personal choice of spouses still further, and especially narrows the scope for female choice. Thus, one might argue, as Crook seems to do, that during the course of human evolution opportunities in which individuals could make their own choices were encountered so infrequently that selection favored sexual indifference and complete acquiescence to the decisions of elders or to the dictates of culture and society. To explain why this did not occur, it is necessary to distinguish

the outward behaviors associated with marriage and copulation from the underlying psychology of sexual choice; to distinguish, that is, between action and desire.

Because sexual emotions are closer to the genes than sexual behaviors are, emotions are central to an evolutionary perspective on sexuality. The organism—at least the human organism—is neither a passive mediator between stimulus and response nor a mindless vehicle of culture, but an active assessor and planner. Psyche becomes important precisely where the external environment is unpredictable or complex. The overwhelming majority of an organism's biological processes and energetic transactions with the external world are unconscious; in fact, it appears that every process—digestion, oxygen transport, breathing, reflex blinking—that can be carried out unconsciously is more efficiently carried out this way, and conscious processes seem to become unconscious whenever possible. In the learning of a complex skill, for example, component movements are practiced until they no longer require attention—until they become automatic, or reflexlike—and consciousness then is freed to monitor larger groupings of components and to plan future strategies. In short, mind is usually about the rare, the difficult, and the future; the everyday becomes unconscious habit. Proust remarked that love, "ever unsatisfied, lives always in the moment that is about to come," and

Montaigne observed that "Nature makes us live in the future, not the present." It is the "us," which is living in the future, rather than the observable body, which is behaving in the present, that is of primary importance in understanding human sexuality. Sexual experience is largely adapted to the exceptional. We react consciously to the rare opportunity or threat, and we fantasize about desired and feared states of affairs, imagining how the former might be realized, the latter coped with or avoided.

The primary issue with respect to sexual choice, then, is not whether our ancestors usually were able to choose their own mates, but whether they sometimes had a voice in mate choice, and, still more important, whether they were occasionally able to choose their sexual partners. All available evidence points to the conclusion that everywhere the complexities of human social life provide scope for the occasional satisfaction of desires, hence selection can be expected to favor the existence of desires, though they may rarely be translated into behavior. In this regard it is crucial to distinguish between sex and marriage. Although the opportunities for individuals to arrange their own marriages—at least their initial marriages—may have been slight, there must have been much more scope for individuals of both sexes to arrange their own copulations. Human sexual dispositions should be considered not so much adaptations to strengthen marriage as adaptations to maximize reproductive success in an environment in which marriage is ubiquitous. Although individual humans constrain one another's sexual activities to an unprecedented degree, the complexities of human social life everywhere provide opportunities for occasionally evading such constraints. One's own evasions must be planned for, the evasions of others guarded against.

If modern ethnographies are reliable guides to the past, in ancestral populations a young person's initial marriage probably was arranged by elders, especially male elders. Now the *ultimate* basis for the decisions that elders made was their own genetic "interests," which could not have been identical with the genetic "interests" of the principals. Trivers (1974) calls attention to the existence of inevitable "conflicts" between parent and offspring owing to the fact that they are imperfectly related genetically. Choice of spouse may constitute one such conflict. Indeed, the literature on preliterate peoples suggests that all the individuals involved in a marriage arrangement attempt to influence the marriage for their own ends. Usually, this means that men use women for barter to get other women, but women themselves exercise whatever influence they can. This point is clearly illustrated in Hart and Pilling's (1960) account of sex and marriage among the Tiwi. Although a Tiwi woman had no power to choose her first mate, after her husband's death she sometimes exercised considerable influence in making subsequent marriages. A young Tiwi male could not exercise control over his mother and sisters because a female was controlled by her husband or father. Later in life, however, a man with power and influence might gain some control over the remarriages of his elderly sisters and mother. Hart and Pilling (1960:24) write:

> Whenever this occurred, although the resulting situation might have the superficial appearance of clan solidarity—with sons, mothers, brothers, and sisters all acting and planning together as a partnership—such surface appearance was illusory. The motivations involved in it were scarcely altruistic desires on the part of the brothers to look after their mothers and elderly sisters, but rather efforts by the brothers to use to advantage, in their intricate political schemes, some women of their own clan.

But when Hart and Pilling write "altruistic desires" and "use to advantage" they are referring to proximate human motives; the relationship of these motives to fitness and ultimate causation is an open question.

Offspring receive many benefits from their parents, and it is possible that in some parent-offspring conflicts there is not, in fact, a great deal of "conflict" in terms of fitness. Adults' far greater knowledge and experience may result, on the average, in a better choice of spouse than an offspring would be likely to make on its own. Williams (1966) has even suggested that the hypertrophy of the human cerebral cortex is not the result of selection for adult intelligence but rather is a by-product of selection for the abilities to understand and to respond to parental verbal commands in childhood. Whether or not this hypothesis is correct (I doubt that it is), it provides a useful corrective to excessive emphasis on parent-offspring conflict. If a child wants to play with the saber-toothed tiger and the child's parent has a different view of the matter, the parent may be 100 percent right and the child 100 percent wrong, even though they share only 50 percent of their genes. Yet it is the existence of an environment containing watchful parents that permitted the evolution of juvenile desires to experiment with playmates.

Until very recently, selection occurred within a fairly narrow range of environments, and impulses selected in one set of circumstances may be maladaptive in others. Consider, for example, the potential parent-offspring conflict Trivers (1974) outlines over weaning. Mothers may be selected to want to wean an offspring when it is X months old, whereas offspring may be selected to want to nurse beyond X months. But if offspring are, in fact, *always* weaned before the theoretical "ideal" age—from their genetic point of view—selection would have no way of "knowing" what the ideal age is, and it might favor the relatively simple infant disposition *always* to resist weaning. If such an infant were raised in an artificial environment in which it was allowed to nurse as long as it liked, its disposition always to resist weaning would certainly prove maladaptive. Similarly, in an environment in which young people have relatively little say in spouse choice, selection might favor strong adolescent emotions about members of the opposite sex, emotions that have been designed by selection specifically to function in a milieu in which an adolescent's actual behavior will be constrained by the necessity to compromise with elders. Just as a child's desire to play with the saber-toothed tiger or always to resist weaning might be adaptive precisely because social constraints and safeguards exist in a natural environment, so an adolescent's desire to marry person A rather than person B (whom the elders favor) might be adaptive even if B is, in many cases, the better mate choice. An adolescent's desires may be designed to function primarily as one important item of information that the elders will consider in reaching their decision. These emotions may prove to be poor guides when adolescents are free to choose their own mates.

Sexual Arousal

Kinsey et al. (1948, 1953) reported that men are sexually aroused far more easily and frequently by visual stimuli than women are, and they pointed out that everywhere and always, pornography is produced for a male audience. Furthermore, Kinsey et al. found that males almost universally fantasize visually during masturbation, and require visual fantasy to orgasm, whereas two-thirds of their female informants did not fantasize during masturbation. But recently, a number of investigators have challenged Kinsey's conclusions: the current trend in the literature on human sexuality is to minimize sex differences in visual arousal and to attribute Kinsey's findings to the sexual repression of women in that era and to Kinsey's reliance on retrospective reports instead of immediate reports or physiological measurement.

As with theories of the evolution of female orgasm and the loss of estrus, much of the recent scientific writing about visual arousal implies that underlying the everyday world—in which there appear to be enormous sex differences in sexual response to, and interest in, visual stimuli—is a deeper reality in which males and females are virtually identical. Some insight into this strange state of affairs can be gained from a major American sex researcher's response to recent findings that women are sexually aroused by pornography: he remarked that these new data eliminate the last claim for human female hyposexuality. In my view, as long as the matter is phrased in terms of hyper- versus hyposexuality (with hypersexuality assumed to be good or desirable), and as long as evidence for sex differences in sexuality is felt to be necessarily detrimental to women, experiments will continue to be designed, and their results interpreted, to emphasize similarities between men and women, and the everyday world will continue to suffer neglect.

According to *The Report of the U.S. Commission on Obscenity and Pornography* (1970), the pornography industry in the United States—including books, periodicals, and motion pictures—grosses between $537 and $574 million annually, almost entirely from men. The Commission characterized patrons of adult bookstores and movie theaters as "predominantly white, middle-class, middle-aged, married males, dressed in business suit or neat casual attire. . . ."[1] The male fantasy realm—"pornotopia"— portrayed in Victorian pornography (Marcus 1966) appears to differ little from the realm portrayed in modern pornography; the major social changes that have occurred during the last century have left pornotopia largely untouched. Written pornography gives scant description of men's bodies (unless, of course, it is aimed at the homosexual market), but describes women's bodies in great detail (Smith 1976). The most striking feature of pornotopia is that sex is sheer lust and physical gratification, devoid of more tender feelings and encumbering relationships, in which women are always aroused, or at least easily arousable, and ultimately are always willing. There is no evidence that a similar female fantasy world exists, and there appears to be little or no female market for pornography.

The intractably male nature of pornography is problematical for those who wish to see men and women as in some fundamental sense sexually identical. Individuals who believe that human sexuality is basically a male sexuality, and thus imagine that sexually liberated women will act and feel as men do, must cope first with the evidence that while many women respond sexually to pornography in an experimental setting, few apparently are motivated to seek it out, and second with the evidence that sex differences in sexual arousal to depictions of nude members of the opposite sex seem to be as substantial as they ever were. On the other hand, individuals like Brownmiller (1975), who imply that human sexuality is basically a female sexuality, and that liberated men will act and feel as women do, generally interpret heterosexual interactions in political rather than in sexual terms; thus Brownmiller avoids directly confronting the challenge pornotopia poses to her theoretical position, yet indirectly acknowledges the difficulties when she states that pornography is *inherently* sexist, and advocates a political solution, viz., the total elimination of pornography.

The recent evidence of women's sexual arousal to pornography has demonstrated, in my view, primarily what was already known: first, that women are capable of being aroused by erotica, mainly via the subjective process of identification with the female participant; and second, that once heterosexual activity is under way, women have the potential to be at least as strongly aroused as men. To the extent that exposure to pornography during scientific experiments simulates anything in a woman's everyday life, it simulates an actual heterosexual interaction to which she has already consented and in which she is a willing and eager participant. I regard a female subject's agreement to participate in an experiment on sexual response as approximately equivalent to her agreement, or decision, to have sexual relations with a man in everyday life; her erotic responses during the experiment simulate her ordinary response during sexual interaction. Men and women differ far less in their potential physiological and psychological responses during sexual activities *per se* than they do in how they negotiate sexual activities and in the kinds of sexual relationships and interactions they are motivated to seek. This may explain the anomaly (from the male point of view) that although women can be strongly aroused by pornography they are unlikely to seek it out. It also may explain women's general lack of sexual response to nude males: a woman may be "interested" in a nude male, in that she evaluates him favorably as a potential sex partner and wishes to become sexually involved with him and to be sexually aroused by him, but a wish for future sex is not the same as immediate arousal.

One observation of the Committee on Obscenity and Pornography may be especially relevant in the present context: "When viewing erotic stimuli, more women report the physiological sensations that are associated with sexual arousal than directly report being sexually aroused."[2] Obviously this finding is subject to a number of possible interpretations, but I believe that the most parsimonious interpretation also is the most likely: I suggest that during such experiments some women experience the physiological changes that prepare their bodies for sexual intercourse without, in fact, experiencing emotional sexual arousal, and that this ability is the result of the unprecedented independence of receptivity and proceptivity in the human female (see Mead 1967). This independence is, I believe, a basic human female adaptation to use sexual intercourse and the possibility of sexual intercourse to advantage in an environment in which males wield physical and political power.

Male-female differences in tendencies to be sexually aroused by the visual stimulus of a member of the opposite sex—whether this stimulus is a drawing, painting, photograph, or actual person—can be parsimoniously explained in terms of ultimate causation, although their proximate bases remain obscure. Because a male can potentially impregnate a female at almost no cost to himself in terms of time and energy, selection favored the basic male tendency to become sexually aroused by the sight of females, the strength of such arousal being proportionate to perceived female reproductive value; for a male, any random mating may pay off reproductively. In other mammals, female reproductive value is revealed primarily by the presence or absence of estrus; that is, by ovulation advertisements. But human females do not advertise ovulation, hence selection favored male abilities to "assess" reproductive value largely through visual cues, as discussed below. Human females, on the other hand, invest a substantial amount of energy and incur serious risks by becoming pregnant, hence the circumstances of impregnation are extremely important to female reproductive success. A nubile female virtually never experiences difficulty in finding willing sexual partners, and in a natural habitat nubile females are probably always married. The basic female "strategy" is to obtain the best possible husband, to be fertilized by the fittest available male (always, of course, taking risk into account), and to maximize the returns on sexual favors bestowed: to be sexually aroused by the sight of males would promote random matings, thus undermining all of these aims, and would also waste time and energy that could be spent in economically significant activities and in nurturing children. A female's reproductive success would be seriously compromised by the propensity to be sexually aroused by the sight of males.

The male's desire to look at female genitals, especially genitals he has not seen before, and to seek out opportunities to do so, is part of the motivational process that maximizes male reproductive opportunities. There is no corresponding benefit for females in wanting to look at male genitals, hence selection has not favored female impulses to become sexually aroused by the sight of male genitals or to seek out opportunities to look at them. If females tended to be sexually aroused by the sight of male genitals, men would be able to obtain sexual intercourse via genital display; but the deliberate male display of genitals to unfamiliar women is understood to be a kind of threat, whereas a similar female display is understood to be a sexual invitation. Although the practice of covering the genitals with clothing is almost universal, the underlying reasons for concealing male and female genitals probably are different.

While the most significant question for an evolutionary analysis is how human dispositions develop in natural environments, it is likely that selection so consistently favored males who were sexually aroused by the sight of females and the female genitals, and so consistently disfavored females who were aroused by the sight of males and the male genitals, that the resulting male-female differences approach "innateness," and are manifested even in artificial, modern environments. I hasten to add that this does not mean that environments could not be designed in which most females would develop malelike dispositions and vice versa; but such environments probably never existed, nor are they likely to exist in the future.

The widespread failure to appreciate the extent of sex differences in sexual arousal has a number of possible explanations. One possibility is the (generally adaptive) human tendency to conceive other minds in terms of one's own. For example, although it is regularly alleged that men believe, and propagate the myth, that women are "hyposexual," in fact, men often grossly misunderstand women's experiences because they imagine women to be repressed men waiting to be awakened. Kinsey *et al.* write:

> We have histories of males who have attempted to arouse their female partners by

showing them nude photographs or drawings, and most of these males could not comprehend that their female partners were not in actuality being aroused by such material. When a male does realize that his wife or girl friend fails to respond to such stimuli, he may conclude that she no longer loves him and is no longer willing to allow herself to respond in his presence. He fails to comprehend that it is a characteristic of females in general, rather than the reaction of the specific female, which is involved in this lack of response.[3]

Women themselves sometimes imagine that their failure to respond as men do is primarily a matter of repression. As Stauffer and Frost (1976) note, the fact that the editors of *Playgirl* magazine copied *Playboy's* format so closely reflects the misconception that liberated women will be like men.

Sexual Attractiveness

Nowhere are people equally sexually attracted to all members of the opposite sex; everywhere sexual attractiveness varies systematically with observable physical characteristics (Ford and Beach 1951). In their review of the social psychological literature on physical attractiveness, Berscheid and Walster (1974) note that this topic has been neglected in part because appearance is closely tied to the genes, hence the importance of physical attractiveness in everyday life is antagonistic to the optimistic environmentalistic bias of American psychology: it seems undemocratic that hard work cannot compensate for genetic happenstance. Berscheid and Walster argue that nonscientists are more likely than scientists to assess accurately the importance of physical attractiveness because nonscientists have not been misled by social science theories:

> ... social scientists have taken longer to recognize the social significance of physical

appearance than have laymen; the accumulating evidence that physical attractiveness is an important variable to take into account if one is plotting the course and consequences of social interaction may be more startling to social scientists than to those who were never exposed to the strong "environmentalist" tradition of psychology, who did not take at face value beliefs of equal opportunity, and who were not aware that an interest in physical appearance variables relegated one to the dustbin of social science (p. 207).[4]

But even Berscheid and Walster may be guilty of an environmentalistic bias when they state that "culture transmits effectively, and fairly uniformly, criteria for labeling others as physically 'attractive' or 'unattractive'" (p. 186).[5] As discussed below, the extent to which criteria of physical attractiveness are transmitted by culture is debatable.

Berscheid and Walster's review indicates: (1) People generally agree very closely in rating the physical attractiveness of others, regardless of the sex, age, socioeconomic status, or geographical region (within a given country) of the individuals doing the rating. (2) Physical attractiveness greatly influences the formation of heterosexual relationships; as Murstein[6] (1972: 11) writes, "physical attractiveness, both as subjectively experienced and objectively measured, operates in accordance with exchange-market rules." Naturalistic studies of heterosexual couples in public places indicate that members of a pair tend to be approximately equal in physical attractiveness. Experimental studies confirm the importance of physical characteristics. For example, men were paired randomly with women (except that the man was always taller than his partner) at a college dance, and subsequently participants were asked how much they liked their partner. Liking proved to be a direct function of the partner's physical attractiveness; every attempt to discover other factors failed. Needless to say, such findings are at variance with young people's statements about what they value most in a member of the opposite sex, which tend to emphasize "personality" and "character."

Berscheid and Walster call attention to the "dazzling variety" of characteristics considered attractive in various societies and in times past and also to the absence of theories capable of bringing order out of this chaos. Although physical attractiveness is both easily assessed and of great importance in everyday life, "an answer to the question of who is physically attractive is neither available currently nor foreseeable on the immediate horizon".[7] They do note, however, that in the West tallness is considered attractive in men, and that people of high socioeconomic status are judged, on the average, to be more attractive than people of low socioeconomic status. In discussing standards of beauty in cross-cultural perspective, Ford and Beach (1951) also emphasize the diversity of standards, both in what characteristics are admired, and in what parts of the body are considered to be most important.

But standards of physical attractiveness may be neither so variable nor so arbitrary as they seem. I suspect that variability and arbitrariness have been overemphasized for the same historical and ideological reasons that physical attractiveness itself has been ignored in the social sciences: physical characteristics are close to the genes and are distributed undemocratically. If standards of attractiveness can be shown to vary arbitrarily, attractiveness itself is made to seem trivial. Thus Rosenblatt (1974), in reviewing cross-cultural standards of physical attractiveness, describes beauty as an "impractical" criterion on which to base mate choice, whereas economic and political gain are said to represent "practical" criteria. I shall argue that the tendency to discriminate physical attractiveness among members of the opposite sex and to be more sexually attracted to some than to others represents an adaptation whose ultimate basis is that people vary in reproductive value. That humans universally assess one another in terms of physical attractiveness and universally desire attractive partners indicates that these assessments and desires—like economic and political considerations—are "practical" in the sense that they are designed to promote reproductive success.

The perception of physical attractiveness seems to originate in three different kinds of psychological mechanisms. These mechanisms do not, of course, operate independently, but they can be considered separately for analytical purposes. First, some physical characteristics, which can be specified in an *absolute* sense, universally indicate high reproductive value. The ability to discriminate these characteristics and the tendency to desire them in a partner are relatively "innate," in that humans who make these discriminations and experience these desires tend to develop in all natural environments and probably in most unnatural environments as well. Second, some physical characteristics, which can be specified only in a *relative* sense (by comparing individuals in the population with one another), universally indicate high reproductive value. The ability to discriminate these characteristics is acquired through experience, but this does not mean that relative standards of physical attractiveness are transmitted from one individual to another, much less from culture to individuals. The mechanisms underlying the learning of these relative standards may be best considered "innate" *rules*, or programs, that specify how standards of physical attractiveness are to be derived from experience; the development of these relative standards may occur completely outside of consciousness, and the standards thus developed may be unavailable to introspection. Third, individuals derive some criteria of physical attractiveness from one another. Whether these "cultural" criteria are systematically related to reproductive value is an open question, but if they are not, selection can be expected to oppose tendencies to adopt other people's standards of physical attractiveness.

Absolute Criteria. Health obviously is very closely associated with reproductive value, and at least some characteristics predictive of good health are universally attractive. As Byron said, "health in the human frame / Is pleasant, besides being true love's essence." Ford and Beach (1951) report that among all peoples good complexion and cleanliness are considered attractive, poor complexion and filthiness unattractive. These characteristics very likely are the most reliable available indices of good health, and tendencies to pay close attention to skin condition and to be attracted by a clear, clean complexion probably are "innate" human dispositions. Furthermore, the ethnographic record suggests that evidences of disease or deformity render individuals less physically attractive. Perhaps many other physical characteristics—clear eyes, firm muscle tone, sound teeth, luxuriant hair, or a firm gait, for example—are reliably associated with health and vigor and are universally attractive, but the topic has yet to be investigated systematically. Social psychologists have not emphasized the importance of indices of health and skin condition on physical attractiveness perhaps in part because their study populations are often middle-class college students who are, on the whole, extremely clean and healthy; the effect of ringworm on physical attractiveness, for example, is unlikely to be disclosed in such a sample. Furthermore, many social psychological studies of physical attractiveness rely on photographs, in which skin condition may be virtually undetectable; in the case of yearbook photographs, blemishes and irregularities may even have been deliberately eliminated.

A human female's age is very closely associated with her reproductive value, and physical characteristics that vary systematically with age appear to be universal criteria of female physical attractiveness; Williams (1975), in fact, remarks that age probably is the most important determinant of human female attractiveness. The correlation of female age and sexual attractiveness is so intuitively obvious that ethnographers apparently take it for granted—as they do the bipedalism of the people they study—and the significance of female age tends to be mentioned only in passing, in discussions of something else.

Since Western studies of physical attractiveness have focused on people of college age or younger, age is seldom mentioned as an important variable, except incidentally, as in Mathews, Bancroft, and Slater (1972), but the waning of female attractiveness with age is well known. Social scientists may also have neglected age as a variable influencing female attractiveness because in the artificial environments of modern Western societies women can maintain a youthful appearance far longer than is possible under more natural conditions. Where women begin their reproductive careers at seventeen, spend most of their lives pregnant and nursing, and engage in strenuous gathering and domestic activities in which they are regularly exposed to the elements of nature—especially to the effects of the sun on skin texture—the aging process is manifested dramatically in physical appearance.

How age affects female sexual attractiveness can be expected to depend on whether the male's (unconscious) mechanism for "evaluating" female physical characteristics has been designed by selection primarily for wife-detecting or primarily for sexual partner-detecting (Williams 1975). Montagu (1957) provides data relevant to this question in his discussion of "adolescent sterility": in cross-cultural perspective, menarche, accompanied by anovulatory cycles, occurs at $13-16 \pm 1$ years of age; nubility, the beginning of fertile, ovulatory cycles, occurs at $17-22 \pm 2$ years of age and is accompanied by high rates of maternal and infant mortality; maturity, in which full growth is attained, occurs at $23-28 \pm 2$ years of age. Hence, "the best time for conception, pregnancy, and childbirth in the human female is, on the average, at the age of 23 ± 2 years and for about 5 years thereafter."[8] If males have been

designed by selection to "evaluate" females primarily as sex partners, males should be attracted most strongly by females of $23-28 \pm 2$ years, since they are most likely to produce a viable infant; but if males have been designed by selection to "evaluate" females primarily as wives, males should be attracted most strongly by females who are just about to become nubile, at $17-22 \pm 2$ years, since a male who marries a female of this age maximizes his chances of tying up her entire reproductive output. In the West, males might be expected to be attracted most strongly by somewhat younger females (depending on what physical characteristics males use to assess age) since the age of menarche (and presumably of nubility and maturity as well) has been steadily dropping for the last century, hence most of the observable signs of fertility appear earlier among Western females.

Among many higher primate species that do not form harems, adult males are known to prefer older females as sex partners; more dominant rhesus males, for example, tend to copulate with older females. Ultimately, this preference is the result of the relative infertility of the younger estrous females. On the other hand, hamadryas baboons form harems, and a hamadryas male may start his harem by "adopting" permanently a prepubescent, two-year-old female (though his motive may not be sexual). While the relevant data on human male preferences have yet to be collected, it seems very likely that the male "evaluative mechanism" has been designed more for detecting the most reproductively valuable wives than for detecting the most reproductively valuable sex partners. The probabilities that a 30-year-old woman and a 20-year-old woman will produce healthy, viable offspring from a given act of intercourse would seem to be far too similar to explain their differential attractiveness; but, in a natural environment, the 30 year old would have completed perhaps half of her reproductive career and hence, other things being equal, would make a far less valuable wife than the 20 year old. Although I have argued that marriage is not primarily based on lust, marriage may sometimes be motivated by lust, and, more importantly, lust may motivate the male's attempt to accumulate young wives. In *Don Juan*, Byron describes a Turkish sultana who is still an overpowering beauty despite her advanced years: "there are forms which Time to touch forbears / And turns aside his scythe to vulgar things." She is twenty-six years old.

There has recently been a good deal of public discussion of romantic relationships in which the woman is substantially older than the man. With respect to the issue of sexual attractiveness, the following points may be pertinent: (1) Humans are flexible, and individual ontogenetic histories vary enormously in modern societies; no doubt some men are most strongly sexually attracted to older women. (2) The competition for older women is much less keen than the competition for younger women, and, as a group, young men—like most young male mammals—are in a weak competitive position. Among rhesus monkeys, for example, young, low-ranking males tend to mate with the youngest females—who are least likely to produce viable offspring—because the dominant males monopolize the older, more fertile females. (3) Physical sexual attractiveness is only one component of a romantic relationship; older women are likely to be much more interesting intellectually, less inhibited sexually, more highly skilled in lovemaking, and, perhaps, less demanding.

The universal, absolute criteria of physical attractiveness associated with health and female age have been neglected by physical attractiveness theorists perhaps because these criteria are obvious and not very interesting; nevertheless, they may account for much of the variance in physical attractiveness within a given population. Anthropologists may have failed to emphasize these criteria because anthropology takes culture to be its subject matter and universals appear to lie outside the province of culture. But, as argued below, some of the standards of physical attractiveness that do vary cross-culturally probably also lie outside the province of culture.

Relative Criteria. The tendencies to find healthy people and young women attractive are relatively "innate" because they are universally associated with reproductive value and because some indices of health and age (such as unblemished and unwrinkled skin) can be specified in an absolute sense. But the reproductive value of most characteristics can be specified only relatively; hence selection may favor "innate" mechanisms that specify the *rules* by which the individual is to develop standards of attractiveness by comparing members of the population with one another.

The human female tendency to detect and to be attracted by high-status males may constitute one such "innate" rule. When the males of a species regularly compete for status, high rank will, on the average, confer reproductive advantage (Wilson 1975). Females of such species might be expected to prefer dominant males—other things being equal—because such males are more likely than low-ranking males to produce reproductively successful sons. Ford and Beach write that, in cross-cultural perspective.

> One very interesting generalization is that in most societies the physical beauty of the female receives more explicit consideration than does the handsomeness of the male. The attractiveness of the man usually depends predominantly upon his skills and prowess rather than upon his physical appearance.[9]

Social psychological studies have found that female "popularity" is more closely correlated with physical attractiveness than is male popularity, and that males are more likely than females to report that physical attractiveness is important to them in evaluating a member of the opposite sex.

The attractiveness of high-status males may shed light on the question of whether the female "evaluative mechanism" is designed primarily to detect husbands or primarily to detect sex partners (assuming, of course, that ancestral females sometimes had some say in choosing their husbands). If male A has higher status or greater hunting ability than male B, A's wife or wives can expect, other things being equal, to be better off than B's wife or wives; but if B's wife has an affair with A (assuming that she receives no material compensation), all she has to gain, ultimately, is the possibility of conceiving a child by A instead of by B. Selection can be expected to favor the female desire for high-status sex partners, as distinct from husbands, only to the extent that the variance in male status has a genetic basis.

The situation is not as clear-cut as the previously discussed effect of age on female attractiveness: from the male's point of view, the ideal age for a wife is different from the ideal age for a sex partner; but from the female's point of view, a high-status male is both the best choice for a husband and for a sex partner. Nevertheless, I suspect that the proportion of the variance in male status that is caused by genetic differences among males is far too small to account for the persistent female interest in male status and prowess and therefore speculate that the human female "evaluative mechanism" has been designed by selection more for detecting the most reproductively valuable husbands than for detecting the most reproductively valuable sex partners.

The human female preference for high-status males is rapidly becoming a sociobiological cliché and perhaps is not worth belaboring. Good data are needed on this question. In gathering such data, it will be important (and difficult) to distinguish between intellectual judgments and actual sexual attraction: there is no question that humans of both sexes can calculate rationally that they are likely to benefit materially from marriage—or even from association—with a high-status member of the opposite sex. But the interesting question is the extent to which the emotion of sexual attraction varies with the status of the individual being evaluated. Berscheid and Walster (1974) report that middle-class people are, on the average, perceived as more physically attractive than working-class people; this may result from class differences in nutrition and medical care; genetic differences between classes arising from the tendency of attractive women to marry high-status men; and/or specific cues associated with social class. Possibly the effect of status on male attractiveness is not linear, but instead, only a few males of the highest status benefit substantially from intense female interest. This possibility should be considered in designing experiments to assess the effects of status on attractiveness.

Rosenblatt (1974) argues that Ford and Beach's finding—that cross-culturally, male attractiveness is based more on prowess than on handsomeness, while female attractiveness is based largely on beauty—is an artifact of women's lack of power in most societies to choose their own mates. He predicts that women will be equally concerned with handsomeness, and equally unconcerned with prowess and status, when they have equal power to choose their own mates. The question of whether there are "innate" male-female differences in the importance of status as a criterion of sexual attractiveness may be resolved in the near future as Western women achieve economic and political equality. My own prediction is that even when men become used to women in high-status positions, and are not emasculated by the fear of such women, and women become used to holding high-status positions, status will not substantially affect women's sexual attractiveness but will continue to affect men's attractiveness. (The rise of the 20th-century groupie is food for thought.) It might prove interesting to study individuals who regularly move between environments in which they have high status and environments in which they are unknown. I suspect that many men experience dramatic fluctuations in their attractiveness to the other sex as a result of such transitions, and that women generally experience little or no such fluctuations.

If high status is desirable in a mate or a sex partner, and humans are disposed to detect and to be attracted by such individuals, the next best thing to possessing high status is appearing to possess it, hence people may imitate signs of status in order to enhance their own attractiveness. "Fashion" in Western societies may be largely status-imitation run amok: change for its own sake must occur constantly at the top because signs of status are constantly being imitated at lower levels and thereby rendered useless. Imitation may, of course, be prevented by penalties, such as those for impersonating an officer, but the existence of penalties among many peoples implies the existence of impulses to violate them.

Health and status are unusual in that there is no such thing as being too healthy nor too high ranking. But with respect to most anatomical features, natural selection produces the population mean, either directly, in that individuals exhibiting the mean tend to be the most reproductively successful, or indirectly, in that the extremes of the population distribution tend to be reproductively less successful. Thus sexual selection can be expected to favor an "innate" mechanism to detect the population mean (or other measure of central tendency) of most physical characteristics and to find it attractive. Cross-cultural variation in standards of physical attractiveness must be in part the result of racial variation; *Homo sapiens* is an extremely polytypic species. Darwin (1871) argued that peoples tend to admire characteristics peculiar to their own race, characteristics, that is, which distinguish their race from others, and that sexual selection would therefore tend to exaggerate racial differences; in fact, Darwin believed that sexual, rather than natural, selection is primarily

responsible for racial differences. It seems more likely, however, that during most of human evolution individuals rarely encountered members of races very different physically from their own, that racial differences are primarily the result of natural selection, and that any tendency to prefer one's own race is an artifact of the tendency to prefer the norm, a norm which is reinforced rather than exaggerated by sexual selection. That is, sexual selection may simply tend to reduce variability by eliminating the tails of the population distribution.

The human beauty-detecting mechanism probably evolved to deal with small, relatively homogeneous groups of people. How this mechanism operates in large communities, often of varied racial composition, provides interesting problems for research. In a small, relatively homogeneous population there may be a single ideal face, but if the averaging mechanism is designed to detect *relations* among facial features, rather than absolute dimensions, in a large, heterogeneous population a number of "ideal" faces may exist, each characterized by a different harmony in the relative proportions of its features. Moreover, one wonders whether humans have completely distinct criteria of attractiveness for different racial groups, or whether exposure to a number of races results in a mutual influence of standards.

According to Berscheid and Walster's (1974) review, tallness is valued in American men, which appears to contradict the hypothesis that the most attractive height will be the population mean. But the evidence on this question is equivocal, and raises a number of interesting issues. How sexual attractiveness varies with male height has not, in fact, been systematically investigated; furthermore, the data Berscheid and Walster cite have more to do with political success and the hiring practices of American businessmen than with male attractiveness to females. Berscheid and Walster report no evidence that men taller than the mean (about seventy inches) are consistently judged to be more sexually attractive than shorter men; according to their discussion, the male's absolute height does not appear to be as important as his height relative to that of the female doing the evaluating. Women clearly prefer men somewhat taller than themselves, but how much taller is not known.

The following points—which are intended to be hypotheses rather than conclusions—may be worth considering. First, humans are designed by selection to live in small, relatively homogeneous groups in which the variability in body height is far less than the variability existing in the United States today. In a natural human habitat, virtually all adult men will be taller than all adult women, so perhaps it is "natural" for women to prefer men somewhat taller than themselves. The problem of a "restricted field of eligibles" faced by tall women and short men in the United States probably is peculiar to modern, heterogeneous societies. Second, although inquiries into the effects on attractiveness of posture, gait, and body carriage have not, to my knowledge, been made, these characteristics probably influence attractiveness and may tend to favor shorter men. Third, although there are no data to show that men taller than seventy inches are considered more attractive than seventy-inch-tall men, it does seem likely that a man whose height is above the mean generally will be considered more attractive than a man who is the same distance from the mean in the other direction. Since at least the beginning of this century, mean body height (for both sexes) in the United States has steadily increased; perhaps it is not too farfetched to imagine that, as a refinement on a mean-detecting mechanism, humans also are able to detect major trends—presumably by comparing members of different generations—and have a tendency to prefer individuals who deviate from the mean in the direction of the trend. Such a mechanism would be adapted to long-term environmental changes; the perceived trend in phenotypes naturally need not be the result of genetic

evolution, but a trend-detecting and -preferring mechanism might lead to genetic tracking (Wilson 1975) of facultative responses.

According to Darwin (1871), the human male's preference for physically attractive females resulted in sexual selection for beauty. Crook[10], however, argues that "since in tribal societies virtually all women marry, the case for differential selection is poor because the less beautiful are not known to be less fecund than the more beautiful." But it is also true that the less beautiful are not known *not* to be less fecund than the more beautiful. Data are lacking. If higher-status males were able to obtain a disproportionate share of physically attractive wives, beautiful women may have had a slight reproductive edge. Nevertheless, if for most anatomical characteristics the population mean is considered most attractive, male preference for beauty would have reinforced natural selection and reduced population variability. Indeed, it is difficult to believe that sexual selection acted very strongly among hominid females, nor is there convincing evidence that the function of any human female anatomical characteristic— such as breasts—is to stimulate males visually. Most likely, female anatomy is stimulating to males owing to evolution in male brains, not female bodies. Consider that in cross-cultural perspective the sight of the female genitals, more than any other feature of female anatomy, is consistently reported to stimulate males, yet no one (to my knowledge) has yet suggested that any part of female genital anatomy was designed by selection for the purpose of visually stimulating males (although artificial elongation of the labia minora is sometimes thought to enhance attractiveness).

Much of the cross-cultural variation in standards of physical attractiveness reported by Ford and Beach (1951) is in body build, especially in the amount of body fat that is considered to be ideal. Among most peoples, plump women are considered more attractive than thin women. Rosenblatt[11] remarks that "in a world where food is often scarce and nutritional and digestive-tract illnesses often epidemic, plumpness is an indication of wealth and health." Tobias (1964) suggests that the characteristic steatopygia of Bushmen women is adaptive in an environment of periodic food shortages, and he notes that Bushmen men prefer women with the fattest bottoms. Body fat is one of the most variable physical characteristics: major intra- and inter-population variation occurs, in part owing to differing nutritional opportunities, and the amount of body fat an individual possesses can change noticeably in the course of a few days. Humans do not seem to have an "innate" preference for a particular body build; rather, individuals learn to associate variation in body build with indices of health and status. Plumpness has gone out of fashion in Western societies during the last century, probably as a result of the changing relationship between body fat and status: when food was scarce for many people, plumpness was a sign of wealth, but as circumstances improved for the majority, the rich began to distinguish themselves through thinness. (A similar argument sometimes is made with respect to suntans.) That a preference for plumpness is not "innate" seems to support arguments that hunter/gatherers (and by inference our Pleistocene ancestors) do not exist in a state of perpetual nutritional insufficiency. Alternatively, humans may have a tendency to prefer plumpness, a tendency that can be overridden by the enormous influence of health and status on standards of physical attractiveness.

Ford and Beach (1951) report substantial cross-cultural variability in the particular anatomical features that are considered to be most relevant to assessing beauty: this group emphasizes the lips, that group the nose, another group the ears, and so forth. I confess to a certain amount of skepticism. Such data are almost always obtained in an unsystematic and haphazard way, and must depend heavily on what features one or a few informants happen to mention. We know from more careful and systematic studies in the West that physical attractiveness—at least facial beauty—is perceived more as a total Gestalt than in isolated features (Berscheid and Walster 1974). Neither is the fact that a people adorn one facial feature and not another convincing evidence for the overriding importance of the former. It would be incorrect to assume, for example, that because many more Western women color their lips than their noses that lips are a more important criterion of beauty than noses are.

None of the foregoing is intended to deny the existence of cultural traditions of beauty that are unrelated to fitness, or of personal idiosyncrasies that result from unusual learning experiences; rather, it is intended to suggest first, that the ability to detect and to be attracted by members of the opposite sex who evidence high reproductive value is an important adaptation, and second, that humans have "innate" preferences for certain physical characteristics (for example, good skin), and "innate" rules by which other preferences are learned (for example, "prefer characteristics associated with high-status people"). If one argues, as so many people continue to do, that behavior must be caused either by the genes or by the environment, and that any exception to a general rule demonstrates environmental causation (unless the exception can be shown to have a genetic basis), one can deny the existence of any genetic influences on human sexual preferences. But if one acknowledges that behavior and psyche result from the interactions of genes and environments, and that human genes were selected on the basis of their ability to perpetuate themselves within a limited range of environmental circumstances, then, despite exceptions, one can interpret the cross-cultural regularities in standards of physical attractiveness as powerful evidence for "innate" dispositions. There is no a priori reason to doubt that a human child could be taught to be sexually attracted to anyone or anything; but this in no way diminishes the significance of the standards of attractiveness that develop in existing human environments.

Sex Differences in the West. In *The Selfish Gene*, Dawkins (1976) ends the chapter on the "battle of the sexes" as follows:

> One feature of our own society which seems decidedly anomalous is the matter of sexual advertisement. As we have seen, it is strongly to be expected on evolutionary grounds that, where the sexes differ, it should be the males who advertise and the females who are drab. Modern western man is undoubtedly exceptional in this respect. It is of course true that some men dress flamboyantly and some women dress drably but, on average, there can be no doubt that in our society the equivalent of the peacock's tail is exhibited by the female, not by the male. Women paint their faces and glue on false eyelashes. Apart from actors and homosexuals, men do not. Women seem to be interested in their own personal appearance and they are encouraged in this by their magazines and journals. Men's magazines are less preoccupied with male sexual attractiveness, and a man who is unusually interested in his own dress and appearance is apt to arouse suspicion, both among men and among women. When a woman is described in conversation, it is quite likely that her sexual attractiveness, or lack of it, will be prominently mentioned. This is true, whether the speaker is a man or a woman. When a man is described, the adjectives used are much more likely to have nothing to do with sex.
>
> Faced with these facts, a biologist would be forced to suspect that he was looking at society in which females compete for males, rather than vice versa. In the case of birds of paradise, we decided that females are drab because they do not need to compete for males. Males are bright and ostentatious because females are in demand and can afford

to be choosy. The reason female birds of paradise are in demand is that eggs are a more scarce resource than sperms. What has happened in modern western man? Has the male really become the sought-after sex, the one that is in demand, the sex that can afford to be choosy? If so, why?[12]

I have tried to show that the ultimate cause of the greater importance of female than of male physical attractiveness is easily explained by the nature of reproductive competition during the course of human evolution: a female's reproductive value can be assessed more accurately from her physical appearance than a male's reproductive value can. Human females compete with one another in the currency of physical attractiveness because that is primarily what males value. (Appearance is enhanced in large measure by making the skin look healthier and younger.) A woman's physical attractiveness is significant not only in heterosexual interactions that may result in sexual intercourse, but in almost any heterosexual interaction in which male sexual interest can be advantageous to the woman or to her employer. Thus women employers are likely to be no less concerned than men about the physical attractiveness of their female employees, since they recognize that beauty is a tangible economic asset. Of course this is true also of male employees, but to a markedly lesser extent.

Furthermore, the fact that most men in modern Western societies wear more drab or conservative clothing than women does not mean that men are uninterested in being sexually attractive to women; on the contrary, this mode of dress is attractive to most women. Drabness connotes a responsible, hard-working family man, and almost all criteria of conservative good taste in men's clothing are simply signs of high status and membership in the upper classes. Men with the most to conserve— that is, those with the most power—tend to be the most conservative and to require conservative appearance of their subordinates. And in any species that typically exhibits both male-male competition and some female choice, visible signs of success in intrasexual competition are also likely to be important determinants of male attractiveness to females. Overt, flamboyant, sexual advertising in male attire is often perceived by women as a sign of promiscuous tendencies, which few women find attractive. As homosexual men are much less likely to be put off by signs of promiscuity in a potential sex partner, they are much freer than heterosexual men to use clothing as sexual advertising.

Dawkins's discussion does, however, raise some interesting questions about the peculiar circumstances of modern societies. Although Western women's concern with physical attractiveness doubtless does in part reflect female intrasexual competition, I trust no one believes that women compete for opportunities to copulate. In the West, as in all human societies, copulation is usually a female service or favor; women compete for husbands and for other relationships with men, not for copulation (when prostitutes compete for customers they are competing for money, not copulation). This competition is artificially magnified in Western societies because, by custom and by law, polygyny has been almost eliminated. Mead writes:

> In modern societies where polygamy is no longer sanctioned and women are no longer cloistered, there is now a new problem to meet, the competition of females for males. Here we have an example of a problem that is almost entirely socially created, a product of civilization itself imposed upon an older biological one. . . . So in those societies in which there are more women than men— our normal Western sex ratio—and in which monogamy is the rule, we find the struggle of women over men also.[13]

There is a second feature of modern Western societies that may conceivably increase female competition. Mead (1967) maintains, in effect, that the desire to be a mother is more "innate"— that is, develops under a wider range of environmental circumstances—than is the desire to be a father. She argues that "men have to learn to want to provide for others, and this behaviour, being learned, is fragile and can disappear rather easily under social conditions that no longer teach it effectively. Women may be said to be mothers unless they are taught to deny their child-bearing qualities."[14] In modern Western societies not only may males be relatively ineffectively taught to want children, but many of the former economic motives for having children have disappeared. If more women than men do desire to have children (a proposition which has yet to be established), female competition may be rendered more fierce. Finally, modern women's sexual emancipation may have the effect of making some men reluctant to form durable heterosexual relationships (thus exacerbating female competition) not because men desire such relationships less strongly than women do, but because more males than females desire sexual variety for its own sake. The opportunities to satisfy this desire probably are greater, for the majority of men, in modern Western societies than in any other time or place, and the opportunities are greatest for the most desirable men.

The male peacock's tail and the bright, ostentatious plumage of male birds of paradise, to which Dawkins refers, were produced by intersexual selection, which results from the combination of individual differences in the males' "power to charm the females" and female choice. Among species in which females have the power and opportunity to choose their mates, if male fitness happens to be reliably associated with an observable physical characteristic, selection favors females who are predisposed to choose males exhibiting this characteristic. As this female predisposition becomes widespread in the population, selection begins to favor males who manifest this characteristic in the most extreme form—that is, males with the most effective advertising—and females who choose such males, since these females produce sons who are differentially chosen as mates. The resulting "run-away" sexual selection exaggerates the male characteristic until sexual selection is eventually halted by the counter-pressure of natural selection (the more flamboyant the male peacock's tail, for example, the more energy is expended in its development, the more conspicuous the male is to predators, and the more his mobility is limited).

There is no evidence that any features of human anatomy were produced by intersexual selection. Human physical sex differences are explained most parsimoniously as the outcome of intrasexual selection (the result of male-male competition) and perhaps natural and artificial selection, not intersexual selection or female choice. Analogies between humans and birds, and the perspective of modern Western societies, both lead to serious overestimation of the importance of female choice in human evolution. Also, the natural desire to have one's views accepted may—given current standards of acceptability—lead evolutionary theorists to exaggerate the importance of female choice: perhaps it is felt that the often unwelcome messages of an evolutionary view of life—an amoral universe and a creative process that is founded on reproductive competition—can be to some extent ameliorated by the welcome news that in the battle of the sexes nature has given females the upper hand.

Although copulation is, and presumably always has been, in some sense a female service or favor, hominid females evolved in a milieu in which physical and political power was wielded by adult males, and the substantial evidence, documented in the ethnographic record, that men will use their power to control women should not be underestimated. In modern Western societies males are severely limited in their opportunities to accumulate wives or to capitalize on their greater strength, and male political dominance is being steadily eroded; hence female choice (of mates and sex partners)—the psychological underpinnings of which presumably have always been present—is now manifested to an unprecedented degree in behavior. Ironically, the social, political, and sexual features of modern societies that have increased women's opportunities to chart the course of their own lives and to choose their own sexual partners and mates are the same features that have increased female intrasexual competition.

A final point: Dawkins writes that "a man who is unusually interested in his own dress and appearance is apt to arouse suspicion," which I take to mean "suspicion of being homosexual." Probably many heterosexual men are, in fact, as concerned with dress and appearance as any homosexual man (although heterosexuals may be more reluctant to admit such concern); nevertheless, homosexual men in general undoubtedly are more concerned with their appearance than heterosexual men in general are. As with all behaviors that characterize homosexuals, this emphasis on appearance provides a powerful insight into the nature of human sex differences. Homosexual men tend to be interested in dress and appearance not because they are, as a group, effeminate, but simply because they face the same problem that heterosexual women face: they wish to be sexually attractive to males, and males assess sexual attractiveness primarily on the basis of physical appearance.

To some extent the artificiality of modern Western environments can be considered to constitute an unplanned experiment. Although most human behavior in such environments is not explicable as adaptation (since the environments have existed for an infinitesimal amount of time), the modern world may dramatically reveal formerly adaptive human dispositions by allowing them, to an unprecedented degree, to be realized in behavior. For example, mate selection tends to be based on physical attractiveness to a much greater extent when young people arrange their own marriages than when marriages are arranged by elders (Rosenblatt 1974). It is a mistake to imagine either, as Rosenblatt does, that beauty is a totally "impractical" criterion, or, as a sociobiological perspective might imply, that young people "know" what is in their reproductive interests, and that elders and principals disagree over mate choice only because elders are "looking out" for their own inclusive fitness at the expense of the principals' inclusive fitness (although this undoubtedly is sometimes the case). Perhaps the typical differences between the criteria of elders and the criteria of the principals in matters of spouse selection can be thought of as a division of labor, elders taking account of factors they are uniquely situated to perceive owing to their age and experience, and principals assessing reproductive value evidenced largely in physical attractiveness, the final choice being a compromise (heavily weighted in favor of the elders).

By the standards of preliterate peoples, modern human communities provide an enormous pool of potential sexual and marital partners, relatively few taboos, unprecedented freedom from parental influences, and thus great scope for personal attraction based on physical appearance. While the choices made under such circumstances perhaps are not often the most adaptive ones possible, the underlying psychological mechanisms that determine physical attractiveness are strikingly illuminated, since they are regularly manifested in behaviors and marriages. These mechanisms represent adaptations to maximize reproductive success in the environments normally encountered during the course of human evolutionary history.

Notes

1 U.S. Commission on Obscenity and Pornography 1970, p. 21.
2 U.S. Commission on Obscenity and Pornography 1970, p. 24.
3 Kinsey et al., 1953, p. 653.
4 Berscheid and Walster 1974, p. 207.
5 Berscheid and Walster 1974, p. 186.
6 Murstein 1972, p. 11.
7 Berscheid and Walster 1974, p. 181.
8 Montagu 1957, p. 193.
9 Ford and Beach 1951, p. 94.
10 Crook 1972, p. 2448.
11 Rosenblatt 1974, p. 87.
12 Dawkins 1976, pp. 177–178.
13 Mead 1976, pp. 196–197.
14 Mead 1967, p. 192.

References

Berscheid, E., & Walster, E. (1974). Physical attractiveness. In L. Berkowitz (Ed.), *Advances in Experimental Social Psychology*, 7 (pp. 157–215). New York: Academic Press.

Brownmiller, S. (1975). *Against Our Will: Men, women and rape*. New York: Simon and Schuster.

Crook, J. H. (1972). Sexual selection, dimorphism, and social organization in the primates. In B. Campbell (Ed.), *Sexual Selection and the Descent of Man 1871–1971* (pp. 231–81). Chicago: Aldine.

Darwin, C. (1871). *The Descent of Man and Selection in Relation to Sex*. London: John Murray

Dawkins, R. (1976). *The Selfish Gene*. Oxford: Oxford University Press.

Ford, C. S., & Beach, F. A. (1951). *Patterns of Sexual Behavior*. New York: Harper & Row.

Hart, C. W., & Pilling, A. R. (1960). *The Tiwi of North Australia*. New York: Holt, Rinehart and Winston.

Kinsey, A. C., Pomeroy, W. B., & Martin, C. E. (1948). *Sexual Behavior in the Human Male*. Philadelphia, PA: W. B. Saunders.

Kinsey, A. C., Pomeroy, W. B., Martin, C. E., & Gebhard, P. (1953). *Sexual Behavior in the Human Female*. Philadelphia, PA: W. B. Saunders.

Lochart, W. B. (1970). *The Report of the Commission on Obscenity and Pornography*. New York: Bantam Books.

Marcus, S. (1966). *The Other Victorians: A study of sexuality and pornography in mid-nineteenth-century England*. New York: Basic Books.

Mathews, A. M., Bancroft, J. H. J., & Slater, P. (1972). The principal components of sexual preference. *British Journal of Social and Clinical Psychology*, 11: 35–43.

Mead, M. (1967). *Male and Female: A study of the sexes in a changing world*. New York: William Morrow and Company.

Montagu, A. (1957). *The Reproductive Development of the Female, with Special Reference to the Period of Adolescent Sterility: A study in the comparative physiology of infecundity of the adolescent organism*. New York: Julian Press.

Murstein, B. I. (1972). Physical attractiveness and marital choice. *Journal of Personality and Social Psychology*, 22: 8–12.

Rosenblatt, P. C. (1974). Cross-cultural perspective on attraction. In T. L. Huston (Ed.), *Foundations of Interpersonal Attraction* (pp. 79–95). New York: Academic Press.

Smith, D. D. (1976). The social content of pornography. *Journal of Communication*, 26: 16–24.

Stauffer, J., & Frost, R. (1976). Male and female interest in sexually-oriented magazines. *Journal of Communication*, 26: 25–30.

Tobias, P. V. (1964). Bushman hunter-gathers: a study in human ecology. In D. H. S. Davis (Ed.), *Ecological Studies in Southern Africa*. The Hague: W. Junk.

Trivers, R. L. (1974). Parent-offspring conflict. *American Zoologist*, 14: 249–264.

US Commission on Obscenity and Pornography (1970). *The Report of the US Commission on Obscenity and Pornography*. New York: Random House.

Williams, G. C. (1966). *Adaptation and Natural Selection: A critique of some current evolutionary thought*. Princeton, NJ: Princeton University Press.

Williams, G. C. (1975). *Sex and Evolution*. Princeton, NJ: Princeton University Press.

Wilson, E. O. (1975). *Sociobiology: The new synthesis*. Cambridge, MA: Harvard University Press.

Chapter 29

John Dupré

THE EVOLUTIONARY PSYCHOLOGY OF SEX AND GENDER

Introduction

The aim of this chapter is to engage in some detail with the nitty-gritty of contemporary evolutionary psychology, especially the evolutionary psychology of sex and gender. It will be helpful to begin with a brief consideration of the distinction just invoked, that between sex and gender. The distinction originates in feminist scholarship with the insistence that gender, the differentiated roles and identities defined for men and women by particular cultures, should be sharply distinguished from sex, the supposedly universal biological differences between men and women. The central claim was simply that sex did not determine gender roles. The support for this claim was a wide variety of empirical investigations of the variability of gender roles both cross-culturally and through human history. Since it was generally assumed that biology was more or less a constant across these diverse contexts,[1] this diversity seemed to show that sex did not determine gender. This led to a positive concern with how gender roles were shaped and maintained, and a political engagement with the question how they might be changed.

Contemporary evolutionary psychologists generally acknowledge some degree of variation among human cultures. This acknowledgement is not without its problems, most notably the difficulty it presents in providing empirical support for their hypotheses. And in fact it is highly characteristic of evolutionary psychology to insist that the extent of diversity has been greatly exaggerated by anthropologists labouring under the illusions of the Standard Social Sciences Model. They delight, for example, in citing Freeman's (1983) claim to have refuted the classic ethnography of Samoa by Margaret Mead (1949), the latter having been the *locus classicus* for claims about the variability of human sexual behaviour. Evolutionary psychologists, in short, admit that variability exists on pain of empirical absurdity, but deny that there is nearly as much of it as their opponents claim.

I do not propose to attempt to adjudicate the question exactly how much variation in gender roles there may be. Fortunately it is admitted on all sides that there is a good deal of it, and this will be sufficient for the purposes of the present discussion. Evolutionary psychologists want to claim, nonetheless, that the key to understanding the various manifestations of gender in human societies is to expose the species-wide psychology of sex on which these various structures are all erected. And it is to this project that I now turn.

The Sociobiology of Sex and Gender: The Classic Story

The starting point for all sociobiological stories about sex and gender is with what is now taken to be the fundamental biological definition of male and female. In sexual species there is generally a large disparity between the size of the gametes (sperms and eggs) that unite to form the zygote which, in turn, develops into a new organism. Males, by definition, are the contributors of the smaller gamete, females of the larger. Introducing an economic metaphor, to which I shall return, males are said to require a much smaller investment in reproduction.[2] In most animal species, of course, this discrepancy in gamete size is only a tiny part of the difference in biological investment in reproduction: for mammals, in particular, the female contribution also includes gestation and, usually, a substantial amount of post-natal care including lactation.

This difference in investment, the story then goes, will lead males and females to pursue radically different strategies in seeking to maximize their reproductive success. Males, whose gametes are cheap and numerous, will seek to mate with as many females as possible. This will lead to various kinds of more or less violent conflict between males over access to females, reluctance to devote much energy to any one female, and, it is often suggested, various deceptive or coercive strategies in seeking matings. As Richard Dawkins puts it, "a male . . . can never get enough copulations with as many females as possible: the word excess has no meaning for a male."[3] Females, on the other hand, have their potential for reproduction much more limited by the large investment demanded by each offspring and, given male psychology, experience no difficulty in acquiring the minimal necessary male contribution to the process. They will, therefore, rather be concerned to obtain male mating partners with the highest quality genes and, if possible, to mate with males who are willing to contribute something to the care of the offspring. Since the male, having made his small contribution to mating, has little evolutionary reason for hanging around, it is generally supposed, however, that the latter desideratum is usually unattainable. So far this story is intended to apply quite generally to sexual organisms, though with greatest force to organisms with the most disparity between the reproductive investment of the two sexes. It is also fair to say that it is a story that has provided some insight into the variety of mating behaviour observed in nature.

It is crucial to emphasize, however, the *variety* of such behaviour. There is enormous diversity among species in the degree of promiscuity or monogamy in both sexes, and enormous diversity in the ways in which different animals select their mates. This variability is fully exhibited by our closest non-human relatives. Whereas chimpanzees are highly promiscuous, fertile females generally being observed to mate with several males, and their close relatives the bonobos have become a byword for polymorphous perversity, silver-back gorillas, the dominant males, enjoy exclusive access to a group of females.[4] Thus it is extremely hazardous to infer what kind of mating behaviour to expect in a species apart from detailed and careful observation of the animals in question. This brings us to the application of all this to humans, and its problems.

Early sociobiologists exhibited varying degrees of caution in the extension of their theories to humans, but some general ideas were widely asserted or insinuated. It was taken as fairly obvious that men are inclined to promiscuity and women to monogamy, and thus that, in the words of one authority, "In . . . all human societies, copulation is usually a female service or favor".[5] Women, but not men, were assumed to have a biological urge to take care of children, whereas men were expected to be out in the forest—or its modern surrogate, the urban jungle—competing with one another for resources and, ultimately, access to more women. In summary, let me quote Wilson himself:

> It pays males to be aggressive, hasty, fickle and undiscriminating. In theory it is more profitable for females to be coy, to hold back until they can identify males with the best

species that rears young, it is also for the females to select males who are likely to stay with them after insemination.

Humans obey this biological principle faithfully.[6]

Needless to say, such pronouncements reflected some widely held stereotypes. However, it was also widely perceived that such stories were extremely simplistic. The evidence on which they were based was often little more than the stereotypic impressions of sociobiologists, and little account was taken of the huge variety of human sexual behaviour, let alone variation across species. Even the underlying model, when analysed in any detail, will give quite different predictions depending upon many specific facts about the ecological situation. For example, will desertion by the male really lead to possibilities of future matings of which the reproductive benefits will outweigh the possible benefits of caring for existing offspring?[7] In fact, Dawkins, sensitive to the variety of human mating practices, remarks uncharacteristically that these suggest "that man's way of life is largely determined by culture rather than genes".[8] A quarter of a century later, however, few such doubts are entertained by evolutionists. It is to these contemporary versions of human sociobiology that I now turn.

Sociobiology Twenty-five Years Later

Épater les Bourgeois

Sociobiologists have always liked to shock. And the picture of the human condition they present is indeed a bleak one. While they usually insist that any possible amelioration of human ills will require the understanding of evolutionary origins, they like to make clear that the origins of these ills are deep and biological. But where twenty-five years ago these pessimistic conclusions tended to be somewhat cautious

and speculative, now they are forthright and uncompromising. And nowhere are these shocking conclusions more striking than in the matter of sexuality, as can be discovered by the most casual glance through the biology section of a contemporary bookshop. One does not even need to open the books: on the cover of a book on the human male by British biologist Ben Greenstein, we read:

First and foremost, man is a fertilizer of women.[9] His need to inject genes into a female is so strong that it dominates his life from puberty to death. This need is even stronger than the urge to kill . . . It could even be said that production and supply of sperm is his only raison d'être, and his physical power and lust to kill are directed to that end, to ensure that only the best examples of the species are propagated. If he is prevented from transmitting his genes he becomes stressed, ill, and may shut down or go out of control. (1993)

Opinions may, I suppose, differ as to what constitute the "best examples of the species". In a slightly more temperate work by the respected evolutionist David Buss (1994; a book which will provide my main focus in much of what follows) we also find a depressing message on the dust jacket:

Much of what I discovered about human mating is not nice . . . In the ruthless pursuit of sexual goals, for example, men and women derogate their rivals, deceive members of the opposite sex, and even subvert their own mates. (1994)

The emphasis on deception in sexual interactions is a major theme in current biological thought. There is little room for sentimental moralizing in a matter of this importance.

More disturbing still, perhaps, are the following remarks by science journalist and enthusiast for evolutionary psychology, Robert Wright: "the roots of all evil can be seen in natural selection . . . The enemy of justice and decency does indeed lie in our genes".[10] It is no doubt true that if we hadn't evolved we wouldn't do anything nasty. But apart from that rather trivial sense of the "roots of all evil", it might seem that there are a lot of more immediate sources. But biology, we discover, teaches us that the derelict inner cities, unemployment, and exploitation that we might naively have thought sources of human evil are at most triggers for eliciting our deeply ingrained natural tendencies.

Uniting the popular themes of sex and violence, Buss suggests that men may have an evolved tendency to kill their unfaithful wives under appropriate circumstances.[11] If he has anyhow lost control of her reproductive resources he can prevent their being diverted to an evolutionary rival. He may mitigate the great loss in status accruing to a cuckold, and status is important for getting other reproductive opportunities. And—plausibly enough—this will serve as a deterrent to other concurrent or future wives. Wilson and Daly (1992) develop this theme in more detail in terms of their elaboration of the evolved tendency of men to treat women as property. They note that some American states until recently treated the killing of a wife discovered in adultery as no crime, and that "the violent rages of cuckolds constitute an acknowledged risk in all societies, and some sort of diminution of their criminal responsibility is apparently universal" (311). Certainly it is not a pretty picture of our evolutionary heritage.

The Political Economy of Sex and Gender

As I have already remarked, the sociobiology of sex differences has been informed from the outset by an economic metaphor, that of "parental investment" (Trivers, 1972). The economistic aspects of the field have grown in recent years, and may now fairly be said to

dominate it. The central locus of quasi-economic interaction has become the decision to mate. Buss (1994; subsequent page numbers are for this work) entitles two major chapters of his book "What Women Want" and "Men Want Something Different". Evidently we have the classic preconditions for exercise of the fundamental human disposition to—in Adam Smith's famous words—"truck, barter, and trade", and an obvious grounding for the treatment of human relations as a marketplace that has inspired some economists interested in these matters. This perspective naturally invites a consideration of the features men and women will be prepared to pay for in a mate, and his book, Buss notes in the introduction, "documents the universal preferences that men and women display for particular characteristics in a mate" (8). Put simply, what men want is sex with as many women of as high a quality as possible,[12] and women want to get paid for it. Prostitution, one might say, is the biologically fundamental form of interaction between men and women.

To consider in more detail what women want, their central problem is one of choice among universally eager men. "Men vary tremendously in the quantity of resources they command—from the poverty of the street bums to the riches of Trumps and Rockefellers".[13] And, needless to say, this problem is greatly exacerbated by the fact that men will do everything in their power to misrepresent the resources they control in the attempt to dupe women into accepting a less affluent contender than they might otherwise have traded their sexual resources to. In addition, men differ in their willingness to devote their resources to one woman and her children, as to whether, as Buss puts it, they are "dads" or "cads". And again, needless to say, the cads will do everything to convince the gullible woman that they are really dads. (What is not always clear is why there should be any honest dads out there.) The main problem for women, then, is to identify and secure the resources of a Rockefeller dad. Thus women are said to look for various cues in men that signal either the possession, or the likelihood of acquiring, resources.[14] In the former category they prefer, for example men in suits to those less expensively dressed,[15–16] and also have some preference for men who are older and consequently better heeled.[17] In predicting future resources, they look for ambition, industry, stability, and intelligence. Women also like a good physical specimen. Apart from the more minimal requirement that their partners be free of open sores and lesions, universally regarded as unattractive[18], women like their men tall. As an extreme illustration of this point, Buss observes that "when the great basketball player Magic Johnson revealed that he had slept with thousands of women, he inadvertently revealed women's preferences for mates who display physical and athletic prowess".[19] (It might be noted that Magic Johnson did also have some modest resources.) Less anecdotally, but relevant, I suppose, to Magic Johnson, Buss quotes research that is said to show that "tall men make more money ... [and] advance more rapidly in their professions".[20] Moreover, they tend to have prettier girlfriends.[21] Apparently this preference for size is not sufficiently explained by the greater resource-acquisition potential of taller men. In addition, women want big men for protection, not a bad idea given the bleak picture of men shortly to unfold.[22]

Finally, in addition to money and size, unless a woman is looking for a fling (something to which I shall return), there is the problem of sorting out the dads from the cads, since the cads, once they have had their way with her, will take off with their resources. What they look for here is signs of love. In all cultures, Buss asserts, women desire love. "Love is universal".[23] "To identify precisely what love is", Buss himself has studied "acts of love".[24] Typical of these are "talking of marriage, and expressing a desire to have children with the person".[25] The somewhat

banal function of these acts of love, when performed by a man, is "to signal the intention to commit resources to one woman and her children". Once again, we might worry that the cads are sure to talk the same talk. Indeed in more traditional accounts, this is just what cads are known for.

Men, as I have noted, want something different. The first few subheadings in Buss's chapter on this topic will leave no doubt what this is. They are: "Youth"; "Standards of Physical Beauty"; "Body Shape"; "Importance of Physical Appearance"; and "Men's Status and Women's Beauty". Men, in short, want their women young, cute, and curvy. Evolutionarily, of course, the claim is that men want good breeding stock; and they are prepared to pay for it, even sometimes the high price of (almost) monogamous commitment. That a younger woman will have the potential of producing more children, at least, is not controversial. More surprising, especially to those who have analysed the cultural construction of standards of beauty, is Buss's insistence that these standards are cross-cultural universals. Our ancestors, apparently, needed to assess women for their youth and health. All they had to go on were such features as "full lips, clear skin, lustrous hair, and good muscle tone ... a bouncy youthful gait, an animated facial expression, and a high energy level".[26] Somewhat more peculiar is the allegedly universal preference for curves; or, more specifically, a ratio of waist-to-hip measurement of about 70 per cent[27] (57; Singh, 1993). Whatever this supposedly optimal body shape may show about youth or health, it does, of course provide some useful evidence that the woman is not already pregnant.

This brings us to the one other thing men care about, fidelity. The evolutionary fate worse than death is to invest one's resources in the offspring of another man's genes. Indeed at one point Buss seems to think it appropriate that cuckolders should be required to pay compensation to the victimized husband since this "reflect[s] an intuitive understanding of human evolutionary psychology: cuckoldry represents the unlawful stealing of another man's resources".[28] Fidelity, however, can be difficult to predict in a potential mate. There is apparently a correlation between premarital and post-marital promiscuity, which suggests that a good cue would be to seek out hitherto chaste women. Oddly, however, while apparently men used to care a lot about this, they do so increasingly less: they still care more in Texas than in California,[29] but in Sweden they now care scarcely at all.[30] But as I have already noted, evolutionary psychologists are now quite complacent about such minor refutations of their theories. Buss seems happy, in this case, to provide an uncharacteristic cultural explanation of these anomalies.

So far I have considered the generic account of the economic trade between men and women, but with my reference above to the political economy of sex and gender I had rather more in mind. This was made strikingly clear a few years ago when in the course of about a year three long articles on the evolution of human sexual behaviour were published in the prestigious journal *Behavioral and Brain Sciences*. The first presents evidence intended to show that men are attracted to younger women, increasingly younger as they age, and that women are attracted to somewhat older men (Kenrick and Keefe, 1992). The second concerns rape. Specifically, it argues that men have a variety of evolved sexual strategies, and one of these, usually resorted to when others fail, is rape (Thornhill and Thornhill, 1992). The third documents the female preference for men of high status (Pérusse, 1993). Putting the three theses together presents a very simple politics of class and gender: with the acquisition of high status, men have increasing access to women, especially the younger ones they prefer; the lower-status men, having little legitimate access to women, will resort to rape.

These class implications of Buss's story occasionally emerge in striking ways. As mentioned above, the status or quality of both men and women is often crucial to the analysis. For example, "Men of high status typically insist on more stringent standards for a spouse than most women are able to meet".[31] However, they are "willing to relax their standards and have sex with a variety of women if the relationship is only short-term and carries no commitment" (50). Occasionally the class markers are more detailed. At one point, for example, Buss describes the predicament of a woman in a singles bar rebuffing the approach of a "beer-drinking, T-shirted, baseball-capped, stubble-faced truck driver or construction worker who asks her to dance".[32] His angry response, "What's the matter, bitch, I'm not good enough for you?", is, of course, exactly correct. Buss, I imagine, hopes that she has secured a sufficiently tall protector if she later encounters this low-class specimen in the alley outside the singles bar. Such class stereotypes will strike many readers as quite as disturbing as the gender stereotypes developed throughout the work.

Methodology

Reading these accounts of male–female relations, one is struck by a mixture of the stereotypic, the outrageous, and the banal. One should not, however, suppose that these are merely the ungrounded speculations of an evolutionist who might better have stuck to ants or seals. I have remarked that evolutionary psychologists do often acknowledge some greater responsibility for presenting empirical data than did earlier sociobiologists, and the claims just cited are constantly buttressed with impressive arrays of empirical data and research. Buss's book synthesizes a thriving and sizeable industry of evolutionary psychological research. Buss reports his own production of thousands of questionnaires on what men and women find attractive in members of the opposite sex, what they take to be significant "acts of love", and so on. In many, though not all, cases data are offered from a variety of developed and developing countries and from tribal societies, grounding claims of the universality of the phenomena he describes. These are not, it seems, the opinions of an isolated researcher.

Having acknowledged this much, however, closer examination of the empirical data often proves rather disappointing. It will be useful to divide this evidence into categories, which I shall label the absurd, the banal, and the mildly interesting. I shall begin with the absurd.

Perhaps the most glaring example of the absurd is the research, widely cited by evolutionary psychologists, on the hypothesis that men have a mental module the function of which is to measure the waist-to-hip ratio of prospective female sexual partners. The conclusion of this research is that men have a consistent preference for a waist-to-hip ratio of 0.7. The evidence for this curious conclusion is derived first by showing men line drawings of women of various shapes, and asking them which they found most attractive. The presupposition that one could make judgements of this sort on the basis of a line-drawing already incorporates a view of sexual attraction on which it is perhaps politer not to dwell. To buttress this important result, researchers spent painstaking hours poring over back runs of *Playboy* magazine measuring the vital statistics of the models there portrayed with calipers, and again discovered the magic number 0.7 for the waist-to-hip ratio. Since, presumably, the selection of these models reflects men's innate ideals of female pulchritude, the daring hypothesis is further confirmed. Sometimes it is asserted that this shape is also correlated with maximal fertility, though I have not seen, and prefer not to imagine, the research on which this is based. The absurdity of the argument from this evidence to the hypothetical mental module is sufficiently obvious from the fact that evolutionary psychologists much more confidently insist that men are hard-wired to prefer women at the beginning of the fertile stage of the life-cycle. Since hourglass figures are commonest among young, sexually mature women, the results in question would be expected simply as an epiphenomenon of this prior assumed preference. It is, I suppose, possible in principle that men estimate waist-to-hip ratio as a way of detecting young fertile females. But apart from the fact that the research does nothing whatever to support this hypothesis, it seems a highly improbable conjecture. One of the more plausible specialized mental functions of the human brain is the ability to analyse human physiognomy, and it seems unlikely that this undoubted facility would not serve to identify a face as belonging to a young female. Perhaps in the case of androgynous young faces, a glance at the overall shape might be of further assistance in disambiguation. This merely points to the hypothesis that there are a variety of physical cues that have some relevance to the classification of people by age and sex, and that very plausibly people have an ability to integrate a range of cues. A module basing this judgement on a single not entirely reliable gross feature of shape seems otiose.

Equally absurd, though rather less innocuous, is some of the research into the claim that men have a module that directs them, under appropriate circumstances, to rape women. One major source for the claim that rape is a natural male mating strategy derives from experiments done mainly on prison inmates (a questionably representative sample of the population?), referred to in the scientific jargon as "objective phallometry" (Thornhill and Thornhill, 1992). In these experiments prisoners were made to watch filmed depictions of coercive sex, with instruments attached to their penises that recorded their sexual response to these movies. One variable found relevant to the degree of response was the extent to which the victim enjoyed the incident, a dimension that many experts on this topic would perhaps not consider very relevant to the real experience of rape. Even ignoring problems such as this and assuming that these prisoners were sexually aroused by plausible depictions of rape, the inference that they were disposed to rape has all the persuasive force of the assumption that overweight middle-aged men showing objective signs of excitement in front of their televisions on a Sunday afternoon are disposed to play professional football. (In fairness I should note that Buss, unlike Thornhill and Thornhill, remains agnostic as to whether an evolved strategy of rape has been clearly established.)[33,34]

Turning from the absurd to the banal, the important point to emphasise in this category is that it consists of claims that most people already believe. The importance of this is that hypotheses that are banal in this sense cannot be taken to illustrate the heuristic usefulness of evolutionary psychology for generating hypotheses. Such hypotheses could just as readily be generated from a casual interview with the person at the next stool in your local bar. In this category are the claims that men prefer somewhat younger female partners and vice versa for women. Of course the fact that such hypotheses are banal doesn't mean that they may not be true, and if they are true it may be a legitimate scientific project to enquire why they are true. I say only "may be" because there is a subcategory of the banal for which the search for explanation seems wholly redundant. I have in mind, for example, Buss's suggestions that evolution has predisposed people of both sexes to prefer partners who are intelligent and kind. The consideration that it might be more amusing to spend a substantial portion of one's life with an intelligent person than with a dullard seems to me to make redundant the speculation that intelligent partners may have been better at distinguishing edible roots or avoiding sabre-toothed cats. But the claims about age preference do seem to provide a sensible occasion for seeking explanation.

The evidence that these preferences are manifestations of innate mental modules is, however, disappointing. The research mentioned above (Kenrick and Keefe, 1992), for example, is based substantially on the analysis of singles advertisements. As with prison inmates, if placers of singles ads form a representative sample of the population, this is something that needs to be demonstrated. But there is a much more fundamental and pervasive problem. These ideas are, as I have said, banal. Most people in most societies think that these kinds of preferences are "normal" or "natural". The media constantly represent couples in which the man is older, often much older. A man of 65 marrying a woman forty years younger excites only mild surprise, and men of that age are sometimes found playing romantic leads in Hollywood movies paired with much younger women. Reversing the gender roles in such scenarios is considered extraordinary. It is reported that typical members of contemporary Western societies watch several hours a day of television, and this points to an obvious way in which such clichés might affect people's assumptions about the normal or the natural. These platitudes might, of course, be platitudes because of imperatives written in our brains by our distant past. But they might also reflect, for example, the fact that men have much greater power in most societies, and the right to youthful partners is one of the exercises of that power. It is not my aim to defend that, or any of an indefinite range of alternative hypotheses one might imagine as to how these social expectations became banal. I want only to point out that the evidence, for example the answers to the questionnaires designed by Buss to elicit the sexual preferences of large numbers of men and women, do nothing to discriminate between these different kinds of explanation. Such raw data are entirely silent on the aetiology of the preferences Buss and others claim to discover. Since in most cases these preferences are clichés—women should be young, narrow-waisted, inexperienced, etc., men should be tall, affluent, sophisticated, perhaps a bit older and more experienced, etc.—it takes little imagination to come up with much simpler explanations than the trials and tribulations of our distant ancestors.

I should perhaps respond at this point to the inevitable tired reaction that I am assuming the Standard Social Sciences Model, a view of the mind as a blank slate on which culture can write as it chooses. I am, of course, assuming nothing of the sort. People certainly have minds of sufficient structural complexity to acquire the dispositions, attitudes, and varieties of behaviour that they in fact acquire. How much structure, and what kind of structure this is, I do not pretend to know. Part of the advantage of my position over that of evolutionary psychologists is just that they do pretend to know. But more important still, there is no reason at all to suppose that a structure that is sufficiently complex to allow human behaviour to be learned will narrowly constrain the kinds of behaviour that can be learned even if, as is by no means uncontroversial, the structure evolved to facilitate fairly specific behaviours that were useful to our Stone Age ancestors. To invoke the computer analogy generally much admired by the scientistically inclined, the fact that the innards of my computer are highly structured doesn't prevent them from carrying out a remarkably diverse set of tasks. And the fact that much of the underlying technology was developed with military applications in mind doesn't entail that my computer is constantly on the verge of planning a nuclear attack, or designing some instrument of mass destruction.

To the obvious objection outlined above, that the evidence adduced in no way favours the hypotheses of evolutionary psychologists over a range of alternative and perhaps intuitively more plausible explanations, one response is to appeal to a range of cross-cultural data. If the same psychological phenomena are found in very diverse cultural contexts, should we not conclude that the phenomena are biologically generated? But this presents problems of its own and although, as I have mentioned, the data that underlie Buss's claims are sometimes collected cross-culturally, very little sensitivity can be discerned to the difficulties of making the relevant cross-cultural comparisons. For example, his insistence that love is a cross-cultural universal is not supported by any discussion of how relevant, and surely quite complex, concepts might be translated unambiguously across cultures. Of course, since he takes love mainly to consist of a disposition to say "I'd like to marry you and have children with you", the problem may seem to be somewhat mitigated. But in fact this raises another deep difficulty. One of the conclusions that evolutionary psychologists would like to establish is that important anthropological concepts such as "marriage" have a universal, cross-cultural meaning, a meaning grounded in our evolved psychology. But this is a thoroughly implausible assumption. Anthropologists describe systems of "marriage" that are monogamous, polygamous, occasionally polyandrous, hypergamous or hypogamous (women marrying up or down in status, though equal status is said to be the commonest case), between people of the same sex, and in some cases as not involving sexual relations at all. And of course there is a wealth of particular rules and expectations surrounding these diverse social institutions. Even within "Western" culture, the implications of marriage in, say, rural Ireland and Southern California are quite different.[35]

I do not take this diversity to rule out the possibility that these various social institutions may nevertheless reflect the same underlying universal psychology. What I do claim is that evidence about marriage in diverse societies offered in support of such a hypothesis cannot, on pain of blatant question-begging, start with the assumption that these different forms of marriage are fundamentally the same thing. It should finally be added that to the extent that relatively straightforward cross-cultural translation of such concepts is legitimate, it is very likely to be because the cultures concerned have had a good deal of mutual interaction. And of course if this is true, then the value of cross-cultural data is proportionately reduced. And surely the large majority of contemporary cultures do share, to a considerable extent, values shaped by exposure to the same transnational media. It is typical of this kind of work that massive collection of data occurs without any real sensitivity to the problems in interpreting the data. Thus the data underlying Buss's story range from the questionable to the ludicrous. As I shall argue in the final part of this chapter, even where the data are clear-cut, there are deep problems in drawing from them the kinds of biological conclusions that Buss wants.

This brings me, finally, to the category of mildly interesting data. Here what I have in mind are empirical results that confirm evolutionary psychological hypotheses that are to some degree surprising (and hence do not belong in the category of the banal). These, as far as I can discover, are thin on the ground. The element of surprise might be in the fact that the hypothesis is confirmed at all, or in the extent of its confirmation. I know of no clear-cut case of the first kind, though probably the best candidate is the research by Leda Cosmides showing that people were much better able to perform simple logical inferences when the subject matter concerned the application of social rules than when it concerned an arbitrary topic. The experiments were a version of the well-known Wason selection task (Wason, 1968). Subjects were given a statement of the form "If P, then Q", and then shown cards on the visible side of which were statements P, not P, Q, and not Q. They were then asked which cards they would need to turn over to see whether the two sides together constituted a refutation of the statement. Since the statement is only refuted by the conjunction P and not Q, logic requires that the cards P and not Q are turned over. In general subjects proved quite bad at solving this problem where the statement involved, for example, geometrical patterns (e.g. "If one side of the card has a square then the other has a circle").

Cosmides was able to show that when the statement under test had the form of a social rule, subjects did much better. For a rule such as "If someone is drinking beer, then they must be over twenty", and shown cards marked "drinking beer", "drinking Coke", "25 years old", "16 years old", subjects generally managed to identify the first and last card as loci of possible violations (Tooby and Cosmides, 1992). Cosmides takes this as confirming her hypothesis that there is a mental module serving social cooperation and specifically designed to detect cheats who violate social rules.

I do not want to deny that this is an interesting result, and one that calls for some explanation. The problems, unfortunately, are ultimately just as serious as for the banal cases. Children are constantly exposed to social rules, criticized for violating them, and praised or rewarded for conforming to them. As Cosmides's results confirm, they become very competent at identifying violations of such rules. How could we infer from this the existence of a specialized mental module that produced this result? Explanations have been constructed that assume no such special-purpose module, for example by Patricia Cheng and Keith Holyoak (1989). Tooby and Cosmides (1992) have attempted to show that their data rule out such interpretations, but Elisabeth Lloyd (1999) makes clear that these arguments fail. As Lloyd shows, ultimately Cosmides's argument must fall back on a claim about what must have, or would have been very likely to have, evolved in conditions supposed to have obtained in the Stone Age. But as I have tried to explain in detail, evolutionary theory just can't do this sort of work. Cosmides's research provides an interesting result for cognitive psychology, but does nothing to settle questions about the extent of innate structure in the brain.

The most striking quantitative surprise claimed to the credit of evolutionary psychology is the data from Daly and Wilson on the discrepancy in the amount of violence to children perpetrated by step-parents and biological parents. No one would be surprised to learn that there was some such discrepancy: most of us are familiar with the sad plight of Cinderella, and the idea that her situation is a not uncommon one perhaps belongs in the category of the banal. Daly and Wilson (1988), however, showed that using actual homicide as an index of violence against stepchildren or adopted children, the occurrence of this was many times that for biological children. There is no doubt that there are social factors that would predict some of this difference. Perhaps there are biological grounds for the prevalence of the view that "blood is thicker than water", but it is at any rate a view widely held to be true. And no doubt it is widely assumed that there is a natural human goal of producing and raising one's biological offspring. Equally true and important is the fact that for every child murdered by its step-parents there are hundreds or thousands brought up by step-parents who provide just as much care and love as most biological parents. So we have a rare but horrible breakdown of the norm of parental care that occurs much more frequently for non-biological than for biological parents. We have some obvious cultural factors that go some way to account for this discrepancy, but perhaps not far enough. Any parent will testify that it is easy enough to see why, if one did not feel affection towards children, one might well murder them. So perhaps there is a biological disposition to feel affection for one's own offspring that helps to prevent this unfortunate outcome. On the other hand, it must be reiterated that in the vast majority of cases this biological deterrent is redundant, as shown by all the non-biological parents who show no disposition to murder their children. It is entirely unclear what inference should be drawn about the nature and action of whatever innate disposition one may have to care about the genetic origins of one's children.

A final point is worth mentioning. Recent research, no doubt disturbing to many men, has suggested that somewhere in the region of 15 per cent of children were not in fact fathered by the men who take themselves to be the biological father. It would, no doubt, be a persuasive bit of evolutionary psychological evidence if these men were found much more likely to commit violence on their children. But in the absence of such evidence, I conjecture that such a correlation would hold only to the extent that these men knew or suspected that they were not the biological fathers. If that is the case, then the phenomena under consideration work through conscious cognition.[36] And that, in turn, suggests that they should be susceptible to the influence of social norms. This is not, of course, an argument against there being a biological component to what is, certainly, an evolutionarily fundamental social relationship. I do want to insist, however, that the evidence under consideration licenses no compelling conclusions about the innate structure of the mind.

Further Reflections on the Poverty of Evolutionary Psychological Inference

In this section I shall further explore the difficulties in the attempt to infer from psychological phenomena to evolved functional components of the mind. First, however, I would like to mention another strategy somewhat notoriously connected with sociobiological thinking, the comparison of human behaviour with that of the behaviour of other species. Sociobiologists have often been accused, and often with justice, of supporting their arguments by appeal to any convenient non-human species that happened to behave in an apparently analogous way. Thus, for example, scorpionflies and ducks have figured largely in discussion of the alleged biological roots of rape.[37] In criticizing such strategies it has been noted first, that the examples were often arbitrarily selected; and second, that only in the crudest analogical sense could, for example, the behaviour of copulating flies be related to that of human rapists. It is fair to say that contemporary evolutionary psychologists depend less heavily on this strategy than their predecessors, in part, of course, because they claim much more data derived directly from the study of humans. However, animal analogies still play an important rhetorical role in this work, and sometimes seem all the more bizarre for their lesser frequency.

To take a few examples from Buss: "Women, like weaverbirds, prefer men with desirable nests";[38] or, "Like the male roadrunner offering up his kill, men offer women resources as a primary method of attraction";[39] and "humans' ways of solving the adaptive problem of keeping a mate are strikingly similar to insects".[40] The latter include such methods as physically carrying the female off to some place less frequented by competitors or, which sounds to me distinctly unlikely as a human strategy, shedding their broken-off genitalia after copulation to seal off the reproductive opening of the female. I shall not dwell on this issue because, as I have noted, it does not play an obviously central role in the kinds of arguments I am considering. No doubt part of the function of this constant ornamentation of the text with these more or less fanciful parallels is to remind the reader that the author is, after all, doing no more than taking seriously the fact that we are ultimately just animals. Whether anything much follows about any specific kind of animal merely from the fact that it is, ultimately, just an animal is another matter.[41]

The empirical detail characteristic of contemporary sociobiology raises a further difficulty that I want to stress. A common objection to earlier variants of sociobiology was that their accounts of human behaviour were massively simplistic. Modern evolutionary psychology has partially responded to this objection, and provided accounts that allow for more complex and varied behavioural strategies. But in doing so it has exposed even more clearly than before

the difficulty, emphasized many years ago by critics such as Gould and Lewontin (1979), that the theory is almost infinitely malleable and consequently empirically empty. To consider one example, early emphasis on the evolution of pair-bonding as well as on a male tendency to promiscuity seemed to some not only simplistic, but also as verging on the inconsistent. The obvious difficulty derives from the tautological, but still sometimes neglected, observation that the total number of matings by males and females is identical. Given that there is an approximately equal number of heterosexual males and females, the average number of matings per male and female will also be the same. (It is true that the proportion of males does tend to decline with age, but not to an extent that is relevant to the general point.) And, since at least the Kinsey Reports, it has been scientifically well established that humans, in both sexes, are variably but moderately promiscuous animals.

The more empirical turn in contemporary evolutionary psychology has taken account of these facts. In place of earlier monolithic theories of the sexual predilections of men and women they have suggested a repertoire of evolved sexual strategies. (The suggestion that rape is an evolved alternative sexual strategy for otherwise unsuccessful men is an example of this manœuvre.) Typically, the idea is that in addition to psychological mechanisms designed to promote pair-bonding, humans have alternative strategies for engaging, under appropriate conditions, in casual sexual liaisons. Within the evolutionary framework it is not difficult to see why men should be said to have evolved this strategy, either before or after engaging in pair-bonding. However, recalling again the tautology mentioned in the previous paragraph, some account is required of why women might cooperate. In fact, without some chance of finding amenable women, there is no evolutionary explanation of the male tendency to casual sex: looking around for opportunities for casual sex when none are to be found is, presumably, a mere waste of resources and should be penalized by evolution. Thus a major growth industry in evolutionary psychology is the provision of explanation for female proclivities towards casual sexual encounters.

Unsurprisingly, the main thrust of such explanations is once again economic. Apart from prostitution in the strict sense, women are perceived as providing themselves with insurance against the provisioning inadequacies of their principle mate. Buss spells out the prehistoric scenario:

> Imagine a food shortage hitting an ancestral tribe thousands of years ago. Game is scarce. The first frost has settled ominously. Bushes no longer yield berries. A lucky hunter takes down a deer. A woman watches him return from the hunt, hunger pangs gnawing. She makes him an offer for a portion of the prized meat. Sex for resources, or resources for sex—the two have been exchanged in millions of transactions over the millennia of human existence.[42]

In slight twists on this simple economic tale, women are said to be providing insurance (their mate may lose status or command of resources or, for that matter, die, so they are establishing connections with possible replacements) or to be setting up a network of provisioners.

A different kind of story suggests that women may perceive that the man who is the best provider that they can secure may not have the best genes they can attract. Thus they might attempt to get their genes from a different source.[43] In support of this hypothesis, empirical evidence is said to show that married women usually have lovers of higher social status than their husbands; that they arrange trysts with their lovers disproportionately while they are ovulating; and that they have more orgasms with their lovers than with their husbands. (Female orgasm is now said to cause more sperm to be retained in the reproductive tract.) Husbands, incidentally, are said to respond by ejaculating higher numbers of sperm when their wives have been out of their sight, thus attempting to swamp the contributions of their suspected competitors.

A rather more bizarre explanation of female promiscuity might be called the self-appraisal theory. In the context of the general economic metaphor, it is important for a woman, especially, to have an accurate idea of her market value. By engaging in a series of casual sexual encounters she can, on this account, "obtain valuable information about the quality of the men she can potentially attract".[44] She thus avoids the twin dangers of selling herself short, and of holding out for more than she can command. (The fact that, according to another part of sociobiological theory, she will, as a consequence of her value-appraisal exercise, also reduce her value by becoming more sexually experienced, creates the sort of problem beloved of mathematical economists.)

These various accounts illustrate plainly the ease with which evolutionary stories can be constructed. Early sociobiological intuitions about female monogamy are readily superseded by a host of complicating adaptive considerations. With sufficient ingenuity multiple possible evolutionary benefits can be imagined for almost any form of behaviour. And this, of course, shows only that such stories should be treated with great scepticism. This scepticism should be amplified when, as in the present case, a whole series of alternative stories are offered for the same supposedly evolved behaviour.

But perhaps an even more important point is the way in which the attempt to accommodate the empirical variability of human behaviour leads to the introduction of ever more flexible, and arguably ad hoc, auxiliary assumptions. If a behaviour is thought to be more or less universal across cultures it is because it evolved. If there is an exception (such as the lack of concern by men about premarital female promiscuity in

Scandinavia) it is because there is sensitivity to cultural influences. As Buss puts it, "some preference mechanisms are highly sensitive to cultural, ecological, or mating conditions, while others transcend these differences in context".[45] It is, of course, equally possible that the social conditions that encourage some of these preferences are currently less variable than those that support others. At any rate, it is clear that once these strategies are admitted to be subject to cultural influence, any amount of variability will be fully explicable within the sociobiological paradigm. And as is a familiar truism in the philosophy of science, a theory that can explain anything explains nothing.

The ease with which evolutionary psychologists can accommodate data is strikingly illustrated in a paper by Bruce Ellis commenting on the fact that in questionnaires women, contrary to evolutionary prediction, claimed to attach little importance to either dominance or social status. Ellis offers four possible explanations: they may mistakenly have supposed that the men were disposed to dominate them rather than other men; they may be reluctant to admit that they prefer such men; they may prefer such men but be unconscious of the preference; or their assumed reference class may only include high-status men, among whom details of status will not be important.[46] Perhaps so. But philosophers of science have long seen such multiplication of auxiliary hypotheses, hypotheses introduced solely to account for a failure of match between theory and actual experience, as the main symptom of a theory in decay. In the terminology of Imre Lakatos (1978), these are the signs of a degenerating research programme—if, indeed, such a judgement does not imply more antecedent progressiveness than is evident.

Let me conclude this section with a brief comment on the great difference between the context in which, according to evolutionary psychologists, the psychology of sex evolved and more modern conditions. Even if our hypothetical cavemen ancestors selected mates solely

on the basis of their reproductive potential, things have got a bit more complicated. So-called trophy wives would not, perhaps, be accounted trophies if there were not some recognized virtue to mere youthful good looks; but a trophy wife seriously deficient in intelligence, charm, good manners, etc. would, I suppose, be as often an embarrassment as a prize. Prudent mate-selection, that is to say, involves a wide range of factors, many of which have nothing whatever to do with purely physical attractiveness. Although evolutionary psychologists do mention a range of such factors, the attempts to explain the importance, for example, of intelligence or kindness[47] in terms of effects on fertility are both implausible and redundant.

Of equal importance is the fact that mate-selection, in the sense of selection of a long-term partner for the bearing and rearing of children, is hardly the sole context in which modern humans make judgements about the attractiveness of other people. Whether or not this was true of our less sophisticated ancestors, contemporary humans are interested at different times in a variety of different kinds of relationships with members of the opposite sex (or, in many cases, the same sex; though how this relates to the present issue is obviously problematic). They may seek friendship, casual sex, a brief romance, lifelong companionship, a co-parent for their children (existing or yet to be born), a status symbol, a domestic drudge, and so on. Presumably the relevance of prehistoric whisperings concerning reproductive potential will vary considerably from one to another of these cases.

These considerations emphasize why, regardless of evolved psychology, we should be in no way surprised that sexual behaviour is highly varied, and hence reinforce the impossibility of inferring the evolved psychology from behavioural data. Suppose, for the sake of argument, that there is indeed a mechanism in the human brain that disposes men to select very young women or girls as ideal mates. Given that this atavistic mechanism provides only one of a range of inputs into actual processes of mate-selection, and given that mate-selection, in the sense assumed by evolutionists, is only one of a range of kinds of behaviour in which this hypothetical machinery might figure, it is not at all clear that identifying such machinery will tell us anything much about the behaviour or even behavioural dispositions of modern humans. At the most, we might learn something about psychopathology: the maladapted mind, the mind unable to function in the conditions in which it finds itself, is perhaps a mind constantly and uncontrollably driven by atavistic urges from its evolutionary past. The healthy mind, the mind that despite its Stone Age origins functions effectively in the complex context of modern life, is another matter.

In summary, then, the evolutionary psychology of sex and gender offers us mainly simplifications and banalities about human behaviour with little convincing illumination of how they came to be banal. It offers us no account of the great differences in behaviour across cultures, which is exactly what we might want to know if we were interested in exercising any measure of control over the changes in these phenomena. It offers no account of why different people develop such diverse sexual proclivities (notoriously, it has nothing but the most absurd evolutionary fantasies to offer in explanation of homosexuality). And it offers no account of how the complex motivations underlying sexual behaviour interact with the pursuit of the many other goals that inform the lives of most humans. In fact it offers us nothing, unless perhaps a spurious sense of the immutability of the behaviours that happen to characterize our own contemporary societies. *unchangeable*

Notes

1 Some feminists later came to question even this assumption, and recognize a relation of mutual determination between sex and gender (see Jaggar,

1983: 109–13). In the 1990s, feminists began to argue that sex was just as much a social construct as gender (e.g. Butler, 1990). Though interesting and important, these developments do not materially affect my present points.

2 This economic conception of the problem was popularized by Trivers (1972).

3 Dawkins 1976, p. 176.

4 It is also noted that the price that gorillas pay for this glittering prize, apart from the high probability of not winning it, is unusually small testes (Short, 1977). Since their sperm is not forced to compete with that of other males for access to the female ovum, there is no advantage to having a lot of it. On the basis of ratio of testis to body weight, human males are judged to lie in between the gorilla and the chimpanzee, and it is inferred that they are by nature moderately promiscuous.

5 Symons 1979, p. 202.

6 Wilson 1978, p. 125.

7 Kitcher 1985, p. 171.

8 Dawkins 1976, p. 177.

9 Connoisseurs of sexist language will find this sentence truly breathtaking. If man (generic, surely) is a fertilizer of women, to what species do these beneficiaries of fertilization belong?

10 Wright 1994, p. 151.

11 Buss 1994, p. 130–131.

12 High- and low-quality people are also a central concept for the explicitly economic treatment of sex by Gary Becker (1981/1991).

13 Buss 1994, p. 23.

14 Buss 1994, p. 101.

15 Buss reports (24) that women value resources in a mate about twice as highly as men do (the exact number is of course an artefact of his survey design). Given, first, that women in most societies have fewer resources and, second, that women often anticipate dependency on the financial resources of their mates, this is not an observation in obvious need of a deep biological explanation.

16 "The same men were photographed wearing either a Burger King uniform with a blue baseball cap and a polo-type shirt or a white dress shirt with a designer tie, a navy blazer, and a Rolex watch" (101). One can't help admiring the attention to detail in the experimental design.

"Based on these photographs women [all women?] state that they are unwilling to date, have sex with, or marry the men in the low-status costumes, but are willing to consider all of these relations with men in high-status garb."

17 Buss 1994, pp. 27–28.

18 Buss 1994, p. 41.

19 Buss 1994, p. 38.

20 Buss 1994, p. 39.

21 Buss 1994, p. 40, quoting Ellis 1992.

22 Though as Philip Kitcher suggested to me (in correspondence), bigger men may also present more of a risk of physical violence to their mates.

23 Buss 1994, p. 42.

24 Buss 1994, p. 43.

25 Buss 1994, p. 43.

26 Buss 1994, p. 53.

27 Buss 1994, p. 57.

28 Buss 1994, p. 140.

29 Buss 1994, p. 67.

30 Buss 1994, p. 69.

31 Buss 1994, p. 50.

32 Buss 1994, p. 144.

33 Buss 1994, p. 163.

34 Miller (2000) argues that rape was unlikely to have been common in the Stone Age. He is required to make this argument, since his central thesis is that sexual behaviour evolved largely in response to female choice among mates, something that would be ineffective if women were commonly subject to coerced sex. Though his arguments here seem plausible enough, I note this fact mainly as an illustration of the ease with which arguments can be made up on both sides of questions about Stone Age life.

35 For nuanced discussions of some of these social arrangements around sexuality and gender see, for instance, Ortner and Whitehead (1981). It is also worth noting that for a substantial proportion of the world's population marriages are arranged by families.

36 If my hunch is wrong, of course, that would indeed provide genuinely persuasive evidence for an unconscious, perhaps even innate, mental mechanism.

37 See Fausto-Sterling (1985) for trenchant criticism.

38 Buss 1994, p. 7.

39 Buss 1994, p. 100.

40 Buss 1994, p. 124.

41 I do not, of course, mean to deny that there is a role for comparative phylogenetic studies in establishing the adaptive nature of traits. But this role requires evidence that a trait is homologous between related species. Trawling through the animal world for analogous traits, as in the examples in the text, has no such value. As Jonathan Kaplan (in correspondence) has emphasized to me, the unusual lack of close relatives of humans makes the legitimate strategy largely unfeasible.

42 Buss 1994, p. 86.

43 This ingenious, if Macchiavellian, strategy, is attributed to various bird species. See Wilson and Daly (1992: 292–7) for an account of avian sexual shenanigans in the swallow and dunnock, and numerous further references.

44 Buss 1994, p. 89.

45 Buss 1994, p. 254.

46 Ellis 1992, p. 282.

47 Buss 1994, pp. 34–35, 45.

References

Barkow, J., Cosmides, L., and Tooby, J. (Eds) (1992). *The Adapted Mind*. New York: Oxford University Press.

Becker, G. S. (1981; enlarged edition 1991). *A Treatise on the Family*. Cambridge, MA: Harvard University Press.

Buss, D. (1994). *The Evolution of Desire*. New York: Basic Books.

Cheng, P. W., & Holyoak, K. J. (1989). On the natural selection of reasoning theories. *Cognition*, 33: 285–313.

Daly, M., & Wilson, M. (1988). Evolutionary social psychology and family homicide. *Science*, 242: 519–524.

Dawkins, R. (1976). *The Selfish Gene*. Oxford: Oxford University Press.

Ellis, B. J. (1992). The evolution of sexual attraction: Evaluative mechanisms in women. In J. Barkow, L. Cosmides and J. Tooby (Eds.), *The Adapted Mind* (pp. 267–288).

Fausto-Sterling, A. (1985). *Myths of Gender*. New York: Basic Books.

Freeman, D. (1983). *Margaret Mead and Samoa: The making and unmaking of an anthropological myth*. Cambridge, MA: Harvard University Press.

Gould, S. J. & Lewontin, R. C. (1979). The spandrels of San Marco and the panglossian paradigm: A critique of the adaptationist programme. *Proceedings of the Royal Society of London*, 205: 581–598.

Kenrick, D. T., & Keefe, R. C. (1992). Age preferences in mates reflect differences in reproductive strategies. *Behavioral and Brain Sciences*, 15: 75–133.

Kitcher, P. (1985). *Vaulting Ambition: Sociobiology and the Quest for Human Nature*. Cambridge, MA: MIT Press.

Lakatos, I. (1978). *The Methodology of Scientific Research Programmes: Philosophical Papers*, vol. 1, Ed. J. Worrall and G. Currie. Cambridge: Cambridge University Press.

Lloyd, E. A. (1999) Evolutionary psychology: The burdens of proof. *Biology and Philosophy*, 14: 211–233.

Mead, M. (1949). *Male and Female*. New York: Morrow.

Miller, G. (2000). *The Mating Mind: How Sexual Choice Shaped the Evolution of Human Nature*. London: William Heinemann.

Ortner, S. B., & Whitehead, H. (1981). *Sexual Meanings: The Cultural Construction of Gender and Sexuality*. Cambridge: Cambridge University Press.

Pérusse, D. (1993). Cultural and reproductive success in industrial societies: Testing the relationship at the proximate and ultimate levels. *Behavioral and Brain Sciences*, 16: 267–322.

Short, R. V. (1977). Sexual selection and the *Descent of Man*. In J. H. Calaby and C. H. Tyndale-Briscoe (Eds.), *Reproduction and Evolution*. Canberra: Australian Academy of Sciences.

Singh, D. (1993). Adaptive significance of waist-to-hip ratio and female physical attractiveness. *Journal of Personality and Social Psychology*, 65: 293–307.

Symons, D. (1979) *The Evolution of Human Sexuality*. New York: Oxford University Press.

Thornhill, R., & Thornhill, N. W. (1992). The evolutionary psychology of men's coercive sexuality. *Behavioral and Brain Sciences*, 15: 363–421.

Tooby, J., & Cosmides, L. (1992). The psychological foundations of culture. In J. Barkow, L. Cosmides, and J. Tooby (Eds.), *The Adapted Mind* (pp. 19–136). New York: Oxford University Press.

Trivers, R. (1972). Parental investment and sexual selection. In B. Campbell (Ed.), *Sexual Selection and the Descent of Man*. New York: Aldine de Gruyter. (pp. 136–179).

Wason, P. C. (1968). Reasoning about a rule. *Quarterly Journal of Experimental Psychology*, 20: 273–81.

Wilson, E. O. (1978). *On Human Nature*. Cambridge, MA: Harvard University Press.

Wilson, M., & Daly, M. (1992). The man who mistook his wife for a chattel. In J. Barkow, L. Cosmides and J. Tooby (Eds.), *The Adapted Mind* (pp. 289–322). New York: Oxford University Press.

Chapter 30

Nathan W. Bailey and Marlene Zuk

SAME-SEX SEXUAL BEHAVIOR AND EVOLUTION

Same-sex sexual behavior has been extensively documented in non-human animals. Here we review the contexts in which it has been studied, focusing on case studies that have tested both adaptive and non-adaptive explanations for the persistence of same-sex sexual behavior. Researchers have begun to make headway unraveling possible evolutionary origins of these behaviors and reasons for their maintenance in populations, and we advocate expanding these approaches to examine their role as agents of evolutionary change. Future research employing theoretical, comparative and experimental approaches could provide a greater understanding not only of how selection might have driven the evolution of same-sex sexual behaviors but also ways in which such behaviors act as selective forces that shape social, morphological and behavioral evolution.

Why Does Same-sex Sexual Behavior Matter?

Same-sex sexual behavior in animals has long fascinated scientists as well as non-scientists. Previous work has emphasized the apparent paradox of selection acting on non-reproductive individuals (Levan et al. 2008; Santtile et al. 2009), but little is known about the evolutionary consequences of such behavior, whether it occurs as exclusive life-long pairing or as a part of other sexual interactions. The variety and ubiquity of same-sex sexual behavior in animals is impressive; many thousands of instances of same-sex courtship, pair bonding and copulation have been observed in a wide range of species, including mammals, birds, reptiles, amphibians, insects, mollusks and nematodes (Table 30.1). These observations are likely to be underestimates of the frequency of such interactions, partly because researchers assume that pairs in sexually monomorphic species that are engaging in sexual behavior must be opposite sexes.

From an evolutionary perspective, same-sex behavior has been viewed as a puzzle requiring a special explanation, rather like suicide or adoption of unrelated infants (Sommer and Vasey, 2006). Why would animals engage in sexual behaviors that do not directly result in reproduction? It is clear that lifelong same-sex orientation is unlikely to evolve and, indeed, few examples of life-long pairings in wild animals exist, but the persistent and well-documented occurrence of same-sex sexual behaviors across nearly all taxonomic groups of animals is worth exploring.

The purpose of this review is to expand our thinking about the evolutionary implications of same-sex behavior in animals. We suggest that the phenomenon needs to be viewed in a broader framework, and whereas many have speculated on adaptive explanations for same-sex sexual behavior, it can have evolutionary consequences that biologists might not have fully

Table 30.1 Representative sampling of same-sex sexual behavior across non-human taxa, ranging from observations in a wild setting to genetic manipulations in the laboratory

Species[a]	Setting	Sex of participants	Description	Refs
African bat bugs (*Afrocimex constrictus*)	Wild	Males	Males traumatically inseminate other males in addition to females, and they possess genital structures which reduce the negative effects associated with traumatic insemination.	Reinhardt et al. (2007)
Bonobos (*Pan paniscus*)	Wild	Females and males	Females spend a considerable amount of time engaged in same-sex sexual behavior, including genito-genital rubbing that can culminate in orgasm. To a much lesser extent, males engage in kissing, fellatio and genital massage. Same-sex sexual behavior might ease social tension and facilitate reconciliation among group members.	Fruth & Hohmann (2006)
Bottlenose dolphins (*Thursiops sp.*)	Wild	Females and males	Bottlenose dolphins show one of the highest rates of same-sex sexual behavior documented in any animal. Male–male mounting, genital contact and "goosing" appear to strengthen alliances between small groups of males and provide practice for later opposite-sex encounters. Female-female sexual behavior also occurs, but to a much lesser extent.	Mann (2006)
Chinstrap penguins (*Pygoscelis antarcticus*)	Captivity	Males	Penguins in captivity can form long-lasting same-sex pair bonds and engage in same-sex sexual behaviors, including copulation.	Zuk (2006)
Common toad (*Bufo bufo*)	Wild	Males	Male toads do not discriminate between the sexes and will amplect males as well as females. Amplected males, however, produce a stereotyped call that quickly induces the other male to release. Sex discrimination might not be favored in this species because male–male amplexus is not very costly.	Rice et al. (1999)

Flour beetles (*Tribolium castaneum*)	Laboratory	Males	Forced male–male mounting and copulation occur frequently, and there is limited evidence that sperm deposited during homosexual mounting can be indirectly transferred to a female during subsequent heterosexual copulation.	Levan et al. (2008
Fruit flies (*Drosophila melanogaster*)	Laboratory	Males	Males with mutations in the gene *genderblind* court other males, as a result of reduced glutamate transmission. Social experience and mutations in other genes such as *fruitless*, *satori* and *white* also cause varying degrees of same-sex courtship and mounting behavior.	Gill (1963), Greenspan & Ferveur (2000) Zhang & Odenwald (1995), McRoberts et al. (2003). Grosjean et al. (2008), Liu et al. (2008), Kultovic et al. (2007), Miyamato & Amrient (2008) Svetec et al. (2005) Lee et al. (2008)
Garter snakes (*Thamnophis sirtalis parietalis*)	Wild	Males	Some males mimic females in size or pheromone attributes, and are courted by other males when females are absent. However, male–male courtship is not likely a result of mistaken sex recognition; attracting male courtship might allow solitary males to thermoregulate and protect themselves.	Shine et al. (2003)
Guppies (*Poecillia reticulata*)	Laboratory	Males	Males maintained in all-male social environments directed more courtship displays toward other males than those kept in mixed-sex environments. This tendency persisted even after females were introduced into the previously all-male tanks.	Field & Waite (2004)
Laysan albatross (*Phoebastria immutabilis*)	Wild	Females	Birds in Hawaiian populations form long-term female–female pair bonds, which include courtship displays, copulation, mutual grooming behavior and egg incubation.	Young et al. (2008)

(Continued overleaf)

Table 30.1 Continued

Species[a]	Setting	Sex of participants	Description	Refs
Marine snails (*Crepidula fornicata*)	Wild and laboratory	Males	All snails of this species start out male, and have weak sex discrimination. If they pair with another male, then one simply changes sex. Flexibility in sex changing allows for a weak sex-discrimination system; in a sister species that is less flexible, male–male pairings are far more rare.	Ambrogio & Pechenik (2008)
Nematodes (*Caenorhabditis elegans*)	Laboratory	Females (hermaphrodites)	To study sex differences in mate-finding behavior, the nervous systems of hermaphrodites, which are essentially female, were masculinized by overexpressing the gene *fem-3*. This caused their attraction to other hermaphrodites, a typically male behavior.	White (2007)
Rams (*Ovis aries*)	Captivity	Males	A small proportion, around 6%, of domesticated rams displays typical male courtship and copulatory behaviors toward other males and can be exclusively male oriented even when estrous females are available.	Perkins & Roselli (2007), Price et al. 1988
Zebra finch (*Taeniopygia guttata*)	Laboratory	Females and males	Females administered estrogen synthesis inhibitors pair bond with other females, and male deprivation during juvenile development can cause opposite-sex partner preferences in both females and males.	Adkins-Regan (2002)

[a] The 14 species listed here are by no means an exhaustive list of animals exhibiting same-sex behavior, but provide a starting point for readers interested in obtaining further information and examples.

considered. Studying these consequences can lead to a richer understanding of both same-sex behavior and the processes through which selection shapes social interactions, reproductive behavior and even morphology, and we identify several research strategies that can be employed to achieve this.

Categories of Same-sex Interactions in Animals

We mainly focus on same-sex behavior *per se*, without inferring anything about the sexual preference or orientation of individuals engaging in the behavior. Sexual behavior, sexual preference and sexual orientation are distinct but often conflated concepts. Confusion among them can undermine the clarity and accurate interpretation of scientific research, so here we emphasize that same-sex sexual behaviors are interactions between same-sex individuals that also occur between opposite-sex individuals in the context of reproduction. For example, many *Drosophila* studies examine genetic mutations that affect pheromone receptors (Box 30.1). Sex-specific pheromones and their accurate detection are crucial for sex recognition in fruit flies, and alterations in sex-recognition pathways can produce males that court other males, females that court females, or males that switch from same-sex to opposite-sex courtship within minutes (Gill, 1963; Greenspan & Ferveur, 2000; Zhang and Odenwald, 1995; McRoberts et al., 2003; Grosjean et al., 2008; Liu et al., 2008; Kurtovic et al., 2007; Miyamoto & Amrien, 2008; Svetec et al., 2005; Lee et al., 2008). In other words, the mutations cause same-sex sexual behavior. However, this behavior often occurs alongside opposite-sex courtship as well, with males mating indiscriminately (Grosjean et al., 2008; Kurtovic et al., 2007; Miyamoto & Amrien, 2008). So although they show same-sex sexual behavior, males might not actually be exhibiting a preference for one sex over the other (see Box 30.1).

Box 30.1 Drosophila: the workhorse of same-sex behavior research

Over the past two decades, *Drosophila* researchers have examined a multitude of candidate genes implicated in the genetic and neurological control of sexual behavior. These studies have provided insights into sexual behavior in general, and as a by-product have illustrated different mechanisms that can independently produce same-sex sexual behavior.

What are these mechanisms, and what can we learn from them?

Mutations in a *Drosophila* gene called fruitless have been known for nearly half a century to cause males to court other males (Gill, 1963). Fruitless codes for transcription factors that yield male-specific courtship behavior, and mutations affecting the functioning of these factors induce varying types and degrees of male–male courtship [5]. However, mutations with similar effects have since been discovered in many other genes, including *dissatisfaction, prospero, quick-to-court, transformer, raised, genderblind* and *white* (Zhang & Odenwald, 1995). The ways these genes exert their effects differ, sometimes subtly. For example, a receptor gene for volatile pheromones, OR67d, and one for non-volatile pheromones, GR32a, were both found to inhibit male–male courtship. Males that lack functional copies of either gene cannot accurately distinguish the sexes using sex-specific pheromones, and therefore court males as well as females. However, the neural pathways and brain centers that are affected differ markedly between the two types of mutants (Kurtovic et al., 2008; Miyamoto & Amrien, 2006). Neurochemical and social factors can also interact with the underlying genetic blueprint of the *Drosophila* brain to induce same-sex behavior (Svetec et al., 2005). For example, a gene named *genderblind* controls levels of the extracellular chemical glutamate, which regulates pheromone information processing in nerve cells in male fly brains (Grosjean et al., 2008). Mutations in *genderblind* disrupt males' chemosensory abilities, so that they misinterpret and overreact to chemical signals that distinguish the sexes (Grosjean et al., 2008). As a result, they court both males and females (Grosjean et al., 2008). Exogenous substances can also induce same-sex behavior, for example, ethanol (Lee et al., 2008). The presence of the neurotransmitter dopamine is critical for the ethanol effect, however, and dopamine in and of itself can elevate levels of male–male courtship (Liu et al., 2008).

Male–male courtship in *Drosophila* is unambiguously influenced by genetic factors. However, what we can truly learn about same-sex sexual behavior from *Drosophila* studies might be limited. The majority of studies focus on genetic mutations that affect the ability of male flies to distinguish sexes through olfactory recognition; as a result, they court males as well as females. This does not imply that they prefer males over females, or that they are same-sex orientated. Olfactory sensing plays an important role in human homosexual orientations (see Box 30.2), but it would be equally untenable to suggest that if researchers eliminated humans' abilities to detect sex differences, then their subsequent indiscriminate mating behavior represented bisexual or homosexual orientations. The intensely studied *Drosophila* system presents unrivalled opportunities for examining the genetic bases of same-sex behavior, preferences and orientation. Admirable strides have been made with the first, and we anticipate that future research will begin to disentangle the remaining related, but distinct, concepts.

Individuals exhibiting a same-sex preference choose to engage in sexual behavior with a member of the same sex, when given the option of engaging in sexual behavior with an opposite-sex individual. Preference implies that the animal has made a choice. Examples of same-sex preferences in non-human animals are far more rare than examples of same-sex behavior.

Nevertheless, in the damselfly *Ischnura elegans*, researchers demonstrated that males exposed to all-male groups preferentially courted other males when they were given a choice between a male and a female (Van Gossum et al., 2005). Their preference for one sex over the other was flexible, and could be switched by manipulating the social context they experienced previously (Van Gossum et al., 2005).

Same-sex orientation implies a more permanent set of preferences—an internal predisposition to desire sexual interactions with members of one sex or another—and although commonly used to describe sexual identity in humans, it is rarely applied to other animals. In part, this is because it is impossible to know what animals "desire"; we can only observe what they do. Individuals in a handful of vertebrate species have been described as having same-sex orientations, among them male chinstrap penguins (*Pygoscelis antarcticus*), which have been documented to form long-term pair bonds in captivity (Zuk, 2006), and some male bighorn sheep (*Ovis canadensis*), which will only mount females if the females adopt male-like behavior (Bagemihl, 1999). Categorizing an individual animal's orientation is fraught with the added difficulty of not knowing for how long an animal must retain its sexual preference to be considered same- versus opposite-sex oriented. Considering sexual orientation using this set of criteria is likely of limited use to biologists studying same-sex behavior in non-human animals.

Causes of Same-sex Sexual Behavior

Published research on same-sex sexual behavior in animals has focused almost exclusively on two areas. The first area describes proximate mechanisms that underlie same-sex sexual behaviors. Such mechanistic studies have used model organisms such as *Drosophila* melanogaster, the nematode *Caenorhabditis elegans* and zebra finches to explore genetic, neurological, hormonal and social foundations of same-sex sexual interactions (Adkins-Regan, 2002; Svetec & Ferveur, 2005; Baum, 2006; Perkins & Roselli, 2007; White, 2007). Not all of these studies explicitly set out to examine same-sex behaviors, but research testing hypotheses about the formation of heterosexual partner preferences or sexual differentiation of the nervous system, for example, has spawned insights into genetic and physiological pathways that influence same-sex sexual behavior. Same-sex sexual behavior in Drosophila is clearly not comparable to that in bonobos, but studies of the neurophysiological control of sexual preferences in one organism can help to identify common mechanisms in other species, such as alteration in olfactory sex recognition or the importance of social experience in shaping subsequent mating behaviors.

The second major area of research has focused on the adaptive significance of same-sex sexual behavior (Table 30.2). The context in which this body of work has developed merits consideration. In the scientific literature, emphasis is often placed on the "apparent paradox" (Levan et al., 2008; Santtile et al., 2009) that same-sex sexual behavior presents. It "appears to be inconsistent with traditional evolutionary theory" (MacFarlane et al., 2007) and "seems to violate a basic 'law' of nature: that of procreation" (Sommer & Vasey, 2006). Attempts are then made to reconcile its existence with traditional selection theory by testing adaptive explanations, and these generally fall into three broad categories, as follows. (i) Same-sex sexual behavior provides the glue that establishes, maintains and strengthens social relationships, such as male alliances in bottlenose dolphins (Mann, 2006). (ii) Same-sex sexual behavior provides a conduit for intensifying or diminishing intrasexual aggression and conflict. In the dung fly Hydromyza livens, for example, males have been hypothesized to mount other males to deny them the opportunity to mate, thereby increasing the likelihood that the mounting male obtains more mating

opportunities (Preston-Mafham, 2006). By contrast, in the viviparous Goodeid fish Girardinichthys multiradiatus, males sometimes display a dark, female-like "pregnancy" spot around their vent. Subordinate males with dark spots attract fewer aggressive maneuvers by dominant males, who appear to mistake them for females and consequently court them (Macías-Garcia and Valero, 2001). This diversion of aggressive behavior into courtship behavior affords subordinate males greater opportunities to sneak copulations with females (Macías-Garcia and Valero, 2001). (iii) Same-sex sexual encounters might provide younger animals with practice for courtship, mounting or other behaviors associated with reproduction, so as to improve their reproductive success when a heterosexual partner becomes available later on. Evidence from Drosophila supports a role of same-sex sexual experience in improving the outcome of later heterosexual mating encounters for young males, but not older males (McRobert & Tompkins, 1988), and pink flamingoes might benefit from same-sex sexual experience by improving their territory-acquisition abilities (King, 2006).

In recent years, a handful of studies have sought to understand the causes of same-sex sexual behavior from a broader evolutionary perspective. MacFarlane et al. (2007) surveyed same-sex sexual behavior in birds, and concluded that male–male sexual behavior was more commonly found in polygamous species, whereas female–female behavior was more likely to be observed in species with precocial young and a monogamous mating system. They suggested that same-sex behavior among males might be facilitated by proximity, as would occur in leks or other communal displays. And in one of the few attempts to model the selective forces that could lead to same-sex sexual behavior, Gavrilets and Rice (2006) developed a set of theoretical predictions about the likely architecture of genes that might influence human homosexuality. The results of their theoretical study have wide-ranging consequences for our understanding of the evolution of same-sex sexual

Table 30.2 Adaptive and non-adaptive explanations for same-sex sexual behavior

Hypothesis	Function or mechanism	Examples of species studied[a]	Refs
Adaptive explanations			
Social glue	Bonds and alliances are formed and maintained through participation in same-sex sexual interactions	Bottlenose dolphins (♂) (*Tursiops spp.*)	Mann (2006)
	Same-sex sexual interactions reduce tension and prevent future conflict	Acorn woodpeckers (♀) (*Melanerpes formicivorous*)	McRoberts & McRoberts (1976)
	Same-sex sexual interactions facilitate reconciliation after conflict occurs	Japanese macaques (♀) (*Macaca fuscata*)	Vasey et al. (1998)
Intrasexual conflict	Same-sex sexual encounters establish and reinforce dominance hierarchies	American bison (♀) (*Bison bison*)	Vervaecke & Roden (2006)
	Individuals might reduce the reproductive success of competitors, and thereby increase their own, through same-sex interactions	Dung fly (♂) (*Hydromyza livens*)	Preston-Mafhan (2006)
Practice	Immature individuals learn more successful courtship or mating skills through same-sex activity with conspecifics	Fruit flies (♂) (*Drosophila spp.*)	McRobert & Tompkins (1988)
Kin selection	Individuals that engage in same-sex sexual behavior provide resources to siblings, thereby increasing their inclusive fitness	Humans (♂♀) (*Homo sapiens*)	Rahman & Hull (2005)
Indirect insemination	Males can indirectly inseminate females by depositing sperm on or in other males, that then transfer it to females during subsequent opposite-sex mating	Flour beetles (♂) (*Tribolium castaneum*)	Levan et al. (2008)
Overdominance	Genes promoting same-sex sexual behavior in a homozygous state confer a selective advantage when in a heterozygous state	Humans (♂♀) (*Homo sapiens*)	Gavrilets & Rice (2006)
Sexually antagonistic selection	Alleles promoting same-sex sexual behavior in one sex increase fitness in the other sex, and are thereby maintained by selection	Humans (♂) (*Homo sapiens*)	Camperio-Ciani et al. (2004)

Non-adaptive explanations

Mistaken identity	Same-sex behavior might occur because of weak sex discrimination	Orange chromide cichlids (♀) (*Etroplus maculates*)	Barlow (2000)
Prison effect	Depriving individuals of members of the opposite sex causes them to engage in sexual interactions with members of the same sex	Damselflies (♂) (*Ischnura elegans*)	Van Gossum et al. (2005)
Evolutionary byproduct	Same-sex sexual behavior arises as a byproduct when selection acts on a separate trait, such as high sexual responsiveness	Japanese macaques (♀) (*Macaca fuscata*)	Vasey et al. (2008)
Maladaptation	Same-sex sexual behavior manifests when organisms are imperfectly adapted to their environment	Many species	[16]
Infection	Infection with an external agent, such as a virus, promotes the expression of same-sex sexual preferences	Postulated in humans	Cochran et al. (2000)

[a] The species listed in this table represent those in which the given hypothesis has been proposed or studied. Empirical studies have delivered varying levels of support for these hypotheses.

behavior in both humans and non-human species. For example, their models indicated a surprisingly wide range of genetic conditions under which genes influencing same-sex orientation in humans could propagate and persist, and predicted that individuals exhibiting both same-sex and opposite-sex sexual behaviors should be common (Gavrilets and Rice, 2006) (see Table 30.2).

Those instances of same-sex sexual behavior that cannot be explained from an adaptationist perspective are often attributed to cases of mistaken identity, especially in invertebrates (Harari et al., 2000; Reinhardt et al., 2007; Ambrogio & Pechenik, 2008).

Evolutionary Consequences of Same-sex Sexual Behavior

There is no lack of hypotheses for how same-sex sexual behavior might be adaptive,

and these hypotheses will vary greatly among species (Table 30.2). However, evolutionary consequences of same-sex sexual behavior have received scant attention. How do same-sex sexual interactions alter evolutionary dynamics within populations or species?

Same-sex sexual behavior is prevalent enough to influence the social dynamics of wild populations in some species but not others. In bottlenose dolphins (*Thursiops sp.*), for instance, roughly half of male sexual interactions are with other males (Mann, 2006). Male–male mountings in the bearded vulture *Gypaetus barbatus* accounted for roughly 11–26% of all mountings in one study (Bertran & Margalida, 2003), and in Japanese beetles (*Popillia japonica*), 1–6% of all observed copulations were between males (Switzer et al., 2004). Recent studies in other wild populations suggest that these behaviors should not be dismissed as unimportant sources of selection (although see Shine et al., 2003).

Consider, for example, Laysan albatross. In 2008, researchers studying a colony of albatross in Hawaii reported that 31% of all pairs consisted of pair-bonded females that courted, allopreened and shared parenting responsibilities (Young et al., 2008). In this socially monogamous species, successfully rearing a chick requires the cooperation of two parents, and although the same-sex female pairs did not enjoy the level of reproductive success as their male–female counterparts, they fared far better than unpaired females (Young et al., 2008). The sex ratio in the population was heavily female biased. If same-sex pair bonding and parenting are part of a flexible breeding strategy that females employ in response to dynamic social conditions such as sex-ratio fluctuations, then the alterations in social structure and social interactions within the population might also impact the evolutionary dynamics of the population.

One intriguing possibility is that female–female pairing increases the potential fitness benefits, and therefore selective advantage of, male extra-pair copulations. This is because there are more females available that can both participate in extra-pair copulations and provide care for the offspring afterward than there would be if all pairs in the population were opposite sex, or even if excess females remained unpaired. In addition, the likelihood of divorce might be weakened in populations where females exhibit the flexibility to form same-sex pairs and produce offspring. Same-sex pairing removes excess females from the population that would, under other circumstances, provide pressure for males in opposite-sex pairs to abandon their partner. The existence of female–female pairs in the albatross population— regardless of its genetic, hormonal or evolutionary causes—might therefore have evolutionary consequences. At any given time, such population-level consequences will depend on the degree of female flexibility and the

population demographic factors that influence female pairing behavior. Furthermore, the importance of same-sex pairings is likely not limited to albatross; similar female–female pairings have been found in several other species, such as Roseate terns (*Sternus dougallii*) and California gulls (*Larus californicus*) (Nisbet & Hatch, 1999; Conover & Hunt, 1984).

It is clear that same-sex sexual behaviors occur in a wide variety of animal taxa, so predicting their evolutionary effects should be a key goal of future research. One way to do this would be to consider whether indirect genetic effects (IGEs) occur as a result of same-sex sexual behavior. IGEs occur when genes expressed in one individual alter the phenotype of another individual (Moore et al., 1997; Wolf et al., 1998). This can happen when two individuals have a social interaction, or when one individual modifies the environment in a way that influences another's phenotype. In the case of same-sex sexual behavior, genes in one individual causing it to direct sexual behavior toward another member of the same sex could exert indirect effects on the second individual. For example, the second individual might experience either increased or reduced reproductive fitness, as in the albatross and dung fly examples, respectively (Young et al., 2008; Preston-Mafham, 2006). Recent theoretical models have suggested that IGEs can, depending on the circumstances, dramatically strengthen or weaken evolutionary responses to selection (Moore et al., 1997; Wolf et al., 1998). In this sense, same-sex sexual behavior is both a trait that is potentially shaped by selection and a *force* that shapes selection on other traits.

For same-sex sexual behavior to be an IGE, however, it must have a heritable genetic basis. We are unaware of any published heritability estimates for same-sex sexual behavior in non-human animals, but estimates for human sexual orientation range as high as 0.74 (Pillard & Bailey, 1998) (see Box 30.2).

Box 30.2 Insights from studies of human homosexual orientation

Since the publication of controversial research by Swaab and Hofman (1990) and LeVay (1991) in the early 1990s that examined brain differences in homosexual versus heterosexual men, insights into the genetic, hormonal, neurophysiological and social contributions to sexual orientation in humans have accumulated rapidly. Humans make unique study organisms, because they can directly communicate with researchers and provide information that differentiates same-sex behavior from sexual orientation. Here we highlight advances in the study of same-sex behaviors in humans that have bearing on research goals addressing the patterns and processes that underlie same-sex behaviors in other animals:

- **Twin/sibling studies**. Studies examining the degree to which monozygotic, dizygotic and adopted siblings share their sexual orientation indicate that the tendency to be gay or lesbian is heritable and can run in families (Pillard & Bailey, 1998), and might confer a reproductive fitness advantage to the relatives of gay men (Camperio-Ciani et al., 2004; King et al., 2005; Rahman et al., 2008; Zeitsch, 2008). However, such studies are limited in their ability to elucidate the genetic architecture of traits such as sexual orientation.

- **Linkage studies**. Early studies on genes influencing sexual orientation suggested an association between male homosexual orientation and a marker on the X chromosome (Hamer et al., 1993; Hu et al., 1995; Hamer, 2002;). Other researchers have had difficulty replicating these findings (Rice et al., 1999) (although see Bocklandt et al., 2006), and a subsequent genome-wide linkage study identified several autosomal regions that potentially influence human sexual orientation (Mustanski et al., 2005).

- **Fraternal birth-order effect**. Having more older brothers increases the likelihood of a male being homosexual (Blanchard & Bogaert, 2004; Blanchard, 2004). This pattern might arise because of the pre-natal environment that fetuses experience, including compounds to which they are exposed in utero (Bogaert, 2006). For example, maternal anti-male antibodies might aggregate during repeated pregnancies where the child is male, which in turn affect the sexual differentiation of a subsequent male fetus's brain.

- **Sexual orientation and pheromones**. In male homosexuals, regions of the brain that are associated with sexual activity activate in response to a testosterone derivative with pheromone-like properties (Savic et al., 2005). An estrogen derivative similarly activated the same brain regions in homosexual women (Berglund et al., 2006). The responses are sex atypical, and researchers have begun to attribute such differences to anatomical features of the brain, for example amygdala connections, that are differentiated with respect to sexual orientation but not biological sex (Savic & Lindström, 2008).

Homosexuality in humans is clearly not equivalent to, for example, male–male mountings in Japanese beetles; but, as with any other trait, it is useful to apply conceptual evolutionary frameworks that have been refined in one animal system, in this case humans, to other systems. For instance, twin studies in humans have provided estimates of the heritability of homosexual orientation, but heritability estimates for the tendency to exhibit same-sex behavior do not exist in any other species, to our knowledge. In model organisms such as flour beetles (Levan et al., 2008), such an approach could clarify whether the tendency to engage in same-sex sexual behavior can be a target of selection and have indirect effects on social evolution.

Generating heritability estimates in a model organism would not only identify same-sex behaviors that are potential targets of selection but would also allow researchers to use quantitative genetic models incorporating IGEs to predict whether same-sex sexual behaviors alter the strength of selection on other traits. These could include behaviors such as courtship in *Drosophila* (Macías-Garcia & Valero, 2001), or morphological features such as the armature found in both male and female African bat bugs (*Afrocimex constrictus*) that protects against traumatic insemination (Reinhardt et al., 2007).

Same-sex Sexual Behavior and Sexual Selection

Sexual selection is characterized by competitive interactions that result in increased variation in mating success, and therefore increased variation in reproductive fitness (Andersson & Simmons, 2006). It manifests either as intrasexual competition for mates or as intersexual mate choice, and can drive the evolution and maintenance of elaborate weaponry (in the case of intrasexual selection) or ornaments (in the case of intersexual selection). Because of its interactive nature, the outcome of sexual selection can be influenced by same-sex sexual behavior in relatively intuitive ways. For

example, some same-sex sexual behaviors appear to play a role in aggressive or dominance interactions, especially in males. In numerous genera and species of cockroaches, for example, males frequently elicit mountings by other males using stereotyped courtship maneuvers, or they might mimic female behaviors and mount courting males (Wendelken & Barth, 1985). Such "pseudofemale" behavior apparently increases the reproductive fitness of the males exhibiting it, because it increases the likelihood that they will mate with the female that had been courted by the displaced male. If a heritable genetic component underlies the tendency to engage in such interactions, the net effect can be to exaggerate or diminish the response to selection of traits that are involved in the interaction (Moore et al., 1997).

Same-sex sexual behavior as a channel for dominance interactions has been documented in other species such as dung flies [24], and although the behaviors might not have evolved as a mechanism of aggression, male–male mating attempts in desert locusts (*Schistocerca gregaria*) and wasps (*Lariophagus distinguendus*) are similarly disadvantageous (Rono et al., 2008; Ruther & Steiner, 2008). The consequence of these behaviors, regardless of their evolutionary cause, is selection for males to inhibit undesired courtship attempts. In the case of the locusts and wasps, this means releasing a pheromone that inhibits courtship by other males (Rono et al., 2008; Ruther & Steiner, 2008). Is it logical, though, to treat these same-sex sexual behaviors as something separate from other behaviors or morphological traits that mediate intrasexual aggression? The only distinction is that they are sexual in character; they would normally be expressed in the context of an opposite-sex courtship or reproductive interaction, but are instead co-opted for another function. Thus, the evolutionary origins of same-sex sexual behaviors can be decoupled from their present function. It does not matter whether they arise as a by-product of selection on other traits, genetic drift or millions of years of carefully honed adaptation driven by selection. They can have the same evolutionary consequences regardless of their independent causes. This highlights a key feature of same-sex sexual behaviors: they are flexibly deployed in a variety of circumstances, for example, as alternative reproductive tactics, as cooperative breeding strategies, as facilitators of social bonding or as mediators of intrasexual conflict. Once this flexibility is established, it becomes in and of itself a selective force that can shape selection on other aspects of physiology, life history, social behavior and even morphology.

Concluding remarks

For many people, the issue of same-sex sexual behavior in animals is more than just academic. Bagemihl's (1999) compendium documenting same-sex behavior in nearly 450 species has been frequently cited in media articles and websites dealing with gay rights issues in humans (Soltaire, 2007; Anonymous blogger, 2008).

It was even referenced by the American Psychiatric Association in evidence submitted to the US Supreme Court for consideration during the 2003 gay rights case *Lawrence v. Texas*, which overturned a Texas law banning homosexual sodomy (Gilfoyle et al., 2003). It is crucial that scientific contributions from animal studies shed more light than heat on the topic of same-sex behavior, so it is useful to define promising directions for future work and identify pitfalls to avoid as the field matures.

Researchers have begun to achieve a firmer grasp on evolutionary explanations for the origin and maintenance of same-sex sexual behaviors. We advocate expanding the contexts in which same-sex sexual behavior is studied by exploring its evolutionary consequences. Same-sex interactions occur in an enormous variety of taxonomic groups, and both the mechanisms producing the behaviors and the outcomes of the behaviors can vary widely among and within species. Regardless of their proximate or evolutionary origins, viewing these behaviors as potential selective agents in and of themselves, and studying their evolutionary effects, would contribute insight into the general principles underlying phenomena such as cooperative breeding, aggression, conflict and sexual selection.

Several approaches appear promising. First, greater communication between researchers working on human sexual behavior and researchers engaged in non-human animal work would enhance the research programs of both (Box 30.2). These two fields can most effectively communicate with each other if efforts are made to avoid politicizing research results and drawing parallels between human sexual identity and animal behavior when they are clearly not merited. Second, models incorporating indirect genetic effects would be especially practical for quantifying the effects of same-sex sexual interactions on the rate and direction of selection, and particular emphasis should be placed on their effects on traits involved in reproductive isolation (Moore et al., 1997). Third, and key to the second approach, heritability estimates for the tendency to engage in same-sex sexual behaviors are necessary to estimate the magnitude of these effects. It might be feasible to derive these from laboratory populations of model organisms that have already been shown to engage in same-sex sexual behaviors. Finally, by combining the above approaches with techniques that have been used to examine the evolutionary consequences of other behavioral or life-history traits, such as quantitative genetic and experimental evolution studies, we can achieve a richer understanding of how same-sex sexual behaviors do—or perhaps do not—contribute to social evolution and genetic and phenotypic diversification.

References

Adkins-Regan, E. (2002). Development of sexual partner preference in the zebra finch: a socially monogamous, pair-bonding animal. *Arch. Sex. Behav.* 31, 27–33.

Ambrogio, O.V. and Pechenik, J.A. (2008). When is a male not a male? Sex recognition and choice in two sex-changing species. *Behav. Ecol. Sociobiol.* 62, 1779–1786.

Andersson, M. and Simmons, L.W. (2006). Sexual selection and mate choice. *Trends Ecol. Evol.* 21, 296–302.

Anonymous blogger (2008). The Agonist 7 November. (http://agonist.org/stirling_newberry/20081106/for_equal_marriage).

Bagemihl, B. (1999). *Biological Exuberance.* St. Martin's Press.

Barlow, G.W. (2000). *The Cichlid Fishes: Nature's Grand Experiment in Evolution.* Perseus.

Baum, M.J. (2006). Mammalian animal models of psychosexual differentiation: when is "translation" to the human situation possible? *Horm. Behav* 50, 579–588.

Berglund, H. et al. (2006). Brain response to putative pheromones in lesbian women. *Proc. Natl. Acad. Sci. U.S.A.* 103, 8269–8274.

Bertran, J. and Margalida, A. (2003). Male-male mountings in polyandrous bearded vultures Gypaetus barbatus: an unusual behaviour in raptors. *J. Avian Biol.* 34, 334–338.

Blanchard, R. (2004). Quantitative and theoretical analyses of the relation between older brothers and homosexuality in men. *J. Theor. Biol.* 230, 173–187.

Blanchard, R. and Bogaert, A.F. (2004). Proportion of homosexual men who owe their sexual orientation to fraternal birth order: an estimate based on two national probability samples. *Am. J. Hum. Biol.* 16, 151–157.

Bocklandt, S. et al. (2006). Extreme skewing of X chromosome inactivation in mothers of homosexual men. *Hum. Genet.* 118, 691–694.

Bogaert, A.F. (2006). Biological versus nonbiological older brothers and men's sexual orientation. *Proc. Natl. Acad. Sci. U.S.A.* 103, 10771–10774.

Camperio-Ciani, A. et al. (2004). Evidence for maternally inherited factors favouring male homosexuality and female fecundity. *Proc. R. Soc. Lond. B Biol. Sci.* 271, 2217–2221.

Cochran, G.M. et al. (2000). Infectious causation of disease: an evolutionary perspective. *Perspect. Biol. Med.* 43, 406–448.

Conover, M.R. and Hunt, G.L., Jr (1984). Experimental evidence that female-female pairs in gulls result from a shortage of breeding males. *Condor* 86, 472–476.

Field, K.L. and Waite, T.A. (2004). Absence of female conspecifics induces homosexual behaviour in male guppies. *Anim. Behav.* 68, 1381–1389.

Fruth, B. and Hohmann, G. (2006). Social grease for females? Same-sex genital contacts in wild bonobos. In *Homosexual Behaviour in Animals* (Sommer, V. and Vasey, P.L., eds), pp. 294–315, Cambridge University Press.

Gavrilets, S. and Rice, W.R. (2006). Genetic models of homosexuality: generating testable predictions. *Proc. R. Soc. Lond. B Biol. Sci.* 273, 3031–3038.

Gilfoyle, N.F.P. et al. (2003). Lawrence v. Texas (Docket no. 02-102). Brief Filed: 1/03. Court: Supreme Court of the United States. Year of Decision: 2003. (http://www.apa.org/psyclaw/lawrence-v-texas.pdf)

Gill, K.S. (1963). *A Mutation Causing Abnormal Mating Behavior, Drosophila.* Information Service.

Greenspan, R.J. and Ferveur, J-F. (2000). Courtship in Drosophila. *Annu. Rev. Genet.* 34, 205–232.

Grosjean, Y. et al. (2008). A glial amino-acid transporter controls synapse strength and courtship in Drosophila. *Nat. Neurosci.* 11, 54–61.

Hamer, D. (2002). Molecular genetics and the human personality. In *Genetics of Sexual Behavior* (Benjamin, J. et al., eds), pp. 257–272, American Psychiatric Publishing.

Hamer, D.H. et al. (1993). A linkage between DNA markers on the X chromosome and male sexual orientation. *Science* 261, 321–327.

Harari, A.R. et al. (2000). Intrasexual mounting in the beetle Diaprepes abbreviatus (L.). *Proc. R. Soc. Lond. B Biol. Sci* 267, 2071–2079.

Hu, S. et al. (1995). Linkage between sexual orientation and chromosome Xq28 in males but not in females. *Nat. Genet.* 11, 248–256.

King, C.E. (2006). Pink flamingos: atypical partnerships and sexual activity in colonially breeding birds. In *Homosexual Behaviour in Animals* (Sommer, V. and Vasey, P.L., eds), pp. 77–106, Cambridge University Press.

King, M. et al. (2005). Family size in white gay and heterosexual men. *Arch. Sex. Behav.* 34, 117–122.

Kurtovic, A. et al. (2007). A single class of olfactory neurons mediates behavioural responses to a *Drosophila* sex pheromone. *Nature* 446, 542–546.

Lee, H-G. et al. (2008). Recurring ethanol exposure induces disinhibited courtship in *Drosophila*. *PLoS ONE* 1, e1391.

Levan, K.E. et al. (2008). Testing multiple hypotheses for the maintenance of male homosexual copulatory behaviour in flour beetles. *J. Evol. Biol.* 22, 60–70.

LeVay, S. (1991). A difference in hypothalamic structure between heterosexual and homosexual men. *Science* 253, 1034–1037.

Liu, T. et al. (2008). Increased dopamine level enhances male–male courtship in *Drosophila*. *J. Neurosci.* 28, 5539–5546.

MacFarlane, G.R. et al. (2007). Same-sex sexual behavior in birds: expression is related to social mating system and state of development at hatching. *Behav. Ecol.* 18, 21–33.

Macías-Garcia, C. and Valero, A. (2001). Context-dependent sexual mimicry in the viviparous fish Girardinichthys multiradiatus. *Ethol. Ecol. Evol.* 13, 331–339.

MacRoberts, M.H. and MacRoberts, B.R. (1976). *Social Organization and Behavior of the Acorn Woodpecker in Central Coastal California* (Ornithology Monographs, Vol. 21), American Ornithologists' Union.

Mann, J. (2006). Establishing trust: socio-sexual behaviour and the development of male-male bonds among Indian Ocean bottlenose dolphins. In *Homosexual Behaviour in Animals* (Sommer, V. and Vasey, P.L., eds), pp. 107–130, Cambridge University Press.

Marco, A. and Lizana, M. (2002). The absence of species and sex recognition during mate search by male common toads. *Bufo bufo. Ethol. Ecol. Evol.* 14, 1–8.

McRobert, S.P. and Tompkins, L. (1988). Two consequences of homosexual courtship performed by *Drosophila* melanogaster and *Drosophila* affinis males. *Evolution Int. J. Org. Evolution* 42, 1093–1097.

McRoberts, S.P. et al. (2003). Mutations in raised *Drosophila* melanogaster affect experience-dependent aspects of sexual behavior in both sexes. *Behav. Genet.* 33, 347–356.

Miyamoto, T. and Amrien, H. (2008). Suppression of male courtship by a *Drosophila* pheromone receptor. *Nat. Neurosci.* 11, 874–876.

Moore, A.J. et al. (1997). Interacting phenotypes and the evolutionary process: I. Direct and indirect genetic effects of social interactions. *Evolution Int. J. Org. Evolution* 51, 1352–1362.

Mustanski, B.S. et al. (2005). A genomewide scan of male sexual orientation. *Hum. Genet.* 116, 272–278.

Nisbet, I.C.T. and Hatch, J.J. (1999). Consequences of a female-biased sex ratio in a socially monogamous bird: female-female pairs in the Roseate tern (*Sterna dougallii*). *Ibis* 141, 307–320.

Perkins, A. and Roselli, C.E. (2007). The ram as a model for behavioral neuroendocrinology. *Horm. Behav.* 52, 70–77.

Pillard, R.C. and Bailey, J.M. (1998). Human sexual orientation has a heritable component. *Hum. Biol.* 70, 347–365.

Preston-Mafham, K. (2006). Post-mounting courtship and the neutralizing of male competitors through "homosexual" mountings in the fly Hydromyza livens F. (Diptera: Scatophagidae). *J. Nat. Hist* 40, 101–105.

Price, E.O. et al. (1988). The relationship of male–male mounting to the sexual preferences of young rams. *Appl. Anim. Behav. Sci.* 21, 347–355.

Rahman, Q. and Hull, M.S. (2005). An empirical test of the kin selection hypothesis for male homosexuality. *Arch. Sex. Behav.* 34, 461–467.

Rahman, Q. et al. (2008). Maternal inheritance and familial fecundity factors in male homosexuality. *Arch. Sex. Behav.* 37, 962–969.

Reinhardt, K. et al. (2007). Female-limited polymorphism in the copulatory organ of a traumatically inseminating insect. *Am. Nat.* 170, 931–935.

Rice, G. et al. (1999). Male homosexuality: absence of linkage to microsatellite markers at Xq28. *Science* 284, 665–667.

Rono, E. et al. (2008). Concentration-dependent parsimonious releaser roles of gregarious male pheromone of the desert locust, Schistocerca gregaria. *J. Insect Behav* 54, 162–168.

Ruther, J. and Steiner, S. (2008). Costs of female odour in males of the parasitic wasp Lariophagus distinguendus (Hymenoptera: Pteromalidae). *Naturwissenschaften* 95, 547–552.

Santtila, P. et al. (2009). Testing Miller's theory of alleles preventing androgenization as an evolutionary explanation for the genetic predisposition for male homosexuality. *Evol. Hum. Behav.* 30, 58–65.

Savic, I. and Lindstrom, P. (2008). PET and MRI show differences in cerebral asymmetry and functional connectivity between homoand heterosexual subjects. Proc. Natl. Acad. Sci. U. S. A. 105, 9403–9408

Savic, I. et al. (2005). Brain response to putative pheromones in homosexual men. Proc. Natl. Acad. Sci. U. S. A. 102, 7356–7361.

Shine, R. et al. (2003). Confusion within "mating balls" of garter snakes: does misdirected courtship impose selection on male tactics? Anim. Behav 66, 1011–1017.

Soltaire, F. (2007). Agora Vox 11 April. (http://www.agoravox.fr/article_tous_commentaires.php3?id_article=22111).

Sommer, V. and Vasey, P.L., eds (2006). Homosexual Behaviour in Animals, Cambridge University Press.

Svetec, N. and Ferveur, J-F. (2005). Social experience and pheromonal perception can change male–male interactions in Drosophila melanogaster. J. Exp. Biol. 208, 891–898.

Svetec, N. et al. (2005). Effect of genes, social experience, and their interaction on the courtship behaviour of transgenic Drosophila males. Genet. Res. 85, 183–193.

Swaab, D.F. and Hofman, M.A. (1990). An enlarged superchiasmatic nucleus in homosexual men. Brain Res. 537, 141–148.

Switzer, P.V. et al. (2004). Effects of environmental and social conditions on homosexual pairing in the Japanese beetle (Popillia japonica Newman). J. Insect Behav. 17, 1–16.

Van Gossum, H. et al. (2005). Reversible switches between male-male and male-female mating behaviour by male damselflies. Biol. Lett. 1, 268–270.

Vasey, P.L. et al. (1998). Mounting interactions between female Japanese macaques: testing the influence of dominance and aggression. Ethology 104, 387–398.

Vasey, P.L. et al. (2008). Courtship behaviour in Japanese macaques during heterosexual and homosexual consortships. Behav. Processes 78, 401–407.

Vervaecke, H. and Roden, C. (2006). Going with the herd: same-sex interaction and competition in American bison. In Homosexual Behaviour in Animals (Sommer, V. and Vasey, P.L., eds), pp. 131–153, Cambridge University Press.

Wendelken, P.W. and Barth, R.H., Jr (1985). On the significance of pseudofemale behavior in the neotropical cockroach genera Blaberus. Archimandrita and Byrsotria. Psyche (Stuttg.) 92, 493–504.

White, J.Q. (2007). The sensory circuitry for sexual attraction in C. elegans males. Curr. Biol 17, 1847–1857.

Wolf, J.B. et al. (1998). Evolutionary consequences of indirect genetic effects. Trends Ecol. Evol. 13, 64–69.

Young, L.C. et al. (2008). Successful same-sex pairing in Laysan albatross. Biol. Lett. 4, 32 3–325.

Zeitsch, B.P. (2008). Genetic factors predisposing to homosexuality may increase mating success in heterosexuals. Evol. Hum. Behav. 29, 424–433.

Zhang, S-D. and Odenwald, W.F. (1995). Misexpression of the white (w) gene triggers male-male courtship in Drosophila. Proc. Natl. Acad. Sci. U. S. A. 92, 5525–5529.

Zuk, M. (2006). Family values in black and white. Nature 439, 917.

PART III

Human Nature and Normality

Topic 10 HEALTH

S OMEONE WITH A COLD is ill; so is someone with the flu, a colon cancer, AIDS, or herpes simplex. What is common to all these conditions? And why isn't our incapacity to synthesize vitamin C a pathological deficiency, while the incapacity to synthesize enough insulin is a widespread pathological condition known as type-I diabetes? Answering such questions requires explaining what makes a condition a disease (where, as is common among philosophers and physicians, "disease" is understood broadly to include injuries—e.g., a broken arm—and disabilities—e.g., deafness). This explanation would also be useful for determining whether a range of grey cases, including aging, mild depression, obesity, or gigantism, are genuine diseases—an important social issue since medical insurances are unlikely to cover treatments for these conditions if they are not diseases.

An influential strategy to determine the nature of diseases is to characterize them as being abnormal and to define the normal by appealing to the notion of human nature. Roughly, one assumes that it is possible to define what is the normal state or function of an organ in the human body, what is the normal functioning of the human mind, and what capacities it is normal to possess. One then proposes that diseases are conditions that deviate from the normal. This approach has a long history, arguably going back to Hippocrates's view that diseases result from particular types of disequilibrium between the four humors that make up the normal human body.

Boorse's essay is an influential implementation of this strategy, and many bioethicists have built on his definition of diseases. As he puts it, he proposes "an empirical notion of the nature of a species, e.g. human nature, to explicate medical normality." As a first approximation, he takes a disease to be a condition that prevents an organ from fulfilling its normal function, where the function of an organ is its species-typical contribution to survival and reproduction. While the human heart has many effects, including making sounds and pumping blood, only the latter is its normal function because only pumping blood contributes to the survival and reproduction of humans in general. According to Boorse, biology objectively identifies these functions, and thus indirectly provides a value-neutral characterization of what diseases are.

Amundson's chapter, which in part builds on Silvers' essay "A fatal attraction to normalizing" (Topic 11), denies that biology defines which functions, conditions, behaviors, or capacities are normal for a given species, such as human beings. According to Amundson, evolutionary biology, developmental biology, and even physiology highlight the differences between conspecifics (e.g., human beings), such as the genetic variation or the many ways in which an organ may develop to fulfill a particular biological function—which cast doubts on whether a normal human phenotype can be objectively defined in light of these sciences. He then argues that Boorse's and others' approach underwrites discriminatory practices against people with disabilities.

In a new chapter, Cooper reviews the strengths and weaknesses of the main conceptions of health and disease developed by philosophers, physicians, and scientists. She also focuses on the distinction between mental and physical diseases, showing that, while the prevalent conceptions of diseases leave little room for this distinction, it is an important notion for the patients themselves.

The articles in this section echo the issues discussed elsewhere in this volume. Particularly, Amundson's article builds on Hull's criticism of the notion of human nature and on Silvers' criticism of the attempts to derive norms from biological sciences. Silvers' article, in turn, criticizes those bioethicists who have been taking Boorse's and others' approach to normality at face value.

Suggested Further Reading

Boorse, C. (1997) A rebuttal on health. In J. M. Humber and R. F. Almeder (Eds.), *What is Disease?* (pp. 3–143). Totowa, NJ: Humana Press.

Cooper, R. (2002) Disease. *Studies in the History and Philosophy of Biology and the Biomedical Sciences*, 33: 263–282.

Margolis, J. (1976) The concept of disease. *The Journal of Medicine and Philosophy*, 1: 238–255.

Murphy, D. (2008) Concepts of disease and health. *Stanford Encyclopedia of Philosophy*, www.plato.stanford.edu/entries/health-disease/

Reznek, L. (1987) *The Nature of Disease*. New York: Routledge.

Wachbroit, R. (1994) Normality as a biological concept. *Philosophy of Science*, 61: 579–591.

Wakefield, J. (1992) The concept of mental disorder. *American Psychologist*, 47: 373–388.

Chapter 31

Christopher Boorse

HEALTH AS A THEORETICAL CONCEPT

It is a traditional axiom of medicine that health is the absence of disease. What is a disease? Anything that is inconsistent with health. If the axiom has any content, a better answer can be given. The most fundamental problem in the philosophy of medicine is, I think, to break the circle with a substantive analysis of either health or disease.

Except for a clause on universal diseases, the analysis I wish to offer is that health is normal functioning, where the normality is statistical and the functions biological. One result of this view is to distinguish sharply between theoretical health, the absence of disease, and practical health, roughly the absence of treatable illness. Practical health is a less demanding ideal. We shall argue that the literature on health misses this distinction, either by ignoring disease altogether or by assuming with Engelhardt that "choosing to call a set of phenomena a disease involves a commitment to medical intervention."[1] On our view disease judgments are value-neutral, which is our second main result. If diseases are deviations from the species biological design, their recognition is a matter of natural science, not evaluative decision.

A strong motivation for trying to sort out various notions of health is the hope of throwing light into the morass of mental-health controversies. But because psychological applications of the health vocabulary are controversial, they will be excluded from the argument below. Our goal in this paper is to analyze health and disease as understood by traditional physiological medicine.[2] The outline of the discussion is as follows. The first two sections introduce the problem by a survey of the main ideas of previous discussions of health (**I**) and some methodological remarks (**II**). The functional account is then presented and defended (**III–IV**).

I. Major Themes in the Literature

There is a large clinical literature and a smaller philosophical one on concepts of health.[3] We will first look at some main lines of this body of work, which I suggest ignores or misrepresents the notion of disease. In a brief survey we cannot discuss individual writers' views except as they illustrate recurrent themes. We can cover seven major themes—elementary ideas that occur frequently in definitions of health—and show that none by itself provides a necessary or sufficient condition for disease. This procedure will expose some problems that a good analysis must solve. It will also give some notion of our functional account's competition, though we naturally cannot go over all the ways one could combine these elements in a complex analysis.

All seven ideas below certainly represent features of fatal or debilitating illnesses such as malaria, smallpox, cholera, tuberculosis, cancer, and so on through the list of famous scourges of mankind. That is, they apply to what one might call the paradigm objects of medical concern. More interestingly, I think one can also say that most of them suggest an underlying assumption that the concept of health can be read off from its role in medical *practice*. This is a natural assumption, since the most obvious fact about medicine is that it is a clinical discipline which treats a special population of patients. One easily supposes that healthy people are those who do not need medical treatment, unhealthy ones those who do. To be a disease is to be the sort of thing doctors (ought to) treat. Some writers take this assumption as a complete analysis, while others go on to try to say *what* sort of thing doctors treat, e.g. painful or disabling conditions. But we shall argue that the assumption does not fit the traditional view of health as the absence of disease at all. According to our account, the judgment that something is a disease is a theoretical judgment that neither entails nor is entailed by any therapeutic judgment about people's need for medical treatment.

1. *Value.* Health is, on the whole, certainly desirable. It is easy to view this value as part of the concept of health, or even as essentially all of it. On the latter view physical health is physical well-being or welfare, an identification often made in discussions of health.

On the one hand, however, there are whole broad classes of undesirable physical conditions, conditions that restrict one's physical well-being, which do not appear as diseases in medical texts. It is undesirable to be mildly below average in any valuable physical quality, e.g. height, strength, endurance, coordination, reflex speed, beauty, etc. It is undesirable to have such universal human weaknesses as a need for sleep and regular access to food and water. These conditions are not diseases. Yet one could never distinguish them from diseases on grounds of disvalue alone. As any short person knows, shortness may reduce a person's quality of life much more, in the long run, than a minor

allergy or viral infection. It cannot be undesirability alone that makes a physical condition a disease. On the other hand, it is clear that diseases can be desirable under some circumstances. Cowpox could save a person's life in the midst of a smallpox epidemic; myopia would be advantageous if it meant avoiding the infantry. Sterility, in a world without contraception, might be a heavenly blessing to parents of large families. It therefore remains to be seen how values can enter into the concept of disease, let alone constitute the whole of it.

2. *Treatment by physicians.* It is often supposed that diseases are, if not undesirable conditions, then undesirable conditions that doctors happen to treat. Certain human ills, for historical or sociological or technical reasons, fall within medical practice. Those that do are *ipso facto* diseases; there is no other content to the notion of disease. As medical practice varies over time with evolving social institutions and values, so will the inventory of unhealthy conditions. But no *a priori* limit is put on this variation by any fixed further analysis of the concept of disease. At best, one can generalize about what kinds of conditions we tend to see as requiring medical treatment (cf. Engelhardt, 1975, 1976, 1977). This view, a sort of medical positivism, is one of the stronger trends in the literature.

It does seem natural to cite realities of medical treatment to explain why certain undesirable conditions do not count as diseases. If there were a standard medical treatment for shortness or the need to sleep, then, surely, these conditions would be diseases. The reason they do not appear in a medical book is that there is no treatment for them. But this explanation does not survive scrutiny. Many recognized diseases are equally untreatable. Actual treatability, the existence of effective therapy, is far too strong a condition on disease. The positivist approach must appeal instead to some broader notion of "falling within medical practice." Yet shortness falls within medical practice in the sense that patients complain of it to their doctors. What seems to be lacking is only the medical judgment that it is a disease, as opposed to a region of the normal range of variation.

In a similar way, medical usage presents a converse difficulty for any practical definition of disease. Besides regarding as disease some conditions they cannot treat, doctors also treat some conditions they do not regard as disease. Among standard medical procedures are circumcision, cosmetic surgery, elective abortions, and the prescription of contraceptives. None of the conditions so altered appears in the AMA *Standard Nomenclature*, the latest attempt at a comprehensive listing of diseases. Nor are they listed as diseases by other medical texts. One will search in vain for such a disease as unwanted pregnancy, and it would be absurd to call foreskins on male babies—a part of normal male anatomy—an innate disease. The performance of sex change operations hardly makes male gender, or female, a disease. The fact is that physicians distinguish, even among conditions they treat, between some they consider pathological and others they do not.[4] In traditional medical thought, a condition does not become pathological as soon as a patient or a society wants it changed. Treatment in medical practice is neither necessary nor sufficient for something to be a disease.

3. *Statistical normality.* In clinical language, diseases or pathological conditions are also called abnormal, and healthy conditions normal. An obvious idea that fits some features of medicine well is to interpret this normality statistically. Textbook normals for clinical variables like height, weight, pulse and respiration, blood pressure, vital capacity, basal metabolism, sedimentation rate, and so on are certainly statistical means surrounded by some range of "normal variation." In some cases, such as our example of shortness, the width of the normal range also seems to be a statistical matter. Where normal variation in height ends and dwarfism or giantism begins may depend only on parameters of the population distribution. In other cases, however, as when a text gives 95mm Hg as maximum normal diastolic blood pressure, the boundary of the normal range may reflect higher morbidity or mortality outside it (McCombs, 1971, p. 539). Medical writers frequently say that their quoted normal values represent, not the average person, but the average healthy person. This seems unfortunate for the project of using statistical normality to analyze health. But there is a persistent intuition that the average person—or at least the average heart, lung, kidney, thyroid, etc.—must be normal, or we would have no way of telling what the normal person or organ should be like.

I will return to this intuition when we construct our functional account. Here we note only that statistical normality fails as a necessary or sufficient condition of health. It cannot be necessary because unusual conditions, e.g., type O blood or red hair, may be perfectly healthy. It cannot be sufficient because unhealthy conditions may be typical. No doubt the average person or organ is healthy in a practical sense of displaying no indications for treatment, but that is not the same as complete freedom from disease. Some of what medical texts consider disease processes are at work in virtually everyone below the level of clinical detection. There are also particular diseases—atherosclerosis, minor lung inflammation, perhaps tooth decay—that are nearly universal. In spite of these difficulties we will give statistical normality an important role in our view, which shows that necessary and sufficient conditions are not the only possible components of an analysis.

4. *Pain, suffering, discomfort.* Another theme of many discussions is that health contrasts with the pain and discomfort of illness. This idea suggests a focus on medical practice rather than theory, and in fact on patients who come complaining of symptoms. Even within medical practice, routine physicals can disclose asymptomatic

disease of many kinds—tuberculosis, diabetes, liver cirrhosis, breast cancer, various forms of heart disease, syphilis, and so on through a long list. As textbooks of medicine constantly mention, a complete absence of "subjective distress" is compatible with severe internal lesions. It has been said that pathologists doing autopsies in cases of sudden death often find it a mystery why the victim was not dead years before. At any rate, there is no reason why a disease process must be evident to its bearer via pain or discomfort. Conversely, pain and discomfort occur in normal processes, e.g., teething, menstruation, and childbirth.

5. *Disability.* If not all diseases cause physical suffering, perhaps any disease must at least tend at some stage to cause disability. The notion of disability is broad enough to have some hope of covering the field of disease and possibly subsumes pain as a special case. The most extreme disability, death itself, one judges to be some sort of analytic opposite of health.

In some manner, an analysis of disease using disability must solve the following sorts of problems. It must be broad enough to include minor skin diseases such as athlete's foot, eczema, and warts, either under the heading of disability or some other one. It must include disabilities like myopia and color blindness, but not the inability to swim, fly, or see in the dark like a cat, though the latter failings could be more harmful than the former. It must count adults, but not babies, abnormal if they cannot walk. If a notion of disability meets these tests and a few others, I think it will converge on our notion of dysfunction below, and so no more will be said about it here.

6. *Adaptation.* For a biologist, the standard abilities of organisms are adaptations to their environments. A growing movement in the literature, shown in the work of writers as diverse as J. A. Ryle (1947), Rene Dubos (1959), and Heinz Hartmann (1958), identifies health outright

with a biological notion of fitness or adaptation. The notion cannot, however, be "Darwinian fitness," or pure reproductive success. Parents hardly become healthier with each successive child, nor would anyone maintain that the healthiest traits are the ones that promote large families. Fitness or adaptation here must be a relation between organism and environment only indirectly related to bearing progeny. These accounts typically emphasize that an organism well adapted to one environment may not be well adapted to another. From this it is concluded that health is relative to environment, and the conclusion is pursued in either of two directions. Adaptation may be made a positive ideal of maximum enhancement of the abilities useful in each person's unique circumstances. Or one may develop the negative theme that conditions which would be intolerable in one person's situation may be tolerable or beneficial in another's. In the negative vein Ryle, for example, writes as follows:

> The small stocky Durham miner—poor though his general physique may appear to be from the combined effects of heredity, malnutrition in childhood, and occupational stress in adolescence—is probably better adapted to underground work and life than would be the more favoured and robust candidate for the Metropolitan police force.
>
> . . . what we call normal or (better) normal variability in biology and medicine must always be related to the work required of the organism or its parts and to the medium in which they have their being.[5]

Although the force of Ryle's example is clear, the moral it illustrates might dismay a miners' union general counsel. The issue is whether Ryle would deny what his case suggests—that some of the Durham miner's adaptations to his work are manifestations of disease. The thesis that a condition is not a disease if it helps you on the job would hardly make a good principle of labor law. On the contrary, it is a medical truism that symptoms of disease, e.g. inflammation, may be adaptive responses to environmental insult. As we saw, on the usual view of disease it is quite possible for diseases like cowpox or myopia to be advantageous in special environments. They do not thereby cease to be diseases, for the judgment that they are is a judgment about types of condition and mentions no particular environment. So Ryle's "normality" is best interpreted as the practical normality of requiring no medical attention. It cannot well be interpreted as the theoretical normality of freedom from disease.

It is still clearer in the positive variations that adaptation is not freedom from disease. All sorts of abilities—violin playing, tightrope walking, impersonating a President—may enhance people's ability to live well in their particular environments. But that does not mean that the lack of these abilities would be pathological for them or anyone else. Ordinary medical thought uses no such notion as "pathological for person X in environment E," though "bad for X in E" of course makes sense. The relativity of adaptation to environment, which is its main attraction, is also what makes it unpromising for an analysis of disease.

7. *Homeostasis.* Finally, the notion of homeostasis has wide, and probably excessive, influence as a clinical concept of health (cf. Engel, 1953). The importance of homeostatic regulating mechanisms in body physiology was emphasized by Claude Bernard (1957) and Walter Cannon (1939). Bernard looked at physiological processes as serving to maintain equilibrium in the milieu intérieur, while disease processes were disruptions of the equilibrium, or homeostatic failures. Certainly many aspects of normal and abnormal physiology fit this model. Countless biological variables like blood temperature, acidity, speed of flow, and composition with respect to innumerable substances and organisms must be kept within narrow limits in a state of health.

Homeostasis cannot, however, profitably be viewed as a general model of biological function. Many life functions are not homeostatic unless one stretches the concept to cover every goal-directed process.[6] Perception, locomotion, growth, and reproduction upset an equilibrium rather than maintain one. To say that their ultimate aim is internal equilibrium is unfounded; it is equally true, or truer, that the ultimate aim of internal equilibrium is perception, locomotion, growth and reproduction. Thus there is no point in trying to view corresponding diseases such as deafness, limb paralysis, dwarfism, or sterility as homeostatic failures. One can see why various equilibria are crucial to life without confusing homeostasis with the broader idea of normal functioning.

All the ideas discussed in this section have, in fact, some connection with normal functioning, i.e. with the typical *modus operandi* of the internal physiological machinery of a species. Breakdowns or malfunctions of this machinery—what we shall argue constitute disease—would tend to diminish health on all seven views. Most of the connections are empirical ones. The mode of internal functioning typical of our species, by definition typical, has by natural selection given us abilities adapted to a way of life in our environment that we value. Most serious failures in these internal functions would cause disability, pain, and suffering undesirable enough to justify seeking medical care. But our discussion suggests that a direct attempt to analyze abnormal functioning will better fit the medical notion of disease than the ideas of this section. Before this attempt is made, some summary remarks may help clarify its goal.

II. Remarks on the Problem

1. *Generic usage of "disease".* Our project is, as we have said, to analyze the notion of *disease* behind the view that health is the absence of disease. It should be clear from the beginning that this view employs a much broader usage of "disease"

than any outside medicine. Until now I have tried to postpone this issue by my choice of cases, perhaps unsuccessfully. But health cannot possibly be the absence of disease unless at least the following are diseases: not only infection syndromes like malaria and syphilis, but also birth defects like spina bifida, growth disorders like cancer, functional impairments like limb paralysis, and all kinds of injuries and causes of death. The AMA *Nomenclature* lists as diseases many conditions to which lay usage would never apply the term: obesity and inanition, seasickness, broken bones, gunshot wounds, foreign bodies in the stomach, supernumerary toes, animal bites, and drowning, electrocution, asphyxiation, incineration, and "general crushing." Some medical sources have separate headings for diseases and injuries; the broad usage of "disease" is not invariable even within medicine. It is, however, well-established—exactly as well-established as the principle that health is the absence of disease.[7] The principle is impossible on any usage that distinguishes diseases from injuries, since it would then imply that one can be perfectly healthy and dead.

In order to analyze the broad medical usage, we will take medical reference works that employ it as more or less authoritative about what counts as a disease. An unusually comprehensive source is the *Nomenclature*, which aims to provide a code number for every disease recognized by clinicians. This book is invaluable as a compendium of thousands of test cases for an analysis of disease. It also includes some perfectly normal conditions, such as emmetropia or correct lens refraction, though perhaps only under codes indicating their normality. This concession to statistical convenience[8] suggests that the *Nomenclature* should not be regarded as completely authoritative about what conditions medical thought sees as diseases. Its evidence must be combined with the usage of "disease" and "health" in the discursive context of medical textbooks and research papers. An analysis of disease should, I think, be viewed as an explanatory theory of this whole body of usage and judged accordingly.

2. *Illness and disease entity.* Besides any lay conceptions of disease, there are at least two other narrower notions from which our generic target idea needs to be distinguished: *illness* and *disease entity.* Neither medical nor lay usage would describe a person with athlete's foot, warts, color blindness, or even all three at once as *ill.* But medical sources do call each of these conditions a disease. This means that some distinction, not a sharp one, is observed in medicine between disease and illness. I have argued elsewhere (Boorse, 1975) that being ill involves having a disease serious enough to be somewhat incapacitating, which thereby supports normative judgments about treatment and responsibility. Not every disease makes its bearer ill.

Roughly corresponding to philosophical debates over universals, there have been recurrent controversies in the history of medicine about whether diseases or only ill patients are real (Engelhardt, 1975; Hudson, 1966). Sometimes the issue was whether diseases are independently existing external entities; at other times it was whether disease taxonomy is artificial or natural. Our legacy from these controversies is the term *disease entity*, used to mean a natural unit of disease classification. Today the strictest definition of a disease entity would be a constellation of signs, symptoms, and pathology with specific etiology and prognosis. It is part of the ideal of a medical nomenclature or textbook to divide the realm of unhealthy conditions into disease entities of this sort. But in practice, because of limitations of medical knowledge, the division can only be carried out so far. Thus conditions like fever, diarrhea, breathing difficulty, or hypoglycemia would not be accepted as specific diagnoses, since they are common to many identifiable diseases, but the *Nomenclature* does reluctantly accept acidosis and glycosuria when no more specific diagnosis can be found. So some of the "diseases" listed in medical sources are surely not disease entities in a strict sense. Our generic notion of disease looks wider than that of disease entity.

Fortunately, if our goal is to understand health as the absence of disease, we can abstract entirely from this problem of individuating diseases. Complete freedom from disease is the same however the field of diseases is split up into units. As a side effect of this abstraction, though, our analysis of disease will include conditions like fever, diarrhea, dyspnea, hypoglycemia, and so on, which are not considered individual diseases by medical sources. In this respect alone we make no attempt to be faithful to the customary extension of "disease". The reader should bear this restriction in mind.

3. *Intrinsic vs. instrumental health.* One last distinction is vital to our target conception. It is convenient to call it the distinction between intrinsic and instrumental health, or between what is a disease and what tends to produce one. The term "unhealthy" is used in both senses, often with no risk of confusion. When one speaks of unhealthy habits, like smoking, or unhealthy environments, like New York, these are of course items that produce poor health, not exemplify it. But among physical states, it is easy to confuse diseases with dispositions to become diseased under certain conditions. A good example of the difference is the vermiform appendix. Having an appendix can be instrumentally unhealthy in the sense that with it one can get appendicitis. But the disease here is appendicitis, not the appendix itself. Although people with appendixes may be less likely to be healthy in the future than people without, their intrinsic health is no less until appendicitis strikes.

This intrinsic-instrumental distinction is often of no consequence in medical practice. Usually physician and patient want to eliminate conditions that are unhealthy in either sense. But failure to draw the distinction is fatal to an analysis of health as the absence of disease. If

whatever can cause disease were itself disease, everything would be a disease, since any causal connection is possible in a special environment. The correct strategy is to deal first with intrinsic health by examining what physicians call disease. An analysis of promoting or conducing to health then automatically follows, but not conversely.

III. A Functional Account of Health

1. *Orientation.* The intuition behind our account of health and disease will be a simple one, as simple as the ideas of section I but distinct from all of them. It is that the normal is the natural. Temkin, in his lucid survey of the history of medical conceptions of disease, finds this idea characteristic of the whole classical medical tradition that culminated in Galen:

> Such a concept of health and disease rests on a teleologically conceived biology. All parts of the body are built and function so as to allow man to lead a good life and to preserve his kind. Health is a state according to Nature; disease is contrary to Nature.[9]

Without being able to discuss any part of the history of medicine here, we will argue that the contemporary inventory of diseases shows this ancient conception still at work.

From our standpoint, then, health and disease belong to a family of typological and teleological notions which are usually associated with Aristotelian biology and viewed with suspicion. Often this suspicion is excessive. Informal thinking in the life sciences constantly uses typological and teleological ideas with profit, and much recent philosophical work has been done on concepts of function and goal-directedness in modern biology. This work suggests that aseptic substitutes can be found for ancient notions that continue to have a scientific use. I think one should see that the analysis below is essentially just such a substitute for the idea that diseases are conditions foreign to the nature of the species. Our version of the nature of the species will be a functional design empirically shown typical of it. The ancient view that an ideal can be simultaneously empirical and normative, which pervades the *Republic* and also more contemporary mental-health literature, will have no role at all below. The denial that health is essentially evaluative may be our largest departure from the classical tradition.

With these preliminary remarks, I now state the proposal of this section to show where the discussion is going. I will then lead up to it by developing each detail in turn. This formulation omits a clause about environmental injuries, which I postpone to the next section because it is more speculative than anything in this one.

1. The *reference class* is a natural class of organisms of uniform functional design; specifically, an age group of a sex of a species.

2. A *normal function* of a part or process within members of the reference class is a statistically typical contribution by it to their individual survival and reproduction.

3. *Health* in a member of the reference class is *normal functional ability*: the readiness of each internal part to perform all its normal functions on typical occasions with at least typical efficiency.

4. A *disease* is a type of internal state which impairs health, i.e. reduces one or more functional abilities below typical efficiency.

2. *Functions.* Biologists regularly use functional language to describe the role of traits in the life of organisms. For example, they report that the function of the peacock's tail is to attract a peahen, the function of gills in fish is respiration, and the functions of the human hypothalamus are too numerous to mention. A large philosophical literature now exists on the problem of analyzing these biological function statements.

To defend any view on the topic is beyond our scope, but at the same time the content of a functional account of health depends on one's view of functions. I will therefore sketch an account of functions that I have elsewhere argued in detail (Boorse 1976; cf. Grim, 1977). This account is typical of the literature in taking biological function statements to be value-free; only a few discussions have made them evaluative (Margolis, 1969; Sorabji, 1964; cf. Wimsatt, 1972). It is also not the only account to see physiological functions as causal contributions to an organism's survival and reproduction.

In my view the basic notion of a function is of a contribution to a goal. Organisms are goal-directed in a sense that Sommerhoff (1950), Braithwaite (1960), and Nagel (1961) have tried to characterize: that is, they are disposed to adjust their behavior to environmental change in ways appropriate to a constant result, the goal. In fact, the structure of organisms shows a means-end hierarchy with goal-directedness at every level. Individual cells are goal-directed to manufacturing certain compounds; by doing so they contribute to higher-level goals like muscle contraction; these goals contribute to overt behavior like web-spinning, nest-building, or prey-catching; overt behavior contributes to such goals as individual and species survival and reproduction. What I suggest is that the function of any part or process, for the biologist, is its ultimate contribution to certain goals at the apex of the hierarchy. That is why the function of the heart is to pump blood rather than to produce heart sounds, and the function of the kidney is to eliminate wastes rather than to keep the bladder full. It is the former effects, not the latter, which typically contribute to the organism's highest-level goals.

To some extent, however, these highest-level goals of organisms are indeterminate and must be determined by a biologist's interests. It is a feature of the Sommerhoff analysis that whenever goal G causes G' within the range of environmental changes for which an organism is directed to G, that organism is also directed to G'. This phenomenon occurs constantly in biology. Most behavior of organisms contributes simultaneously to individual survival, individual reproductive competence, survival of the species, survival of the genes, ecological equilibrium, and so forth. As a result, it appears that different subfields of biology (e.g., genetics and ecology) may use different goals as the focus of their function statements. But it is only the subfield of physiology whose functions seem relevant to health. On the basis of what appears in physiology texts, I suggest that these functions are, specifically, contributions to individual survival and reproduction. This assumption has definite consequences for our health concept and should therefore be kept in mind. Whatever goals are chosen, function statements will be value-free, since what makes a causal contribution to a biological goal is certainly an empirical matter.

3. *Reference class and species design.* We assume, then, that the physiological functions of a trait are causal contributions it makes to its bearer's survival and reproduction. For a definition of physiological function, we need at least one further qualification. Clearly physiological function statements are about a trait's *standard* contribution in some population or reference class, e.g. a species. A text may say that the function of the human lens is to focus light on the retina. This claim is not falsified by the existence of people with cataracts, or no lens at all. Similarly, one case of an animal's life being saved by some character would not be enough to make this effect a biological function. One squirrel might catch its tail in a crack *en route* to being run over by a car, but that would not make defense against cars a function of the squirrel tail. The statement about the human lens is true because it is overwhelmingly typical of members of the population for their lens to contribute to their survival and reproduction in that way. In general, function statements describe species or population characteristics, not any individual plant or animal.

As a result, the subject matter of comparative physiology is a series of ideal types of organisms: the frog, the hydra, the earthworm, the starfish, the crocodile, the shark, the rhesus monkey, and so on. The idealization is of course statistical, not moral or esthetic or normative in any other way. For each type a textbook provides a composite portrait of what I will call the *species design*, i.e. the typical hierarchy of interlocking functional systems that supports the life of organisms of that type. Each detail of this composite portrait is statistically normal within the species, though the portrait may not exactly resemble any species member. Possibly no individual frog is a perfect specimen of *rana pipiens*, since any frog is bound to be atypical in some respect and to have suffered the ravages of injury or disease. But the field naturalist abstracts from individual differences and from disease by averaging over a sufficiently large sample of the population. The species design that emerges is an empirical ideal which, I suggest, serves as the basis for health judgments in any species where we make such judgments.

It would be a mistake to think that this notion of a species design is inconsistent with evolutionary biology, which emphasizes constant variation. The typical result of evolution is precisely a trait's becoming established in a species, only rarely showing major variations under individual inheritance and environment. On all but evolutionary time scales, biological designs have a massive constancy vigorously maintained by normalizing selection. It is this short-term constancy on which the theory and practice of medicine rely. Medical diagnosis and treatment of, say, pancreatitis requires confidence that the patient is enough like other people to have a pancreas, located near the stomach, and secreting specific digestive enzymes that can attack the organ itself, producing such signs and symptoms as abdominal pain, diarrhea, weight loss, jaundice, hyperglycemia, and steatorrhea. Our species and others are in fact highly uniform in structure and function; otherwise there would be no point to the extreme detail in textbooks of human physiology. This uniformity of functional organization I call the species design. To deny its existence on Darwinian grounds would be to miss the forest for the trees.

Polymorphic functional traits, no one form of which is yet fixed in the population, can actually be included in the species design disjunctively. Thus it is typical of human blood to be either A or B or AB or O, typical of human irises to be either blue, brown, or green, typical of human skin to have some amount of pigmentation from small to great. But there are other intraspecific differences which cannot be handled disjunctively, and they are striking enough to generate several distinct species designs. These differences are of sex and age. Only a poor observer would be satisfied with noting that human beings typically have either ovaries or testicles, either wombs or penises, either large or small breasts, etc. The female characters occur together and constitute a single coherent functional design, as do the male's. Hence a disjunctive treatment of sex is inadequate. Less obviously in our species, functional design varies with age (Timiras, 1972). This phenomenon is unmistakable in species whose life stages are as dissimilar as caterpillars, pupas, and butterflies. But there are functions performed in the human infant and not in the adult, e.g. enlargement of the skeleton, and also the reverse, e.g. sperm production or ovulation. Thus species design seems to be relative both to sex and to age.

For these reasons, physiology should probably be viewed as making its statistical abstractions from reference classes smaller than species. In medical applications the operative class seems to be an age group of a sex of a species, e.g., human male neonates or, say, 7–9 year old girls. In other contexts, perhaps even in medicine itself, one would have to factor in race as well, since in some respects the different races have different functional designs. Despite this contraction of the reference class to a fraction of a species, the term "species design" is still convenient and seems unlikely to cause confusion.

4. *Normal functioning.* Our interest in species design is that we wish to analyze health as conformity to it. It will simplify the exposition to introduce first a notion of normal functioning, which will develop into our final analysis of health by two modifications. The two modifications are a shift from functioning to functional readiness (III.5) and a clause on environmental injuries (IV.2). But aside from details, the idea is that diseases are internal states that interfere with functions in the species design.

> *Normal functioning* in a member of the reference class is the performance by each internal part of all its statistically typical functions with at least statistically typical efficiency, i.e. at efficiency levels within or above some chosen central region of their population distribution.

Three comments are necessary on this definition. First, its final clause says "within or above" because superior functioning is consistent with health. The unusual cardiovascular ability of a long-distance runner is not a disease. Secondly, the definition tries to avoid confusion between different uses of "function". In one sense, sometimes used with clinical tests, a function is the concrete process that makes a physiological contribution, e.g. thyroid secretion. In this sense there can be too much thyroid function, i.e. hyperthyroidism. This is not our usage, since for us the function is the contribution to physiological goals, and too much thyroid secretion damages these goals as much as too little. To put it another way, the function of the thyroid is not merely to secrete hormones, but to secrete the right amount of them for current metabolic needs. For us there is no such thing as excessive function. But to keep the formulation unambiguous, I use the term "efficiency". What health always allows is unusual efficiency of a process in serving physiological goals, not unusually much of the process itself. The latter may be a disease. The population distribution to which the definition refers is the one for a function's efficiency. Abnormal functioning occurs when some function's efficiency falls more than a certain distance below the population mean. My third comment is that this distance can only be conventionally chosen, as in any application of statistical normality to a continuous distribution. The precise line between health and disease is usually academic, since most diseases involve functional deficits that are unusual by any reasonable standard.

I must now defend this claim that diseases involve interferences with normal functioning in the sense of the definition. It seems clearly true of any disease process serious enough to cause manifest illness. In such cases there are gross disturbances far enough up in the functional hierarchy that the patient feels their effect. Tuberculosis or emphysema, when actual illnesses, make respiration unusually ineffective. Cardiovascular diseases interfere with blood circulation and thereby greatly depress muscular function during physical activity. Common symptoms of acute illness such as fever, vomiting, and loss of appetite imply failures of such functions as temperature maintenance and digestion. And so on. The connection between overt illness and abnormal functioning, like the connection between overt illness and virtually every account of health ever proposed, is fairly clear without argument.

More significantly, latent or asymptomatic disease also seems to involve atypical functioning at lower levels of the functional hierarchy. Diabetes, whether or not it is evident to its bearer, consists of an unusual deficiency in insulin secretion and therefore in sugar metabolism. Hepatic cirrhosis, nephritis, pancreatic cancer, and countless other pieces of local pathology can progress for a long time without

depressing gross functions enough to be detected. They do, however, make standard tissue functions decline and fail in the affected part of the organ. Such localized dysfunction is also characteristic of the various minor skin diseases. To the biologist or physician, the skin is a highly versatile organ, with a complex structure designed for such functions as sensation, excretion, temperature regulation, and protection from environmental agents. In general, there is clearly some plausibility in the claim that the history of medical theory is nothing but a record of progressive investigation of normal functioning on the organismic, organic, histologic, cellular, and biochemical levels of organization, and of the increasingly subtle kinds of pathology this investigation reveals.

5. *Functional readiness.* With a small modification, normal functioning now becomes the analysis of health from the beginning of this section. The modification is required because biological functions are usually performed on appropriate occasions, not continuously. What occasions are appropriate is an empirical fact about the reference class. Thus vision occurs when the eyes are open, digestion when food is in the alimentary canal, adrenalin secretion under stress, sweating when temperature is rising, blood-clotting after a wound, and so on.

At any one time an organism might be functioning normally with respect to its current situation, yet be incapacitated from doing so on occasions yet to arise. It is then less than a perfect specimen of its species and so, by our original idea, not in perfect health. Medicine again seems to conform to this view. An inability to perform a function remains a disease even if the occasion to perform it never arises. Hemophiliacs who are protected from all injury, or diabetics who take daily insulin, are still diseased. One could, of course, say that what maintains functional readiness for the future, e.g. clotting factor in the blood, is itself a function in the present. But it seems clearer to replace the idea of normal functioning with normal functional ability or readiness. The change preserves all previous argument, since failure of function entails failure of functional readiness. The only effect of the revision is to count new conditions as diseases. So the result of the section is to support the following proposal.

1. The *reference class* is a natural class of organisms of uniform functional design; specifically, an age group of a sex of a species.

2. A *normal function* of a part or process within members of the reference class is a statistically typical contribution by it to their individual survival and reproduction.

3. *Health* in a member of the reference class is *normal functional ability*: the readiness of each internal part to perform all its normal functions on typical occasions with at least typical efficiency.

4. A *disease* is a type of internal state which impairs health, i.e., reduces one or more functional abilities below typical efficiency.

6. *Limits of the proposal*. Our guiding principle has been the species-relativity of health. We have supposed that the basic notion is "X is a healthy Y"—that it is by comparing X with its reference class Y that one distinguishes the way X does function from the way it ought to. This comparison presupposes enough uniformity in the species to generate a statistically typical species design. When the uniformity breaks down—as with polymorphic or continuously distributed traits like eye color, blood type, height, metabolism, body build—no one version of the trait can be required for health. Correspondingly, no version is a disease unless it depresses some function far below the group mean. As long as the efficiency of all functions exceeds a minimum, any value of these traits is as healthy as any other. In this way our definition allows variation within the normal, recognizing a wide range of individual differences of equal intrinsic health.

Thus our account abstracts from the intraspecific variability which is the raw material of evolutionary change. Judgments about what promotes species members' success in different environments are not, for us, judgments of intrinsic health. This seems inevitable in a definition of health as absence of disease, since medicine does not regard failure to be in the evolutionary vanguard as a disease. Diseases are, so to speak, failures to get as far as the rest of the species has been for millennia. On the other hand, some judgments about differential adaptation are judgments of instrumental health. Individual differences may be irrelevant to health in that none is a disease, but relevant in that they make a person more likely to get a disease under certain conditions. There is some evidence that even blood types carry different risks of various diseases, e.g. stomach cancer and diabetes.[10] There is no doubt that individual variations of body build affect the probability of cardiovascular disease or complications in childbirth.

IV. Successes and Failures of the Account

The last section proposed an empirical notion of the nature of a species, e.g. human nature, to explicate medical normality. In this section we will try to generalize about how well the explication works. The thesis that health is normal functioning is essentially a medical truism, some such formula appearing in many dictionaries. We merely specified the notion of function as biological and the notion of normality as statistical. As compared with other views, our proposal has at least the following advantages in fidelity to standard disease classifications.

1. *Successes*. First, it explains the divergence between judgments of disease and those of desirability or treatability. As we noted, some undesirable conditions but not others are diseases. Hemophilia is, while an inability to

regenerate severed limbs or damaged brain tissue is not. The reason seems clear: blood-clotting in wounds is a typical human function, limb and brain regeneration are not. If we were one of the species that regenerate their limbs, a person lacking this ability would undoubtedly count as diseased. Similarly, health requires a person to manufacture insulin but not vitamin C, since our species does make one and not the other.[11] Controlled diabetes remains a disease; to control scurvy is to eliminate it. Partial color blindness is probably fatal to fewer people each year than smell blindness to carbon monoxide, but the former is still a disease and the latter is not. It is hard to imagine explaining these judgments without appeal to what is typical of the human species. Our account further explains why a condition once a disease is always so, regardless of its harmful, neutral, or beneficial effects in an individual case. Cowpox, myopia, and hemophilia are diseases because they involve functioning below the species norm, but the effect of a deficit varies with a person's situation.

Second, our account seems to capture the medical view of traits with a continuous distribution in the population. It provides a unified treatment of *extremal diseases*, i.e. those associated with the tails of a statistical distribution. Its appeal to function explains why the spectrum of some traits contains two extremal diseases (hyperemia and anemia, hyperthyroidism and hypothyroidism, galactorrhea and agalactia) and that of others only one (night blindness, mental deficiency). At the same time, its appeal to statistics yields a reasonable level of minimal normal function. Night blindness is an unusual inferiority to the species norm for night vision; we do not all suffer from it by virtue of failing to meet the standard set by cats. At bottom, according to our account, all diseases are extremal diseases. Above the minimal level of normal functions, our view also matches medicine by making individual differences consistent with present health, and at the same time differentially relevant to future health in a given environment.

Third, our view makes health judgments independent of the gross output of the organism. It recognizes latent asymptomatic diseases like intestinal polyps, and other minor diseases like eczema which may have no effect on a person's overall ability to function. It also recognizes that the same effect on gross output may or may not be produced by a disease. Thus a man unable to lift a heavy weight may be either a normal individual or a strong man with Addison's disease. If the disease were a stable condition, the two states, normal musculature and underlying disease, could be equally undesirable, equally disabling, equally maladaptive, and so on through most accounts of the nature of health. Our account explains the difference by pointing to the abnormality of a microfunction, adrenocortical secretion, in Addison's disease. The distinction between normal variation and underlying disease is one of the most important features of medical theory, though in practice it is often hard to draw because so much clinical evidence is gross output.

Fourth, our view explains how biologists can apply the notion of disease so readily to animals and plants, and why its application by veterinarians to commercial animals does not simply reflect commercial interests. What a healthy hen or cow is like is a biological fact; it is not an economic one.

Finally, for reasons sketched at the end of **I**, our account explains the partial successes of others. Organisms being what they are, important breakdowns of internal functions, homeostatic or otherwise, tend to be signaled by discomfort, to disturb the abilities on which the organism's adaptation to its environment rests and hence, in our case, to be judged bad. But these ideas seem too broad-gauged to follow medical judgments of disease into the fine structure of human physiology. To penetrate that structure, the notion of normal functioning on every level of organization is ideal. We have also given this notion enough content that its success cannot be ascribed to its vacuity. On the contrary, our account excludes at least two classes of recognized diseases.

2. *First anomaly: structural diseases.* The first class of diseases our account excludes are the entries in the Nomenclature that seem to be purely structural disorders. Some cases of this sort may have dysfunctional varieties or be included on the assumption that the affected part has an unknown function. Examples are congenital absence of the appendix, perhaps dextrocardia, and calcification of the pineal gland. But the Nomenclature also lists minor deformities, especially of the nose, the ear, and, mysteriously, the hymen. Many of these deformities disturb no normal function, and there may also be some internal tumors of which the same is true.

One might wonder why these structural disorders cannot be handled by making the whole disease concept structural rather than functional. Certainly physicians have a working assumption that structural abnormalities underlie functional ones, i.e. that pathology underlies disease. An empirical notion of normal structure could be derived from the reference class in the same way as our normal functioning. Unfortunately such an account would count superior as well as inferior functioning as disease, since structural abnormality occurs in one as much as the other. Thus it seems that no correct account can make structural deviation a sufficient condition of disease. As a necessary condition it is redundant and would not help with the problem of deformity. Despite the few structural disorders in the Nomenclature, therefore—and the tendency of reference works to define health by formulas like "the structural and functional integrity of the human body"[12]— it is hard to see how structure plays any direct role in the concept of disease. The contrary evidence may illustrate the power of the species-design idea over the medical mind, even where species-typical structure loses all connection with function. Major deformities and tumors involve deviations from the functional design as well as the structural one. Some of the minor ones, e.g. macacus ear or absence of the earlobe, may appear in the Nomenclature for convenience in record-keeping. Any structural disorders that do not fit these two categories remain as anomalies in an otherwise intelligible scheme of classification.

3. *Second anomaly: universal diseases.* Another way in which our definition diverges from medical usage is by excluding some universal diseases. Dental caries, lung irritation, atherosclerosis, and benign hypertrophy of the prostate in old men are diseases typical of the whole population or a sex or age group. It is clear that medicine is prepared to view the entire reference class as functioning abnormally. On the other hand, such cases are so few that it is hard to decide among various explanations. To begin with, our definition already covers some universal diseases. For normal functioning it required every body part to function in its typical way. Because of this requirement, which was introduced to handle local pathology with no systemic effects, the only problem arises when everyone has the same disease in the same location. Dental caries are vitiligo of the teeth, conceptually speaking, and atheromas may be vitiligo of the arteries. Unless there are specific body locations which are typically carious or atheromatous, these conditions are diseases on our account. The universal diseases which violate the definition seem to be those which are evenly distributed, e.g. lung irritation due to environmental pollution or arterial thickening after a certain age.

These remaining cases seem to show that the above explanation is, if not sophistical, inadequate to understanding the medical acceptance of universal disease. The case of lung irritation suggests that we might revise our definition of health to count all environmental injuries diseases. I favor this modification because it is an obvious extension of the principle that normality lies in the nature of a species. If one is after a species design, one would wish to subtract limitations on functional ability directly caused by environmental agents, leaving only the inherent defects of the organism itself. It is common in biology to draw such a distinction of degree between external and internal causation; this is done, for example, whenever a trait is said to be under genetic control. Perhaps the change might be made as follows:

> 3. A *disease* is a type of internal state which is either an impairment of normal functional ability, i.e. a reduction of one or more functional abilities below typical efficiency, or a limitation on functional ability caused by environmental agents.
>
> 4. *Health* is the absence of disease.

The revised definition covers conditions like lung irritation and provides an alternate explanation of tooth decay. What there cannot be, on this view, is a universal genetic disease.

Exactly that, however, may be implied whenever medical authors list progressive dysfunctions of normal aging as diseases. When senile decline of function is caused from within, our account will not allow it to be a disease. That is because of the age-relativity which we built into the account to reflect differences between child and adult. Apart from childhood, one might be tempted to take the adult as the species type and old age as its disintegration. Yet the same functional limitations viewed as diseases in old age may count as normal in childhood. Much of senility is only regression to earlier stages of development. The puzzle is why old age is not always seen as a stage with its own statistical norms of healthy functioning. Lacking a solution to this puzzle, our account ends up differing from some medical sources over whether minor deformities and normal aging constitute disease.

It would be a mistake, I think, to take such differences to invalidate our general approach to defining health. Instead they should be viewed as anomalies deserving continued analysis. The best course, I think, is to continue trying to accommodate the anomalies within our view or to find another view of comparable explanatory power. If both efforts fail, a reasonable conclusion is that minor deformities and aging do not fit the traditional medical conception of disease.

Notes

1   Engelhardt 1975, p. 137.
2   The results of the present paper are applied to mental health in Boorse (1975, 1976).
3   Two excellent guides to the clinical literature, with emphasis on mental health, are Jahoda's *Current Concepts of Positive Mental Health* (1958) and Offer and Sabshin's *Normality* (1966). Philosophers who have written extensively on health and disease include Engelhardt (1975, 1976, 1977), Flew (1973), Macklin (1972, 1973), and Margolis (1966, 1969, 1976).
4   The pathology of a disease is its morbid anatomy, i.e. the structural changes in body tissues that underlie its signs and symptoms. "Pathological", however, can be a synonym for "diseased" and "abnormal". The two usages are related by the medical assumption that every disease has some pathology, known or unknown.
5   Ryle 1947, pp. 3, 4.
6   The difference between homeostasis and goal-directedness is discussed by Sommerhoff (1950, pp. 196–197).
7   According to the historical sketch in World Health Organization (1967), the broad usage dates back at least to 1855. In that year William Farr, the first official British medical statistician, employed it in his proposal to the Paris Congress. It would be interesting to have further information on its history.
8   Despite such concessions, in hospital record-keeping the *Nomenclature* lost out to a version of the *International Statistical Classification* (World Health Organization, 1967), which proved more efficient. The introduction repeatedly stresses that a statistical classification does not try to be a nomenclature. Perhaps the *Nomenclature* should not have tried to be a statistical classification.
9   Temkin 1973, p. 398; cf. Moravcsik 1976.

10   Smith 1968, p. 245.
11   Dobzhansky 1962, p. 43.
12   Szasz 1960, p. 114.

References

Bernard, C. Introduction to the Study of Experimental Medicine. Translated by H. C. Green. New York: Dover, 1957.

Boorse, C. On the distinction between disease and illness. Philosophy and Public Affairs, (Fall 1975) 5: 49–68.

Boorse, C. Wright on functions. Philosophical Review, 85 (1976): 70–86.

Boorse, C. What a theory of mental health should be. Journal for the Theory of Social Behaviour, 6 (1976): 61–84.

Braithwaite, R. B. Scientific Explanation. New York: Harper, 1960.

Cannon, W. B. The Wisdom of the Body. New York: Norton, 1939.

Dobzhansky, T. Mankind Evolving. New Haven: Yale, 1962.

Dubos, R. Mirage of Health. New York: Harper, 1959.

Engelhardt, H. T., Jr. The concepts of health and disease. In Evaluation and Explanation in the Biomedical Sciences. Edited by Engelhardt and Spicker. Dordrecht: Reidel, 1975.

Engelhardt, H. T., Jr. Ideology and Etiology. Journal of Medicine and Philosophy, 1 (1976): 256–68.

Engelhardt, H. T., Jr. Is there a philosophy of medicine? In PSA 1976². Edited by Suppe and Asquith. East Lansing: Philosophy of Science Association, 1977. Quotation from pre-publication manuscript.

Flew, A. Crime or Disease? New York: Barnes and Noble, 1973.

Grim, P. Further notes on functions. Analysis, 37 (1977): 169–76.

Hartmann, H. Ego Psychology and the Problem of Adaptation. Translated by D. Rapaport. New York: International Universities Press, 1958.

Hudson, R. P. The Concept of Disease. Annals of Internal Medicine, 65 (1966): 595–601.

Jahoda, M. Current Concepts of Positive Mental Health. New York: Basic Books, 1958.

Macklin, R. Mental health and mental illness: Some problems of definition and concept formation. Philosophy of Science, 39 (1972): 341–65.

Macklin, R. The medical model in psychotherapy and psychoanalysis, Comprehensive Psychiatry 14 (1973): 49–69.

Margolis, J. Psychotherapy and Morality. New York: Random House, 1966.

Margolis, J. Illness and medical values. The Philosophy Forum, 8 (1969): 55–76.

Margolis, J. The concept of disease. Journal of Medicine and Philosophy, 1 (1976): 238–55.

McCombs, R. P., Fundamentals of Internal Medicine, 4th ed. Chicago: Year Book Medical Publishers, 1971.

Moravcsik, J. Ancient and modern conceptions of health and medicine. Journal of Medicine and Philosophy, 1 (1976): 337–48.

Nagel, E. The Structure of Science. New York: Harcourt, Brace and World, 1961.

Offer, D. & Sabshin, M. Normality. New York: Basic Books, 1966.

Ryle, J. A. The meaning of normal. Lancet, 252 (1947): 1–5.

Smith, A. The Body. New York: Walker, 1968.

Sommerhoff, G. Analytical Biology. London: Oxford, 1950.

Sorabji, R. Function. Philosophical Quarterly, 14 (1964): 289–302.

Szasz, T. S. The myth of mental illness. American Psychologist, 15 (1960): 113–118.

Temkin, O. Health and disease. In Dictionary of the History of Ideas, 2, 395–407. New York: Scribner's, 1973.

Timiras, P. S. Developmental Physiology and Aging. New York: Macmillan, 1972.

Wimsatt, W. C. Teleology and the logical structure of function statements. Studies in History and Philosophy of Science, 3 (1972): 1–80.

World Health Organization. Manual of the International Statistical Classification of Diseases, Injuries, and Causes of Death. Eighth revision. Geneva: WHO, 1967.

Chapter 32

Ron Amundson

AGAINST NORMAL FUNCTION

The concept of normality has been the target of criticism in recent years. Social critics claim that the term carries ideological baggage. Describing individuals or groups as "abnormal" is seen as marginalizing them by use of a falsely objective criterion. This paper will continue that tradition. It will examine the concept of *normal function*, said by many philosophers to be objectively grounded in the practice of biological and biomedical science. This concept is used in discussions of health care policy, quality-of-life assessments, and even radical "treatments" such as assisted suicide. The core of this paper will be an examination of the biological legitimacy of the concept of functional normality. Social concerns aside, does current biology imply a concept of functional normality, and a distinction between normal and abnormal function? I will argue that it does not. In the last sections of the paper I will introduce the social context of this issue, emphasizing the disadvantages experienced by people whose function is assessed as abnormal. I will distinguish between the *level* of an individual's functional performance and the *mode* or style by which that performance is achieved. This distinction will help reveal that the doctrine of biological normality is itself one aspect of a social prejudice against certain functional modes or styles. The disadvantages experienced by people who are assessed as "abnormal" derive not from biology, but from implicit social judgments

about the acceptability of certain kinds of biological variation.

1. Normality as Race

We humans have innumerable ways of categorizing ourselves, of managing the variation among us. Some but not all of these categories are taken to reflect a biological reality. Differences between men and women are believed to be biologically real in a way that differences between Lutherans and Catholics are not. Until quite recently the category of *race* was taken to reflect biological reality. There were scientific debates about the number of human races, the characteristics that typify each race, and whether races were incipient species. Racial traits were invoked to explain the differences in accomplishment among groups of people, and the dominance of some groups over others.

During this century the assumption that races are biologically real has been called into question. Biologists no longer see race as a biological category (Lewontin, 1995; Marks, 1995; AAPA, 1996). There is more variation within the traditionally named races (Caucasian, Negroid, etc.) than between them. The tradition of naming races, assigning individuals to them, and then treating individuals differently depending on their racial assignment had no factual basis in biology. Today the study of "race" is a study of the far-reaching social consequences of that old, biologically confused tradition. We were not carving nature at its joints when we partitioned human variability into races.

I consider the concept of *normal function* to be similar to the traditional concept of race. Like the concept of race, the concept of biological normality is invoked to explain certain socially significant differences, such as unemployment and segregation. Like the concept of race, the concept of normality is a biological error. The partitioning of human variation into the normal versus the abnormal has no firmer biological footing than the partitioning into races. Diversity of function is a fact of biology.

2. Functional Determinism and Naturalism about Disease

The topic of biological normality is related to a philosophical debate on the concept of disease. Naturalists consider disease to be a straightforward, non-evaluative, theoretical concept within the sciences of medicine and physiology. Normativists consider disease concepts to embody evaluative judgments of the conditions designated as diseases. Much of the present paper is an argument for the normativity of the concept of functional normality, at least as the concept is currently used. Naturalists and normativists agree that certain disease concepts in the past ("diseases" such as homosexuality and masturbation) were ideologically tainted. The difference is that naturalists believe that such taint can be avoided by careful science, and normativists do not. My purpose is to show that the normative taint is not avoided in current discussions of biological normality.

Christopher Boorse's Biostatistical Theory (BST) of disease is the most influential naturalistic account (Boorse, 1975, 1997). It provides a foundation in the philosophy of science for most of the writers on health care ethics discussed in Section 7 and Section 8. Boorse uses a technical definition of disease that covers such conditions as blindness, paralysis, and limb loss.

My interest is in these permanent and stable conditions, commonly called disabilities, rather than in the more episodic or life-threatening conditions commonly called diseases (e.g. measles and cancer). Boorse's account of disease is founded on the concept of biological normality. Normativists have challenged the biological foundation of Boorse's theory, but they mostly question his definition of disease in terms of biological normality. They do not challenge the concept of biological normality itself.[1] If my critique of normality is forceful, it will presumably have implications for Boorse's account of disease, but I will not explore those implications here. Boorse's naturalism about normality can be seen in the background assumptions behind two definitions:

(1) The *reference class* is a natural class of organisms of uniform functional design; specifically, an age group of a sex of a species.

(2) A *normal function* of a part or process within members of the reference class is a statistically typical contribution by it to their individual survival and reproduction.[2]

Points 3 and 4 in this list go on to define "disease" as reduction in normal function, and "health" as the absence of disease. The expressions "typical contribution to … survival and reproduction" and "species typical function" are used by Boorse and his followers as synonyms for *normal function*. In this paper I will use the term "typical" not as a synonym for "normal", but in the colloquial sense of common, usual, or frequent. On my usage a "typical" trait may be merely the least unusual, and an atypical trait need not be abnormal. This convention allows the discussion of typical and atypical traits without assuming that they are respectively normal and abnormal. It should also be noted that, as with other quasi-statistical uses of the concept of normality, abnormality is usually to be read as subnormality. Better-than-average function is not usually labeled as abnormal even though it is statistically atypical.

Boorse's two definitions imply that natural species have a certain statistical characteristic: the variations of function among their members is sufficiently narrow to justify a dichotomy between normality and abnormality based on the distribution alone. Obviously not all species members function in exactly the same way. We can treat them as if they do by labeling as abnormal any non-conforming species members. This labeling is statistically justified only if the bell curve of functional design is very steep, i.e. there are many uniformly designed individuals and only a few scattered individuals with novel functional design. I will refer to this statistical claim about functional diversity within species as *functional determinism*. I will challenge the claim, and argue that the facts of functional variation do not support functional determinism.

Boorse and other functional determinists recognize the existence of at least some "normal" variation. "[T]he BST can accommodate normal polymorphisms, and, of course, admits normal statistical variation . . .".[3] Eye color and blood type are customarily cited as examples of normal variation. Boorse gives no account of how normal variation is differentiated from abnormal variation. One suspects that normal variation simply means *functionally equivalent* variation, like eye color and blood type. No examples are given of functionally distinct but still normal variation.

To set the stage, let us dissect functional determinism a bit. It is useful to distinguish between the *level of performance* of a function and the *mode* of its performance.[4] Functional mode is the manner in which a functional outcome or performance is achieved. Performance level is the quantitative degree of the functional performance, such as the speed or the strength of a motion. In addition, we can identify functions at different organizational levels of the biological hierarchy.[5] Functions can be seen as occurring at genetic and physiological levels of the hierarchy, at the level of limb movements, and even in ecological interactions (e.g. "obtain food"). Whatever the hierarchical level,

functional determinism states that functions take place in a uniform mode at a relatively uniform performance level by a statistically distinctive portion of the members of a species. These are the normals.

Discussion of functional determinism will consider information from evolutionary biology, developmental biology, physiology, and anatomy. First, evolution.

3. Darwin

Variation among individuals in a species can be seen as arising from two sources. One is the genetic variation that exists in all natural species, and on which natural selection operates. The other is developmental plasticity, the variability of the traits that an organism actually develops during its lifetime due to influences other than its genome. From an evolutionary perspective, this distinction is rather artificial. It is a version of the infamous nature/nurture contrast. Developmental plasticity itself evolves by natural selection, and genomes only determine phenotypic traits within the context of developmental plasticity. But for present purposes I will treat nature and nurture as distinct. This section will deal with heritable variation in natural populations, and what modern evolutionary theory has to say about it. The following section will discuss developmental plasticity.

Current evolutionary theory considers natural species to contain very large amounts of heritable variation. This contradicts certain earlier doctrines about "pure lines" and "the wild type", that considered natural species to be relatively genetically homogenous. The first influential proponent of the modern view was Theodosius Dobzhansky.[6] Based on his beliefs in high degrees of genetic variation, Dobzhansky had this to say about normality: "The use of the word 'normal' poses a semantic problem. No end of misconceptions and lax thinking is caused by the belief in something called 'normal man' or 'normal human nature' ".[7] Is the

Darwinian view of rich ranges of variation consistent with the notion of a determinate species design?

Boorse and Robert Wachbroit recognize and comment on the contrast between the Darwinian doctrine of variability and their own doctrines of a determinate species design. Both acknowledge that functional determinism might be seen as a typological or essentialistic theory, and so as antithetical to Darwinian population thinking. Wachbroit argues that biological normality is theoretically grounded in biomedical science. He appears simply to accept the contrast with Darwinian evolution in his comment that "tensions between established scientific doctrines are not uncommon".[8] He does seem to attempt a reconciliation, however: "Of course, some variations will be abnormal from the perspective of physiology, while others, understood in evolutionary terms, will be ascribed to speciation, where variation constitutes a different, not abnormal, physiology" (ibid.). If this is intended as a reconciliation, it is unsuccessful. Variation is not confined to speciation events in evolutionary biology. Variation is ubiquitous. It is always "different, not abnormal" simply because there is no Darwinian interpretation of abnormality.

Boorse makes more detailed comments on the tension. One response is similar to Wachbroit's; the BST analysis is based on contemporary physiology, and any typology comes from the present state of the science.[9] A second is the assertion that evolution typically drives traits to fixation in a species, and the traits thereafter are kept from varying by normalizing selection (a very aptly named phenomenon if this is what it accomplishes). A third is that essentialism usually involves a claim about the causal powers of the essential traits, and the BST has no such implications.

I will briefly comment on these defenses in turn. First, current physiology may not be as typological as the determinists believe. And if it is, it might well be wrong in its typology. These points will be argued in Section 6. Second, I am willing to consider it an open empirical question whether evolution results in the kind of functional uniformity that would license normality definitions. Frankly I doubt it, but theoretical considerations do not suffice to answer the question. Third, I agree that the concept of normality invokes no essentialist causal powers, in that the functional type does not explain biological form. I am concerned, however, that once the concept is introduced and reified, it is itself used in causal explanations of social phenomena. It is used to explain and rationalize the social disadvantages of people labeled abnormal.

My own opinions about the tension between evolution theory and functional determinism tend towards those of David Hull. Hull argues that no set of traits can be constructed so as to characterize all and only members of a natural species, that species are rife with variation, and that this is an unavoidable outcome of Darwinian biology. ". . . [A]ttempts to argue away this state of affairs by reference to 'potentiality' and 'normality' have little if any foundation in biology".[10] I doubt, however, that the refutation of functional determinism can be achieved on the basis of evolutionary theory alone. Evolution is a process that gave rise to tapeworms and elephants. It could surely give rise to species members as functionally alike as paper clips, and to species members as functionally diverse as . . . well, as human beings.

If we base our estimate of functional diversity on genetic diversity, there seems to be plenty available in the human species. Studies of a group of over four hundred distinct species of cichlid fishes in Lake Victoria have shown that there is less genetic variation among the cichlid species than within the single species Homo sapiens. The four hundred cichlid species show wide variations in functional organization (Stiassny and Meyer, 1999). So one cannot argue that human beings share a single functional design based on the lack of genetic variance.

High genetic variance creates at least a potential, if not a proof, of functional variability. Evidence from developmental biology gives further evidence of variability.

4. Developmental Plasticity and Integration

Boorse recently explicated his naturalistic concept of health by connecting it with the concept of the goal-directedness of life processes.[11] He takes goal-directedness to be expressed in the notion of *species design*. I agree with the goal-directedness of life, but I consider Boorse's version of it unnecessarily narrow. Functional determinism does not follow from life's goal-directedness. In fact, certain goal-directed biological processes make the notion of a determinate design seem presumptuous.

Two pre-evolutionary concepts of teleology illustrate the contrast between my preferred notion of goal-directedness and Boorse's. Functional determinism was anticipated in the tradition of British natural theology, with William Paley as the traditional spokesperson. Body parts of an organism are specifically designed to adapt the organism to its environment, and each member of a species is functionally identical. A contrasting pre-evolutionary sense of teleology existed in the Continental tradition of developmental morphology. Teleology was seen not in the external fit of the organism into its environment, but in the internal directedness of the processes of embryological development.

The Kantian concept of biological directedness focuses on the processes of embryological, ontogenetic development, which are directed towards the development of functioning adults. These processes are remarkably plastic and resilient to perturbation. If the genome actually were a set of blueprints or instructions for building a body, as some modern metaphors have it, the slightest perturbation would throw off the end result. Any embryo that could not be built to fit

the determinate design would be non-viable. But in fact functioning adults can develop in an indefinitely large number of ways. The goal-directedness seen in developmental plasticity renders the concept of *species design* highly suspect. Development yields adults that *function*, but not adults that *function identically*. Functional diversity is a product of developmental plasticity.

The processes of ontogeny bring about the functional integration of the organism. As various body parts and systems develop, they adjust to each other. This integration occurs during the development of every organism, whether the organism is destined to be statistically typical or atypical of its species. The lens of the eye is not determined to develop in the location it does by its position on some genetic blueprint. Rather, the already-formed optic vesicle induces the ectoderm that overlays it to differentiate into the lens (after an earlier and more complex series of tissue interactions).[12] If some trauma happened to relocate an optic vesicle to an unusual position on the head, lens induction would still proceed and result in a functioning eye. A more familiar aspect of developmental plasticity is the ontogenetic adaptation of an organism to its external environment. Development of use-enlarged muscles and protective calluses are customary examples of this kind of phenomenon.

These facts of developmental biology do not conclusively refute functional determinism. But they do make it seem unnecessary. A non-typical but viable phenotype is not *broken* by its failure to comply with some imagined blueprint for its species. It will function anyhow, in spite of its atypicality. It will owe its function to the same developmental processes of integration and adaptation responsible for the function of typical organisms of its species. Section 5 will list several examples of developmental plasticity that challenge functional determinism. I will later argue that the kind of functional diversity that follows from developmental plasticity is also an ordinary part of everyday life.

5. Examples of Developmental Plasticity

5.1 Slipjer's Goat

In the 1940s the biologist E. J. Slipjer studied a goat that was born without forelegs.[13, 14] The goat learned to walk bipedally, showing that individuals of the same species can perform a function like walking using different means. But this is not the whole significance of the example. Slipjer's goat had many other deformities (relative to the statistical norm) in its skeletal and muscular anatomy. It had an S-shaped spine, an atypically broad neck, many atypically shaped bones and atypically positioned muscles. Its thorax was oval shaped, unlike the V-shaped cross section of the typical goat. By this census of 'abnormalities' it was a radical departure from its species design, and each abnormality pulls it further from the norm. By the species design criterion of goal-directedness, Slipjer's goat was a notable failure. By the developmental criterion it was a roaring success. The goat's skeletal and muscular abnormalities were, each of them, adaptively suited for life as a biped. They mimic the body conformation of kangaroos and humans.

Slipjer's goat illustrates the inadequacy of the metaphor of the genetic blueprint. Ontogenetic processes are epigenetic. The genome provides developmental resources for ontogeny; it is not a preformed image of the adult body (Nijhout, 1990). "No one would maintain that goats have genes for developing an S-shaped spine, 'just in case'. What we see here is a basic mammalian potential emerging from the self-righting properties of the skeleto-muscular systems of all mammals, and the sort exploited by our hominid ancestors".[15] Many of the mechanisms that gave rise to the bipedal goat are well understood.

These secondary modifications occurred because muscles which are used grow bigger, tendons grow along lines of tension, bone grows along lines of compression, and so on.

The relevance of such developmental flexibility is that a single major change—for example the loss of the forelegs—instead of being a disaster may be compatible with life.[16]

It is important to recognize that the self-righting properties of the mammalian developmental system are not emergency measures that only kick in when pathology is present. They are exactly the same processes involved in the generation of more typical quadrapedal goats and bipedal humans under different circumstances. Without these morphogenetic processes, well-functioning mammals would never develop at all. Biological "types" are unified not by the functional identity of their eventual phenotypes, or the common blueprint from which they were built. Rather they are unified by their shared developmental processes. These processes generate phenotypes that are functionally diverse, both between and within species.

5.2 Is Your Brain Really Necessary?

Hydrocephaly can lead to profound physical and mental disabilities. A backup of cerebrospinal fluid causes the ventricles of the brain to balloon to many times their usual size. The resulting pressure leads to enlargement of the cranium and/or reduction in the volume of brain tissue. In the most severe category, ventricle expansion fills 95% of the cranium. This category includes some profoundly disabled people. But half of this severely affected group has IQs over 100.[17] Usually associated with spina bifida, hydrocephaly can also occur subclinically in people who show no signs of abnormal function. The people in the subclinical category have heads of average or slightly above average size. In an article entitled "Is Your Brain Really Necessary?" Roger Lewin describes a University student in the UK who has an IQ measured at 126, a normal social life, and "virtually no brain". He was tested only because his professor was familiar with a colleague's ongoing study of subclinical hydrocephaly, and the student had a large head. The student was functionally indistinguishable from his colleagues, but had no more than 10% of the average person's brain tissue. Accounts of similar phenomena are common in medical literature. "[A] substantial proportion of patients appear to escape functional impairment in spite of grossly abnormal brain structure" (*ibid.*). The mode of function of these persons is statistically "abnormal", even though their level of performance is statistically average.

5.3 How to Handicap a Basketball Player

The sport of wheelchair basketball began during World War II and has steadily increased in popularity and competitiveness. Variation in physical ability among players is extensive, with large differences in arm and abdomen musculature, and in upper body balance in two planes. In order to allow fair competition among players with different physical abilities, a system of ranking of players was devised. Rankings go from 1 to 3 points, with more points assigned to players with more upper body control. Teams are allowed to have no more than a specified number of ranking points on the court at one time. In this way a skilled but more disabled player can be of more value to a team than a less disabled player. (This is "handicapping" in the original sporting sense of the term. Less disabled players have to carry the handicap of a higher point ranking.) A medical committee originally administered the ranking system, with medical specialists assigning ranks based on physical examinations of each athlete. Athletes were ranked by their usable musculature, based on the assumption that athletes with identical musculature would function identically. The results were unsatisfactory. Medical assessments of the athletes did not match their performance on the court. Athletes that were judged equal in

physical ability by the doctors were seen to differ significantly by the players and coaches. With much resistance from the medical committee, the sport switched over to a system of assessment based on observation of actual on-court performance (Craven, 1990). The assumption that *mode* of function determined *level* of performance was falsified. Different athletes achieved different performances with the same musculature. For example, some athletes with a given abdominal muscular loss achieved balance in the lateral plane, and some did not. Conversely, athletes who achieved the same function did so by different modes. Athletes who possessed the typical musculature for achieving lateral balance did so in a different way from those with atypical musculatures. Clearly the athletes with high function but low musculature were achieving their performance via a different mode from their similarly-ranked but differently-muscled competitors.

5.4 Signed Languages

Since about 1960 two major innovations have modified our understanding of human language. The first, begun by Noam Chomsky (1966), is the notion that human natural languages are extremely highly structured in hierarchical levels of organization, and are acquired by means unlike the learning of other human skills and abilities. Chomsky and others believe that major aspects of language learning are hardwired into our cognitive equipment. The second innovation, begun by William Stokoe (1960), is the realization that the sign languages used within many deaf communities are themselves natural human languages. They are not mere pidgins, or signal systems, or substitutes for 'real' (spoken) language. They have the full structural complexity, and the cognitive and expressive powers of spoken languages. It has even been shown that brain injuries that cause certain kinds of aphasias in spoken languages have similar affects on signed languages (Poizner *et al.*, 1987).

It has not been widely recognized what an incongruous pair of doctrines these two are. The ability to learn language is as innate to, and as distinctive of the human species as any biological trait. Modern linguistic analyses of spoken languages are strongly tied to phonology, the perceptual analysis of spoken sounds. Nevertheless, it turns out that human language can be manifested in a completely distinct sensory and performance modality, namely manual gesture. Unless modern linguistics is grossly mistaken, there exists *some* human capacity specific to the learning of language. In statistically typical humans (those of average hearing abilities growing up in typical linguistic environments) this capacity gives rise to a spoken language. But the capacity cannot be purely the capacity for *spoken* language, because the same capacity also gives rise to signed languages in a minority of people (those growing up in signing environments). It is as if we were to discover a population of honeybees that were unable to secrete wax, but built fully functional honeycombs out of clay they dredged from river bottoms.

There are two ways of interpreting this anomaly. First, the language capacity might actually be innately and evolutionarily tied to vocal sound, as has usually been assumed. If this is so, then humans have an astonishing flexibility in applying an innate capacity to a domain that is foreign to it. Second, the language capacity might not be innately tied to vocal sound at all, but be abstract enough to apply indiscriminately to signed or spoken language. This has very intriguing evolutionary implications (Armstrong *et al.*, 1994). Neither case gives any succor to functional determinists. In the first case, developmental plasticity greatly dilutes any claim of the privilege of normality for spoken language. In the second, both language modalities are equally "normal" insofar as biology is concerned.

Ian Hacking dates the origin of the concept of normality to the rise of statistics in the nineteenth century. He says that normality ". . . uses

a power as old as Aristotle to bridge the fact/value distinction, whispering in your ear that what is normal is also right".[18] There was no time lost in exploiting this shortcut between facts and values. Many nineteenth-century educators of deaf people used the new concept of statistical normality to suppress a highly functional minority adaptation.[19] In certain schools deaf children were forbidden to use sign. They were trained according to a doctrine called "oralism". They were taught to lip-read and to speak aloud, two skills that are extremely difficult to learn and of marginal value for most profoundly deaf individuals. Biology, then as now, gives no legitimacy to this practice. Lip-reading and speaking may be useful to a deaf signer in a crowd of English speakers, but no more so than sign would be useful to a non-signing English speaker in a crowd of signers.

In summary, the goal-directed processes of biological development are not finely tuned towards the production of functionally identical species members. Their inherent flexibility can be expected to generate a rich diversity of functional modes.

6. Physiology and Anatomy

Recall that Boorse and Wachbroit claim that contemporary medicine and physiology imply functional determinism, even if it is not implied by evolutionary biology. We will now consider dissenting opinions, two criticisms of the concept of normality taken from within the sciences of physiology and anatomy. Each concludes that the range of functional variability is too wide to justify a concept of biological normality.

Jiří Vácha has written a series of papers on the notion of normality of physiological function (Vácha, 1978, 1982, 1985). Like other authors (e.g. Davis and Bradley, 1996) Vácha emphasizes the multiplicity of meanings for "normality" in medicine, and especially the "intermingling of normality in the statistical and value sense, which is typical of current practice".[20] He considers the common use of "normality" to be typological and idealistic in that it assumes that "the frequent [is] the [normal] and, besides that, the healthy".[21] A part of this idealism is the unstated assumption that health and illness are distinct alternative body states. In fact there is a multidimensional continuum of states of health. The health/illness and normal/abnormal dichotomies are illusions. A high degree of variability exists among individuals on any physiological measurement, with even the most extreme values found within healthy individuals. Extreme values of physiological parameters, associated with disease in some individuals, are compensated for in others. Indeed, the constellation of other parameters in an individual may directly require the extremeness of a particular character for good health. "Immense variability has been found in the manner in which individuals in the population attain health".[22] Functional integration at the physiological level gives rise to a range of differently functioning, but comparably successful physiological systems. Physiological analogs to Slipjer's goat are walking among us.

Vácha, following the German medical theorist L. R. Grote, suggests that the concept of species normality be replaced by a concept of individual normality or "responsiveness". Rather than testing a patient's statistical conformity, medical judgments should assess

> that congruence between physiological performance of the individual and the performance necessary for him. . . . An individual may be healthy—responsive—without regard to the quality or quantity of the morphology and function which the statistical norm would wish to prescribe for him.[23]

Notice that the concept of responsiveness (individual normality) abandons the statistical and comparative basis of normality, replacing it with an assessment of the relation between individual performance and needs. There is no need for a species design.

Variation in human anatomy is the subject of a remarkable Internet document-in-progress entitled *Illustrated Encyclopedia of Human Anatomic Variation* (Bergman et al., 1992–1998). Part I, "The Muscular System", is complete at this writing. Additional sections on the skeletal, cardiovascular, nervous, and organ systems are in progress. The document summarizes medical reports since antiquity on observed variations in human musculature, categorized by specific muscle and muscle group. There is no easy way to summarize the richness of variation; one must browse the reports on individual muscle groups. These authors show no patience with labels of normality. Any variation consistent with viability is accepted as 'normal' ". . . however imperfect or monstrous by Galen's and Vesalius' definition".

> Many or most variations are totally benign. . . . Some of these variations may seriously compromise parts of the muscular, vascular, nervous, skeletal and/or other organ systems. . . . What we are trying to convey to interested readers is that the things we describe here are "normal" even though they may differ from the mean or usual. They are found in "normal" long-lived individuals, and they are statistically (for the most part) predictable. Man is not machine-made but rather more subjectively fashioned with many developmental and environmental factors intervening in the process.

The *Encyclopedia* gives no information on functional differences among the variants, although such variation surely exists. One would expect the large variability of muscle and tendon positioning in the hand, for example, to correlate with level of strength or dexterity in certain kinds of manual tasks. Do better violin players tend to have a common configuration of hand musculature, or one that is unusual? Do people with the best and worst penmanship tend to have certain configurations? These questions seem meaningful, but they do not draw us towards a robust concept of "normality". We always knew that people varied in their manual abilities, and now we know that they differ in musculature as well. Perhaps muscular variation maps onto the variation in manual skills. If so, so what? Skills in penmanship and musicianship are so various that no one seriously thinks there are "normal" ranges here. There is no reason that discovering a biological explanation for variations in functional performance should cause us to declare certain performances abnormal.

The views of Vácha and the *Encyclopedia* are a challenge to Boorse and Wachbroit's claims that functional determinism is implied by contemporary biomedical science. If medical textbooks emphasize average or typical cases, there may well be pragmatic reasons to do so. It would be a mistake to infer from this that diversity constitutes abnormality. Nevertheless, functional determinism remains an underlying assumption of certain discussions of health care ethics, to which we now turn.

7. The Reification of Abnormality in Health Care Ethics

Human beings are distinctive among species in their extensive use of tools and in the degree to which they modify their environment. A weak person using an atlatl can throw a spear farther than a strong person without one. A weak person can walk faster on pavement than a strong person can walk on a sandy beach. Such improvements are entirely typical of human beings, in the statistical sense that everyone does them. Tool use and environmental design change the modes and levels of human function. From a broad biological perspective these changes can be seen as an extension of the principle of functional integration. Richard Dawkins has suggested that tools and environmental modifications could be seen as an organism's *extended*

phenotype (Dawkins, 1982). We saw in Section 4 that an individual does not possess in its genome a preformed determinate design, but rather develops its adult phenotype (and its functional potential) through ontogenetic growth processes that include functional integration and adaptation. The present point is that even if we assume a fixed bodily phenotype, the functional potential of an individual human being is not fixed. The speed at which a given human walks and the distance she can throw a spear depend on the surfaces and tools available to her, her "extended phenotype". Nevertheless, the notion of a fixed species design with determinate limits on functional potential still plays a dominant role in discussions of health care ethics.

Norman Daniels argues that the preservation and restoration of normal function is a primary goal of health care. "[T]he kinds of [health care] needs picked out by reference to normal species functioning are objectively important because they meet this high-order interest persons have in maintaining a normal range of opportunities".[24] The goal of normality is seen as especially legitimate, because it is fixed by nature rather than by human convention; ". . . we can take as fixed, primarily by nature, a generally uncontroversial baseline of species-typical [i.e. normal] functioning".[25] Daniels proposes three levels of health care provision. The first is preventive health care. The second is curative and rehabilitative—returning people to species-normal functioning. The third level is services for the people who cannot be normalized, "extended medical and social support services for the (moderately) chronically ill and disabled and the frail elderly".[26] Silvers points out that Daniels's schema implies that mode of function has a higher priority than level of performance, apparently because mode of function receives its objective validation from nature itself.[27]

Daniels does not actually argue for the reality of species-normal functioning. He cites Boorse, and accepts it as an obvious fact. He goes beyond Boorse in one important respect: the linkage between normality and opportunity. Abnormals have reduced opportunity, and so maintenance of normality is maintenance of opportunity. Health care sustains normality, and normality sustains opportunity. Normality is the crucial objective link between health care and opportunity. And since normality is determined by objective science, judgments based on it carry a high authority.

The link between normality and opportunity may help us recognize the hierarchical level at which biological normality is conceived to operate. A person with unusually low blood pressure, or an unusual muscle configuration in the hand, may experience no direct loss of opportunity. So a socially oriented functional determinist like Daniels might not be concerned about the variability documented in Section 6. But people who are blind or paraplegic do experience a reduction of opportunity. It is probably this level, the level of "basic personal abilities" that draws the functional determinist's attention.[28] All *normal* humans can see and walk. Those whose opportunities are diminished by their inability to see and walk have their own abnormality to blame. Their status as abnormals is a fact of nature; the associated opportunity loss seems likewise to be entirely natural.

The tight linkage between opportunity and normality reappears in Dan Brock's analysis of the concept of quality of life. "[Q]uality of life must always be measured against normal, primary functional capacities for humans . . .".[29] This is taken to follow from Daniels's position that the "normal opportunity range" is only available to functionally normal humans. One might think that quality of life would be measured by the satisfaction and fulfillment actually experienced by those living those lives. This would allow an empirical test of the identification of quality of life with functional normality. If the linkage is empirically correct, then functionally atypical people would report low qualities of life. Unfortunately, the data do not support this identification. Atypical people

typically report a high quality of life. There is a great deal of empirical evidence that people with even serious disabilities report a quality of life averaging only slightly lower than that reported by non-disabled people. Physicians in particular estimate the quality of the lives of their disabled patients to be much lower than do the patients themselves (Bach and Tilton, 1994).

Brock is aware of the mismatch between biological normality and the reported quality of people's lives. If we were discussing a genuinely empirical hypothesis, such a mismatch would be taken as evidence that one's biological normality is irrelevant to the quality of one's life. After all, if happiness doesn't correlate with normality, then normality doesn't measure quality of life. But Brock argues exactly the reverse. Since normality doesn't correlate with happiness, happiness itself does *not* measure quality of life! In order to protect from refutation the link between normality and quality of life, Brock distinguishes *ad hoc* between the *subjective* and *objective* aspects of quality of life.[30] Subjective aspects are the degree of happiness and satisfaction that a person experiences. Objective aspects include the person's own objective abnormality and the opportunity associated with it. Abnormal people who report a high quality of life are simply mistaken about the quality of their own lives. Their quality of life is merely *subjectively* high. Objectively, it is low.

How does Brock account for the mismatch between high subjective quality and low normality-defined ("objective") quality? He offers only one explanation. Functionally abnormal people who report a high quality of life have lower expectations than functionally normal people. Lowered expectations are more easily satisfied, and the easy satisfaction of low expectations yields a high subjective quality of life. This, to Brock, is not *real* quality of life. "To be satisfied or happy with getting much less from life, because one has come to expect much less, is still to get *less* from life or to have a less good life".[31]

I do not deny that people labeled as abnormal have a reduced range of opportunity. And I agree that equality of opportunity is an important moral value. But the discussion of opportunity takes a very different form in the context of supposed biological abnormality than in other contexts. Racism and sexism, for example, cause very serious reductions of opportunity. Moral discussion of these problems centers on how opportunity should be restored to the disadvantaged groups, by changing social institutions if necessary. We are well past the time when academic discussion of race and sex was centered on rationalizations of how the disadvantages experienced by certain races and genders were caused by nature itself. But the normality discussions do just that. The abnormals are said to be disadvantaged by nature itself. If a black woman today considered herself to have a fulfilling life, would a moral philosopher be likely to suggest that her happiness only results from lowered expectations, and she is really getting *less* from life than a white male? I doubt it. But the abnormals can still receive this patronizing treatment.

The present unequal distribution of opportunities among people with varying biological traits can only appear to be fixed by nature if we ignore the fact that *all* human beings use tools and live in built environments, and that the design of tools and environments is an outcome of human choices. Given the appropriate technology and environment, blind people can read and paralyzed people can be mobile. The disadvantage that attaches to blindness and paralysis derives not from the atypicality of one's biology, but from the absence of appropriate tools and environments. This simple fact goes unnoticed by philosophical commentators on normality. We consider the social prohibition of hiring based on race or sex to be a remedy for the disadvantages caused by racism and sexism. But we do not consider the social provision of appropriate tools and environments to be a remedy for the disadvantages of abnormal people. Why not? In Section 8 I will argue that it

is because the tools and environments that enable atypical people to function at a high level are *themselves* stigmatized by social prejudices against the conditions they ameliorate.

The concept of normality, and not the concept of function, controls current thought about the disadvantages caused by biological atypicality. If we thought merely about *level* of functional performance, rather than the mode, fashion, or style of function, the disadvantages of disability would not seem so natural and inevitable. High levels of function are possible for very atypical people when they use atypical modes of functioning. A concern with functional normality is less a concern with the level of performance than with cosmetic aspects of functional mode. The widespread fascination with normality of functional mode is itself a hindrance to functional performance.

8. Unfashionable Function

During the past three decades the concept of disability has undergone critical evaluation and reconceptualization. The customary way of thinking about disability is based on what is now called the Medical Model. Disability is thought of as a biomedical condition of an individual, an abnormality that is naturally associated with disadvantages. Disability activists began in the 1970s to think of disabled people as an oppressed minority, and to demand civil rights parallel to the rights earlier won by "racial" minorities and women (Eisenberg et al., 1982). As a part of this movement, the Medical Model is being replaced by the Social Model of disability (Oliver, 1990; Shakespeare et al., 1996). It was long recognized that the disadvantages experienced by people with disabilities were at least partly caused by the social context in which they lived, if only by the widespread negative stereotypes of disabled people. The Social Model makes disability *entirely* an issue of social context, arising as it does from the disabling ways in which certain kinds of human variation are dealt with in society.

Section 7 asserted that high levels of function were possible for atypical people using atypical modes. It intimated that functional determinists were more concerned with the cosmetic issue of the mode of function than the pragmatic issue of the level of function. If this is so, the aversion to atypical modes of function is a simple prejudice, and not an objective scientific assessment. What evidence is there that functional mode is favored over level of performance?

There is abundant social evidence that atypical modes of function are stigmatized. Many disabled people attempt to hide their disability. Some refuse to use tools that would make their disability more apparent, even though the tools would greatly enhance their level of function. A large population of survivors of the polio epidemics of the 1940s and 1950s are now experiencing Post-Polio Syndrome, a condition that causes increased weakness and discomfort with exertion. Many were *passers* for most of their life (a term significantly borrowed from the racial context to mean a disabled person who passes for non-disabled). It is common wisdom in this group that most passers will resist the use of new assistive devices (canes, crutches, wheelchairs, or ventilators, depending on the nature and extent of the paralysis) even though their waning strength would make the devices extremely useful. These people voluntarily suffer increasing pain and limitations on their activities just to avoid acknowledging their muscular weakness. Exclamations of joy can be seen on Internet lists as individuals finally give in and discover how much the adaptive equipment liberates them and increases their level of function. The same is true of other gradually acquired disabilities, such as resistance to the use of a hearing aid or a white cane. Publicly acknowledging one's own disability is often a personally momentous 'coming out' similar to acknowledging one's homosexuality, or one's unacknowledged ethnic background.

The fact that individuals try to hide their disability has usually been interpreted patronizingly,

as evidence of the failure to accept one's own limitations. It should instead be seen as a recognition on the part of disabled people of a deep social prejudice against them. Cosmetic normality at the cost of functional performance has been an acknowledged goal of many rehabilitation programs. As cited above, many schools for deaf children forbade the use of sign among their students, just as government schools for Native Americans forbade the use of indigenous languages. Oralism produced a lower level but more cosmetically normal performance.

Wheelchairs are another example of the stigmatization of an unfashionable performance mode. Many people with mobility impairments are taught not to use wheelchairs if there is any way to avoid it. This is true even if avoiding the wheelchair means walking with difficulty, pain, and very low efficiency. Depending on the environment and the task at hand, a wheelchair user can function at or above the level of a person with bipedal mobility. The world's record for a marathon race is 45 minutes faster for a wheelchair user than for a runner. Nevertheless, the phrases "wheelchair-bound" and "confined to a wheelchair" are used as synonyms for paralysis. The irony is that wheelchairs are tools of mobility, not confinement devices. The people who are genuinely confined are paraplegic people who do not *have* a wheelchair, or who have one but live in an environment filled with barriers to its use. The stigmatization of wheelchairs is another example of a higher level of performance sacrificed to cosmetic normality. Upright walking is socially approved over wheelchair use, no matter how painful and inefficient the walking.

This is not a mere popular prejudice from which academics are immune. Brock discusses three assessment instruments designed to measure what he describes as "functions of the 'whole person'" (Brock, 1993, p. 298).[32] They actually measure something quite different. One such instrument has a scale for "mobility" and a scale for "physical activity". These scales illustrate the bias towards fashionable normality of mode over level of functional performance. The "physical activity" scale scores 4 points for walking freely, 3 points for walking with limitations (using a cane or crutches), and 2 points for moving independently in a wheelchair. A walking person scores higher in physical activity than a person who uses a wheelchair, even if the walker manages only slow and painful steps and the wheelchair user is a marathon racer. Cosmetic normality wins over functional performance. Recall that Brock refers to these very measures as the "objective" components of genuine quality of life. The post-polio population is filled with people who can attest that wheelchair use improves not only their level of physical activity, but also their quality of life. The wheelchair is a stigmatized tool, and the stigma is reinforced by the doctrine of biological normality.

The "mobility" scale of this instrument awards 5 points for using public transportation alone, 4 points for requiring assistance to use public transportation, and 3 points for needing assistance to go outside (*ibid.*). Consider how a physically fit paraplegic wheelchair user would score on this assessment. If there were barriers between his living quarters and the street (e.g. stairways without elevators), he would score 3. If there were no such barriers but his city's public transportation was inaccessible to wheelchairs, he would score 4. If his living quarters and his public transportation were both wheelchair-accessible, he would score 5. The differences in score depend not on the biological traits of the person, but on the environment he is living in. Does this scale measure "functions of the whole person"? Not in the least. It measures the accessibility of the person's environment. To conceive of these criteria as measuring the functional traits *of a person* is the crudest of prejudices. The design of the environment is the cause of the disadvantage. The doctrine of biological normality obscures this cause.

9. Conclusion

Causal attribution is a complicated thing. We pick out one antecedent event or condition and baptize it as *the cause* of a phenomenon. Different perspectives, different theoretical orientations, or different prejudices can lead to the baptism of different antecedent events or conditions as *the cause*. The Social Model of disability never identifies the biomedical condition of a person as *the cause* of that person's disadvantages. The causes of disadvantage are always identified in the environment and the social context. A critic might dismiss this approach as politically motivated and therefore not scientifically objective.

But consider the alternative. Functional determinism, the doctrine that biological normality is a part of the real natural world, is presented as an objective scientific claim. Philosophers and medical practitioners alike have used the category to conclude that the disadvantages of disabled people result from their own abnormality; they have only themselves (and nature) to blame. Is *this* assessment scientific and objective? Or does it merely reflect a preference for "ways of doing things that are preferred by the dominant classes and to which we have therefore become accustomed".[33] If the latter, then "policies of normalizing threaten not to equalize but to preserve existing patterns of functional dominance and privilege" (*ibid.*).

When an inaccessible environment causes the confinement of a wheelchair user, the abnormality of the wheelchair user is identified as the cause of the confinement. The doctrine of biological normality (Boorse and Wachbroit), the linkage of normality to opportunity (Daniels) and thence to quality of life (Brock) rationalizes this assessment. The opportunity losses of abnormal people are theorized to be not only natural and obvious, but morally innocuous.

In past years, versions of biological determinism have buttressed racist and sexist doctrines. Celebrated for their scientific objectivity, they had little objective biological foundation. Their plausibility was enhanced by their congruence with the social prejudices of their time. Functional determinism, the reificiation of functional normality and abnormality, is typical of this genre. The ideology it supports and is supported by has been labeled "ablism", the chauvinism of the non-disabled. It has little else to recommend it.

Notes

1 Boorse 1997, p. 41.
2 Boorse 1997, p. 7.
3 Boorse 1997, p. 39.
4 Silvers 1998, p. 101.
5 Wachbroit 1994b, p. 237.
6 Mayr 1980, p. 128.
7 Dobzhansky 1962, p. 126.
8 Wachbroit 1994a, p. 590.
9 Boorse 1997, p. 33.
10 Hull 1986, p. 4.
11 Boorse 1997, p. pp. ff.
12 Gilbert 1997, pp. 665 ff.
13 Maynard Smith 1975, p. 317.
14 Rachoonin and Thomson, 1981, p. 184.
15 Rachoonin and Thomson, 1981, p. 184.
16 Maynard Smith 1975, p. 317.
17 Lewin 1980, p. 1232.
18 Hacking 1990, p. 160
19 Baynton 1996, Chapter 6.
20 Vácha 1978, p. 23.
21 Vácha 1978, p. 730.
22 Vácha 1978, p. 339.
23 Vácha 1978, p. 826.
24 Daniels 1987, p. 301.
25 Daniels 1987, p. 303.
26 Daniels 1987, p. 48.
27 Silvers 1998, p. 101.
28 Amundson 1992, p. 107.
29 Brock 1993, p. 308.
30 Brock 1993, p. 306.
31 Brock 1993, p. 309.
32 Brock 1993, p. 298.
33 Silvers 1998, p. 108.

References

American Association of Physical Anthropologists (1996). Statement on biological aspects of race. *American Journal of Physical Anthropology*, 101: 569–570.

Amundson, R. (1992). Disability, handicap, and the environment. *Journal of Social Philosophy*, 23: 105–118.

Armstrong, D. F., Stokoe, W. C., & Wilcox, S. E. (1994). Signs of the origin of syntax. *Current Anthropology*, 35: 349–358.

Bach, J. R., & Tilton, M. C. (1994). Life satisfaction and well-being measures in ventilator assisted individuals with traumatic tetraplegia. *Archives of Physical Medicine and Rehabilitation*, 75: 626–634.

Baynton, D. C. (1996). *Forbidden Signs: American Culture and the Campaign against Sign Language*. Chicago, University of Chicago Press.

Bergman, R. A., Afifi, A. K., & Miyauchi, R. (1992–1998) *Illustrated Encyclopedia of Human Anatomic Variation* (Iowa City: University of Iowa Health Care, http://www.vh.org/Providers/Textbooks/AnatomicVariants/AnatomyHP.html).

Boorse, C. (1975). On the distinction between disease and illness. *Philosophy and Public Affairs*, 5: 49–68.

Boorse, C. (1997). A rebuttal on health. In J. M. Humber and R. F. Almeder (Eds.), *What is Disease* (pp. 3–134), Totowa, NJ: Humana Press.

Brinkman, C. & Porter, R. (1983). Plasticity of motor behavior in monkeys with crossed forelimb nerves. *Science*, 220: 438–440.

Brock, D. W. (1993). *Life and Death*. Cambridge: Cambridge University Press.

Chomsky, N. (1966). *Cartesian Linguistics: A chapter in the history of rationalist thought*. New York: Harper and Row.

Craven, P. L. (1990). The development from a medical classification to a player classification in wheelchair basketball. In *Adapted Physical Activity: An Interdisciplinary Approach* (pp. 81–86), Berlin: Springer-Verlag.

Daniels, N. (1985). *Just Health Care*: Cambridge: Cambridge University Press.

Daniels, N. (1987). Justice and Health Care. In D. Van deVeer and T. Regan (Eds.), *Health Care Ethics* (pp. 290–325) Philadelphia: Temple University Press.

Davis, P. V., & Bradley, J. G. (1996). The meaning of normal. *Perspectives in Biology and Medicine*, 40: 68–77.

Dawkins, R. (1982). *The Extended Phenotype*. Oxford: Oxford University Press.

Dobzhansky, T. (1962). *Mankind Evolving*. New Haven: Yale University Press.

Eisenberg, M. G., Griggins, C., & Duval, R. J. (Eds.) (1982). *Disabled People as Second-Class Citizens*. New York: Springer.

Gilbert, S. F. (1997). *Developmental Biology, Fifth Edition*. Sunderland, MA: Sinauer Associates, Inc.

Hacking, I. (1990). *The Taming of Chance*. Cambridge: Cambridge University Press.

Hull, D. L. (1986). On human nature, *PSA 1986, Vol. 2* (pp. 3–13) East Lansing, MI, Philosophy of Science Association.

Lewin, R. (1980). Is your brain really necessary? *Science*, 210: 1232–1234.

Lewontin, R. C. (1995). *Human Diversity*. New York: W.H. Freeman.

Marks, J. B. (1995). *Human Biodiversity: Genes, race, and history*. New York: Aldine de Gruyter.

Maynard Smith, J. (1975). *The Theory of Evolution, Third Edition*. Cambridge: Cambridge University Press.

Mayr, E. (1980). The role of systematics in the evolutionary synthesis. In M. Ernst and W. Provine (Eds.), *The Evolutionary Synthesis* (pp. 123–136) Cambridge: Harvard University Press.

Nijhout, H. F. (1990). Metaphors and the role of genes in development. *BioEssays*, 12: 441–445.

Oliver, M. (1990). *The Politics of Disablement*. Basingstoke: Macmillan.

Poizner, H., Klima, E., & Bellugi, U. (1987). *What the Hands Reveal about the Brain*. Cambridge, MA: MIT Press.

Rachootin, S. P., & Thomson, K. S. (1981). Epigenetics, paleontology, and evolution. In G. G. E. Scudder and J. L. Reveal (Eds.), *Evolution Today* Pittsburg: Hunt Institute.

Shakespeare, T., Gillespie-Sells, K., & Davies, D. (1996). *The Sexual Politics of Disability: Untold desires*. London: Cassell.

Silvers, A. (1998). A fatal attraction to normalizing. In Erik Parens (Ed.), *Enhancing Human Traits: Ethical and social implications* (pp. 95–123) Washington, DC: Georgetown University Press.

Stiassny, M. L. J., & Meyer, A. (1999). Cichlids of the Rift Lakes. *Scientific American*, 280: 64–69.

Stokoe, W. C. (1960). *Sign Language Structure: An outline of the communication systems of the American deaf*: Studies in Linguistics Occasional Papers 8.

Vácha, J. (1978). Biology and the problem of normality. *Scientia*, 113: 823–846.

Vácha, J. (1982). The problem of so-called normality in anthropological sciences. *Anthropos*, 22: 73–85.

Vácha, J. (1985). German constitutional doctrine in the 1920s and 1930s and pitfalls of the contemporary conception of normality in biology and medicine. *Journal of Medicine and Philosophy*, 10: 339–367.

Wachbroit, R. (1994a). Normality as a biological concept. *Philosophy of Science*, 61: 579–591.

Wachbroit, R. (1994b). Distinguishing genetic disease and genetic susceptibility. *American Journal of Medical Genetics*, 53: 236–240.

Chapter 33

Rachel Cooper

WHAT'S SPECIAL ABOUT MENTAL HEALTH AND DISORDER?

Glance through the *Diagnostic and Statistical Manual of Mental Disorders* published by the American Psychiatric Association (2000), but influential worldwide, and one gets some idea of the variety of conditions that are considered "mental disorders." One finds not only codes for types of schizophrenia and depression, but also for types of substance abuse and addiction; dementias; conditions that normally manifest in childhood, such as dyslexia, autism, and bedwetting; anxiety disorders, including post-traumatic stress disorder and phobias; sexual problems—which range from erectile dysfunction to pedophilia; personality disorders—deeply entrenched problems in personality, including schizoid and antisocial personality disorders; and sleep disorders, such as nightmare disorder and insomnia. What, if anything, unites this collection? Is there something special about mental health and disorder?

During the 1960s and 70s many held that mental disorders were disorders of an especially problematic type; antipsychiatrists mounted powerful challenges to the legitimacy of psychiatry as a branch of medicine (Foucault, 1971; Laing & Esterson, 1970; Szasz, 1972; Rosenhan, 1973). At the extreme, mental illness was claimed to be a myth (Szasz, 1972). These debates have now died down. The pendulum has swung the other way to the extent that those writing on the concept of mental disorder now tend to think that mental disorder is much like physical disorder. In current debates the important issue, it is assumed, is whether a condition is a disorder, or some non-pathological state (a normal variation, or a moral failing, for example). The question of what distinguishes mental and physical disorders is considered to be of only secondary importance, and is dealt with, if at all, as an afterthought.[1] Those who do examine the question of what distinguishes mental from physical disorders generally conclude that a clear-cut and meaningful distinction cannot be drawn and that the distinction should either be abandoned, or merely tolerated for book-keeping purposes (e.g., it is useful to have some agreement as to the conditions that psychiatrists will treat).

Notably, this "ivory tower" view meets with little agreement amongst those at the sharp end of diagnosis. To many patient groups it matters a very great deal whether "their label" is taken to indicate a physical or mental disorder. Recently, for example, researchers who suggest that Chronic Fatigue Syndrome/M. E. may have a psychological cause have received death threats from some patient activists who are convinced that the causes must be physical (Feilden, 2011). The insurance industry and some lawmakers also continue to see a sharp division between mental and physical disorders.

This chapter examines how it is that academics and those directly affected by diagnoses can have reached such very different conclusions. How could a distinction that academics consider to be of little importance matter on the ground, and who is right? I will first consider work in the philosophy of medicine, and then go on to consider the views of patient groups.

"Mental Disorder" According to the Academics

Academics interested in the concept of mental disorder have generally worried about the disorder part first, and the mental, if at all, only afterwards. The big problem has been taken to be how we might distinguish between the normal and the pathological. As it happens, much of the impetus for this work arose from debates about mental health issues during the 1970s, which centred on the challenges posed by the antipsychiatry movement and the debate about the normality or otherwise of homosexuality. Mental health issues sparked interest in the question of what distinguishes the normal from the pathological, but the accounts of disorder that were developed are either explicitly intended to encompass both mental and physical conditions, or can easily be adapted to cover both. In this section I will show how it is that current philosophy of medicine manages to consider mental and physical disorders together. I examine current accounts of disorder, and their problems, and show that the issues that arise apply equally to physical and mental disorders.

The best known account of disorder is that proposed by Christopher Boorse (Chapter 31 this volume, 1975, 1976, 1977, 1997). Boorse holds that we can think of the human organism as being made up of various subsystems (which include solid organs, such as kidneys, and also more diffuse systems such as the nervous system). Each subsystem has a normal function, which is whatever it normally does in comparable organisms that contributes to survival and reproduction. For example, the

function of my teeth is to chew food. This is what teeth do in most humans of my age and sex that contributes to survival. If my teeth fail to enable me to chew, then there is a dysfunction, and I have a disorder. Boorse adopts an account of normal function that claims that the normal function of a subsystem is whatever is statistically normal for organisms of the same sex and age. However, amongst philosophers of biology there is no agreement that this is the correct account of biological normal function.[2] Evolutionary accounts, which claim that the normal function of a biological subsystem is whatever it was selected to do, are also popular. Those tempted by the basic idea that disorders are dysfunctions, but skeptical of Boorse's account of normal function, can adopt a variant of Boorse's account by accepting his claim that disorders are dysfunctions, but adopting an evolutionary account of normal function. On such an account, my non-chewing teeth will still be said to be dysfunctioning, but now past selective pressures provide the justification for saying that the function of my teeth is to chew food.

Either version of the disorder as dysfunction account might be hoped to apply also to mental disorders. With the rise of evolutionary psychology it has become commonplace to think of the mind as being made up of various mental modules each of which has one or more particular functions (Tooby & Cosmides, 1992). One might conceive of mental disorder as occurring when one or more of these modules fails to function (with dysfunction being understood in either statistical or evolutionary terms). Indeed this pattern of explanation has become popular, most famously in the case of autism, which Simon Baron-Cohen (1995) has hypothesized stems from a failure in the theory of mind module.

However, the notion that disorders can simply be equated with dysfunctions, as Boorse claims, has come in for widespread criticism. The most influential case in this regard is homosexuality.

Homosexuality was considered a disorder by the American Psychiatric Association until 1973, when its members voted to remove it from the classification of mental disorders (Bayer, 1981). The case of homosexuality causes problems for accounts that claim that all biological dysfunctions are disorders. The problem is that, though the causes of homosexuality are debated, it might turn out to be the case that homosexuality occurs as the results of some biological dysfunction. Maybe, for example, there is some mental mechanism that normally functions so as to ensure that people are attracted to members of the opposite sex, and something goes wrong with this in cases of homosexuality. If one claims that dysfunctions are disorders, one is forced to conclude that homosexuality may be a disorder. For many participants in the debates about homosexuality, this was an unacceptable conclusion. Many claimed that whatever the biological origins of homosexuality it would not count as a disorder because it is not a bad thing. Following the debates about homosexuality, Jerome Wakefield's account of mental disorder, that claims that a disorder must not only be a dysfunction but also be harmful, became the most influential account of disorder amongst those interested in mental health.[3] Although homosexuality is the case that convinced most commentators, and although Jerome Wakefield proposed his account with mental disorder specifically in mind, it is worth noting that cases where a biological dysfunction does no harm, and should plausibly not be considered a disorder, also occur in physical medicine.[4]

On accounts that claim that disorders are harmful dysfunctions, dysfunction is no longer sufficient for disorder, but it remains necessary. Some consider even this to be a mistake. Although many mental disorders can be thought of as biological dysfunctions, there are problematic cases. Evolutionary psychopathologists have been struck by the fact that many mental disorders appear to have a genetic basis and yet occur at rates that are too high to merely be the result of random mutations. Examples include manic-depression, sociopathy, obsessive-compulsivity, anxiety, drug abuse, and some personality disorders (Wilson 1993). This implies that such disorders have at some stage conferred a selective advantage. For example, on some accounts the aggression and promiscuous behavior of psychopaths may make biological sense for low-status men born into hostile environments (Mealey, 1995). If this is the case then being a psychopath is no dysfunction, and yet we would still want to consider it a disorder. For such reasons the idea that disorders can be considered biological dysfunctions has perhaps been particularly contested in psychiatry. However, similar problems can also occur in the case of physical health—consider the "thrifty phenotype" account of Type-2 diabetes, for example (Hales & Barker, 1992). Here again it looks like some disorders arise because of a mismatch between the environment in which traits were selected and the current environment in which we live. Such cases suggest that biological dysfunction may not be necessary for disorder.

If dysfunction is abandoned as either being sufficient or necessary for disorder, the field opens up for the development of a whole range of alternative accounts of disorder. One family of accounts focuses on the fact that disorders limit a human's ability to live a good life. Chris Megone has developed an Aristotelian account claiming that a healthy human is one in which physical and mental sub-systems function in ways that enable the human to live a flourishing life (Megone, 1998, 2000). Somewhat similarly, both Leonard Nordenfelt's (1995) *On the Nature of Health* and Kenneth Richman's (2004) *Ethics and the Metaphysics of Medicine* propose that an individual is healthy if their body and mind is such that they can reasonably hope to achieve important goals (though Richman and Nordenfelt differ in exactly how this should be understood). The fundamental worry for such accounts is that they risk being over-inclusive. The problem is that there are states that limit flourishing but that we do not want to count as diseases (vices, lack of education, etc.) and these accounts struggle to respect this distinction.[5]

Another family of accounts holds on to the idea that disorders are necessarily harmful, but adds some other criteria in an attempt to more clearly demarcate disorders from other sorts of problem (educational problems, housing problems, and so on) (Reznek, 1987; Cooper, 2002). The extra criteria vary from author to author but may include requirements such as that disorders have to be potentially medically treatable, that sufferers have to be unlucky, that diseases must be statistically infrequent, that disorders have to have some biological basis. As I see it, the main difficulty with such complex accounts is that to date none has been developed in any detail, and as the devil is so often in the details, a final assessment of such accounts must wait until a fully developed account has been produced.[6]

For our purposes here the main point to note is that although the correct account of disorder is contested, all accounts that are currently being developed can apply equally to both mental and physical disorders. As such any distinction that can be drawn between mental and physical disorders will not simply emerge naturally out of a satisfactory account of disorder. Rather, even if a satisfactory account of disorder is developed, the problem of working out how mental and physical disorders can be distinguished will remain as a separate task.

In practice, mental disorders are frequently taken to be circumscribed by the *Diagnostic and Statistical Manual of Mental Disorders* (better known as the D.S.M.), but even the authors of the D.S.M. are not too interested in the distinction between mental and physical conditions. The current edition states:

> Although this volume is titled the *Diagnostic and Statistical Manual of Mental Disorders*, the term mental disorder unfortunately implies a distinction between "mental" disorders and "physical" disorders that is a reductionistic anachronism of mind/body dualism. A compelling literature documents that there is much "physical" in "mental" disorders and much "mental" in "physical" disorders. The problem raised by the term "mental" disorders has been much clearer than its solution, and, unfortunately, the term persists in the title of DSM-IV because we have not found an appropriate substitute.[7]

The D.S.M.'s claim that only dualists can accept a distinction between mental and physical disorders is a philosophical blunder. Physicalists hold that all is ultimately physical, but still they may think that different varieties of ultimately physical stuff can be distinguished. Tables and chairs, and apples and pears, are all physical, but can be differentiated. The mental and the non-mental physical might also be distinguishable, for example on the basis of some feature such as consciousness or intentionality.

Still, though physicalists can hold that there is some distinction between physical and mental disorders, figuring out what it might be is far from easy. As the D.S.M. notes, at the level of causes and of symptoms the distinction between physical and mental disorders is far from clear-cut. "Mental" disorders frequently have multifactorial causes that, though including psychological factors such as stress, also include physical factors such as genetic susceptibility, complications at birth, and drug use. Similarly, many physical conditions are affected by psychological factors. For example, studies show that the optimistic have better outcomes in some cancers (Allison et al., 2003). At the level of symptoms there is also much overlap. Mental disorders can have some physical symptoms, for example, fatigue and pain in depression, and many physical disorders can make us moody and irrational.

Traditionally it has been claimed that intentionality is the "mark of the mental." Intentionality has to do with the "aboutness" of mental states— a belief is a belief about something, a desire is a desire for something, a fear is a fear of something. Derek Bolton (2001) suggests that this can be used to distinguish physical from mental disorders. He points out that intentionality is subject to normative constraints; beliefs are more or less well grounded, emotions more or less appropriate. Mental disorders, he suggests, occur where there is a radical failure to respect these constraints. Someone with delusions has ungrounded beliefs; someone with a mood disorder has inappropriate emotions. The primary difficulty with Bolton's suggestion is that there are many conditions in the D.S.M. that it is hard to characterize in terms of dysfunctional intentionality. Consider conditions such as insomnia or erectile dysfunction, for example. If you have problems sleeping, or sustaining an erection, where's the problem with intentionality? In later work, Bolton suggests that we might use the criteria of intentionality-failure to pick out a somewhat narrower class of conditions than those currently treated by psychiatrists.[8] Call his narrower class "madness" or "insanity." Here, though, Bolton's interests diverge from our own, for we are considering what if anything is special about mental disorders characterized as the rather broad range of conditions that psychiatrists currently treat.

Where does this leave us? With perhaps the dominant view being that there is no clear-cut distinction that can be drawn between physical and mental disorder. Dominic Murphy considers that contingent historical pressures have led to psychiatrists dealing with a jumble of conditions. He concludes: "We are left with a mess."[9] In an influential 2001 article in the *British Journal of Psychiatry*, Robert Kendell goes so far as to claim that the view that mental disorders are "fundamentally different from other illnesses" has been "abandoned by all thinking physicians."[10] He holds that differences between mental and physical disorders are "no more profound than the differences between disease of the circulatory system and those of the digestive system, or between kidney diseases and skin diseases."[11]

The Mental/Physical Distinction on the Ground

While psychiatrists and philosophers have been relaxed about the distinction between mental and physical disorders, to many patients the distinction is a matter of grave concern. Here, in seeking to get a sense of the issues, I will focus on the debates that surround two contested conditions: Tourette's and M.E./C.F.S. Through looking at these cases I hope to gain insight into what it means to patients to receive a mental disorder diagnosis.

Border Skirmishes 1: *Tourette's Syndrome*

Tourette's syndrome is characterized by multiple motor and verbal tics. Stereotypically someone with Tourette's swears uncontrollably and has an oddly jerking body. Until comparatively recently Tourette's was considered a rare condition. Estimated prevalence was once 1–2 per thousand,[12] but is now 1–2 percent (Swerdlow, 2005). As milder cases come to be diagnosed, the proportion of patients who exhibit the more extreme symptoms has decreased. Coprolalia, the involuntary shouting of swear words, was once taken as the defining symptom, but is now considered rare.[13] Tourette's is normally diagnosed in childhood, and often becomes most severe during adolescence.

In the United States the most vocal patient group is the Tourette Syndrome Assocation (T.S.A.) founded in 1972. Since their founding the T.S.A. has sought to present Tourette's as a neurological as opposed to a psychological condition. Public information adverts issued by the Association have consistently taken this line. One in the mid-1970s informed readers that "Most victims accept it as an emotional problem, which it is not. Many doctors, too, misdiagnose it as mental disorder. But it is physical!"[14] The T.S.A. formed alliances with researchers who postulated organic etiologies for the disorder. In his histories of Tourette syndrome, Howard

Kushner (1999, 2004) argues that the activities of the Tourette Syndrome Association have been highly effective. He suggests that the reason that researchers in the U.S. now believe that the disorder has an organic basis, while in other countries, such as France, psychodynamic explanations still predominate, can be traced to the activities of the Association.

Those who argue that Tourette's has an organic basis commonly point out that family studies suggest a genetic component to the disorder (Swerdlow, 2005). Some theorists suggest that the condition may be caused by some problem with the basal ganglia, a brain region that is thought to play a role in inhibiting unwanted behaviors (Mink, 2001). However, other features of the disorder are more suggestive of a psychological element. Tourette's is frequently co-morbid with attention deficit hyperactivity disorder or obsessive compulsive disorder, making links with these conditions a possibility (Robertson 1989; Swerdlow, 2005). As with so many conditions, the severity of symptoms can vary over time, often becoming worse with stress. Sufferers can often control their tics to the extent that they can hold tics back for some period of time, maybe 20 minutes, before discharging them at a later point (some describe the urge to tic as being similar to the urge to sneeze). Many patients report that releasing a tic feels voluntary (Leckman et al., 1993). While most motor tics are apparently meaningless, some verbal tics bear at least some of the hallmarks of intentionality, for example, "fat pig" may be shouted only in the presence of the obese, or "nigger" only in the presence of black people.

Claiming that Tourette's is neurological has become important to patients both at a personal level and in lobbying for various changes to public policy. At the personal level it is common to find patients and their parents speak of their "relief" at hearing that Tourette's is a physical disorder.[15] In part, to claim that Tourette's is a physical disorder is to make a claim about what

it is not. For some, a physical disorder is specifically not the sort of condition that can be explained by psychoanalytic theory, or by other psychological models that trace disordered behavior to faulty upbringing. Many parents and patients can recall unhappy experiences with psychoanalysts in the seventies and eighties. One mother recalls "the really tragic part of it was that the psychiatrists we went to would all blame me for Bill's problems. Right in front of me, they would ask him, 'What has you mother been doing to you'."[16] More recently the jacket of a biography written by another parent proclaims that the neurological diagnosis means that "His behaviour is NOT OUR FAULT!"[17] To claim that Tourette's is physical rather than mental is to claim that no-one—neither the child-patient, nor their parents—can be blamed for it.

At the level of public policy, claiming that Tourette's is a neurological condition has become important in a number of debates. Newman (2009) analyses the rhetoric employed by the T.S.A. in a recent campaign to ensure that children with Tourette's receive particular accommodations in schools. In the U.S., the legislation that ensures that disabled children receive special education makes the type of educational adjustment dependent on the type of disability. There are only a limited number of categories of disability, meaning that children with Tourette's must be placed in one pigeon-hole or another. In many cases, children with Tourette's had been classified as emotionally disturbed, a decision that led to children with Tourette's being placed in special classrooms for emotionally disturbed children, and in some cases being subjected to programs that aim to adjust behavior via systems of rewards and punishments. The T.S.A. campaigned to have children with Tourette's instead classified as Other Health Impaired, a classification that encompasses children with epilepsy, A.D.H.D., asthma, and rheumatic fever. The legislation was due to be revised in 2003, and the T.S.A. lobbied for Congress to facilitate the reclassification of children with Tourette's. The letters directed to decision-makers emphasised that Tourette's is a "neurobiological disorder." This lobbying eventually succeeded and Tourette syndrome is now explicitly mentioned as an example of Other Health Impaired.

What should we make of these debates? The debates about Tourette's show clearly how the distinction between mental and physical disorders can make a difference to patients. First, a mental disorder diagnosis opens up the possibility of blame. While those who suffer from physical conditions may be conceived of as being blameless victims, the moral status of those diagnosed with mental disorders and their families may be more ambiguous. Second, whether Tourette's is considered mental or physical matters because such categories play a role in organizing bureaucracies—those with physical disorders are processed differently than those with mental disorders. In this case, school children will be treated differently depending on whether their diagnosis is conceived of as a physical or mental disorder.

Border Skirmishes 2: Myalgic Encephalomyelitis (M.E.)/Chronic Fatigue Syndrome (C.F.S.)/ Chronic Fatigue Immune Dysfunction (C.F.I.D.)

Everything about M.E./C.F.S./C.F.I.D. is controversial. Starting with the name: Patient groups frequently prefer terms that are suggestive of a biological cause—myalgic encephalomyelitis (in the U.K.) or chronic fatigue immune dysfunction (in the U.S.). In contrast, chronic fatigue syndrome, a term frequently used by medics, has no overtones of organicity. Here I will follow the terminology that has become commonplace in much of the literature and refer to the condition as C.F.S./M.E. The disorder is characterized by fatigue, associated with somatic complaints such as joint pains and headaches, which last at least six months. In part, the diagnosis is made on the basis of exclusion—by definition no organic cause for the syndrome

must be found. The condition can be extremely disabling. Many sufferers are forced to give up work and may be bed-bound.

The causes of the condition are unknown. Some believe that some sort of virological or immunological cause is likely. Others think the condition is psychosomatic. Mixed views hold that the condition may have an organic origin and then be made worse by psychological factors. Controversy rages over the use of treatments that include cognitive behavioral therapy and graded exercise programs. Some patient groups take such psychological and behavioral treatments to be suggestive of the idea that the condition is psychological. The studies proving such treatments effective are contested (Jason et al., 1997). One area of debate concerns the diagnostic criteria that should be used to select subject groups for study. These debates are entangled with debates about the supposed origins of the disorder, and so resolving them is far from straightforward. Those who think that C.F.S./M.E. is allied to other psychosomatic conditions favor broad definitions of the condition. They think that patients with C.F.S./M.E. are basically the same as those with other medically unexplained somatic complaints (Wessely et al., 1999). Using such criteria some studies have found that interventions such as graded exercise have been useful. However, those who think the condition likely organic favor a tighter definition (Jason, 2011). They think that a core group of C.F.S./M.E. sufferers have a condition with an organic cause, and that these patients need to be distinguished from look-a-likes who suffer from psychologically-caused syndromes. Researchers who adopt narrower criteria find interventions such as graded exercise programs to be of less use (Jason et al., 1997).

The debates between those favoring a biological cause and those who suspect a psychological cause have become unusually heated and personal. I suggest two major reasons why the debates about C.F.S./M.E. are so very problematic. First, C.F.S./M.E. can be an extremely debilitating and chronic condition. This means that there are major economic issues tied up with how it is classified and perceived. Insurance companies have an interest in the condition being dismissed as somehow unworthy of consideration. On some insurance programs it makes a difference whether a condition is considered a mental or physical condition. Recent parity laws introduced in the U.S., which require certain forms of insurance to cover mental and physical disorders equally, mean that this is less of a problem than it used to be, but the scope of the legislation is limited, and in many cases insurance continues to pay out less for mental than for physical conditions (Hitt, 2010). Here making the disorder appear mental has major economic implications.

Secondly, and tied up with the economic issue, patients with C.F.S./M.E. are frequently suspected of malingering—that is claiming to have symptoms that they do not for financial gain. Estimates of levels of malingering amongst benefits applicants who claim to have C.F.S./M.E. are up to 35 percent (Mittenberg et al., 2002). Such statistics need to be treated critically. On the one hand, it is certainly the case that some patients claiming to have C.F.S./M.E. are malingerers. Some applicants are caught out by video surveillance; they may claim to be unable to walk, but are videoed jogging (DeLuca, 2008). On the other hand, many of the large numbers of patients who are suspected of malingering are suspected solely because their physician thinks their symptoms fishy—whether this suggests that the patient is a malingerer or that the physician is unsympathetic to those with C.F.S./M.E. is anyone's guess. Furthermore the hurdles around claiming benefits are such that legitimately sick patients may find they can only be gained via "acting sick". Obtaining benefits can be a hit and miss affair. It thus helps if one self-presents in a particular way – it is better to look scruffy than well-presented for hearings, better not to fill in forms in an overly neat way, better to rate symptoms on bad days. Advice on such matters is shared on online support groups (Davis, 2002; Dumit, 2006). A sick patient may have to act sick to maximize her chances of receiving the benefits that are legitimately hers, but still onlookers might find something about her behavior suspicious. In response to concerns about malingering, some insurance providers in the U.S. have introduced a category of disorders known as "self-reported" or "subjective" which covers disorders that are diagnosed on the basis of self-reported symptoms (Dumit, 2006). The insurance pays out at a lower rate for these conditions. Such a category enables these insurers to sidestep the question of whether C.F.S./M.E. is physical or mental.

The fundamental problem for patients with C.F.S./M.E. is that there is no biomarker for the condition. The non-objectivity of their symptoms means that C.F.S./M.E. sufferers are treated with suspicion not only by insurance companies, but also by some medics and lay people. Patients thus face a constant battle to prove the legitimacy of their claims to illness. In this context, for C.F.S./M.E. patients a good doctor is not necessarily one who offers treatment, but is one who "believes in ME" and fills in forms for benefits (Guise et al., 2010). "Believing in M.E." tends to be equated with holding that the disorder may well turn out to have an organic basis. In this conflation of the question of whether C.F.S./M.E. has a physical origin and the question of whether it is a "real" disorder, we see an example of what Nicholas Rose (2007) has characterized as a recent "flattening" of psychological space. His suggestion is that while in the first half of the twentieth century lay conceptions of the mind came to embrace notions of the unconscious, and thus psychological space came to have depth, by the end of the twentieth century notions of the psychological had flattened. Now the perceived options for the causes of behavior are limited—either behavior is intended or it has an organic cause. In such a context, it is understandable that patients with C.F.S./M.E. are often highly resistant to any suggestion that it might be a psychological condition. They tend to present their disorder as somatic, often tracing onset to some post-viral state, and describing fatigue and aches and pains as being of organic origin (Banks & Prior, 2001). As medics often hold that the disorder is psychogenic, this can lead to tension in consultations.

At the political level too, C.F.S./M.E. patient groups are keen to present the condition as having an organic basis. The condition is not currently included in the D.S.M., and is in the W.H.O. classification under Disorders of the Nervous System. However, the condition's status as a neurological disorder is fragile. In one study, 84 percent of British neurologists said that they did not consider C.F.S./M.E. to be a neurological condition (Wojcik et al., 2011). Patient groups are alert in monitoring any changes to classification systems that mean that C.F.S./M.E. might come to be classified as mental. In recent consultations about plans for the forthcoming D.S.M.-5, various patient groups wrote to the American Psychiatric Association to express concern over a proposed category, Complex Somatic Symptom Disorder, which they feared could be used to give C.F.S./M.E. sufferers a psychiatric label (McCleary, 2010).

What can we draw from this debate? The essential problem for patients with C.F.S./M.E. is the non-objectivity of the symptoms and the lack of a biomarker. This leads to claims for benefits being denied or only grudgingly granted, and to patients being treated with suspicion. Even when the patient is agreed to have a "real disorder" the benefits that are paid to those who suffer from "mental disorders" or "subjective disorders" are often lower than those paid to those who suffer from physical disorders. There are various historical reasons why insurance in the U.S. has traditionally given only reduced benefits for "mental disorders."[18] However, one obvious reading of why it is that such limitations have been tolerated for so long is that both "mental disorders" and "disorders characterized by subjective symptoms" are considered to be only dubiously disorders. In this respect "mental disorders" and "subjective disorders" are only half-way medicalized—and patients are granted the sick-role only grudgingly and to a limited extent. Given that society treats mental disorders as only being dubiously disorders, it is understandable that patients with C.F.S./M.E. hear suggestions that the condition may be psychological as being dangerously close to claiming that it is unreal.

Conclusions: What's Special about Mental Health and Disorder?

While academics have tended to think of the distinction between mental and physical disorders as being of little importance, patient groups disagree. In this chapter I set out to determine who is right. Now we can see that both sides have some justification for their claims. The academics are right in saying that there is no one common feature that all and only mental disorders share. On the other hand, patient groups are right to care whether their condition is counted as a mental disorder. While a tradition amongst academics has it that there is no genuine distinction between mental and physical disorders, and that thus any differences in treatment are down purely to prejudice, I will suggest this view is incorrect. I suggest that mental disorders are treated differently from physical disorders in part because amongst them are many that are particularly troubling. Many amongst the mental disorders are only dubiously disorders, and for this reason it comes to be stigmatizing for one's condition to be labeled a mental disorder.

Disorders can be only dubiously disorders for two main reasons. First there are conditions that shade into normality; here, we find it hard to know whether a condition is normal or not. Of course, there are physical disorders that shade into normality, such as high blood pressure, and obesity. However, in physical medicine the boundaries of such conditions tend to be policed by the introduction of an arbitrary and yet objectively measurable cut-off point; only those with a blood pressure reading of X, or a B.M.I. index of Y will be said to suffer from a medical condition and will receive treatment.

On the other hand, many mental disorders are problematic in that they both shade into normality, and also do not have an objectively measurable cut-off point. While there are scales that will provide scores for depression or anxiety, these are all too clearly based on what a patient reports, and so lack the authority of a quantifiable bodily measure. The problem of shading into normality affects most mental disorders: depression, personality disorders, anxiety, substance abuse, insomnia, A.D.H.D.—in their milder forms, all clearly merge into the normal.

Disorders also become dubious when they shade into moral failings. Problems with this dimension are far more common with mental disorders than physical disorders. While some think that smoking lung-cancer sufferers bring it on themselves, here we have only moralizing regarding the cause of the disorder. In contrast, in some mental disorders it is genuinely unclear whether the condition itself is a disorder or a vice. This ambiguity is clearest with the personality disorders. Personality disorders are life-long conditions that are highly resistant to treatment. Many are characterized in distinctly moral terms. Those with antisocial personality disorder "frequently lack empathy and tend to be callous, cynical, and contemptuous of the feelings, rights and sufferings of others."[19] Symptoms of narcissistic personality disorder include "a grandiose sense of self-importance" and taking advantage of others.[20] Certain disorders of childhood are also uncomfortably close to moral problems. Children can be diagnosed with conduct disorder if they persistently engage in behaviors that are aggressive, destructive of property, deceitful, and violate accepted norms and rules. Oppositional defiant disorder is a diagnosis for children who oppose authority.

Problems also emerge with alcoholism and the drug addictions. While some addicts would very much like to be rid of their addictions, others drink or take drugs because these activities have become central to a lifestyle that they value (Fingarette, 1988).

To add to those conditions that are clearly on the borderline between vices and disorders, the psychoanalytic tradition comes very close to blaming patients, or their parents, for conditions that superficially appear blameless. For example, traditional accounts of psychosomatic disorders have it that secondary gains (for example, being looked after by relatives) provide the motivation for the patient to be ill. While analysts may seek to avoid blaming their patients despite holding such theories,[21] it is hard for lay people to follow suit.

Many mental disorders are problematic in that it is unclear whether they are disorders or moral failings. In contrast, the only physical disorder I can think of where the condition itself rather than merely the cause is subject to such moralizing might be obesity (Townend, 2009).

A powerful line of academic thought claims that although mental illness tends to be more stigmatized than physical illness this is merely because of prejudice, and can be remedied by educational efforts (Byrne, 2000; Kendell, 2001; Rüsch et al., 2005). I suggest that this is not the case. Consider the specific types of mentally ill people that lay people would prefer to avoid: top of the list are antisocial personality, pedophilia, factitious disorder, exhibitionism, voyerism, cocaine dependence (Feldman & Crandall, 2007). Such disorders are genuinely perplexing, in that it is unclear whether they should be considered disorders or moral failings or both. In addition, persons with these conditions genuinely do exhibit behaviors that make it prudent to avoid them.

I hold that some mental disorders are intrinsically morally problematic. However, following a suggestion by Charlotte Blease (2012), I also think that we have a tendency to impute moral failing to those who suffer from some mental illnesses unfairly. Blease considers lay responses to depression. Blease suggests that we find the existence of depression threatening to the optimistic worldview that we prefer to adopt. We want to believe that life is generally good and meaningful, and that we will get what we deserve. Depressed people threaten this belief. In an effort to avoid drawing the obvious conclusion—that life can be horrible for some people through no fault of their own—we tend to clutch at other hypotheses—that depressed people are whining and their life isn't really so bad, or that they are somehow to blame for their condition. Such thinking is plausibly part of a broader pattern of commonplace psychological defenses, which come into play when our belief in a just and benevolent world is threatened. In a series of experiments, Melvin Lerner found that when we are faced with suffering that we cannot alleviate we have a tendency to unfairly blame the victim for their predicament or underestimate the extent of their suffering (Lerner, 1980). Following Blease, I suggest that the awfulness of severe mental illness, and our relative powerlessness in the face of it, can thus lead us to unfairly suspect that such conditions are only dubiously disorders, and that sufferers are morally responsible or exaggerating their suffering.

To conclude, in this chapter I set out to examine what, if anything, is special about mental health and disorder. While academics who have examined the issue frequently suggest that the distinction is meaningless and should be abandoned, many patient groups are deeply concerned to avoid a mental health label for "their" condition. I have argued that both the academics and the patient groups are correct. There is no clear-cut way of distinguishing mental from physical disorders. Those disorders that are considered mental have come to be so considered for a mish-mash of frequently contingent historical reasons. This being said, the desire of many patient groups to avoid being diagnosed as suffering from a mental disorder is completely

understandable. Amongst those disorders that are considered mental are a disproportionate number that are only dubiously disorders, either because they shade into normality or because it is unclear whether they should be considered disorders or moral failings. As some mental disorders are only dubiously disorders, mental disorders as a class have come to be stigmatized and only partially medicalized.

Notes

1 A recent article on the distinction between mental and physical disorders even starts with the claim that "it is of far greater practical importance how we draw the line between the pathological and the nonpathological than how we draw the line between mental and somatic disorders" (Brülde and Radovic, 2006).
2 For an overview of the debates, see Garvey, 2007, Chapter 7.
3 Wakefield (1992a, 1992b, 1999) adopts an evolutionary account of normal function.
4 Amundson, Chapter 32 this volume.
5 Cooper (2007) develops this argument against Aristotelian accounts. Parallel arguments can be developed against the other accounts in this family.
6 I am currently working on fully developing the account proposed in Cooper, 2002.
7 A.P.A. 2000.
8 Bolton 2008, pp. 251–252, also notes that the conditions covered by the DSM are diverse.
9 Murphy 2006, p. 71.
10 Kendell 2001, p. 491.
11 Kendell 2001, p. 491.
12 Roberston 1989, p. 148.
13 Swerdlow 2005, p. 330.
14 Kushner 1999, p. 181.
15 Kushner 1999, p. 176.
16 Kushner 1999, p. 176.
17 Hughes 1990, capitals in original.
18 Cooper 2005, pp. 127–129.
19 APA 2000, p. 703.
20 APA 2000, p. 717.
21 See Pickard 2011 for an interesting account of how it is possible for therapists to hold patients responsible, but not blame them.

References

Allison, P., Guichard, C., Fung, K., & Gilain, L. (2003). Dispositional optimism predicts survival status 1 year after diagnosis in head and neck cancer patients. *Journal of Clinical Oncology*, 21: 543–548.

American Psychiatric Association (2000). *Diagnostic and Statistical Manual of Mental Disorders*, 4th ed. Text revision. Washington, DC: American Psychiatric Association.

Banks, J., & Prior, L. (2001). Doing things with illness: the micro-politics of the CFS clinic. *Social Science and Medicine*, 52: 11–23.

Baron-Cohen, S. (1995). *Mindblindness: An essay on autism and theory of mind*. Cambridge, MA: MIT Press.

Bayer, R. (1981). *Homosexuality and American Psychiatry*. New York: Basic Books Inc.

Blease, C. (2012). Stigmatising depression: Folk theorising and "the Pollyanna backlash". In H. Carel and R. Cooper (Eds.), *Contemporary Topics in Philosophy of Medicine* (pp. 181–196). Stocksfield: Acumen.

Bolton, D. (2001). Problems in the definition of "mental disorder". *The Philosophical Quarterly*, 51: 182–199.

Bolton, D. (2008). *What is Mental Disorder?* Oxford: Oxford University Press.

Boorse, C. (1975). On the distinction between disease and illness. *Philosophy and Public Affairs*, 5: 49–68.

Boorse, C. (1976). What a theory of mental health should be. *Journal of Social Behaviour*, 6: 61–84.

Boorse, C. (1977). Health as a theoretical concept. *Philosophy of Science*, 44: 542–573.

Boorse, C. (1997). A rebuttal on health. In J. Hunter and R. Almeder (Eds.), *What is Disease?* (pp. 1–134). Totowa, NJ: Humana Press.

Brülde, B., and Radovic, F. (2006). What is mental about mental disorder? *Philosophy, Psychiatry and Psychology*, 13: 99–116.

Byrne, P. (2000). Stigma of mental illness and ways of diminishing it. *Advances in Psychiatric Treatment*, 6: 65–72.

Cooper, R. (2002). Disease. *Studies in History and Philosophy of Biological and Biomedical Sciences*, 33: 263–282.

Cooper, R. (2005) *Classifying Madness*. Dordrecht: Springer.

Cooper, R. (2007). Aristotelian accounts of disease— what are they good for? *Philosophical Papers*, 36: 427–442.

Davis, S. (2002). Completing disability forms. Available at http://www.anapsid.org/cnd/disability/complete forms.html.

DeLuca, J. (2008). Chronic fatigue syndrome and malingering. In J. Morgan and J. Sweet (Eds.), *Neuropsychology of Malingering Casebook* (pp. 245–253). New York: Psychology Press.

Dumit, J. (2006). Illnesses you have to fight to get: Facts as forces in uncertain, emergent illnesses. *Social Science and Medicine*, 62: 577–590.

Feilden, T. (2011). "Torrent of abuse" hindering ME research. *BBC News*, 29 July 2011, available at http:www.bbc.co.uk/news/science-environment-14326514?print=true.

Feldman, D. B., & Crandall, C. S. (2007). Dimensions of mental illness stigma: What about mental illness causes social rejection? *Journal of Social and Clinical Psychology*, 26: 137–154.

Fingarette, H. (1988). *Heavy Drinking: The myth of alcoholism as a disease*. Berkeley, CA: University of California Press.

Foucault, M. (1971). *Madness and Civilisation*. London: Routledge.

Garvey, B. (2007). *Philosophy of Biology*. Stocksfield: Acumen.

Guise, J., McVittie, C. and McKinlay, A. (2010). A discourse analytic study of ME/CFS (Chronic Fatigue Syndrome) sufferers' experiences of interactions with doctors. *Journal of Health Psychology*, 15: 426–435.

Hales, C. and Barker, D. (1992). Type 2 (non-insulin-dependent) diabetes mellitus: the thirfty phenotype hypothesis. *Diabetologia*, 35: 595–601.

Hitt, E. (2010). Law requiring parity of mental and substance abuse health insurance benefits implemented. *Medscape medical news*, January 29. Available at http://www.medscape.com/viewarticle/716208.

Hughes, S. (1990). *Ryan: A mother's story*. Duarte, CA: Hope Press.

Jason, L., Richman, J., Friedberg, F., et al. (1997). Politics, science and the emergence of a new disease: The case of chronic fatigue syndrome. *American Psychologist*, September: 973–983.

Jason, L. (2011). Small wins matter in advocacy movements: giving voice to patients. *American Journal of Community Psychology*. Published online 20 August 2011.

Kendell, R. (2001). The distinction between mental and physical illness. *British Journal of Psychiatry*, 178: 490–493.

Kushner, H. (1999). *A Cursing Brain? The histories of Tourette syndrome*. Cambridge, MA: Harvard University Press.

Kushner, H. (2004). Competing medical cultures, support groups, and Tourette syndrome. In M. Randall, Packard, P., Brown, J., Berkelman, R., & H. Frumkin (Eds.), *Emerging Illness and Society: Negotiating the Public Health Agenda* (pp. 71–101). Baltimore: John Hopkins University Press.

Laing, R. D. and Esterson, A. (1970 [1964]). *Sanity, Madness and the Family*. Harmondsworth: Penguin.

Leckman, J., Walker, D. and Cohen, D. (1993). Premonitory urges in Tourette's syndrome. *American Journal of Psychiatry*, 150: 98–102.

Lerner, M. (1980). *The Belief in a Just World: A fundamental delusion*. New York: Plenum press.

McCleary, K. (2010). Letter to the DSM-5 task force from the CFIDS association of America. Available at http://www.cfids.org/advocacy/2010/dsm5-statement.pdf.

Mealey, L. (1995). The sociobiology of sociopathy: An integrated evolutionary model. *Behavioural and Brain Sciences*, 18: 523–541.

Megone, C. (1998). Aristotle's function argument and the concept of mental illness. *Philosophy, Psychiatry, Psychology*, 5: 187–201.

Megone, C. (2000). Mental illness, human function and values. *Philosophy, Psychiatry and Psychology*, 7: 45–65.

Mink, J. (2001). Basal ganglia dysfunction in Tourette's syndrome: A new hypothesis. *Pediatric Neurology*, 25: 190–198.

Mittenberg, W., Patton, C., Canyock, E. and Condit, D. (2002). Base rates of malingering and symptom exaggeration. *Journal of Clinical and Experimental Neuropsychology*, 24: 1094–1102.

Murphy, D. (2006). *Psychiatry in the Scientific Image*. Cambridge, MA: MIT Press.

Newman, S. (2009). Irreconcilable differences? Tourette syndrome, disability, and definition in democratic policy debates. *Disability Studies Quarterly*, 29: available at http://www.dsq-sds.org/article/view/934/1114.

Nordenfelt, L. (1995). *On the Nature of Health: An action-theoretic approach*. Dordrecht: Kluwer.

Pickard, H. (2011). Responsibility without blame: Empathy and the effective treatment of personality disorder. *Philosophy, Psychiatry, Psychology*, 18: 209–224.

Reznek, L. (1987). *The Nature of Disease*. London: Routledge and Kegan Paul.

Richman, K. (2004). *Ethics and the Metaphysics of Medicine*. Cambridge, MA: MIT Press.

Robertson, M. (1989). The Gilles de la Tourette syndrome: the current status. *British Journal of Psychiatry*, 154: 147–169.

Rose, N. (2007). *The Politics of Life Itself*. Princeton, NJ: Princeton University Press.

Rosenhan, D. (1973). On being sane in insane places. *Science*, 179: 250–258.

Rüsch, N., Angermeyer, M. and Corrigan, P. (2005). Mental illness stigma: Concepts, consequences and initiatives to reduce stigma. *European Psychiatry*, 20: 529–539.

Swerdlow, N. (2005). Tourette syndrome: Current controversies and the battlefield landscape. *Current Neurology and Neuroscience Reports*, 5: 329–331.

Szasz, T. (1962) [1972]. *The Myth of Mental Illness*. St Albans: Paladin.

Tooby, J. and Cosmides, L. (1992). The psychological foundations of culture. In J. Barkow, L. Cosmides and J. Tooby (Eds.), *The Adapted Mind* (pp. 19–136). Oxford: Oxford University Press.

Townend, L. (2009). The moralizing of obesity: A new name for an old sin? *Critical Social Policy*, 29: 171–190.

Wakefield, J. (1992a). The concept of mental disorder: On the boundary between biological facts and social value. *American Psychologist*, 47: 373–388.

Wakefield, J. (1992b). Disorder as harmful dysfunction: A conceptual critique of D.S.M-III-R's definition of mental disorder. *Psychological Review*, 99: 232–247.

Wakefield, J. (1999). Evolutionary versus prototype analyses of the concept of disorder. *Journal of Abnormal Psychology*, 108: 374–399.

Wessely, S., Nimuan, C. and Sharpe, M. (2001). Functional somatic syndromes: one or many? *The Lancet*, 354: 936–939.

Wilson, D. (1993). Evolutionary epidemiology: Darwinian theory in the service of medicine and psychiatry. In S. Baron-Cohen (Ed.) (1997), *The Maladapted Mind* (pp. 39–55). Hove: Psychology Press.

Wojcik, W., Armstrong, D. and Kanaan, R. (2011). Chronic fatigue syndrome: Labels, meanings and consequences. *Journal of Psychosomatic Research*, 70: 500–504.

Topic 11 POLITICS AND THE CONCEPT OF HUMAN NATURE

THE CONCEPT OF HUMAN nature has often been used to justify the oppression of various social groups on the grounds either that their behavior or characteristics (e.g., homosexuality) were abnormal ("they go against human nature") or that these groups (e.g., women) were by nature inferior (e.g., "women are unable to learn"). Thus, Rousseau asserts that "if you want right guidance, always follow the leadings of nature. Everything that characterizes sex should be respected as established by nature." Kant agrees, writing that "laborious learning or painful pondering, even if a woman should greatly succeed at it, destroy the merits of her sex."

One may wonder whether such oppressive uses of the notion of human nature are misuses of this notion or whether there is something in it that promotes the justification and rationalization of social injustices. Some, such as the Swedish sociologist Gunnar Myrdal in his classic book *An American Dilemma*, perhaps even suspect that appeals to human nature are always oppressive and reactionary. Alternatively, while some ways of thinking about human nature may be intrinsically reactionary, other approaches may not invite oppressive misuses. But, then, what are these? How do they differ from oppressive ways of thinking about human nature? Furthermore, in light of these past oppressive uses of the notion of human nature, we should also be wary that unbeknownst to us current uses are oppressive too (see Amundson's article in Topic 10). We may also wonder whether scientific (or, some may hold, pseudo-scientific) research on human nature should be encouraged. After all, we may be better off being ignorant of some things. And, if this is going too far, it may still be that our epistemic standards should be stricter for research on human nature than for other scientific research.

This section is dedicated to an assessment of the notion of human nature in light of these oppressive uses. Silvers' essay is a frontal attack on the traditional ways of thinking about human nature in light of their oppressive uses. She introduces an important distinction between the mode and the level of functioning of an individual, arguing that traditional notions of human nature have focused on the modes of functioning instead of the level of functioning. This focus has underwritten social and educational policies that have harmed people with disabilities, a claim illustrated by several examples in her essay. Silvers holds, as Amundson does in his essay (Topic 10), that interventions meant to help people with disabilities should take the level of functioning into consideration and acknowledge the role of the environment to high-level functioning.

Antony acknowledges the oppressive uses of the notion of human nature with a particular focus on the oppression of women. In response, feminists could adopt one of the following two positions: They could reject the notion of human nature or they could develop a distinct notion of human nature, compatible with scientific progress and consistent with their feminist agenda. In this chapter, Antony favors the latter option and develops an original notion of human nature.

Finally, in a new chapter, Holmstrom reviews the feminist debates about the notion of human nature in great detail, and defends the view that the notion of human nature is important for feminists. This chapter will help the reader navigate this very active area of debate.

Suggested Further Reading

Antony, L. M. (2000) Natures and norms. *Ethics*, 111: 8–36.

Chomsky, N. and Foucault, M. (2006) *The Chomsky–Foucault Debate: On human nature*. New York: The New Press.

Curti, M. (1980) *Human Nature in American Thought: A history*. New York: John Wiley.

Degler, C. N. (1991) *In Search of Human Nature: The decline and revival of Darwinism in American social thought*. New York: Oxford University Press.

Dewey, J. (1922) *Human Nature and Conduct*. New York: Henry Hold and Company.

Fausto-Sterling, A. (1985) *Myths of Gender: Biological theories about women and men*. New York: Basic Books.

Holmstrom, N. (1984) A Marxist theory of women's nature. *Ethics*, 94: 456–473.

Jaggar, A. M. (1983) *Feminist Politics and Human Nature*. Lanham, MD: Rowman & Littlefield Publishers.

Kant, I. (1764). Observations on the feelings of the beautiful and the sublime. Quoted p. 167 of M. Baron, Kantian ethics and claims of detachment. In R. M. Schott (Ed.), *Feminist Interpretations of Immanuel Kant* (pp. 145–172). University Park, PA: The Pennsylvania State University Press.

Kitcher, P. (2001) *Science, Truth, and Democracy*. New York: Oxford University Press.

Myrdal, G. (1944) *An American Dilemma: The negro problem and modern democracy*. New York: Harper & Row.

Roughley, N. (2000) *Being Human: Anthropological universality and particularity in transdisciplinary perspectives*. New York: De Gruyter.

Rousseau, J.-J. (1972/2009) *Émile*. In K. J. Warren (Ed.), *An Unconventional History of Western Philosophy: Conversations Between Men and Women Philosophers* (p. 295). Lanham, MD: Rowman & Littlefield publishers.

Chapter 34

Anita Silvers

A FATAL ATTRACTION TO NORMALIZING
Treating Disabilities as Deviations from "Species-Typical" Functioning

Health Care as a Social Good

In the late twentieth century, (bio)medical ethics bifurcated into micro- and macro-studies, the former devoted to probing singular cases suffused with difficulties, the latter committed to finding some common good(s) to invoke so as to resolve hard as well as clear cases. Being clear about what kind of good health care represents, it was argued, enables us to decide who, in what circumstance, deserves it. To this way of thinking, while health is a personal good, health care is a social good. And it is not how to secure the former, but when to provide the latter, that is the challenge in morally difficult cases. Accordingly, macro-(bio)medical ethics developed an account of how to judge right and wrong in caring for patients, namely, by proposing what kind of health care, in what circumstances, a just society allocates.

Macro-(bio)medical ethics enthusiasts think that if we had a just system of health care, the right interventions would be evident. Once health care is cast as a social good, principles drawn from political morality will guide us in assessing the propriety and priority of various kinds of medical interventions. Just principles will enable us to see what should be provided for particular patients.[1] It is the nature of justice to illuminate the difference between obligatory and merely beneficial interventions, that is, between necessary treatment and salutary enhancement.

The latter may be privileging or not, depending on how the patient is circumstanced relative to other people. But the former is always equalizing, suggests Norman Daniels in presenting his immensely influential theory, which is meant to place the provision of health care on the firm foundation of democratic values that, by tradition, inform our public policy. What makes a medical intervention a treatment for Daniels, and what makes treatments equalizing vehicles is that they aim at preventing or remedying the disadvantages that people would otherwise suffer as the result of accident or disease.

> None of us deserves the advantages conferred by accidents of birth . . . It is . . . important to use resources to counter the natural disadvantages introduced by disease . . . This does not mean we are committed to the futile goal of eliminating or "leveling" all natural differences between people . . . [But] health care has normal functioning as its goal: it concentrates on a specific class of obvious disadvantages and tries to eliminate them.[2]

The notion of "leveling" that Daniels introduces here is a traditional theme in American political morality. Dissenting religious groups like the Quakers urged that society be arranged to show more respect for the commonalities of human nature, our essential humanity, than for artificial distinctions of class, caste, or role. Those committed to "leveling" were motivated by the conviction that all souls were equally valuable to God; therefore, all souls should have an equal voice in the community. The accidents of wealth and birth ought not to disadvantage people by limiting their opportunities for social participation.

Traditional leveling theories did not propose that all souls were identical, of course, but only that they have equal opportunity for community involvement and influence. Nor did these theories propose to eliminate the natural differences among people, only those accidental disadvantageous differences attendant on wealth and birth. Indeed, the argument for diminishing the importance assigned to wealth and birth (that is, to inherited rank) was that these socially constructed characteristics should not be allowed to obscure or impede the expression of natural talents and traits, the properties that naturally differentiate one individual from another.

In this tradition, Daniels's policy proposes that health care should eliminate, to the degree possible, the disadvantageous adventitious differences that occur when poor health impairs physical, sensory, or cognitive functioning. People should not be leveled in every way, for they naturally differ in skills and talents: only artificially disadvantageous differences should be eliminated. One of Daniels's important contributions to the traditional discussion is to suppose us to have become so proficient in the practice of medicine that the disadvantageous differences attributable to unrepaired poor health are artificial as when people remain in ill health due to an unjust system of distributing effective medical interventions. If the disadvantages associated with poor health are thus as much a social as a natural product, our "leveling" tradition urges that deficiencies in people's functioning that result from poor health should be remedied so as not to diminish the opportunities their skills and talent would otherwise secure for them. Daniels writes:

We are obliged to help others achieve normal functioning, but we do not "owe" each other whatever it takes to make us more beautiful, strong, or completely happy.[3] . . . The uses of health care that most of us believe we are obliged to make available to other are uses that maintain or restore normal functioning, not simply any use that enhances our welfare. . . . This distinction between the treatment of disease and disability and the enhancement of otherwise normal appearance or capabilities is reflected in the health care benefit package of nearly every national health insurance system, whether public or mixed, around the world.[4]

And as he concludes in another text, "If people have a higher-order interest in preserving . . . opportunity, . . . then they will have a pressing interest in maintaining normal species functioning by establishing institutions—such as health care systems that do just that."[5]

On this (bio)ethical emendation to political morality, medical treatment has a public value because it is an instrument of the state's commitment to protect all citizens equally against arbitrary disadvantage. Interventions that merely enhance the welfare or well-being of individuals in respects in which they are not disadvantaged do not have a similar public value.

> The central function of health care services is to keep us functioning as close to normal as possible. Since maintaining normal functioning protects the range of opportunities open to people, by providing an appropriate set of health care services, we make a significant contribution to preserving equality of opportunity.[6]

Treatments, then, are those interventions that are used to reduce or remedy whatever disadvantage is occasioned by abnormal functioning that is associated with ill health. Because treatments are so defined, they are necessarily equalizing, in the sense that to be treatments they must be aimed at preventing or rectifying disadvantageous functioning and, consequently, at reducing or eliminating a specific kind of disadvantage the patient has in comparison with normally functioning individuals. Treatments can be prospective as well as retrospective on this view. For example, as the purpose of vaccination programs is to prevent some individuals from becoming disadvantaged by the sequelae of disease, to vaccinate children against polio or measles is to treat them.

Treatments are processes, however, and a process that has a definitive objective may not always succeed in reaching it. For example, it can be accurate to describe what we do in relation to our students as "educating them" even if some of the students are not educated. Similarly, treating someone may not always succeed in restoring that individual to the desired mode and/or level of functioning. But the key to a medical process's being a treatment is the plausibility of our casting it as a procedure to eliminate a disadvantage by restoring functioning.

For example, breast reductions often count as treatments now that a convincing case for the disadvantageousness of very large breasts is made; for example, she can't buy clothes that fit, she can't run because of their weight, they make her an object of derision in the workplace. But we can imagine social contexts in which it is much harder to make this case. If women custom-made their own clothes, rarely ran (because society insisted it isn't lady-like to run) and never, never pursued careers in the workplace (because fathers and husbands did not want women to work outside the home), it would be harder to argue that the breast reduction procedure remedies disadvantages rather than merely increases a woman's comfort. For in that context women would not normally engage in the performances the procedure rehabilitates or restores. But this does not totally resolve the issue, for some women may desire to transform the roles females are permitted to adopt and so may argue that breast reductions remove one of the barriers to women's assuming such roles. They might argue that in their case breast reduction is not merely a means of enhancing the welfare of large breasted women with unfashionable preferences for comfort over sexual attractiveness; rather, it responds to a legitimate need to eliminate a social disadvantage.

Considerations such as these raised by the breast reduction procedure lead to questions about the neutrality of appealing to normal fashions of functioning. Sometimes, people who function in the normal fashion are, for that very reason, confined to roles that are disadvantageous and detract from their flourishing. This restriction has surely been the case for women in societies in which women have been assigned to disadvantageous roles on the ground that their normal fashion of functioning prohibited their achieving in more highly valued roles. Since the goal of treatment is to remove disadvantage, but normal fashions of functioning can be disadvantageous, why does Daniels believe that (maintaining or restoring) functioning in a normal fashion is the standard for determining whether an intervention is a treatment?

Normalizing

Whether or not I am an individual whose disadvantage is reduced because I receive treatment, social arrangements providing for the reduction of undeserved disadvantage occasioned by physical, sensory, or cognitive dysfunction are for the public good, Daniels says, and thus for my good insofar as I am a community member. Daniels comments:

> I abstract from the special effects that derive from an individual's conception of the good. This level of abstraction seems appropriate given our search for a measure of the social importance, for claims of justice, of impairments of health. My conclusion is that we

should use impairment of the normal . . . as a measure of the relative importance of health care needs.[7]

Because treatment is a public good, the condition which occasions or invites it should be objective and independent of transitory social accidents, Daniels believes.[8] What he takes to be the natural difference between normal functioning and functioning corrupted by illness or accident suggests to him a fixed and objective, and therefore an appropriately public, standard for ascertaining the occasions when treatment should occur. "Where we can take as fixed, primarily by nature, a generally uncontroversial baseline of species-typical functioning," we can show, he thinks, "which principles of justice are relevant to distributing health care services."[9] Daniels thinks that the way the species typically functions constitutes a natural and therefore a neutral standard to which the public can assent.

First, all "people have a fundamental interest in protecting their share of the normal range of opportunities."[10] Second, maintaining "normal species functioning" is necessary to protect this high order interest persons have in maintaining a normal range of opportunities: "Life plans we are otherwise suited for and have a reasonable expectation of finding satisfying or happiness-producing are rendered unreasonable by impairments of normal functioning . . ."[11] Third, and crucial to Daniels's argument, is his assumption that normal functioning is natural and thereby neutral in that the criteria for determining what functioning is normal are biological rather than social. "The basic idea is that health is the absence of disease, and diseases (I here include deformities and disabilities that result from trauma) are deviations from the natural functional organization of a typical member of a species."[12] This step of the argument is critical, for it is here that we are told why not functioning as people typically do is disadvantageous. When disease is the reason individuals do not function in typical fashion, their resulting performances must be inferior to those that issue from individuals whose natural functional organization has not been corrupted by disease.

Of course, this argument leaves open what counts as being diseased. Daniels thinks that the line between disease and its absence generally is noncontroversial and publicly ascertainable through the methods of the biomedical sciences.[13] Others argue to the contrary, of course. For example, Susan Sherwin points out that some elements of women's lives for instance, menstruation, pregnancy, menopause, body size and feminine behavior—have been medicalized and treated as diseases because they have been viewed as disruptive of normal functioning.[14] In the same vein, genetic conditions that result in what we think is inferior functioning are equated with disease. These examples suggest that not disease but functioning in the normal fashion is the controlling notion here.

John Rawls, on whose theory Daniels relies to scope out justice in health care and other domains, gives us a political perspective on normal functioning. He remarks:

> [A] person is someone who can be a citizen, that is, a fully cooperating member of society over a complete life . . . [F]or our purposes . . . I leave aside permanent physical disabilities or mental disorders so severe as to prevent persons from being normal and fully cooperating members of society in the usual sense.[15]

Here is an additional reason to think of a policy of normalizing functioning as an instrument that secures the ends of democratic political morality. For on the view that being a well-functioning individual is critical to performing the social responsibilities of citizens, normalizing is seen as qualifying functionally defective individuals for citizenship by repairing them so they can execute the usual social interactions and sustain common social responsibilities. To do so they must conduct themselves normally and be able to comply with other people's natural expectations of them. For whoever cannot perform competently as a cooperating and contributing and, therefore, an equal, social partner is fully neither citizen nor person.

The Right to (Normalizing) Treatment

The prescription is clear: although interventions that enhance a patient's functioning so that it departs from what is normal may be advisable for the patient when they enhance the patient's welfare, only interventions that normalize command a broader social warrant. That is because normalizing interventions restore or maintain individuals as cooperative, contributing citizens.

To understand what is at stake, we should notice that at least two aspects of functioning, the mode and the level, affect whether the performance of a function is normal. A function's mode is the way it is accomplished. To illustrate, the normal mode in which we execute the function of reading a document is by seeing the text. This function can be executed in other ways, for instance, tactilely if the text is brailled, aurally if the text is scanned into a computer with a voice output screen reader. These alternative or adaptive modes may support a normal level of functioning. If the individual is adept, she may still read at normal speed and comprehension. Or she may function in the alternative mode above or below the normal level. According to Daniels, restoring individuals who have suffered impairment of functioning through illness or accident to the normal mode and level of functioning takes priority. If treatment fails, the next step is adaptation.

> One important function of health care services ... is to restore handicapping dysfunctions (e. g., of vision, mobility, and so on). The medical goal is to cure the diseased organ or limb when possible. When a cure is

impossible, we try to make function as normal as possible, through corrective lenses or prosthesis and rehabilitative therapy. But when restoration of function is beyond the ability of medicine per se, we begin another area of services, nonmedical support services.[16]

It is important to notice that this system gives mode of functioning precedence over level of functioning. On it, we first attempt to restore the patient's ability to function in the customary mode, seeing or walking or hearing the way other people do. Afterward, if a cure proves impossible, we apply prostheses—corrective lenses, artificial limbs and physical therapy, hearing aids, and lipreading lessons. These prostheses may restore the patient to the typical level of functioning (or enhance it, remember the Bionic Man) but not (quite) to the normal mode: lipreading requires that those engaged in dialogue face each other, artificial limbs demand both stump and prosthesis maintenance, corrective lenses must be put on and removed.

Parenthetically, Daniels complains that social support services are allocated fewer resources than restorative treatment. Given Daniels's account up to this point, his preferred explanation is curious. He hypothesizes:

> Yet for various reasons, probably having to do with the profitability and glamor of personal medical services and careers ... as compared with services for the handicapped, our society has taken only slow and halting steps to meet the health care needs of those with permanent disabilities.[17]

It is odd for him to think that the reason society does not provide sufficient social support services is because doing so is not sufficiently personally profitable or glamorous for professionals. His own account provides a more persuasive explanation, namely, that the initial response to defective functioning, which consequently has first call upon resources, is restorative treatment. On his own account, normalizing interventions do and should take precedence over interventions with any other kind of impact because their outcomes are assigned a higher social or political value.

This priority is because normal functioning appears to be a firm and impersonal, yet compelling, goal, whereas we have no reliable standard of what counts as satisfactory if an individual does not function normally. Normal functioning is a clear standard as well, Daniels supposes, because to determine what normal function is, we need only observe the natural functional organization of human beings. This task, he says "falls to the biomedical sciences . . . since claims about the design of the species and its fitness to meeting biological goals underlie at least some of the relevant functional ascriptions,"[18] So neither the predominant functional modes nor the modal functional levels are artifactual, he thinks. Because the functioning that typifies a species seems so expressive of its nature, species-typical functioning appears to be a self-justifying standard, nature's way of deducing how we ought best to conduct ourselves given what kind of creature we are.

Further, what could be a more modest and natural expectation of individuals than the prospect of functioning as their species typically does? Given these considerations, all individuals equally are found to have a natural stake in social arrangements designed to prevent or repair anomalous conditions that interfere with species-typical functioning. Concomitantly, relatively few individuals would have an interest in preserving or promoting any specific functional anomaly or singularity. So it seems as if the broadest based public support very naturally will go to social arrangements that reduce whatever anomalies or singularities hinder adherence to the species typical functional standard.

The protean character of two of the notions pivotal to Daniels's argument, namely, those marked by the designations "natural" and "normal," is striking. Absent the suggestion that these are virtually interchangeable characters, in that our normal fashions of functioning are those that are natural rather than acquired, there would be no obvious connection between normalizing modes of functioning and equalizing opportunity. For there is nothing unusual in equally healthy people experiencing vast differences in the opportunities available to them, nor in people in different states of health enjoying similar scopes of opportunity. But our species has evolved a natural functional organization so well-suited to realizing these goals, Daniels thinks, that an individual's falling away from this organizational standard by not functioning normally cannot help but diminish his or her options for desirable achievement.

What apparently is important here is not actualized opportunities. Rather, what is supposed to be equalized is the amplitude of options that each individual has available for achieving our species biological goals. It might seem, then, that nature determines what normal species functioning is (a biological premise) and in doing so specifies the mode and level of functioning individuals need to exhibit if they are to enjoy meaningful equality of opportunity (a social conclusion).

Yet when we probe more deeply into Daniels's account of just health care, we find that it is a social rather than a biological value that informs and validates reparative interventions. Indeed, it is not even a sociobiological value, for rather than surrendering individual benefit to the species' collective evolutionary good, the value to which Daniels appeals is simply an extension of the liberal sociopolitical commitment to preserving equal access to opportunity for the individual.

Daniels's standard is biological, but the principle that implements it clearly is not. For biology tends to eliminate truly dysfunctional individuals, not repair them. The principle that advises us to restore people's normal functioning through health care is also not an expression of an impersonal sociobiological drive of individuals to maintain their species. At most it is an intersubjective principle with the potential to unify the personal interests individuals have in maintaining a competitive position. It suggests that we should be suspicious of claims that there is a biological mandate that accredits policies of normalizing people by restoring them to typical or familiar modes and levels of functioning.

"Normalizing" has a passionate component, of course, namely, our tribal preferences to congregate with individuals like ourselves. But our attraction to the company of our counterparts, which can be intense, is not usually thought to justify a public commitment to allocate resources to repair those who do not measure up. Simply avoiding or excluding those who fall away from the common standard is the usual concomitant of our passion for congregating with those who most resemble us. The difficulty with thinking of a policy of normalizing as a component of democratic political morality becomes even more evident when we notice that normalizing is sometimes privileging rather than equalizing. For instance, interventions that help some individuals more closely approach species typical functioning may deprive, disadvantage, or otherwise reduce opportunities for individuals who function normally already. And, as we saw when we considered the value of breast reductions, making normalizing our policy can also be unfair if it worsens the position, or otherwise oppresses, the very individuals whose functioning it purports to repair by, for instance, depriving them of anomalous but effectively adaptive alternative modes of functioning.

We should be wary of policies that cloak privileging certain fashions of functioning in the mantle of the "normal." Normalizing then is not the self-evidently right thing to do. Nor can we justly allocate health care without careful attention to the circumstances of whoever is normalized.

What Is Being Normal?

How useful is the concept of normalizing in warranting medical interventions considered case by case? Whether, in fact, there is much clarity about what normalizing is raises a second kind of concern about its compatibility with egalitarian ends, for there is a tendency to equivocate to a dangerous degree as to the meaning of this admittedly circumstantial standard. In "The Meaning of Normal," Phillip Davis, and John Bradley comment:

> Medicine uses the word normal to express . . . various meanings. . . . In medicine, normal can refer to a "defined standard," such as normal blood pressure: a "naturally occurring state," such as normal immunity: . . . "free from disease," as in a normal pap smear . . . "balanced" as in a normal diet, "acceptable" as in normal behavior, or it can be used to describe a stable physical state. In all these meanings . . . normal is used to describe an "ordinary finding" or an "expected state." But medicine allows another meaning . . . that differs significantly from the ordinary. [M]edicine has come to understand normal as a "description of the ideal." . . . Defining the norm as an ideal leads to significant problems. . . . Disease and ill health are a normal part of the human condition. The constant pursuit of health . . . leads easily to blaming those who bear the burden of illness. . . . More important . . . are the problems that result from defining variation from the ideal as "abnormal." . . . Accepting the ideal as the norm begs the question of how uncommon something must be to be considered abnormal.[19]

Current practice assigns pathological conditions the role of being signifiers of unhealth. But because it is not cost effective to intervene wherever pathology occurs—that is, to conduct an all-out campaign to normalize all parts of all people—current practice takes a further conceptual step by identifying some departures from the norm as incapacitating, while others are tolerated as benign. Davis and Bradley observe: "When the ideal is taken as the norm, variation becomes defined as disease—an especially peculiar circumstance insofar as much variation has no particular clinical significance or biological consequence."[20]

Christopher Boorse suggests that it is usual on current practice to assess departures from the norm as warranting intervention if they cause death, disability, discomfort, or deformity.[21] Interventions are made not on the ground of the rarity of the condition but rather its disruption of function. But while death indubitably is incapacitating, disability, discomfort, and deformity need not always be so. To define such conditions as necessarily dysfunctional and consequently as demanding intervention begs the question.

Surely, any measure used to sanction intervention should distinguish what is not normal and thereby harmful from what is not normal but merely unusual or anomalous. This is to avoid justifying every culture's every intercession into anomalies regarded by that culture as pathological. For instance, for the Punan Bah of Borneo, the birth of twins is a greater social disgrace than the birth of a spastic, blind, or retarded child. It is so socially disturbing and disadvantageous a condition that it is also dysfunctional, for after twin births, one twin always dies (unless it is given to another family living distantly enough to achieve the concealment of its twinhood).

Normal Quality of Life

To distinguish such prescientific practices to remove anomalies from modern medical practices to abate defects in individuals, Dan Brock very usefully attempts to say more about the damage that departures from being normal can do. In *Life and Death* (1993) Brock correctly eschews offering an absolute standard for knowing when medical intervention properly remedies abnormality.

The dominant conception of the appropriate aims of medicine focuses on medicine as an intervention aimed at preventing, ameliorating, or curing and thereby restoring, or preventing the loss of, normal function or of life. Whether the norm be that of the particular individual, or that typical in the particular society or species, the aim of raising people's function to above the norm is not commonly accepted as an aim of medicine of equal importance in restoring function up to the norm. Problematic though the distinction may be, quality of life measures in medicine and health care consequently tend to focus on individuals' or patients' dysfunction and its relation to some such norm.[22]

How does dysfunction present itself as a diminution of quality of life? Brock observes: "At a deep level, medicine views bodily parts and organs, individual human bodies, and people from a functional perspective."[23] But what one must go on to grapple with is the difficulty of connecting, let alone commensurating, different kinds or levels of functional descriptions. An increasingly familiar component of medical judgment, so-called quality of life scales are meant to quantify well-being to determine for what and on whom health care dollars are best expended.

Brock cites such a "Quality of Well-Being Scale"[24] to illustrate a discussion about containing high-cost but low-benefit treatments. Of almost equal weight on the scale are what are designated as the patient's physical activity level, namely, how competently the patient executes the performances of daily living, and (assigned just slightly more importance) the patient's functional level, that is, what the patient achieves through engagement in daily life performances.

But these rankings do not reflect the subtleties of what can be achieved despite impairment.

In the physical activity category of the scale Brock cites, mobilizing by walking, albeit with a feeble gait, ranks higher than using a wheelchair to be mobile. But which mode actually facilitates mobility more effectively is not nearly as clear as this scale makes it out to be. For while wheelchair users are more limited in the types of sites they can access, they exceed the customary level in respect to the speed at which and distance from where they travel to those sites. Individuals who mobilize by walking can climb into many more types of sites but only those they have the time and stamina to reach.

The physical activity category assesses the modes individuals adopt to perform a function and then assigns the patient a rank that reflects the degree to which his mode of functioning diverges from the customary mode. Walking very feebly more closely resembles our customary mode of mobilizing than wheeling very vigorously, so the individual who uses the former mode is assessed as enjoying a higher quality of life than the individual who uses the latter. On the other hand, the functional category addresses interactions between the patient and the environment. For whether someone who uses a wheelchair can get into a car or use public transportation, for instance, is as much a question about the availability of appropriately designed vehicles as it is about the patient.

This abstracting from complex differences between kinds of limits suggests that the scale is more responsive to the mere fact of an individual's being limited than to how functionally devastating or benign the limit might be. We should discount any scale that arbitrarily fixes the relative effectiveness of different modes of performing any function, any scale that equates what is most common with what is best, and equally any scale that illegitimately naturalizes such rankings by appeal to biological imperatives. For mechanically aided functioning is not necessarily inferior to unassisted activity, no more is driving twenty miles to be disparaged as the crutch of subnormal hikers, and no more

than manually signed communication is categorically inferior to speech. In general, we should mistrust any scale of well-being that purports to measure life's quality by comparing modes of functioning in a way that obscures how modes that are not the common fashion can nevertheless be fully functional.

Moreover, we should distrust any summative process that commensurates fixed and variable elements while disregarding the contexts to which the latter are relativized. The degree to which either personal or environmental limitations result in social limitations—that is, prevent an individual from normal social achievement like having a family and earning a living—is the outcome of complex interactions between the individual's limits and the limits of his or her environment. It is therefore difficult not only to predict the degree to which, but also to comprehend the process whereby, physical or environmental dysfunction leads to social dysfunction.

Brock himself recognizes that even serious physical limitations do not always lower quality of life if the disabled persons have been able or helped sufficiently to compensate for their disabilities so that their level of primary functional capacity remains essentially unimpaired; in such cases it becomes problematic even to characterize those affected as disabled.[25]

As the individuals Brock describes just prior to writing this passage are persons without arms and legs, this remark is revealing. If their eating, driving, painting pictures, raising a family—the functions of a good life that Brock portrays them as achieving—makes it problematic to describe them as disabled, then underachieving must be part of the definition of disability. And if being disabled is tied so firmly to lowered achievement, then even very marked deviation from species-typical functioning has only circumstantial connection to disability.

For it is far from clear that deviations from normal functioning mean either lowered productivity or decreased quality of life. Far from being the natural way of conducting ourselves, the modes of functioning that typify our species may merely be ways of doing things that are preferred by the dominant classes and to which we have therefore become accustomed. To the extent that this preference is the case, policies of normalizing, however well-intentioned, threaten not to equalize but to preserve existing patterns of functional dominance and privilege, a problem exacerbated by an absence of clarity in the practice of medicine in regard to establishing what is normal.

A Social Instrument for Normalizing

Accordingly, we need to clarify the nature and consequences of a public policy that gives expression to a mandate to normalize, an inquiry that I propose to pursue by exploring an analogous sphere, the domain of education. At least two reasons compel us to consider what we can learn from comparing analogous practices in education and health care. First, our current public policy intersects the two domains by legislating entitlements to preventative health education and rehabilitative special education within the public educational system. Indeed, a surprisingly large amount of what Daniels describes as basic health care needs are served by the public education system. Given that it is an egalitarian value, equalizing opportunity, that ultimately justifies the allocation of health care on Daniels's view, he is relatively expansive in delineating what is needed

to maintain, restore, or provide functional equivalents (when possible) to normal species functioning. These include adequate nutrition and shelter, safe and unpolluted living and working conditions, preventative and rehabilitative personal medical services, and nonmedical personal (and social) support services.[26]

Using public education to deploy preventative, curative, and rehabilitative health care

services is, of course, a very familiar practice. During the past century, day and residential schools in this country have, to give some examples, enforced preventative vaccination policies; promoted safe, sanitary, unpolluted, and tobacco-free living; ensured that children are given the basic principles of nutrition; instructed students about maintaining the health of their reproductive systems; identified and referred children in need of reparative care for vision, hearing, and other impairments; and offered rehabilitative speech, psychological, and other therapies, or adaptive education for blind children or deaf children, on their premises. Second, Daniels himself not only finds the analogy between educational and medical benefit apt but relies on it to argue for social support for (universal) health care:

[T]here is an important analogy between health care and education. Both are strategically important contributors to fair equality of opportunity. Both address needs that are not equally distributed among individuals. Various social factors . . . may produce special learning needs; so too may natural factors, such as the broad class of . . . disabilities. . . . [E]ducational needs, like health care needs, differ from other basic needs . . . Both at the national level and in many states, legislation to meet special educational needs . . . is justified by reference to the opportunities it protects.[27]

Daniels construes education as a reparative technology. The difference between their views lies in whether, as Daniels thinks, our educational priority should be to teach all children the knowledge and skills normally required to be participating, contributing citizens, or whether, as Brock has it, our educational priority should be to advance the widest array of children's cognitive abilities so as to nourish their different talents and give each appropriate personal opportunities for flourishing. In education as in health care, then, there is a question about the priority to assign to engendering normal functioning.

The Ascendancy of the Normal

In this regard, the battles that raged for nearly a hundred years about how best to educate deaf children provide an opportunity to assess the benefits of giving priority to normalizing. In the late nineteenth century, educators of the deaf bifurcated into two camps, one that passionately supported and one that vehemently opposed educating deaf children in the language of manual signs. Each charged the other with protracting the dysfunctionality of deaf people and consequently with unfairly constricting their opportunity. At the heart of this debate lay another divide, namely, an unbridgeable chasm that separated two very different beliefs about the relationship between biology and opportunity.

As Douglas Baynton writes in *Forbidden Signs: American Culture and the Campaign Against Sign Language*:

> The real battle (over sign language) was fought on a . . . rarefied plane, encompassing such questions as the larger purposes of education in a democratic and industrializing society . . . and the locus and character of cultural authority in America. Indeed, occupying a central place in the fight was a late-nineteenth century debate over the nature of nature itself.[28]

That deaf individuals talk by means of manual signs has been recognized since antiquity. Plato refers to this mode of communicating in the *Cratylus* (422e). In the early part of the nineteenth century manual sign language schools were established to equalize deaf people's access to the Word, understood to be the conveyance of that moral and religious knowledge which is the goal of human imagination, intelligence, and understanding. Because manual signing was thought to rely on natural symbols that were self-interpreting, Sign was believed to engage the intelligence directly and lucidly, and to stimulate the moral sense. Sign therefore was the instrument to repair deaf people's dysfunction and permit them to develop to greatest perfection. America followed Europe in becoming fascinated by signing. Teachers were imported to systematize and disseminate the gestural communication used by the deaf in this country.

Manualists considered deaf people to be a singular class, distanced from the transient fashions of speech and therefore less corruptible, out of the ordinary, remarkable, unique. Citing such eighteenth-century sources as Daniel Defoe and Denis Diderot, Lennard Davis writes in *Enforcing Normalcy: Disability, Deafness and the Body* that, for different reasons and in different respects, both the blind and the deaf were often thought to exhibit certain heightened and purer sensibilities than the ordinary person.[29] Far from being roleless, deaf people were assigned a special place in the eighteenth- and early nineteenth-century imagination.

But, as Baynton observes, "by the late nineteenth century, naturalness as an ideal was being challenged and eventually was not merely defeated but colonized by the competing ideal of 'normality.' "[30] For one thing, naturalness had lost its status as a trait independent of and superior to the artifice, convention, and craft characteristic of social organization. "This intellectual and indeed moral shift in American culture was crucial to the reversal in attitudes toward sign language and the deaf community," Baynton adds.[31]

An 1884 speech by oralist Alexander Graham Bell shows how naturalizing the preferred behaviors of the dominant class propelled a program of normalizing, where this meant conforming the behaviors of deaf children to those of the hearing majority:

> I think we should aim to be as natural as we can. I think we should get accustomed to

treat our deaf children as if they could hear.... We should try ourselves to forget that they are deaf. We should teach them to forget that they are deaf. We should ... avoid anything that would mark them out as different from others.[32]

By 1899 we find the President of Amherst College, John Tyler, folding the mantle of science around these normalizing practices. Tyler assured a convention of oralists that America would "never have a scientific system of education until we have one based on ... the grand foundation of biological history.... [T]he search for the ... goal of education compels us to study man's origin and development."[33] Such scientifically based or biologized education would maintain the functional strategies that seemed to place speech higher on the scale of evolutionary development than the expressive gestures of lower primates. The political morality of the time made it a moral and social obligation to increase the opportunities of both deaf signers and gesticulating foreigners by repairing them, a duty which a scientific system of educating them in the language and communication behaviors of the dominant class could help discharge.

It is important to understand that the fundamental division here is between competing ideas of what organizes a well-ordered society. The eighteenth-century's ideal of individualized moral perfection had given way to an ideal of communal or social participation by people who functioned dialogically in common in the public sphere. Where once language's highest function had been to engage individuals with ideas understood as transcendent sources of right belief and right conduct, now its most important use was to engage people with one another in productive commercial and civic interaction.

Arguing against the idea that deaf people could flourish with a language of their own, an oralist insisted. "To go through life as one of a peculiar class is the sum of human misery. No other misfortune is comparable to this."[34] This thought typifies the shift of priorities from personal to social improvement, and the correlated elevation of the importance of collective over idiosyncratic individualistic identities.

This urge to create fair opportunity by leveling the players rather than the playing field is a theme which has come more and more to dominate American egalitarianism over the past hundred years. What is striking is that systematically "normalizing" how deaf people communicate (and many other rehabilitation strategies) may amplify anomalous individuals' opportunities by making them more fit to pursue these, but concomitantly may make them less able to perform alternatively or adaptively. By devaluing alternative or adaptive modes of functioning, the policy transgresses liberal political theory's requirement that the state remain neutral between different citizens' ideas of the good life. Oralism's defense of its violation of this dictum was that, until deaf individuals communicated and consequently contributed in the normal mode, they could not be qualified for the protection due citizens.

Normalizing is played out in both medical and educational programs that intervene to repair or restore or revise members of nondominant groups so they qualify as citizens. In education, normalizing has been expressed as a mandate to assimilate the children of immigrant families to the dominant culture, and to impose the practices and preferences of males upon females. In being presented with arguments for normalizing deaf children, the public was invited to decide whether the management of "deaf schools" should be awarded to hearing people who promised to assimilate deaf children. By allocating resources to educational techniques intended to normalize deaf people, public policy imposed a conception of the good under which they did not flourish. We need to ask now whether there are some people who may not flourish, or whose well-being will be compromised, if normalizing similarly warrants and consequently guides the allocation of resources that go to health care.

A Cost/Benefit Assessment of Normalizing

Normalizing has costs. If maintaining or restoring normal function is of such public significance that a system of benefits is made available for this purpose, it is hard to resist supposing that those whose functioning is anomalous ought to acknowledge the system by assigning the same priority to being restored. Baynton reminds us: "Oralism meant that many deaf people had access only to limited or simplified language during the crucial early years of language development."[35] For fear they would fall back to communicating in a more convenient but "abnormal" or "unnatural" way, deaf children were often not taught to write unless they had mastered intelligible speaking. This practice left a legacy of reduced literacy among deaf people.

Interventions that reduce rather than expand already limited functionality surely extract too high a price, but such is the history of oralism in the education of the deaf. "Oralism failed," Baynton concludes, "and sign language survived, because deaf people themselves chose not to relinquish the autonomous cultural space that their community and language made possible." That is, for many people who do not hear, the opportunity of communicating fully within a limited group appears to be more satisfying, more equalizing and more meaningful than the opportunity of communicating in a limited way with the larger community. This is not to say that all deaf and hard of hearing people make this choice, but merely to point out that the alternative to normalizing often is not a limitation of full functioning but merely a limitation in the expanse of environment in which one functions successfully.

Tribalism, our partiality for interacting with those most like us, undoubtedly influences us to assign preeminence to (the appearance of) normalcy. But to the degree it corrupts the positive balance of benefits over personal and public costs, serious questions about whether the policy of normalizing compromises fair opportunity rather than promotes it must be addressed.

The Canadian Health Care system's intervention in the cases of children born with missing or shortened limbs because their pregnant mothers took thalidomide illustrates this last point. In their treatment, appearing more normal was the priority, so much so that large public sums were expended to design dysfunctional painful prostheses which actually decreased their dexterity and mobility. They could walk with these, but only painfully and slowly. Reminiscent of the oralist ban on signing, they were forbidden to roll or crawl, although these modes offered much more functionality, at least within their home environments.

The direction of resources to fund artificial limb design and manufacture rather than wheelchair design was influenced by the supposition that walking makes people more socially acceptable than wheeling does. As the children became independent adults, less vulnerable to the aggressive elements of institutionalized health care, they discarded the dysfunctional prosthetics in favor of wheelchairs, some made to their own designs. Here is another case (among many such examples I could adduce) in which the tyranny of the normal cost anomalous individuals to sacrifice an effective level of functioning at the alter of social preference for a particular mode of functioning, and in so doing compromised rather than equalized their opportunities.

We should not underestimate the coercive potential of policies that validate a particular mode of functioning by directing resources to efforts to restore that mode. When oralism dominated in schools for the deaf, deaf children could either try to lip read and speak, or have no education at all. For the Canadian children with no usable lower limbs, mechanical limbs were the only mobility option offered because policy directed the resources to institutions that designed and engineered limb like prostheses, not wheelchairs. More generally, then, to commit public policy to restoring individuals to species-typical modes of functioning diminishes public recognition of, and consequently resources for, alternative modes of functioning.

So far, we have seen that normalizing equalizes opportunity primarily for those who can be maintained in or restored to the image of the dominant group. But no natural biological mandate nor evolutionary triumph assures that the functional routines of this group are optimally efficient or effective. Rather, the members of this group have the good fortune to find themselves in a social situation that suits them.

For others, there is the choice of limited functionality in an ordinary environment, or ordinary functionality in a limited environment. How much opportunity need be absent from the former alternative, or sacrificed by the latter, depends upon how expansive the nonhostile environment can be made. Replacing staircases with spiral ramps for wheelchair users, adding captions to televised programs for deaf viewers, alt-tags to computer icons so that the screen readers used by people who are blind can identify them, all these make the constructed environment less hostile to and more inclusive of people who function in anomalous, alternative, or adaptive modes.

The main ingredient of being (perceived as) normal lies in finding or creating social situations that suit one. Contrary to Daniels's claim, normalizing is no self-warranting process that deserves the allocation of resources because it furthers democratic values. For individuals with disabilities, for example, such values are better advanced by developing social environments accustomed to people like one's self. The record of their history does not support assuming that broad social or moral benefits accrue to normalizing interventions. The attractiveness of war-

ranting health care interventions that maintain/restore normal functioning on the ground that they are instruments of justice therefore appears to be much dimmer than the initial enthusiasm of macro-(bio)medical ethics for normalizing suggests.

Disability, Self-Respect, and Lowered Quality of Life

Nothing said so far should be interpreted to mean that interventions to maintain or restore familiar modes of functioning never enhance individuals' welfare. But as we have seen, no clear difference in social benefit, or strict difference in obligation, separates these interventions, ones Daniels would call treatments, from interventions that enhance already average functionality. Then why is functioning normally of such value that maintaining or restoring this level becomes a decisive standard?

A critical component of a good quality of life, Dan Brock says, depends on each of us measuring our capacities and capabilities favorably against the standard of normal human functioning.[36] That is, whether we function normally or not influences how we rate ourselves in comparison to others and consequently affects our confidence and self esteem. This observation suggests that the paramount benefit of being normal is to maintain the psychosocial well-being of tribalism.

Brock may well be correctly describing a self-reflective process our current cultural standards promote. But this is not sufficient to defend the process as reliable or otherwise reasonable. We have seen that normal functioning is hardly a firm and reliable mark of the quality of our performance. Indeed, it is so fragile a standard that Brock worries about how easily a program of genetic intervention might shatter it. Brock, and others, are alarmed by the potential genetic intervention has for disrupting our confidence in the standard of normalcy.

First, if we manipulate genes to raise the level of performances that typify our species, any pretense that typical functioning is a natural rather than manipulated standard vanishes. Heretofore, a social structure that privileges some people to control communications and construction to suit themselves has determined what modes of functioning are considered normal. Henceforth, a social structure that privileges some people to influence genetic research and the allocation of genetic interventions might determine what levels of functioning become normal. What is feared is that our current confidence in a firm and impersonal, because natural, standard of normality will be undermined by a new and widespread recognition of seemingly normal functioning as being merely the artifactual expression of the interests of whichever members of our species are positioned to deploy technology.

Will such an eventuality constrict rather than enlarge opportunity? Applying genetic technology that increases disparities of access to opportunity initially appears to be inconsistent with a democratically informed health care system, regardless of how much personal welfare the applications might bestow. Consequently, justice appears to advise constraining, or even prohibiting, these important broad applications of genetic technology.

For instance, genetic intervention could result in improving how some people function, so that someone who performs at a level that was comfortable for his species-average parents might find that the naturally good genes he inherited from them are surpassed by great genes installed in his competitors as a compensatory or even as a privileging measure. Constraining applications of this technology so that no individual can acquire an abnormally large number of desirable characteristics may seem advisable. But it is hardly an implementable policy, for the desirability of many of our characteristics is itself provisional and dependent on environment. Whether, and how, adding specific characteristics benefits the recipient—whether it privileges, equalizes, or just makes

one more comfortable must be decided with regard to the context in which the patient will function.

Brock is also concerned about whether, as we come to understand genetic structures accurately enough to identify the potentially anomalous functioning consequent on every species' member's inheritance, some members of the species will find themselves devalued by their own futures. Although performing splendidly at the time, they will be labeled, and consequently marginalized, as being at greater risk than others of deteriorating function. So, for instance, those at risk of Alzheimer's would be rejected as mates by whoever wanted the services of a spousal caretaker, while employers desiring to keep medical insurance costs down would not hire individuals genetically disposed to developing various kinds of cancer.

With the widespread use of genetic testing, he worries:

> [P]eople who feel healthy and who as yet suffer no functional impairment will increasingly be labeled as unhealthy or diseased. . . . For many people, this labeling will undermine their sense of themselves as healthy, well-functioning individuals and will have serious adverse effects both on their conceptions of themselves and the quality of their lives.[37]

Notice that, at this point, the idea, rather than the reality, of nonnormal functioning has become the signifier of whether someone is equally well off, or is advantaged or disadvantaged in comparison to others. This observation suggests that it is one's psychosocial rather than physical functioning that is most vulnerable to variations from accustomed states or normal prognoses—that is, to deviations from what is typical of our species. Brock describes how this occurs: "Generally it is when we have noticed an adverse effect or change in our normal functional capacity that we contact health care professionals and begin the process which can result in our being labeled as sick or diseased. . . ."[38] An adverse outcome of a genetic test could trigger this same process, though deterioration in physical functionality has not been and perhaps never will be manifested. Here being labeled as likely to become nonnormal initiates psychosocial processes that themselves are dysfunctional. The perception of being disadvantaged thus precedes and causes, rather than follows upon, dysfunction.

So the standard constructed to identify who is disadvantaged itself becomes the facilitator of disadvantage. Applying genetic technology then is merely the occasion, not the cause, of an unjust constriction of opportunity. It need not be categorically constrained for fear it will do so. For notice now how the disconnect between actually functioning differently and being disadvantaged has opened even wider. In the case about which Brock worries, individuals are functioning normally but are disadvantaged by having a significant potential, perhaps never to be actualized, for anomalous functioning. Here the social convention of the sick role, rather than the realities of effective performance, determines what modes and levels of functioning are advantageous, indifferent to advantage, or disadvantageous.

The prospect of increasing the power of the standard of species-typical functioning to consign individuals to the sick role undoubtedly is alarming. However, it is not the standard, but the science that could extend its applications, that is typically attacked. So Adrienne Asch and Gail Geller express their concern that "the Human Genome Initiative could turn out to make 'species-typical functioning' a guide to joining or remaining part of the human community."[39]

To counter these worries about genetic research, we should turn from policies of normalizing to approaches that make us more receptive to alternative ways of functioning. The strategy of protecting against discrimination

those who function differently, are genetically disposed to function differently in future, or are perceived as functioning differently is of great help here. The 1990 Americans with Disabilities Act offers one strategic example; another is the recent stream of legislation protecting patients against disclosure of the results of genetic testing.

Normalizing, What Priority?

Because there may be no firm answer as to whether a health care intervention does or does not level social advantage, we often cannot deduce from principles of justice whether a medical intervention effects treatment or enhancement. Consequently, even in a just system—indeed, especially in a just system—this distinction is unlikely to guide us in determining what should be provided for particular patients.

Of course, health care's primary mission is to keep us functioning. But what kind of intervention is most just remains an issue. To justly liberate group members' many talents, its members could be altered to better satisfy the expectations that pervade their social environment. On the other hand, altering the environment to better support their flourishing may correct their disadvantage equally well.

This last consideration remains too much neglected by prominent strategists of health-care justice. As we have seen, our normal modes and levels of functioning are, to an extent that often goes unrecognized, socially relative constructions rather than independent biological facts. Adjusting the environment so anomalous individuals can better flourish can be as compensatory as leveling them. Moreover, enhancing individuals or their groups by magnifying their exemplary performance in some domains can, under some circumstances, sometimes compensate for there being barriers to their performance in other domains of functioning. Wherever strategies that equalize the amount of opportunity individuals have available rather than homogenize the kinds of opportunities they can access are feasible, there is even less reason to suppose that restoring anomalous individuals to normal modes of functioning is a better instrument of justice than enhancing the effectiveness of their anomalous modes.

In positing justice as the regulatory ideal of health care, macro-(bio)medical ethics initially proposed a deductive model on which principles of justice would inform our picking out and prioritizing those medical interventions that further equality. Interventions that qualify as treatments because they aim effectively at restoring normal function were, on this model, to take precedence in the allocation of resources. As we have seen, however, endorsing maintenance or restoration of normal functioning as the standard for allocation can itself, all too readily, prolong disadvantage. Macro-(bio) medical ethics must therefore overcome its fatal attraction to normalizing in order to open itself to other strategies for advancing justice.

Notes

1   Daniels 1987, pp. 290–93.
2   Daniels 1987, p. 312.
3   Daniels et al. 1996, pp. 25–26.
4   Daniels et al. 1996, p. 21.
5   Daniels 1987, p. 301.
6   Daniels et al. 1996, p. 41.
7   Daniels 1987, p. 306.
8   Daniels 1987, p. 300.
9   Daniels 1987, p. 303.
10 Daniels 1987, pp. 306–307.
11 Daniels 1987, p. 301.
12 Daniels 1987, p. 302.
13 Daniels 1987, p. 303.
14 Sherwin 1992, p. 179.
15 Rawls 1985, pp. 233–234.
16 Daniels 1987, p. 318.
17 Daniels 1987, p. 318.
18 Daniels 1987, p. 302.
19 Davis and Bradley 1996, pp. 69–70.
20 Davis and Bradley 1996, p. 70.
21 Boorse 1987, p. 368.
22 Brock 1993, p. 297.
23 Brock 1993, p. 297.
24 Brock 1993, p. 346.
25 Brock 1993, p. 307.
26 Daniels 1987, p. 304.
27 Daniels 1985, p. 46.
28 Baynton 1996, p. 107.
29 Davis 1995, pp. 53, 57–59.
30 Baynton 1996, p. 110.
31 Baynton 1996, p. 110.
32 Baynton 1996, p. 136.
33 Baynton 1996, p. 36.
34 Baynton 1996, p. 145.
35 Baynton 1996, p. 1.
36 Brock 1994, p. 31.
37 Brock 1994, p. 29.
38 Brock 1994, p. 29.
39 Asch and Geller 1996, p. 330.

References

Asch, A. & Geller, G. (1996). Feminism, bioethics and genetics. In S. M. Wolf (Ed.), *Feminism and Bioethics* (pp. 318–350). Oxford: Oxford University Press.

Baynton, D. (1996). *Forbidden Signs: American culture and the campaign against sign language.* Chicago, IL: University of Chicago Press.

Boorse, C. (1987). Concepts of health. In D. VanDeVeer and T. Regan (Eds.), *Health Care Ethics: An introduction* (pp. 359–393). Philadelphia, PA: Temple University Press.

Brock, D. (1993). *Life and Death.* New York: Cambridge University Press.

Brock, D. (1994). The Human Genome Project and human identity. In R. Weir, S. Lawrence and E. Fales (Eds.), *Genes and Human Self-Knowledge: Historical and philosophical reflections on modern genetics* (pp. 18–33). Ames, IA: University of Iowa Press.

Daniels, N. (1985) *Just Health Care.* Cambridge: Cambridge University Press.

Daniels, N. (1987). Justice and health care. In D. VanDeVeer and T. Regan (Eds.), *Health Care Ethics: An introduction* (pp. 290–325). Philadelphia, PA: Temple University Press.

Daniels, N., Light, D., & Caplan, R. (1996). *Benchmarks if Fairness for Health Care Reform.* Oxford: Oxford University Press.

Davis, L. (1995) *Enforcing Normalcy: Disability, deafness and the body*. London: Verso.

Davis, P., & Bradley, J. (1996). The meaning of normal. *Perspectives in Biology and Medicine*, 40(1): 68–77.

Rawls, J. (1985). Justice as fairness: Political not metaphysical. *Philosophy and Public Affairs*, 14: 223–251.

Sherwin, S. (1992). *No Longer Patient*. Philadelphia, PA: Temple University Press.

Chapter 35

Louise M. Antony

"HUMAN NATURE" AND ITS ROLE IN FEMINIST THEORY

Philosophical Appeals to "Human Nature"

Essentially positive conceptions of human nature have figured prominently in the normative theories of Western philosophers: Aristotle, Rousseau, Kant, and many others based their general ethical and political systems on substantive assumptions about the capacities and dispositions of human beings. Many of these views have been interpreted as affirming the inherent moral value and essential equality of all human beings, and a few have provided inspiration for emancipatory movements, including feminism.

Nonetheless, for anyone who would find in these theories a message of universal equality, there is one immediate difficulty: none of the major philosophers intended their claims about the natural entitlements of "man" to be applied to women.[1] Contrary to what's maintained by many contemporary exegetes, it's unlikely that the philosophers' use of masculine terms in the framing of their theories was a "mere linguistic convenience."[2] For if one looks at the (very few) places at which the major philosophers explicitly discuss women, one finds that women are expressly denied both the moral potentialities and the moral perquisites that are supposed to accrue to "man" in virtue of "his" nature.[3] If "man" is generic, and women are "men," then how could this be?

It's possible that the philosophers in question believed that men and women did not share a nature at all, in which case all their talk of "man" would be simply and literally talk of *men*. But this seems unlikely. Philosophers have not really wanted to claim that men and women are members of distinct kinds. Aristotle, Rousseau, and Kant, for example, who all made the possession of reason criterial of humanity, agreed that women could not plausibly be claimed to be utterly devoid of rationality.[4] Alternatively, then, the view must have been that men and women shared some sort of "human" nature, even while women differed from men in morally relevant respects. On this view, it would not be the generic human nature per se that grounded the celebrated virtues and rights but rather something in the specifically male realization of that nature. If so, the distinction between a generic and a non-generic sense of "man" can be preserved; yet as long as "man's" virtues and rights still turn out to be identical with *men's*, it will be a distinction without a difference.[5]

In fact, the philosophers had a problem. They did not, as I said, wish to count women and men as distinct species. Still, if the differences between men and women were to rationalize differences in moral status, such differences would have to be, in some sense, matters of kind rather than of degree. For if mere quantitative differences could warrant assignments of different roles and virtues, then such distinctions would have to be made also among men, who differ from each other in quantitative ways.[6] The solution to this problem, independently embraced by Aristotle, Rousseau, and Kant, was to first affirm that women and men shared a nature but to then add the qualification that women were—by nature—unable to realize it fully.[7] Men thus became, by some kind of natural necessity, the only *proper* exemplars of "man." On this view, because women are still "men," the characteristics of "man" remain normative for women, despite their natural inability to instantiate them.

Aristotle, Rousseau, and Kant all made some effort to present the situation as one in which man and woman are separate but equal, with different but complementary roles, virtues, and forms of flourishing. But the not-so-benign reality is revealed in the fact that it is always *man's* nature alone, rather than some combination or disjunction of his nature with woman's, that is canonized as "human" nature. Furthermore, despite the fact that women's distinctive nature is supposed to yield a distinctive set of virtues, these virtues are clearly viewed as inferior to men's.[8] The upshot is that women can be good only insofar as they are considered *as women*; considered *as human* (i.e., according to the standards set by men), they are *necessarily* inferior. Women are human, but only in the way a broken wing is a wing; they are at best *defective* tokens of the human type.

It would be bad enough if all this signified nothing but the sexism of some of the Western world's greatest philosophers. But, unfortunately, it signifies much more. The theories and ideas articulated by these thinkers have had and continue to have a powerful influence on the lives of real women, by providing theoretical rationalization for the almost universal domination of women by men. While the nature of "man" has grounded lofty demands for moral equality or political independence, the particular nature of *woman* has grounded nothing but preemptory prohibitions and demeaning prescriptions. Leading philosophers agree: *because*

of their natures, women should be denied serious educations and given only limited opportunities to develop physical strength. They should be barred from political or commercial activity and restricted entirely to the domestic sphere. They are not to aspire to any achievements—not even moral achievements—but what fit the character and scale of the domestic realm. In sum, *because of their natures*, women's entire lives are to be oriented toward pleasing and serving men.

What's gone wrong? Theories that seemed to promise a grounding for universal equality transmute before our eyes into rationalizations for the exploitation of women by men. In fact, there is nothing unusual here. Historically, it's been a standard strategy for explaining and justifying oppressive social hierarchies to appeal to alleged differences between the "natures" of oppressors and oppressed. The strategy is extraordinarily labile, exploiting in turn each of the various normative and modal connotations carried by the notion of "the natural," depending on the point that needs making. The trick is in picking the right stratagem at the right time.[9]

As a first move, it's best to try to represent the status quo as morally optimal. Thus counsels Rousseau: "If you want right guidance, always follow the leadings of nature. Everything that characterises sex should be respected as established by nature."[10] But should anyone be so bold as to disapprove of some aspect of nature's arrangements, the second stratagem can be brought into play: emphasize the futility of attempting to breach the laws of nature. Kant, for example, who can "hardly believe that the fair sex is capable of principle,"[11] warns that "whatever one does contrary to nature's will, one always does very poorly."[12] If it's pointed out that certain alleged laws have in fact been breached, the final stratagem must be deployed: show that success in some unnatural pursuit threatens one's well-being—even one's *identity*. Kant thus admonishes any would-be Elizabeths that "Laborious learning or painful pondering, even if a woman should greatly succeed in it, destroy [sic] the merits that are proper to her sex. . . . The fair can leave Descartes his vortices to whirl forever without troubling themselves about them."[13] Of course, this maneuver comports neatly with the notion that women have distinctive virtues and forms of flourishing.

The concession that it is possible, though not desirable, to alter or thwart the course of nature is necessitated by an internal tension in ideological appeals to natures. The problem is this: if nature is straightforwardly deterministic, if the social status quo is simply a neutral unfolding of the laws of nature, then why do we need prescriptions and warnings in order not to disturb it? As John Stuart Mill pointed out, there is no need to legislate against that which is anyway impossible, and no point in promoting what will happen all by itself.[14] If it's conceded, however, that the maintenance of the status quo does depend partly upon contingent human choices, an epistemological question arises: How do we know that the qualities we see displayed by men and women are due to differences in natures, rather than to the differences we engineer in their circumstances?[15] Furthermore, once it's granted that gender roles are not strictly determined by nature, the question of their justice can once again be opened, and must be otherwise forestalled. Hence the "normative determinism" exemplified in the quotations from Kant: natures may not dictate what you will become, nor even what you will want to become, but they do dictate what will make you a good thing of your kind.

The same tensions emerge in the modern appeals to nature as in the classical ones: if women are naturally incapable of performing certain roles, why is it necessary to socially engineer against their attempting them? And given that the social engineering is necessary, how do we know that that is not what's responsible for the apparent differences in capacities? The answer, once again, is that such engineering is really a way of preserving a woman's own unique identity, of sparing her the frustration of her inevitable failure should she try to enter the world of men. The epistemology of such claims is left mysterious.

Consider, for example, Steven Goldberg, who contends that men's naturally higher levels of testosterone make them more aggressive, giving them a uniform competitive advantage over women. Goldberg has to confront the objection that girls appear to be less aggressive than boys even before puberty, when the relevant hormonal difference first appears. He admits that this difference must be attributable to different socialization but discounts the significance of this, arguing that it's rational and humane to train girls away from those highly valued activities where, in competition with boys, they'd certainly fail. How do we know they would certainly fail, given that we don't give them the opportunity to try? Because they're naturally less aggressive—aren't you paying attention?[16]

With eerie regularity, popular media in the United States trumpet "new" findings that purportedly establish completely biological—and hence "natural"—explanations for observed gender differences.[17] Paradoxically, though predictably, all this proof that gender roles are biologically mandated becomes the basis of support for discriminatory socialization, and for opposition to efforts to provide equality of opportunity. Here's John Stossel as the voice of reason on an ABC News special "Boys and Girls Are Different": "If we deny what science knows about human nature, how can we create sensible social policies? Isn't it better to act on the basis of what is true, rather than maintaining it has no right to be true?"[18]

Let us stop and take stock. Where does all this leave the feminist theorist with respect to the notion of human nature? One response to these difficulties would be to claim all and only the liberatory conceptions, and then insist on their proper extension to women and other denigrated groups. This strategy, favored by those feminists who see value in preserving what they see as the "humanism" at the core of liberal moral and political theory, strives to demonstrate the empirical falsity of negative claims that philosophers and others have made about the natures of women, and men of color, while leaving in place central assumptions about the theoretical and practical value of a substantive theory of human nature. Increasingly, however, feminist theorists are rejecting this line of response. Such theorists have come to the conclusion that careful analysis of the problems outlined here reveals that the notion of "human nature" is, from the theoretical point of view, conceptually bankrupt, and from the practical political point of view, inevitably pernicious. They argue, accordingly, that the long-standing philosophical project of characterizing "human nature" should not be refurbished, reformed, or revised but rather simply abandoned.

In the remainder of this chapter, I would like to argue for a revival of the first strategy. I think that feminist theory needs an appeal to a universal human nature in order to articulate and defend its critical claims about the damage done to women under patriarchy, and also to ground its positive vision of equitable and sustaining human relationships.[19] Nonetheless, I accept the legitimacy of much of the recent feminist critique of appeals to "human nature" and of the philosophical strategies that prompt them. So in the next section, I'll explain the central elements of the critique that has emerged from feminist reflection on the problems cited earlier. In the third section, I'll try to demonstrate how the approach to the investigation of human nature that I favor takes account of the feminist critique. In the final section of the chapter, I'll fill out and defend my claim that a theoretical appeal to a universal human nature is both possible and desirable as a grounding for feminist theory.

Feminist Critique

Leslie Stevenson, a philosopher at the University of St. Andrews, is the author of a book called

Seven Theories of Human Nature (1987) and editor of a collection of readings called *The Study of Human Nature* (1981). Both the monograph and the collection treat only the works of male theorists, and except for a few sentences here and there (a paragraph in an excerpt from Freud's *Question of Lay Analysis* in the collection, and a passing reference to Freud's theory of penis envy in the monograph), there is no discussion of women or girls in either book.[20] Neither one mentions, much less discusses, any of the problematic writings about women that we've been looking at. It is clear that Stevenson wishes his readers to form the impression that the theories he discusses are unproblematically applicable to women. Perhaps he even believes that their authors wished them to be so understood (although it should be clear that this is decidedly not so in at least three cases).

Stevenson appears to be genuinely sensitive to feminist criticism that his treatment of theories of human nature has ignored women. In the introduction to the second edition of the monograph, he comments perceptively on the use of "generic" language: "The use of the masculine word 'man' here is very convenient for brevity of question and statement, and . . . it has been very common practice. But straight away many of us will want to protest that what is involved is more than mere linguistic convenience, that some distinctive features and problems of women's nature have all too often been overlooked by the common assumption that the concept *man* can represent the whole human species."[21] But having evinced this much apprehension of the feminist critique, he reveals in his very next statement that he has, despite his good intentions, quite missed the point. "This book does not attempt any systematic discussion of feminist issues: it presents some rival theories of general *human* nature." Stevenson believes it possible that there exist "distinctive features and problems of women's nature," which "have all too often been overlooked," and yet he feels that such matters can be safely ignored within the context of a discussion of "human nature."[22] These are "feminist issues," matters of *special* interest to women and their champions, important but peripheral.[23]

Stevenson is certainly right that the character, cause, and significance of gender differences are matters of intense interest among feminist scholars and activists—necessarily so, since, as we saw in the last section, appeals to "women's nature" have been used to justify the subordination of women throughout Western history. But the issue feminists are trying to raise when we speak of philosophy's failure to "take account of gender" is independent of any of the detailed questions that can be raised about exactly how and why men and women are different, and it is more fundamental. The real issue concerns the *treatment of "difference"* itself.[24]

How is it, we ask, that someone like Stevenson can allow the possibility that women are importantly different from men and yet think that theorizing about "human nature" can proceed without attending to that fact? Why, indeed, is the situation conceptualized as one in which it is *women's* situation that bears "distinctive features and problems"? Are not men's situations equally "distinctive" relative to women's? The same questions arise, though more pointedly, for those philosophers we've been looking at who do explicitly discuss women: if women are supposed to have different properties than men, what then justifies the canonization of the distinctively *male* properties as the properties constitutive of full humanity? By what process of reasoning does a theorist who thinks that at least half the members of the species lack authoritative reason decide that it is precisely authoritative reason that is the distinctive mark of the species?

Ironically, questions of this sort arise even within feminist theory itself, for "mainstream" feminists (i.e., white, heterosexual, middle-class feminists) often canonize their own circumstances and concerns, while either ignoring or treating as peripheral the lives and problems of women who are "different." Liberal feminist discussion of liberation, marriage, motherhood, and work has been vigorously and properly criticized by black and Third World feminists, as well as by socialist feminists, for its failure to recognize both that the options middle-class women enjoy with respect to motherhood, domestic work, and paid employment are not available to most women and that the significance of these matters can vary enormously among women of different races, cultures, and sexual orientations.[25]

Similarly, radical feminists like Catherine MacKinnon, who make pornography and sexual violence the organizing points of their theories of oppression, have been criticized by black feminists like Angela Harris for ignoring the very different meanings such phenomena have for nonwhite and non-Western women.[26] Elizabeth Spelman emphasizes how even Simone de Beauvoir, who wrote so brilliantly about the process by which the dominant construct the subordinate as "the Other," failed to check the very same tendencies in her own theorizing, acknowledging the variety of women's circumstances on the one hand but then on the other making her own specific circumstances the basis of her analysis of women's oppression *as women.*[27]

Questions and observations like these have prompted many feminists to take a serious look at the circumstances in which philosophers have produced theories of "generic" human nature, at the methodologies they've employed, and at the background assumptions and values that have funded such projects. The regularity that emerges immediately is that the problematic treatments of difference always appear when individuals who are in some kind of *privileged* position undertake to theorize about some larger group of which they are the dominant members. This has led to speculation that the particular theories of human nature produced within Western philosophy, together, possibly, with the very idea that such a thing as human nature exists, reflect or express the privileged viewpoints of their authors.

Feminist elaborations of this idea have looked both at traditional philosophical method and at the specific content of theories of human nature. The methodological critiques begin by noting an important interaction between the aprioristic character of philosophical method and the privileged position of its most prominent practitioners. A method for discovering the qualities distinctive of humanity that depends heavily on reflection and introspection carries several inherent risks. One is that there will be a biased selection of traits—theorists may fasten on qualities that are particular to them rather than on qualities that are common to every member of humankind. A second danger is that the traits selected, whether or not they happen to be traits that all human beings possess, may nonetheless be traits that are not universally *valued*. Finally, theorists may mistake contingent properties for essential properties, treating as inherent qualities that are in fact the result of highly variable circumstances. Every one of these risks is increased when the theorists form a socially homogeneous group, since that makes it more likely that one theorist's hasty generalization will tend to confirm the others.'

So much follows just from familiar canons of empirical investigation. But many feminists, drawing on Marxist standpoint theory, have argued that the danger of distortion is further heightened when the homogeneous group of theorists is *privileged*. People in dominant social positions tend to be successful in limiting the range of views that are available for contention in the public domain, partly through their greater access to education and their monopoly over effective means of publication, and partly because of their ability to coerce at least the appearance of agreement among subordinates. Because consensus is often taken as a sign of objectivity, the absence of views that conflict with the theorist's own is taken, at least tacitly, as additional confirmation, and the absence of any

stimulus to produce explicit defenses of the dominant view facilitates the illusion that the view is self-evident, enhancing the theorist's faith in the reliability of his own a priori method.[28]

Against this highly conceptual background, we must also remember the altogether mundane ways in which bias can operate. Remember that privileged individuals frequently have a stake in the outcome of theories of human nature. To the extent that his or her own position depends upon the exploitation or oppression of someone else, the theorist has a strong motive for discovering some way of justifying the status quo. As we have seen, theories that can trace inequalities within a society back to "natural" differences among its members have enormous ideological value, since they make social hierarchies seem at once fair, good, and inevitable. It is an empirical question whether or not any given philosopher was actually moved, consciously or unconsciously, by such venal considerations, but it cannot be denied that the risk is there.[29]

I have surveyed some of the mechanisms feminists have proposed by which theorizing about human nature *might* have been distorted by the conditions under which it has been conducted. Two questions remain, however: first, have any of these distortions actually occurred, and second, could such distortions be guarded against or corrected by changes in the way we conduct our theorizing? I'll review feminists' answers to these questions in turn.

Although feminists are divided on the first issue, many theorists, reflecting on the contents of the theories of "human" nature that philosophy has produced, believe that such distortions have occurred. Some theorists, particularly those working within ethical and political theory, believe that there are significant differences between the ways men and women think about themselves in relation to others, and that traditional normative theories have been based exclusively on the forms typical of men. The most famous of these theorists is probably Carol

Gilligan (1982), who (in what always seems to me an eerie echo of Kant) holds that men are more likely to adopt the "perspective of justice" and women the "perspective of care." Traditional normative theories, she claims, have overvalued the former and ignored the latter. Virginia Held (1990), Nell Noddings (1984), and Sara Ruddick (1989) have argued, in a kind of ethical analogue to standpoint epistemology, that the biological and social roles occupied by women provide a better starting point than those of men for the development of normative theories. Annette Baier thinks that traditional theories have ignored the moral significance of the emotions, the passions, and the affections, and have devalued them largely because of their association with femininity and the female.[30] Susan Okin has argued that liberal theory, in recognizing a public-private distinction that identifies the interests of an entire family with the interests of its "head," renders invisible the primary site of women's oppression.[31]

Other feminist theorists see the tradition's emphasis on "reason" and mentality, and its devaluation of the physical, as reflecting both the values and the situation of privileged individuals. Genevieve Lloyd has pointed out that the kind of mental activity canonized as "reason," and held to be most supremely human by Plato, Aristotle, Descartes, Kant, and others, is in fact a kind of activity that can be enjoyed on a regular basis only by those who are relatively free of mundane cares and responsibilities. Indeed, Lloyd contends, the very notion of "reason" has been constructed within theology and philosophy in explicit contrast to the properties displayed (or thought to be displayed) by the people to whom such responsibilities were standardly assigned: women, and men of lower class, caste, or race. The valuation of cognitive skills over manual skills may also be a reflection of class and gender privilege, since only those with material means can afford to neglect manual skills for the sake of pursuing the life of the mind.[32]

Feminists' answers to the second of my two questions—whether some less distorted theory is possible—are much more difficult to discern. Many of the critiques outlined here are at least compatible with the idea that there exists some kind of universal "human" nature. Even those like Gilligan's and Chodorow's, which assume the existence of relatively stable gender differences, do not attribute these to differences in male and female *natures*, but rather to stable regularities in the social situations of males and females. Since the distortions that feminists have claimed to find are held to be artifacts of a situation we have independent reason to hope will change, perhaps there is at least the possibility of developing an *adequate* characterization of the basic nature that we all share, necessarily, as human beings.[33]

On the other hand, what positive reason is there to think that there *is* a "human nature" out there to be discovered? If there is any single point to emerge from all the critiques we have surveyed, it is this: differences among human beings, whatever their cause, are theoretically important for understanding ourselves and our relations with others. What reason, then, is there for assuming that if we abstract away from all those differences, there will be anything left? We should note, too, that such differences as *have* been noticed or posited have tended to be viewed as immutable *natural* differences rather than reflections of physical or social contingencies. Why, then, think that *any* of our properties are attributable to our *natures* rather than to the contingencies of our existence?

These two questions have led many feminists to suspect that the categories "human being" and "woman"—at least in the sense of these terms that's relevant for normative theory—are not *natural* categories at all but are, rather, "socially constructed." To say that a category is socially constructed is to say, first, that the existence of such a category is not determined by nature, and, second, that the criteria for membership in the category are sensitive to the interests and viewpoints of intentional beings. Since these interests and perspectives are not all identical, and since they tend to shift over time, the membership criteria for socially constructed categories may not be stable, and different things may be counted members at different times and places. Socially constructed categories may be thought of as similar to Lockean "nominal essences" in that they represent contingent, subjectively determined groupings that may or may not correspond to any "deeper" or more stable underlying commonality—in a sense, members of socially constructed kinds owe their membership to our agreement to call them all by the same name.

This does not mean that socially constructed categories are unreal, nor that the properties on which they are (contingently) based are without real causal power. And it does not mean that the categories are indefinable; at any given time, we may be perfectly able to identify the criteria determined by the relevant social and intentional activity. Catherine MacKinnon, for example, holds that "woman" is a socially constructed kind, but still is happy to give necessary and sufficient conditions. According to MacKinnon, one's status as a man or a woman is determined not by natural differences in reproductive capacities, but rather by one's location in a particular power hierarchy: one is a man if one is a sexual objectifier, and a woman if one is sexually objectified. There is nothing *natural* that women can be presumed to have in common with other women—a "woman" in MacKinnon's sense may even be biologically male, as she thinks is the case with certain male homosexuals—but there is nonetheless something very real that all women share.[34]

But as we've noted, MacKinnon's theory has been criticized on the grounds that it improperly universalizes an experience of sexuality that is typical of only a small group of women. Similar criticisms have been raised against Chodorow, Gilligan, Ruddick, and others who have offered general accounts of gender based

on some presumably common feature of women's situations. Postmodernist feminists have argued that these theories all suffer from a common defect, which they share with the traditional theories of "human nature" they are meant to replace: they all yield to the impulse to "*essentialize*." That is to say, as Nancy Fraser and Linda Nicholson put it, such theories "project onto all women and men qualities which develop under historically specific social conditions."[35] To avoid this defect, postmodernists argue, it's not enough to recognize that such categories as "man" and "woman" are not fixed by nature. It is necessary to go further and recognize that they are not fixed "*by anything*" at all.[36]

According to postmodernists, the very project of seeking a theory of gender, not to mention the project of seeking a theory of human nature, has at its core the dogmatic assumption that there is always some single thing—an essence, a definition, a nature—that can be found to underlie and explain observed diversity. As Iris Young explains it (borrowing a term from Adorno), this assumption reflects the "logic of identity": a mode of thought that attempts to impose a single static and abstract order onto the multiple and constantly shifting patterns of concrete events. Such thinking always leads to a pernicious normalization of the thinker's own characteristics, by the following process. It first denies difference, in its drive to reduce all diversity to an underlying unity; but then, ironically, difference is reintroduced in a new form: the normative dichotomy. "Since each particular entity . . . has both similarities and differences with other particular entities . . ., the urge to bring them into unity under a category or principle necessarily entails expelling some of the properties of the entities or situations. Because the totalizing movement always leaves a remainder, the project of reducing particulars to a unity must fail. Not satisfied then to admit defeat in the face of difference, the logic of identity shoves difference into dichotomous hierarchical oppositions."[37]

The postmodernist challenge, because it threatens not only the possibility of a theory of *human* nature but the possibility of a theory of (even socially constructed) *gender* as well, has generated enormous controversy among feminists. Many feminists feel that the availability of gender as an analytical category is vital to progress toward feminist goals, and they remain optimistic that there is some conception of "gender" that can survive the postmodernist challenge. Elizabeth Rapaport (1993), defending Catherine MacKinnon, asserts the "utility of theoretical illuminations of aspects of women's common experience" and argues that such a theory need not fall prey to the serious problems identified by Harris, Spelman, and others. Similarly, Susan Bordo, although very sympathetic to postmodernism overall, still worries that giving up "gender analytics" entails the loss of a powerful analytical tool, without which we may "cut ourselves off from the source of feminism's transformative possibilities."[38]

I want to say the same thing about "human nature."

Toward a New Understanding of "Natures"

Clearly some of the problems associated with normative appeals to "natures" stem from inequitable distributions of power and epistemic authority within the societies that produce them. But I believe that many of the problems that feminists have found with philosophical theories of "nature" and "essence" have a different source. Such problems stem, I believe, from particular difficulties that we face in conceptualizing the products of certain kinds of theoretical analyses. I'd like to suggest that the notion of a *disposition* may be of help both in outlining these difficulties, and in pointing a way to their solution.

Let's start by looking somewhat more closely at the notion of a "nature" or "essence." Contemporary philosophical conceptions of essence are informed by two central ideas. The first, deriving from Aristotle, is that natures should be, in some sense, "definitional"—a nature should be that which makes a thing the kind of thing it is; a specification of a nature should tell you what it is to be that thing. "Natures," then, are properties with certain modal features: at a minimum, any property that is part of an individual object's nature is a property that that object has *necessarily*, and any property that is part of the nature or essence of a kind is a property that is *necessary* for being an object of that kind. From Locke, we get the second idea of essence as an underlying explanatory structure: natures are, in this sense, *intrinsic* and *fundamental*. Locke contrasted these *"real essences"* with "nominal essences," which are simply any set of sensible qualities stably enough associated together to be given a name. Real essences were "hidden" structures, possibly unknowable, but nonetheless causally responsible for the object's observable properties and behavior.

On certain assumptions, these two notions of "nature" may appear to be in conflict: if we think of definitions as word meanings, and we think of meanings as introspectively available to competent speakers, then it would appear that essences could be discovered by a priori means. But Locke's essences were knowable, if at all, only by abductive inference from empirically determined regularities. If essences could be discovered through conceptual analysis, how could they yield empirical explanations? But if they could only be discovered through empirical investigation, how could they entail *necessities*? Work by Hilary Putnam and Saul Kripke in the 1970s suggested a resolution. Wittgenstein, Quine, and others had already challenged the model of language and linguistic knowledge implicit in the preceding assumptions about definitions; it remained for Putnam and Kripke to make a case for *a posteriori necessities*. They argued that our modal judgments about identity conditions for objects and natural kinds do not depend on their superficial qualities but, rather, on deeper structural or historical properties, properties that we assume to exist but may be unable to characterize in advance of scientific investigation. A thing's "definition," then, is not the dictionary "definition" associated with the thing's name but, rather, a theoretical specification of what, as a matter of empirical fact, the thing is.

Which of a thing's properties are candidates for being its essence? First, let's consider what *kinds* of properties there are. A standard distinction made in the philosophy of science is that made between "dispositional" properties and nondispositional, or what might be called "categorical," properties.[39] Roughly, a categorical property is a property attributable to an object in virtue of its current or actual state or behavior, whereas a dispositional property is a property attributable to an object in virtue of the state it *would* be in, or the behavior it *would* display under certain (typically nonactual) circumstances. For example, the salt currently in my saltshaker has the categorical property of solidity: it is right now in a solid state. At the same time, it has the dispositional property of solubility: it *would* dissolve if placed in water. The attribution of a dispositional property to an object is thus equivalent to the assertion of a certain conditional: if such and such circumstances obtain, *then* the object will display this or that categorical property. We can call the circumstances specified in the antecedent the "activating circumstances" and the categorical property cited in the consequent the "associated categorical." Now which, if any, of the salt's properties should be considered part of its essence? Clearly, many of the categorical properties of an object can change over time—the salt in my saltshaker is *now* solid, but I could easily change that by emptying the shaker into a pot of water. Solidity, therefore, cannot be part of the salt's essence; solidity is only the state that salt is in *under certain conditions*.

But what about the *dispositional* property of *solubility*? This seems more promising; it does seem to be a necessary feature of salt that it

dissolves under certain conditions, and, indeed, that it remain solid under certain (different) conditions. But this can't be all there is to the story. Essences are supposed to be *explanatory* as well as definitive, and attributing solubility to salt seems to be just a way of saying *what* salt does rather than *why* it does it. What explains the disposition?

This is one of several good reasons for thinking that dispositional properties are always "grounded" in categorical properties.[40] Here's another: recall that a dispositional property can be correctly ascribed to an object even if the object is not, has never been, and will never be in the activating circumstances, and even if it does not, has never, and never will instantiate the associated categorical. But this then raises a question: What can or could be true of an object *now* that determines what it will or would do under nonactual conditions? This is a metaphysical, not an epistemological, matter, but the epistemology of dispositions points in the same direction. Our warrant for ascribing a dispositional property to one object is most often the observed behavior of objects we judge to be relevantly similar—this practice could only work if the objects we judge to have the same dispositions really do have something objectively in common.

Such a "grounding categorical," if it exists, would have a very good claim to being regarded as a nature or real essence. Since the advent of atomic theory and the reductionist paradigm in the physical sciences, it's been a working hypothesis that these real essences, at least in the case of physical objects, consist in quantitative and structural features of the objects' microstructures. The molecular structure of table salt explains not only its dispositional properties, like its solubility, but also many of its observable categorical properties: its solidity at room temperature and its crystalline structure when solid. It also expresses the objective feature that all salt has in common—it says "what it is to be" salt. Taking molecular structure to be the nature of salt, then, unifies the Lockean notion of real essence as hidden explanatory structure with the Aristotelian notion of essence as real definition.

This, then, is the general picture of "natures" that I wish to endorse: a nature is a (possibly hidden) categorical property that grounds dispositions and explains observable categorical properties. I do not mean to suggest that all natures are atomic or molecular structures—it's both possible and likely that different kinds of kinds will have different kinds of natures. The natures of biological kinds may consist in genomes; the nature of psychological kinds may consist in functional organizations. Nor do I wish to beg any questions against the social constructionists. It may turn out that some "kinds"—perhaps the kind "person" among them—have no natures in this sense at all and constitute groupings only because of features that are contingently of interest to some group at some time in some place. For all that, I do want to maintain that an inquiry that seeks a "human nature" in my sense will not be marred by the defects that have inspired feminist and progressive criticism of the traditional projects.

To see why this is so, I must point out two important features of this model of natures. The first thing to note is that when a real essence, in the sense of a grounding categorical, is found, it is always a *distinct property* from any of the categoricals associated with the dispositions it grounds. Thus, salt does not have a "dissolving nature"—rather, it has a nature *such that* it will, if placed in water, dissolve. "Natures" are thus *functional*, in the mathematical sense: they can be thought of as things that "yield" categorical properties *given* a specific set of circumstances. This fact about natures means that they are frequently difficult to characterize substantively—they are, in effect, hard to *name*. If and when there is developed a theoretical articulation of the grounding characteristics, natures can be named, but in advance of any such theory, it is difficult to conceptualize a nature, except by reference to one

or more of the dispositions it grounds (consider the infamous *virtus dormitiva* possessed by Molière's secret sleeping preparation). These, in turn, tend to get conceptualized and named in terms of their associated categoricals: this is how a person who behaves aggressively in certain circumstances comes to have "an aggressive nature." I will call this difficulty in conceptualizing the grounding categoricals the "naming problem."

But, of course, even a person who is said to be "naturally aggressive" is not displaying aggression *all the time*. That brings us to the second important point: dispositional properties are only fully specified if the *activating circumstances* are fully specified. If they are not, then there is a danger either that the ascription of a disposition will be empty or ill defined, or else that it will be extremely apt to mislead. Often, the activating circumstances can be safely assumed to be understood, and needn't be explicitly mentioned. We all understand the term "soluble" to mean "soluble *in water*." Knowing this, we also know that if we want to say of something that it will dissolve in a fluid other than water, we must specify that fluid in the ascription: "soluble in alcohol."

Sometimes when the activating conditions are left unspecified, there's a presumption that they are simply the "normal" conditions. This is a much trickier assumption. Generally, the idea is that we are, in such cases, talking about "normalcy" in some flatly descriptive *statistical* sense—that is, the conditions that most frequently obtain. Sometimes the activating conditions are *so* prevalent that it's possible to forget that the instantiation of the associated categorical is *dependent* upon those conditions. We then stop bothering to express the dispositional property as such, and may even begin to conflate the property with its associated categorical. As noted earlier, many objects that we think of simply as "solid" or "liquid" are only contingently so—water is liquid *at some temperatures* but solid at others. In our standard characterizations of water and salt, we simply take for granted the presence of the activating conditions under which those substances appear in those states. Thus, the fact that the activating conditions for a dispositional property can be the (statistically) normally prevailing ones can effectively make us forget that many of the properties that we may think of as "belonging to the nature" of a thing— its apparent color, its shape, its physical state— are actually the result of an *interaction* of that thing's nature with the thing's environment.

This process partly accounts, I think, for the feeling many have that *any* attribution of "natures" is going to entail an unacceptable kind of determinism. When an associated categorical, like "aggression" or "intelligence," is treated not as the result of a certain nature in interaction with a particular environment but as itself part of the nature, it's easy to think that the aggression or intelligence is something that's there *all* the time, independently of circumstances. The *contingency* of the display of some particular categorical property becomes invisible—giving us, therefore, what I'll call the *problem of the invisibility of contingencies*.

This problem is exacerbated when the "normalcy" being presumed is not the relatively innocuous statistical sort of normalcy but is, rather, prescriptive—*ideal* or *optimal* conditions. There is nothing inherently wrong with the use, even the tacit use, of such a sense of normalcy. This is the use of "normal" in which it can make sense to say that some very large percentage of a population is above or below "normal"—we might, for example, document the extent of malnutrition in some war-torn region by pointing out that most of the children in the region are significantly below "normal" in height and weight. The "norm" appealed to here is obviously not merely the statistical average of the children's heights, nor even the average of their heights pooled with the heights of children elsewhere. Rather, it involves some notion of the *optimal* height and weight for human children of certain ages. Still, the introduction of an evaluative element into notions of normalcy is potentially problematic.

Sometimes there is and sometimes there is not a clear principle for the selection of "optimal" conditions. Height and weight norms, as I suggested, reflect assumptions about the *health* of the organism. Yet even this apparently clear and uncontroversial principle is not as straightforward as it might at first appear. Even if all our questions about empirical dependencies could be answered (At what weight is cardiovascular function most efficient? Does limiting fat in the diets of young children retard brain development?), there would still be difficult issues to resolve about what constitutes "good health": Is *length* of life the only determinant of the ultimate healthiness of the organism, or must length be weighed against *quality* of life? If so, who or what determines what counts as quality?

Sometimes all these issues are sidestepped by implicitly appealing to the status quo—that is, what is sometimes taken to be *normatively* normal is simply whatever we're used to. Because this assumption, when it's made, is generally implicit, the status quo is not frequently scrutinized in this context for either *desirability* or *mutability*. If, however, the presumption that the status quo is or ought to be stable *were* to be explicitly examined, it's likely that it would rarely hold up.

Note the *status quo* incorporates lots of differently caused regularities. Some of these, like the climate, are largely independent of human agency (which is, of course, not to say that human agency cannot largely mitigate the *effects* of climate). Other regularities, like war and poverty, are extremely sensitive to human agency. But the invisibility of contingencies can lead to the idea that natures that are expressed *one* way under the de facto prevailing conditions are *inevitably* expressed the same way, so that phenomena that are quite amenable to human control are written off as due to "laws of nature." (It may, in the end, be true that the poor will be with us always, but, if so, it will only be because those of us who aren't poor chose to do nothing about it.)

Another misconception that arises from the invisibility of contingencies is the completely unfounded idea that natures somehow set the "strength" of tendencies toward the display of some categorical property, even if they don't determine it, where strength is measured either in terms of the number of environments in which the categorical property will be expressed or in terms of the "difficulty" of suppressing the expression of the property. Thus, according to much current opinion, if intelligence is "natural," then it will shine through no matter how deprived the environment; and for "natural" stupidity, there is no environmental remedy.[41]

There is a concept from biology that can help dismantle this particular confusion—the concept of a "norm of reaction."[42] Remember that biologists distinguish the genotype of an organism from its phenotype. The *genotype* is the organism's particular genetic configuration; it is the biological analogue of molecular structure (or at least it can be so regarded for present purposes). The *phenotype* is the set of properties the organism actually displays: in general, the phenotype is a function of the genotype, the environment, and random factors. The genotype, then, can be regarded as the grounding categorical for the organism's disposition to display certain phenotypic properties in certain environments. My genotype, for example, makes me disposed to turn bright red if I'm exposed to an hour or more of direct sunlight.[43] Now it's possible, for some organisms, to chart, for a given genotype, the effects of the manipulation of a particular environmental variable on a particular phenotypic trait. Such a chart is called the "norm of reaction" (or "range of reaction") for that genotype.

In order to develop a norm of reaction for a genotype, several conditions must be satisfied: first, there must be available a large number of exemplars of the genotype; second, the environmental variable must be a factor that can be precisely quantified; and third, the phenotypic trait must also be a factor that can be precisely quantified. Because it is difficult to contrive (much less find) situations where all three conditions are satisfied, very few actual norms of reaction have been plotted. But we do know at least the following:

(i) One cannot in general extrapolate any one part of the norm of reaction from any other. Norms of reaction are not necessarily neat, and are rarely linear. It needn't be true even that a particular environmental factor that produces an increase in some phenotypic property for part of the range will continue to do so throughout the range. It is, in short, impossible to predict, just from the known parts of the norm of reaction, the phenotypic effects of a novel environmental alteration. (ii) The norm of reaction for *one* genotype cannot in general be used to predict the norm of reaction for another. The environment that produced optimal growth for one genotype may be stunting for another. Anything that is known about the *general* requirements or behavior of kinds of living things must be known either through old-fashioned empirical sampling and inductive generalization (with all the attendant risks) or through some abductive argument for a presumed universal (an example of which—the "poverty of the stimulus" argument—I'll discuss later). (iii) Difference in phenotypic properties does not entail difference in genotype, and similarity of phenotypic properties does not entail sameness of genotype.

This brings us to an extremely important point concerning the difference between *species* natures and *individual* natures. An individual nature can be thought of as a genotype grounding a norm of reaction. A species nature is then a generalization *over* genotypes. The first thing it's crucial to realize is that such a generalization is not the same as a generalization over observed phenotypic properties, nor as an abstraction from observed phenotypic differences. It is, rather, a generalization over *dispositions*. It is misleading to say that *language use* is part of the human essence. What's actually meant by-such a claim is the empirical generalization that every human being is disposed to acquire language under an extremely large range of "normal" human environments. The same can be said for having two legs, ten toes, and so forth—our saying that such characteristics are determined by the human genome should be understood to mean "by almost every human genotype under the known range of environmental variation."

Frequently, the reliable generalizations that can be drawn from empirical observation concern extremes. We pretty much know the effects of both starvation and glutting on most animals, but we also know that, within a large range of "normal" consumption, the same number of calories consumed by different bodies (even different bodies within the same species) will have different effects on both size and health. We know a lot about the kinds of environments that produce various impairments and pathologies in human beings—we know that severe malnutrition produces mental retardation, for example, and we have evidence that extreme and sustained physical abuse produces dissociative personality disorders—but we don't have even the beginnings of serious theories about the role the environment plays in accounting for the variation we observe among people with "normal" personalities and intellects. We know that children who are completely deprived of social interaction with other human beings up until the age of puberty never acquire certain linguistic abilities; we know nothing, however, about the role of environmental variables—if there is one—in accounting for individual differences in normal linguistic development.

Altogether, what we know about norms of reaction tells us this: there are individual differences in *natures* (understood as genotypes) and also individual differences in phenotypes. But we cannot infer anything about the former directly from the latter. In carefully controlled conditions, where we have large numbers of genetically identical individuals and a precisely defined environmental variable that can be readily manipulated, it is possible to construct a norm of reaction for a single genotype. But outside such rare conditions, we are not entitled to assume that we know anything about any individual's *nature*.

In short, the very notion of a "nature/ nurture" dichotomy is confused. It's considered good form in nature/nurture controversies, whichever side one is on, to concede that there might well be *some* natural/environmental "component" to whatever trait is being discussed. But such concessions miss the point. There is *always* a genetic "component" and always an environmental "component" in the genesis of a phenotypic trait, and there is no meaningful way to apportion *causal responsibility* between them. The genotype is just as "active" in an environment in which it produces one phenotype as it is in any other. What nongeneticists probably *mean* when they say things like "Eighty percent of intelligence is inherited" is probably something like this: changing the environment can only alter intelligence by about 20 percent—the genes are four times "stronger" than the environment. But *this* claim embodies another misconception.

As Richard Lewontin has explained, there is a huge difference between the *analysis of variance* and the *analysis of causes* (Lewontin, 1976). We can explain the variance in phenotypic traits within a given population as being n percent due to genetic variation and m percent due to variations in the environment, but this is hardly the same as saying that n percent of the trait was caused by the individual's intrinsic nature while m percent was caused by the environment. Heritability estimates must always be relativized to populations and environments—that is why it is such a blatant fallacy to infer, as Herrnstein, Jensen, and Murray all do (despite persistent criticism on this point),[44] from the heritability of intelligence within one group to a genetic explanation of average differences in measured intelligence *between* groups.

Let me summarize, then, what all this tells us about the notion of *nature* and its use and abuse within both philosophy and science. I claim that the naming problem, which stems from the functional character of natures, together with the problem of the invisibility of contingencies, result in a problematic conflation of natures with particular categorical properties. When this conflation occurs against a background in which only privileged individuals are engaged in theorizing, we get the sorts of objectionable methods and results that feminist theorists have criticized: the activating circumstances that are tacitly privileged as "normal" become those that are typical of or are highly valued by the theorists themselves. The categorical properties that the theorists display in those circumstances then become the properties that are reified as "natures." Because the contingency of these circumstances is invisible, and because the conflation of the associated categorical with nature itself is wholly unnoticed, the absence of the selected categorical property in others is treated as a difference in *nature*.

Understanding that a nature does not determine a phenotypic property, but rather grounds a complex set of dispositions, can also help us to avoid problematic reifications of analytical parameters and to check the correlative tendency to think of some individuals in some circumstances as displaying "purer" expressions of these parameters than others. A nature, conceived as a grounding categorical, can *never* be expressed in some "pure" form: *any* expression of any genotype must be mediated by some environment. There may be some environments that are more *typical*, in the statistical sense, than others, and some that are more *optimal*, relative to some set of values, but there is no way to "factor out" the effects of "extrinsic" or "artificial" or "disturbing" influences so as to reveal nature in its pure form. (This also reveals the fundamental absurdity of the notion of "following the dictates of nature.") Furthermore, a category like "gender" can only refer to some genotypic

parameter, some feature of the genotype. And individual parts of genotypes can no more receive "pure" expression than whole genotypes can.

A quick case study: let's analyze Stephen Goldberg's claim that men are "naturally" more aggressive than women, one of the most persistent claims about differences in the "natures" of men and women. We can see now that it's far from clear even what's meant by this: sometimes people seem to mean that there's some actual substance, "aggression," that men have more of than women (as some snakes store more venom than others); at other times they seem to mean that men are, given any particular situation, more likely to act aggressively than are women. The evidence cited for this claim (if indeed any evidence is cited) generally consists in facts about the relative number of aggressive acts committed by men and by women, or, as in Goldberg's case, about the connection between some biological factor presumed to be more prevalent in men (like testosterone) and the commission of aggressive acts.

But we can see now that none of this makes any sense. Let us grant that there is an observed regularity that men display more aggressive behavior than do women. That in itself tells us nothing about the underlying natures of men and women. It is, in fact, consistent with their having *identical* natures. What we would need to know in order to draw any conclusions about differences or similarities in natures is this: how men and women act when they grow up in the *same circumstances*, where this includes, crucially, being presented with the same set of behavioral options. The idea of an option is affected by utility—if women's and men's incentive structures are different, that's enough for their *options* to be different (Baber 1994).

The important lesson here is that regularities, even remarkably stable regularities in the observed behavior of the two genders, are not necessarily (and, given what we know, not even probably) evidence of a difference in natures.

Neglect of this very important qualification in talk about men's "natural" aggression or women's "natural" tendency to nurture probably reflects either an indifference to, or approval of, whatever system of circumstances *produces* these regularities.[45]

The Need for Natures

Perhaps if the foregoing is right, the notion of "nature" can be recovered and rendered innocuous. But why should we bother? Can this notion of nature do any of the work natures were supposed to do? And do we really want such work done anyway? There are really two aspects to the question of whether we "need" a notion of human nature. One aspect I take to be purely empirical: Are there, or are there not theoretically significant properties that all human beings share, that appear to be nearly invariantly expressed under a large range of circumstances? If there are such "universals," then whether we need it or not, there is such a thing as "human nature." I don't think that anyone has ever seriously doubted the existence of *biological* universals in this sense. The presence of one heart, two kidneys, two lungs, two arms with five digits each—though not absolutely universal—is taken, at least by biologists, to be *normal* and *natural* for human beings. I am not saying that such assumptions are wholly unproblematic: only that, properly understood, they seem to be *true*. And any problems that attend talk of "normalcy" and "naturalness" in this instance, I claim, stem from conflation of statistical and evaluative senses of these terms.

But in addition to biological natures, there is increasing evidence of the existence of a *cognitive* nature, of what Steven Pinker (1994) thinks of as a set of human *instincts*. Instincts are not strict programs that determine behavior; they are, rather, programs that determine *dispositions*. The activating conditions for instincts can be quite specific or highly diverse; the associated categorical properties—overt behavior, in the case

of these dispositions—can be quite rigid or highly plastic. The "language instinct" in humans, for example, is such that the child requires human social contact, and a modicum of linguistic input, but nothing in the way of explicit instruction in order for it to be triggered.[46] The "behavior" that's triggered is itself a grounding categorical (a grammar) for a highly complex disposition (a language). The general form of the grammar is dictated by the human genome, but within that form there is all the variation that can be found across human languages.

Thus, while we cannot say that *all* human beings, without exception, speak a language, and while there is no "universal language" spoken by all human beings, and while no one language can sensibly be thought closer to "natural" than any other,[47] it is still the case that there is, in the case of language, a genuine human universal. What's universal is a certain *capacity*: we are able to converge onto a grammar for any language that displays certain very abstract formal properties ("universal grammar") to which we are given a short exposure during a critical period of our youth. This means *any* human language is potentially acquirable by *any* human infant; in practical terms, it means that we can communicate a potential infinity of richly structured thoughts, and we can *intercommunicate*, at least potentially, with every other member of our species.

Surely this is a morally significant fact. The ability to communicate is *valuable*. It is not just *useful*—it is centrally connected to nearly everything human beings have ever claimed to value about themselves, everything from our capacity for abstract thought (so emphasized in the philosophical tradition) to our capacities for social affiliation and cultural creation. That we have language is, in short, a *good thing*. But if we can agree on this very minimal evaluative claim, then we are on our way to seeing how facts about *natures* can legitimately ground normative claims. Our capacity for language may in itself make us morally valuable creatures, as certain philosophers have claimed (though it surely would be only a sufficient and not a necessary condition). But even if that's not so, the fact that *language* is valuable, together with the fact that human beings have a capacity to acquire it, provides part of a nonarbitrary conception of what Aristotle called "human flourishing." If it's good for humans to develop and exercise their capacities for linguistic communication, then it counts as *damage* to human beings to impede or prevent this development.

I claim that some such conception of human flourishing, grounded in assumptions about a shared set of capacities, in fact lies behind feminism's protest against the treatment of women.[48] Feminists do not want to say *simply* that women are unhappy under patriarchy—for one thing, not all women are. Rather, I take it to be feminism's position that women under patriarchy are systematically *dehumanized*—treated in ways that prevent or impede the full development of their *human* capacities. Without a nonarbitrary background notion of human flourishing, the notion of *damage* makes no sense. And if feminists cannot make out the case that patriarchy *damages* women, then we are properly open to the charge, leveled at us often enough by our critics, that we are simply trying to impose on others our own parochial views of how life should be lived.

Notice that the need for appeal to *human* universals does not beg any questions against those who think that there are systematic differences between men and women. I have made no argument against this, although I think the considerations raised in the preceding section should make clear how hard it would be to properly justify any such claim. But consider what such a claim must mean once we understand natures properly as the grounds of complex dispositions. To say that boys "have better spatial abilities than girls" turns out to be many ways ambiguous. The (probably) intended meaning is that, in the standard curriculum, boys do better

than girls. But suppose it so—it hardly follows that there are no curricula in which girls do as well as boys, or even better! And, of course, that environment could be provided to girls *without* disadvantaging boys: what is to prevent us as a society from providing girls with the environment that will permit *them* to flourish, and boys the environment that will permit *them* to flourish?

Nothing but *will*. This is already the scheme that's followed when the children in question are deemed truly valuable. In colleges and universities, in private elementary and secondary schools, and in the more affluent public schools, instructors labor mightily to provide "individualized instruction" to students with a variety of "special needs." Deficits in middle- and upper-class students are attributed to the environment; innate stupidity and laziness are found only in the poor. The idea that "natures" and "natural differences" are the only, or even *an important*, determinant of levels of human flourishing should be exposed for the self-serving nonsense that it is. It means nothing more or less than the patently abhorrent claim that the human flourishing of some individuals—men, white people, affluent people, English-speaking people, Christian people, straight people—is more valuable than that of others.

Questions of difference aside, however, there is a more fundamental point. As long as women and men share certain morally relevant capacities—the capacity for rationally directed action, the capacity to form emotional attachments, the capacity to communicate—general norms of human flourishing will still apply equally to both. It is impossible for me to imagine discoverable differences between men and women that could swamp the significance of these commonalities. The properties we manifestly share are sufficient to make clear that there can be no justification for separating men and women—or, indeed, any two groups of human beings—into "rulers or things ruled by Nature's direction."[49]

Notes

1 With the possible exceptions of Plato and Descartes, but see Lloyd 1984; Bordo 1987 and Scheman 1993.

2 Stevenson 1987, pp. 3 and viii. I'll discuss Stevenson's discussion of the use of masculine "generics" in detail in the next section.

3 Most of what the major Western philosophers had to say about women can be found in the invaluable collection *Philosophy of Woman*, edited by Mary Mahowald. References are to the third 1994 edition unless otherwise noted.

4 In all three casts, the concession was made not because women were manifestly capable of rational thought (philosophy has never been seriously constrained by what's obvious) but rather because women would need a modicum of rationality to fulfill their proper roles. See ibid., 30 (Aristotle); 91, 93–95 (Rousseau); 103 (Kant).

5 For further discussion see Moulton 1977.

6 Aristotle explicitly recognizes and struggles with precisely these difficulties. See Mahowald 1994, p. 30. For further discussion of Aristotle's views of women see Lange 1983; Spelman 1983 and Spelman 1988. For discussion of Rousseau and Kant, see Lloyd 1984.

7 See Mahowald 1994, pp. 31 (Aristotle); 89 (Rousseau); 102 (Kant).

8 Kant, for example, allows that "[t]he fair sex has just as much understanding as the male," but adds the notorious qualification "it is a *beautiful understanding*, whereas ours ['ours'?!—LA] should be a *deep understanding*, an expression that signifies identity with the sublime" (Mahowald 1994, p. 103). "Her philosophy is not to reason, but to sense" (p. 104). And Rousseau announces baldly: "What would be defects in men are good qualities in women, which are necessary to make things go on well" (p. 90). Evidently the goodness of the feminine virtues lies mainly in their instrumental value to men. Kant concurs: "The content of woman's great science ... is humankind, and among humanity, men" (p. 104). See also Christine Garside-Allen, "Can a Woman Be Good in the Same Way as a Man?" *Dialogue* 10 (1971): 534–544.

9 See Pierce 1994; Trebilcot 1994.

10 Mahowald 1994, p. 90. Speaking of women's sensitivity to shame, Kant argues that "since it has the voice of nature on its side, [it] seems always to agree with good moral qualities even if it yields to excess" (p. 106).

11 Ibid., p. 105. Similarly, Aristotle's slaves *could not* rule because they lacked the deliberative faculty (p. 31).

12 Ibid., p. 111.

13 Ibid., p. 103. A personal note: my own experience and that of countless other women my age attests to the durability of Kant's view. Most of us have bitter memories of someone admonishing us to disguise or downplay our intelligence if we ever wanted to get dates. Judging from my students' reports, a distressing number of girls are *still* being told that boys just don't like smart girls. Yet to my knowledge, not a single one of the studies of sex differences in math and science emerging around puberty takes account of this extremely potent social message. How well would boys do at calculus if you told them—credibly—that they would never get to have sex if they mastered differential equations?

14 Mill 1994, see especially pp. 153–157.

15 See ibid. and also Wollstonecraft 1994; Taylor Mill 1994 especially pp. 113–115, 171–173.

16 Goldberg 1978, pp. 81–86.

17 *Time and Newsweek* feature cover stories on the "naturalness" of gender differences every few years. See, for example, *Time*'s cover story entitled Sizing up the sexes (1/20/92) and *Newsweek*'s The new science of the brain: Why men and women think differently (3/27/95).

18 ABC News Special Report: Boys and girls *are* different: Men, women and the sex difference, February 1, 1995.

19 In this I concur with Charlotte Witt, who defends a version of this claim in her essay Feminist metaphysics, Witt 1993.

20 This is to the best of my knowledge. There is no index for the edited collection, and in the monograph's index the only relevant entries are five page citations under "Female, feminism," three of which refer to Stevenson's discussions of his own neglect of the issue of gender differences, added in the second edition.

21 Stevenson 1987, p. 3.

22 Or, as the characters in *Charlotte's Web* innocently sing, in a Hanna-Barbera video: "We've got lots in common where it . . . really counts! Where it . . . really counts!" (Thanks to my daughter, Rachel Antony-Levine, for bringing this song to my attention.)

23 Stevenson 1987, p. 3.

24 I would like to acknowledge here my enormous debt to the writings of bell hooks and Elizabeth Spelman, whose works—especially hooks's *Feminist Theory* and Spelman's *Inessential Woman*—have informed this entire section. The tacit exclusion of women of color by white feminist theorists is a central critical theme among black feminist and "womanist' writers. See, for example, Londe 1984; Omoladc 1980; and Joseph 1981.

25 See, for example, bell hooks's discussion of Betty Freidan, hooks 1984, pp. 1–3, and Chapter 4.

26 See Harris 1990, p. 588.

27 Spelman 1988, pp. 57–79.

28 For an important early statement of the view that the material conditions of femininity constitute an epistemic standpoint in this sense, see Hartsock 1983. For a more recent development of such a view, see Schott 1993. For a critique of universal theories of human nature that draws on standpoint theory, see Scheman 1995, pp. 177–190, 199–200.

29 It is difficult to believe that some of them were not. It is a little hard to swallow; for example, that Locke could have seriously believed his own apology for the enslavement of Africans within the colonies: they had been captives in a "just war" who had forfeited their lives "by some Act that deserves death." As Peter Laslett remarks in his notation to section 24 of the *Second Treatise on Government*, Locke's justification of slavery "may seem unnecessary, and inconsistent with his principles, but it must be remembered that he writes as the administrator of slave-owing colonies in America" (Locke 1963, p. 325). (Laslett does not comment on Locke's inconsistency in granting husbands a natural right to prevail over their wives.) For further examination of colonial-era discussions of slavery and the natural rights of "man," see Bailyn 1967. For more on Locke's view of race, see Bracken 1973.

30 Baier (1987) does not condemn all the canonical philosophers: she thinks that Hume's empiricism provides a promising basis for both a feminist ethics and a feminist epistemology.

31 Okin 1989. See also Okin 1990 for a survey and discussion of the range of feminist views on the matter of gender differences in moral thinking.

32 Lloyd 1984. Marcia Homiak (1993) defends Aristotle against the charge that his conception of a life governed by reason is elitist in Feminism and Aristotle's rational ideal.

33 Although most of the theorists I have discussed are skeptical that the minimally necessary conditions for successful theorizing are even close to being realized. See, for example, Scheman 1995.

34 See MacKinnon 1989. For discussion, see Haslanger 1995, 1996 pp. 95–125; and Babbitt 1995, p. 6.

35 Fraser and Nicholson 1990, p. 28. Fraser and Nicholson are not here criticizing the particular theories I referred to, though I think they would agree that the criticism applies. I am simply borrowing their gloss of the term "essentialist."

36 Donna Haraway explains and explores the implications of this absence of fixity through the metaphor of a *cyborg*—a being that defies all distinction between male and female, between animal and machine, and between natural and artificial. See Haraway 1985.

37 Young 1990, p. 99.

38 Bordo 1993, p. 243.

39 The term "categorical" as a name for nondispositional properties was suggested to me by Stephen Yablo.

40 See Quine 1969, pp. 114–138. To be more precise, the standard view is that attributions of dispositional properties, *to the extent that they are determinate*, are grounded in some categorical fact about the object.

41 Actually, middle- and upper-class American parents have somewhat incoherent attitudes about intelligence. On the one hand, they have a great deal invested in the idea that their children are inherently smarter (i.e., better) than poorer kids; on the other hand, they are not about to risk leaving their kids' natural intelligence to flourish on its own, so they demand for their own children the most highly enriched educational environment that tax dollars can buy. George Bush used to publicly opine that quality of education had nothing to do with how much was spent per

student. His parents then must have been real
suckers to shell out the bucks it cost to send him
to Andover, which spends eleven thousand dollars
per student. See Kozol 1991.

42 I rely here on Lewontin 1976.

43 Despite this, I'm classified as "white"—a good
example of the naming problem (the complex
dispositional property of being pale if not exposed
to sunlight is conflated with the associated categorical of being pale), aided and abetted by the invisibility of contingencies—"normal" here being
partially statistical (I am mostly not in the sun) and
normative (what's statistically true for me, an
urban professional, is tacitly taken as the standard).

44 See Block and Dworkin 1976 and also the discussion of heritability and its abuse in the IQ debate
in Lewontin, Rose and Kamin 1984, Chapter 5.

45 Nancy Holmstrom makes the same point but
argues for a conception of "nature" on which such
properties that depend on such stable regularities
are counted as part of the thing's nature. See
Holmstrom 1982.

46 Although the social contact may be more important than the language. "There are cases of spontaneously invented languages: see the discussion of
creoles and of invented sign language among
congenitally deaf twins", Pinker 1994, pp. 32–39.

47 Although see Stephen Jay Gould 1995, for an
intriguing countersuggestion. Gould argues that
certain creoles, because they do not carry the
syntactic accretions and alterations that appear
during the histories of most languages, may
provide insight into "default" settings of the
parameters specified by Universal Grammar. There
is no consensus among linguists as to whether
such default settings exist.

48 Cf. Witt 1993.

49 Aristotle in Mahowald 1994, p. 31.

References

Antony, L. and Witt, C. (Eds.) (1993). *A Mind of One's
Own*. Boulder, CO: Westview Press.

Babbitt, S. (1995). *Impossible Dreams: Rationality, integrity, and
moral imagination*. Boulder, CO: Westview Press.

Baber, H. (1994). Choice, Preference and Utility: A
response to Sommers. Paper presented at APA
Eastern Division Meetings, December 1994.

Baier, A. (1987). Hume, the women's moral theorist?
In E. Feder Kittay and D. T. Meyers, (Eds.), *Women and
Moral Theory* (pp. 37–56). Totowa, NJ: Rowman and
Littlefield.

Bailyn, B. (1967). *The Ideological Origins of the American
Revolution*. Cambridge, MA: Belknap Press of Harvard
University Press.

Block, N., & Dworkin, G. (1976). *The IQ Controversy*. New
York: Pantheon Books.

Bordo, S. (1987). *The Flight to Objectivity*. Albany, NY:
State University of New York Press.

Bordo, S. (1993). Feminism, postmodernism, gender
skepticism. In S. Bordo, *Unbearable Weight: Feminism,
western culture and the body*. Berkeley and Los Angeles,
CA: University of California Press.

Bracken, H. (1973). Essence, accident and race.
Hermathena, 16(winter): 81–96.

Fraser, N., & Nicholson, L. (1990). Social criticism
without philosophy. In L. Nicholson (Ed.), *Feminism/
Postmodernism* (pp. 132–136). London and New York:
Routledge.

Garside-Allen, C. (1971). Can a woman be good in the
same way as a man?, *Dialogue* 10: 534–44.

Gilligan, C. (1982). *In a Different Voice: Psychological theory
and women's development*. Cambridge, MA: Harvard
University Press.

Goldberg, S. (1978). The inevitability of patriarchy. In
A. Jaggar and P. Rothenberg Struhl (Eds.), *Feminist
Frameworks* (pp. 81–86). New York: McGraw-Hill.

Gould, S. J. (1995). Speaking of snails and scales. *Natural
History*, May: 14–23.

Haraway, D. (1985). A manifesto for cyborgs: Science,
technology, and socialist feminism in the 1980's.
Socialist Review 15(80: 65–107.

Harding, S., & Hintikka, M. (Eds.) (1983). *Discovering
Reality*. Dordrecht: U. Reidel.

Harris, A. (1990). Race and essentialism in feminist
legal theory. *Stanford Law Review*, 42: 588.

Hartsock, N. (1983). The feminist standpoint:
Developing the ground for a specifically feminist
historical materialism. In S. Harding and M.
Hintikka (Eds.), *Discovering Reality* (pp. 283–310).
Dordrecht: U. Reidel.

Haslanger, S. (1995). Ontology and social construction. *Philosophical Topics*, 23(2).

Haslanger, S. (1996). *Feminist Perspectives on Language,
Knowledge, and Reality*. Fayeteville, AR: University of
Arkansas Press.

Held, V. (1990). Feminist transformations of moral theory. *Philosophy and Phenomenological Research*, 50(nos. 3–4, supplement): 321–344.

Holmstrom, N. (1982). Do women have a distinct nature? *Philosophical Forum*, 14 (1: 25–42.

Homiak, M. (1993). Feminism and Aristotle's rational ideal. In L. Antony and C. Witt (Eds.), *A Mind of One's Own* (pp. 1–17). Boulder, CO: Westview Press.

hooks, b. (1984). *Feminist Theory: From margin to center*. Boston, MA: South End Press.

Joseph, G. (1981). The incompatible menage à trois: Marxism, feminism, and racism. In L. Sargent (ed.), *Women and Revolution: a discussion of the unhappy marriage of Marxism and feminism* (pp. 91–107). Boston, MA: South End Press.

Kozol, J. (1991). *Savage Inequalities*. New York: Crown.

Lange, L. (1983) Woman is not a rational animal. In S. Harding and M. Hintikka (Eds.), *Discovering Reality* (pp. 1–15). Dordrecht: U. Reidel.

Lewontin, R. (1976). The analysis of variance and the analysis of causes. In N. Block and G. Dworkin (Eds.), *The IQ Controversy* (pp. 107–112) New York: Pantheon Books.

Lewontin, R. C., Rose, S. & Kamin, L. J. (1984). *Not in Our Genes*. New York: Pantheon.

Lloyd, G. (1984). *The Man of Reason: "Male" and "female" in western philosophy*. Minneapolis, MN: University of Minnesota Press.

Locke, J. (1963). *Two Treatises of Government*, edited and with introduction and notes by Peter Laslett. Cambridge and New York: Mentor Books of Cambridge University Press.

Londe, A. (1984) *Sister Outsider*. Trumansburg, NY: Crossing Press.

MacKinnon, C. (1989). *Toward a Feminist Theory of the State*. Cambridge, MA and London: Harvard University Press.

Mahowald, M. (Ed.) (1994). *Philosophy of Woman*. Indianapolis, IN: Hackett, 1978 2nd ed., 1983 3rd ed.

Mill, J. S. (1994). On the subjection of women. In M. Mahowald (ed.), *Philosophy of Woman* (pp. 151–170). Indianapolis, IN: Hackett.

Moulton, J. (1977) The myth of neutral "man". In M. Vetterling, F. Elliston and J. English (Eds.), *Feminism and Philosophy*. Totowa, NJ: Littlefield, Adams.

Noddings, N. (1984) *Caring: A feminine approach to ethics and moral education*. Berkeley and Los Angeles, CA: University of California Press.

Okin, S. (1989). *Justice, Gender and the Family*. New York: Basic Books.

Okin, S. (1990). Thinking like a woman. In D. L. Rhode (Ed.), *Theoretical Perspectives on Sexual Difference* (pp. 145–159). New Haven, CT: Yale University Press.

Omoladc, B. (1980). Black women and feminism. In H. Eisenstein and A. Jardine (Eds.), *The Future of Difference* (pp. 247–257). Boston, MA: G. K. Hall.

Pierce, C. (1994). Natural law language and women. In M. Mahowald (Ed.), (pp. 356–368). Indianapolis, IN: Hackett.

Pinker, S. (1994). *The Language Instinct*. New York: William Morrow.

Quine, W. V. O. (1969). Natural kinds. In W. V. O. Quine, *Ontological Relativity and Other Essays* (pp. 114–138). New York and London: Columbia University Press, 1969.

Rapaport, E. (1993). Generalizing gender: Reason and essence in the legal thought of Catherine MacKinnon. In L. Antony and C. Witt, *A Mind of One's Own*, (pp. 127–143). Boulder, CO: Westview Press.

Ruddick, S. (1989). *Maternal Thinking: Toward a politics of peace*. Boston, MA: Beacon Press.

Scheman, N. (1993). Though this be method, yet there is madness in it: Paranoia and liberal epistemology. In L. Antony and C. Witt (Eds.), *A Mind of One's Own* (pp. 145–70). Boulder, CO: Westview Press.

Scheman, N. (1995). Feminist epistemology and reply to Antony. *Metaphilosophy* 26 (3): 177–190, 199–200.

Schott, R. (1983). Resurrecting embodiment: Toward a feminist materialism. In In L. Antony and C. Witt (Eds.), *A Mind of One's Own* (pp. 171–184). Boulder, CO: Westview Press.

Spelman, E. (1983). Aristotle and the politicization of the soul. In S. Harding and M. Hintikka (Eds.), *Discovering Reality* (pp. 17–30). Dordrecht: U. Reidel.

Spelman, E. (1988) *Inessential Woman*. Boston, MA: Beacon Press.

Stevenson, L. (1981). *The Study of Human Nature*. New York and Oxford: Oxford University Press.

Stevenson, L. (1987). *Seven Theories of Human Nature*, 2nd ed. New York and Oxford: Oxford University Press.

Taylor Mill, H. (1994). Enfranchisement of women. In M. Mahowald (ed.), *Philosophy of Woman* (pp. 170–185). Indianapolis, IN: Hackett.

Trebilcot, J. (1994). Sex roles: The argument from nature. In M. Mahowald (Ed.), *Philosophy of Woman* (pp. 349–356). Indianapolis, IN: Hackett.

Witt, C. (1993). Feminist metaphysics. In L. Antony and C. Witt (Eds.), *A Mind of One's Own* (pp. 273–288). Boulder, CO: Westview Press.

Wollstonecraft, M. (1994). Vindication of the rights of woman. In M. Mahowald (Ed.), *Philosophy of Woman* (pp. 112–128). Indianapolis, IN: Hackett.

Young, I. (1990). *Justice and the Politics of Difference*. Princeton, NJ: Princeton University Press.

Chapter 36

Nancy Holmstrom

IS HUMAN NATURE IMPORTANT FOR FEMINISM?[1]

According to Noam Chomsky,

Any serious social science or theory of social change must be founded on some concept of human nature. A theorist of classical liberalism such as Adam Smith begins by affirming that human nature is defined by a propensity to truck and barter, to exchange goods: that assumption accords very well with the social order he defends. If you accept that premise (which is hardly credible), it turns out that human nature conforms to an idealized early capitalist society, without monopoly, without state intervention, and without social control of production. If, on the contrary, you believe with Marx or the French and German Romantics that only social cooperation permits the full development of human powers, you will then have a very different picture of a desirable society. There is always some conception of human nature, implicit or explicit, underlying a doctrine of social order or social change.[2]

Similarly, Charles Taylor has argued:

human needs, wants and purposes have an important bearing on the way people act, and . . . therefore one has to have a notion . . . that is not too wildly inaccurate if one is to establish the framework for any science of human behavior, that of politics not excepted. A conception of human needs thus enters into a given political theory and cannot be considered something extraneous which we later add.[3]

Alison Jaggar's masterful *Feminist Politics and Human Nature* (1983) is premised on this view. A comprehensive analysis of feminist writings from both scholarly and activist sources, Jaggar distinguishes four feminist frameworks: Liberal, Traditional Marxism, Radical Feminism, and Socialist Feminism, and argues in favor of the last. One could, as always, question the classificatory scheme, but what is most interesting here is that first, all the different feminist frameworks assume that women and men share a common human nature, and, secondly, that their differing politics are intimately connected to their particular understandings of that common nature.

But much has changed since Jaggar wrote her book in the heyday of the women's movement, when "women's liberation" was the goal, and "feminism" was too tame a word. For a variety of very different reasons, many feminists came to reject the idea of a—by definition—*universal* human nature, or at least to deny its importance for feminism. Recently some feminists have returned to notions of human nature as an important grounding for feminist theory and politics, although this is by no means an uncontested move. I will argue that the reasons given for rejecting human nature do not hold, and hence that this is the correct position for feminists to take, especially for feminists of a radical political persuasion.

Some Historical Antecedents

The best known feminist voices from the past relied on notions of human nature: liberal feminists, Marxists, and (despite their disclaimers) the Existentialists. Mary Wollstonecraft, inspired by the French Revolution, wrote *A Vindication of the Rights of Women* in 1790 clearly influencing John Stuart Mill's better known classic of liberal feminism, *The Subjection of Women* a century later (Mill, 1988). Physical qualities, sex-differentiated or not, are not important to them, morally, but rather, what distinguishes human beings from other animals—"the simple power . . . of discerning truth . . ."[4] Thus, reason is the essential quality of human nature, all others accidental, a normative dualist conception[5] typical of liberal feminism (though arguably less so today). Both frankly acknowledge that women and men display different attributes, even describing women as "almost sunk below the standard of rational creatures."[6] But Mill describes the "hothouse" manner in which women are raised and contends that what is called the nature of women is "an eminently artificial thing." Are men and women essentially the same then? Though sometimes they take an agnostic position, which suffices to argue for equal opportunity, they often take a stronger position. "A wild wish has just flown from my heart to my head . . .," Wollstonecraft says, "to see the distinction of sex confounded in society."[7] This "wild wish" can be defended on the grounds on methodological simplicity. As Mill says,

> however great and ineradicable the moral and intellectual differences between men and women might be, . . . those only could be inferred to be natural which could not possibly be artificial—the residuum, after deducting every characteristic of either sex which can admit of being explained from education or external circumstances.[8]

On the liberal view, then, all normal human beings share the essential capacity to reason and the desire to be free, if these have not been extinguished by repression. For Wollstonecraft, these facts are the basis of natural rights, which are inconsistent with rigid sex roles. For Mill, sexual restrictions are wrong on Utilitarian grounds because "After . . . food and raiment, freedom is the first and strongest want of human nature."[9]

Marxists deepened the critique of essentialist justifications of hierarchical sexual relations. Rejecting liberalism's normative dualism, they start, they say, with real material beings, who, in all modes of production, must eat and have shelter and must labor to satisfy these needs. Humans are also the only animals who engage in free conscious activity (their "species being") and can satisfy animal needs in distinctly human ways. "The cultivation of the five senses is the work of all previous history."[10] Thus the idea of trans-historical needs and capacities—human nature—is important for Marxists, although they criticized abstractions like Humanity, and conservative characterizations of that nature. However, this human nature is always exemplified in specific social historic forms; thus, the biological and social are co-instantiated. In one passage in *Capital*, Marx refers to the "exclusively human form of labor," and also says, "by acting on the external world and changing it [man] changes his own nature."[11] Engels calls absurd the idea that women have always been slaves to men, contending instead that male domination came into existence at a certain stage of the history of property forms (the "world historic defeat of the female sex") and would go out of existence with socialism. Though Marx and Engels seem inconsistent in treating the reproductive roles of the sexes simply as "natural" without qualification, they did not believe the biological facts would, or should lead to invariable gender roles. The family, they stressed, is not only a biological, but a social relationship, hence historically variable. In socialism, where labor is under conscious collective control, both sexes would engage in free conscious activity, and there is no suggestion that this labor would take sex-differentiated forms. Thus women and men are understood as sharing the same fundamental human nature.

Simone de Beauvoir's groundbreaking *The Second Sex* opens with one of the most famous statements in feminist literature, "one is not born, but rather becomes, a woman."[12] However, de Beauvoir saw women's reproductive function as an obstacle to their realizing the radical freedom Existentialists believe humans have to determine one's own essence. Relying on Hegel's master-slave narrative, she contended that men were able to define women as the Other because men were often required to put their lives into danger, which raised them above the animal. To the idea that giving birth is the most fundamentally creative act, de Beauvoir replied that giving birth and suckling are not activities at all, but "natural functions; no project is involved . . ."[13] Raising a child could be a valid project if it were freely chosen, but this is next to impossible in a male-dominated world. Women's increasing freedom consisted primarily, she maintained, in the fact that women were increasingly able to escape the "slavery" assigned to them by their reproductive role. Though existentialists say they reject human nature, what they really reject is static predetermined conceptions, holding instead a normative dualist view of human nature whose most important aspect is radical freedom.

Feminist Challenges to Human Nature

Within the ever-evolving variety of opinion among feminists since the women's liberation movement, challenges to ideas of human nature came from several sides, challenging both their scope and content. Many critics pointed out how biased most conceptions were. Both Wollstonecraft's and Mill's liberal conception and de Beauvoir's existentialist one extolled activities associated with men[14] and denigrated those associated with women and bodies. The negative portrayal of childbirth and motherhood typified by de Beauvoir and carried to more extreme conclusions by radical feminist Shulamith Firestone (1970) reflected a dualist bias against the body common throughout the history of Western thought; others saw a more specific distaste for *women's* bodies (Jaggar, 1983; Spelman, 1988). Although neither problems of scope or content entail that the concept of human nature should be rejected, this was the inference that was drawn. Iris Young (1990) characterized these critiques as a distinct perspective, "gynocentric feminism", as opposed to the earlier humanist feminism. Many in this period emphasized biological differences between the sexes. Poet Adrienne Rich argued that what women needed was not liberation from *motherhood*, but liberation from *male domination of motherhood*. Rather than women's bodies being an obstacle to realizing their most human potentialities, on the contrary, women's reproductive functions make them better able to realize a uniquely human potential of rationality and physicality (Rich, 1976).

Some gynocentric writers went further, putting forward theories of essential differences between women's and men's cognitive and emotional attributes sufficiently important to be called sex-differentiated natures. Particularly influential were Mary Daly (1978) and Susan Griffin (1978), radical feminists whose views had evolved into a distinct perspective called "cultural feminism." To Daly and Griffin, women's bodies and sexuality made them closer to nature, and therefore more intuitive and creative. A familiar anti-feminist theme, what defines these thinkers as feminist is their reversal of the usual (male) evaluation of these (alleged) male-female differences. Women's bodies were celebrated rather than deprecated, and seen as the source of superiority, intellectual and moral, rather than inferiority. In order to become whole persons, women must free themselves not of their femaleness, but of the artificial femininity imposed by men and must each get in touch with her wild natural self. It is not clear why Daly supposes that there is this true self beneath women's socialized one, why she does not allow the same possibility for men, and why the "true self" must be a distinctively female one. More generally, one can ask how gender essentialists can avoid biological determinism, or if not, why it is any more defensible when they propound it than when conservatives do. While gender essentialists offer a thoroughgoing critique of male-domination, they have no basis for opposing "separate-but-equal" sex roles, a less radical position than Wollstonecraft's "wild wish" to deny any social importance to the sex distinction.

Most contemporary feminists have opposed the idea of sex-differentiated natures and the biological determinism on which it rests. Mill's argument from methodological simplicity has been buttressed by scientists who have subjected the allegedly scientific claims to detailed critique, both on specific and methodological grounds.[15] According to Stephen Jay Gould, the chief problem with biological determinism is that it is a theory of limits rather than potentials, all these critics stressing that genes cannot determine physical properties directly, but only in interaction with environmental conditions, which of course vary. Radicals extended the concept of environmental conditions to include the social/political system in which the science is embedded (Gould, 1991; Rose, Lewontin & Kamin, 1984). Philosophers have shown the extent to which political theories rest on theories of human nature and in turn how much theories of human nature and women's nature are influenced by political and other normative

theories. Radical scientists have shown that this is true of scientific theories as well.[16] Alison Jaggar and others, including myself (Holstrom 1982a, 1994), have argued against identification of the natural with the biological and a too simple contrast of the biological and the social. In fact the two interpenetrate. While human biological needs and capacities certainly have influenced the societies humans have constructed, so also have social conditions influenced human biology, for example, our size, shape, and even our reproductive capacities. Thus, sex is not a pure biological substratum beneath a socially constructed gender, as is sometimes assumed.

Criticisms of human nature came also from the opposite corner, from extreme social constructionists who extended the anti-essentialist arguments to sex as well as gender (Dworkin 1974; Wittig, 1981, 1982; MacKinnon 1987; Butler, 1990). Recognizing that there is no pure biological sex uncontaminated by society, thinkers like Monique Wittig and Andrea Dworkin go further, contending that "gender created anatomical sex (Wittig, 1982)." Since human nature is understood as partly a biological concept, this entails its rejection. Dworkin, ironically, rests her case for androgyny at the social level only because she believes in it at a biological level. Given that several aspects of sex identity do not always fit together, but nevertheless everyone is neatly divided into two and only two sexes, she concurs with Wittig that this shows that the basis is political, namely, its usefulness for heterosexism. Influenced by Foucault and deconstructionists, Judith Butler argued that there is no body prior to its construction by phallocentric significations.

Extreme social constructionism is problematic since nothing is a "given fact of nature" in the sense presupposed. Social elements enter into decision-making in all science and classifications are not so neat in natural sciences either. Classifications, in both natural and social science, are not on the basis of similarity and differences of properties alone, but how important the common properties are. Why else would German Sheperds belong to the same species as Chihuahuas, and not wolves? The actual distribution of properties among organisms is such that, contrary to the Aristotelian view, most taxa names can only be defined disjunctively. Any of the disjuncts is sufficient and the few necessary properties are far from sufficient, making most concepts of so-called natural kinds what are called "cluster concepts." Thus whether women (and men) have distinct natures depends, first, on their properties and, second, on the importance of these properties. But "importance" can only be evaluated within a specific theoretical context (Holmstrom, 1982b). Given that the sex difference is what allows for reproduction of humans and most other kinds of things, the division into two sexes has great importance for biological theory. Why then should it not be considered a natural or biological division, taking these terms to means something like "the object of biological theory?"[17] That there are different ways of representing reality, which can yield new discoveries and practical applications, in no way proves that there is no reality that sets constraints on the ways of understanding that can yield such discoveries and applications. Human beings can never, obviously, get beyond our human-influenced approaches to reality, but we can strive to eliminate, at least to reduce distorted ways of conceiving it. Intellectual and political struggle is crucial to bringing those changes, as will be discussed later.

Extreme social constructionism is also deficient politically. The political importance of the revelation that supposedly natural categories like race and gender are actually social in origin is greatly diminished if everything turns out to be social (Haslanger, 1995). Furthermore, it has a decidedly idealist character, neglecting the fact that humans are embodied beings; how does one support the demand for reproductive rights as especially critical for women except in virtue of their distinctive bodies?[18]

Yet other factors led to the rejection of human nature. Just as gender essentialists rejected the idea of a common human nature as being overly abstract and biased, theories regarding "women" were criticized for ignoring important differences among women, and being implicitly biased towards the speaker/writer who was usually white and middle class (Baca Zinn, 1986; Hill Collins, 1990; Spelman, 1988). Marxists had long made this point with respect to class, and lesbians had objected to heterosexual presumptions, but it was primarily women of color who pushed this issue to the foreground, especially in the United States. The emphasis on "difference" meant a turn away from such a universal concept as human nature as it was held to be impossible, in practice, to achieve a bias-free perspective. Postmodernism, highly influential in this period, held it to be impossible even in principle. So-called "totalizing" theories like liberalism or Marxism were rejected, and the stress was on "particularity" and "location." The popularity of relativism, of all kinds, in this period also precluded such theorizing.

The problem of implicit bias is very real and must be struggled against continually. Logically speaking, however, there is no inconsistency between the concept of human nature and the recognition of all its many variations, both physical and psychological.[19] If there were, we could not use *any* general terms, as there are always more specific terms included in the concept. Methodologically the critique of human nature is ill conceived as well. Human beings evolved to have different physical properties in different physical environments. Similarly, it is the flexibility of the human brain that allows human beings to adapt psychologically to different social environments, being, for example, more egoistic in some sets of social relations and more cooperative in others. Differences amongst human beings exist *because, not in spite of,* a biologically based common human nature.

New Feminist Humanisms

In recent years, a number of voices have been heard again defending the validity and importance of general concepts like sex, gender, and human nature. One could even speak of a new feminist humanism. In response to criticisms of universalistic projects like her theory of "humanist justice," Susan Moller Okin has argued forcefully for the political importance of the category gender, by which she means that

> it is possible to generalize about many aspects of inequality between the sexes. From place to place, from class to class, from race to race, and from culture to culture, in their causes and effects, though not in their extent or their severity.[20]

Jane Flax (1995) criticized her for assuming that gender and race are separable and that gender is internally undifferentiated and conflict-free. However, neither of these assumptions is necessary to Okin's conclusion. As discussed, general names can be usefully employed even if there are only family resemblances among their instantiations. Attention to differences and generalizing about commonalities should not be counter-posed.

The 1948 International Declaration of Human Rights premised on commonalities of needs, desires and capacities amongst all human beings, was a great historical achievement. In recent years activists and attorneys have had some success on the international level arguing that violations of women's rights are not a particularistic problem, as typically understood, but are violations of human rights (Peters & Wolper, 1995). *The Human Rights Watch Global Report on Women's Rights* of 1995 documents some abuses unique to women because of their bodies, e.g., forced pregnancy and virginity exams, and others that primarily affect women, e.g., rape and sexual servitude. Many kinds of violence against women that have been ignored because

they are allegedly "private" (domestic violence) or "cultural practices" (female genital mutilation) are argued to be violations of the human right not to be tortured. Other less sex-specific abuses like denial of the right to employment also serve to maintain women's subordination. Without the ideas of sexual difference on the one hand, and of a human nature common to women and men on the other, it is not clear how such arguments could be made.

Martha Nussbaum has been an influential voice in favor of the new humanism. In a series of papers over the past couple of decades[21] she has developed in an explicitly Aristotelian direction, later integrated with Rawlsian liberalism, what is called the capabilities approach pioneered by economist and philosopher Amartya Sen. He developed this approach as an alternative to preference-based welfarist measures of well-being which, among other faults, fail to take account of the fact that preferences and beliefs can be distorted by oppression, even on the most basic matters such as whether or not one's body needs food (Sen 1982, 1985, 1993, 1999. Nussbaum argues that a conception of a human being and human functioning is an important part of a theory of justice and the best way to evaluate women's position around the world. Although Aristotle denied that women shared this human nature, Nussbaum calls this a problem of the scope of the concept, rather than the concept itself, saying it is both "thick" and "vague" enough to accommodate historical and cultural variations in its exemplification. Starting with the intuitive idea that human capabilities "exert a moral claim that they be developed,"[22] she distinguishes two thresholds of capabilities: the first, below which a life would not count as human at all, and a higher threshold for a good human life. The capabilities in the latter conception, which is strikingly similar to Marx's conception of fully human flourishing, are all individually necessary and include the following items: (1) "being able to have good health, . . . nourish(ment), . . . shelter, . . . opportunities for sexual satisfaction and choice in matters of reproduction" and (2) "being able to use the senses, . . . being able to imagine, to think and to reason . . . and to do these in a way informed and cultivated by an adequate education."[23] Arguing that there is no basis for the claim that there should be different norms for human functioning for women and men or that they should be exercised in different ways, Nussbaum recommends specific legal rights and political policies to secure equal capabilities for women— although, respecting the value of autonomy, these should allow that not every woman will choose to exercise them. The capabilities approach has both influenced and been influenced by debates within developmental policy at the United Nations and has undoubtedly been a positive force.

Criticisms of Nussbaum's approach have, however, been raised by feminists on both political and philosophical grounds. Alison Jaggar, for example, though agreeing with the importance of a conception of human nature for feminism, questions the superiority of the capabilities approach over the longer-established human rights approach, and she urges Western philosophers to focus more on their own governments' complicity in the denial of these rights and capabilities worldwide. She has in mind here international economic policies and institutions like the World Bank and the International Monetary Fund as well as Western governments' support of dictatorships around the world (Jaggar, 2002). She also doubts that Nussbaum can resolve the epistemological question of whether, as "keeper of the list" of capabilities in highly unequal conditions, she is not, despite her best intentions, simply projecting her own views on her informants (Jaggar, 2006).

Louise Antony has other worries, which challenge not only Nussbaum, but all those who believe in the importance of human nature for the feminist project. Although she had previously shared this view (Antony, 2011) she came to believe that "there is no plausible notion of

human nature that can do quite this sort of normative work."[24] Claims about a human nature common to all people can be understood in different ways, she explains. Understood as a scientific claim, they have the advantage of being objective, independent of anyone's values, thereby giving a solid ground to whatever follows, but then, she argues, they cannot yield ethical conclusions. On the other hand, if one is simply appealing to shared beliefs about the nature of human beings and values as to what makes a life truly human, then this cannot give the "hard constraints" for one's ethics that one hopes to get from human nature. And, if it is fundamentally a normative claim, she argues, then whether or not these traits are part of our human nature is irrelevant morally. Antony contends that Nussbaum is inconsistent, relying mostly on the second interpretation of human nature claims, but, here and there, seeming to appeal to the stronger scientific/metaphysical interpretation for support.

In her reply to Antony, Nussbaum denies that she ever appeals to the stronger interpretation of human nature claims and makes even more explicit than she had before that her theory of capabilities is an ethical one. Like Rawls, she says, "the provisional 'fixed points' in our judgments are all evaluative, indeed ethical, and the theories we test against them are evaluative, indeed ethical, also."[25] For this reason she prefers not to speak of human nature, but rather the "human being," which is more like "person" (a word that debates about abortion and euthanasia make clear is an ethical concept). Scientific facts about the world simply set constraints on what would be a plausible political project. While Nussbaum's approach may be strategically wise, I believe most feminists both are and should be committed to a stronger position than Nussbaum's regarding human nature and feminist politics. After explaining why, I will come back to Antony's criticism.

Metaphysical realism, even when it is distinguished from foundationalism, is indeed difficult to establish to everyone's satisfaction. Scientific facts, when not understood in an explicitly realist manner, get more general agreement, but these too can be contested. Feminist scientists have to spend most of their time refuting other scientists as well as popular pundits. But Nussbaum's strategy first of all, yields a weaker conclusion and second, is not easy to establish either. While it is always useful to try to show that one's opponents actually share one's own views, there are serious limits to Nussbaum's approach of trying to show that in practice, in close contact, people do presume that women and other oppressed people have the qualities they deem distinctive of human beings. Men have lived in intimate contact with women throughout history, yet failed to recognize, or perhaps to acknowledge, that they shared the same capabilities. This is less true today where social, economic, and historical changes have put women and men in relations of greater equality. Similarly, in the southern United States white people lived in close contact with black people for centuries, but failed to recognize or again, perhaps, to acknowledge, their full humanity. It was the civil rights movement that established greater equality, which then caused the perceptions to begin to change. In these cases it was not only the ethical views about how people ought to be treated that changed, but the views of the majority about the facts. To some extent the facts about people (their "nature," some would call it) actually do change in conditions of greater equality. But the fundamental facts regarding their potential to do so had not changed; it was always true that people in all these groups shared a common human nature. It was the minority of people acting on this belief that brought about the conditions in which others could see the truth.[26]

Feminism, Human Nature, and Freedom

As discussed, variations in human behavior, emotions, and bodies do not prove there is no human nature, any more than changes in climate prove there are no fundamental laws of non-human nature. Can any reason be given for crediting some particular expressions of human nature as closer to, or more truly human than others? I think there is, and the reason has to do with freedom, as I shall attempt to explain. But first let us appreciate the constants that underlie all variations.

The basic biological facts regarding birthrates of male and female humans and their nutritional and medical needs allowed Amartya Sen to demonstrate that one hundred million women are missing due to neglect of these needs.[27] I suspect it was the facts that were most crucial in showing that this is a tragic injustice, rather than convincing people of the ethical premise that females also have a right to life. Similarly, the fact that humans suffer and seek to avoid pain should be sufficient to condemn the routine infliction of pain on women and girls. It is also demonstrably true that people throughout the world suffer permanent mental and physical damage from malnutrition and lack of access to clean water. Conflicts over scarce resources and mass migrations follow, and will only get worse due to the fact that global warming is rapidly destroying the bases of human life on Earth. Though even these examples involve the "entanglement of fact and value," that Hilary Putnam (1993) stresses is part of real-life ethical discussions, the near-universal consensus on the basic values involved make discovering and educating people about the facts the principal *intellectual* task involved in changing them. (Even more important is political struggle against them and here the connection of values and facts is very difficult to untangle, e.g. over private versus common property.) Thus stressing the basic biological needs of human beings—a most fundamental aspect of what we mean by human nature—is fundamentally important from a feminist point of view, whether or not their deprivation is gendered.

Harms due to deprivation of needs, capabilities, or desires beyond such basic physical ones are not as easy to establish, due to their complexity and the greater entanglement of facts and values involved in assessing well-being. However, they are presumed in most feminist critiques. For feminists typically say that women are oppressed not only because of the egregious facts of deprivation and violence against women around the world, but because of "normal" hierarchical gender roles.[28] To say that these constitute oppression of women implies, I contend, that these subordinate gender roles are, first of all, not due to women's inherent (in) abilities and secondly, that they did not freely choose those roles.[29] I will explain in order each of these conditions, which turn out to be connected.

The first condition denies that women fill these roles because of their "natures," as typically claimed in their defense. It might very well be the case that women in particular social conditions do have abilities especially suited to their subordinate social roles (they are better than men at household and caring tasks) and moreover, that they lack the abilities to do much else. Nevertheless, they are oppressed because these (in)abilities are not inherent; the conservative claim has been disproven, even if it is continually reasserted. They might not feel at all oppressed either, but this is neither necessary nor sufficient for being oppressed. The concept of a happy slave is not contradictory. Nor is a king oppressed who feels oppressed by his role, or else the concept loses all its political import. Now, if it were possible to remove male domination but retain the roles, as proposed by the last Papal Encyclical on the role of women in the Roman Catholic Church, according to which their "vocation" is to be mothers or virgins, would women still be oppressed? I would say that the answer depends on whether the above two conditions are met.[30] If women (and men) are not in fact limited—either by God or by inherent (in)abilities—to those roles, then restriction to them is oppressive—unless that is, they freely chose them.

This is why the second condition of the analysis of oppression is necessary in order for feminists to sustain their critique, for it is possible that some might choose to limit themselves to such roles, and if it was a genuinely free choice, then they would not be oppressed. Nuns of Mother Theresa's order choose lives that everyone else struggles to avoid, but their situation does not constitute oppression because they don't have to live as they do. In many parts of the world still today, women have absolutely no choice about the matter; they are clearly forced into subordinate gender roles. (As sometimes they are still children, the word "females" would be better than "women.") Other times, however, there is some choice and they may feel that they are voluntarily choosing their roles. However, choice does not necessarily mean an action is free; people make choices even in concentration camps. The question is how free is the choice?— and this is a matter of degree. But to acquiesce is not to freely choose, and choices many women feel are voluntary are more like acquiescing. True, they had choices, but if they were limited and all bad, then the offer they accepted can be called a "forcing offer."[31] Given the options, such choices may be entirely rational, as such roles typically have the advantage of security that women outside them lack. And sometimes these roles have the compensation that as women get older, their power in the family increases (power, that is, over other women in the family). Thus some writers talk of "patriarchal bargains," a phrase indicating that there is some choice, some room for "negotiation," and that women are acting as agents, not simply victims (Kandiyoti, 2002). Conceiving of them as bargains helps to explain why women sometimes make choices that feminists find puzzling. This analysis also applies to American anti-feminist women, as many seem motivated by a desire for security and stability they think are best provided by "traditional" 1950s-style marriages. But patriarchal bargains are still patriarchal. They are bargains made by

women in the context of male-dominated societies that accept subordination as better than the
alternative. Moreover, as people in subordinate
positions usually accept the prevailing justifications of the existing arrangements and furthermore, as they adapt their preferences to them,
these beliefs and desires act as additional internal
constraints on genuinely free choices.

Though there is not the space to defend
further this analysis of freedom, my principal
contention here is simply that feminists' understanding of oppression commits them to something like the above. If feminists want to claim
that women who make patriarchal bargains,
whether in North Africa or the United States, are
oppressed, they must argue that in conditions of
greater freedom, fewer would make that choice.
This brings out the interconnection between the
two conditions I have offered for oppression:
that their positions are not based on inherent
qualities, and not freely chosen. Though human
nature can take many forms, i.e., humans adapt
to all sorts of conditions, there are good reasons
then to say that the forms expressed in conditions of greater freedom, as opposed to subordinate positions within hierarchical power
structures, are more truly expressive of human
nature. Only free of domination can each individual actively define her/his own individual
variant of human nature (Hirschmann, 2003;
Holstrom, 1975, 1977). That should be the goal
of feminism.

Acceptance of (something like) the above
analysis of what it means to say that women are
oppressed ought also, I contend, to lead one to
challenge all other systems of power relations,
such as racism and, more controversially, class.
For the economic inequalities in capitalism are
far greater than the inequalities between women
and men, and lead to similar constraints, objective and internal, on peoples' ability to make
genuinely free choices about how to live. If one
does not believe that these class inequalities are
rooted in nature, then what is the justification of
the power that a tiny minority has to determine

so much in the lives of everyone else on the
planet? Feminists who are unwilling to take this
further step undercut their critique of traditional gender roles.[32]

The preceding line of argument may put me
in disagreement with Louise Antony, but I am
not sure. There might just be a difference in
emphasis or words, or perhaps on the fact/value
issue. Antony agreed that the many commonalities among human beings "still ha[ve] deep
significance for ethics and politics," but she
contended "that such human universals as exist
are due to our *nature* is itself of no ethical significance"[33] and again, "etiology is morally insig-
nificant."[34] She is certainly correct that simple
facts about people do not directly entail any
ethical conclusions. We need values to evaluate
the facts. But the human sciences are not value-
free, and our conceptions of a good life—for
human beings—must include conceptions of
what human beings are like, their needs, wants,
and purposes. It makes intuitive sense for a
moral/political theory (for humans—who
else?) to give these moral weight, and to give
the highest value to the most distinctly human
capacities and dispositions. (If moral realism is
true, then the connection is even tighter.) In any
case, since freedom is a central value in Western
thought, surely the etiological question of the
degree to which traits were acquired freely and
would or would not be expressed in conditions
of freedom is not morally irrelevant.

However, freedom/self-realization is not in
itself decisive since not all human capacities are
positive. But it can be a central value and help to
organize other values. So, for example, since
humans' capacity for violence threatens peoples'
lives, and ipso facto freedom/self-realization,
happiness, etc., it must be constrained, whether
violent tendencies are innate, socially acquired,
or a mix. On the other hand, as the human
capacities for empathy, solidarity, and reciprocity
are the basis for the self-realization of all individuals, they should be encouraged. This position, reminiscent of both Mill's delineation of

the private sphere of freedom, and Marx's vision of a society where "the free development of each is the condition for the free development of all," provides a plausible basis for a moral/ political theory—based on certain assumptions. For, as I have been arguing, assumptions— consider them competing hypotheses—about the *degrees of equality of human capacities*, and about the *nature of those capacities* underlie different political philosophies. If people really were as egoistic by nature as Hobbes believed, then they would be incapable of living in a more cooperative and egalitarian society and would be unhappy if they tried. This would be a powerful argument against it. And if, on the other hand, most people have enormous potentials that are unrealized and would make them happier and more fulfilled if they were realized (which is implied by saying that it is part of their nature), then this is a powerful argument in favor of a society organized to encourage them, and to encourage the traits of empathy, solidarity, and reciprocity requisite for their realization. Now, if people were naturally very unequal in basic capacities, we *could* still decide to make social arrangements to equalize opportunities as much as possible, as we do, e.g., via special education classes and sidewalk cuts. However, it would clearly make a radically egalitarian society much more difficult and therefore a much less plausible goal— thereby going a long way to justifying our current very unequal arrangements. Thus, certain presumptions about human nature are not only necessary, but very important politically as they serve to motivate (or to discourage) people about possible change.

At present the idea that human beings have such core needs and capacities is a hypothesis; although I submit, it is a plausible one, we do not know if it is the case, and we certainly do not know the biological and functional bases that underlie them if they do exist. But for feminists who are committed to women's liberation from *all* systems of domination, not only gender, a commitment to such a hypothesis is especially

important. As they are arguing for something quite different from what has been realized throughout history and hence from what we observe, it is easy to dismiss their position as utopian. And indeed this has always been the response to calls for radical change, whether it was the end of slavery or equality for women. Nevertheless, as our knowledge has advanced throughout history, so has the scope of morality expanded, and it is not utopian to think this could continue.[35] The possibilities can be glimpsed in those rare occasions when structures of domination are forced open and other ways of living and being seem possible. The recent revolts known as the Arab spring provide inspiring examples. One woman in Yemen completely covered in black came to her first demonstration, and then returned to play an increasingly assertive role, saying she never thought it was possible. Participatory budgeting in Brazil has involved more than 100,000 people showing that ordinary people are capable of radical democracy (Wainwright, 2003). The wealth of unrealized human potentials is suggested in normal times by the Suzuki method of teaching violin. While most people would think a high level of musical proficiency requires a special gift, this is belied by the success of this method, which is premised on the denial of that assumption. Starting at age three, thousands of ordinary children around the world are playing Vivaldi by ten, and achieve orchestra-proficiency by young adulthood.

So in conclusion: to answer the question posed in the title of this essay, yes, human nature is important for feminists. Not just a *conception* of human nature, but the claim that this conception is in fact true. As Cornel West said recently, it's important to stress against those defending the status quo that people who believe in liberation have truth on their side—"truth in an ordinary sense, not Absolute Truth, as we are but weak vessels (Left Forum, 2011)." This conviction can both help us envision a different and better society and also help motivate people to try and achieve it, thereby proving that it is true. This is especially true of feminists who do not just want equality with men in this unequal and unjust system, but who have a more radical emancipatory vision.

Notes

1 I wish to thank Louise Antony for her stimulating comments on this paper.
2 Chomsky 2006, p. 126.
3 Taylor 1972, p. 155.
4 Wollstonecraft 1975, p. 303.
5 Alison Jaggar's term.
6 Wollstonecraft 1975, p. 287.
7 Wollstonecraft 1975, p. 397.
8 Wollstonecraft 1975, p. 24.
9 Wollstonecraft 1975, p. 95.
10 Marx 1964, p. 161.
11 Marx 1972, p. 177.
12 de Beauvoir 1973, p. 201.
13 de Beauvoir 1973, p. 71.
14 There is an extensive debate about "reason," which has been seen as inherently masculine (abstract, egoistic, and elitist) by some feminists, while others include emotions, sociality, and practice within the concept.
15 Groundbreaking work was done by feminist scientists like Ruth Bleier and Ruth Hubbard. The best current source is Fausto-Sterling 1992.
16 Sohn-Rethel 1978, and others.
17 Their argument does apply however to the roughly 4% of people who do not fit neatly into either sex. Anne Fausto-Sterling, 2000, The five sexes, revisited, *Sciences*, 40, 18–23.
18 Assiter 1996) and May Schott 2002 both stress this point. Given the importance of bodies in determining one's gender identity, Assiter goes on to identify this as a female nature. However, this does not follow.
19 Particularly clear on these points are Jane Roland Martin, 1994 and Sabina Lovibond, 1989. For an excellent discussion of the political import of intersecting "differences," see "A Black feminist statement" by the Combahee River Collective, in Hull, Scott, and Smith 1982.
20 Moller Okin, 1995, p. 294.
21 Nussbaum 1995, pp. 61–104, among others.
22 Sen 1995, p. 88.
23 Sen 1995, p. 83f.
24 Antony 2000, p. 11.
25 Nussbaum 2000, p. 118.
26 Consider the signs saying "I am a Man" held by striking sanitation workers in Memphis in 1968, the campaign on which Martin Luther King was working when he was assassinated.
27 Sen 1990. Sometimes, Sen stresses, different people need *different* resources to satisfy the *same* biological needs; for instance, pregnant women have higher nutritional needs.
28 Feminists make these claims *in general, i.e. about women as a group*; they need not apply to all individuals.
29 I defended this analysis in an unpublished paper "Feminism, women's nature and freedom." On this analysis, "oppression" carries a clear implication of injustice, but is not itself a moral term. Some feminists include a moral term like "unfair" in the analysis of the concept of oppression, but the justification of this claim I believe makes the same two assumptions.
30 Mackinnon 1987 includes male domination in the very definition of gender, so this would not even make sense from her point of view.
31 This term comes from Ezorsky 2007.
32 See Cudd and Holmstrom 2011. Conceiving of rationality simply as instrumental rationality, which is typical of liberal philosophy, also limits feminist critique.
33 Antony 2000, p. 12.
34 Antony 2000, p. 30.
35 See Alan Gilbert's moral realist argument along these lines in *Democratic Individuality* (Cambridge: Cambridge University Press, 1990).

References

Antony, L. (1998). "Human nature" and its role in feminist theory. In J. Kourany (Ed.), *Philosophy in a Feminist Voice* (pp. 63–91). Princeton, NJ: Princeton University Press.

Antony, L. (2000). Natures and norms. *Ethics*, 111: 8–36.

Assiter, A. (1996). *Enlightened Women*. New York: Columbia University Press.

Butler, J. (1990). *Gender Trouble*. New York: Routledge.

Chomsky, N. (2006). A philosophy of language. Reprinted in The Chomsky–Foucault Debate on Human Nature. New York: The New Press.

Combahee River Collective (1982). A Black feminist statement. In G. T. Hull, P. B. Scott and B. Smith (Eds.), But Some of Us Were Brave (pp. 13–22). New York: Feminist Press.

Cudd, A. and Holmstrom, N. (2011). Capitalism For & Against: A feminist debate. Cambridge: Cambridge University Press.

Daly, M. (1978). Gyn/Ecology: The metaethics of radical feminism. Boston, MA: Beacon.

de Beauvoir, S. (1973). The Second Sex, trans. and ed. H. M. Parshley. New York: Bantam Books.

Dworkin, A. (1974). Woman-Hating. New York: Dutton.

Ezorsky, G. (2007). Freedom in the Workplace? New York: Cornell University Press.

Fausto-Sterling, A. (1992). Myths of Gender. New York: Basic Books.

Fausto-Sterling, A. (2000). The five sexes, revisited. Sciences, 40: 18–23.

Firestone, S. (1970). The Dialectic of Sex. New York: William Morrow.

Flax, J. (1995). Race/gender and the politics of difference. Political Theory, 23: 500–510.

Gilbert, A. (1990). Democratic Individuality. Cambridge: Cambridge University Press.

Gould, S. J. (1981). The Mismeasure of Man. New York: Norton.

Griffin, S. (1978). Woman and Nature: The roaring inside her. New York: Harper and Row.

Haslanger, S. (1995). Ontology and social construction. Philosophical Topics, 23: 95–125.

Hill Collins, P. (1990). Black Feminist Thought. New York: Routledge.

Hirschmann, N. (2003). The Subject of Liberty: Towards a feminist theory of freedom. Princeton, NJ: Princeton University Press.

Holmstrom, N. (1975). Free will and a Marxist concept of natural wants. Philosophical Forum, vi: 423–446.

Holmstrom, N. (1977). Firming up soft determinism. The Personalist, 58: 39–51.

Holmstrom, N. (1982a). A Marxist theory of women's nature. Ethics, 94: 456–473

Holmstrom, N. (1982b). Do women have a distinct nature? Philosophical Forum, xiv: 25–42.

Holmstrom, N. (1994). Humankind(s). Canadian Journal of Philosophy, Supplementary Volume, 20: 69–105.

Jaggar, A. (1983). Feminist Politics and Human Nature. Totowa, NJ: Rowman & Allanheld.

Jaggar, A. (2002). Challenging women's global inequalities: Some priorities for Western philosophers. Philosophical Topics, 30: 229–253.

Jaggar, A. (2006). Reasoning about well-being: Nussbaum's methods of justifying the capabilities. Journal of Political Philosophy, 14: 301–322.

John Stuart Mill, J. S. (1988). The Subjection of Women. Indianapolis, IN: Hackett.

Kaniyotti, D. (2002). Bargaining with patriarchy. In N. Holmstrom (Ed.), The Socialist Feminist Project (pp. 137–151). New York: Monthly Review Press.

Left Forum (2011). New York City, March 18, 2011.

Lovibond, S. (1989). Feminism and postmodernism. New Left Review, 178: 5–28.2.

MacKinnon, C. (1987). Feminism Unmodified. Cambridge, MA: Harvard University Press.

Marx, K. (1964). Economic and philosophical manuscripts In T. B. Bottomore (Ed.), Karl Marx: Early Writings. New York: Prentice Hall.

Marx, K. (1972). Capital, vol. I. New York: Penguin.

Moller Okin, S. (1995). Inequalities between the sexes in different cultural contexts. In M. Nussbaum and J. Glover (Eds.), Women, Culture and Development. Oxford: Clarendon.

Nussbaum, N. (1995). Human capabilities, female human beings. In M. Nussbaum and J. Glover (Eds.), Women and Human Development: A study of capabilities. Oxford: Oxford University Press.

Nussbaum, N. (2000). Aristotle, politics and human capabilities. Ethics, 111: 102–140.

Peters, J. and Wolper, A. (Eds.) (1995). Women's Rights, Human Rights. New York: Routledge.

Putnam, H. (1993). The science-ethics distinction. In M. Nussbaum and A. Sen (Eds.), The Quality of Life (143–157). Oxford: Oxford University Press

Rich, A. (1976). Of Woman Born: Motherhood as experience and institution. New York: Norton.

Roland Martin, J. (1994). Methodological essentialism, false difference, and other dangerous traps. Signs, 19: 630–657.

Rose, S., Lewontin, E., & Kamin, L. J. (1984). Not in Our Genes: Biology, ideology and human nature. New York: Pantheon.

Schott, R. M. (2002). Resurrecting embodiment: Toward a feminist materialism. In L. Antony and

C. Witt (Eds.), *A Mind of One's Own: Feminist essays on reason and objectivity*, 2nd edn. Boulder, CO: Westview.

Sen, A. (1982). *Choice, Welfare and Measurement*. Cambridge, MA: MIT Press.

Sen, A. (1985). *Commodities and Capabilities*. Amsterdam: North Holland.

Sen, A. (1990). One hundred million women are missing. *New York Review of Books*, Christmas issue.

Sen, A. (1993). Capability and well-being. In M. Nussbaum and A. Sen (Eds.), *The Quality of Life* (30–53). Oxford: Oxford University Press.

Sen, A. (1999). *Development as Freedom*. New York: Alfred Knopf.

Sohn-Rethel, A. (1978). *Intellectual and Manual Labor: A critique of epistemology*. London: Macmillan & Co.

Spelman, E. (1988). *Inessential Woman*. Boston, MA: Beacon Press.

Taylor, C. (1972). Neutrality in political science. In A. Ryan (Ed.), *The Philosophy of Social Explanation*. New York and Oxford: Oxford University Press.

Wainwright, H. (2003). *Reclaim the State: Experiments in popular democracy*. London: Verso.

Wittig, M. (1981). One is not born a woman. *Feminist Issues*, 1: 47–54.

Wittig, M. (1982). The category of sex. *Feminist Issues*, 2: 63–38.

Wollstonecraft, M. (1790). *A Vindication of the Rights of Women*. London: Penguin, 1975).

Young, I. M. (1990). Gynocentric vs. humanist feminism. In I. M. Young, *Throwing Like a Girl and other Essays* (73–91). Bloomington, IN: Indiana University Press.

Zinn, M. B. (1986). The costs of exclusionary practices in women's studies. *Signs*, 11: 290–303.

Topic 12 TRANSHUMANISM

FOR THE FIRST TIME, in 2011, Oscar Pistorius, a South-African athlete whose two legs were amputated and who is running with two carbon-fiber blades (whence his nick-name "Blade Runner"), was allowed to run with typical athletes at the World Championship, where he reached the semi-finals of the 400m sprint. It is plausible that in a few years prostheses will allow some athletes with so-called disabilities to beat typical athletes. Beware, Usain Bolt, the future may belong to Pistorius and his likes! Already, 20 percent of scientists who answered a 2008 survey run by the prestigious journal *Nature* acknowledged taking drugs such as Ritalin and Provigil to stimulate their productivity (particularly by improving concentration), most of them daily, and more than a third of the respondents felt that they would give such drugs to their children if they learned that other children received them! Add to this that genetic engineering and synthetic biology are among the cutting edges of contemporary pharmaceutical research.

In light of such technological progress, one may speculate that it will be soon possible either to modify human nature (e.g., by means of genetic engineering) or to reject its shackles (e.g., by means of pharmaceutical enhancement). Far from being our heritage, our children or grandchildren will be able to construct human nature or to build their own capacities.

Transhumanists welcome this possibility. They typically hold that there is no decisive moral or prudential consideration against using these "human enhancement technologies" (as Bostrom calls them) and against making them broadly available; they also believe that using these technologies is a matter of individual choice and that the state should interfere as little as possible with these decisions.

By contrast, bioconservatives are worried by the possibility of modifying or rising above human nature by means of pharmaceutical, genetic, synthetic–biological, etc., technologies. Their concerns are multifarious: Some object to the development or broad availability of human enhancement technologies on prudential groups, others on moral grounds.

Kass's chapter is a famous statement of the bioconservative position. After reviewing several arguments, which he finds defective, he argues that the use of human enhancement technologies would amount to rejecting a crucial characteristic of the human condition, which gives meaning to our existence: We need to work and labor to bring about desired outcomes.

Bostrom's chapter defends transhumanism against several objections developed by bioconservatives. It also gives a useful overview of the controversy between transhumanists and bioconservatives.

Suggested Further Reading

Agar, N. (2004) *Liberal Eugenics: In Defence of Human Enhancement*. Malden, MA: Blackwell.

Bostrom, N. (2003) Human genetic enhancements: A transhumanist perspective. *Journal of Value Inquiry*, 37: 493–506.

Bostrom, N. (2005) A history of transhumanist thought. *Journal of Evolution and Technology*, 14: www.jetpress.org/volume14/bostrom.pdf

Buchanan, A. (2009) Human nature and enhancement. *Bioethics*, 23: 141–150.

Fukuyama, F. (2002) *Our Posthuman Future: Consequences of the biotechnology revolution*. New York: Farrar, Strauss and Giroux.

Habermas, J. (2003) *The Future of Human Nature*. Oxford: Blackwell.

Harris, J. (2007) *Enhancing Evolution: The ethical case for making better people*. Princeton, NJ: Princeton University Press.

Kamm, F. M. (2005) Is there a problem with enhancement? *American Journal of Bioethics*, 3: 5–14.

Kass, L. (2002) *Life, Liberty, and Defense of Dignity: The challenge for bioethics*. San Francisco, CA: Encounter Books.

Lewens, T. (2009) Enhancement and human nature: The case of Sandel. *Journal of Medical Ethics*, 35: 354–356.

Liao, S. M. (2008) Selecting children: The ethics of reproductive genetic engineering. *Philosophy Compass*, 3: 973–991.

Ruder, W. C., Lu, T. and Collins, J. J. (2011) Synthetic biology moving into the clinic. *Science*, 333: 1248–1252.

Sandel, M. J. (2004) The case against perfection. *The Atlantic Monthly*, 292: 50–62.

Sandel, M. J. (2007) *The Case Against Perfection: Ethics in the age of genetic engineering*. Cambridge, MA: Harvard University Press.

Savulescu, J. and Bostrom, N. (Eds.) (2009) *Human Enhancement*. Oxford: Oxford University Press.

Chapter 37

Leon R. Kass

AGELESS BODIES, HAPPY SOULS
Biotechnology and the Pursuit of Perfection

Let me begin by offering a toast to biomedical science and biotechnology: May they live and be well. And may our children and grandchildren continue to reap their ever tastier fruit—but without succumbing to their seductive promises of a perfect, better-than-human future, in which we shall all be as gods, ageless and blissful.

As nearly everyone appreciates, we live near the beginning of the golden age of biotechnology. For the most part, we should be very glad that we do. We are many times over the beneficiaries of its cures for diseases, prolongation of life, and amelioration of suffering, psychic as well as somatic. We should be deeply grateful for the gifts of human ingenuity and cleverness, and for the devoted efforts of scientists, physicians, and entrepreneurs who have used these gifts to make those benefits possible. And, mindful that modern biology is just entering puberty, we suspect that the finest fruit is yet to come.

Yet, notwithstanding these blessings, present and projected, we have also seen more than enough to make us anxious and concerned. For we recognize that the powers made possible by biomedical science can be used for non-therapeutic or ignoble purposes, serving ends that range from the frivolous and disquieting to the offensive and pernicious. These powers are available as instruments of bioterrorism (e.g., genetically engineered drug-resistant bacteria or drugs that obliterate memory); as agents of social control (e.g., drugs to tame rowdies or fertility-blockers for welfare recipients); and as means of trying to improve or perfect our bodies and minds and those of our children (e.g., genetically engineered super-muscles or drugs to improve memory). Anticipating possible threats to our security, freedom, and even our very humanity, many people are increasingly worried about where biotechnology may be taking us. We are concerned about what others might do to us, but also about what we might do to ourselves. We are concerned that our society might be harmed and that we ourselves might be diminished, indeed, in ways that could undermine the highest and richest possibilities of human life.

The last and most seductive of these disquieting prospects—the use of biotechnical powers to pursue "perfection," both of body and of mind—is perhaps the most neglected topic in public and professional bioethics. Yet it is, I believe, the deepest source of public anxiety about biotechnology, represented in the concern about "man playing God," or about the Brave New World, or a "post-human future." It raises the weightiest questions of bioethics, touching on the ends and goals of the biomedical enterprise, the nature and meaning of human flourishing, and the intrinsic threat of dehumanization (or the promise of super-humanization). It compels attention to what it means to *be* a human being and to be active *as* a human being. And it gets us beyond our often singular focus on the "life issues" of abortion or embryo destruction, important though they are, to deal with what is genuinely novel and worrisome in the biotechnical revolution: not the old crude power to kill the creature made in God's image, but the new science-based power to remake him after our own fantasies.

This is, to be sure, a very difficult topic and one not obviously relevant to current public policy debate. Compared with other contemporary issues in bioethics, the questions connected with biotechnological "enhancement" seem abstract, remote, and too philosophical, unfit for political or other action. The concerns it raises are also complicated and inchoate, hard to formulate in general terms, especially because the differing technologically based powers raise different ethical and social questions. Finally, bothering oneself about this semi-futuristic prospect seems even to me precious and a touch self-indulgent, given that we live in a world in which millions are dying annually of malaria, AIDS, and malnutrition for want (in part) of more essential biotechnologies, and when many of our fellow Americans lack basic healthcare. Yet this push toward bio-engineered perfection strikes me as the wave of the future, one that will sneak up on us before we know it and, if we are not careful, sweep us up and tow us under. For we can already see how the recent gains in health and longevity have produced not contentment but rather an increased appetite for more. And, from recent trends in the medicalization of psychiatry and the study of the mind, it seems clear that the expected new discoveries about the workings of the psyche and the biological basis of behavior will greatly increase the ability and the temptation to alter and improve them. Decisions we today are making—for instance, what to do about human cloning or sex selection and genetic selection of embryos, or whether to get comfortable prescribing psychotropic drugs to three-year-olds, or how

vigorously to pursue research into the biology of senescence—will shape the world of the future for people who will inherit, not choose, life under its utopia-seeking possibilities. It is up to us now to begin thinking about these matters.

The Marvels of Biotechnology

What exactly are the powers that I am talking about? What kind of technologies make them possible? What sorts of ends are they likely to serve? How soon will they be available? They are powers that affect the capacities and activities of the human body, powers that affect the capacities and activities of the mind or soul, and powers that affect the shape of the human life cycle, at both ends and in between. We already have powers to prevent fertility and to promote it; to initiate life in the laboratory; to screen our genes, both as adults and as embryos, and to select (or reject) nascent life based on genetic criteria; to insert new genes into various parts of the adult body, and someday soon also into gametes and embryos; to enhance muscle performance and endurance; to replace body parts with natural or mechanical organs, and perhaps soon, to wire ourselves using computer chips implanted into the body and brain; to alter memory, mood, and attention through psychoactive drugs; and to prolong not just the average but also the maximum human life expectancy. The availability of some of these capacities has been demonstrated only with animals, but others are already in use in humans.

It bears emphasis that these powers have not been developed for the purpose of producing perfect or post-human beings. They have been produced largely for the purpose of preventing and curing disease, and of reversing disabilities. Even the bizarre prospect of machine-brain interaction and implanted nanotechnological devices starts with therapeutic efforts to enable the blind to see and the deaf to hear. Yet the "dual use" aspects of most of these powers, encouraged by the ineradicable human urge toward "improvement" and the commercial interests that see market opportunities for non-therapeutic uses, means that we must not be lulled to sleep by the fact that the originators of these powers were no friends to the Brave New World. Once here, techniques and powers can produce desires where none existed before, and things often go where no one ever intended.

So how are we to organize our reflections? One should resist the temptation to begin with the new techniques or even with the capacities for intervention that they make possible. To do so runs the risk of losing the human import and significance of the undertakings. Better to begin with the likely ends that these powers and techniques are destined to serve: ageless bodies, happy souls, better children, a more peaceful and cooperative society. Leaving aside the pursuit of optimum babies or better citizens, I will concentrate on the strictly personal goals of self-improvement: those efforts to preserve and augment the vitality of the body and to enhance the happiness of the soul. These goals are, arguably, the least controversial, the most continuous with the aims of modern medicine and psychiatry (better health, peace of mind), and the most attractive to most potential consumers—probably indeed to most of us. It is perhaps worth remembering that it was these goals, now in the realm of possibility, that animated the great founders of modern science: flawlessly healthy bodies, unconflicted and contented souls, and freedom from the infirmities of age, perhaps indefinitely.

With respect to the pursuit of "ageless bodies," we can replace worn out parts, we can improve upon normal and healthy parts, and, more radically, we can try to retard or stop the entire process of biological senescence. With respect to the first biotechnical possibility, we must keep in mind organ transplantation and the prospect of regenerative medicine, where decayed tissues are replaced with new ones produced from stem cells. With respect to the second possibility, we must consider precise genetic modifications of muscles, through a single injection of a growth-factor gene, that keep the transformed muscles whole, vigorous, and free of age-related decline (a practice already used to produce mighty mouse and super rat, and soon to be available for treatment of muscular dystrophy and muscle weakness in the elderly, but also of interest to football coaches and to the hordes of people who spend two hours daily pumping iron and sculpting their "abs"). And with respect to the last possibility, we need to keep in mind recent discoveries in the genetics of aging that have shown how the maximum lifespan of worms and flies can be increased two- and three-fold by alterations in a *single* gene, a gene now known to be present also in mammals.

With respect to the pursuit of "happy souls," we can eliminate psychic distress, we can produce states of transient euphoria, and we can engineer more permanent conditions of good cheer, optimism, and contentment. Already, there are drugs available that, administered promptly at the time of memory formation, dull markedly the painful emotional content of the newly formed memories of traumatic events (so-called "memory blunting," a remedy being sought to prevent post-traumatic stress disorder). There are simple euphoriants, like Ecstasy, the forerunner of Huxley's "soma," now widely used on college campuses; and, finally, there are powerful yet seemingly safe anti-depressant and mood brighteners like Prozac, capable in some people of utterly changing their outlook on life from that of Eeyore to that of Mary Poppins.

The Problem of Terminology

Accurate description is crucial to moral evaluation. One should try to call things by their right names. One should not encumber thought by adopting fuzzy concepts. And one should not try to solve the moral question by terminological sleight of hand—the way that some scientists today try to win support for cloning-for-biomedical-research by denying that the cloning of embryos is cloning or that the initial product is an embryo. In this area especially the terminological question is crucial, but also hard. And, I confess at the start, although I have tried to find one, I have no simple solution: I see no clear way of speaking about this subject using simple, trouble-free distinctions.

Among the few people who have tried to address our topic, most have approached it through a distinction between "therapy" and "enhancement": "therapy," the treatment of individuals with known diseases or disabilities; "enhancement," the directed uses of biotechnical power to alter, by direct intervention, not diseased processes but the "normal" workings of the human body and psyche (whether by drugs, genetic engineering, or mechanical/computer implants into the body and brain). Those who introduced this distinction hoped by this means to distinguish between the acceptable and the dubious or unacceptable uses of biomedical technology: therapy is always ethically fine, enhancement is, at least *prima facie*, ethically suspect. Gene therapy for cystic fibrosis or Prozac for psychotic depression is fine; insertion of genes to enhance intelligence or steroids for Olympic athletes is not. Health providers and insurance companies, by the way, have for now bought into the distinction, paying for treatment of disease, but not for enhancements.

But this distinction, though a useful shorthand for calling attention to the problem, is inadequate to the moral analysis. Enhancement is, even as a term, highly problematic. Does it mean "more" or "better," and, if "better," by what standards? Can both improved memory and selective erasure of memory both be "enhancements"? If "enhancement" is defined in opposition to "therapy," one faces further difficulties with the definitions of "healthy" and "impaired," "normal" and "abnormal" (and hence, "super-normal"), especially in the area of "behavioral" or "psychic" functions and activities. "Mental health" is not easily distinguished from "psychic well-being" or, for that matter,

from contentment or happiness. And psychiatric diagnoses—"dysthymia," hyperactivity, "oppositional disorder," and other forthcoming labels that would make Orwell wince and Soviet psychiatry proud—are notoriously vague. Furthermore, in the many human qualities (like height or IQ) that distribute themselves "normally," does the average also function as a norm, or is the norm itself appropriately subject to alteration? Is it therapy to give growth hormone to a genetic dwarf but not to a very short fellow who is just unhappy to be short? And if the short are brought up to the average, the average, now having become short, will have precedent for a claim to growth hormone injections. Needless arguments about whether or not something is or is not an "enhancement" get in the way of the proper question: What are the good and bad uses of biotechnical power? What makes a use "good," or even just "acceptable"? It does not follow from the fact that a drug is being taken solely to satisfy one's desires that its use is objectionable. Conversely, certain interventions to restore what might seem to be natural functioning wholeness—for example, to enable postmenopausal women to bear children or 60-year-old men to keep playing professional ice hockey—might well be dubious uses of biotechnical power. The human meaning and moral assessment are unlikely to be settled by the term "enhancement," any more than they are settled by the nature of the technological intervention itself.

This last observation points to the deepest reason why the distinction between healing and enhancing is of limited ethical or practical value. For the human whole whose healing is sought or accomplished by biomedical therapy is by nature finite and frail, medicine or no medicine. The healthy body declines and its parts wear out. The sound mind slows down and has trouble remembering things. The soul has aspirations beyond what even a healthy body can realize, and it becomes weary from frustration. Even at its fittest, the fatigable and limited human body rarely carries out flawlessly even the ordinary desires of the soul. Moreover, there is wide variation in the natural gifts with which each of us is endowed: some are born with perfect pitch, others are born tone-deaf; some have flypaper memories, others forget immediately what they have just learned. And as with talents, so too with desires and temperaments: some crave immortal fame, others merely comfortable preservation. Some are sanguine, others phlegmatic, still others bilious or melancholic. When Nature deals her cards, some receive only from the bottom of the deck. Conversely, it is often the most gifted and ambitious who most resent their limitations: Achilles was willing to destroy everything around him, so little could he stomach that he was but a heel short of immortality.

As a result of these infirmities, human beings have long dreamed of overcoming limitations of body and soul, in particular the limitations of bodily decay, psychic distress, and the frustration of human aspiration. Dreams of human perfection—and the terrible consequences of pursuing it—are the themes of Greek tragedy. Until now these dreams have been pure fantasies, and those who pursued them came crashing down in disaster. But the stupendous successes over the past century in all areas of technology, and especially in medicine, have revived the ancient dreams of human perfection. Like Achilles, the major beneficiaries of modern medicine are less content than worried well, and we regard our remaining limitations with less equanimity, to the point that dreams of getting rid of them can be turned into moral imperatives. For these reasons, thanks to biomedical technology, people will be increasingly tempted to realize these dreams, at least to some extent: ageless and ever-vigorous bodies, happy (or at least not unhappy) souls, and excellent human achievement (with diminished effort or toil).

Why should anyone be worried about these prospects? What could be wrong with efforts to improve upon human nature, to try, with the help of biomedical technology, to gain ageless bodies and happy souls? A number of reasons have been offered, but looked at closely, they do not get to the heart of the matter.

Three Obvious Objections

Not surprisingly, the objections usually raised to the uses of biomedical technologies that go "beyond therapy" reflect the dominant values of modern America: health, equality, and liberty.

In a health-obsessed culture, the first reason given to worry about any new biological intervention is safety, and that is certainly true here. Athletes who take steroids will later suffer premature heart disease. College students who take Ecstasy will damage dopamine receptors in their basal ganglia and suffer early Parkinson's disease. To generalize: no biological agent used for purposes of self-perfection will be entirely safe. This is good conservative medical sense: anything powerful enough to enhance system A is likely to be powerful enough to harm system B, the body being a highly complex yet integrated whole in which one intervenes partially only at one's peril. Yet many good things in life are filled with risks, and free people if properly informed may choose to run them, if they care enough about what is to be gained thereby. If the interventions are shown to be *highly* dangerous, many people will (later if not sooner) avoid them, and the FDA or tort liability will constrain many a legitimate purveyor. It surely makes sense, as an ethical matter, that one should not risk basic health trying to make oneself "better than well." On the other hand, if the interventions work well and are indeed highly desired, people may freely accept, in trade-off, even considerable risk of later bodily harm. Yet, in the end, the big issues have nothing to do with safety; as in the case of cloning children, the real questions concern what to think about the perfected powers, assuming that they may be safely used. And the ethical issue of avoiding risk and bodily harm is independent of whether the risky intervention aims at treating disease or at something beyond it.

A second obvious objection to the use of personal enhancers, especially by participants in competitive activities, is that they give those who use them an unfair advantage: blood doping or steroids in athletes, stimulants in students taking the SATs, and so on. Still, even if everyone had equal access to brain implants or genetic improvement of muscle strength or mind-enhancing drugs, a deeper disquiet would remain. Not all activities of life are competitive: it would matter to me if she says she loves me only because she is high on "erotogenin," a new brain-stimulant that mimics perfectly the feeling of falling in love. It matters to me when I go to a seminar that the people with whom I am conversing are not psychedelically out of their right minds.

The related question of distributive justice is less easily set aside than the unfairness question, especially if there are systematic disparities between who will and who will not have access to the powers of biotechnical "improvement." The case can be made yet more powerful to the extent that we regard the expenditure of money and energy on such niceties as a misallocation of limited resources in a world in which the basic health needs of millions go unaddressed. As a public policy matter, this is truly an important consideration. But, once again, the inequality of access does not remove our disquiet to the thing itself. And it is, to say the least, paradoxical in discussions of the dehumanizing dangers of, say, eugenic choice, when people complain that the poor will be denied equal access to the danger: "The food is contaminated, but why are my portions so small?" It is true that Aldous Huxley's Brave New World runs on a deplorable and impermeably rigid class system, but would you want to live in that world if offered the chance to enjoy it as an Alpha (the privileged caste)? Even an elite can be dehumanized, and even an elite class can dehumanize itself. The central matter is not equality of access, but the goodness or badness of the thing being offered.

A third objection, centered around issues of freedom and coercion, both overt and subtle, comes closer to the mark. This is especially the case with uses of biotechnical power exercised by some people upon other people, whether for social control—say, in the pacification of a classroom of Tom Sawyers—or for their own putative improvement—say, with genetic selection of the sex or sexual orientation of a child-to-be. This problem will of course be worse in tyrannical regimes. But there are always dangers of despotism within families, as parents already work their wills on their children with insufficient regard to a child's independence or real needs. Even partial control over genotype—say, to take a relatively innocent example, musician parents selecting a child with genes for perfect pitch—would add to existing social instruments of parental control and its risks of despotic rule. This is indeed one of the central arguments against human cloning: the charge of genetic despotism of one generation over the next.

There are also more subtle limitations of freedom, say, through peer pressure. What is permitted and widely used may become mandatory. If most children are receiving memory enhancement or stimulant drugs, failure to provide them for your child might be seen as a form of child neglect. If all the defensive linemen are on steroids, you risk mayhem if you go against them chemically pure. As with cosmetic surgery, Botox, and breast implants, the enhancement technologies of the future will likely be used in slavish adherence to certain socially defined and merely fashionable notions of "excellence" or improvement, very likely shallow, almost certainly conformist.

This special kind of restriction of freedom—let's call it the problem of conformity or homogenization—is in fact quite serious. We are right to worry that the self-selected non-therapeutic uses of the new powers, especially where they become widespread, will be put in the service of the most common human desires, moving us toward still greater homogenization of human society—perhaps raising the floor but greatly lowering the ceiling of human possibility, and reducing the likelihood of genuine freedom, individuality, and greatness. (This is Tocqueville's concern about the leveling effects of democracy, now augmented by the technological power to make them ingrained and perhaps irreversible.) Indeed, such homogenization may be the most important society-wide concern, if we consider the aggregated effects of the likely individual choices for biotechnical "self-improvement," each of which might be defended or at least not objected to on a case-by-case basis.

For example, it would be difficult to object to a personal choice for a life-extending technology that would extend the user's life by three healthy decades, or for a mood-brightened way of life that would make the individual more cheerful and less troubled by the world around him. Yet the aggregated social effects of such choices, widely made, could lead to the Tragedy of the Commons, where genuine and sought for satisfactions for individuals are nullified or worse, owing to the social consequences of granting them to everyone. (I will later argue such a case with respect to the goal of increasing longevity with ageless bodies.) And, as Huxley strongly suggests in *Brave New World*, biotechnical powers used to produce contentment in accordance with democratic tastes threaten the character of human striving and diminish the possibility of human excellence. Perhaps the best thing to be hoped for is preservation of pockets of difference (as on the remote islands in *Brave New World*) where the desire for high achievement has not been entirely submerged in the culture of "the last man."

But, once again, important though this surely is as a social and political issue, it does not settle the question for individuals. What if anything can we say to justify our disquiet over the individual uses of performance-enhancing genetic engineering or mood-brightening drugs? For even the safe, equally available, non-coerced and non-faddish uses of these technologies for "self-improvement" raise ethical questions, questions that are at the heart of the matter: the disquiet must have something to do with the essence of the activity itself, the use of technological means to intervene in the human body and mind not to ameliorate disease but to change and (arguably) improve their normal workings. Why, if at all, are we bothered by the voluntary *self*-administration of agents that would change our bodies or alter our minds? What is disquieting about our attempts to improve upon human nature, or even our own particular instance of it?

It is difficult to put this disquiet into words. We are in an area where initial repugnances are hard to translate into sound moral arguments. We are probably repelled by the idea of drugs that erase memories or that change personalities; or of interventions that enable 70-year-olds to bear children or play professional sports; or, to engage in some wilder imaginings, of mechanical implants that enable men to nurse infants or computer-body hookups that would enable us to download the *Oxford English Dictionary*. But is there wisdom in this repugnance? Taken one person at a time, with a properly prepared set of conditions and qualifications, it is going to be hard to say what is wrong with any biotechnical intervention that could give us (more) ageless bodies or happier souls. If there is a case to be made against these activities—for individuals—we sense that it may have something to do with what is natural, or what is humanly dignified, or with the attitude that is properly respectful of what is naturally and dignifiedly human.

I will come at this question from three directions: the goodness of the ends, the fitness of the means, and the meaning of the overarching attitude of seeking to master, control, and even transform one's own given nature. Three human goods will figure prominently in the discussions: modesty and humility, about what we know and can do to ourselves; the meaning of aging and the human life cycle;

and the nature of human activity and human flourishing, and the importance of exercising the first and seeking the second through fitting means. My aim here is only to open the questions, starting with the matter of proper attitude.

The Attitude of Mastery

A common man-on-the-street reaction to these prospects is the complaint of "men playing God." An educated fellow who knows Greek tragedy complains rather of *hubris*. Sometimes the charge means the sheer prideful presumption of trying to alter what God has ordained or nature has produced, or what should, for whatever reason, not be fiddled with. Sometimes the charge means not so much usurping God-like powers, but doing so in the absence of God-like knowledge: the mere playing at being God, the hubris of acting with insufficient wisdom.

The case for respecting Mother Nature, and the critique of rushing in where angels fear to tread in order to transform her, has been forcefully made by environmentalists. They urge upon us a precautionary principle regarding our interventions into all of nature—usually, by the way, with the inexplicable exception of our own nature. Go slowly, they say, you can ruin everything. The point is certainly well taken. The human body and mind, highly complex and delicately balanced as a result of eons of gradual and exacting evolution, are almost certainly at risk from any ill-considered attempt at "improvement." There is not only the matter of unintended consequences already noted, but also the question about the unqualified goodness of our goals—a matter to which I shall return.

But for now, I would observe that this matter about the goodness of the goals is insufficiently appreciated by those who use the language of "mastery," or "mastery and control of nature," to describe what we do when we use knowledge of how nature works to alter its character and workings. Mastery of the means of intervention without knowing the goodness of the goals of intervening is not, in fact, mastery at all. In the absence of such knowledge of ends, the goals of the "master" will be set rather by whatever it is that happens to guide or move his will—some impulse or whim or feeling or desire—in short, by some residuum of nature still working within the so-called master or controller. To paraphrase C. S. Lewis, what looks like man's mastery of nature turns out, in the absence of guiding knowledge, to be nature's mastery of man. There can, in truth, be no such thing as the full escape from the grip of our own nature. To pretend otherwise is indeed a form of hubristic and dangerous self-delusion.

Although this is not the time and place to develop this point further, it is worth noting that attempts to alter our nature through biotechnology are different from both medicine and education or child-rearing. It seems to me that we can more-or-less distinguish the pursuit of bodily and psychic perfection from the regular practice of medicine. To do so, we need to see that it is not true, as some allege, that medicine itself is a form of mastery of nature. When it functions to restore from deviation or deficiency some natural wholeness of the patient, medicine acts as servant and aid to nature's own powers of self-healing. It is also questionable to conflate child-rearing and education of the young with the attitude that seeks willful control of our own nature. Parents do indeed shape their children, but usually with some at least tacit idea—most often informed by cultural teachings that have stood the test of time—of what it takes to grow up to live a decent, civilized, and independent life. The multiplicity of such cultural teachings should, of course, make us modest about the superior wisdom of our own way. But in any decent society, the rearing of children would seem to be closer to teaching young birds to fly than to training an elephant to tap dance.

So how, returning to the problem of "men playing God," are we to understand this particular form of disquiet about biotechnology?

Michael Sandel, in a working paper prepared for the President's Council on Bioethics, has offered a very interesting version of the hubris objection. The problem with biotechnological efforts at enhancement and re-creating ourselves is what he calls "hyperagency, a Promethean aspiration to remake nature, including human nature, to serve our purposes and to satisfy our desires." The root of the difficulty seems to be both cognitive and moral: the failure properly to appreciate and respect the "giftedness" of the world.

> To acknowledge the giftedness of life is to recognize that our talents and powers are not wholly our own doing, nor even fully ours, despite the efforts we expend to develop and to exercise them. It is also to recognize that not everything in the world is open to any use we may desire or devise. An appreciation of the giftedness of life constrains the Promethean project and conduces to a certain humility. It is, in part, a religious sensibility. But its resonance reaches beyond religion.

As a critique of the Promethean attitude of the enhancers, Sandel's suggestion is on target. For the manipulator, appreciating that the given world—including his natural powers to alter it—is not of his own making could induce an attitude of modesty, restraint, humility. But the giftedness of nature also includes smallpox and malaria, cancer and Alzheimer's disease, decline and decay. And, to repeat, nature is not equally generous with her gifts, even to man, the most gifted of her creatures. Modesty born of gratitude for the world's "givenness" may enable us to recognize that not everything in the world is open to any use we may desire or devise, but it will not *by itself* teach us *which* things can be fiddled with and which should be left inviolate. The mere "giftedness" of things cannot tell us which gifts are to be accepted as is, which are to be improved through use or training, which are to be housebroken through self-command or medication, and which opposed like the plague.

The word "given" has two relevant meanings, the second of which Sandel's account omits: "given," meaning "bestowed as a gift," and "given" (as in mathematical proofs), something "granted," definitely fixed and specified. Most of the given bestowals of nature have their given species-specified *natures*: they are each and all of a given *sort*. Cockroaches and humans are equally bestowed but differently natured. To turn a man into a cockroach—as we don't need Kafka to show us—would be dehumanizing. To try to turn a man into more than a man might be so as well. We need more than generalized appreciation for nature's gifts. We need a particular regard and respect for the special gift that is our own given nature (and, by the way, also that of each of our fellow creatures).

In short, only if there is a human givenness, or a given humanness, that is also *good* and worth respecting, either as we find it or as it could be perfected without ceasing to be itself, does the "given" serve as a *positive* guide for choosing what to alter and what to leave alone. Only if there is something precious in the given—beyond the mere fact of its giftedness—does what is given serve as a source of restraint against efforts that would degrade it. When it comes to human biotechnical engineering, only if there is something inherently good or dignified about, say, natural procreation, human finitude, the human life cycle (with its rhythm of rise and fall), and human erotic longing and striving; only if there is something inherently good or dignified about the ways in which we engage the world as spectators and appreciators, as teachers and learners, leaders and followers, agents and makers, lovers and friends, parents and children, and as seekers of our own special excellence and flourishing in whatever arena to which we are called—only then can we begin to see why those aspects of our nature need to be defended. (It is for this reason why a richer bioethics will always begin by trying to clarify the human good and aspects of our given humanity that are rightly dear to us, and that biotechnology may serve or threaten.) We must move from the hubristic attitude of the powerful designer to consider how the proposed improvements might impinge upon the nature of the one being improved. With the question of human nature and human dignity in mind, we move to questions of means and ends.

"Unnatural" Means

How do, and how should, the excellent ones become excellent? This is a notorious question, famously made famous by Plato's Meno at the start of the dialogue bearing his name:

> Can you tell me, Socrates, whether human excellence is teachable? Or is it not teachable, but to be acquired by practice (training)? Or is it neither acquired by practice nor by learning, but does it originate in human beings by nature, or in some other way?

Teaching and learning, practice and training: sources in our power. Natural gift or divine dispensation: sources not in our power. Until only yesterday, these exhausted the (sometimes competing, sometimes complementary) alternatives for acquiring human excellence, perfecting our natural gift through our own efforts. But perhaps no longer: biotechnology, a high art based on knowledge of nature, may be able to do nature one better, even to the point of requiring no teaching and less training or practice to permit an improved nature to shine forth. The insertion of the growth-factor gene into the muscles of rats and mice bulks them up and keeps them strong and sound without the need for nearly as much exertion. Drugs to improve memory, alertness, and amiability could greatly relieve the need for exertion to acquire these powers, leaving time and effort for better things.

Some people, not thinking very hard, will object to these means because they are artificial or unnatural. But the man-made origin of the means cannot alone be the problem. Beginning with the needle and the fig leaf, man has from the start been the animal that uses art to improve his lot. By his very nature, man is the animal constantly looking for ways to better his life through artful means and devices; man is the animal with what Rousseau called "perfectibility." Supplementing healthy diet, rest, and exercise, ordinary medicine makes extensive use of artificial means, from drugs to surgery to mechanical implants. If the use of artificial means is absolutely welcome in the activity of healing, it cannot be their unnaturalness alone that upsets us when they are used to make people "better than well."

Yet in those areas of human life in which excellence has until now been achieved only by discipline and effort, the attainment of those achievements by means of drugs, genetic engineering, or implanted devices looks to be "cheating" or "cheap." We believe—or until only yesterday believed—that people should work hard for their achievements. "Nothing good comes easily." Even if one prefers the grace of the natural athlete, whose performance deceptively appears to be effortless, we admire those who overcome obstacles and struggle to try to achieve the excellence of the former, who serves as the object of the latter's aspiration and effort and the standard for his success or failure. This matter of character—the merit of disciplined and dedicated striving—though not the deepest basis of our objection to biotechnological shortcuts, is surely pertinent. For character is not only the source of our deeds, but also their product. People whose disruptive behavior is "remedied" by pacifying drugs rather than by their own efforts are not learning self-control; if anything, they are learning to think it unnecessary. People who take pills to block out from memory the painful or hateful aspects of a new experience will not learn how to deal with suffering or sorrow. A drug to induce fearlessness does not produce courage.

Yet things are not so simple, partly because there are biotechnical interventions that may assist in the pursuit of excellence without cheapening its attainment, partly because many of life's excellences have nothing to do with competition or adversity. Drugs to decrease drowsiness or increase alertness, sharpen memory, or reduce distraction may actually help people interested in their natural pursuits of learning or painting or performing their civic duty. Drugs to steady the hand of a neurosurgeon or to prevent sweaty palms in a concert pianist cannot be regarded as "cheating," for they are not the source of the excellent activity or achievement. And, for people dealt a meager hand in the dispensing of nature's gifts, it should not be called cheating or cheap if biotechnology could assist them in becoming better equipped—whether in body or in mind. Even steroids for the proverbial 97-pound weakling help him to get to the point where, through his own effort and training, he can go head-to-head with the naturally better endowed.

Nevertheless, there is a sense that the "naturalness" of means matters. It lies not in the fact that the assisting drugs and devices are artifacts, but in the danger of violating or deforming the deep structure of natural human activity. In most of our ordinary efforts at self-improvement, either by practice or training or study, we sense the relation between our doings and the resulting improvement, between the means used and the end sought. There is an experiential and intelligible connection between means and ends; we can see how confronting fearful things might eventually enable us to cope with our fears. We can see how curbing our appetites produces self-command. Human education ordinarily proceeds by speech or symbolic deeds, whose meanings are at least in principle directly accessible to those upon whom they work. Even where the human being is largely patient to the formative action—say, in receiving praise and blame, or reward and punishment—both the "teacher" and the "student" can understand both the content of the means used and their relation to the conduct or activity that they

are meant to improve. And the further efforts at self-improvement, spurred by praise and blame, will clearly be the student's own doing.

In contrast, biomedical interventions act directly on the human body and mind to bring about their effects on a subject who is not merely passive but who plays no role at all. He can at best feel their effects *without understanding their meaning in human terms*. (Yes, so do alcohol and caffeine and nicotine, though we use these agents not as pure chemicals but in forms and social contexts that, arguably, give them a meaning different from what they would have were we to take them as pills.) Thus, a drug that brightened our mood would alter us without our understanding how and why it did so—whereas a mood brightened as a fitting response to the arrival of a loved one or an achievement in one's work is perfectly, because humanly, intelligible. And not only would this be true about our states of mind. All of our encounters with the world, both natural and interpersonal, would be mediated, filtered, and altered. Human experience under biological intervention becomes increasingly mediated by unintelligible forces and vehicles, separated from the human significance of the activities so altered. (By contrast, the intelligibility of a scientific account of the mechanism of action of the biological agent would not be the intelligibility of human experience.) The relations between the knowing subject and his activities, and between his activities and their fulfillments and pleasures, are disrupted. The importance of human effort in human achievement is here properly acknowledged: the point is less the exertions of good character against hardship, but the manifestation of an alert and self-experiencing agent making his deeds flow intentionally from his willing, knowing, and embodied soul. The lack of "authenticity" sometimes complained of in these discussions is not so much a matter of "playing false" or of not expressing one's "true self," as it is a departure from "genuine," unmediated, and (in principle) self-transparent human activity.

To be sure, an increasing portion of modern life is mediated life: the way we encounter space and time, the way we "reach out and touch somebody" via the telephone or Internet. And one can make a case that there are changes in our souls and dehumanizing losses that accompany the great triumphs of modern technology. But so long as these technologies do not write themselves directly into our bodies and minds, we are in principle able to see them working on us, and free (again, in *principle*) to walk away from their use (albeit sometimes only with great effort). But once they work on us in ways beyond our ken, we are, as it were, passive subjects of what might as well be "magic." It makes little difference to the point if we choose by ourselves to so subject ourselves: the fact that one chooses to drink alcohol or to take a mood-brightening drug does not make one the agent of the change that one thereby undergoes (though the law, with good reason, may hold us responsible).

The same point can perhaps be made about enhanced achievements as about altered mental states: to the extent that an achievement is the result of some extraneous intervention, it is detachable from the agent whose achievement it purports to be. "Personal achievements" impersonally achieved are not truly the achievements of persons. That I can use a calculator to do my arithmetic does not make me a knower of arithmetic; if computer chips in my brain were to "download" a textbook of physics, would that make me a knower of physics? Admittedly, this is not always an obvious point to make: if I make myself more alert through Ritalin or coffee, or if drugs can make up for lack of sleep, I may be able to learn more using my unimpeded native powers in ways to which I can existentially attest that it is I who is doing the learning. Still, if human flourishing means not just the accumulation of external achievements and a full curriculum vitae but a life-long *being-at-work* exercising one's *human* powers *well* and without great impediment, our genuine happiness requires that there be little gap, if any, between the dancer and the dance.

This is not merely to suggest that there is a disturbance of human agency or freedom, or a disruption of activities that will confound the assignment of personal responsibility or undermine the proper bestowal of praise and blame. To repeat: most of life's activities are noncompetitive; most of the best of them—loving and working and savoring and learning—are self-fulfilling beyond the need for praise and blame or any other external reward. In these activities, there is at best no goal beyond the activity itself. It is the deep structure of unimpeded, for-itself, human being-at-work-in-the-world, in an unimpeded and wholehearted way, that we are eager to preserve against dilution and distortion.

In a word, one major trouble with biotechnical (especially mental) "improvers" is that they produce changes in us by disrupting the normal character of human being-at-work-in-the-world, what Aristotle called *energeia psyches*, activity of soul, which when fine and full constitutes human flourishing. With biotechnical interventions that skip the realm of intelligible meaning, we cannot really own the transformations nor experience them as genuinely ours. And we will be at a loss to attest whether the resulting conditions and activities of our bodies and our minds are, in the fullest sense, our own as human. To the extent that we come to regard our transformed nature as normal, we shall have forgotten what we lost.

Dubious Ends

But now we must step back yet again. By considering first the questionable means for pursuing excellence, we have put the cart before the horse. Socrates, you may recall, refuses to answer Meno's question about how excellence is acquired because, he says, he is ignorant of the answer to the prior question: what human excellence itself really is? The issue of good and bad means must yield to the question about good and bad ends.

How are we to think about the goals themselves—ageless bodies and happy souls? Would their attainment in fact improve or perfect our lives *as* human beings? These are very big questions, too long to be properly treated here. But the following initial considerations seem to merit attention.

The case for ageless bodies seems at first glance to look pretty good. The prevention of decay, decline, and disability, the avoidance of blindness, deafness, and debility, the elimination of feebleness, frailty, and fatigue, all seem to be conducive to living fully as a human being at the top of one's powers—of having, as they say, a "good quality of life" from beginning to end. We have come to expect organ transplantation for our worn-out parts. We will surely welcome stem cell-based therapies for regenerative medicine, reversing by replacement the damaged tissues of Parkinson's disease, spinal cord injury, and many other degenerative disorders. It is hard to see any objection to obtaining a genetic enhancement of our muscles in our youth that would not only prevent the muscular feebleness of old age but would empower us to do any physical task with greater strength and facility throughout our lives. And, should aging research deliver on its promise of adding not only extra life to years but also extra years to life, who would refuse it? Even if you might consider turning down an ageless body for yourself, would you not want it for your beloved? Why should she not remain to you as she was back then when she first stole your heart? Why should her body suffer the ravages of time?

To say no to this offer seems perverse. But I want to suggest that it may not be—that there are in fact many human goods that are inseparable from our aging bodies, from our living in time, and from the natural human life cycle by which each generation gives way to the one that follows it. Because this argument is so counterintuitive, we need to begin not with the individual choice for an ageless body, but with what the individual's life might look like in a world in which everyone made the same choice. We need to make the choice universal, and see the meaning of that choice in the mirror of its becoming the norm.

What if everybody lived life to the hilt, even as they approached an ever-receding age of death in a body that looked and functioned—let's not be too greedy—like that of a 30-year-old? Would it be good if each and all of us lived like light bulbs, burning as brightly from beginning to end, then popping off without warning, leaving those around us suddenly in the dark? Or is it perhaps better that there be a shape to life, everything in its due season, the shape also written, as it were, into the wrinkles of our bodies that live it? What would the relations between the generations be like if there never came a point at which a son surpassed his father in strength or vigor? What incentive would there be for the old to make way for the young, if the old slowed down little and had no reason to think of retiring—if Michael could play until he were not forty but eighty? Might not even a moderate prolongation of life span with vigor lead to a prolongation in the young of functional immaturity—of the sort that has arguably already accompanied the great increase in average life expectancy experienced in the past century? One cannot think of enhancing the vitality of the old without retarding the maturation of the young.

I have tried in the past to make a rational case for the blessings of finitude. In an essay entitled "L'Chaim and Its Limits: Why Not Immortality?," I suggest that living with our finitude is the condition of many of the best things in human life: engagement, seriousness, a taste for beauty, the possibility of virtue, the ties born of procreation, the quest for meaning. Though the arguments are made against the case for immortality, they have weight also against even more modest prolongations of the maximum lifespan, especially in good health, that would permit us to live as if there were always tomorrow. In what I take to be the two most important arguments of that essay, I argue that the pursuit of perfect bodies and further life-extension will deflect us from real-izing more fully the aspirations to which our lives naturally point, from living well rather than merely staying alive. And I argue that a concern with one's own improving agelessness is finally incompatible with accepting the need for procre-ation and human renewal: a world of longevity is increasingly a world hostile to children. Moreover, far from bringing contentment, it is arguably a world increasingly dominated by anxiety over health and the fear of death. In this connection, Montaigne suggests why it is only decline and decay that enable us to accept mortality at all:

> I notice that in proportion as I sink into sick-ness, I naturally enter into a certain disdain for life. I find that I have much more trouble digesting this resolution when I am in health than when I have a fever. Inasmuch as I no longer cling so hard to the good things of life when I begin to lose the use and pleasure of them, I come to view death with much less frightened eyes. This makes me hope that the farther I get from life and the nearer to death, the more easily I shall accept the exchange . . . If we fell into such a change [decrepitude] suddenly, I don't think we could endure it. But when we are led by Nature's hand down a gentle and virtually imperceptible slope, bit by bit, one step at a time, she rolls us into this wretched state and makes us familiar with it; so that we find no shock when youth dies within us, which in essence and in truth is a harder death than the complete death of a languishing life or the death of old age; inas-much as the leap is not so cruel from a painful life as from a sweet and flourishing life to a grievous and painful one.

In other words, even a modest prolongation of life with vigor, or even only a preservation of youthfulness with no increase in longevity,

could make death less acceptable and would exacerbate the desire to keep pushing it away.

Those who propose adding years to the human lifespan regard time abstractly, as physi-cists do, as a homogeneous and continuous dimension, each part exactly like any other, and the whole lacking shape or pattern. Yet, the "lived time" of our natural lives has a trajectory and a shape, its meaning derived in part from the fact that we live as links in the chain of genera-tions. For this reason, our flourishing as individ-uals might depend, in large measure, on the goodness of the natural human life cycle, roughly three multiples of a generation: a time of coming of age; a time of flourishing, ruling, and replacing of self; and a time of savoring and understanding, but still sufficiently and intimately linked to one's descendants to care about their future and to take a guiding, supporting, and cheering role.

What about pharmacologically assisted happy souls? Painful and shameful memories are disquieting; guilty consciences disturb sleep; low self-esteem, melancholy, and world-weariness besmirch the waking hours. Why not memory blockers for the former, mood bright-eners for the latter, and a good euphoriant—without risks of hangovers or cirrhosis—when celebratory occasions fail to be jolly? For let us be clear: if it is imbalances of neurotransmitters—a modern equivalent of the medieval doctrine of the four humors—that are responsible for our state of soul, it would be sheer priggishness to refuse the help of pharmacology for our happi-ness, when we accept it guiltlessly to correct for an absence of insulin or thyroid hormone.

And yet, there seems to be something misguided about the pursuit of utter psychic tranquility, or the attempt to eliminate all shame, guilt, and painful memories. Traumatic memo-ries, shame, and guilt, are, it is true, psychic pains. In extreme doses, they can be crippling. Yet they are also helpful and fitting. They are appropriate responses to horror, disgraceful conduct, and sin, and, as such, help teach us to avoid them in the future. Witnessing a murder *should* be remembered as horrible; doing a beastly deed should trouble one's soul. Righteous indignation at injustice depends on being able to feel injustice's sting. An untroubled soul in a troubling world is a shrunken human being. More fundamentally, to deprive oneself of one's memory—including and especially its truthfulness of feeling—is to deprive oneself of one's own life and identity.

Second, these feeling states of soul, though perhaps accompaniments of human flourishing, are not its essence. Ersatz pleasure or feelings of self-esteem are not the real McCoy. They are at most shadows divorced from the underlying human activities that are the essence of flourishing. Not even the most doctrinaire hedonist wants to have the pleasure that comes from playing baseball without swinging the bat or catching the ball. No music lover would be satisfied with getting from a pill the pleasure of listening to Mozart without ever hearing the music. Most people want both to feel good and to feel good about themselves, but only as a result of being good and doing good.

Finally, there is a connection between the possibility of feeling deep unhappiness and the prospects for achieving genuine happiness. If one cannot grieve, one has not loved. To be capable of aspiration, one must know and feel lack. As Wallace Stevens put it: Not to have is the beginning of desire. There is, in short, a double-barreled error in the pursuit of ageless bodies and factitiously happy souls: human fulfillment depends on our being creatures of need and finitude and hence of longings and attachment.

I have tried to make a case for finitude and even graceful decline of bodily powers. And I have tried to make a case for genuine human happiness, with satisfaction as the bloom that graces unimpeded, soul-exercising activity. The first argument resonates with Homeric and Hebraic intuitions; the second resonates with the Greek philosophers. One suspects that they might even be connectable, that genuine human flourishing is rooted in aspirations born of the kinds of deficiencies that come from having limited and imperfect bodies. To pursue this possibility is work for another day.

A flourishing human life is not a life lived with an ageless body or untroubled soul, but rather a life lived in rhythmed time, mindful of time's limits, appreciative of each season and filled first of all with those intimate human relations that are ours only because we are born, age, replace ourselves, decline, and die—and know it. It is a life of aspiration, made possible by and born of experienced lack, of the disproportion between the transcendent longings of the soul and the limited capacities of our bodies and minds. It is a life that stretches towards some fulfillment to which our natural human soul has been oriented, and, unless we extirpate the source, will always be oriented. It is a life not of better genes and enhancing chemicals but of love and friendship, song and dance, speech and deed, working and learning, revering and worshipping. The pursuit of an ageless body is finally a distraction and a deformation. The pursuit of an untroubled and self-satisfied soul is deadly to desire. Finitude recognized spurs aspiration. Fine aspiration acted upon is *itself* the core of happiness. Not the agelessness of the body, nor the contentment of the soul, nor even the list of external achievement and accomplishments of life, but the engaged and energetic being-at-work of what nature uniquely gave to us is what we need to treasure and defend. All other perfection is at best a passing illusion, at worst a Faustian bargain that will cost us our full and flourishing humanity.

Chapter 38

Nick Bostrom

IN DEFENSE OF POSTHUMAN DIGNITY

Transhumanists vs. Bioconservatives

Transhumanism is a loosely defined movement that has developed gradually over the past two decades, and can be viewed as an outgrowth of secular humanism and the Enlightenment. It holds that current human nature is improvable through the use of applied science and other rational methods, which may make it possible to increase human health-span, extend our intellectual and physical capacities, and give us increased control over our own mental states and moods (Bostrom, 2003). Technologies of concern include not only current ones, like genetic engineering and information technology, but also anticipated future developments such as fully immersive virtual reality, machine-phase nanotechnology, and artificial intelligence.

Transhumanists promote the view that human enhancement technologies should be made widely available, and that individuals should have broad discretion over which of these technologies to apply to themselves (morphological freedom), and that parents should normally get to decide which reproductive technologies to use when having children (reproductive freedom) (Bostrom, 2003). Transhumanists believe that, while there are hazards that need to be identified and avoided, human enhancement technologies will offer enormous potential for deeply valuable and humanly beneficial uses. Ultimately, it is possible that such enhancements may make us, or our descendants, "posthuman", beings who may have indefinite health-spans, much greater intellectual faculties than any current human being – and perhaps entirely new sensibilities or modalities – as well as the ability to control their own emotions. The wisest approach vis-à-vis these prospects, argue transhumanists, is to embrace technological progress, while strongly defending human rights and individual choice, and taking action specifically against concrete threats, such as military or terrorist abuse of bioweapons, and against unwanted environmental or social side-effects.

In opposition to this transhumanist view stands a bioconservative camp that argues against the use of technology to modify human nature. Prominent bioconservative writers include Leon Kass, Francis Fukuyama, George Annas, Wesley Smith, Jeremy Rifkin, and Bill McKibben. One of the central concerns of the bioconservatives is that human enhancement technologies might be "dehumanizing". The worry, which has been variously expressed, is that these technologies might undermine our human dignity or inadvertently erode something that is deeply valuable about being human but that is difficult to put into words or to factor into a cost-benefit analysis. In some cases (for example, Leon Kass) the unease seems to derive from religious or crypto-religious sentiments, whereas for others (for example, Francis Fukuyama) it stems from secular grounds. The best approach, these bioconservatives argue, is to implement global bans on swathes of promising human enhancement technologies to forestall a slide down a slippery slope towards an ultimately debased, posthuman state.

While any brief description necessarily skirts significant nuances that differentiate between the writers within the two camps, I believe the above characterization nevertheless highlights a principal fault line in one of the great debates of our times: how we should look at the future of humankind and whether we should attempt to use technology to make ourselves "more than human". This paper will distinguish two common fears about the posthuman and argue that they are partly unfounded and that, to the extent that they correspond to real risks, there are better responses than trying to implement broad bans on technology. I will make some remarks on the concept of dignity, which bioconservatives believe to be imperiled by coming human enhancement technologies, and suggest that we need to recognize that not only humans in their current form, but posthumans too could have dignity.

Two Fears About the Posthuman

The prospect of posthumanity is feared for at least two reasons. One is that the state of being posthuman might in itself be degrading, so that by becoming posthuman we might be harming ourselves. Another is that posthumans might pose a threat to "ordinary" humans. (I shall set aside a third possible reason, that the development of posthumans might offend some supernatural being.)

The most prominent bioethicist to focus on the first fear is Leon Kass:

> Most of the given bestowals of nature have their given species-specified natures: they are each and all of a given *sort*. Cockroaches and

humans are equally bestowed but differently natured. To turn a man into a cockroach – as we don't need Kafka to show us – would be dehumanizing. To try to turn a man into more than a man might be so as well. We need more than generalized appreciation for nature's gifts. We need a particular regard and respect for the special gift that is our own given nature.[1]

Transhumanists counter that nature's gifts are sometimes poisoned and should not always be accepted. Cancer, malaria, dementia, aging, starvation, unnecessary suffering, and cognitive shortcomings are all among the presents that we would wisely refuse. Our own species-specified natures are a rich source of much of the thoroughly unrespectable and unacceptable – susceptibility for disease, murder, rape, genocide, cheating, torture, racism. The horrors of nature in general, and of our own nature in particular, are so well documented (Glover, 2001) that it is astonishing that somebody as distinguished as Leon Kass should still in this day and age be tempted to rely on the natural as a guide as to what is desirable or normatively right. We should be grateful that our ancestors were not swept away by the Kassian sentiment, or we would still be picking lice off each other's backs. Rather than deferring to the natural order, transhumanists maintain that we can legitimately reform ourselves and our natures in accordance with humane values and personal aspirations.

If one rejects nature as a general criterion of the good, as most thoughtful people nowadays do, one can of course still acknowledge that particular ways of modifying human nature would be debasing. Not all change is progress. Not even all well-intentioned technological intervention in human nature would be on balance beneficial. Kass goes far beyond these truisms, however, when he declares that utter dehumanization lies in store for us as the inevitable result of our obtaining technical mastery over our own nature:

The final technical conquest of his own nature would almost certainly leave mankind utterly enfeebled. This form of mastery would be identical with utter dehumanization. Read Huxley's *Brave New World*, read G. S. Lewis's *Abolition of Man*, read Nietzsche's account of the last man, and then read the newspapers. Homogenization, mediocrity, pacification, drug-induced contentment, debasement of taste, souls without loves and longings – these are the inevitable results of making the essence of human nature the last project of technical mastery. In his moment of triumph, Promethean man will become a contented cow.[2]

The fictional inhabitants of *Brave New World*, to pick the best known of Kass's examples, are admittedly short on dignity (in at least one sense of the word). But the claim that this is the *inevitable* consequence of our obtaining technological mastery over human nature is exceedingly pessimistic – and unsupported – if understood as a futuristic prediction, and false if construed as a claim about metaphysical necessity.

There are many things wrong with the fictional society that Huxley described. It is static, totalitarian, caste-bound; its culture is a wasteland. The brave new worlders themselves are a dehumanized and undignified lot. Yet posthumans they are not. Their capacities are not super-human but in many respects substantially inferior to our own. Their life expectancy and physique are quite normal, but their intellectual, emotional, moral, and spiritual faculties are stunted. The majority of the brave new worlders have various degrees of engineered mental retardation. And everyone, save the ten world controllers (along with a miscellany of primitives and social outcasts who are confined to fenced preservations or isolated islands), are barred or discouraged from developing individuality, independent thinking, and initiative, and are conditioned not to desire these traits in the first place. *Brave New World* is not a tale of human

enhancement gone amok, but is rather a tragedy of technology and social engineering being deliberately used to cripple moral and intellectual capacities – the exact antithesis of the transhumanist proposal.

Transhumanists argue that the best way to avoid a Brave New World is by vigorously defending morphological and reproductive freedoms against any would-be world controllers. History has shown the dangers in letting governments curtail these freedoms. The last century's government-sponsored coercive eugenics programs, once favored by both the left and the right, have been thoroughly discredited. Because people are likely to differ profoundly in their attitudes towards human enhancement technologies, it is crucial that no single solution be imposed on everyone from above, but that individuals get to consult their own consciences as to what is right for themselves and their families. Information, public debate, and education are the appropriate means by which to encourage others to make wise choices, not a global ban on a broad range of potentially beneficial medical and other enhancement options.

The second fear is that there might be an eruption of violence between unaugmented humans and posthumans. George Annas, Lori Andrews, and Rosario Isasi have argued that we should view human cloning and all inheritable genetic modifications as "crimes against humanity" in order to reduce the probability that a posthuman species will arise, on grounds that such a species would pose an existential threat to the old human species:

> The new species, or "posthuman," will likely view the old "normal" humans as inferior, even savages, and fit for slavery or slaughter. The normals, on the other hand, may see the post-humans as a threat and if they can, may engage in a preemptive strike by killing the posthumans before they themselves are killed or enslaved by them. It is ultimately this predictable potential for genocide that makes

species-altering experiments potential weapons of mass destruction, and makes the unaccountable genetic engineer a potential bioterrorist.[3]

There is no denying that bioterrorism and unaccountable genetic engineers developing increasingly potent weapons of mass destruction pose a serious threat to our civilization. But using the rhetoric of bioterrorism and weapons of mass destruction to cast aspersions on therapeutic uses of biotechnology to improve health, longevity, and other human capacities is unhelpful. The issues are quite distinct. Reasonable people can be in favor of strict regulation of bioweapons, while promoting beneficial medical uses of genetics and other human enhancement technologies, including inheritable and "species-altering" modifications.

Human society is always at risk of some group deciding to view another group of humans as being fit for slavery or slaughter. To counteract such tendencies, modern societies have created laws and institutions, and endowed them with powers of enforcement, that act to prevent groups of citizens from enslaving or slaughtering one another. The efficacy of these institutions does not depend on all citizens having equal capacities. Modern, peaceful societies can have large numbers of people with diminished physical or mental capacities along with many other people who may be exceptionally physically strong or healthy or intellectually talented in various ways. Adding people with technologically enhanced capacities to this already broad distribution of ability would not need to rip society apart or trigger genocide or enslavement.

The assumption that inheritable genetic modifications or other human enhancement technologies would lead to two distinct and separate species should also be questioned. It seems much more likely that there would be a continuum of differently modified or enhanced individuals, which would overlap with the continuum of as-yet unenhanced humans. The scenario in which "the enhanced" form a pact and then attack "the naturals" makes for exciting science fiction, but is not necessarily the most plausible outcome. Even today, the segment containing the tallest ninety percent of the population could, in principle, get together and kill or enslave the shorter decile. That this does not happen suggests that a well-organized society can hold together even if it contains many possible coalitions of people sharing some attribute such that, if they ganged up, they would be capable of exterminating the rest.

To note that the extreme case of a war between humans and posthumans is not the most likely scenario is not to say that there are no legitimate social concerns about the steps that may take us closer to posthumanity. Inequity, discrimination, and stigmatization – against, or on behalf of, modified people – could become serious issues. Transhumanists would argue that these (potential) social problems call for social remedies. One example of how contemporary technology can change important aspects of someone's identity is sex reassignment. The experiences of transsexuals show that Western culture still has work to do in becoming more accepting of diversity. This is a task that we can begin to tackle today by fostering a climate of tolerance and acceptance towards those who are different from ourselves. Painting alarmist pictures of the threat from future technologically modified people, or hurling preemptive condemnations of their necessarily debased nature, is not the best way to go about it.

What about the hypothetical case in which someone intends to create, or turn themselves into, a being of such radically enhanced capacities that a single one or a small group of such individuals would be capable of taking over the planet? This is clearly not a situation that is likely to arise in the imminent future, but one can imagine that, perhaps in a few decades, the prospective creation of superintelligent machines could raise this kind of concern. The would-be creator of a new life form with such surpassing capabilities would have an obligation to ensure that the proposed being is free from psychopathic tendencies and, more generally, that it has humane inclinations. For example, a future artificial intelligence programmer should be required to make a strong case that launching a purportedly human-friendly superintelligence would be safer than the alternative. Again, however, this (currently) science fiction scenario must be clearly distinguished from our present situation and our more immediate concern with taking effective steps towards incrementally improving human capacities and health-span.

Is Human Dignity Incompatible with Posthuman Dignity?

Human dignity is sometimes invoked as a polemical substitute for clear ideas. This is not to say that there are no important moral issues relating to dignity, but it does mean that there is a need to define what one has in mind when one uses the term. Here, we shall consider two different senses of dignity:

1. Dignity as moral status, in particular the inalienable right to be treated with a basic level of respect.
2. Dignity as the quality of being worthy or honorable; worthiness, worth, nobleness, excellence.

On both these definitions, dignity is something that a posthuman could possess. Francis Fukuyama, however, seems to deny this and warns that giving up on the idea that dignity is unique to human beings – defined as those possessing a mysterious essential human quality he calls "Factor X"[4] – would invite disaster:

> Denial of the concept of human dignity – that is, of the idea that there is something unique about the human race that entitles every member of the species to a higher moral status than the rest of the natural world – leads us down a very perilous path. We may be compelled ultimately to take this path, but we should do so only with our eyes open. Nietzsche is a much better guide to what lies down that road than the legions of bioethicists and casual academic Darwinians that today are prone to give us moral advice on this subject.[5]

What appears to worry Fukuyama is that introducing new kinds of enhanced person into the world might cause some individuals (perhaps infants, or the mentally handicapped, or unenhanced humans in general) to lose some of the moral status that they currently possess, and that a fundamental precondition of liberal democracy, the principle of equal dignity for all, would be destroyed.

The underlying intuition seems to be that instead of the famed "expanding moral circle", what we have is more like an oval, whose shape we can change but whose area must remain constant. Thankfully, this purported conservation law of moral recognition lacks empirical support. The set of individuals accorded full moral status by Western societies has actually increased, to include men without property or noble decent, women, and non-white peoples. It would seem feasible to extend this set further to include future posthumans, or, for that matter, some of the higher primates or human-animal chimaeras, should such be created – and to do so without causing any compensating shrinkage in another direction. (The moral status of problematic borderline cases, such as foetuses or late-stage Alzheimer patients, or the brain-dead, should perhaps be decided separately from the issue of technologically modified humans or novel artificial life forms.) Our own role in this process need not be that of passive bystanders. We can work to create more inclusive social structures that accord appropriate moral recognition and legal rights to all who need them, be they male or female, black or white, flesh or silicon.

Dignity in the second sense, as referring to a special excellence or moral worthiness, is something that current human beings possess to widely differing degrees. Some excel far more than others do. Some are morally admirable; others are base and vicious. There is no reason for supposing that posthuman beings could not also have dignity in this second sense. They may even be able to attain higher levels of moral and other excellence than any of us humans. The fictional brave new worlders, who were subhuman rather than posthuman, would have scored low on this kind of dignity, and partly for that reason they would be awful role models for us to emulate. But surely we can create more uplifting and appealing visions of what we may aspire to become. There may be some who would transform themselves into degraded posthumans – but then some people today do not live very worthy human lives. This is regrettable, but the fact that some people make bad choices is not generally a sufficient ground for rescinding people's right to choose. And legitimate countermeasures are available: education, encouragement, persuasion, social and cultural reform. These, not a blanket prohibition of all posthuman ways of being, are the measures to which those bothered by the prospect of debased posthumans should resort. A liberal democracy should normally permit incursions into morphological and reproductive freedoms only in cases where somebody is abusing these freedoms to harm another person.

The principle that parents should have broad discretion to decide on genetic enhancements for their children has been attacked on the grounds that this form of reproductive freedom would constitute a kind of parental tyranny that would undermine the child's dignity and capacity for autonomous choice; for instance, by Hans Jonas:

Technological mastered nature now again includes man who (up to now) had, in technology, set himself against it as its master . . .

But whose power is this – and over whom or over what? Obviously the power of those living today over those coming after them, who will be the defenseless other side of prior choices made by the planners of today. The other side of the power of today is the future bondage of the living to the dead.[6]

Jonas is relying on the assumption that our descendants, who will presumably be far more technologically advanced than we are, would nevertheless be defenseless against our machinations to expand their capacities. This is almost certainly incorrect. If, for some inscrutable reason, they decided that they would prefer to be less intelligent, less healthy, and lead shorter lives, they would not lack the means to achieve these objectives and frustrate our designs.

In any case, if the alternative to parental choice in determining the basic capacities of new people is entrusting the child's welfare to nature, that is blind chance, then the decision should be easy. Had Mother Nature been a real parent, she would have been in jail for child abuse and murder. And transhumanists can accept, of course, that just as society may in exceptional circumstances override parental autonomy, such as in cases of neglect or abuse, so too may society impose regulations to protect the child-to-be from genuinely harmful genetic interventions – but not because they represent choice rather than chance.

Jürgen Habermas, in a recent work, echoes Jonas' concern and worries that even the mere *knowledge* of having been intentionally made by another could have ruinous consequences:

We cannot rule out that knowledge of one's own hereditary features as programmed may prove to restrict the choice of an individual's life, and to undermine the essentially symmetrical relations between free and equal human beings.[7]

A transhumanist could reply that it would be a mistake for an individual to believe that she has no choice over her own life just because some (or all) of her genes were selected by her parents. She would, in fact, have as much choice as if her genetic constitution had been selected by chance. It could even be that she would enjoy significantly *more* choice and autonomy in her life, if the modifications were such as to expand her basic capability set. Being healthy, smarter, having a wide range of talents, or possessing greater powers of self-control are blessings that tend to open more life paths than they block.

Even if there were a possibility that some genetically-modified individuals might fail to grasp these points and thus might feel oppressed by their knowledge of their origin, that would be a risk to be weighed against the risks incurred by having an unmodified genome, risks that can be extremely grave. If safe and effective alternatives were available, it would be irresponsible to risk starting someone off in life with the misfortune of congenitally diminished basic capacities or an elevated susceptibility to disease.

Why we Need Posthuman Dignity

Similarly ominous forecasts were made in the seventies about the severe psychological damage that children conceived through *in vitro* fertilization would suffer upon learning that they originated from a test tube – a prediction that turned out to be entirely false. It is hard to avoid the impression that some bias or philosophical prejudice is responsible for the readiness with which many bioconservatives seize on even the flimsiest of empirical justifications for banning human enhancement technologies of certain types but not others. Suppose it turned out that playing Mozart to pregnant mothers improved the child's subsequent musical talent. Nobody would argue for a ban on Mozart-in-the-womb on grounds that we cannot rule out that some psychological woe might befall the child once she discovers that her facility with the violin had been prenatally "programmed" by her parents. Yet when, for example, it comes to genetic

enhancements, eminent bioconservative writers often put forward arguments that are not so very different from this parody as weighty, if not conclusive, objections. To transhumanists, this looks like doublethink. How can it be that to bioconservatives almost any anticipated downside, predicted perhaps on the basis of the shakiest pop-psychological theory, so readily achieves that status of deep philosophical insight and knockdown objection against the transhumanist project?

Perhaps a part of the answer can be found in the different attitudes that transhumanists and bioconservatives have towards posthuman dignity. Bioconservatives tend to deny posthuman dignity and view posthumanity as a threat to human dignity. They are therefore tempted to look for ways to denigrate interventions that are thought to be pointing in the direction of more radical future modifications that may eventually lead to the emergence of those detestable posthumans. But unless this fundamental opposition to the posthuman is openly declared as a premise of their argument, this then forces them to use a double standard of assessment whenever particular cases are considered in isolation: for example, one standard for germ-line genetic interventions and another for improvements in maternal nutrition (an intervention presumably not seen as heralding a posthuman era).

Transhumanists, by contrast, see human and posthuman dignity as compatible and complementary. They insist that dignity, in its modern sense, consists in what we are and what we have the potential to become, not in our pedigree or our causal origin. What we are is not a function solely of our DNA but also of our technological and social context. Human nature in this broader sense is dynamic, partially human-made, and improvable. Our current extended phenotypes (and the lives that we lead) are markedly different from those of our hunter-gatherer ancestors. We read and write, we wear clothes, we live in cities, we earn money and buy food from the supermarket, we call people on the telephone, watch television, read newspapers, drive cars, file taxes, vote in national elections, women give birth in hospitals, life-expectancy is three times longer than in the Pleistocene, we know that the Earth is round and that stars are large gas clouds lit from inside by nuclear fusion, and that the universe is approximately 13.7 billion years old and enormously big. In the eyes of a hunter-gatherer, we might already appear "posthuman". Yet these radical extensions of human capabilities – some of them biological, others external – have not divested us of moral status or dehumanized us in the sense of making us generally unworthy and base. Similarly, should we or our descendants one day succeed in becoming what relative to current standards we may refer to as posthuman, this need not entail a loss dignity either.

From the transhumanist standpoint, there is no need to behave as if there were a deep moral difference between technological and other means of enhancing human lives. By defending posthuman dignity we promote a more inclusive and humane ethics, one that will embrace future technologically modified people as well as humans of the contemporary kind. We also remove a distortive double standard from the field of our moral vision, allowing us to perceive more clearly the opportunities that exist for further human progress.

Notes

1   Kass 2003, p. 1.
2   Kass 2002, p. 48.
3   Annas et al. 2002, p. 162.
4   Fukuyama 2002, p. 149.
5   Fukuyama 2002, note 8, p. 160.
6   Jonah 1985.
7   Habermas 2003, p. 23.

References

Annas, G., Andrews, L., & Isasi, R. (2002). Protecting the endangered human: Toward an international treaty prohibiting cloning and inheritable alterations. *American Journal of Law and Medicine; 28*(2&3): 162.

Bostrom, N. (2003a). *The Transhumanist FAQ, v. 2.1.* World Transhumanist Association. www.transhumanism.org/resources/FAQv21.pdf

Bostrom, N. (2003b). Human genetic enhancements: A transhumanist perspective. *Journal of Value Inquiry, 37*(4): 493–506.

Fukuyama, F. (2002). *Our Posthuman Future: Consequences of the biotechnology revolution.* New York: Farrar, Strauss and Giroux.

Glover, J. (2001). *Humanity: A moral history of the twentieth century.* New Haven, CT: Yale University Press.

Habermas, J. (2003). *The Future of Human Nature* Oxford: Blackwell.

Jonas, H. (1985). *Technik, Medizin und Ethik: Zur Praxis des Prinzips Verantwortung.* Frankfurt am Main: Suhrkamp.

Kass, L. (2003). Ageless bodies, happy souls: Biotechnology and the pursuit of perfection. *The New Atlantis, 1.*

Kass, L. (2002). *Life, Liberty, and Defense of Dignity: The challenge for bioethics.* San Francisco, CA. Encounter Books.

Simpson, J. A., & Weiner, E. (Eds.) (1989). *The Oxford English Dictionary,* 2nd edn. Oxford: Oxford University Press.

Index

Acknowledgments

The editors and publisher would like to thank the following copyright holders for their permission to reprint material:

Amundson, Ron. "Against normal function." *Studies in History and Philosophy of the Biological and Biomedical Sciences*, 31, pp. 33–53. Copyright © 2000 Elsevier. Reprinted with permission.

Antony, M. Louise. "'Human nature' and its role in feminist theory." In Janet Kourany (Ed.), *Philosophy in a Feminist Voice: Critiques and Reconstructions*, pp. 63–91. Copyright © 1998 Princeton University Press. Reprinted by permission of Princeton University Press.

Bailey, Nathan W. and Marlene Zuk. "Same-sex sexual behavior and evolution." *Trends in Ecology and Evolution*, 24, pp. 439–446. Copyright © Elsevier 2009. Reprinted with permission.

Bateson, Patrick. "Behavioral Development and Darwinian Evolution". In Oyama, Susan, Paul E. Griffiths, and Russell D. Gray. (Eds.) *Cycles of Contingency: Developmental Systems and Evolution*, pp. 147–161, Copyright © 2001 Massachusetts Institute of Technology. Reprinted with permission.

Bolnick, Deborah A. "Individual ancestry inference and the reification of race as a biological phenomenon." In Barbara A. Koenig, Sandra Soo-Jin Lee, and Sarah S. Richerson (Eds.), *Revisiting Race in the Genomic Age*, pp. 56–69. Copyright © 2008 Rutgers, the State University. Reprinted by Permission of Rutgers University Press.

Bolstrom, Nick. "In defense of posthuman dignity." *Bioethics*, 19, 202–214. Copyright © 2005 John Wiley and Sons. Reprinted with permission.

Boorse, Christopher. "Health as a theoretical concept." *Philosophy of Science*, 44, pp. 542–573. Copyright © University of Chicago Press. Reprinted by permission of University of Chicago Press.

Bouchard, Thomas Jr. "Genetic influence on human psychological traits: A survey." *Current Directions in Psychological Science*, 13, 148–151. Copyright © 2004, Sage Publications. Reprinted with permission.

Brown, Donald E. "Incest avoidance and other human universals," *Human Universals*, Donald E. Brown. McGraw-Hill. Chapters 5 and 6, pp. 118–141. Copyright © 2012 Donald E. Brown. Reprinted by permission of Donald E. Brown.

Buller, David J., *Adapting Minds: Evolutionary Psychology and the Persistent Quest for Human Nature*, pp. 420–457, Copyright © 2005 Massachusetts Institute of Technology. Reprinted by permission.

Cosmides, Leda and Tooby, John (1997), "Evolutionary psychology: A primer." http://www.psych.ucsb.edu/research/cep/primer.html. Online.

Downes, Stephen M. "The basic components of the human mind were not solidified during the Pleistocene epoch." In F. Ayala and R. Arp (Eds.) *Contemporary Debates in Philosophy of Biology*, Copyright © 2009. Wiley-Blackwell. Reprinted by permission of the publisher.

Dupré, John (2003). *Human Nature and the Limits of Science* Chp.2 "The Evolutionary Psychology of Sex and Gender." pp.44–69. Copyright © John Dupré 2001. Reprinted by permission of Oxford University Press.

Edwards, A.W.F. "Human genetic diversity: Lewontin's fallacy." *BioEssays*, 25, pp. 798-801. Copyright © 2003 John Wiley and Sons. Reprinted with permission.

Fessler, Daniel M.T. and Edouard Machery, "Culture and cognition." In Eric Margolis, Richard Samuels, and Stephen P. Stich (Eds.), *The Oxford Handbook of Philosophy of Cognitive Science* (pp. 503–527). Copyright © 2012 Oxford University Press.